OXFORD STUDIES IN EUROPEAN LAW

Series Editors

PAUL CRAIG

Professor of English Law at St John's College, Oxford

GRÁINNE DE BÚRCA

Professor of Law at New York University School of Law

EU Powers Under External Pressure

OXFORD STUDIES IN EUROPEAN LAW

Series Editors
Paul Craig, Professor of English Law at St John's College, Oxford, and
Gráinne de Búrca, Professor of Law at New York University School of Law

The aim of this series is to publish important and original research on EU law. The focus is on scholarly monographs, with a particular emphasis on those which are interdisciplinary in nature. Edited collections of essays will also be included where they are appropriate. The series is wide in scope and aims to cover studies of particular areas of substantive and of institutional law, historical works, theoretical studies, and analyses of current debates, as well as questions of perennial interest such as the relationship between national and EU law and the novel forms of governance emerging in and beyond Europe. The fact that many of the works are interdisciplinary will make the series of interest to all those concerned with the governance and operation of the EU.

OTHER TITLES IN THIS SERIES

Frontex and Human Rights
Responsibility in 'Multi-Actor Situations' under the ECHR and EU Public Liability Law
Melanie Fink

EU Equality Law
The First Fundamental Rights Policy of the EU
Elise Muir

Subnational Authorities in EU Law
Michèle Finck

Accessing Asylum in Europe
Extraterritorial Border Controls and Refugee Rights under EU Law
Violeta Moreno-Lax

National Parliaments after the Lisbon Treaty and the Euro Crisis
Resilience or Resignation?
Davor Jančić

Environmental Integration in Competition and Free-Movement Laws
Julian Nowag

EU Agencies
Legal and Political Limits to the Transformation of the EU Administration
Merijn Chamon

Coherence in EU Competition law
Wolf Sauter

Foreign Policy Objectives in European Constitutional Law
Joris Larik

Private Regulation and the Internal Market Sports, Legal Services, and Standard Setting in EU Economic Law
Mislav Mataija

EU Powers Under External Pressure

How the EU's External Actions Alter its Internal Structures

CHRISTINA ECKES
Professor of European Law, University of Amsterdam

OXFORD
UNIVERSITY PRESS

OXFORD
UNIVERSITY PRESS

Great Clarendon Street, Oxford, OX2 6DP,
United Kingdom

Oxford University Press is a department of the University of Oxford.
It furthers the University's objective of excellence in research, scholarship,
and education by publishing worldwide. Oxford is a registered trade mark of
Oxford University Press in the UK and in certain other countries

First Edition published in 2019

Impression: 1

Published in the United States of America by Oxford University Press
198 Madison Avenue, New York, NY 10016, United States of America

British Library Cataloguing in Publication Data
Data available

Library of Congress Control Number: 2018956531

ISBN 978–0–19–878554–5

Printed and bound by
CPI Group (UK) Ltd, Croydon, CR0 4YY

Series Editors' Preface

This book addresses the important question of how the European Union's growing external dimension affects the internal constitutional structures and functioning of the EU.

The expanding international powers and external relations of the EU has been a steadily growing phenomenon since the time of the Maastricht Treaty and indeed before, and was consolidated in many of the provisions of the Lisbon treaty.

Christina Eckes sets out to examine the external relations law of the European Union with particular emphasis on how it affects the division of powers between the EU and its member states, and the EU's internal structures and functioning more generally. Her analysis seeks to interrogate what effect the intensification of EU international relations law and policy has on the legitimacy and effectiveness of the EU and EU law, with specific concern for its effects on the relationship between individuals and the EU—or what the author calls 'the structures of bonding' that connect the citizen to the EU. She defines these structures of bonding as 'formal legal principles, rules and rights that allow the Union to justify its actions to its citizens and allow individuals to rely on EU law and to participate in its adoption' and suggests that these structures of bonding enhance the Union's legitimacy.

The book identifies the risk of increasing centralization of EU external relations powers at a time when the EU is already struggling on multiple fronts, and enjoys less support at present from its various member states and citizens than it has for many years. There are individual chapters examining the principle of loyalty or sincere cooperation, the principles of subsidiarity, primacy, and coherence, and a chapter on the significance of the choice of legal basis in external relations. There is also an analysis of the growing role of the European parliament in EU external lawmaking, and the significance of that development for the legitimacy of the EU, the role of national parliaments, and the relationship between citizens and the EU more generally. The implications of the jurisdiction of international courts and tribunals for the autonomy of the EU legal order is considered in Chapter 6, before conclusions are drawn in the final chapter.

This book should be of interest to students and teachers of EU law, and particularly those interested in external relations law, as well as to international relations scholars with an interest in legal issues.

Paul Craig
Gráinne de Búrca

Acknowledgements

I have been very fortunate in having colleagues who generously shared their time with me and helped me to better understand my own thoughts. I benefitted in particular from the critiques and comments of Marija Bartl, Chantal Mak, Steven Blockmans, Marcus Klamert, Jan-Herman Reestman, Martijn Hesselink, Ingo Venzke, Laurens Ankersmit, Thomas Vandamme, Annette Schrauwen, Wiebe Hommes, Filipe Brito Bastos, Or Brook, and Anne Thies. I also benefitted from the discussions of earlier drafts with members of the Amsterdam Centre for European Law and Governance (ACELG) and Law and Justice Across Borders. Minke de Haan helped me beyond expectation to prepare a presentable manuscript.

The work presented here builds on the research carried out as part of the project 'Outside-In: Tracing the Imprint of the European Union's External Actions on Its Constitutional Landscape', which was between 2012 and 2015 financially supported by the *Netherlands Organisation for Scientific Research (NWO).* It also draws from the work I did as Emile Noël Fellow-in-residence at New York University in 2012/2013.

Writing this book took longer than anticipated. It was delayed by the joy of my son Dorian and my daughter Leonore joining my family and the grief of losing my mother. I am most indebted to my partner, Dennis, for his love, support and endurance.

Table of Contents

Table of Cases xiii
Table of Legislation xxi
List of Abbreviations xxxi

Introduction: External Relations as a Constitutional Challenge 1
Objective of the Book 2
Relevance of EU Law 4
Dilemma 7
Fear of EU External Actions? 8
Terminological Clarifications 9
Structure of the Book 10

1. Conceptual Toolkit: Bonding Structures, Autonomy, Effectiveness, and Legitimacy 15
1. Introduction 15
2. Structures of Bonding 16
2.1 EU law as source of rights and obligations 17
2.2 Representation within the Union 18
2.3 Legal structures and politics 19
3. Autonomy and Effectiveness 22
3.1 The Court's narrative of the autonomous legal order 23
3.2 Interlocking embrace 24
3.3 Institutional backbone 25
3.4 Fragility of an interlocking embrace 26
3.5 Fragility of otherness 30
4. Legitimacy 32
4.1 Different aspects 32
4.2 The link between autonomy and legitimacy 37
4.3 External relations as purpose? 39
5. Conclusions 41

2. EU Loyalty: Framing Legal Relationships 45
1. Introduction 45
2. The Principle of Sincere Cooperation: Taking Stock 47
2.1 Codifications 47
2.2 Sincere cooperation in the case law: subjects, objects, and integrative force 48
2.3 Limits 52
3. Beyond the Law: What is Loyalty? 54
3.1 A conceptual approach 54
3.2 Institutional loyalty 56
3.3 Framing force and limits 57
4. Loyalty and External Relations 59
4.1 Exclusivity and pre-emption 59
4.2 Mixed agreements: differences between internal and external actions 61

4.3 Information and communication obligations 65
4.4 Unity of international representation as an independent source of distinct obligations 66
4.5 Protecting autonomous actions of the Union in the future 70
5. The Transformative Effect of EU Loyalty 71
5.1 Loyalty: justified choice 72
5.2 Stricter EU loyalty in external relations 74
6. Conclusions 77

3. Organizational Principles Under External Pressure: Subsidiarity, Primacy, and Coherence 81
1. Introduction 81
2. Subsidiarity Under External Pressure 82
2.1 Constitutional framework and interpretation 82
2.2 A revealing example: externalities in environmental law 87
2.3 Rebuttable presumption that Union action in external relations is needed? 89
3. Primacy Under External Pressure 92
3.1 Meaning and interpretation within the EU 92
3.2 A revealing case of external pressure: UN counter-terrorist sanctions 94
3.3 Primacy: relevance for external relations 97
4. Coherence Through Ambiguity 98
4.1 Constitutional framework and interpretation 98
4.2 Coherence in external relations 99
4.3 Institutional ambiguity 100
4.4 Ambiguity triggers litigation and extends jurisdiction 104
4.4.1 Mutual non-affection clause 104
4.4.2 Horizontal objectives 105
4.4.3 Procedural prerogatives before the court 107
4.4.4 Enforceability and constitutionalization 108
5. Conclusions 109

4. Consequences of Choosing an External Legal Basis 113
1. Introduction 113
2. Choice of Legal Basis: Relevance and Principles 114
3. Consequences and Function of (External) Legal Bases 118
3.1 Parallel competences in external relations 118
3.2 Geographical scope 120
3.3 Signalling function 121
4. Integrating Effects of Union External Actions 124
4.1 The case of environmental law: minimum or maximum harmonization? 124
4.2 Common commercial policy: ever more inclusive? 127
4.3 Ripple effect of Union positions in international organizations 131
5. External Pressures on the Foundations 132
5.1 Legal bases for cross-Treaty policies 132
5.1.1 Pre-Lisbon third pillar cases 132
5.1.2 Cross-Treaty legal basis post-Lisbon 134
5.1.3 International treaties 136

5.2 European sanctions as an exceptional bridge between CFSP and TFEU policies 138
6. Vesting International Obligations with the Bite of EU Law: The Case of the Aarhus Convention 140
6.1 *Slovak Bears* 140
6.2 Further case law 143
7. Conclusions 145

5. Institutional Powers in External Relations 149

1. Introduction 149
2. Shifting Powers Within a Setting of Executive Dominance and Institutionalized Diffusion 150
2.1 External relations as the domain of the executive 151
2.2 Counterbalancing the executive: Parliament's increased role in external relations 153
2.2.1 Formal Treaty powers 154
2.2.2 Information is power: formal rules 155
2.2.3 Parliament's dual role 157
2.3 CFSP as a policy apart 157
3. Affirming Powers in Practice: The European Parliament 158
3.1 Refusal of consent 158
3.1.1 TFTP agreement 159
3.1.2 ACTA 161
3.2 'Business as usual': information, influence, and inter-institutional cooperation post-Lisbon 162
3.2.1 Institutional involvement: EU–US Personal Name Record (PNR) Agreement and new generation free trade agreements 162
3.2.2 Veto powers, institutional involvement, and substantive influence 165
3.3 Struggle for (external) visibility 168
3.4 CFSP agreements 169
4. Facultative Mixity 170
5. The European Parliament's Acts of Contestation as Claim to External Representation 173
5.1 Representation as structures of bonding 173
5.2 Parliament's symbolic function 175
5.3 Is the European Parliament the better alternative? 178
5.4 Potential implications of Parliament's claim 181
6. Conclusions 183

6. International Courts or Tribunals and the Autonomy of the EU Legal Order 185

1. Introduction 185
2. International Courts or Tribunals 186
2.1 The European Court of Human Rights 189
2.1.1 Relevance of EU accession to the European Convention on Human Rights 189
2.1.2 Draft accession agreement and Opinion 2/13 190

2.2 Investor-State Dispute Settlement and the Investment Court System 191
2.2.1 Investment Court System 192
2.2.2 Remaining criticism 194
2.2.3 The future of ISDS and the ICS 196
2.3 Aarhus Convention and its compliance committee 198
2.3.1 Reception and rejection of ACCC findings 198
2.3.2 Deference and bite of the ACCC 200
3. Is the Autonomy of the EU Legal Order Under Pressure? 201
3.1 Contestation from the inside 202
3.2 Article 267 TFEU 204
3.3 Policy choices and division of competences 205
3.4 Standing 207
3.5 EU law as fact 209
4. The Special Case of the ECHR 210
4.1 Elevated status within the European legal order 210
4.2 Triangle of ECHR, EU law, and national law post-accession 212
4.3 ECHR accession and the autonomy of the European legal order 214
4.4 Post-accession scenario: 'what-if?'-considerations 215
5. Relevant Characteristics of International Courts or Tribunals 216
6. Conclusions 219

Conclusions: Internal Structures Under External Pressure 223

External Pressure is Stronger 224
Bonding Structures, Autonomy, Effectiveness, and Legitimacy 227
Better Representing EU Citizens in External Relations? 228
Organizational Principles Under Pressure 230
The Higher Purpose of EU Loyalty 231
External Legal Bases Frame Political Power Struggles and Trigger Integration 232
A Normative Case for the Autonomy of the European Union 233
Integrative Force of EU External Relations 236
The Union, the National, and the Other 237

Index 239

Table of Cases

EUROPEAN UNION

European Court of Justice - Decisions

Case 9/56, Meroni & Co., Industrie Metallurgiche, SpA v High Authority of the European Coal and Steel Community [1958] EU:C:1958:7 . . . 172
Case 6/60 Humblet v Belgium ECR 559 . . . 50–51
Case 26/62, Van Gend en Loos [1963] ECLI:EU:C:1963:1 . . . 23–24
Joined Cases 90/63 and 91/63, Commission v Luxembourg and Belgium [1964] EU:C:1964:80 . . . 60
Case 6/64, Flaminio Costa v ENEL [1964] EU:C:1964:66 . . . 17 18, 23, 50–51, 92–93
Case 9/65, Acciaierie San Michele SpA (in liquidation) v High Authority of the ECSC [1965] EU:C:1965:63 . . . 92–93
Case 11/70, Internationale Handelsgesellschaft mbH v Einfuhr- und Vorratsstelle für Getreide und Futtermittel [1970] EU:C:1970:114 . . . 23–24, 92–93
Case 22/70, Commission v Council (ERTA) [1971] EU:C:1971:32 . . . 2, 59–61, 117
Case 48/71, Commission of the European Communities v Italian Republic [1972] EU:C:1972:65 . . . 92–93
Joined Cases 21/72 to 25/72, International Fruit Company and Others v Produktschap voor Groenten en Fruit [1972] EU:C:1972:115 . . . 128
Case 30/72, Commission v Italy [1973] EU:C:1973:16 . . . 50–51
Case 39/72, Commission v Italy [1973] EU:C:1973:13 . . . 50–51
Case 34/73, Fratelli Variola S.p.A. v Amministrazione italiana delle Finanze [1973] EU:C:1973:101 . . . 92–93
Case 166/73, Rheinmühlen-Düsseldorf v Einfuhr- und Vorratsstelle für Getreide und Futtermittel (Rheinmühlen II) [1974] EU:C:1974:3, . . . 93–94
Case 181/73, R. & V. Haegeman v Belgium [1974] EU:C:1974:41 . . . 140
Case 8/74, Procureur du Roi v Benoît and Gustave Dassonville [1974] . . . 84–85
Case 38/75, NV Nederlandse Spoorwegen [1975] EU:C:1975:154, . . . 128
Case 33/76, Rewe-Zentralfinanz [1976] EU:C:1976:188 . . . 49–50
Case 41/76, Donckerwolcke [1976] EU:C:1976:182 . . . 172
Case 106/77, Amministrazione delle Finanze dello Stato v Simmenthal SpA [1978] EU:C:1978:49 . . . 23–24, 49–51
Case 104/81, Hauptzollamt Mainz v Kupferberg [1982] EU:C:1982:362 . . . 140
Case 230/81, Luxembourg v Parliament [1983] EU:C:1983:32 . . . 47, 48–50
Case 283/81, Srl CILFIT and Lanificio di Gavardo SpA v Ministry of Health [1982] EU:C:1982:335 . . . 209
Joined Cases 205/82 and 215/82, Deutsche Milchkontor [1983] EU:C:1983:233 . . . 49–50
Case 44/84, Hurd v Jones (Her Majesty's Inspector of Taxes) [1986] EU:C:1986:2 . . . 104
Case 186/85, Commission v Belgium [1987] EU:C:1987:208 . . . 50–51
Joined Cases 358/85 and 51/86, France v Parliament [1988] EU:C:1988 . . . 49–50
Case 45/86, Commission v Council [1987] EU:C:1987:163 . . . 116
Case 204/86, Greece v Council [1988] EU:C:1988:450 . . . 49–50
Case 70/87, Fediol v Commission [1989] EU:C:1989:254 . . . 199
Case 2/88 Imm., Zwartveld and Others [1990] EU:C:1990:440 . . . 49–50
Case 5/88, Wachauf [1989] EU:C:1989:321 . . . 53
Case 70/88, Parliament v Council (Chernobyl I) [1990] EU:C:1990:217 . . . 126
Case 103/88, Costanzo [1989] EU:C:1989:256 . . . 50, 75–76
Case C-69/89, Nakajima [1991] EU:C:1991:186 . . . 199
Case C-106/89, Marleasing [1990] EU:C:1990:395 . . . 49–50
Case C-234/89, Stergios Delimitis [1991] EU:C:1991:91 . . . 49–50
Case C-251/89, Athanasopoulos and Others [1991] EU:C:1991:242 . . . 48–50
Case C-260/89, Elliniki Radiophonia Tileorassi [1991] EU:C:1991:254 . . . 53

Case C-300/89, Commission v Council (Titanium dioxide) [1991] EU:C:1991:244. . . . . 116–17, 125
Joined Cases C-6/90 to C-9/90, Francovich and Others [1991] EU:C:1991:428 50–51
Case C-33/90, Commission v Italy [1991] EU:C:1991:476. 48–49
Joined Cases C-63/90 to C-67/90, Portugal and Spain v Council [1992] EU:C:1992:381 . . . . . 75, 104
Case C-70/90, Spain v Council [1992] EU:C:1992:382 104
Case C-71/90, Spain v Council [1992] EU:C:1992:383 104
Case C-295/90, Parliament v Council [1992] EU:C:1992:294. 116
Case C-165/91, Van Munster [1994] EU:C:1994:359. 49–50
Joined Cases C-46/93 and C-48/93, Brasserie du Pêcheur SA [1996] EU:C:1996:7. . . . 194–95, 205
Case C-65/93, Parliament v Council [1995] EU:C:1995:91 . . . . 49–50, 155
Case C-312/93, Peterbroeck [1995] EU:C:1995:437 49–50
Case C-426/93, Germany v Council [1995] EU:C:1995:367 83
Case C-16/94, Dubois and Cargo v Garonor [1995] EU:C:1995:148 51–52
Case C-25/94, Commission v Council (FAO) [1996] EU:C:1996:114 . . . . . .65–67, 68–69, 167–68
Case C-84/94 UK and Northern Ireland v Council (Working Time Directive) [1996] EU:C:1996:431. 83
Case C-265/95, Commission v France (Spanish Strawberries) [1997] EU:C:1997:595. 50–51
Case C-53/96, Hermès International [1998] EU:C:1997:539, Opinion of AG Tesauro. 144–45
Case C-129/96, Inter-Environnement Wallonie [1997] EU:C:1997:628 49–50
Case C-170/96, Commission v Council (Airport Transit Visa) [1998] 104
Joined Cases C-10/97 to C-22/97, Ministero delle Finanze v IN.CO.GE.'90 [1998] EU:C:1998:498 92–93
Case C-202/97, Fitzwilliam Executive Search (FTS) [2000] EU:C:2000:75 49–50
Case C-319/97, Kortas [1999] EU:C:1999:272. 49–50
Case C-62/98, Commission v Portugal [2000] EU:C:2000:358 70–71
Case C-84/98, Commission v Portugal [2000] EU:C:2000:359 70–71
Case C-170/98, Commission v Belgium [1999] EU:C:1999:411 70–71
Joined Cases C-300/98 to C-392/98, Parfums Christian Dior and others [2000] EU:C:2000:688. . . . . 49–50, 74–75
Case C-376/98, Federal Republic of Germany v European Parliament and Council of the European Union (Tobacco Advertising) [2000] EU:C:2000:324. . . . . 84–85, 116
Case C-377/98, Netherlands v EP and Council (Biotechnology Directive) [2001] EU:C:2001:523 84–85
Case C-467/98, Commission v Denmark [2002] EU:C:2002:625. 59–60
Case C-476/98, Commission v Germany [2002] EU:C:2002:631 59–60
Case C-13/00, Commission v Ireland (Berne Convention) [2002] EU:C:2002:184. 140
Case C-50/00 P, Unión de Pequeños Agricultores v Council (UPA) [2002] EU:C:2002:462. . . . . 144, 207, 235
Case C-326/00, Idryma Koinonikon Asfaliseon (IKA) [2003] EU:C:2003:101. 49–50
Case C-339/00, Ireland v Commission [2003] EU:C:2003:545. 47
Case C-453/00, Kühne & Heitz [2004] EU:C:2004:17. 49–50
Case C-224/01, Gerhard Köbler v Republik Österreich [2003] EU:C:2003:513 25–26
Case C-281/01, Commission v Council (Energy Star Agreement) [2002] EU:C:2002:761 126–27
Case C-491/01, British American Tobacco (Investments) and Imperial Tobacco [2002] EU:C:2002:741 . . . . 85, 87–88, 91
Case C-494/01, Commission v Ireland [2005] EU:C:2005:250. 48–49
Case C-105/02, Commission v Germany [2006] EU:C:2006:637. 48–49
Case C-277/02, EU-Wood-Trading [2004] EU:C:2004:810 48–49
Case C-377/02, Van Parys [2005] EU:C:2005:121 186–87
Case C-6/03, Deponiezweckverband Eiterköpfe [2005] EU:C:2005:222 124–25
Case C-94/03, Commission v Council (Rotterdam Convention) [2006] EU:C:2006:2 . . . . 121, 126–27
Case C-105/03, Pupino [2005] EU:C:2005:386 49–50
Case C-176/03, Commission v Council (Environmental Crime) [2005] EU:C:2005:542 104–5
Case C-178/03, Commission v Parliament and Council (Dangerous Chemicals) [2006] EU:C:2006:4. 125
Case C-239/03, Commission v France (Étang de Berre) [2004] EU:C:2004:598. 140
Case C-266/03, Commission v Luxembourg [2005] EU:C:2005:341 73–74

Case C-433/03, Commission v Germany [2005] EU:C:2005:462 . . . . 48–49, 63, 73
Case C-459/03, Commission v Ireland (Mox Plant) [2006] EU:C:2006:345 . . . . 47–49, 74–75, 140, 187–89
Case C-519/03, Commission v Luxembourg [2005] EU:C:2005:234 63
Case C-144/04, Mangold [2005] EU:C:2005:709 29
Joined Cases C-317/04 and C-318/04, Parliament v Council and Commission [2006] EU:C:2006:346 68
Case C-355/04 P, Segi and Others v Council [2007] EU:C:2007:116 . . . . 48–49, 136–37
Case C-432/04, Commission v Édith Cresson [2006] EU:C:2006:455 210–11
Case C-526/04, Laboratoires Boiron [2006] EU:C:2006:528 49–50
Case C-91/05, Commission v Council (ECOWAS) [2008] EU:C:2008:288 . . . . 106, 116–17, 135–36
Case C-119/05, Lucchini [2007] EU:C:2007:434 50
Case C-229/05 P, Osman Ocalan, on behalf of the Kurdistan Workers' Party (PKK) and Serif Vanly, on behalf of the Kurdistan National Congress (KNK) v Council [2007] EU:C:2007:32 210–11
Case C-284/05 Commission v Finland [2009] EU:C:2009:778 67–68
Case C-294/05 Commission v Sweden [2009] EU:C:2009:779 67–68
Case C-337/05 Commission v Italy [2008] EU:C:2008:203 67–68
Case C-372/05 Commission v Germany [2009] EU:C:2009:780 67–68
Case C-378/05 Commission v Italy [2006] EU:C:2006:581 67–68
Joined Cases C-402/05 P and C-415/05 P, Yassin Abdullah Kadi and Al Barakaat International Foundation v Council of the European Union and Commission [2008] EU:C:2008:461 . . . . 23–24, 94–96, 96, 97, 182, 204, 210, 215–16, 230
Case C-409/05 Commission v Greece [2009] EU:C:2009:782 67–68
Case C-431/05, Merck Genéricos [2007] EU:C:2007:496 142
Case C-461/05 Commission v Denmark [2009] EU:C:2009:783 67–68
Case C-157/06 Commission v Italy [2008] EU:C:2008:530 67–68
Case C-205/06, Commission v Austria (BITs) [2009] EU:C:2009:118 . . . . . . 47–48, 49–50, 70–71
Case C-239/06 Commission v Italy [2009] EU:C:2009:784 67–68
Case C-249/06, Commission v Sweden [2009] EU:C:2009:119 70–71
Case C-308/06, Intertanko [2008] EU:C:2008:312 187
Case C-411/06, Commission v Parliament and Council [2009] EU:C:2009:518 . . . . 116, 126
Case C-45/07, Commission v Greece [2009] EU:C:2009:81 . . . . 47, 60, 63–64, 67–68
Case C-118/07, Commission v Finland [2009] EU:C:2009:715 70–71
Case C-118/07, Commission v Finland [2009] EU:C:2009:525, Opinion of AG Maduro 70–71
Case C-155/07, Parliament v Council (European Investment Bank Guarantees) [2008] EU:C:2008:605 116
Case C-188/07, Commune de Mesquer v Total France and Total International Ltd., Judgment of the Court (Grand Chamber) of 24 June 2008 [2008] ECR I-4501 97
Joined Cases C-200/07 to C-201/07, Marra [2008] EU:C:2008:579 49–50
Case C-246/07, Commission v Sweden (PFOS) [2010] EU:C:2010:203 . . . . . 11,48, 62, 64–65, 76, 144
Case C246/07, Commission v Sweden (PFOS) [2010] EU:C:2009:589, Opinion of AG Maduro 63–64, 66–67, 73
Joined Cases C-261/07 and C-299/07, VTB-VAB and Galatea [2009] EU:C:2009:244 49–50
Case C-555/07, Seda Kücükdeveci v Swedex GmbH & Co. KG [2010] EU:C:2010:21 . . . . 29, 151–52
Case C-47/08, Commission v Belgium [2011] EU:C:2011:334 50
Case C-58/08, Vodafone and Others [2010] EU:C:2010:321 . . . . 84, 85
Case C-73/08, Bressol and Others [2009] EU:C:2009:396, Opinion of AG Sharpston 49–50
Case C-263/08, Djurgården-Lilla Värtans Miljöskyddsförening [2009] EU:C:2009:631 143
Case C-301/08, Irène Bogiatzi v Deutscher Luftpool, Société Luxair, European Communities, Luxembourg, Foyer Assurances SA, Judgment of the Court (Fourth Chamber) of 22 October 2009' (2010) 47 CML Rev 899 97
Case C-355/08, WWF-UK Ltd. v Council [2009] EU:C:2009:286 200
Case C-444/08, Região autónoma dos Açores v Council [2009] EU:C:2009:733 200
Case C-34/09, Gerardo Ruiz Zambrano v Office national de l'emploi (ONEm) [2011] EU:C:2011:124 84–85

Case C-115/09, Bund für Umwelt und Naturschutz Deutschland [2011] EU:C:2011:289 143
Case C-176/09, Luxembourg v Parliament and Council [2011] EU:C:2011:290 84
Case C-240/09, Lesoochranárske zoskupenie VLK (Slovak Bears) [2011] EU:C:2011:125. . . . . 140, 141–42, 142–43, 144, 145
Case C-240/09, Lesoochranárske zoskupenie VLK (Slovak Bears) [2011] EU:C:2011:125, Opinion of AG Kokott. 142
Case C-399/09, Marie Landtová [2011] EU:C:2011:415 29
Case C-524/09, Ville de Lyon (trading emission allowances) [2010] EU:C:2010:822 . . . . 143–44, 198–99
Case C-524/09, Ville de Lyon (trading emission allowances) [2010] EU:C:2010:613, Opinion of AG Kokott. 198–99
Case C-71/10, Office of Communications (mobile phone base) [2011] EU:C:2011:525 143–44
Case C-130/10, Parliament v Council (UN Sanctions) [2012] EU:C:2012:472 . . . . 104–5, 106, 115–16, 134–36, 139, 145–46, 223–24
Case C-130/10, UN Sanctions [2012] EU:C:2012:50, Opinion of AG Bot 106
Case C-364/10, Hungary v Slovakia [2012] EU:C:2012:124, Opinion of AG Bot 49–50
Case C-400/10 PPU, JMcB v LE [2010] EU:C:2010:582. 189
Case C-571/10, Kamberaj [2012] EU:C:2012:233 212
Joined Cases C-584/10, C-593/10, and C-595/10 P, Commission, Council and UK v Kadi [2013] EU:C:2013:518. 182
Case C-615/10 Insinööritoimisto Ins Tiimi Oy [2012] EU:C:2012:324. 67–68
Case C-617/10, Åkerberg Fransson [2013] EU:C:2013:105 . . . . 49–51, 53, 212
Case C-260/11, Edwards v Environment Agency [2012] EU:C:2012:645, Opinion of AG Kokott 198–99
Case C-414/11, Daiichi Sankyo and Sanofi-Aventis Deutschland [2013] EU:C:2013:520. 128
Case C-431/11, United Kingdom v Council [2013] EU:C:2013:589 120
Case C-518/11, UPC Nederland BV [2013] EU:C:2013:709 48–49
Case C-530/11, European Commission v United Kingdom (WWF-UK) [2014] EU:C:2014:67 200
Case C-540/11, Levy and Sebbag [2012] EU:C:2012:581 67–68
Case C-656/11, United Kingdom v Council (Switzerland-EEA Social Security Coordination) [2014] EU:C:2014:97. . . . . 115–16, 120, 134, 223–24
Case C-658/11, Parliament v Council (Piracy Agreement I (Mauritius)) [2014] EU:C:2014:2025 . . . . 104–5, 107, 107, 134–35, 169–70, 223–24
Case C-658/11, Parliament v Council (Piracy Agreement I (Mauritius)) [2014] EU:C:2014:41, Opinion of AG Bot 106, 155
Case C-28/12, Commission v Council [2015] EU:C:2015:282 . . . . 11, 69, 115–16, 152–53, 223–24
Case C-28/12, Commission v Council [2015] EU:C:2015:43, Opinion of AG Mengozzi, ...69–70
Case C-93/12, ET Agrokonsulting-04-Velko Stoyanov [2013] EU:C:2013:432. 48–49
Joined Cases C-105/12 to C-107/12, Essent and Others [2013] EU:C:2013:677 130
Case C-114/12, Commission v Council (Broadcasting Organisations) [2014] EU:C:2014:2151 . . . . 2, 59–60, 61, 114–16
Case C-114/12, Commission v Council (Broadcasting Organisations) [2014] EU:C:2014:224, Opinion of AG Sharpston 67–68
Case C-137/12, Commission v Council (Broadcasting Rights) [2013] EU:C:2013:675 . . . . 115–16, 128, 223–24
Case C-137/12, Commission v Council (Broadcasting Rights) [2013] EU:C:2013:441, Opinion of AG Kokott. 130
Case C-274/12 P, Telefónica SA v Commission [2013] EU:C:2013:852. 207–8
Case C-290/12, Della Rocca [2013] EU:C:2013:235 68
Case C-298/12, Confédération paysanne [2013] EU:C:2013:630 49–51
Case C-370/12, Pringle v Ireland [2012] EU:C:2012:756 114–15
Case C-377/12, Commission v Council [2014] EU:C:2014:1903 . . . . 115–16, 119, 129, 152–53, 223–24
Case C-390/12, Pfleger [2014] EU:C:2014:281 53
Case C-399/12, Germany v Council (OIV) [2014] EU:C:2014:2258 . . . . 60–61, 65, 66–67, 67–68, 76, 115–16, 223–24

Joined Cases C-401/12 P to C-403/12 P, Council and Others v Vereniging Milieudefensie and Stichting Stop Luchtverontreiniging Utrecht [2015] EU:C:2015:4 . . . . 199, 200
Joined Cases C-404/12 P and C-405/12 P, Council and Commission v Stichting Natuur en Milieu [2015] EU:C:2015:5. . . . . 199, 200
Case C-446/12, Willems [2015] EU:C:2015:238. 53
Case C-66/13, Green Network SpA v Autoritá per l'energia elettrica e il gas [2014] EU:C:2014:156, Opinion of AG Bot 66–67, 114–15
Case C-81/13, United Kingdom v Council [2014] EU:C:2014:2449 120
Case C-81/13, United Kingdom v Council [2014] EU:C:2014:2114, Opinion of AG Kokott 124
Case C-198/13, Hernandéz and Others [2014] EU:C:2014:2055. 53
Case C-206/13, Cruciano Siragusa [2014] EU:C:2014:126 53
Case C-270/13, Iraklis Haralambidis [2014] EU:C:2014:1358, Opinion of AG Wahl 57–58
Case C-425/13, Commission v Council (Emission Trading System) [2015] EU:C:2015:483 . . . . 115–16, 149–50, 223–24
Case C-439/13 P, Elitaliana SpA v Eulex Kosovo [2015] EU:C:2015:753. 103
Case C-439/13 P, Elitaliana SpA v Eulex Kosovo [2015] EU:C:2014:2416, Opinion of AG Jääskinen, ... 47, 103
Case C-456/13 P, T & L Sugars Ltd and Sidul Açúcares, Unipessoal Lda v Commission [2015] EU:C:2015:284. 207–9
Case C-640/13, Commission v United Kingdom [2015] EU:C:2014:2457 50–51
Case C-660/13, Council v Commission (Memorandum of Understanding) [2016] EU:C:2016:616 . . . . 115–16, 149–50, 152–53, 223–24
Case C-660/13, Council v Commission (Memorandum of Understanding) [2015] EU:C:2015:787, Opinion of AG Sharpston 49–50
Case C-662/13, Surgicare [2015] EU:C:2015:89 49–50
Case C-48/14, Parliament v Council [2015] EU:C:2015:91 152–53
Case C-62/14, Gauweiler [2015] EU:C:2015:7, Opinion of AG Cruz Villalon 49–50
Case C-73/14, Council v Commission (ITLOS) [2015] EU:C:2015:663 . . . . 23–24, 48–49, 66, 116–17, 149–50
Case C-102/14, Taricco and others (Taricco I) [2015] EU:C:2015:555. 25–26
Joined Cases C-132/14 to C-136/14, European Parliament and Commission v Council [2015] EU:C:2015:813 119
Case C-222/14, Konstantinos Maïstrellis v Ypourgos Dikaiosynis, Diafaneias kai Anthropinon Dikaiomaton [2015] EU:C:2015:473 151
Case C-263/14, Parliament v Council (Piracy Agreement II (Tanzania)) [2016] EU:C:2016:435 . . . . 104–5, 113, 115–16, 134–35, 170, 223–24
Case C-263/14, Parliament v Council (Pirates Agreement II (Tanzania)) [2015] EU:C:2015:729, Opinion of AG Kokott. 156–57
Case C-441/14 Dansk Industri, acting on behalf of Ajos A/S v Estate of Karsten Eigil Rasmussen, [2016] EU:C:2016:278 29
Case C-455/14 P, H v Council and Commission EU:C:2016:569 103–4
Case C-600/14, Germany v Council [2017] ECLI:EU:C:2017:935 . . . . 115–16, 223–24
Case C.72/15, Rosneft [2017] EU:C:2017:236. . . . . .134–35, 138–39
Case C-176/15, Riskin [2016] EU:C:2016:488 67–68
Case C-243/15, Lesoochranárske zoskupenie VLK (Slovak Bears II) [2016] EU:C:2016:838 . . . . .49–50, 199–200
Case C-243/15, Lesoochranárske zoskupenie VLK (Slovak Bears II) [2016] EU:C:2016:491, Opinion of AG Kokott. 62
Case C-327/15, TDC [2016] EU:C:2016:974 48–49
Case C-389/15, Commission v Council (Lisbon Agreement on Appellations of Origin and Geographical Indications) [2017] EU:C:2017:798. . . . . 115–16, 223–24
Joined Cases C-626/15 and C-659/16, Commission v Council (pending) 115–16, 223–24
Joined Cases C-626/15 and C-659/16, Commission v Council [2018] EU:C:2018:362, Opinion of AG Kokott. 113, 223–24
Case C-687/15, Commission v Council (CMR-15) [2017] ECLI:EU:C:2017:803 . . . . 115–16, 223–24
Case C-16/16 P Belgium v Commission [2018] EU:C:2018:79 48–49
Case C-64/16, Associação Sindical dos Juízes Portugueses [2018] EU:C:2018:117 26

Case C-284/16, Slovak Republic v Achmea BV [2018] EU:C:2018:158 . . . . .12–13, 25, 187–89, 193–94, 196, 197, 197, 205
Case C-414/16, Vera Egenberger v Evangelisches Werk für Diakonie und Entwicklung e.V. [2018] EU:C:2018:257 29
Case C-470/16, North East Pylon Pressure Campaign Limited Maura Sheehy v An Bord Pleanála Minister for Communications, Climate Action and Environment, Ireland Attorney General, Ireland and Joined party EirGrid Plc [2018] EU:C:2018:185 199
Case C-42/17, MAS, MB (Taricco II) [2017] EU:C:2017:936 . . . . .25–26, 52
Case C-82/17 P, TestBioTech eV, European Network of Scientists for Social and Environmental Responsibility eV, Sambucus eV v Commission (pending) 199
Case C-411/17, Inter-Environnement Wallonie asbl, Bond Beter Leefmilieu Vlaanderen vzw v Conseil des ministers (pending) 143–44

European Court of Justice - Opinions

Opinion 1/75 (International agreements – conclusion by EEC) [1975] EU:C:1975:145. 76
Opinion 1/76 (Draft Agreement establishing a European laying-up fund for inland waterway vessels) [1977] EU:C:1977:63 187–89
Opinion 1/91 (creation EEA I) [1991]EU:C:1991:490 . . . . .185–86, 187–89
Opinion 1/92 (creation EEA II) [1992] EU:C:1992:189. 185–86
Opinion 2/91 (Convention No 170 of the International Labour Organisation concerning safety in the use of chemicals at work) [1993] EU:C:1993:106 . . . . 61, 62, 66–67, 68–69, 89, 124–25
Opinion 1/94 (WTO agreement) [1994] EU:C:1994:384 68–69
Opinion 2/94 (Accession by the Community to the European Convention for the Protection of Human Rights and Fundamental Freedoms) [1996] EU:C:1996:140 . . . .185–86, 187–89
Opinion 1/00 (Proposed agreement between the European Community and non-Member States on the establishment of a European Common Aviation Area) [2002] EU:C:2002:231, ...187–89
Opinion 2/00 (Cartagena Protocol) [2001] EU:C:2001:664 . . . . 113, 116, 126
Opinion 1/03 (Lugano Convention) [2006] EU:C:2006:81 . . . . .52, 115–16, 117–18
Opinion 1/09 (European and Community Patents Court) [2011] EU:C:2011:123 . . . . 25, 26, 185–86, 187–89
Opinion 1/13 (Hague Convention) [2014] EU:C:2014:2303. 2, 61, 117–18
Opinion 1/13 (Hague Convention) [2014] EU:C:2014:2392, Opinion of AG Jääskinen 67–68, 114–15
Opinion 2/13 (Accession to ECHR) [2014] EU:C:2014:2454. . . . 11, 23, 24–25, 62, 66–67, 185–86, 187–89, 191 , 235
Opinion 1/15 (EU–Canada PNR Agreement) [2017] EU:C:2017:592. .164
Opinion 2/15 (EU-Singapore Free Trade Agreement) [2016] EU:C:2017:376 . . . . 128, 185–86, 196, 197
Opinion 2/15 (EU-Singapore Free Trade Agreement) [2016] EU:C:2016:992, Opinion of AG Sharpton 129, 129, 130
Opinion 1/17 (Request for an Opinion on CETA), pending 167, 185–86, 187–89

Court of First Instance/General Court

Case T-93/95, Laga v Commission [1998] EU:T:1998:22. 75–76
Case T-94/95, Landyut v Commission [1998] EU:T:1998:23. 75–76
Case T-306/01, Yusuf and Al Barakaat International Foundation v Council and Commission [2005] EU:T:2005:331 94–95
Case T-315/01, Kadi v Council and Commission [2005] EU:T:2005:332 94–95
Case T-338/02, Segi and Others [2004] EU:T:2004:171 136–37
Case T-37/04, Região autónoma dos Açores v Council [2008] EU:T:2008:236 200
Joined Cases T-236/04 & T-241/04, European Environmental Bureau (EEB) and Stichting Natuur en Milieu v Commission of the European Communities [2005] EU:T:2005:426 200
Case T-91/07, WWF-UK Ltd. v Council [2008] EU:T:2008:170. 200
Case T-338/08, Stichting Natuur en Milieu v Commission [2012] EU:T:2012:300. . . . . . . 199, 200
Case T-85/09, Yassin Abdullah Kadi v European Commission [2010] EU:T:2010:418 31

Case T-529/09, Sophie in 't Veld v Council [2012] EU:T:2012:215 160
Case T-271/10, H v Council EU:T:2014:702 103–4
Case T-301/10, Sophie in 't Veld II [2013] EU:T:2013:135 . . . . 161–62, 167–68
Case T-369/11, Diadikasia Symbouloi Epicheiriseon A v Commission and EU Delegation to Turkey [2011] EU:T:2012:425 102–3
Case T-395/11, Elti d.o.o. v Delegation of the European Union to Montenegro [2011] EU:T:2012:274 102–3
Case T-213/12, Elitaliana v Eulex Kosovo, [2013] EU:T:2013:292 103
Case T-177/13, TestBioTech eV and Others v European Commission [2016] ECLI:EU:T:2016:736 199
Case T-721/14, Belgium v Commission [2015] EU:T:2015:829 48–49

Civil Service Tribunal

Case F-65/07, Aayhan and Others v Parliament [2009] EU:F:2009:43 47

INTERNATIONAL COURTS AND TRIBUNALS

European Court of Human Rights

A, B and C v Ireland (2011) 53 EHRR 13 226
Al-Jedda v UK App no 27021/08 (7 July 2011) 215–16
Behrami & Behrami v France App No 71412/01 (2 May 2007) 215
Bosphorus Hava Yollari Turizm veTicaret AS v Ireland App no 45036/98 (30 June 2015) 202, 215
Loizidou v Turkey (Preliminary Objections) App no 15318/89 (23 March 1995) 215
Nada v Switzerland App No 10593/08 (12 September 2012) 215–16
Saramati v France, Germany and Norway App No 78166/01 (13 June 2006) 215
Segi and Gestoras Pro-Amnistia and Others v 15 States of the EU (decision) App Nos 6422/02 and 9916/02 (23 May 2002) 211

Human Rights Committee

Mellet v Ireland, Communication No 2324/2013, UN Doc CCPR/C/116/D/2324/2013, (2016) 226
Whelan v Ireland, Communication No 2425/2014, UN Doc CCPR/C/119/D/2425/2014 (2017) 226

International Court of Justice

LaGrand (Germany v United States of America) (Provisional Measures) [1999] ICJ Rep 9 144–45
Military and Paramilitary Activities in and against Nicaragua (Nicaragua v United States of America) [1986] ICJ Rep 1986 5–6

ICSID

AES v Hungary, Case No ARB/07/22 (Award) (23 September 2010) 203
Electrabel S.A. v Hungary, Case No ARB/07/19 (Decision on Jurisdiction, Applicable Law and Liability) (30 November 2012) 98
RREEF Infrastructure (G.P.) Limited and RREEF Pan-European Infrastructure Two Lux S.à r.l. v. Kingdom of Spain, Case No. ARB/13/30 (Decision on Jurisdiction) (6 June 2016) 98

Permanent Court of Arbitration

Achmea B.V. v The Slovak Republic (UNCITRAL, PCA Case No 2008-13, award on jurisdiction, 7 December 2012) 205
European American Investment Bank AG (EURAM) v Slovak Republic (UNCITRAL, PCA Case No 2010-17, European Commission, Amicus Curiae submission, 13 October 2011) 205

Permanent Court of International Justice

German Interests in Polish Upper Silesia: Germany v Poland PCIJ (ser. A) No 6 (August 1925) 209

NATIONAL CASES

Czech Republic

Constitutional Court (Ústavní soud), Pl. S 5/12, plenary judgment of 31 January 2012 (Holubec). 29

Denmark

Supreme Court, Case 15/2014, 6 December 2013 (Dansk Industri (DI) acting for Ajos A/S v The estate left by 'A') 29
Supreme Court, Case 361/1997, 6 April 1998 (Treaty of Maastricht), summary translated in (1999) 3 CMLR 854 28–29

Germany

Federal Constitutional Court – BVerfG 12, 205, 28 February 1961 (Rundfunkentscheidung) 56–57
BverfG 34, 216, (JZ 1973, 361), 30 January 1973 (Coburg-Fall) 56–57
BVerfG, 2 BvR 2134/92, 12 October 1993 (Treaty of Maastricht judgment) 28–29, 105
BVerfG, 2 BvR 1877/97, 31 March 1998 176
BVerfG,2 BvR 1481/04, 14 October 2004 (Görgülü; ECHR decision) 212–13
BVerfG, 2 BvR 2253/06 (Constitutional complaint, declared inadmissible on 27 January 2010) 28–29
BVerfG, 2 BvE 2/08 (Treaty of Lisbon judgment) 95, 176
BVerfG, 2 BvR 1022/08, 30 June 2009 (Treaty of Lisbon judgment) 28–29, 178–79
BVerfG, 2 BvR 471/09 (Constitutional complaint, not accepted for decision on 13 August 2009) 28–29
BVerfG, 2 BvR 2136/09 (Constitutional complaint, not accepted for decision on 22 September 2009) 28–29
BVerfG, 2 BvR 2365/09, 2 BvR 740/10, 2 BvR 2333/08, 2 BvR 1152/10, 2 BvR 571/10, 4 May 2011 (Preventive Detention) 212–13
BVerfG, 2 BvR 1368/16, 2 BvR 1444/16, 2 BvR 1823/16, 2 BvR 1482/16, 2 BvE 3/16 (CETA) 122–23
BVerfG, 'Solange' judgments 28–29

Hungary

Constitutional Court, Decision No 22/2016. (XII.6.) AB on the Interpretation of art E(2) of the Fundamental Law 28–29

Netherlands

Hoge Raad 6 March 1959, NJ 1962, 2 (Nyugat) 212–13

Spain

Constitutional Tribunal, Declaration 1/2004 (Constitutional Treaty), case no 6603-2004 28–29

United Kingdom

A, K, M, Q, G v HM Treasury [2008] EWCA Civ 1187 95–96
HM Treasury v Ahmed [2010] UKSC 2. . . . . . . 95–96, 97
R (Quark Fishing Ltd) v Secretary of State for Foreign and Commonwealth Affairs [2006] 1 AC 529, ... 96
R v Horncastle and others [2009] UKSC 14. 212–13

United States

Medellín v Texas, 552 US 491 (2008). 215

Table of Legislation

INTERNATIONAL AND REGIONAL INSTRUMENTS

Anti-Counterfeiting Trade Agreement (ACTA) 158–59, 161–62, 165–66, 170, 178–79, 180, 181–82
Arms Trade Treaty (ATT) 226
Cartagena Protocol on Biosafety to the Convention on Biological Diversity . . . 126
Convention on Access to Information, Public Participation in Decision-making and Access to Justice in Environmental Matters (Aarhus Convention) . . . 124–25, 140–41, 142–44, 198–200, 201, 208, 235
Art 9(1) 143
Art 9(2) 143
Art 9(3) 141–43, 144, 199, 200–1
Art 9(4) 144, 200–1
Art 10. 199
Art 12 199
Art 19. 142
Convention on the Conservation of European Wildlife and Natural Habitats (Bern Convention). 198
Energy Charter Treaty (ECT) 98, 216
Art 26.3.b(ii) 206–7
European Convention on Human Rights (ECHR) 12–13, 31, 62, 96, 97, 121, 183, 185–86, 187–89, 190, 191–92, 202, 203, 204, 209, 210–11, 212–13, 214, 215, 219, 221, 234
Art 1(5) 202
Art 34 211
Art 35. 190
Art 35(1) 202
Art 46 190–91
Art 55. 202
Protocol 7, Art 2(1). 210–11
Protocol 8, Art 2(2) 212
Protocol 15, Art 1. 190
ICSID Convention
Art 54(1) 195
International Convention for the Safety of Life at Sea (SOLAS) 60
International Convention on Civil Liability for Oil Pollution Damage. 68–69
Kyoto Protocol. 88
Netherlands - Indonesia BIT 191–92
Netherlands - Slovakia BIT 196
North American Free Trade Agreement (NAFTA)
Chapter 19. 186–87
Paris Agreement 2015 194–95
Protocol of 12 February 2004 to amend the Paris Convention of 29 July 1960 on Third Party Liability in the Field of Nuclear Energy 68
Stockholm Convention on Persistent Organic Pollutants. 64, 124–25
Annex A. 62
Trade-Related Aspects of Intellectual Property Rights (TRIPS) Agreement
Art 27 128
UN Charter. 94–96, 97, 215–16
Chapter VII. 94–95, 110, 204, 215, 216
Art 2(2) 45
Art 103. .95, 96, 215
UN Convention against Transnational Organized Crime (Palermo Convention) 2000 132–33
UN Convention on Contracts for the International Sale of Goods (CISG) 1980 226
UN Convention on the Law of the Sea (UNCLOS) 187
Annex IX. 121–22
UN Convention on the Recognition and Enforcement of Foreign Arbitral Awards 1958 (New York Convention) 195
Vienna Convention on the Law of Treaties
Preamble 45
Art 26 45

EUROPEAN UNION TREATIES

Amsterdam Treaty. 154–55, 165–66
Protocol 30 85
Charter of Fundamental Rights. 97, 183
Art 52(3) 189, 210, 214
Art 53. 93, 189, 214
Community Charter of Fundamental Social Rights of Workers 151
Lisbon Treaty. 1, 7, 11–12, 19, 28–29, 52–53, 75, 83, 86, 99, 100, 101, 102, 104–5, 107–9, 110, 113, 114–17, 132, 134–35, 136–38, 150, 151, 152–53, 154–55, 159–60, 161–63, 166–67, 170, 172–73, 176, 178, 179–80, 181–83, 185–86, 200, 223, 231, 233
Protocol 1, Art 9. 85
Protocol 2 52–53
Art 4(1) 84
Art 5 84
Art 7 . . . . 19, 52–53, 84
Art 8 84

Lisbon Treaty (cont.)
Protocol 8 189
Protocol 21. .120, 134
Protocol 30 189
Declaration 1. 189
Declaration 13. . . . . .8–9, 108
Declaration 14. . . . . .8–9, 108
Declaration 17. 17–18
Declaration 41. 100–1
Declaration 53. .189
Declaration 61 189
Declaration 62. .189
Single European Act 87
Treaty Establishing the European Atomic Energy Community (Euratom Treaty) . . . 85
Art 102. 61–62
Treaty Establishing the European Community (TEC) 85, 94–95
Part 3, Title IV. 132–33
Arts 61*ff*. 132–33
Art 95 . . . . .133–34, 154–55
Art 133. . . . . .126–27, 154–55
Art 175(1). 126–27
Arts 177*ff*. 132–33
Art 189. 19
Art 213(2) .210–11
Art 230(4) 207, 235
Art 296 132–33
Art 300 126–27
Art 308 154–55
Treaty Establishing the European Economic Community (Treaty of Rome) 154
Art 5 66–67
Art 100A 125
Art 130(4) 87
Art 130S 125
Treaty on European Union (TEU – Maastricht Treaty version) 28–29, 165–66, 176
Art 11. 106
Art 24 159–60
Art 34(2)(a) 132–33
Art 38 159–60
Art 47 104
Treaty on European Union (TEU – Lisbon Treaty version) 85, 135–37
Preamble 21
Title III 149–50
Title V. 124
Art 1 6
Art 1(1) .45, 86, 100
Art 1(2) 72, 83–84
Art 3 223
Art 3(2) 60
Art 3(5) 40, 129, 139
Art 4 52
Art 4(2) 52–53, 83, 93
Art 4(3) 46, 47, 68–69, 108
Art 5 88
Art 5(1) 114–15
Art 5(2) 113, 114–15
Art 5(3) 19, 82–83, 89, 90–91
Art 6 . . . . .97, 189
Art 6(1) 189
Art 6(2) 189, 210, 211
Art 6(3) 189, 214
Art 10(1) 173, 176–77
Art 10(2) 18–19, 176–77, 178
Art 10(3) 19
Art 11(1). 40, 105–6
Art 13 . . . . .98–99, 151
Art 13(2) 47, 100, 113, 116–17, 149–50, 152–53, 155
Art 14(1) 179–80
Art 14(2) 19
Art 15. . . . . 18–19, 151
Art 15(1). 151
Art 15(3) 151
Art 15(5) 151
Art 15(6) 151
Art 16. 18–19
Art 16(6) 98–99
Art 17(1). 152
Art 17(2) 152
Art 17(7) 179–80
Art 17(8) 179–80
Art 18. . . . . .101, 102
Art 18(2) 183
Art 18(4) 98–99
Art 21. . . . . 40, 70, 105–7, 115–16, 124, 129, 139, 145–46, 218, 219–20, 223
Art 21(2) 106
Art 21(3) 98–99, 101
Art 22 151
Art 23 139
Art 24 139
Art 24(1) 89–90, 100–1, 135–36
Art 24(3) 48, 98–99, 108
Art 26(2) .98–99, 151
Art 27(3) 101, 158
Art 31. 135–36
Art 31(1). 100–1
Art 31(2) 135–36
Art 32 48
Art 36 135–36
Art 37 138
Art 40 . . . . 100, 102, 104–5, 106–7, 108, 134–35, 138–39
Art 40(2) 106
Art 41(2) 103
Art 41(3) 135–36
Art 42(7) 98–99
Art 48 . . . . .27–28, 99
Art 48(6) 114–15

Protocols and Declarations *see* Lisbon Treaty
Treaty on the Functioning of the European Union (TFEU) . . . 98, 99, 100–1, 104–5, 106–7, 108–9, 110, 114, 116–17, 128, 132, 135–37, 138, 139, 145–46, 152, 158, 169–70, 231
Part 5 . . . 124
Arts 2 to 6 . . . 115–16, 117–18
Art 2(2) . . . 119–20
Art 3 . . . 117–18
Art 3(1) . . . 90–91
Art 3(2) . . . 2, 60–61, 89, 115–16, 117–18
Art 4(2)(e) . . . 124–25
Art 4(3) . . . 47–48, 118–19
Art 7 . . . 98–99
Art 8 . . . 98–99
Art 11 . . . 98–99
Art 12 . . . 98–99
Art 13(2) . . . 171
Art 16 . . . 136–37
Art 21(1) . . . 40
Art 23 . . . 18
Art 43 . . . 131
Art 4(4) . . . 118–19
Art 48 . . . 120
Art 48(6) . . . 8
Art 75 . . . 135
Art 77 . . . 136–37
Arts 77*ff*. . . . 134
Art 79(2)(b) . . . 120
Art 79(3) . . . 119
Art 82(1)(d) . . . 134
Art 83(1) . . . 57–58
Art 87(2)(a) . . . 134
Art 91 . . . 119
Art 100 . . . 119
Art 114 . . . 8, 84–85, 125, 126, 128, 129, 133–34, 154–55
Art 130(4) . . . 98–99
Art 168 . . . 47–48
Art 191(1) . . . 124
Art 191(4) . . . 8, 119
Art 192 . . . 125, 126
Art 192(1) . . . 116–17, 125, 126–27
Art 192(2) . . . 125
Art 193 . . . 64, 124–25
Art 196(1) . . . 98–99
Art 207 . . . 119, 124, 125, 126–27, 129, 138
Art 207(1) . . . 129
Art 207(2) . . . 138, 154–55
Art 207(4) . . . 185–86
Art 207(6) . . . 8, 127, 130
Art 208 . . . 129
Arts 208*ff*. . . . 132–33
Art 209 . . . 8, 118–19
Art 209(2) . . . 118–19
Art 210(1) . . . 47–48
Art 212 . . . 8, 98–99, 118–19, 138
Art 212(2) . . . 138
Art 212(3) . . . 118–19
Art 214 . . . 98–99
Art 215 . . . 105, 135, 138–39
Art 215(2) . . . 106
Art 216 . . . 203–4
Art 216(1) . . . 2, 90, 115–16, 117–18, 124
Art 216(2) . . . 140
Art 217 . . . 119, 120
Art 218 . . . 18–19, 69, 107, 126–27, 138, 151, 154, 155, 169–70, 183
Art 218(5) . . . 138
Art 218(6) . . . 107, 134, 138, 155, 158–59, 189
Art 218(6)(a) . . . 154, 183
Art 218(8) . . . 152–53, 189
Art 218(9) . . . 131–32
Art 218(10) . . . 107, 154, 155, 183
Art 218(11) . . . 8, 121, 158
Arts 223*ff*. . . . 18–19
Art 230(2) . . . 179–80
Art 253 . . . 205–6
Art 254 . . . 205–6
Art 258 . . . 152
Art 263 . . . 102, 208–9, 211
Art 263(4) . . . 200, 207–8, 211
Art 267 . . . 25–26, 204, 208–9, 235
Art 275 . . . 103–4
Art 275(1) . . . 103
Art 275(2) . . . 108
Art 290 . . . 152
Art 329(2) . . . 98–99
Art 344 . . . 47–48, 72–73, 191
Art 345 . . . 130
Art 346 . . . 67–68, 132–33
Art 349 . . . 119
Art 351 . . . 30–31, 97, 210
Art 351(2) . . . 47–48, 70
Art 352 . . . 100–1, 154–55
Art 352(4) . . . 100–1
Protocols and Declarations *see* Lisbon Treaty

EUROPEAN UNION INTERNATIONAL AGREEMENTS

Agreement between Canada and the European Union on the Transfer and Processing of Passenger Name Record (EU–Canada PNR) . . . 164
Agreement between the European Union and Australia on the processing and transfer of Passenger Name Record (PNR) data by air carriers to the Australian Customs and Border Protection Service (EU–Australia PNR Agreement) [2012] OJ L 186/4 . . . 164

Agreement between the European Union and the Republic of Mauritius on the Conditions of Transfer of Suspected Pirates and Associated Seized Property from the European Union-led Naval Force to the Republic of Mauritius and on the Conditions of Suspected Pirates after Transfer (Piracy Agreement I – Mauritius) [2011] OJ L 254/1 169–70
Agreement between the European Union and the United Republic of Tanzania on the Conditions of Transfer of Suspected Pirates and Associated Seized Property from the European Union-led Naval Force to the United Republic of Tanzania (Piracy Agreement II – Tanzania) [2014] OJ L 108/3 170
Agreement between the European Union and the United States of America on the processing and transfer of Financial Messaging Data from the European Union to the United States for purposes of the Terrorist Finance Tracking Programme (TFTP 1 agreement 2010) [2010] OJ L 8/11 . . . . 158–60, 162, 170, 178–79, 180, 181–82
Agreement between the European Union and the United States of America on the processing and transfer of Financial Messaging Data from the European Union to the United States for purposes of the Terrorist Finance Tracking Programme (TFTP 2 agreement 2010) [2010] OJ L 195/5 160–62
Agreement between the European Community and the United States of America on the processing and transfer of PNR data by Air Carriers to the United States Department of Homeland Security, Bureau of Customs and Border Protection (1st EC–US PNR Agreement 2004) [2004] OJ L 183/84 . . . . 132–34, 151–52, 162–63
Agreement between the European Union and the United States of America on the processing and transfer of PNR data by Air Carriers to the United States Department of Homeland Security, Bureau of Customs and Border Protection (3rd EU–US PNR Agreement 2007) [2007] OJ 204/16. . . 133–34, 136–37, 162–63, 168–69
Agreement between the European Union and the United States of America on the processing and transfer of PNR data by Air Carriers to the United States Department of Homeland Security, Bureau of Customs and Border Protection (4th EU–US PNR Agreement 2011) 134, 162–64, 178–79, 181–82
Agreement between the United States of America and the European Union on the protection of personal information relating to the prevention, investigation, detection, and prosecution of criminal offences (EU–US Data Protection Umbrella Agreement) [2016] OJ L 336/1 181–82
Air Transport Agreement between the US, the EU, Norway, and Iceland 152–53
Anti-Counterfeiting Trade Agreement between the European Union and its Member States, Australia, Canada, Japan, the Republic of Korea, the United Mexican States, the Kingdom of Morocco, New Zealand, the Republic of Singapore, the Swiss Confederation, and the United States of America (ACTA) [2013] OJ C 349E/552 161–62
Comprehensive Economic and Trade Agreement between the EU and its Member States on the one hand and Canada on the other (EU–Canada Comprehensive Economic and Trade Agreement – CETA) [2017] OJ L 11/23 . . . . 167, 180–81, 185–86, 192–93, 194–95, 196, 197, 209
Chapter F. 187–89
Art 8.1 194–95
Art 8.9 194–95
Art 8.10 194–95
Art 8.22 (1)(f) and (g) 197
Art 8.27 193
Art 8.27(4). 193
Art 8.27(7). 193
Art 8.28 193
Art 8.30 193
Art 8.31 . . . . .197, 203–4, 206–7, 209
Art 8.31(2) 203
Art 8.41 195
Art 8.41 (2) 194–95
Art 30.7(3)(c) 122–23, 154–55
EU–Singapore Free Trade Agreement (EUSFTA) 194–95, 197, 218
Art 9.1(1)(g) 194–95
Art 9.18 193
Art 9.4(1) 194–95
Art 9.4(2)(e) 194–95
Art 9.4(5) 194–95
Art 13.16 218

EU–Singapore Investment Protection Agreement 128, 129, 154–55, 170–71, 185–87
Partnership and Cooperation Agreement between the EU and the Philippines 119, 129

EUROPEAN UNION REGULATIONS

Council Regulation (EEC) 3254/91 prohibiting the use of leghold traps in the Community and the introduction into the Community of pelts and manufactured goods of certain wild animal species originating in countries which catch them by means of leghold traps or trapping methods which do not meet international humane trapping standards [1991] OJ L 308/1 125
Council Regulation (EC, Euratom) 1605/2002 on the Financial Regulation applicable to the general budget of the European Communities [2002] OJ L 248/1 103
Parliament and Council Regulation (EC) 725/2004 on enhancing ship and port facility security [2004] OJ L 129/6
Art 10(4) 60
Council Regulation (EC) 2252/2004 on standards for security features and biometrics in passports and travel documents issued by Member States [2004] OJ L 385/1 53
Commission Regulation (EC) 842/2006 on certain fluorinated greenhouse gases [2006] OJ L 161/1 125
Parliament and Council Regulation 1013/2006 on shipments of waste [2006] OJ L 190/1 126
Parliament and Council Regulation (EC) 1367/2006 on the application of the provisions of the Aarhus Convention on Access to Information, Public Participation in Decision-making, and Access to Justice in Environmental Matters to Community institutions and bodies [2006] OJ L 264/1 . . . . 141, 199
Parliament and Council Regulation (EC) 1905/2006 establishing a financing instrument for development cooperation [2006] OJ L 378/41
Recital 16 151
Parliament and Council Regulation (EU, Euratom) 966/2012 on the financial rules applicable to the general budget of the Union and repealing Council Regulation (EC, Euratom) No 1605/2002 [2012] OJ L 298/39
Art 65(6) 102–3
Parliament and Council Regulation (EU) 1257/2013 on ship recycling and amending Regulation (EC) No 1013/2006 and Directive 2009/16/EC [2013] OJ L 330/1
Recital 22 90–91
Parliament and Council Regulation (EU) 912/2014 establishing a framework for managing financial responsibility linked to investor-to-state dispute settlement tribunals established by international agreements to which the European Union is party [2014] OJ L 257/121 206–7
Parliament and Council Regulation (EU) 2017/852 on mercury, and repealing Regulation (EC) No 1102/2008 [2017] OJ L 137/1
Recital 34 87
Parliament and Council Regulation (EU) 2017/2394 on cooperation between national authorities responsible for the enforcement of consumer protection laws and repealing Regulation (EC) No 2006/2004 [2017] OJ L 345/1
Recital 53 84–85

EUROPEAN UNION DIRECTIVES

Council Directive (EEC) 85/337 on the assessment of the effects of certain public and private projects on the environment [1985] OJ L 175/40 143
Council Directive (EEC) 92/43 on the conservation of natural habitats and of wild fauna and flora [1992] OJ L 206/7 141–43
Parliament and Council Directive (EC) 95/46 on the protection of individuals with regard to the processing of personal data and on the free movement of such data 133–34
Parliament and Council Directive 98/84/EC on the legal protection of services based on, or consisting of, conditional access [1998] OJ L320/54 128
Parliament and Council Directive (EC) 2003/35 providing for public participation in respect of the drawing up of certain plans and programmes relating to the environment and amending with regard to public participation and access to justice [2003] OJ L 156/17 143

Council Directive 2003/87 establishing a scheme for greenhouse gas emission allowance trading within the Community and amending Council Directive 96/61/EC [2003] OJ L 275/32 143–44
Parliament and Council Directive (EC) 2004/101 amending Directive 2003/87/EC establishing a scheme for greenhouse gas emission allowance trading within the Community, in respect of the Kyoto Protocol's project mechanisms [2004] OJ L 338/18 88
Council Directive (EC) 2005/35 on ship-source pollution and on the introduction of penalties for infringements [2005] OJ L 255/11. 88
Council Directive (EC) 2006/66 on batteries and accumulators and waste batteries and accumulators and repealing Directive [2006] OJ L 266/1. 125
Parliament and Council Directive (EU) 2015/2193 on the limitation of emissions of certain pollutants into the air from medium combustion plants [2015] OJ L 313/1
Recital 33. 87
Parliament and Council Directive (EU) 2016/680 on the protection of natural persons with regard to the processing of personal data by competent authorities for the purposes of the prevention, investigation, detection or prosecution of criminal offenses or the execution of criminal penalties, and on the free movement of such data, and repealing Council Framework Decision 2008/977/JHA [2016] OJ L 119/89 164
Parliament and Council Directive (EU) 2016/681 on the use of PNR data for the prevention, detection, investigation, and prosecution of terrorist offences and serious crime [2016] OJ L 119/132. 134

EUROPEAN UNION COUNCIL DECISIONS

Council Decision (EC) 2001/748 concerning the signing on behalf of the European Community of the United Nations Protocol on the illicit manufacturing of and trafficking in firearms, their parts, components, and ammunition, annexed to the Convention against transnational organized crime [2001] OJ 280/5. . .132–33
Council Decision (EC) 2003/822 on the accession of the European Community to the Codex Alimentarius Commission [2003] OJ L209/14
Annex III. 65
Council Decision (EC) 2004/496 on the conclusion of an Agreement between the European Community and the United States of America on the processing and transfer of PNR data by Air Carriers to the United States Department of Homeland Security, Bureau of Customs and Border Protection [2004] OJ L 183/83. . . . . .132–33, 178–79
Council Decision (EC) 2004/294 authorising the Member States which are Contracting Parties to the Paris Convention of 29 July 1960 on Third Party Liability in the Field of Nuclear Energy to ratify, in the interest of the European Community, the Protocol amending that Convention, or to accede to it [2004] OJ L 97/53
Recitals 8 to 10. 68
Council Decision (EC) 2005/370 on the conclusion, on behalf of the European Community, of the Convention on access to information, public participation in decision-making and access to justice in environmental matters, OJ [2005] L 124/1 . . . . .140–41, 142
Council Decision (EC) 2006/616 on the conclusion, on behalf of the European Community, of the Protocol Against the Smuggling of Migrants by Land, Sea and Air, supplementing the United Nations Convention Against Transnational Organised Crime concerning the provisions of the Protocol, in so far as the provisions of this Protocol fall within the scope of Articles 179 and 181a Treaty establishing the European Community (TEC) [2006] OJ L 262/24. 132–33
Council Decision (EC) 2006/617 on the conclusion, on behalf of the European Community, of the Protocol Against the Smuggling of Migrants by Land, Sea and Air, supplementing the United Nations

Convention Against Transnational Organised Crime concerning the provisions of the Protocol, in so far as the provisions of the Protocol fall within the scope of Part III, Title IV of the Treaty establishing the European Community (TEC) [2006] OJ L 262/34. 132–33
Council Decision (CFSP) 2007/551 on the signing, on behalf of the European Union, of an Agreement between the European Union and the United States of America on the processing and transfer of PNR data by air carriers to the United States Department of Homeland Security (DHS) (2007 PNR Agreement) [2007] OJ 204/16. 136–37
Council Decision (CFSP) 2010/199 on the EU–Montenegro Agreement on the participation of Montenegro in the European Union military operation to contribute to the deterrence, prevention, and repression of acts of piracy and armed robbery off the Somali coast (Operation Atlanta) [2010] OJ L 88/1 137–38
Council Decision (EU) 2010/427 establishing the organization and functioning of the European External Action Service [2010] OJ L 201/30
Recital 1. . . . . 101, 157
Recital 2. 101
Recital 3. 102
Recital 13. 101
Art 1(2) 102
Art 2 101
Art 2(1) 102
Art 3 102
Art 5(3) 101
Art 8(1) 102–3
Council Decision (CFSP) 2011/133 on the signing and conclusion of the EU–Montenegro Agreement establishing a framework for the participation of Montenegro in European Union crisis management operations [2011] OJ L 57/1 137–38
Council Decision (EU) 2011/199 amending art 136 of the Treaty on the Functioning of the European Union with regard to a stability mechanism for Member States whose currency is the euro [2011] OJ L 91/1
Art 8(1) 114–15
Council Decision (CFSP) 2011/318 on the US-EU Framework Agreement on the participation of the United States of America in European Union crisis management operations [2011] OJ L 143/1. 137–38
Council Decision (CFSP) 2011/640 on the EU–Mauritius Agreement on the conditions of transfer of suspected pirates and associated seized property from the European Union-led naval force to the Republic of Mauritius and on the conditions of suspected pirates after transfer [2011] OJ L 254/1 137–38
Council Decision (EU) 12195/2011 on the conclusion of the Anti-Counterfeiting Trade Agreement between the European Union and its Member States, Australia, Canada, Japan, the Republic of Korea, the United Mexican States, the Kingdom of Morocco, New Zealand, the Republic of Singapore, the Swiss Confederation, and the United States of America [2013] OJ C 349E/552 161–62
Council Decision (CFSP) 2012/315 on the EU–New Zealand Agreement establishing a framework for the participation of New Zealand in European Union crisis management operations [2012] OJ L 160/1. 137–38
Parliament and Council Decision (EU) 1386/2013 on a General Union Environment Action Programme to 2020 'Living well, within the limits of our planet' [2013] OJ L 354/171
Recital 38. 85–86
Council Decision (EU) 2015/798 Authorizing the European Commission to Negotiate, on Behalf of the European Union, Amendments to the Vienna Convention for the Protection of the Ozone Layer and the Montreal Protocol on Substances that Deplete the Ozone Layer [2015] OJ L 127/19
Art 8(1) 115–16
Council Decision (EU) 2016/402 concerning the signing and conclusion of the Agreement between the Council of Ministers of the Republic of Albania and the European Union on security procedures for exchanging and proTreaty establishing the European Community (TEC) ting classified information [2016] OJ L 74/1. 137–38

Council Decision (EU) 2016/437 on the signing, on behalf of the European Union, and provisional application of the Agreement between the European Union and the Republic of Peru on the short-stay visa waiver [2016] OJ L 78/2 136–37
Council Decision (CFSP) 2016/602 on the signing and conclusion of the Participation Agreement between the European Union and the Swiss Confederation on the participation of the Swiss Confederation in the European Union Advisory Mission for Civilian Security Sector Reform Ukraine (EUAM Ukraine) [2016] OJ L 104/1 137–38
Council Decision (CFSP) 2016/1783 on the signing and the conclusion on behalf of the Union of the Agreement in the form of an Exchange of Letters between the European Union and the Islamic Republic of Afghanistan on the extension of the agreement on the status of the European Union Police Mission in Afghanistan (EUPOL AFGHANISTAN) [2016] OJ L 273/1 137–38
Council Decision (EU) 2016/1888 on the signing, on behalf of the Union, and provisional application of the Agreement between the European Union and Solomon Islands on the short-stay visa waiver [2016] OJ L 292/1 136–37
Council Decision (EU) 2016/1946 concerning the signing and conclusion of the Agreement between the European Union and Georgia on security procedures for exchanging and proTreaty establishing the European Community (TEC)ting classified information [2016] OJ L 300/1 137–38
Council Decision (EU) 2016/2079 on the signing, on behalf of the European Union, and provisional application of the Partnership Agreement on Relations and Cooperation between the European Union and its Member States, of the one part, and New Zealand, of the other part [2016] OJ L 321/1. 138
Council Decision (EU) 2016/2220 on the conclusion, on behalf of the European Union, of the Agreement between the United States of America and the European Union on the protection of personal information relating to the prevention, investigation, detection, and prosecution of criminal offences [2016] OJ L 336/1, ... 136–37
Council Decision (CFSP) 2017/718 concerning the signing and conclusion of the Agreement between the European Union and the Republic of Moldova on security procedures for exchanging and protecting classified information [2017] OJ L 106/1 137–38
Council Decision (EU) 2017/1346 on the position to be adopted, on behalf of the European Union, at the sixth session of the Meeting of the Parties to the Aarhus Convention as regards compliance case ACCC/C/2008/32 [2017] OJ L 186/15. 201
Council Decision (CFSP) 2017/2322 concerning the signing and conclusion of the Agreement between Canada and the European Union on security procedures for exchanging and protecting classified information [2017] OJ L 333/1 137–38

NATIONAL LEGISLATION

Belgium

Constitution
Art 42 174–75

France

Constitution
Art 53. 178–79
Art 88-1 to 88-7. 212

Germany

Constitution
Art 23 212
Art 38(1) 174–75
Gesetz über die Zusammenarbeit von Bundesregierung und Deutschem Bundestag in Angelegenheiten der Europäischen Union (EUZBBG) vom 12. März 1993 (BGBl. I S. 311, 1780) 178
Gesetz über die Zusammenarbeit von Bundesregierung und Deutschem Bundestag in Angelegenheiten der Europäischen Union (EUZBBG), vom 4. Juli 2013 (BGBl. I S. 2170). 178
Gesetz zu dem Vertrag vom 2. März 2012 über Stabilität, Koordinierung und

Steuerung in der Wirtschafts- und Währungsunion vom 13. September 2012 (BGBl. II S. 1006). 178
Gesetz zur Änderung des EUZBBG vom 22. September 2009 (BGBl. I S. 3026) . . .178

Italy

Constitution
Art 67. 174–75

Netherlands

Constitution
Art 50 174–75
Art 94 212–13

Slovak Republic

Constitution
Art 7(2) 212

United Kingdom

Human Rights Act 1998 . . . . .96, 212–13
s 2 212–13
s 2(1) 212–13
Art 21(1). 96

List of Abbreviations

ACCC	Aarhus Convention Compliance Committee
ACTA	Anti-Counterfeiting Trade Agreement
AFSJ	Area of Freedom, Security and Justice
ALDE	Alliance for Liberals and Democrats for Europe
BITs	bilateral investment treaties
CAP	Common Agricultural Policy
CCP	Common Commercial Policy
CETA	EU–Canada Comprehensive Economic and Trade Agreement
CFI	Court of First Instance (now General Court)
CFSP	Common Foreign and Security Policy
CJEU	Court of Justice of the European Union
COSAC	Conference of Parliamentary Committees for Union Affairs of Parliaments of the European Union
CSDP	Common Security and Defence Policy
DHS	Department of Homeland Security
ECHR	European Convention on Human Rights
ECOWAS	Economic Community of West African States
ECtHR	European Court of Human Rights
EEA	European Economic Area
EEAS	European External Action Service
EP	European Parliament
ETS	Emissions Trading System
EULEX Kosovo	European Union Rule of Law Mission in Kosovo
Euratom	European Atomic Energy Community
FAO	Food and Agriculture Organization
FEU	Functioning of the European Union
FTA	Free Trade Agreement
GC	General Court
GFCC	German Federal Constitutional Court
HRA	Human Rights Act
ICJ	International Court of Justice
ICS	Investment Court System
ICSID	International Centre for Investment Disputes
ICTs	international courts and tribunals
ILO	International Labour Organization
IMO	International Maritime Organization
ISDS	Investor-State Dispute Settlement
ITLOS	International Tribunal for the Law of the Sea
LIBE	Civil Liberties, Justice and Home Affairs
MEPs	Members of the European Parliament
MoP	Meeting of the Parties
OIV	International Organisation of Vine and Wine
ORCON	originator's consent rule
PCA	Partnership and Cooperation Agreement
PCIJ	Permanent Court of International Justice
PKK	Kurdistan Workers' Party
PNR	passenger name record
REIO	regional economic integration organization

SWIFT	Society for Worldwide Interbank Financial Telecommunication
TEU	Treaty on European Union
TFEU	Treaty on the Functioning of the European Union
TFTP	Terrorist Finance Tracking Programme
TRIPS	Trade-Related Aspects of Intellectual Property Rights
TTIP	Transatlantic Trade and Investment Partnership
UN	United Nations
UNCLOS	UN Convention on the Law of the Sea
UNECE	United Nations Economic Commission for Europe
UNHRC	UN Human Rights Committee
WTO	World Trade Organization

Introduction

External Relations as a Constitutional Challenge*

The European Union seems to operate in a perpetual state of crisis.[1] A series of crises, which all had some trigger outside the territory and jurisdiction of the Union and which, combined with the growing internal disenchantment with the European integration project, have merged into one lingering crisis that the Union still has to shake off. Above all, this crisis is a democratic challenge. Citizens experience a lack of ownership, which is perceived as particularly problematic when the Union is not able to adequately solve the problems with which it is confronted. The most vividly discussed question in this context is: should the response be more Europe or less Europe?

With regard to external relations,[2] the Member States and the EU institutions have opted for more Europe. The Lisbon Treaty (2009) transferred more powers to the Union. It extended the Union's formal competences, for example, to include services, trade-related aspects of intellectual property, and foreign direct investment, as part of the common commercial policy.[3] It also, more importantly, aimed to increase the formal logic and coherence of EU external actions by vesting the Union with legal personality and making it the entity behind all external actions, abolishing the split between the second and third pillar, partially integrating the second pillar, and codifying existing case law, for example on implied external powers.[4] The Union's increased international role is hence the direct consequence of the political decision to extend its legal powers. However, it is also a consequence of an evolution by stealth of international law that has led to the increasing acceptance of non-state actors as international legal subjects and allows international law to have increasing regulatory effects, including in domestic legal orders.

The Union, while externally trying to assert the role of one single international actor, remains internally a complex and compound legal order in which numerous actors, that is, Member States and different EU institutions, participate and struggle for visibility. The apparent contradiction between the Union's ambition to create one uniform international presence and the many internal actors and complex structures is not new but tensions have significantly increased as a result of the Union's extended powers and

* All the weblinks have been checked; last accessed 3 October 2018.

[1] While in 2005 a series of books was published hailing the European way (eg Jeremy Rifkin, *The European Dream: How Europe's Vision of the Future Is Quietly Eclipsing the American Dream* (Tarcher Perigree 2005)), in 2017 books are published questioning not only the legitimacy but also the sustainability of the European project (eg Ivan Krastev, *After Europe* (UPP 2017); Desmond Dinan, Neill Nugent, and William Paterson, *The European Union in Crisis* (Macmillan 2017); Natalia Chaban and Martin Holland (eds), *Communicating Europe in Times of Crisis: External Perceptions of the European Union* (Palgrave Macmillan 2014)).

[2] The terms 'external relations' (emphasis on the law and political interaction between international actors) and 'external actions' (emphasis on the Union's participation and contribution in this), while expressing a different nuance, are used interchangeably.

[3] See for more details Chapter 4 on the consequences of the choice of an external legal basis.

[4] On the Union's strive for coherence see Section 4 of Chapter 3.

ambitions, as well as the political climate within and beyond the Union. These tensions not only influence the Union's external capacity and actions, they also have an impact on the Union's internal constitutional structures. Some of the Union's external actions profoundly change its internal mode of operation and transform the relationship between the Union and its Member States. They influence the settled understanding of certain organizational principles and the Union's division of powers. The role of the EU institutions changes as a result of the EU's external actions. The resulting changes cannot easily be translated into an overall extension or reduction of powers but have more nuanced implications.

External competences are largely considered to develop in parallel to internal competences, both explicitly when indicated in the EU Treaties and implicitly when developed as a result of exercising internal competences.[5] This is reflected in Articles 3(2) and 216(1) TFEU.[6] This is also the position of the Court of Justice of the European Union (CJEU), starting in the 1970s with *ERTA/AETR*.[7] In 2014, the Court prominently confirmed this view of supportive parallelism by ruling that a system of EU internal cooperation justified the need for an exclusive external competence.[8] This book demonstrates, among others, that the opposite is also true, namely that the Union's intensified external exposure has an influence on its delicate internal constitutional structures.

Objective of the Book

This book pursues a twofold objective. First, it identifies nuanced internal legal consequences flowing from EU external actions and second, it connects these legal consequences to the broader debate on the democratic crisis, by engaging with the effects of EU external actions on the deep tissue of the EU, that is, its basic constitutional structures, and the Union's relations with its citizens.

The focus of this book is on the 'outside-in' effects of EU external relations. More specifically, the book aims to shed light on how the Union's external actions influence the making and interpretation of EU law and, more importantly, whether and how this affects the power division between the EU and its Member States, the structures that shape the relationship between the Union and its citizens, as well as the autonomy, effectiveness, and legitimacy of EU law. To this end the book introduces the concept of 'structure of bonding', namely, the deep tissue of the Union, including the formal legal principles and rules that have the potential to frame and affect the Union's relations with its citizens.[9] The concept of bonding structures draws on Jürgen Habermas' work on citizens as dual sovereign, acting as EU citizens and as national citizens at the same time and being represented within the European Union in both capacities.[10]

[5] The Union of course also has external competences that have not developed in parallel to internal ones, such as the Common Foreign and Security Policy, development, and humanitarian aid.

[6] Consolidated Version of the Treaty on the Functioning of the European Union [2008] OJ C115/47 (hereafter TFEU).

[7] Case C-114/12, *Commission v Council (ERTA)* [1971] EU:C:1971:32 (hereafter *ERTA*).

[8] Opinion 1/13 [2014] EU:C:2014:2303, see eg para 74.

[9] Often, but not always, these structures also offer the Union the possibility to justify its actions, purpose, and added value. See Chapter 1 for a conceptualization.

[10] Jürgen Habermas, 'Democracy in Europe: Why the Development of the EU into a Transnational Democracy is Necessary and How it is Possible' (2015) 21 ELJ 546. See also Section 4.1 of Chapter 1.

The following questions guide the inquiry: *What are the implications of the Union's external actions for its internal constitutional structures? What structural transformative changes are triggered by EU external actions?* How do the Union's external actions influence the relations and interactions between the Member States and the Union? How do they affect the emerging structures of bonding between the Union and individuals as EU citizens, as well as the autonomy, effectiveness, and legitimacy of EU law?

In order to adequately address these questions, the legal inquiry in this book is enriched and contextualized by references to broader conceptual studies of loyalty, autonomy, and legitimacy, and is supported by engagement with practices of, for example, the EU institutions and individual politicians. This contextualization introduces a critical distance to the law, case law, and practices of the European Union, as well as the selection of materials.

This book aims to demonstrate that EU external relations have more and (more) far-reaching consequences for the European integration process than is prima facie apparent. These consequences are highly relevant because of the Union's tremendously increased external ambitions and actions. Every Treaty amendment has vested the Union with more comprehensive external competences. Politicians actively emphasize that the Union may have a role to play in ensuring the continuous relevance of Europe in a globalized world.[11] Indeed, external relations offer great possibilities to the Union to make a comprehensible claim of purpose and added value compared to any Member State. The Union has greater capacity than any Member State to retain and regain power over globalizing forces that also impose harmful and unjust consequences on individuals. With its central concept of 'structure of bonding', the book highlights that the Union has something to offer in external relations that goes beyond the argument of greater economic power. Not only because of its size but also because of its institutional set up, commitment to connect to its citizens, autonomy, effectiveness, and legitimacy, the Union has at least the potential to offer its citizens an opportunity to exercise self-determination on the international plane.

The role of the Union in the context of globalization is twofold. On the one hand, Europeanization, that is, EU law setting limits to and determining the content of national law and the legal position of individuals, is a regional expression of globalizing forces, which limits national autonomy. On the other hand, the Union offers Member States and EU citizens a means to amplify their voice in a global context and remain able to influence their own course of action, albeit as part of a bigger group. This leads to a dilemma. How can the Union meet its own ambitions of being an effective external actor without unduly restraining Member States powers, both internally and externally?

This book highlights the emerging formal legal structures of bonding that create a potential for self-determination, participation, and ownership of EU citizens in external relations. It demonstrates how and where organizational principles and rules could be interpreted in a way that strengthens these structures of bonding and clarifies and makes more transparent who is in charge for what. This book also identifies factors that currently weaken clarity and transparency of purpose and responsibility in the context of EU external actions.

Formal legal structures of bonding are not about cultural engineering. Whether they result in practice in a transformation of mentality is not relevant for pointing out their

[11] See for example, Commission President Jean-Claude Juncker, 'The Hour of European Sovereignty', State of the Union 2018 https://ec.europa.eu/commission/news/state-union-2018-hour-european-sovereignty-2018-sep-12_en.

existence. Identification of citizens with the Union is a *possibility* within these legal framework conditions; *not a necessary or perhaps even likely result*. Structures of bonding can and should make the possibility of 'voice' and ownership within the system apparent.[12] This can make an inherent contribution to democratic legitimacy, irrespective of any sense of bonding with the Union or fellow EU citizens. Hence, while it seems unconvincing, both in abstract and in the context of the particular European experience, that law can have a significant *identity creating force* in and of itself, structures of bonding are understood to create formal links between a polity and its citizens, which hold the potential to be filled with an actual sense of bonding.

External relations, however, are particular. They offer, among other things, a possibility of an essentializing dichotomy that allows for an easily palatable and emotionally powerful political narrative of insiders and outsiders. Within the Union, political struggle is often reduced to and portrayed as struggles along nationality lines, with the position and interests of national citizens of one Member State opposed to the position and interests of the national citizens of another Member State. Externally, the position and interests of EU citizens are naturally also opposed to the position and interests of citizens of non-EU countries. The potential of this 'us' and 'them' narrative to contribute to identity forming exists, irrespective of the desirability of developing and deploying it.

Relevance of EU Law

The focus of this book is EU *law*. The underlying assumption is that law is highly relevant to the Union's functioning and legitimacy, and therefore also its crisis. This requires further explanation.

More specifically, this book focuses on EU constitutional and external relations law with particular emphasis on the power-conferring rules and principles that govern the relations between the Union and its Member States and among the EU institutions, as well as the legal structures that relate the Union to its citizens. The legal focus of this book and the lack of engagement with the empirical facts of how citizens actually relate to the Union requires justification. It begs the question: can potential and existing legal formal structures of bonding say anything relevant about the actual relationship of the Union and its citizens and EU citizens among themselves? This book is based on the understanding that bonding structures can say more about citizens' conceptions of the world than one would expect.

Law sets the rules of the power game that is inherent in any human interaction. The more effectively it does so, the less room there is for brute politics, acting on preferences and interests. The EU has been identified as 'a lawyer's paradise'.[13] Law has occupied[14] and continues to occupy an exceptional place within the EU integration project. The relevance of legality is what distinguishes *EU law* from *international relations*. Stricter judicial enforcement is one of the features that distinguishes EU law from *public international law*.

[12] Franz Mayer, 'The Transformation of Europe: Loyalty Lost, Democracy Lost?' in Miguel Poiares Maduro and Marlene Wind (eds), *The Transformation of Europe: Twenty-Five Years On* (CUP 2017) 274ff.

[13] Antoine Vauchez, *Brokering Europe: Euro-Lawyers and the Making of a Transnational Polity* (CUP 2015) 1.

[14] See eg Walter Hallstein, *Europe in the Making* (Charles Roetter tr, Norton 1972).

The ability to adopt secondary law relatively autonomously from the will of individual Member States is what allows the EU—to a certain extent—to live a life of its own, pursue its own path, determine its own destiny, and develop and explicate preferences that—at times—openly contradict preferences voiced by certain Member States. This autonomy is protected by and exercised through EU law. Next to the broad range of policies falling within the scope of EU law and their arguable spill-over effect, the EU's autonomy is one of the features that distinguishes it from international organizations. However, even with its very broad range of powers, EU competences are substantively limited. Common policies in some policy fields and not in others result in a patchwork of EU and national regulation that complements, overlaps, and potentially contradicts each other. This, rather than offering a seamless and coherent coverage of a whole policy field, results in a legal construction that is suboptimal as regards legal certainty, predictability, coherence, and the avoidance of legal gaps.[15] The particular need for flexibility in the Union as a complex and compound legal order with many autonomous actors leads to minimum harmonization, waivers, safeguard-clauses, transition periods, mutual recognition, and optional clauses. All these technical legal constructions are prone to creating internal tensions and increasing inconsistencies.

Institutionally, the Commission and the CJEU are the most relevant institutions reinforcing and pushing forward the centrality of law. The Commission, with its largely exclusive right of initiative, is the driving power behind secondary legislation.[16] Its role and mandate are to act as the guardian of the Treaties and hence the guardian of primary EU law. The CJEU is the institution that is most independent from national political forces. It has set out the originality and autonomy claim of EU law.[17] Yet the CJEU demonstrates awareness of its dependencies on national courts.[18] It has been careful to avoid a parallel of the International Court of Justice's (ICJ) 'Nicaragua moment', when the ignorance and disobedience of a ruling of the Court undermined the credibility, effectiveness, and added value of the whole institution.[19]

Ordering and objectifying are two of the core tasks of law. When cast in law, a certain position is to some extent removed from current political debate. Within the Union, law and politics[20] stand in a particular tension. Law's ordering function is particularly strong. This tension is rooted in the compound or multilevel nature of the European Union and has been explained and theorized, for example under the labels of 'integration through law'[21] and 'overconstitutionalization'.[22] Integration through law identified

[15] Thomas Moellers, 'The Role of Law in European Integration' (2000) 48 AJCL 679, 683. Gráinne de Búrca, 'Rethinking Law in Neofunctionalist Theory' (2006) 12 JEPP 310.

[16] In the context of crisis, the dispersed executive power within the Union (see Chapter 5), where most of the political executive power lies with the European Council, comes into play. The Commission may at times be disenfranchised and reacting to 'invitations' from the European Council. At the same time, Juncker's 'political' Commission has also weakened its role as guardian of the Treaties.

[17] See Chapter 1, Section 3.1. [18] See Chapter 1, Section 3.3.

[19] Military and Paramilitary Activities in and against Nicaragua *(Nicaragua v United States of America)* [1986] ICJ Rep 1986. In this case, the ICJ accepted jurisdiction against a super power with the consequence that the US withdrew its optional clause accepting its compulsory jurisdiction.

[20] To the extent that the distinction makes sense. Law refers to a solidified and formalized expression of political will (constitutional law; legislation) or a judicial decision (case law) of the past, adopted pursuant to specific procedural rules and expressing a particular normative claim. Politics refer to political struggle (see also Chapter 1). Law adopted in the past has a framing and constraining force on present politics, including law-making.

[21] eg Renaud Dehousse and Joseph Weiler, 'The Legal Dimension' in William Wallace (ed), *The Dynamics of European Integration* (Pinter 1990).

[22] Dieter Grimm, 'The Democratic Costs of Constitutionalisation: The European Case' (2015) 21 ELJ 460.

law as the object and motor of integration. The term overconstitutionalization engages with the hierarchy of norms within the EU legal order, in which the CJEU's case law enjoys a semi-constitutional status, de facto benefiting from a certain protection from politics. Only Treaty amendments can consciously depart from the Court's case law and require a joint action by all the Member States, including national ratification. This removes decisions of the Court, including those on 'ordinary' regulatory issues, from the politics within the EU institutions. The cumbersome Treaty amendment procedures further cement a political compromise. Secondary law, translating primary law into rules and regulation, benefits from primacy over national law, including national constitutional law—from the perspective of the CJEU.

Furthermore, three inherent features of EU law favour integration, to some extent irrespective of political will. First, all law, including EU law, is inherently hierarchical. The main aim of legal interpretation and doctrine is to create a logical and coherent system in which lower norms conform to higher norms. This creates a natural bias towards centralization at a 'higher' (in practice: EU) level.[23] Second, EU law was the consciously chosen means to tame national politics, it has been set up as the motor of the European integration project. Third, EU law imposes an economic perspective on policymaking that favours internal market concerns over non-economic concerns,[24] which in a circular logic then justifies EU regulation of the given field. All three features create an inherent bias in favour of EU law as opposed to national law. This makes law and the use and application of law factors that cannot be disregarded in research that engages with powers shifts between the Union and the Member States.

However, analysing the role of law within the Union does not yet address the question of how these basic structures and dynamics are relevant to the individual's relationship with the Union. Legal structures of bonding tell us something relevant about reality because of the normativity of law. The normative power of law in general, and of these basic structures of the legal order in particular, has the ability to affect the real world. Legal structures of bonding do not (at least not necessarily) establish rights or duties. However, they have an influence on how individuals form views, understandings, and opinions about the world around them. Most individuals are at least to some degree and some of the time influenced by the law, not only in their actions[25] but also in their understanding of the world. Law offers the formal structures for interaction as recognized rights holders. It takes decisions about such recognition and political links a priori for individuals and thus frees them to a large extent from having to evaluate their relations both with other individuals and the collective.

Law also plays an important role in the opinion of citizens about the legitimacy of decisions and actions of those in power. Neil MacCormick pointed out that 'political power is rarely independent of legal power'.[26] He further explained that this is the case because 'legitimacy is largely dependent on the possession of power or authority conferred by legal order'.[27] In particular, structures of justification, as a subcategory of

[23] See the Preamble and art 1 TEU: '... the process of creating an ever closer union among the peoples of Europe ...'.

[24] Gareth Davies, 'Democracy and Legitimacy in the Shadow of Purposive Competence' (2015) 21 ELJ 2.

[25] Neil MacCormick develops the notion of *homo juridicus* (parallel to the *homo economicus*) as an ideal-typical person whom he supposes to act with regard to legal requirements, permissions, and empowerments in Neil MacCormick, 'Powers and Power-Conferring Norms' in Stanley Paulson (ed), *Normativity and Norms: Critical Perspectives on Kelsenian Themes* (OUP 1999) 505.

[26] ibid, 497. [27] ibid.

bonding structures, have the potential to contribute to the justifiability and hence legitimacy of Union actions.[28]

This book identifies and explains the influence of the Union's external actions on these structures of bonding, which shape the way citizens perceive the Union and the legitimacy of the Union's actions.

Dilemma

This book demonstrates the internal (de-)centralizing legal consequences of *EU external actions* and argues that the *centralizing effects of law are exacerbated in the context of external relations*. This leads to the dilemma that the Union's external actions increase the influence of the collective in a globalized world, while restricting the autonomy of the Member States. This makes external relations a constitutional challenge for the Union, which might even trigger dynamics that drive the Union apart.

In other words, the analysis of this book raises the question of whether the Union is in danger of falling prey to its own success. Its external powers have increased tremendously because of spill-over effects from national policies and the realization that the Union is in many contexts better placed to represent joint interests. However, this book argues that EU external actions result in an acceleration of national politics being locked into a tightening net of EU law. It demonstrates the nuanced legal consequences of the Union's increased (exercise of) external powers, which seem not to be widely accepted by the Member States and potentially were not fully thought through when the Lisbon Treaty was negotiated. It raises questions such as: how can the multiplicity of actors and interests be coordinated within EU external relations without triggering a centralizing effect through 'unintentional constitutionalization of power-sharing' and 'the routinization of practices'?[29]

Integration contains and channels unilateral national action. This may trigger counter-constitutionalization dynamics, in which incumbents act outside the established structures. Already in 1991, Joseph Weiler predicted the tendency of Member States to flee a constitutional structure that allows less and less national deviation and warned us not to understand the centralization of power in the EU context as a straightforward zero-sum game in which national power is lost.[30] The strengthening of the Union's mandate and competences in external relations, both gradually through the case law of the CJEU and in formal leaps in Treaty amendments, most recently under the Treaty of Lisbon, again raises these fundamental issues of the relationship between the political and the legal sphere, the ability of the Member States to determine their own course of action, and the creation of formal structures of bonding that may (or may not) allow for identification of citizens with the Union as representing them.

Weiler framed Member States' actions intended to avoid the institutional structures and constraints of the Union in terms of voice and exit.[31] This raises particular questions in the context of external relations. Voice can only be exercised internally. Any exercise of voice on the international plane, with third parties involved, in particular if it carries legally binding consequences for the Union, is by definition a form

[28] Section 4 of Chapter 1 develops the book's approach to legitimacy.

[29] Rey Koslowski, 'Understanding the European Union as a Federal Polity' in Thomas Christiansen, Knud Erik Jorgensen, and Antje Wiener (eds), *The Social Construction of Europe* (SAGE 2001) (hereafter Koslowski, 'European Union as a Federal Polity').

[30] Joseph Weiler, 'Transformation of Europe' (1991) 100 Yale LJ 2403.

[31] ibid.

of exit from the joint endeavour. For Member States to act jointly under international law, as they have done, for example, in the context of the financial and economic crises, is a formal collective form of exit from the EU structures. However, the Treaty Establishing the European Stability Mechanism only involves EU Member States as parties. Involvement of non-EU parties would be significantly more problematic in terms of potential international responsibility, entrenchment, and the involvement of parties, who do not share the same interdependent stakes in the functioning of the EU legal order. The Union's increased external actions and their constraining effects on the Member States' ability to act autonomously are particularly prone to trigger exit-strategies on the part of national actors, which may ultimately have disintegrating consequences.

Fear of EU External Actions?

In external relations, more than in any other context, the Member States have codified their concerns that the Union's actions may incrementally limit their powers and margin of manoeuvre. This is the consequence of the dilemma developed above. It is also an indication that Member States are to some extent aware of the hidden integrative forces of the Union's external actions.

Member States submit changes to the Union's external relations powers to national ratification by excluding them from the simplified revision procedure in Article 48(6) TFEU. The Court has the power to review envisaged international agreements (Article 218(11) TFEU) to avoid external (entrenched) commitments that run counter to EU law. More specific examples of codified containment clauses are Articles 191(4) and 207(6) TFEU and Declarations 13 and 14, as well as the protection of the position of Member States in international organizations and of their ability to negotiate international agreements in Articles 209 and 212 TFEU.

Article 191(4) TFEU on environmental policy limits actions by the Union and the Member States explicitly to 'their respective spheres of competence' and expresses that Union action is 'without prejudice to Member States' competence to negotiate in international bodies and to conclude international agreements'. Similarly, aiming to contain a competence creep through the exercise of external powers by the Union, Article 207(6) TFEU stipulates that the exercise of common commercial policy competences 'shall not affect the delimitation of competences between the Union and the Member States and shall not lead to harmonisation of legislative or regulatory provisions of the Member States in so far as the Treaties exclude such harmonisation'. The latter point aims to protect the Member States from harmonization through international agreements that would be excluded in internal market legislation under Article 114 TFEU.[32]

Both Declarations 13 and 14 aim to confine Union powers under the Common Foreign and Security Policy (CFSP). Declaration 13 'underlines' that the CFSP, 'including the creation of the office of High Representative [...] and the establishment of an External Action Service, do not affect the responsibilities of the Member States, as they currently exist, for the formulation and conduct of their foreign policy nor of their national representation in third countries and international organisations'.[33] Declaration 14 adds that CFSP provisions 'will not affect the existing legal basis, responsibilities, and powers of each Member State in relation to the formulation and

[32] See Chapter 4 for more details on this point.
[33] See specifically for the EEAS Section 4 of Chapter 3.

conduct of its foreign policy, its national diplomatic service, relations with third countries and participation in international organisations, including a Member State's membership of the Security Council of the United Nations'. It further 'notes that the provisions covering the [CFSP] do not give new powers to the Commission to initiate decisions nor do they increase the role of the European Parliament'. In these two declarations, Member States highlighted their concern regarding international visibility (representation in third countries and international organizations; diplomatic relations) and continuous presence, in particular in the UN Security Council. They also specified that the role and influence of the EU political institutions that are most autonomous from Member States' influence (Commission and Parliament) should not increase.

The Treaties themselves consequently provide ample reason to doubt the parallelism between internal and external powers of the Union. Rather, they draw attention to what this book sets out to demonstrate: EU external actions have more and (more) far-reaching effects on the division of powers within the Union than is widely acknowledged.

Terminological Clarifications

'Internal' and 'external' in the context of the European Union may require further explanation, as the Union has an ambiguous relationship with territoriality. On the one hand, EU defines its jurisdiction and hence the reach of its law in a territorial way. EU law applies to the territories of the Member States. On the other hand, the EU shares a territory with its Member States. This raises particular issues in the context of international law, which considers the Union to be an international organization that does not possess sovereignty over a territory. 'Internal' in the present book refers to relations within the EU's jurisdiction. 'External' refers to law and actions beyond the jurisdiction of the Union. EU external actions are subject to the rules of international law and usually involve 'external' actors, that is, non-EU states or international organizations.

European 'integration' is understood broadly in this book. It comprises Ernst Haas' conception as a process of shifting 'loyalties, expectations and political activities to a new *centre*, whose institutions possess or demand jurisdiction over pre-existing national states',[34] but goes beyond shifts of loyalties, expectation, and political activities from the Member States to the EU, also including shifts from institutions that are less independent of the Member States (e.g. the Council) to institutions that are more independent of the Member States (e.g. European Parliament; Court), as well as cooperation of the Member States within EU legal structures that have the effect of submitting Member States to EU rules.

'Federalist theory' grapples with the same (de-)centralizing forces that this book examines in the specific context of external relations. As early as 1964, William Riker argued that federal systems either centralize or decentralize but cannot remain stable.[35] Giandomenico Majone coined the catchy phrase 'federalize or perish' to describe this centralization phenomenon.[36] In its general and ideal-type form, federalist theory underpins and protects compound legal orders, with numerous autonomous units.

[34] Ernst Haas, *The Uniting of Europe: Political, Social, and Economic Forces 1950–57* (SUP 1958) 16 (emphasis added).

[35] William Riker, *Federalism: Origin, Operation and Significance* (Little Brown 1964) 7.

[36] Giandomenico Majone, *Europe as the Would-Be World Power* (CUP 2009) 46.

Its objective is not achieving a higher level of effectiveness,[37] but rather protecting unity as well as diversity within one polity,[38] including value-pluralism, diversity, and, most importantly, autonomy of the constituting units. The constituting units must have the power to protect the overall distribution of powers between the central and the constituent units.[39] Scholars have explicitly identified the specific nature of the Union as a 'federation in the becoming'[40] or a 'federation of states',[41] as well as the particularities of the federal traits of the Union.[42] However, those scholars, who refer to 'shared sovereignty of the people(s)', 'compound of constitutions' (*Verfassungsverbund*) or 'demoicracy'[43] in the context of the Union and who identify and endorse gradual integration without compromising the genuine 'statehood',[44] also follow a federalist logic more implicitly. This book uses federalist theory to highlight the fundamental nature of the challenge: the autonomy and effectiveness of the federal level almost inevitably seems to lead to centralization. Federalism is explicitly understood in a non-state-centric way; yet the Union is *contrasted* with federal *states* in order to highlight particular difficulties that it faces because of these differences.

Structure of the Book

This book investigates how the Union's external actions affect the internal constitutional structures of the Union. It explores these effects on foundational concepts, power relations, and bonding structures. This includes shifts of actual power and changes in the understanding of who is in charge and who represents the rights and preferences of individuals.

Chapter 1 sets out the conceptual framework for the rest of the book. It first and foremost develops the meaning and relevance of bonding structures that formally legally connect the Union and its citizens. One prominent example is the European Parliament's legal mandate to represent EU citizens. The chapter further identifies the autonomy and effectiveness of the EU legal order as the unique features that set it apart from international organizations and international law. The potential of structures of bonding depends on these features. Chapter 1 also develops the mutually dependant relationships of autonomy, effectiveness, structures of bonding, and the legitimacy of the Union and its actions. It identifies different dimensions of legitimacy and emphasizes, drawing on Habermas, justifiability or, even more precisely, worthiness of recognition (*Annerkennungswürdigkeit*) as the core of legitimacy. Justification to individuals, as EU citizens and national citizens, returns in all the following chapters as a necessary precondition for legitimacy and as the core potential of bonding structures.

[37] Anna Gamper, 'A Global Theory of Federalism: The Nature and Challenges of the Federal State' (2005) 6 Ger LJ 1297, 1310 (hereafter Gamper, 'Theory of Federalism').

[38] WS Livingston, 'A Note on the Nature of Federalism' (1952) 67 PSQ 81, 88.

[39] Gamper, 'Theory of Federalism' (n 37) 1307.

[40] For a short historic overview of the federalist persuasion: Chapter 2 'Federalism Old and New' in Majone, *Europe as the Would-Be Power* (n 36) 46ff.

[41] Robert Schütze, *From Dual to Cooperative Federalism: The Changing Structure of European Law* (OUP 2009).

[42] Phillip Dann, *Parlamente im Exekutivföderalismus* (Springer-Verlag 2004).

[43] Kalypso Nicolaïdis, 'European Demoicracy and Its Crisis' (2012) 51 JCMS 351.

[44] eg discussed by: Stefan Oeter, 'Federalism and Democracy' in Armin von Bogdandy and Jürgen Bast (eds), *Principles of European Constitutional Law* (2nd edn, Hart Publishing 2009).

Chapters 2 and 3 focus on organizational principles, which establish and guide the process and the scope for institutional action in the EU.[45] They are determinative for the interpretation of the procedural rules of how power is exercised. Hence they have a high indirect relevance for the division of powers. The CJEU has made this most explicit with regard to the principle of sincere cooperation: it does not change the existence or boundaries of powers under the Treaties, but it legally restrains the institutions and the Member States in their ability to exercise these powers.[46] The effects for the division of powers are quite apparent for sincere cooperation (Chapter 2), subsidiarity and primacy (Chapter 3). For coherence this may be prima facie less apparent and is explained in more detail in the introduction to Chapter 3. Other principles that one may expect in this context, such as the principle of conferral and the institutional balance are not discussed in their own right but more indirectly in Chapter 4 on the choice of the correct legal basis (conferral) and Chapter 5 on inter-institutional power shifts (institutional balance).

Chapter 2 discusses the legal consequences and deeper meaning of EU loyalty. It identifies specific active and passive obligations flowing from the principle of sincere cooperation in the context of EU external relations and argues that they are best understood as forming part of a comprehensive duty of loyalty, which endows EU membership with a distinctive meaning. EU loyalty is central to imposing a quasi-federal discipline and making sovereign states 'Member States of the EU'. It legally restrains Member States from exercising their rights as independent international actors in a way that finds no parallel beyond the European Union. It may require placing the common Union interest above the national interests. The concept of unity of international representation has a particular capacity to deepen and widen the obligations flowing from EU loyalty. It amplifies the effects of EU loyalty on the scope of legal action of the Member States, including in the field of reserved competences. It is also part of the explanation of why loyalty has more stringent consequences externally rather than internally. This in turn means that the duty of loyalty has a particular integrative force in the context of external relations. Chapter 2 also argues that this stringent understanding of EU loyalty is justified by the nature of external relations and that this justification should be (better) explicated by the EU institutions and the Member States.

Chapter 3 identifies how the principles of subsidiarity, primacy, and coherence are interpreted in the context of external relations. When Union action gives effect to international law, for example, this is portrayed by the EU institutions as amounting in certain circumstances to an assumption that the requirements of subsidiarity are met. However, subsidiarity is regularly reduced to an economic concept focused on increasing effectiveness. The chapter highlights the democratic legitimacy dimension of subsidiarity. It argues that, in particular, the principle of subsidiarity forms part of the bonding structures because it offers a formal legal opportunity to justify Union action and explicate that the Union is better placed to represent its citizens externally. With regard to primacy, Chapter 3 demonstrates that this principle is the necessary precondition for both the autonomy and effectiveness of the EU legal order. The chapter then explains how EU external relations may put primacy under pressure. It gives a glimpse

[45] This book focuses on organizational principles that are particularly relevant for the power relations between the Union and the Member States and among the EU institutions, rather than among the Member States.

[46] Case C-28/12, *Commission v Council* [2015] EU:C:2015:282; Case C-246/07, *Commission v Sweden (PFOS)* [2010] EU:C:2010:203.

of why national courts may rebel against the primacy of EU law because of this external pressure. Finally, Chapter 3 turns to the principle of coherence. It argues that the Lisbon Treaty made a choice for coherence through ambiguity, which empowers the Court and contributes to the opaqueness of decision-making in the context of external relations. It then argues that (perceived) coherence and predictability are necessary preconditions for bonding structures to realize their potential. Justifiability and hence legitimacy require a certain level of coherence and predictability.

Chapter 4 discusses the constitutional consequences of the choice of legal basis in the context of external relations. The Union and its Member States are interlocked in a tight embrace, which leads to a far more complicated power division than may appear from a straightforward reading of the Treaty provisions on competences. The choice of the appropriate legal basis is the legal emanation of internal power struggles between the Member States and the Union and among the EU institutions. The chapter identifies situations, in which the fact that law-making moves from the internal EU sphere to the external, that is, international, sphere places more far-reaching restrictions on the Member States' exercise of powers than would apply internally. It also argues that clarity in attributing responsibilities is a foundational requirement for bonding structures in a divided representative democracy, in which individuals are represented as EU citizens and national citizens. An adequate level of clarity on who is responsible for what is a necessary, albeit insufficient, condition for feeling represented and for limiting the ability of representatives to deny responsibilities. Finally, the chapter illustrates how the international obligations of the Member States are vested with the particular bite, namely, effectiveness, of EU law when the Union becomes next to the Member States a contracting party to an international agreement, that is, when a mixed agreement is concluded. This limits the scope of manoeuvre of Member States as international actors.

In Chapter 5, the book turns to the institutional relationships within the European Union. It identifies power shifts between the EU institutions that take place when the Union acts under international law and in cooperation with third countries or international institutions, rather internally. The focus is, in particular, on the role of the European Parliament. The fact that the conclusion of EU international agreements depends on the consent of Parliament gives EU citizens a voice in international relations, which, with all its flaws, draws on a source of democratic legitimation that is independent and separate from the EU Member States. Parliament's position in negotiating and concluding international agreements and its ability to represent EU citizens (and also non-economic interests) in external relations is analysed as an emerging formal structure of bonding.

The final chapter, Chapter 6, examines the consequences of the Union's submission to the jurisdiction of international courts and tribunals (ICTs) for the autonomy of the European legal order. In fact, no discussion of the effects of external relations on the internal constitutional structures would be complete without considering the specific and ever-increasing external pressure from ICTs that led the Court to take a rather protective and controversial position, for example, in Opinion 2/13 (EU accession to the European Convention on Human Rights (ECHR)) and the case of *Achmea* (investment arbitration).[47] It concentrates on three ICTs that have, in the eyes of the Court or the Commission, raised particular issues for the autonomy of the EU legal order: investor-state dispute settlement (ISDS) mechanisms, the Aarhus Convention

[47] Opinion 2/13 (Accession to ECHR) [2014] EU:C:2014:2454; Case C-284/16, *Slovak Republic v Achmea BV* [2018] EU:C:2018:158.

Compliance Committee, and the European Court of Human Rights after the EU's accession to the ECHR. The chapter draws the conclusion that, under certain circumstances, the CJEU's concern that ICTs may threaten the autonomy of the EU legal order is plausible and links this conclusion to the potential of emerging structures of bonding within the EU legal order, as well as the effectiveness and legitimacy of the Union and its actions. Simply put, conceptual legal autonomy is needed for all three. Indeed, the very potential of structures of bonding depends on autonomy. One can only bond with an autonomous entity.

The Conclusions bring the findings of the previous chapters together and articulate them in a consistent narrative that EU external relations not only have specific legal consequences but also affect the Union's constitutional structures at a deeper level. The Union has established itself as an autonomous legal entity in multiple ways, whose law enjoys a unique effectiveness in practice and established numerous direct links with its citizens that create formal legal structures of bonding. These structures could and should serve as structures of justifiability, in which the Union directly addresses its citizens and explicates its purpose and added value, including in terms of democratic representation in external relations.

On a final note, I should add that this book is written from a position that is strongly sympathetic towards the European integration project. It is motivated by genuine concern for the project. At the same time, I do not argue for or against increasing the competences or influence of the European Union in any particular policy field. The question of what the balance of competences should be does not concern me in this book. I simply want to bring to light the oft-hidden effects of EU external actions on the power divisions within the European Union and, in a second step, draw conclusions about how these effects may influence the links between the Union and its citizens, as well as the Union's autonomy, effectiveness, and legitimacy. I do argue in favour of strengthening the Union's bonds with its citizens, and explicating and justifying its actions and purpose, in order to increase its legitimacy.

Any evaluation of the EU, its ability to connect to and represent individuals, and to represent EU interests internationally, should be aware of an important pitfall: using the state paradigm as the starting point or an implicit comparison entails the danger of applying an unsuited standard. Furthermore, state paradigms refer to ideal types, while in practice states fall short of these ideals in many ways, including their ability to represent, their effectiveness, and legitimacy. The explicit perspective of this book is that the EU is not a state and neither does it nor should it aspire to become a (super) state, including in external relations.

1

Conceptual Toolkit

Bonding Structures, Autonomy, Effectiveness, and Legitimacy

1. Introduction

National and EU law interlock in a tight embrace. Legal, economic, and social interdependencies are both amplified and mitigated within the Union. EU citizens are directly affected by EU law and directly represented in the Union's political structures. The EU legal order makes a claim to autonomy and takes the role of an independent international actor. While many of the core principles that govern the functioning of the EU legal order, such as primacy, direct effect, or sincere cooperation, are not unique to EU law and also exist in a different form and shape in international law, the EU legal order is *unique* in its ability to give effect to EU law within the national legal orders and create direct links with its citizens (structures of bonding).

This chapter first conceptualizes 'structures of bonding', understood as formal legal connections between individuals and the Union through EU law, which prima facie entail a potential for bonding between EU citizens and the Union, as well as among individuals as EU citizens. The potential of legal structures of bonding depends on, and can only be reasonably spoken about because of, the unique effectiveness of EU law. The Union's ability to change the legal position of individuals is what makes it possible for individuals to experience the Union and its law as directly relevant. This immediate relevance does not require active engagement, such as voting, participating, becoming politically involved. It exists for every EU citizen and anyone present within the territories of the Member States via *national* law, courts, and administrations. Individuals simply cannot avoid contact with EU law.

The extraordinary level of effectiveness and the autonomous, that is, self-referential, character of EU law on which this effectiveness depends is the second focus of this chapter. Effectiveness is understood as the ability to determine the law of the land, including the legal situation and relations of individuals, not only with regard to the state but also with regard to each other. It depends on the ability of the Court of Justice (CJEU) to interpret EU law effectively and uniformly in a self-referential fashion. It is solely because EU law is authoritatively interpreted as self-referential and hence not depending on national or international law that it can deploy its unique effectiveness, and immediately and ultimately determine the legal situations of individuals. If EU law depended for its validity on national or international law, it could not determine what the law of the land is in the same way as it does at present.

Third, the chapter sets out different aspects of legitimacy. The presumption is that any exercise of public power must be legitimate, in particular, however, those that have tangible and far-reaching legal effects and directly determine the legal situation of individuals. Structures of bonding offer the potential for explicit justification of Union action towards its citizens, which is a central form of legitimation. Both autonomy and effectiveness also depend on the willingness of national actors, above all courts, but also politicians and citizens, to rely on and comply with EU law, interpreted as autonomous and effective by the CJEU. This willingness is directly connected to the (perceived) legitimacy of EU law and the understanding that it is the law of a polity to which these actors see themselves as belonging. The potential sense of belonging closes the circle of structures of bonding.

Bonding structures, as well as the effectiveness and legitimacy of EU law are not integration neutral. They directly and indirectly influence the power division between the Union and its Member States. This is most apparent for the effectiveness of EU law, which has an inherent centralizing force. For EU law to be effective, it relies inter alia on primacy and direct effect, which lead to setting aside conflicting national law. This is a form of integration in practice, even if the national norm remains valid. Structures of bonding may also entail centralizing dynamics when they establish autonomous direct links between the Union and its citizens, which no longer involve the Member States as intermediates. Similarly, they contribute to legitimacy by allowing the Union to directly justify its action towards its citizens. Autonomy as such is a precondition for the Union's ability to act effectively and justifiably and, ultimately, to bond with its citizens. It does not necessarily trigger integrating dynamics; however, in its broad interpretation of the Court, it also protects the ability of the EU institutions to act autonomously from Member State interference and hence the supranational nature of these institutions.

This first chapter serves as a toolkit for the remaining five chapters of the book. It is structured as follows. Section 2 explains the notion of formal legal 'structures of bonding'. It then identifies some structures of bonding under EU law that confer on individuals the role of subjects of the EU legal order. Individuals are the ultimate point of reference for the legitimacy of EU action. They are the holders of rights and obligations under EU law. Union action must be justified to them. The notion of bonding structures is used in the rest of the book to identify effects of Union external relations on the deeper tissue of the EU legal order. Section 3 argues that autonomy and effectiveness of EU law are the two interdependent characteristics that distinguish it from international law and that vests structures of bonding under EU law with the potential to facilitate actual bonding. Section 3.1 introduces the CJEU's autonomy narrative, which is in practice accepted because of the interlocking embrace among all internal actors and legal spheres, as explained in Section 3.2. Section 3.3 sets out the preliminary ruling procedure as the institutional backbone of the autonomy and effectiveness of EU law. Sections 3.4 and 3.5 discuss the fragility of the interlocking embrace and of the 'otherness', that is, autonomy of the EU legal order, respectively. Section 4 distinguishes different aspects of the legitimacy of EU law (Section 4.1) and explicates the links between legitimacy and autonomy (Section 4.2). Section 4.3 purports that the Union's ability to allow representation of its citizens in external relations is a powerful justification for the Union's existence and could as such serve as a potential source to strengthen its legitimacy. Section 5 concludes.

2. Structures of Bonding

This book focuses on the power relations within the European Union. Prima facie this appears to place the institutions and Member States, rather than EU citizens, in the centre of the discussion. However, since the very inception of the European integration project, individuals have played a highly relevant role in the dynamic power relations within the European legal order. The remainder of this section sets out structures of bonding between the Union and its citizens, with a focus on how they experience EU law as a source of rights and obligations and view the Union (potentially) as a political entity that represents them. It closes by relating these legal structures to politics.

The European Treaties offer individuals a sufficiently stable institutional framework that formally allows for safe and durable input and participation as *subjects*, that is, active shapers of the rules of the polity rather than just objects of the rules of others. They create formal structures of reference (*Bezugsstrukturen*) and structures of bonding (*Bindungsstrukturen*) that have the potential of allowing individuals to be and feel represented in decision-making, and to directly participate and experience (a sense of) self-determination. *Structures of bonding* are legal mechanisms, principles, and rules that allow for an emerging core political affiliation. This also entails some potentially centralizing effects, moving some affiliation towards the Union. Law permits the establishment of formal, general, and anonymous structures of mutual recognition for rights holders and participants, which create systemic relationships and unburden individuals from having to take specific decisions involving integration. Law is also a central tool of political self-determination.

The term 'bonding structures' is focused on revealing the political dimension of legal phenomena.[1] Bonding structures are, for example, formal channels for providing input, applying control, and exercising rights. They express voluntary choices of loyalty towards a polity and fellow citizens and make visible links of legitimation and representation. They refer not only to vertical relationships between institutions and individuals, but also have the potential to trigger bonding between individuals within a given collective (here the EU). Individuals relate to each other when they exercise political power within an institutional system—communicate through media or public deliberation. Different structures of bonding may have different potential in this respect. Arguably, relying on EU law to enforce individual rights (direct effect) is different in this respect from participation in a political system. This is why rights are fundamentally important but other bonding structures may have a greater potential to create bonds of collectivity. The next two subsections in turn discuss rights under EU law and representation within and throughout the European Union.

2.1 EU law as source of rights and obligations

The original Treaties have established only a tenuous formal link between EU law and individuals as holders of rights and obligations. The CJEU established this (missing) link over time, followed by widespread compliance but only very weak codification.[2] In its most foundational case law of Member States it spoke of having 'created a body of law which *binds both their nationals* and themselves'.[3] It held that the Treaty obligation in question 'is [...] legally complete in itself and is consequently capable of producing direct effects on the relations between Member States and individuals' and that it 'became an integral part of the legal system of the Member States, forms part of the law

[1] See on this political dimension: Martin Loughlin, 'What is Constitutionalisation?' in Petra Dobner and Martin Loughlin (eds), *The Twilight of Constitutionalism?* (OUP 2010) (hereafter Loughlin, 'What is Constitutionalisation?'), as well as Martin Loughlin, *Foundations of Public Law* (OUP 2010).

[2] A reference to direct effect is still absent in the Treaties; on primacy, see Declaration 17, which is essentially a codified reference to the Court's case law.

[3] Case 6/64, *Flaminio Costa v ENEL* [1964] EU:C:1964:66 593–94 (hereafter Case 6/64, *Costa v ENEL*) (emphasis added).

of those States and directly concerns their nationals, in whose favour it has created individual rights which national courts must protect'.[4] The Court hence emphasized the direct link between the EU legal order and individuals ('nationals' rather than nations or peoples of the Member States) and established a triangular relationship, in which the EU shares a direct link both with the Member States and with individuals, and in which EU law also changes the relationship between Member States and their nationals. Individuals are vested with enforceable rights by the combined effect of the CJEU's doctrines of primacy and direct effect, supported by the formalized judicial discourse under the preliminary ruling procedure.[5]

The very origins of the EU's creation of rights of individuals lie within the internal market. Free movement provisions offered individuals 'constitutional rights', enforceable against Member States, protected from national political intervention and enforced by the national judiciary.[6] Furthermore, nowadays, 'European citizenship' is a key element in the process of European integration, which brings political rights to all EU citizens, including those who have not exercised their free movement rights. It is one of the most prominently discussed structures of bonding, both between the Union and its citizens and among citizens. Externally, citizenship entails 'the right to enjoy, in the territory of a third country in which the Member State of which they are nationals is not represented, the protection of the diplomatic and consular authorities of any Member State on the same conditions as the nationals of that State . . .'.[7] This is a direct and practical added value of EU citizenship for citizens abroad.

Structures of bonding, however, do not necessarily confer rights or impose obligations on individuals. Some structures of bonding are simply formal legal occasions that allow and require the Union to publicly justify its actions. The next section discusses representation of citizens within the Union as a necessary element to justify Union action.

2.2 Representation within the Union

The European Treaties express the Union's commitment that 'the functioning of the Union shall be founded on representative democracy'.[8] The Union provides EU citizens with possibilities of direct and indirect input into Union decision-making. 'Direct input' refers to the ability of citizens to voice their position in the institutional context of the EU (eg in elections to the European Parliament or through participation in 'citizen initiatives'). 'Indirect input' refers to the ability of citizens to voice their positions in and through national structures (eg national parliaments; referendums). Article 10(2) s.1 TEU explains that 'Citizens are directly represented at Union level in the European Parliament'.[9] This is the most robust and comprehensive channel of direct legitimation of Union action, because of the influential role of Parliament in most decision-making procedures, for example, co-legislator under ordinary legislative

[4] ibid, 596 (emphasis added).

[5] Christina Eckes, 'The Court of Justice's Participation in the Judicial Discourse: Theory and Practice' in Marise Cremona and Anne Thies (eds), *The European Court of Justice and External Relations: Constitutional Challenges* (Hart Publishing 2014).

[6] Poiares Maduro, *We, the Court* (Hart Publishing 1998); Loïc Azoulai, 'The Court of Justice and the Social Market Economy: The Emergence of an Ideal and the Conditions for its Realisation' (2008) 45 CML Rev 1335, 1342–43.

[7] Consolidated Version of the Treaty on the Functioning of the European Union [2008] OJ C115/47 (hereafter TFEU), art 23.

[8] Art 10(1) TEU.

[9] This is further detailed in arts 223ff TFEU.

procedure and consent giver for the conclusion of most international agreements.[10] It is an independent (and internationally unique) source of supranational legitimacy that is not rooted in a technocratic, but a democratic justification. Article 10(2) s 2 TEU sets out the two main channels of *indirect* legitimation:[11] Member States are represented in the European Council by their Heads of State or Government and in the Council by their governments, which are accountable to their national parliaments and citizens.

The two strands of direct and indirect representation, and hence legitimacy, run parallel; they do not depend or build on each other. This places Parliament in a *partnership* position with the Council rather than in the position of a loyal majority provider or a direct instance of control.[12] Furthermore, the Treaty of Lisbon explicated the institutional powers and legitimation of the European Parliament. Article 14(2) TEU states that '[t]he European Parliament shall be composed of representatives of the Union's citizens'. This is a reference to a collective unity that did not exist before.[13] Pre-Lisbon, the European Parliament was referred to as the representative body of the *peoples of the States brought together in the Community*.[14] At the same time, the current procedures for the elections to the European Parliament may not be seen as fully decoupled from the peoples of the Member States.

'Every citizen shall have the right to participate in the democratic life of the Union. Decisions shall be taken as openly and as closely as possible to the citizen.'[15] This relates democratic legitimacy to the principle of subsidiarity.[16] National parliaments also have a limited direct role in EU decision-making in the context of subsidiarity,[17] adding a layer of autonomous legitimation through state structures in which citizens act as national citizens. Formally, the Union can hence trace its actions in many ways back to its citizens. The next section relates the formal legal structures of identity forming and political struggle within the EU.

2.3 Legal structures and politics

Legal structures of bonding frame *politics*, understood as sites for deliberation, as well as political struggle. At the same time, they allow for symbolism of the *political*, understood as an image of the polity, for example, as a community of fate.[18] The political interacts and is interconnected with politics as the (antagonistic) struggle for power among different actors. At the same time, the two must necessarily be distinguished.

EU law remains close to, if not dependent on, state-dominated power politics. Amending the European Treaties is the privilege of the Member States. The European Council, as a strongly intergovernmental institution, has in the past decade assumed the role of determining not only the direction but also the pace and means to achieve this. At the same time, EU law as it is construed by the Court and also often by scholars of EU law remains an ideological project, which considers, without much further supporting argument, unity as a value elevated above politics. The Union however, as every political system, takes decisions that produce winners and losers. Substantive

[10] Art 218 TFEU. See Chapter 5 for more details.
[11] This is further detailed in arts 15 and 16 TEU.
[12] Philipp Dann, *Parliamente im Exekutivföderalismus* (Springer-Verlag 2004) 7.
[13] See also: Jörg Gerkrath, 'Representation of Citizens by the EP' (2005) 1 ECL Rev 73, 75.
[14] Art 189 EC. [15] Art 10(3) TEU.
[16] Art 5(3) TEU. See Chapter 3 for the links between subsidiarity and democratic legitimation in the context of external relations.
[17] Protocol 2 on subsidiarity and proportionality, in particular art 7.
[18] See the following discussion.

disagreement and potential conflict are therefore inevitable. This requires the EU to allow for political struggle in order to permit individuals to feel ownership for contestable decisions. Politicization of the Union may feel like stemming the tide. However, lack of ownership and the resulting feeling of being exposed to decisions that one cannot influence is perceived as a risk by individuals and the national polity. Any domestic polity must fight against such a risk of heteronomy, as an act of sovereign rearing up.

The political, in contrast to politics, has been conceptualized as institutionalized power that has the ability to draw people together in a consensual way.[19] It is rooted in trust and requires constraints and controls exercised by those drawn together over those who govern. The political is also the way the polity develops and presents its own unity both vis-à-vis itself and vis-à-vis external actors.[20] This image is influenced by and to some extent a reflection of the internal and external struggles. The political consists of social and personal relations of a lasting duration.[21] These relations are constructed both consensually (formation of a common identity) and in contrast with the other (distinct from others).

In the understanding presented here, both politics and the political are necessary for a democratic polity. In fact, democracy keeps the vacuum empty, following Lefort, that has emerged from the fact that sovereignty is no longer of divine origin and will. This is the first and foremost characteristic of the political in a democracy.[22] This is possible through politics, through the continuous struggle of actors, visions, and positions. This continuous struggle rejects establishing any one unified image. It hence resists any one singular position or image filling the empty space. If political struggle is so inherently important to a democracy, this begs the question of whether the EU, with its many institutional structures and tactics to avoid politics and present an image of unity,[23] is at all able to function as a democracy that keeps the space of power empty.

Potentially, the formal structures of bonding could contribute to understanding the Union—from the perspective of the individual—as a bonding community (*Bindungsg emeinschaft*)[24] and hence help to frame political struggle as part of seeking a joined way forward (voice), rather than a rejection of cooperation all together (exit). This potential exists, irrespective of whether bonding is possible with several entities or, as some argue, that inevitably the strongest form of identification (*Bindung*) can only emerge with *one* entity, which is at present the state.[25] The latter position does not exclude, as a matter of principle, a development in which the EU could take the position of the entity with the strongest identification for individuals. This is only excluded if one necessarily and inextricably links sovereignty of the people to state sovereignty, as national constitutional courts do.[26] Others have argued that democratic legitimacy of the EU, if it reaches a certain level, will actually trigger the very exclusionary processes that the EU wanted to work against.[27]

[19] See Loughlin (n 1).

[20] See for the distinction: Claude Lefort, 'The Political and the Social' in Claude Lefort, *Complications: Communism and the Dilemmas of Democracy* (Julian Bourg tr, Col UP 2007) 113–14.

[21] Claude Lefort, 'The Permanence of the Theologico-Political?' in Claude Lefort, *Democracy and Political Theory* (Polity 1988) 217–21.

[22] Martin Loughlin, 'The Concept of Constituent Power' (2013) 13 Eur J Pol T 218, 233–34, referring to 'the people-as-one' as 'the hallmark of totalitarianism', with a reference to Claude Lefort's work.

[23] eg the absence of dissenting opinions in the CJEU; the consensus-seeking mentality in Council meetings.

[24] See for the German terminology: Stefan Haack, *Verlust der Staatlichkeit* (Mohr Siebeck 2007).

[25] ibid. [26] See Section 2.3 above.

[27] Floris de Witte, *We, the People of Europe* (PUP 2004), citing Balibar. See also: Anand Menon and Steven Weatherill, 'Democratic Politics in a Globalising World: Supranationalism and Legitimacy in

The potential of 'othering' is particularly inherent in EU external relations. Othering is a powerful identity shaper.[28] The us- and them-narratives shift as compared to internal EU politics. Internally, inclusiveness is the default within the Union; yet conflicts are framed as interests of the nationals of one Member State clashing with those of the nationals of another Member State. Externally the us- and them-narratives are very different. EU citizens are legally structurally represented as one 'we' through the EU institutions. Any sense of being European is logically linked to what is not European. This is true not only for cultural identity but also for civic identity. At the community and ultimately identity-forming level, the external is relevant not only because of who is in and who is out, but also who one is by distinction.[29] Only outside Europe is being European a distinguishing characteristic.

The political emerges as *distinction over time,* as seeing oneself by contrast to the 'other' or 'foreign'.[30] It may also change over time. This connects to Anderson's well-known understanding of collectivity and polity as an 'imagined community',[31] and hence 'not an inevitable one'.[32] *Legal* structures of bonding however emerge in a jurisdiction and hence presuppose a choice of who forms part of the community and who does not. This solidifies—as law does by definition—the *status quo* and works against the fluidity of Anderson's concept of an 'imagined community'. In any event, the Union's actual success in establishing itself as an imagined community remains highly contentious.[33] The voter turnout in the direct elections to the European Parliament has declined each time since 1979 and finally stabilized at the low level of 42%.[34] This seems to indicate that the legal potential for bonding and creating a framework for politics and democratic deliberation has not been realized in practice, irrespective of the increasing formal powers of the European Parliament. At the same time, the 87th

the European Union' LSE Law, Society and Economy Working Paper 13/2007 http://www.lse.ac.uk/law/working paper series/2007-08/WPS13-2007MenonandWeatherill.pdf.

[28] See fundamentally Carl Schmitt's essentialist conception of politics as making a distinction:

> Die Unterscheidung von Freund und Feind hat den Sinn, den äußersten Intensitätsgrad einer Verbindung oder Trennung, einer Assoziation oder Dissoziation zu bezeichnen [...]. Der politische Feind braucht nicht moralisch böse, er braucht nicht ästhetisch häßlich zu sein [...]. Er ist eben der andere, der Fremde, und es genügt zu seinem Wesen, daß er in einem besonders intensiven Sinne existenziell etwas anderes und Fremdes ist, so daß im extremen Fall Konflikte mit ihm möglich sind, die weder durch eine im voraus getroffene generelle Normierung, noch durch den Spruch eines 'unbeteiligten' und daher 'unparteiischen' Dritten entschieden werden können.

Carl Schmitt, *Der Begriff des Politischen* (Duncker & Humblot GmbH 1932) 27. For a translation, see *The Concept of the Political* (George Schwab tr, Chicago Press 2007).

[29] The reference to European identity in the Preamble of the TEU refers explicitly to the external (and, strikingly, is framed in the context of a possible common *defence*).

[30] In that sense it is similar to identity: Anthony Smith, *National Identity* (UNP 1991) 8.

[31] See Benedict Anderson, *Imagined Communities: Reflections on the Origin and Spread of Nationalism* (Verso 1983). Anderson argues that the development of printed press provided the foundation for the development of national consciousness by creating a common, standardized language. This form of communication essentially allowed previously disconnected people to connect on an imaginative level and see themselves as part of a larger community.

[32] John Boli, 'Sovereignty from a World Polity Perspective' in Stephen Krasner (ed), *Problematic Sovereignty: Contested Rules and Political Possibilities* (CUP 2001) 54.

[33] Ulrich Haltern, 'On Finality' in Armin von Bogdandy and Jürgen Bast (eds), *Principles of European Constitutional Law* (Hart Publishing 2006).

[34] From 61.99% in 1979 to 42.61% in 2014. Arguably the decline between 2009 and 2014 was only 0.36% http://www.europarl.europa.eu/elections2014-results/en/turnout.html.

Standard Eurobarometer in 2017 celebrated the highest percentage ever of citizens feeling that they are *also EU citizens* (68%).[35]

Most important in the present context is that the actual emergence of a political image of the Union is not determinative for the discussion of the existence and emergence of formal legal structures of bonding in the remainder of this book. The book identifies how the law creates formal framework conditions of potential bonding. It does not address the empirical, sociological question of whether actual bonding takes place. It does, however, assume that the process of making bonding structures visible, such as using veto powers in the conclusion of international agreements, increases the potential of these structures and that this also increases the potential for allowing politics within these structures.

This section conceptualized and set out structures of bonding within the EU legal order. It also emphasized the need for allowing politics and an exchange of arguments within and about these bonding structures. The next section sets out two unique features of the Union that make it reasonable to assume that structures of bonding between the Union and its citizens hold potential for actual bonding.

3. Autonomy and Effectiveness

The potential of the structures of bonding within the EU rests on two combined unique characteristics of EU law: its autonomy and its effectiveness. These two characteristics are discussed together because, while they can be and will be conceptually distinguished, they depend on each other and are inseparably connected. The effectiveness of EU law allows it to ensure its uniform application within the legal orders of the Member States and directly determine the legal position of individuals. This effectiveness is the source of the Union's legal power, which can be defined as 'the legally conferred ability to alter the legal situations or relationships of legal persons'.[36] The effectiveness of EU law in the national legal order, including in situations of conflicts between EU and national law, have by definition an integrative effect.

The effectiveness of EU law flows above all from the teleological, purposive interpretation by the CJEU of a combination of legal doctrines, such as direct effect, primacy, and sincere cooperation, but also the doctrine of implied powers. It can only be maintained based on the internal validity of the narrative of the autonomous legal order. Effectiveness hence depends on autonomy, that is, the self-referential nature, of the EU legal order. Autonomy is an a priori presumption; however, the ability of the CJEU to maintain the autonomy narrative depends on the effectiveness of EU law, in particular the willingness of national courts to vest EU law with effect within the national legal order and so confirm its autonomy and primacy.

The CJEU considers the autonomy and effectiveness of EU law to be Razian second-order reasons (trumping meta-considerations), which displace all first-order reasons (other legal considerations).[37] EU law does not actually possess any formal codified

[35] Standard Eurobarometer 87, based on interviews conducted between 20 and 29 May 2017 http://ec.europa.eu/commfrontoffice/publicopinion/index.cfm/Survey/getSurveyDetail/instruments/STANDARD/surveyKy/2142.

[36] Neil MacCormick, 'Powers and Power-Conferring Norms' in Stanley Paulson (eds), *Normativity and Norms: Critical Perspectives on Kelsenian Themes* (OUP 1999) 500.

[37] Raz calls first-order considerations: 'reasons for action' that have been drawn directly from 'considerations of interest, desire or morality' and second-order considerations: 'reason[s] to act on or refrain from acting on a reason', see Joseph Raz, *Practical Reason and Norms* (OUP 1975) 34and 39, respectively. Raz's framework of first and second-order considerations is often used in the human

characteristics that would categorically distinguish it from international law. It can only maintain its uniqueness, or otherness as compared to both national and international law, based on internal validity of the interpretation of EU law by the CJEU. This is the core reason why the Court is so protective of its own monopoly of jurisdiction and the functioning of the formal structures of judicial dialogue in the preliminary ruling procedure, which in combination form the very basis of autonomy of the EU legal order. The following two subsections set out the autonomy narrative of the CJEU and the institutional backbone that allows the Court to maintain this narrative.

3.1 The Court's narrative of the autonomous legal order

The Court construes EU law as autonomous, that is, not depending on *national* or *international* law for its validity. It considers that protecting the autonomy of the EU legal order requires, above all, protecting its own ability to maintain *from the authoritative perspective of EU law* the narrative that EU law 'stems from an *independent source of law*'.[38]

The Court established the autonomy of the EU legal order by using sovereigntist language. It did so both explicitly ('the Member States have limited their *sovereign rights*, albeit within limited fields, and have thus created a body of law which binds both their nationals and themselves'[39]) and implicitly ('the law stemming from the treaty, an *independent source of law*, [that] could not because of its *special* and *original* nature, be overridden by domestic legal provisions, however framed, without being deprived of its character as Community law and without the *legal basis of the Community itself* being called into question'[40]). The essence of this autonomy boils down to an understanding of EU law as being of a *separate independent origin* that derives from sovereign rights transferred from and by the Member States, which, after this transfer, is no longer rooted in the sovereignty of the Member States but in the autonomy of the Union. Autonomy and sovereignty share the assumption of an ability to exercise jurisdiction over a territory in a self-referential and formally independent manner. Ultimately, the Court thus bases its reasoning in a sovereigntist self-conception.

Vis-à-vis national law, the CJEU insists on an autonomous interpretation of EU law, independent from the legal concepts used by the different national legal orders of the Member States.[41] The main purpose of this internal autonomy is to guarantee the effectiveness and uniform application of EU law across the EU in the different national contexts. Vis-à-vis international law, the CJEU has repeatedly defended the Union's autonomy, both at the institutional and at the substantive level, by stating that obligations under international agreements can neither 'affect the allocation of powers fixed by the Treaties',[42] nor can they 'have the effect of prejudicing the constitutional

rights context as an argument against balancing and a justification for giving rights priority over other considerations, see eg Richard Pildes, 'Avoiding Balancing: The Role of Exclusionary Reasons in Constitutional Law' (1994) 45 Hastings LJ 711. See for the CJEU's interpretation following Section 3.1 and Chapter 6.

[38] Opinion 2/13 [2014] EU:C:2014:2454 (hereafter Opinion 2/13), para 166 (emphasis added).

[39] Case 6/64, *Costa v ENEL* (n 3) 593–94 (emphasis added).

[40] ibid, 585 (emphasis added).

[41] Established in Case 26/62, *Van Gend en Loos* [1963] ECLI:EU:C:1963:1; Case 11-70, *Internationale Handelsgesellschaft mbH v Einfuhr- und Vorratsstelle für Getreide und Futtermittel* [1970] EU:C:1970:114; Case 106/77, *Amministrazione delle Finanze dello Stato v Simmenthal SpA* [1978] EU:C:1978:49.

[42] Joined Cases C-402/05 P and C-415/05 P, *Yassin Abdullah Kadi and Al Barakaat International Foundation v Council of the European Union and Commission* [2008] EU:C:2008:461, para 282.

principles of the [Treaties]'.[43] The Court's autonomy concern has come to the fore with the greatest clarity in the context of international courts and tribunals (ICTs), which are seen as a particular threat to the judicial monopoly of the CJEU.[44] Yet the autonomy of EU law is not only related to the Court's powers but requires the autonomy of the Union's institutions more broadly.[45] The Court explicitly protects institutional autonomy, for example the autonomy of the Commission as representor and negotiator of the Union in external relations.[46] This reading by the Court is very close to the position of the early federalists, represented in powerful positions within the institutions and leading the academic debate in the first decades of European integration.[47]

One means by which legal orders protect their own relevance, unity and ultimately their existence is their self-referential character. This self-referential character is *formally complete*, i.e. absolute. It is protected by an independent judiciary. It protects the effects and relevance of the decisions taken within the legal and procedural framework of that legal order. While the legal order can vest any external norm with exceptional normative force, this force depends on the acceptance by that legal order. This continues to be the case even if the exceptional force of the external norm sets aside internal norms. The CJEU constructs in this legal conceptual sense the autonomy of the EU legal order as *absolute*. EU law refers to national and international law, for example, the common constitutional traditions of the Member States and the European Convention on Human Rights, and draws from national concepts. Yet this does not as such undermine the self-referential character of EU law as the CJEU constructs it. At all times, national and international law are at arm's length and cannot determine the validity of EU law. This understanding is also the basis for making a distinction between normative and factual effects. Only normative effects can interfere with the self-referential character, which is the basis for the autonomy of a legal order. The next section explains the reason why national actors, in practice, go along with the CJEU's narrative of the absolute autonomy of EU law and do not challenge it more forcefully.

3.2 Interlocking embrace

One of the 'essential characteristics' of the EU legal order is the 'mutually interdependent legal relations' between the EU and its Member States and the Member States with each other.[48] Member States have permitted their interests to become so entangled that they all have high stakes in the well-functioning of the system. In fact, European integration and the effectiveness of EU law are based on the realization of interconnected stakes and the result-oriented willingness to cooperate. Playing by the rules and in this way coming to a decision and maintaining the problem-solving capacity of the system is advantageous for all participants. This makes loyal behaviour rational and explains it also from a pragmatic point of view.[49] Individual disobediences

[43] ibid, para 285.

[44] Chapter 6 examines the plausibility of the CJEU's autonomy concerns in the context of international courts and tribunals (ICTs) in more detail.

[45] René Barents, *The Autonomy of Community Law* (Kluwer Law International 2004) 226. See also fairly explicitly: Opinion 1/00 [2002] EU:C:2002:231, para 12: 'the preservation of the autonomy of the Community legal order requires [. . .] that the essential character of the powers of the Community and its institutions as conceived in the Treaty remain unaltered'.

[46] eg Case C-73/14 *Council v Commission* [2015] EU:C:2015:663.

[47] See above all the prominent legal scholar and first Commission President Walter Hallstein with *Die echten Probleme der Europäischen Integration* (Kieler Vorträge 1965) and 'L'Évolution des Communautés Européennes' (1959) 6 Annuaire Européen 1 (hereafter Hallstein, 'L'Évolution').

[48] Opinion 2/13 (n 38) paras 165–67.

[49] See Chapter 2 for more details.

do not challenge the system as such. Problematic, however, would be systematic disobedience, which would in turn make loyalty and compliance irrational.

The Union could be characterized as the most serious attempt of transnational problem-solving without domination. Internally, the EU is about inclusion. Under EU law, citizens of different Member States enjoy legal rights that allow them to be included in the societies of other Member States. This is also the normative appeal of European integration, which was termed as 'inclusion of the other'[50] or constitutional tolerance,[51] but is also based more practically on mitigating externalities, including vulnerabilities towards regulatory failures in other Member States.

Without wanting to dismiss the potential of emerging structures of bonding to evoke something that does not immediately depend on self-interest, vested interests in cooperation could be characterized as the most decisive difference between the internal and external sphere of the European Union. Externally, non-EU actors are not subject to the same level of interdependencies. This has practical consequences for their willingness to maintain the CJEU's autonomy conception. The next section introduces the institutional cooperation that allows the CJEU to call on national courts to maintain its claim as regards the autonomy of EU law.

3.3 Institutional backbone

In institutional practice, the autonomy and effectiveness of EU law rely heavily on the willingness of national courts to give effect to EU law as interpreted by the CJEU. Institutionally, it hinges on the functioning of the preliminary ruling procedure. National courts give effect to the CJEU's interpretation of EU law, including its reading of the relations of national, European, and international law. In the words of the Court: 'In order to ensure that the specific characteristics and the autonomy of the EU legal order are preserved, the Treaties have established a judicial system intended to ensure consistency and uniformity in the interpretation of EU law.'[52] The preliminary reference procedure is the 'keystone' of the EU judicial system, 'which, by setting up a dialogue between one court and another, [...] has the object of securing uniform interpretation of EU law [...], thereby serving to ensure its consistency, *its full effect* and its *autonomy* as well as, ultimately, the *particular nature* of the law established by the Treaties [...]'.[53] The Court hence identifies protecting the effectiveness, autonomy, and particular (domestic) nature of EU law as the very purpose of the preliminary ruling procedure.

The preliminary ruling procedure in Article 267 TFEU is a formal, institutionalized form of judicial *cooperation* between the CJEU and national courts. The relationship is not hierarchical in a way that the CJEU could repeal rulings of national courts. While the CJEU has threatened the state with liability if highest national courts, which are

[50] Jürgen Habermas, Cronin and De Greiff (eds) *The Inclusion of the Other. Studies in Political Theory* (Ciaran P. Cronin and Pablo De Greiff eds, MIT Press 2000).

[51] Joseph Weiler, 'In Defence of the Status Quo: Europe's Constitutional Sonderweg' in Joseph Weiler and Marlene Wind (eds) *European Constitutionalism beyond the State* (CUP 2003).

[52] Case C-284/16, *Slovak Republic v Achmea BV* [2018] EU:C:2018:158, para 35, with reference to: Opinion 2/13 (n 38) para 174.

[53] Opinion 2/13 (n 38) para 176 (emphasis added). Earlier, in Opinion 1/09 (European and Community Patents Court) [2011] EU:C:2011:123 (hereafter Opinion 1/09) paras 77ff: the CJEU rejected an ICT—the formation of the European and Community Patent Court—because it considered that the mechanism was susceptible of adversely affecting the position and powers of national courts within the preliminary ruling procedure.

under an EU law obligation to refer, do not do so,[54] this is a much more indirect means of putting pressure than the power to repeal. The CJEU depends on national courts' willingness to cooperate. Member States also hold the power to refer repeatedly and potentially in order to enter into a debate on the right outcome.[55] In federal states by contrast, the hierarchy of the judiciary and the federal court's powers to repeal decisions of the federate courts ensure the completeness of the self-referential character of the federal legal order.

In order to protect the formalized judicial dialogue under the preliminary ruling procedure and allow individuals to benefit from their rights under EU law, EU law protects the independence of any national court or tribunal that could potentially be asked to rule on matters of EU law.[56] Cooperation under the preliminary ruling procedure, despite all legal rules and obligations, requires a level of trust between the CJEU and national courts, as well as between courts of different Member States. This trust, however, requires autonomy, not only of the CJEU but of all participating actors. The Court emphasized that 'the tasks attributed to the national courts and to the [CJEU] respectively are indispensable to the preservation of the very nature of the law established by the Treaties'.[57] From the perspective of individuals, the core value of the rule of law based on the independence of the judiciary is that they are subject to pre-established and general laws, applied by courts, rather than ad hoc executive decisions. Furthermore, only a uniform application of EU law can ensure equal treatment of individuals under EU law, equal opportunity to benefit and put into practice rights under EU law. The uniform application of EU law is, in this sense, a necessary precondition of equality before the law. It is also what gives rights the potential of general bonding structures, by creating abstract stable links with the public actors adopting, interpreting, and enforcing these rights and with other EU citizens benefiting from the same uniformly interpreted rights.

The preliminary ruling procedure is used and the CJEU's interpretation is largely accepted (at least not openly challenged) because of the ever more tightening interlocking embrace between national and European law and the increasing interdependent stakes of all involved actors. The preliminary ruling procedure lies at the very core of what makes the EU unique, that is, its ability to vest EU law with *extraordinary effectiveness* within the national legal order. The dependence on the support by national courts inherent in the procedure also means that an inter-judicial conflict has greater potential to fundamentally challenge the authority of EU law than a conflict of non-compliance by national political actors. The following two sections discuss actual and potential contestation that may challenge the EU legal order.

3.4 Fragility of an interlocking embrace

> [T]he autonomy of EU law is not absolute but relative; it does not mean that EU law has ceased to depend, for its validity and effective application, on the national law of its member states, nor that it has ceased to belong to international law.[58]

[54] Case C-224/01, *Gerhard Köbler v Republik Österreich* [2003] EU:C:2003:513.

[55] See eg Case C-102/14, *Taricco and others (Taricco I)* [2015] EU:C:2015:555 and Case C-42/17, *M.A.S., MB (Taricco II)* [2017] EU:C:2017:936.

[56] Case C-64/16, *Associação Sindical dos Juízes Portugueses* [2018] EU:C:2018:117, para 40.

[57] Opinion 1/09 (n 53) para 84.

[58] Bruno de Witte, 'European Union Law: How Autonomous is Its Legal Order?' (2010) 65 Zeitschrift für öffentliches Recht 141, 142.

This quote expresses a conception of the autonomy of EU law that is very different from the one of the CJEU. The Court has built and protected its own narrative of the EU legal order as autonomous, that is, self-referential, with great care. This is of course not to say that the Court's creation of the EU as a polity with original rights is either uncontested or incontestable. On the contrary, it is essentially contestable.

This inherent contestability distinguishes the EU from federal states. One decisive difference between federal states and the EU is that in the former the federal level, usually with some involvement of the federate units, holds the authority to make changes to the constitution, while in the EU this authority lies with the Member States collectively, subject to the procedure in Article 48 TEU.[59] The Member States hence have collectively the power to determine in the codified 'constitutional' structure of the EU the division of competences and the relationship between EU law and international law. However, because of the fact that any Treaty amendment requires unanimity and national ratification (and to a lesser degree because of the involvement of the institutions and procedures set out in Article 48 TEU), the *status quo* exercises a locking-in effect that goes beyond the locking-in effect of typical constitutional reform, in particular when 28 Member States are involved. Furthermore, while federate units may politically challenge the federal level, they are part of a hierarchical legal and judicial structure, in which the validity of their laws depends on compliance with federal law. They do not—as long as they are part of the federation—enjoy an independent status as subjects of international law for purposes of state responsibility. This also means that federate units cannot actively rely on international law to challenge the status or existence of the federal level. Member States, by contrast, can be and are individually subject to state responsibility claims and could be brought before international courts and tribunals. They can hence be forced to take a legally binding stance in an external forum on how they construct the relationships between international, EU, and national law.

Another difference with federal states is that the EU lacks—as has often been pointed out—*Kompetenz-Kompetenz* (powers to change its own legal powers).[60] To some extent however, this position should be nuanced in light of the following chapters, which demonstrate that the combination of EU exercise of power (in particular in the area of external relations) and the CJEU's monopoly of interpretation of EU law vest the Union with the far-reaching ability to determine the scope of its own powers.[61] One may conclude that the absence or presence of *Kompetenz-Kompetenz* depends—at least as a matter of degree—on whether one focuses on the formal legal rules, such as the principle of conferral, or on their interpretation in practice as well, as on whether one takes the perspective of the CJEU or national constitutional courts. The Member States could abolish the EU (despite the CJEU's autonomy narrative) but as long as it exists, Article 48 TEU authoritatively lays down the procedure to amend the Treaties. The EU adopts legal and judicial acts binding on the Member States but implementation, execution, and enforcement often lie with the Member States, in principle without the

[59] See similarly Christian Calliess, *Die neue Europäische Union nach dem Vertrag von Lissabon* (Mohr Siebeck 2010) 352–54.

[60] See in particular the German scholarly debate following the German Constitutional Court. For an example of this debate in English: Paul Kirchhof, 'The Legal Structure of the European Union as a Union of States' in Armin von Bogdandy and Jürgen Bast (eds), *Principles of European Constitutional Law* (2nd edn, Hart Publishing 2011) 765–802. In German: Dieter Grimm, 'Wer ist souverän in der europäischen Union?' in Dieter Grimm (ed), *Die Zukunft der Verfassung II* (Suhrkamp 2012).

[61] Constellations in which this becomes apparent are implied powers, sincere cooperation in external relations, and mixed agreements.

EU having direct control over the process. Hence, law adoption and enforcement often fall to two different entities. This power split is decisive from the perspective of the individual, who is not subject to the monopoly of coercive power by the Union but who remains subject to the monopoly of coercive power by their state. Yet the Union also has a degree of control over the legitimate use of force, exemplified by Frontex. From the perspective of the individual, the split of adoption and enforcement powers connects to her role as dual sovereign, that is, acting as national citizen and as EU citizen.[62]

National constitutions vest national constitutional courts with the mandate to ensure the continuous existence of the polity, as constructed in the constitution. This includes protecting the sovereignty and the autonomy of the national polity.[63] This also flows from the very nature of state sovereignty. It is inherent in sovereignty that the sovereign ultimately fights against being made irrelevant, against usurpation by external forces.[64] National constitutional courts adhere to a conception of sovereignty that is necessarily and inextricably connected to statehood. The German Federal Constitutional Court (GFCC) is the most vocal national constitutional court in reviewing EU-related cases and in explicating limits to integration as it sees them flowing from the German Constitution. The *Solange* rulings of the GFCC, as well as the *Maastricht* decision, were warning shots. Yet while they had an impact on the development of fundamental rights protection within the European legal order,[65] they did not change the reception of European law within Germany as a matter of principle. The *Lisbon* decision by contrast, had immediate practical consequences.[66] It increased the power of the German parliament over the executive[67] and opened the door to new arguments that European law goes beyond the limits set by the German Constitution.[68] The Danish Supreme Court explicitly considered in its Maastricht Treaty decision that if too many competences were transferred to the EU, Denmark's statehood would be threatened.[69] Similarly, the Spanish Constitutional Tribunal stated that the Spanish constitution imposes substantive limits to what competences can be transferred to the EU and that this is what protects Spanish sovereignty.[70] In other words, the constitutional case law

[62] See Section 4.1 below.

[63] See Dieter Grimm's interpretation of the Lisbon Treaty ruling of the German Constitutional Court: Dieter Grimm, *Souveränität: Herkunnft un Zukunft eines Schlüsselbegriffs* (BUP 2009) 122–23.

[64] See also in the EU context: Konrad Schiemann, 'Europe and the Loss of Sovereignty' (2007) 56 ICLQ 475, 475ff.

[65] See Damian Chalmers and others, *European Union Law* (CUP 2006) 234ff, also referring to support of the *BVerfG*'s position by the Italian Constitutional Court.

[66] See above all the BVerfG, 2 BvE 2/08 (Treaty of Lisbon judgment).

[67] Compare the *Gesetz über die Zusammenarbeit von Bundesregierung und Deutschem Bundestag in Angelegenheiten der Europäischen Union* as amended on 17 November 2005 with the version amended on 22 September 2009. First applied in the landmark vote on Iceland EU membership. See Valentina Pop, 'German House in Landmark Vote on Iceland EU Membership' (*euobserver*, 22 April 2010) http://euobserver.com/15/29913. See also the discussion on whether the Government breached the new law by not involving the Bundestag sufficiently in the decision on the Greek loan http://www.das-parlament.de/2010/20/Titelseite/29786365/307868.

[68] See eg 2 BvR 2253/06, constitutional complaint, declared inadmissible on 27 January 2010; 2 BvR 2136/09 constitutional complaint, not accepted for decision on 22 September 2009; 2 BvR 471/09 constitutional complaint, not accepted for decision on 13 August 2009.

[69] The Supreme Court of Denmark, Case 361/1997, Decision of 6 April 1998 *(Maastricht)* (summary translated in (1999) 3 CMLR 854); See also for further examples Leonard Besselink and others, 'National Constitutional Avenues for Further EU Integration' (European Parliament, Committee on Legal Affairs and Constitutional Affairs Committee of the European Parliament, DG for Internal Policies Study 2014) 28 http://www.europarl.europa.eu/RegData/etudes/etudes/join/2014/493046/IPOL-JURI_ET(2014)493046_EN.pdf.

[70] Spanish Constitutional Tribunal, Declaration 1/2004 (Constitutional Treaty) in case no 6603-2004 https://www.tribunalconstitucional.es/ResolucionesTraducidas/Declaration%201-2004.pdf.

of a large majority of Member States is based on the understanding that the transfer of powers to the EU has taken place on conditions expressed under national constitutional law. This national reading presumes that national law imposes absolute limits on the EU legal order. However, potentially the greatest danger flows from a combined political and judicial challenge, which has so far been the exception. In 2017, the Hungarian constitutional court ruled on the relocation of asylum seekers and announced that it could review EU law in light of Hungarian constitutional identity.[71] This is above all an attempt of a Member State and its courts to abuse the concept of national identity as a means to escape the normative force of EU law, after they were outvoted under the internal decision-making procedures.

In exceptional circumstances, individual highest national courts have also flatly refused to give effect to a preliminary ruling without any immediate repercussions. In the case of *Ajos*, the Danish Supreme Court openly refused to accept the CJEU guidance in a preliminary ruling, because it considered the CJEU's ruling as being *ultra vires*.[72] This is the most direct and confrontational judicial challenge so far.[73] The Danish Court's reference concerned the CJEU's development of the general principle prohibiting discrimination on grounds of age[74] and was interpreted as an invitation to the CJEU to reconsider its previous case law.[75] The CJEU did not take up this invitation in its *Ajos* ruling (2016).[76] The Court also confirmed and further explicated this line of case law in *Egenberger* (discrimination on grounds of religion, 2018) *after* the Danish Supreme Court's *pushback* against *Ajos* in 2016.[77] The CJEU took the position that some constitutional foundations of the Union are so important that all actors should be bound by them. These contestations demonstrate both the vulnerability of the system and the absence of hierarchical control of the CJEU over national courts.

The CJEU's unilateral claim to autonomy of the EU legal order, while remaining unconfirmed by national constitutional courts, is central to the balance of powers within the EU legal order. The irreconcilable narratives of the CJEU on the one hand and national constitutional and supreme courts on the other depend on the ability of each of the judicial actors to make their own claims within the logic of their own legal order. Each narrative is internally consistent but unable to relate to an 'objective'

[71] Hungarian Constitutional Court, Decision No 22/2016. (XII.6.) AB on the Interpretation of art E)(2) of the Fundamental Law, English summary https://www.cambridge.org/core/journals/american-journal-of-international-law/article/decision-222016-xii-5-ab-on-the-interpretation-of-article-e2-of-the-fundamental-law/DAF1B924228F065716B274BAF54B024C/core-reader.

[72] For the preliminary reference: The Supreme Court of Denmark, Case no 15/2014, (Ajos, decision of 6 December 2013) English translation http://www.supremecourt.dk/supremecourt/nyheder/pressemeddelelser/Documents/Judgment%2015-2014.pdf. For the disobedience: Danish Supreme Court no 15/2014, discussed in English at: Sune Klinge, 'Dialogue or Disobedience Between the European Court of Justice and the Danish Constitutional Court? The Danish Supreme Court Challenges the Mangold-Principle' (*eulawanalysis* 13 December 2016) http://eulawanalysis.blogspot.com/2016/12/dialogue-or-disobedience-between.html.

[73] Earlier, the Czech Constitutional Court (Ústavní soud) had also held that a ruling of the CJEU was *ultra vires*: Pl. S 5/12 *(Holubec)* (plenary judgment, 31 January 2012). The case was a response to Case C-399/09, *Marie Landtová* [2011] EU:C:2011:415.

[74] See Case C-144/04, *Mangold* [2005] EU:C:2005:709, para 75 and Case C-555/07, *Kücükdeveci*]2010] EU:C:2010:21, para 21.

[75] Urška Šadl and Sabine Mair, 'Mutual Disempowerment: Case C-441/14 Dansk Industri, acting on behalf of *Ajos A/S v Estate of Karsten Eigil Rasmussen* and Case no.15/2014 *Dansk Industri (DI) acting for Ajos A/S v The estate left by A*' (2017) 13 Eur Con L Rev 347, 349.

[76] Case C-441/14 *Dansk Industri (DI), acting on behalf of Ajos A/S, v Estate of Karsten Eigil Rasmussen*, [2016] EU:C:2016:278.

[77] Case C-414/16, *Vera Egenberger v Evangelisches Werk für Diakonie und Entwicklung e.V.* [2018] EU:C:2018:257.

external mutual point of reference. Each narrative tells how the domestic law of the narrator relates to and affects the law of the others. The national position denies implicitly both the intrinsic unity and autonomy of EU law. It also severs the link between EU law and EU citizens, as well as between EU law and the territories of the Member States. The internal logic of the EU narrative and of its national counterpart is necessary to preclude a hierarchy between them.[78] The existence of incommensurable narratives, one of which is the autonomy narrative of the CJEU, is necessary, if not constitutive, for the EU to rely on pluralist sources of legitimacy.[79] It is what maintains the irreconcilable pluralist legal situation, in which, in the words of Neil MacCormick, '[n]one of the Member States is indebted to the union for the terms or the provisions of its constitution. Each has a constitution whose roots and whose basic legitimacy are independent of any grant by the Union. [. . .] Conversely, the validity of the Union's constitution and legal order is not derivative from the validating power of any state's constitutional order'.[80]

I should add that I do not argue that the CJEU's reading of the original validity of EU law is any more convincing than the national narratives. I only argue that the EU's internal status quo is built on an equilibrium of irreconcilable claims about the nature of EU law. It requires the pluralism of competing claims to autonomy to continue to exist in the way that it functions at present. Several points can be raised to demonstrate that institutionally and also formally legally the autonomy of the EU legal order is not absolute, but that elements of interlocking dependence and possibilities for pressure exist in practice. Yet this does not make the *conceptual legal* autonomy a matter of gradation; it rather means that each side has the formal legal possibility to highjack or challenge the status quo, in which different narratives coexist. Member States possess the political power and national courts possess the institutional power to reign in the EU and the CJEU. The CJEU possesses the legal power to determine the interpretation of EU law. Substantive convergence is possible and is happening. However, the absence of normative hierarchy excludes unity of law and makes real conflict between the norms of both legal orders possible. The next section links the autonomy of EU law to its dualist nature.

3.5 Fragility of otherness

The CJEU's narrative is also a narrative of 'otherness', that is, EU law differs from international law because of the transfer of 'sovereign' powers and its direct relationship with individuals.[81] The Court emphasizes the distinctiveness and separateness of EU law from international law. This also allows it to claim the primacy of EU law over all international law relations of the Member States, which is indirectly apparent in the exception under Article 351 TFEU for prior international agreements of the Member States. In the words of the Court: 'Member States have, by reason of their membership of the European Union, accepted that relations between them as regards the matters covered by the transfer of powers from the Member States to the European Union are governed by EU law, to the *exclusion*, if EU law so requires, of any other law'.[82]

[78] See also René Barents, 'The Precedence of EU Law from the Perspective of Constitutional Pluralism' (2009) 5 Eur Con L Rev 421, 428.

[79] See Section 4.2 below for more details on the link of autonomy and legitimacy.

[80] Neil MacCormick, 'The New European Constitution: Legal and Philosophical Perspective' (Lecture in Honour of L Petrazycki, Warsaw 2003).

[81] Section 3.1 below develops this in more detail.

[82] Opinion 2/13 (n 38), para 193 (emphasis added).

Vis-à-vis non-EU actors, the Court's strict stand on autonomy may be read as a form of exclusion, which stands in stark contrast with the above-discussed inclusion that the Union practices internally.

Violeta Moreno-Lax and Paul Gragl seem to identify a dynamic: '[A]s the distance from traditional international law augmented, the EU legal order became more "domestic" or "internal" in nature as a result'.[83] However, as explained, the CJEU's narrative of the normative autonomy of EU law is best understood as absolute and hence as a binary choice rather than a matter of degree. Opinion 2/13, in which the CJEU rejected the draft agreement of EU accession to the European Convention on Human Rights (ECHR), was characterized by some as a new era of closing-off and isolationism of the EU legal order.[84] Six years earlier, however, in response to the *Kadi* case, scholars had already criticized the CJEU for taking the European legal order as the one and only frame of reference, changing its international law-friendly attitude and moving to a more 'dualist' position than before.[85] I would argue that the Court has in all these cases taken the same standpoint, namely, that the EU legal order is autonomous, only the specific circumstances and consequences differ in the individual case.

The Court's ability to act as a domestic court, applying a dualist logic to international law, depends on the validity of its autonomy narrative within the logic of EU law. Kaarlo Tuori's European Constitutionalism claims in this regard that one of the key functions of a constitution is to position itself vis-à-vis other polities and constitutional entities. In this light, one could well doubt if we could even speak of EU constitutional law without a claim to autonomy.[86]

The autonomy narrative allows the CJEU to depart in *all its case law* from the standpoint that EU law is domestic law. This becomes particularly apparent in its case law concerning the autonomy vis-à-vis international law because only this assumption that EU law is of a domestic nature allows the CJEU to introduce dualist elements into the reception of international law within the EU legal order.

Monism and dualism are conceptual tools to describe the relationship between different legal orders, usually international and domestic. Theoretically, the concepts of monism and dualism developed from debates on 'the nature of law, nature of international law, the overlap between international law and domestic law, constitutional law, and more importantly, on the authority of international law'.[87] 'The main feature of dualism appears to be that international law and [domestic] laws are viewed as separate legal systems, which may be defined as self-contained, because within each system the only existing rules are those that are part of the system. Rules which are

[83] Violeta Moreno-Lax and Paul Gragl, 'Introduction: Beyond Monism, Dualism, Pluralism. The Quest for a (Fully-Fledged) Theoretical Framework: Co-implication, Embeddedness, and Interdependency between Public International Law and EU Law' (2016) 35 YEL 455.

[84] ibid.

[85] See Gráinne de Búrca, 'The European Court of Justice and the International Legal Order after Kadi' (2010) 51 Harvard ILJ 1, 4, criticizing the ECJ for expressing 'important parts of its reasoning in chauvinist and parochial tones'; Jan Klabbers, *Treaty Conflict and the European Union* (CUP 2009) 219, criticizing the ECJ to act like an 'ostrich'. See also the very critical remarks of the General Court in Case T-85/09, *Yassin Abdullah Kadi v European Commission* [2010] EU:T:2010:418, paras 114–22. For other cases in which the CJEU displayed dualist elements in its approach to international law: Mox Plant: Nikos Lavranos, 'Protecting Its Exclusive Jurisdiction: The Mox Plant-Judgment of the ECJ' (2006) 5(3) LAPE 479; for Van Parys: Piet Eeckhout, 'Does Europe's Constitution Stop at the Water's Edge?' (Fifth Walter van Gerven Lecture, Europa Law Publishing 2005) 15 http://www.iuscommune.eu/html/pdf/wvg/wvg5.pdf.

[86] Kaarlo Tuori, *European Constitutionalism* (CUP 2015).

[87] Basak Çali, *The Authority of International Law: Obedience, Respect, and Rebuttal* (Chapter 4, 'Beyond Monism and Dualism', OUP 2015) 137.

not created within the system may nevertheless be relevant for the system if they are referred to by a rule included in the system.'[88] Dualism could be seen as 'the easiest and most drastic form of norm conflict avoidance'.[89] It allows domestic courts in essence to ignore 'external' legal orders. The pluralism discourse that has attracted quite some attention among EU legal scholars, raises in many respects the same conceptual issues as the monism/dualism debate.[90] Pluralism draws attention to plurality of voices in the debate, the merit of this plurality, the system inherent possibilities of contestation that flows from this plurality, and often to the normative value of this plurality of voices. Dualism by contrast focuses on the position of the individual interlocutor, that is, the individual legal orders.

As with most national constitutions, the EU Treaties leave many questions open. What is different is that the 'domestic' nature of the EU legal order is essentially contested; yet it is necessary for any dualistic approach and even more basically to disconnect from general rules of international law, as well as international legal obligations of the EU and of its Member States. Significant authoritative claims, both internally and externally, deny the EU's domestic nature.[91] The potential pressure from international law to dissolve EU law into international law and make it subject to international law rules, increases with the increasing interaction between EU law and international, that is, with increased EU external actions. The next section sets out different aspects of legitimacy in the EU context and how they are conceptualized in the literature.

4. Legitimacy

The normative potential of the legal structures of bonding rests not only on the effectiveness of EU law. It also depends on the legitimacy of the Union and its actions. In fact, structures of bonding can and should serve as a means through which the Union can justify its purpose and actions. This section develops justifiability as the core of legitimacy. It serves as the background for the legitimacy discussions in the remainder of this book.

4.1 Different aspects

Any restriction of rights and freedoms raises questions of legitimacy. Different forms of legitimacy are present and discussed in the EU context. Political scientists often make a distinction between the legitimacy of input, that is, participation by citizens, and output, that is, effectiveness for citizens. Fritz Scharpf is probably the most prominent scholar making a case for the relevance of the latter.[92] Similarly, Giandemenico Majone argues in favour of assessing the Union's legitimacy as a 'regulatory state'.[93] The output

[88] Giorgio Gaja, 'Dualism: A Review' in Janne E Nijman and André Nollkaemper (eds), *New Perspectives on the Divide Between National and International Law* (OUP 2007) 52.

[89] Marko Milanovic, 'Norm Conflict in International Law: Whither Human Rights?' (2009) 20 DJCIL 69, 102.

[90] Stefan Griller, 'International Law, Human Rights and the European Community's Autonomous Legal Order: Notes on the European Court of Justice Decision in Kadi' (2008) 4 ECLR 528, 550.

[91] See Chapter 6 for more details.

[92] Fritz Scharpf, 'Economic Integration, Democracy and the Welfare State' (1997) 4 JEPP 18; Fritz Scharpf, *Governing in Europe: Effective and Democratic?* (OUP 1999).

[93] Giandomenico Majone, 'Europe's "Democratic Deficit": The Question of Standards' (1998) 4 ELJ 5; Giandomenico Majone, 'The European Commission: The Limits of Centralization and the Perils of Parliamentarization' (2002) 15 Governance 375.

legitimacy of the Union has come under considerable pressure since and because of the financial and economic crisis in Europe.[94] However, the growing disenchantment with the Union, which cannot be separated from the growing perception that it fails to reach a sufficiently high level of 'problem-solving', rather confirms that output played a role in the acceptance and support of European integration. This is often referred to as social legitimacy, that is, whether the EU is *perceived* as legitimate. At the same time, the Brexit vote raises strong doubts about the ability of output legitimacy as the single most important factor of sociological legitimacy (acceptance). After all, a (small) majority of Brits voted in the referendum on 23 June 2016 in favour of 'taking back control' and against economic growth.[95] Output legitimacy within the EU also suffers from a distinct expectation-delivery gap. EU citizens regularly voice expectations of the Union in areas in which it has no or only very limited competence.

Input legitimacy predominantly refers to the democratic quality of decision-making. Within the EU, the body of literature on the democratic deficit engages with input legitimacy. More recently, more attention is paid to what has been coined 'throughput' legitimacy, focusing on the processes between the input and output, that is, their inclusiveness and transparency. While throughput legitimacy concentrates in particular on the complex processes of exchange and public deliberation, input legitimacy focuses more on the opportunities for citizens and society actors to be involved.

The work of more theoretically oriented scholars, such as Jürgen Habermas and Rainer Forst, gives helpful guidance on the nature of legitimacy applicable to all the different stages of decision-making.[96] Habermas, in particular, argues that the exercise of public power must be subject to reason-giving public and political practices that engage with the distinctive normative views of those subject to the rights restrictions. His conception of legitimacy is, at its very core, based on discourse as an idealized argumentative process of reaching genuine understanding, which is based on the communicative potential of the more reasonable argument.[97]

Rainer Forst has developed a theory of human rights as originating in a right to justification.[98] Human rights play in the reason-giving process the role of a language of critique ('*Sprache der Kritik*'), which protects citizens from unjustified societal and political circumstances of oppression. Forst argues that being a person ('*Personsein*') depends on being treated as a being with a right to justification ('*Rechtfertigungswesen*').[99] This requires that all individuals be treated as persons whose rights and interests are respected both in the process of decision-making and in the substantive decision.[100] As a consequence of the right to justification, those exercising public power in a way that restricts rights have to offer their citizens legitimate reasons.[101] Forst distinguishes three

[94] See eg Giandomenico Majone, *Rethinking the Union of Europe Post-Crisis: Has Integration Gone Too Far?* (CUP 2014).

[95] See on this debate: Clarke and others, *Brexit: Why Britain Voted to Leave the European Union* (CUP 2017).

[96] See for Habermas a selection of his impressive body of work in the following footnotes. For Rainer Forst see above all: *Recht auf Rechtfertigung. Elemente einer konstruktivistischen Theorie der Gerechtigkeit* (Surhkamp Verlag 2007) (hereafter: Forst, *Recht auf Rechtfertigung*) and *Kritik der Rechtfertigungsverhältnisse. Perspektiven einer kritischen Theorie der Politik* (Suhrkamp Verlag 2011) (hereafter: Forst, *Kritik der Rechtfertigungsverhältnisse*). Jürgen Neyer has comprehensively engaged with the legitimacy of the European Union on the basis of Forst's work on the right to justification: Jürgen Neyer, *The Justification of Europe: A Political Theory of Supranational Integration* (OUP 2012).

[97] The oft-cited passage of the 'eigentümlich zwanglose Zwang des besseren Argumentes', see for some context: Habermas, *Theorie des Kommunikativen Handelns. Handlungsrationalität und gesellschaftliche Rationalisierung. Band I* (2nd edn, Suhrkamp 1982) 45ff.

[98] Forst, *Kritik der Rechtfertigungsverhältnisse* (n 96) 54. [99] ibid, 67.

[100] ibid, 77. [101] ibid, 76.

dimensions of justification: an ethical, a moral, and a third dimension that justifies loyalty and belonging to a group.[102] The third dimension is relevant in the context of the justification of EU loyalty.[103]

Habermas considers that a polity, in order to be legitimate, must be worthy of being recognized as legitimate ('*Annerkennungswürdigkeit*'). This condition is met through the deliberative process as described above. Habermas' conception focuses consequently on procedural legitimacy. He highlights that his understanding of democracy draws from the liberal and the republican understanding, that is, from the republican understanding which accepts that the individual is the subject of a polity and that the subject and the polity make each other possible and determine each other.[104] This leads to a conception of a dialectic democracy, based on the 'intersubjectivity' of its subjects, that is, an 'intersubjectively shared form of life', where the ' "self" of the self-organizing legal community [...] disappears in the subjectless form of communication'.[105] This connects to the 'empty space' discussed above, which is here filled with (subjectless) communication rather than an image of the sovereign or polity.

Politics, however, is not so much portrayed as a struggle in Habermas' work but the ideal type interaction of deliberation. What both the concept of the 'empty space' and 'subjectless form of communication' share is that they reject an image of one people or of one collective will. In this view, even the right to vote is (also) a means to build communicative legitimacy. Transparency is generally accepted to play an important role in allowing citizens to understand and control the exercise of public power. In the Habermasian reading of legitimacy, it also has the important function of connecting the discourse among the public and in the media to the discourse within the institutional structures of the EU.

Sovereignty in the Habermasian understanding is dispersed and present only in the subjectless form of communication.[106] This is the background against which one should read Habermas' development of the 'divided sovereignty' (in other contexts: '*Pouvoir Constituant Mixte*'[107]), in which the very same subject, that is, the individual citizen, acts in two capacities, namely, as citizen of their state and as citizen of the Union.[108] Habermas identifies existing elements of this divided sovereignty, including for example in the equal legislative powers of the Council, representing the peoples of the Member States, and the European Parliament, which goes some way in the direction of representing the citizenry of Europe as such.[109]

The Union in its legal institutional construction under the European Treaties lays direct links with individual citizens. In his later writing, Jürgen Habermas defends the idea of a 'sovereignty that is divided in its root',[110] that is, at the very source of the entity that is to be constituted. Modern constitutions relate in the last instance

[102] Forst, *Recht auf Rechtfertigung* (n 96) 28–29.

[103] See Chapter 2.

[104] This is the core of the republican understanding of democracy, but also comes back in Habermas dialectic conception, ibid.

[105] Jürgen Habermas, 'Three Normative Models of Democracy' (1994) 1 Constellations 1, 10.

[106] Jürgen Habermas, *Zur Verfassung Europas. Ein Essay* (Suhrkamp 2011) 52 (hereafter: Habermas, *Zur Verfassung Europas*).

[107] Jürgen Habermas, 'Citizens and State Equality in a Supranational Political Community: Degressive Proportionality and the Pouvoir Constituant Mixte' (2017) 55 JCML 171.

[108] Habermas, *Zur Verfassung Europas* (n 106) 69. Compare above Section 3.2 on direct and indirect representation.

[109] Jürgen Habermas, 'Democracy in Europe: Why the Development of the EU into a Transnational Democracy is Necessary and How It is Possible' (2015) 21 ELJ 546.

[110] Die Idee einer an der Wurzel geteilten Volkssouveränität, see Habermas, *Zur Verfassung Europas* (n 106) 62–82.

to individuals as subjects of rights. Within the European Union, individuals or rather their representatives have agreed that the democratic substance of their states continues to exist within the ever-closer Union. State guarantees of civil liberties, democracy, and solidarity are achievements that people fear to lose through the continuous power shifts to the Union. This agreement should be honoured, as long as no other agreement is made, following a public discourse that would vest this agreement with sufficient legitimacy. Individuals vote, elect, challenge, and support the establishment and exercise of public power as national citizens and as EU citizens.

Habermas criticizes those that conflate sovereignty of the people with state sovereignty.[111] At the same time, his process-focused subjectless conception of sovereignty has attracted the criticism that it makes the clear attribution of political decisions and responsibility excessively difficult. Indeed, Habermas' discursive understanding of democracy (and ultimately sovereignty) has both the advantage of decoupling power from territory, which makes it particularly applicable to the EU, and the disadvantage that this decoupling and emphasizing of affectedness as a criterion of inclusion is difficult to put into practice. While it entails a risk of disembedding power, it has the advantage that it allows the decoupling of democracy from the nation state, while allowing a continuous legitimizing role for the nation state in the proceduralized process.

In Habermas' conception of legitimacy as worthiness of recognition, established in a discursive process in which the claim to worthiness of recognition must be justified, law creates the necessary conditions for communication.[112] Law, and in particular fundamental rights and principles of the modern *Rechtsstaat*, institutionalizes the demanding conditions for communication as formulated by Habermas.[113] Law benefits from systematic justification, binding interpretation, and enforcement. It constitutes an important element of societal institutional structures. Habermas sees in the democratic legalization of decision-making processes across national borders as a central part the EU's legitimacy,[114] which requires but also builds a diffuse loyalty of the masses.[115] Law is hence central to Habermas conception of legitimacy. It is also the central tool of European integration.

Habermas does not engage with the potential of discourse as a means to increase the effectiveness of decision-making (output legitimacy). One important aspect of Habermas' position is that the justification of exercising public power must connect to existing moral commitments, that is, fundamental rights. Moreover, justifiability requires compliance with the legal and procedural framework for decision-making, the conditions for free deliberation, sufficiently clear responsibilities, a certain level of transparency, but also effectiveness. The division of competence is part of the constitutional structure of polities, which should be determined and adequately understood by the addressees of the exercise of public power.

In this book, I place the different voices in the legitimacy debate and in particular the work of Habermas as the background against which the legal developments are

[111] ibid, 52.

[112] Jürgen Habermas, *The Crisis of the European Union: A Response* (Polity 2012) 110: 'only those statutes may claim legitimacy that can meet with the assent of all citizens in a discursive process of legislation that in turn has been legally constituted' and 449: 'citizens should always be able to understand themselves also as the authors of the law to which they are subject as addressees' (hereafter Habermas, *The Crisis of the European Union*).

[113] eg Habermas, 'Drei normative Modelle der Demokratie' in *Die Einbeziehung des Anderen. Studien zur politischen Theorie* (1st edn, Suhrkamp 1996).

[114] ibid, 53: 'auf demokratische Weise verrechtlicht'.

[115] Jürgen Habermas, *Legitimationsprobleme im Spätkapitalismus* (Suhrkamp 1983) 72.

examined. This is based on an understanding that a plurality of sources of legitimacy can do the combined work of legitimizing the exercise of public power, as well as a system as a whole. In fact, the different legitimacy sources strengthen each other and depend on each other. The legitimacy question becomes the question of whether and how the Union's role and actions can be justified convincingly. What purpose can justify the Union in broad terms within the existing institutional and constitutional structures and power division—subject to reasoned and reasonable reform and reconsideration of interpretation?

Habermas and the broader family of liberal egalitarian theories[116] are salient for the present inquiry about the law and politics of EU external relations because they pursue the objective of reconciling in particular individual rights and democracy. Furthermore, their image of the reasonable person, who seeks social cooperation, perceives of the polity as a 'we' rather than a 'they' and places an emphasis on deliberation and listening.

However, I should also express some caveat. Inspired by Chantal Mouffe's concept of 'agonistic politics',[117] I acknowledge the value of political struggle in a different way than Habermas. While I am convinced by the centrality of rational deliberation, I believe in the necessity of introducing a framed scope for real political controversy, based on an assumption that not all positions can be reconciled in rational deliberation. I share Mouffe's criticism that a 'post-political' vision of society—which is, in my reading, very present in the Union's consensus-seeking structures of governance, as well as its rhetoric of functional arguments—ultimately deprives citizens of a real choice. This is an argument in favour of politicizing the European Union. Making visible political positions that are not reflected in a given EU policy, but that could be reflected in a future EU policy, has the potential of contributing to addressing the disenchantment with the European integration project.

Furthermore, this book attaches more value to indirect legitimation than Habermas seems to do, in particular in his later writings.[118] It assumes that the agreement that Member States must continue to have a legitimizing role should be honoured (as long as it is not replaced by a new sufficiently explicated and legitimized agreement). Bonding structures between the Union and its citizens, as developed above, are meant to allow individuals to give input *as EU citizens in addition to their input as national citizens*. Citizens continue to be formally required to act in their dual role as EU and national citizens.

The EU must continue to draw from classic forms of democratic legitimation of the Member States and the national *demos,*[119] which—irrespective of any growing elements of a European public—remains relevant as a 'decision-making community of individuals, holding citizenship and sharing a commitment to the polity'—a voluntary community, rather than an essentialist community of fate.[120] Habermas acknowledges the relevance of indirect legitimation, not only implicitly by the considerable importance that he attaches to the 'linguistic bonds' of communities of communication and

[116] Forst and Neyer (n 96).

[117] Chantal Mouffe, *The Democratic Paradox* (Verso 2009); see also: Chantal Mouffe, *On the Political* (Routledge 2005).

[118] Habermas, *Zur Verfassung Europas* (n 106).

[119] While 'people' may be understood to refer both to *demos* and *ethnos*, it is here used, together with the Greek terminology *demos*, in the meaning of this former word.

[120] Francis Cheneval, 'The People in Deliberative Democracy' in Samantha Besson and José Marti (eds), *Deliberative Democracy and its Discontents* (Aldershot Ashgate 2006) 161.

law,[121] but also explicitly, for example when he refers to the necessity of the EU to rely on resources of legitimacy of the national state,[122] when he argues in favour of a balance of competences between the Council and the Parliament in all policy areas,[123] as well as when he points out that the Union recognizes and benefits from 'the historical achievements of a level of justice embodied in the nation-states', which remain in their 'democratic-constitutional substance' intact in the Union.[124] At times, Habermas even seems to lean towards a stronger role for the Member States: 'The citizens of the Union have a justified interest in their respective nation states continuing to perform their proven role as guarantors of law and freedom also in their role as member states. The nation states are more than just embodiments of national cultures worthy of preservation; they vouch for a level of justice and freedom which citizens want to see preserved.'[125] The difference to the position taken here is that in Habermas' work, the Union's need to draw from Member States' legitimacy sources appears to be a *temporary* condition, due to its weak denationalized constitutionalization, which could be overcome through a strengthening of the legitimacy of the EU sphere.[126] This book departs from an understanding rooted in federal theory that demands that both the federate units (Member States) and the federal level (Union) must continue to remain autonomous entities in order to ensure that the federal construction benefits from (sufficient) legitimacy that originates in separate sources.[127] Individuals must be able to support and challenge public decision-making within the Union as national citizens via their Member States and as EU citizens via the EU structures. However, the role of the Member States could, in principle, be limited to participation within the internal decision-making structures and implementation of EU law and international law by which the Union is bound. It does not necessarily require external visibility and representation of the Member States.

4.2 The link between autonomy and legitimacy

Structures of bonding that serve justification and so enhance the Union's legitimacy as developed above require conceptual autonomy. Indeed, the autonomy of the EU legal order, understood as its ability to make a claim to self-referential validity of its law, is a central and necessary basis for the legitimacy of the Union as a system and for the exercise of its powers. The legitimacy of the EU rests both on direct and indirect legitimacy, which exist and necessarily must exist alongside each other without being dependent on each other. The width and depth of the exercise of EU powers can no longer be justified exclusively through national structures (indirect legitimacy). It requires additional meaningful legitimation of the EU legal sphere through individuals acting as

[121] 'Was Rechtsgenossen assoziiert, ist letztlich das linguistische Band, das jede Kommunikationsgemeinschaft zusammenhält', see Jürgen Habermas, *Faktizität und Geltung. Beiträge zur Diskurstheorie des Rechts und des demokratishen Rechtsstaats* (1st edn [1998], Suhrkamp 2017) 372.

[122] Jürgen Habermas, 'Konstitutionalisierung des Völkerrechts und die Legitimationsprobleme einer verfassten Weltgesellschaft' in Winfried Brugger (ed), *Rechtsphilosophie im 21. Jahrhundert* (Suhrkamp 2009) 362, citing Ingeborg Maus: '[...] Notwendigkeit des Zugriffs Überstaatlicher Politik auf Nationalstaatliche Legitimationsressourcen'.

[123] Habermas, *Zur Verfassung Europas* (n 106) 73.

[124] ibid, 11.

[125] Habermas, *The Crisis of the European Union* (n 112) 41.

[126] Jürgen Habermas, *Der Gespaltene Westen. Kleine Politische Schriften X* (Suhrkamp 2004) (hereafter Habermas, *Der Gespaltene* Westen) 140.

[127] This was explicated from the very beginning and even by the early federalists. See above all: Hallstein, 'L'Évolution' (n 47) 6–7: 'les Communautés n'ont jamais été conçues comme devant faire disparaître les États, mais comme une forme d'union entre eux'.

EU citizens. These structures of bonding can only serve to legitimize the Union and its actions to the extent that they are indeed capable of offering autonomous justification.

Autonomy is the basis to claim credit and be held responsible for any particular policy outcome. Justification in terms of giving reason, that is, explicating the substantive considerations that motivated a decision, is only convincing if the person exercising public power had the discretion to choose between different means and objectives. Input is only relevant if it can (co-)determine the outcome. Self-determination of both the EU *demos* or national *demoi* through the EU is only possible if the EU enjoys a certain degree of political autonomy, albeit relative. It must be able to take decisions at a certain distance from international and national legal and political constraints in order to be able to claim and take responsibility for its actions and be able to exert an influence on the other. Representatives can only be held responsible for political action if they could also have chosen a different possible course of action.

Drawing on the writings of Habermas,[128] collective autonomy of a polity is understood here as both *analogous to* and *dependent on* individual autonomy. *In analogy* to individual autonomy, collective autonomy does not require that it must be free of all legal or factual constraints but it must be able to steer its own course of action. The polity can consequently commit to external legal constraints without losing its autonomy; yet it must remain able to determine the political course that the policy takes.[129] Habermas' conception of divided sovereignty is based on the understanding that 'only those statutes may claim legitimacy that can meet with the assent (*Zustimmung*) of all citizens in a discursive process of legislation that in turn has been legally constituted,'[130] that is, are worthy of recognition. For citizens, however, to be able to express valid assent they must have a sufficient degree of freedom. Democratically legitimate procedure requires that this freedom is guaranteed. This emphasizes the Union's responsibilities vis-à-vis its citizens. For the Union to benefit from direct democratic legitimacy, it must also protect the autonomy of its citizens (and their ability to enforce individual rights through an autonomous national judiciary), including against their own Member States. The recent case on the rights of UK citizens in the Netherlands after Brexit may shed additional light on the view of the CJEU of this direct autonomous link between the Union and its citizens after a Member State supported by its citizens as national citizens severs the link with the Union.[131]

Constitutional and judicial review by unelected judges stands in essential tension with, and may even pose a threat to, autonomous will-forming. Yet it also forms part of the construction that ensures collective autonomy. It ensures that the collective will is formed pursuant to pre-established (constitutional) rules, including both procedural and substantive rules that allow the equal and free participation of all in the collective

[128] See Section 4.1 above.

[129] This presupposes the distinction introduced by Rousseau between the will of all (aggregation of all individual wills) and the collective will (common will formed in a deliberative process). Habermas' disperse understanding of sovereignty does not presume an impersonated collective will.

[130] Original text: Jürgen Habermas, *Faktizität und Geltung, Beiträge zur Diskurstheorie des Rechts und des demokratischen Rechtsstaats* (Suhrkamp 1992); Quote taken from the English translation: Jürgen Habermas, *Between Facts and Norms: Contributions to a Discourse Theory of Law and Democracy* (MIT Press 1996) (Hereafter, Habermas, *Between Facts and Norms)* 110.

[131] Lisa O'Carroll, 'Britons Living in EU Can Take Case to ECJ Arguing Existing Rights Cannot Be Removed After Brexit' (*The Guardian*, 7 February 2018) https://www.theguardian.com/politics/2018/feb/07/british-group-wins-right-to-take-brexit-case-to-european-court. The reference to the Dutch case referring to the CJEU: Rechtbank Amsterdam, C/13/640244 / KG ZA 17-1327, 7 February 2018.

will-forming.[132] Constitutional and judicial review is, hence, a functional and fundamental requirement. On the one hand, constitutional and judicial review protects the framework conditions for collective will-forming and, on the other hand, it ensures that all participants are treated as individually autonomous. Informative in this regard is Habermas' procedural account of democratic legitimacy, which presumes that a collective will can only be formed in a legally structured political community.[133] In this legally structured political community, courts guarantee equal subjective liberties, equal membership rights and legal protection of these rights.[134] Constitutionalism and the rule of law are a precondition for democratic legitimacy.

However, creating 'politics', understood as political struggle, remains a challenge for the Union. The European way of constitutionalization through rulings by the CJEU centralizes value choices and lifts them with the force of primacy above politics. The challenge for the Union remains to create space for politics without creating legal ambiguities that result in an increase of judicial power settling political struggles. This is also a convincing criticism of the CJEU's autonomy narrative, which portrays everything as converging in one point of power: the judicial monopoly of the CJEU. This point of view may be explicable in light of the fact that the uniqueness and otherness of EU law hinges on its ability to be extraordinarily effective, which in turn is based on the purposive interpretation of the CJEU, largely accepted by national courts. The explicability however does not counter the criticism. Politics at the EU level should be able to disrupt the at least potentially totalizing nature of law, including the rulings of the CJEU. Politics adds the views of those who disagree with the law. It relativizes legal positions. It also allows contestation of the basic structures, including the purpose of the polity.

4.3 External relations as purpose?

> [T]he implementation of the process of integration [...] is the raison d'être of the EU itself.[135]
>
> No normative order is [...] ever adequately legitimated by necessities imposed at lower levels of the hierarchy of control—e.g. by the fact that things *must* be done in a *specific* way because the stability or even survival of the system is at stake.[136]

The two quotes beg the question of whether (the process of) integration suffices as *raison d'être* for the European Union. Two specific and interrelated ways in which the EU could justify its existence with a particular purpose and added value as compared to the nation state have repeatedly been highlighted. First, it possesses a unique capacity to deal with unavoidable externalities and second, it allows EU citizens and Member States to have greater influence on international decision-making processes, that is, to play a more important role in a world. As to the first, externalities of decision-making

[132] This follows roughly Habermas, *Between Facts and Norms* (n 130). See for a detailed analysis of Habermas' stand on democracy and judicial review, Christopher Zürn, 'Deliberative Democracy and Constitutional Review' (2002) 21 Law and Philosophy 467 (hereafter Zürn, 'Deliberative Democracy and Constitutional Review').

[133] See Jürgen Habermas, *Between Facts and Norms* (n 130) 448.

[134] See, for a detailed account and analysis of the extent and intensity of constitutional review foreseen by Habermas, Zürn, 'Deliberative Democracy and Constitutional Review' (n 132).

[135] Opinion 2/13 (n 38) para 172.

[136] Talcot Parsons, *Societies: Evolutionary and Comparative Perspectives* (Prentice Hall 1966) 11.

exist and increase in a globalizing world independently from the European Union.[137] The EU has a particular capacity to deal with these externalities, but it also drives the process of ever-closer interlocking of legal spheres, which increases potential and actual externalities.[138]

As to the second, it has become more prominent in recent years and is also confirmed by the quantitative and qualitative increase of Union powers in external relations under the Lisbon Treaty.[139] The European Treaties confirm this need for autonomous external action by the Union. Externally, the underlying rationale of the objectives under the European Treaties is that the EU must assume the role of an autonomous actor in order to achieve them. The EU's foreign policy objectives after Lisbon clearly go beyond any supportive or supplementary character. This is obvious in the area of the Common Foreign and Security Policy (CFSP) and Common Security and Defence Policy (CSDP) but can also be sensed in Article 21(1) TFEU.[140] This provision not only aims to construct a coherent and complementary European foreign policy but also indicates objectives of influencing its surroundings. Indeed, it does not take a neutral perspective but aims at shaping international relations and law pursuant to the moral conviction that a rule-based international order reflecting universal normative values would lead to a better world. Article 3(5) TEU requires the Union to uphold and promote its values in its relations with the wider world. Article 21 TEU sets out the objectives that the Union shall pursue externally, including developing relations and building partnerships with third countries, as well as promoting multilateral solutions to common problems. The two provisions taken together create an image of the EU as an autonomous international actor. The EU must also logically enjoy a certain autonomy from international law in order to be able to uphold and promote EU values and interests under international law and in order to contribute to the development of international law.

Jose Barroso's State of the Union Address of 2012, for example, repeatedly made one point: the Union is a way of ensuring sovereignty in the sense of self-determination of states and citizens in a globalized world.[141] Emmanuel Macron should be read as stating in 2017 that Member States have already lost their ability to autonomously determine their fate and that the European integration project is the way to regain their sovereignty internationally.[142] He even spoke of the 'sovereignty' of the European Union.[143] This was both hailed as visionary or rejected as delusional at the time.[144]

[137] In Habermas' words in 'Hat die Konstitutionalisierung des Völkerrechts noch eine Chance?' in Habermas, *Der Gespaltene Westen* (n 126) 175: 'In räumlicher, sozialer und sachlicher Hinsicht belasten sich Nationalstaaten gegenseitig mit den externen Effekten von Entscheidungen, die sich reziprok auf andere, am Entscheidungsprozess Unbeteiligte auswirken.'

[138] This is most visible in the internal market context.

[139] See Introduction.

[140] More clearly than in ex-art 11(1) TEU.

[141] José Manuel Barroso, 'State of the Union Address 2012' (Speech 2012/596): 'A political union also means doing more to fulfil our global role. Sharing sovereignty in Europe means being more sovereign in a global world.'; 'A democratic federation of nation states that can tackle our common problems, through the sharing of sovereignty in a way that each country and each citizen are better equipped to control their own destiny. This is about the Union with the Member States, not against the Member States. In the age of globalisation pooled sovereignty means more power, not less.' http://europa.eu/rapid/press-release_SPEECH-12-596_en.htm.

[142] Emmanuel Macron, 'Initiative for Europe' (Sorbonne speech, 26 September 2017) (hereafter Macron, Sorbonne speech) http://international.blogs.ouest-france.fr/archive/2017/09/29/macron-sorbonne-verbatim-europe-18583.html.

[143] Macron, Sorbonne speech (n 142). He uses sovereign* 24 times.

[144] See eg 'The Guardian View on Macron's Europe Speech: A Bold Vision' (*The Guardian*, 26 September 2017) https://www.theguardian.com/commentisfree/2017/sep/26/the-guardian-view-on-macrons-europe-speech-a-bold-vision and Steven Erlanger, 'Emmanuel Macron's Lofty Vision for

In September 2018, the Commission President Jean-Claude Juncker entitled his last State of the Union: 'The Hour of European Sovereignty'.[145] He emphasized the Union's global responsibility in the contemporary geopolitical circumstances and its commitment to multilateralism. He also flagged trade and security as areas where the EU has a particular and identifiable added value.

Several scholars have made the argument that the Union's ability to make a meaningful difference on the international plane is the *raison d'être* of the European integration project.[146] Similarly, Jürgen Habermas has portrayed the EU as the answer to globalization.[147]

This book emphasizes in a non-exclusive fashion the added value of the European Union as an international actor that increases the ability of Member States to shape an effective political course of action and the capacity of individuals to be represented as EU citizens in international relations. States remain the most powerful international actors; yet the range of their lawful actions has decreased tremendously over time—as a result of economic entanglement, international law, and, for EU Member States, also as a result of EU law. The nation state possesses fewer and fewer effective political means and room to manoeuvre. This also limits its ability to represent its citizens internationally. In the context of external relations, the extension of mechanisms of democratic participation to the EU creates a particular potential for a narrative of purpose. It also arguably allows making an argument for counterbalancing some of the executive dominance in international relations. A narrative of purpose about the added value of the Union for the democratic representation in external relations may contribute to justifying an interpretation of principles and rules examined in Chapters 2 to 6 that favours Union action.

5. Conclusions

This chapter developed the notion of *structures of bonding*, which are formal legal channels of interaction and justification between the Union and its citizens. The potential of bonding structures depends heavily on the autonomy, effectiveness, and legitimacy of EU law. The European legal order has incrementally established and strengthened direct links to its citizens, through the case law of the CJEU, Treaty amendments, and through the practices of the institutions.[148] Its actions have direct and far-reaching consequences for the legal situation of individuals, who in turn have a right to justification of this determination of their rights and obligations. When national courts enforce individual rights under EU law against the Member States, the effective realization of these rights allows the Union to relate directly to its citizens. Similarly, EU citizens are directly represented within the Union. Because of the normative authority of EU law, the identification of (potential) formal legal structures of bonding is relevant,

Europe Gets Mixed Reviews' (*The New York Times*, 28 September 2017) https://www.nytimes.com/2017/09/28/world/europe/france-macron-european-union-reforms.html.

[145] Jean-Claude Juncker, 'The Hour of European Sovereignty', State of the Union 2018, https://ec.europa.eu/commission/news/state-union-2018-hour-european-sovereignty-2018-sep-12_en.

[146] See Gráinne de Búrca, 'Europe's *raison d'être*' in Dimitry Kochenov and Fabian Amtenbrink (eds), *The European Union's Shaping of the International Legal Order* (CUP 2014) 21–37; See also: Ian Manners, 'Normative Power Europe: A Contradiction in Terms?' (2002) 40 JCMS 235, 244.

[147] Jürgen Habermas, *The Postnational Constellation* (CUP 2000).

[148] In the 2014 elections to the European Parliament, the Parliament put forward *Spitzenkandidaten* for the office of the Commission President. See Chapter 5 for other institutional practices.

irrespective of whether and to what extent the actual sociological phenomenon of bonding takes place.

Effectiveness, that is, the normative force, of EU law lies at the core of the potential of these formal legal structures of bonding. Any legal structure within the EU legal order can only have or develop potential vis-à-vis individuals because of the Union's unique success of vesting its law with effect within the national legal orders and so directly impacting on the legal position of individuals. This extraordinary effectiveness of EU law depends conceptually on the internal validity of the CJEU's autonomy narrative and in practice on cooperation of numerous actors, whose perspective and mandate are framed by their own autonomous legal orders. By definition, when EU law is vested with effect in the national legal order, including when it contradicts national law, this is a form of integration.

The *autonomy* of the EU legal order is essentially contested. National constitutional courts reason from the assumption that EU law depends in its validity on national law and claim the final say on its validity. Both the functioning and the legitimacy of the European legal order, internally and externally, depend on the CJEU's ability to counter this claim with its own internally valid narrative of the autonomy of EU law. This narrative assumes that EU law is valid in and of itself and that it does not depend on the authority of national or international law for its validity. The parallel existence of these different narratives and perspectives vests the Union with the ability to draw legitimacy from a number of autonomous sources. In this understanding, the legitimacy of the Union also requires continuous reliance on the legitimacy of the Member States. This is conceptualized in Habermas' work as divided sovereignty, presuming the existence of structures that allow individuals to vest the Union with legitimacy both as EU and national citizens.

Legitimacy, framed as justifiability or worthiness of recognition (*Anerkennungswürdigkeit*), requires the possibility to argue convincingly that the Union's existence and actions can be met with the assent of all citizens, as EU citizens and as national citizens, in a discursive process. This also requires the ability to make a convincing claim to a reasonable level of autonomy in decision-making. It relies on explicating the normative positions of participating actors in a way that allows an exchange about the underlying norms of existing practices. In other words, legitimacy requires justifiability in a discourse from the participant perspective.

This book departs from an understanding of the Union as a construction that cannot plausibly be characterized as an international organization, nor as an oversized replica of the nation state to be. Its legitimacy must necessarily rest on both participation of national citizens through state structures and the participation of EU citizens in decision-making in the EU context. In this reading, legitimacy requires a level of autonomy of federate units, as well as the federal unit. In other words, this understanding of legitimacy protects the federate units from complete integration. It requires maintaining the divided sovereignty in the Habermasian sense. This book aims to further develop how external relations put pressure on the delicate balancing act of maintaining autonomy of all units, and hence the divided sovereignty.

The remainder of this book addresses how the Union's external actions influence (emerging) legal structures of bonding, as well as the autonomy, effectiveness, and legitimacy of EU law. The Union's legal links with individuals are both strengthened and hindered when the Union takes external actions. Ultimately, the choice under the Lisbon Treaty to strengthen the EU's role in external relations was also a choice in favour of stricter constraints on Member States. When the EU takes external actions, these constraints tighten and individuals are, among other things, empowered to use EU law in order to enforce their rights under international law vis-à-vis the Member States. The effects of the Union's external actions on its autonomy, effectiveness, and legitimacy make exposure to the outside world a constitutional moment for the Union.

2

EU Loyalty

Framing Legal Relationships

1. Introduction

The duty of loyalty is the 'systemic' organizational principle of EU law[1] that transforms sovereign states into 'Member States of the EU'.[2] It serves to establish and preserve the unity of the Union by imposing a (quasi-)federal[3] discipline on the different autonomous units and actors that make up the Union. It also requires Member States to accept and respect the autonomy of the Union and its unity of international representation, with the result of legally restraining the exercise of Member States' rights as independent international actors. The latter gives it a potentially very strong integrating force.[4] This chapter demonstrates among others that this force is particularly strong in EU external relations.

The duty of sincere cooperation is in essence a good faith obligation in the same form as we find it under public international and national civil law.[5] The historic origins and some of the specific obligations flowing from the principle of sincere cooperation under EU law are very similar or even identical to those flowing from the good faith principle under public international law.[6] This is in particular the case with regard to negative obligations. However, the EU loyalty forms an *inherent* and *necessary* part of the rule-based framework of EU law. It finds specific and stringent expression in the European Treaties.

[1] Takis Tridimas, *The General Principles of EU Law* (OUP 2006) 5.

[2] See art 1(1) TEU, which contains the only reference to the 'High Contracting Parties' immediately followed by a reference to the Member States. The latter term is then used throughout the Treaties. Consolidated Version Treaty on European Union [2016] OJ C 202/01 (hereafter TEU).

[3] See already: Ole Due, 'Article 5 du traité CEE. Une disposition de caractère fédéral?' in Frank Emmert (ed), *Collected Courses of the Academy of European Law Vol. I—Book 2: The Protection of Human Rights in Europe* (Nijhoff 1991).

[4] Marcus Klamert, *The Principle of Loyalty in EU Law* (OUP 2014) 63 (hereafter Klamert, *Principle of Loyalty*).

[5] Good faith or bona fide obligations exist in different formulations in (nearly) all legal systems and legal cultures. In their essence, they express an anthropological proposition of contractual legal conduct and require the addressee to act with sincere belief or motive, without malice or the desire to defraud others. They are expressed in abstract and comprehensive formulations in very different contexts, in national civil law (eg paras 242 and 932 of the German BGB), and under public international law, eg art 2(2) UN Charter or Preamble and art 26 of the Vienna Convention on the Law of Treaties (1969). See also the uniform commercial code (sections 1-201(9) and 2-403). In France, by contrast, the duty of good faith is often understood as a duty of loyalty and in the Draft Common Frame of Reference, the duty to cooperate includes a duty of loyalty: IV.E.–2:201 (Co-operation): 'The parties to a contract within the scope of this Part of Book IV must collaborate actively and loyally and co-ordinate their respective efforts in order to achieve the objectives of the contract.' See also Martijn Hesselink arguing that good faith is normatively empty: 'The Concept of Good Faith' in Arthur Hartkamp and others (eds), *Towards a European Civil Code* (Kluwer Law International 2004).

[6] Geert de Baere and Timothy Roes, 'EU Loyalty as Good Faith' (2015) 64 ICLQ 829 (hereafter De Baere and Roes, 'EU Loyalty').

EU Powers Under External Pressure: How the EU's External Actions Alter its Internal Structures. Christina Eckes © Christina Eckes 2019. Published 2019 by Oxford University Press.

This chapter develops the core difference between the principle of good faith and the duty of EU loyalty, which is that the latter requires devotion to the ultimate and overarching cause of making the Union a union. Inherent in the concept of loyalty is that it requires a particular level of devotion by the 'loyal person' towards the 'object of loyalty', which in the EU context is the functioning and unity of the Union. This may require the loyal person or entity to align their interests to serving an ultimate and overarching cause taking shape in the object of loyalty. By contrast, the principle of good faith under international law, while imposing cooperation obligations, does not aim to commit actors to any additional cause.

The codifications of the principle of sincere cooperation in Article 4(3) TEU and elsewhere in the Treaties are an expression of the general duty of loyalty within the European Union. This duty of loyalty binds both the Member States and the EU institutions, including among each other. The focus of this chapter is its application to the relationship between the Member States and the EU. The chapter identifies the transformative force of EU loyalty in external relations, shows how it preserves the autonomy of the Union, and impacts on the scope of action of Member States on the international plane. It also demonstrates that EU loyalty potentially takes the role of a structure of bonding in the relationship between the Union and its citizens.

This chapter is structured as follows. Section 2 gives an introduction to the different appearances and guises of sincere cooperation in the European Treaties (Section 2.1), its interpretation in the case law of the CJEU (Section 2.2), and its limits and interrelations with other EU law principles (Section 2.3).

Section 3 introduces the notion of loyalty, identifies its core conceptual features, including its potential to shape relations, interests, and identity (Section 3.1). Section 3.2 moves from loyalty in general to 'institutional loyalty'. Section 3.3 engages with the framing effects of loyalty and its limits in the EU context.

Section 4 concentrates on the application of EU loyalty in the context of external relations. It explains its relevance for determining exclusive EU competences and pre-emption of Member States' action (Section 4.1). The different consequences triggered by internal as opposed to external actions of the Member States are discussed in the context of mixed agreements and mixed membership (Section 4.2). EU loyalty triggers specific *internal* information and communication obligations, which support the conceptual understanding that it is indeed a duty of loyalty (Section 4.3). Loyalty in the external relations context is intensified by the requirement of unity of international representation (Section 4.4). Section 4.5 introduces that Member States are also required to protect the *future* scope for autonomous Union action, which underlines the durable nature of loyalty.

Section 5 takes distance from and reflects on the case law of the CJEU (Section 5.1). It discusses the duty-based (deontological) nature and ordering function of EU loyalty. Section 5.2 compares internal and external obligations flowing from EU loyalty and explains why the transformative effect is present in particular in the context of external relations. It further argues that this is justified from a pragmatic perspective.

Section 6 concludes and relates the findings of the previous sections to the overarching conceptual framework of the book, by discussing their consequences for formal legal structures of bonding, as well as for the autonomy, effectiveness, and legitimacy of the Union and its law. This also brings the discussion back to the tension between law and politics that underlies the concept of bonding structures.[7]

[7] See Section 2 of Chapter 1.

2. The Principle of Sincere Cooperation: Taking Stock

2.1 Codifications

The principle of sincere cooperation appears in different forms in the Treaties, from the general and mutual principle in Article 4(3) TEU to numerous more specific forms, addressed to the Member States alone, as well as to the institutions alone. The inclusion of the general principle of sincere cooperation in the TEU confirms that it is applicable across all Union policies, including the Common Foreign and Security Policy (CFSP).[8] It is a mutual obligation ('the *Union* and the Member States shall'); however, while the Union is only addressed in the general part (sentence 1), the following more detailed clauses (sentence 2 and 3) set out only duties of the Member States. Article 13(2) TEU emphasizes the principle of sincere cooperation among the EU institutions, which is not literally covered by the wording of Article 4(3) s 1 TEU. However, arguably such a duty could already be indirectly derived from the general obligation of the Union towards the Member States,[9] because even if the characterization that disputes between the institutions are battles between the Union and its Member States with substitutes[10] may seem exaggerated, any dispute between the institutions is certainly relevant for the power division between the Union and its Member States. This chapter argues that the specific codifications are not the source but a codified expression of the general constitutional duty of loyalty within the EU legal order.[11] This reading also helps to better understand the case law of the CJEU and the limits and more specific obligations flowing from EU loyalty.

Particularly relevant for external relations is Article 351(2) TFEU. It specifically addresses the meaning of loyalty in the context of prior agreements of the Member States.[12] It is hence an expression of a conflict norm reconciling international law obligations into which the States entered before becoming EU Member States with EU law. It may, under specific circumstances, require Member States to renegotiate, adjust, or even terminate prior international agreements. It also calls upon Member States to assist each other and adopt a common attitude where this is necessary.[13] Equally highly relevant in the external relations context is that the CJEU has found the predecessor of Article 344 TFEU, which expresses an obligation of the Member States to respect the exclusive jurisdiction of the CJEU for all matters of EU law, to be 'a specific

[8] See also: Case C-439/13 P, *Elitaliana SpA v Eulex Kosovo* [2015] EU:C:2014:2416, Opinion of AG Jääskinen, para 28.

[9] Case 230/81, *Luxembourg v Parliament* [1983] EU:C:1983:32, para 37 (hereafter Case 230/81, *Luxembourg v Parliament*); Case C-45/07, *Commission v Greece* [2009] EU:C:2009:81, paras 25–26 (hereafter C-45/07, *Commission v Greece*); Case C-339/00, *Ireland v Commission* [2003] EU:C:2003:545, paras 71–76. See also the judgment in Case F-65/07, *Aayhan and Others v Parliament* [2009] EU:F:2009:43, paras 118–19.

[10] Koen Lenaerts, 'EU Federalism in 3-D' in Elke Cloots, Geert de Baere, and Stefan Scottiaux (eds), *Federalism in the European Union* (Hart Publishing 2012) 24.

[11] See also: J Temple Lang, 'Article 10 EC: The Most Important "General Principle" of Community Law' in Ulf Bernitz and others (eds), *General Principles of EC Law in a Process of Development* (Wolters Kluwer 2008) 76.

[12] See for further codifications of the principle of sincere cooperation between Member States: arts 168 and 210(1) of the Consolidated Version of the Treaty on the Functioning of the European Union [2008] OJ C115/47 (hereafter TFEU).

[13] See for more detail: Pieter Jan Kuijper and others (eds), *The Law of EU External Relations. Text, Cases, Materials, and Commentary on the EU as an International Legal Actor* (2nd edn, OUP 2015) 801with a reference to: Case C-205/06, *Commission v Austria (BITs)* [2009] EU:C:2009:118, paras 1–3 and 16–45 (hereafter Case C-205/06, *Commission v Austria*).

expression of Member States' more general duty of loyalty resulting from Article [now 4(3) TFEU]'.[14]

Finally, Article 24(3) TEU specifically sets out the principle of sincere cooperation for CFSP, despite the fact that Article 4(3) TEU after its relocation also applies to the CFSP.[15] Article 24(3) TEU is worded more strictly and limited to the Member States. It requires Member States to 'support the Union's external and security policy actively and unreservedly in a spirit of *loyalty* and *mutual solidarity* and shall comply with the Union's action in this area'.[16] This focus on the Member States reflects the more intergovernmental nature of CFSP. The specific mention of loyalty and solidarity expressly introduces a subjective and moral dimension.[17] This extra-legal dimension is also present in Article 4(3) TEU in most of the language versions of the EU Treaty,[18] while the English language version is an exception in not referring to loyalty.

2.2 Sincere cooperation in the case law: subjects, objects, and integrative force

The true meaning of the cooperation duty under EU law, as well as the spectrum of appearances and nuances of the different obligations flowing from this duty emerge only from the case law of the CJEU. The CJEU has used a range of different expressions to capture the content of the cooperation duty under EU law, ranging from simply 'principle of cooperation',[19] to 'duty to cooperate in good faith',[20] 'the obligation to cooperate in good faith',[21] and 'principle of cooperation in good faith';[22] to 'duty of genuine cooperation'[23] 'obligation of genuine cooperation'[24] and 'spirit of genuine cooperation';[25] as well as 'mutual duties of sincere cooperation'[26] and finally 'duty of loyalty',[27] and 'principle of loyal cooperation'.[28] The Court hence sometimes, but only sometimes, refers to 'loyalty' or 'loyal cooperation'. Sometimes, it also refers to 'good

[14] Case C-459/03, *Commission v Ireland (Mox Plant)* [2006] EU:C:2006:345, para 169 (hereafter Case C-459/03, *Mox Plant*).

[15] See also the consultation duties in art 32 TEU as a particular expression of the principle of sincere cooperation.

[16] Emphasis added.

[17] See Section 3 below for the subjective dimension of loyalty.

[18] Examples are the Germanic (Danish: 'I medfør af princippet om loyalt samarbejde respekterer'; Dutch: 'Krachtens het beginsel van loyale samenwerking respecteren'; German: 'Nach dem Grundsatz der loyalen Zusammenarbeit achten') and Romanic languages (French: 'En vertu du principe de coopération loyale'; Spanish: 'Conforme al principio de cooperación leal'; Italian: 'In virtù del principio di leale cooperazione'), as well as Finnic languages (eg Estonian: 'Kooskõlas lojaalse koostöö põhimõttega abistavad') and Slavic languages (eg Polish: 'Zgodnie z zasadą lojalnej współpracy').

[19] Case C-277/02, *EU-Wood-Trading* [2004] EU:C:2004:810, para 48.

[20] Case C-251/89, *Athanasopoulos and Others* [1991] EU:C:1991:242, para 57 (hereafter Case C-251/89, *Athanasopoulos*); Case C-355/04 P, *Segi and Others v Council* [2007] EU:C:2007:116, para 52.

[21] eg Case C-246/07, *Commission v Sweden (PFOS)* [2010] EU:C:2010:203, para 77 (hereafter Case C-246/07, *PFOS*).

[22] eg Case C-327/15, *TDC* [2016] EU:C:2016:974, para 90 (hereafter C-327/15, *TDC*).

[23] eg Case C-33/90, *Commission* v *Italy* [1991] EU:C:1991:476, para 20; Case C-433/03, *Commission v Germany* [2005] EU:C:2005:462, para 64 (hereafter Case C-433/03, *Commission v Germany*).

[24] Case C-105/02, *Commission v Germany* [2006] EU:C:2006:637, para 87.

[25] Case C-494/01, *Commission v Ireland* [2005] EU:C:2005:250, para 45.

[26] Case 230/81, *Luxembourg v Parliament* (n 9) para 37. This may be where the formulation in art 4(3) TEU comes from (De Baere and Roes, 'EU loyalty' (n 6)).

[27] Case C-459/03, *Mox Plant* (n 14) para 169; Opinion 2/13 [2014] EU:C:2014:2454, para 202 (hereafter Opinion 2/13).

[28] Case C-93/12, *ET Agrokonsulting-04-Velko Stoyanov* [2013] EU:C:2013:432, para 36.

faith'. Parties equally refer sometimes to 'loyalty' obligations[29] or the spirit of 'loyalty',[30] or even request clarification of the scope and consequences of 'Union loyalty'.[31]

In line with some other voices in the literature, this chapter identifies a general duty of *loyalty*,[32] which leads to more specific cooperation obligations for both the Member States[33] and the EU. EU institutions have obligations to cooperate among themselves[34] and with the Member States.[35] Cooperation obligations require the EU institutions to act coherently and disclose their position in advance of taking action.[36] In particular under the preliminary ruling procedure, sincere cooperation obligations also apply between national courts and the CJEU.[37] For the Member States, the duty of sincere cooperation applies to all emanations of the state. It extends to the national legislator, the executive, and the judiciary.[38] An example is the obligation of the national legislator to 'refrain from taking any measures liable seriously to compromise the result prescribed' by a given directive, including during the period of transposition.[39] In administrative law, the duty of sincere cooperation justifies and motivates that the national authorities are in charge of implementing Union law.[40] Particularly strict cooperation duties are imposed on the national judiciaries.[41] In settled case law, the principle of sincere

[29] Appeal brought on 11 January 2016 by Belgium (Case C-16/16 P) against the order of the General Court Case T-721/14, *Belgium v Commission* [2015] EU:T:2015:829. For the Danish court see C-327/15, *TDC* (n 22). Preliminary reference http://curia.europa.eu/juris/document/document.jsf?text=&docid=166632&pageIndex=0&doclang=en&mode=lst&dir=&occ=first&part=1&cid=1466187

[30] See also the Commission, Case C-73/14, *Council v Commission* [2015] EU:C:2015:663, para 88 (hereafter Case C-73/14, *Council v Commission*).

[31] Case C-518/11, *UPC Nederland BV* [2013] EU:C:2013:709; however, neither the Court nor the AG phrased their replies in terms of 'loyalty'. See also the Danish court in: C-327/15, *TDC* (n 22).

[32] eg Klamert, *Principle of Loyalty* (n 4); De Baere and Roes, 'EU loyalty' (n 6).

[33] Judgments in Case C-251/89, *Athanasopoulos* (n 20) para 57; Case C-165/91, *Van Munster* [1994] EU:C:1994:359, para 32; Case C-326/00, *Idryma Koinonikon Asfaliseon (IKA)* [2003] EU:C:2003:101; and Case C-202/97, *Fitzwilliam Executive Search (FTS)* [2000] EU:C:2000:75, paras 51 and 56. See also the Case C-73/08, *Bressol and Others* [2009] EU:C:2009:396, Opinion of AG Sharpston, para 154 and Case C-364/10, *Hungary v Slovakia* [2012] EU:C:2012:124, Opinion of AG Bot, paras 58–60.

[34] Art 13(2) TEU; see eg for communication duties: Case C-65/93, *Parliament v Council* [1995] EU:C:1995:91, para 23; Case 204/86, *Greece v Council* [1988] EU:C:1988:450, para 16.

[35] See eg Case 230/81, *Luxembourg v Parliament* (n 9) para 37 (Seat and Working Place of the Parliament); Joined cases 358/85 and 51/86, *France v Parliament* [1988] EU:C:1988:431, paras 34–35; Case C-2/88 Imm., *Zwartveld and Others* [1990] EU:C:1990:440 (hereafter Case C-2/88 Imm., *Zwartveld*). For mutual diligence obligations under a notification scheme: Case C-319/97, *Kortas* [1999] EU:C:1999:272, para 35 (hereafter Case C-319/97, *Kortas*).

[36] See in this regard, eg Case C-660/13, *Council v Commission* [2015] EU:C:2015:787, Opinion of AG Sharpston, para 124.

[37] Joined Cases C-300-392/98, *Parfums Christian Dior and others* [2000] EU:C:2000:688, paras 36-38 (hereafter Joined Cases C-300-392/98, *Dior*). See most explicitly on the duty of the CJEU: Case C-62/14, *Gauweiler* [2015] EU:C:2015:7, Opinion of AG Cruz Villalon, para 64.

[38] For notification duties of the executive, see eg Case C-319/97, *Kortas* (n 35).

[39] Case C-129/96, *Inter-Environnement Wallonie* [1997] EU:C:1997:628, para 45—the case concerned an order from the Walloon Council.

[40] Joined Cases 205 and 215/82, *Deutsche Milchkontor* [1983] EU:C:1983:233, para 17.

[41] Case C-2/88 Imm., *Zwartveld* (n 35) para 18. Case C-106/89, *Marleasing* [1990] EU:C:1990:395, para 8; Case C-312/93, *Peterbroeck* [1995] EU:C:1995:437 (hereafter Case C-312/93, *Peterbroeck*); Joined Cases C-300-392/98, *Dior* (n 37); Case C-453/00, *Kühne & Heitz* [2004] EU:C:2004:17, paras 24–27; Case C-526/04, *Laboratoires Boiron* [2006] EU:C:2006:528, paras 55 and 57; Joined cases C-261-299/07, *VTB-VAB* and *Galatea* [2009] EU:C:2009:244, para 39; Joined cases C-200-201/07, *Marra* [2008] EU:C:2008:579, para 41; Case C-234/89, *Stergios Delimitis* [1991] EU:C:1991:91 (Commission vis-à-vis national judiciary); Case C-205/06, *Commission v Austria* (n 13) para 44 (Commission must facilitate cooperation between Member States); Case C-298/12, *Confédération paysanne* [2013] EU:C:2013:630, para 37 (hereafter Case C-298/12, *Confédération paysanne)*, citing to that effect the judgments in Case 106/77, *Simmenthal* [1978] EU:C:1978:49, para 24 (hereafter Case 106/77, *Simmenthal*) and Case

cooperation requires national judges to ensure effective judicial protection of rights under EU law[42] and sometimes even to raise EU law of their own motion.[43] Sincere cooperation has further been used by the CJEU to justify limiting national procedural autonomy.[44]

In the case of *Costanzo,* EU loyalty has even been interpreted as prevailing over the relations of loyalty *within the state*.[45] In this case, the CJEU explicitly referred to primacy and loyal cooperation to hold that national administrators must set aside national legislation that is contrary to EU law. This triggered a stream of protests from administrative lawyers—especially from Germany—because this would erode the principle of administrative legality, and with it the loyalty of the executive to the legislative branch.[46] Furthermore, the CJEU construes institutions typically associated with loyalty to the (nation) state, as for example (certain) oaths by public officials, in the light of EU law as being open to nationals of other Member States.[47] The Court found Belgium, for example, in breach of EU law for imposing a nationality condition for access to the profession of civil-law notary. Hence, the concept of loyalty within the (nation) state is to some extent Europeanized. It is extended for EU citizens as necessarily allowing loyalty to their host Member State.

Sincere cooperation or loyal cooperation, as it is called in most language versions, plays an important role in the realization of the Union's constitutional ambitions. Indeed, the duty of loyalty is closely interrelated with the principles of primacy,[48] effectiveness,[49] coherence,[50] and mutual trust,[51] which all significantly facilitate the

C-617/10, *Åkerberg Fransson* [2013] EU:C:2013:105, para 45 (hereafter Case C-617/10, *Åkerberg Fransson*); Case C-105/03, *Pupino* [2005] EU:C:2005:386, para 42–43 (principle of loyal cooperation applicable in the former third pillar and in particular on the national courts). See also: Marise Cremona, 'Defending the Community Interest: The Duties of Cooperation and Compliance' in Marise Cremona and Bruno de Witte (eds), *EU Foreign Relations Law: Constitutional Fundamentals* (Hart Publishing 2008) 158 (hereafter Cremona, 'Cooperation and Compliance').

42 Case C-243/15, *Lesoochranárske zoskupenie VLK (Slovak Bear II)* [2016] EU:C:2016:838, para 50. See on the ambiguous use of effectiveness and effective judicial protection in the case law: Johanna Bergström, 'The Principle of Effective Judicial Protection After the Lisbon Treaty' (2011) 4 Rev EAL 53.

43 Case C-312/93, *Peterbroeck* (n 41).

44 Case 33-76, *Rewe-Zentralfinanz* [1976] EU:C:1976:188, para 5 ('impossible in practice'); Case C-662/13, *Surgicare* [2015] EU:C:2015:89 ('impossible in practice or excessively difficult').

45 Case 103/88, *Costanzo* [1989] EU:C:1989:256. See also: Case C-119/05, *Lucchini* [2007] EU:C:2007:434, in which the Court, drawing on loyal cooperation, held that the duty of the Member States, eg national governments, to recover illegal state aid could justify ignoring the principle of *res judicata*. This could be read as an erosion of the power of national courts over the other branches of government.

46 I would like to thank Filipe Brito Bastos for discussing this with me.

47 Case C-47/08, *Commission v Belgium* [2011] EU:C:2011:334, para 141ff.

48 In the landmark case of Case 6-64, *Costa v ENEL* [1964] EU:C:1964:66 (hereafter Case 6-64, *Costa v ENEL*), the CJEU referred to sincere cooperation as one of a number of principles justifying primacy. In Case C-298/12, *Confédération paysanne* (n 41) para 37, the Court exclusively bases primacy on 'cooperation in good faith'. Yet the two rulings to which the Court refers in this paragraph do not refer to sincere cooperation: Case 106/77, *Simmenthal* (n 41) para 24 and Case C-617/10, *Åkerberg Fransson* (n 41) para 45.

49 The principle of sincere cooperation is the origin of the principle of effectiveness, see Case C-640/13, *Commission v United Kingdom* [2015] EU:C:2014:2457, para 32. See also for supremacy and effectiveness: Eleftheria Neframi, 'The Duty of Loyalty: Rethinking its Scope Through Its Application in the Field of EU External Relations' (2010) 47 CML Rev 323, 325ff (hereafter Neframi, 'Duty of Loyalty').

50 Christophe Hillion, 'Mixity and Coherence in EU External Relations: The Significance of the "Duty of Cooperation"' (2009) CLEER Working Paper 02/2009 (hereafter Hillion, 'Duty of Cooperation').

51 The principle of sincere cooperation is at the origin of the constitutional principle of mutual trust, which is not codified in the Treaties but forms the background of the principle of mutual

workings of the EU legal order and ultimately ensure its functioning. The duty of loyalty is foundational for the unique effectiveness of the (increasing interlocking embrace between the EU institutions, EU law, and the CJEU on the one hand and Member States, national law, and national courts on the other).[52] Landmark cases such as *Costa ENEL* (*primacy*) and *Francovich (Member State liability)* explicitly relied on sincere cooperation when establishing their bold constitutional principles.[53] In the case of *Francovich,* the CJEU further referred to ex-Article 5 EEC as the 'basis for the obligation of Member States to make good such loss and damage' and 'the obligation to nullify the unlawful consequences of a breach of Community law'. [54] Hence, sincere cooperation justified Member State civil liability towards individuals for non-implementation of directives. The CJEU drew on sincere cooperation to conclude that Member States cannot rely on national law as a reason not to give effect to EU law,[55] that they need to consult with the EU institutions before passing laws that affect them,[56] and that they have an active obligation 'to adopt all necessary and proportionate measures in order to prevent the free movement of [goods] from being obstructed by actions by private [parties]'.[57] In short, sincere cooperation can serve as an independent legal basis for distinct obligations.[58] It also transforms Treaty rules to extend further than they otherwise would. Effectiveness is in this sense a direct 'manifestation of loyalty'.[59] Both are *inherent* in the EU legal order.[60] When principles inherent in the legal order as a whole are the source of other principles, as the EU loyalty is the source of effectiveness, this allows them to develop a particular ability and reach to reinforce EU legal structures.

Purposive interpretation has never explicitly been linked by the Court to EU loyalty or sincere cooperation. Advocate General La Pergola, by contrast, argued explicitly that the principle of sincere cooperation 'provides a sound legal basis for condemning as unlawful any conduct by a Member State which, although complying with the literal requirements of a provision of the Treaty, nevertheless runs counter to the aim pursued by that provision'.[61] He concluded that sincere cooperation is 'dealing with indirect

recognition within the Area of Freedom Security and Justice (AFSJ). See Christina Eckes, 'Mutual Trust and the Future of Fundamental Rights Protection in the EU's Compound Legal Order' in Loïc Azoulai, Nehal Bhuta, and Marise Cremona (eds), *Collected Courses of the Academy of European Law* (OUP 2019 *forthcoming*). The link between the principle of sincere cooperation and this principle is explicitly made in secondary law: eg Parliament and Council Directive (EC) 2005/36 on the recognition of professional qualifications [2005] OJ L 255/22.

[52] See Chapter 1, Section 3 for more explanation on the effectiveness of EU law, the interlocking embrace, and the relation between the two.

[53] Case 6-64, *Costa v ENEL* [1964] (n 48) refers to art 5(2) EEC, which sets out the negative duty of Member States to 'abstain from any measures likely to jeopardise the attainment of the objectives of this Treaty'.

[54] Joined cases C-6-9/90, *Francovich and Others* [1991] EU:C:1991:428, para 36, with reference to 'the analogous provision of Article 86 of the ECSC Treaty, the judgment in Case 6/60 *Humblet v Belgium* ECR 559'.

[55] Case 30-72, *Commission v Italy* [1973] EU:C:1973:16, para 11 (Premiums for grubbing fruit trees). See also the judgment in Case 39-72, *Commission v Italy* [1973] EU:C:1973:13, paras 24–25 (Premiums for slaughtering cows).

[56] Case 186/85, *Commission v Belgium* [1987] EU:C:1987:208, paras 39–40.

[57] Case C-265/95, *Commission v France (Spanish Strawberries)* [1997] EU:C:1997:595, para 66.

[58] Klamert, *Principle of Loyalty* (n 4) Chapter 12.

[59] ibid, Chapter 13.

[60] See Chapter 1.

[61] Case C-16/94, *Dubois and Cargo v Garonor* [1995] EU:C:1995:148, Opinion of AG La Pergola, para 12.

failure to observe tenets or principles implicit in the Treaty',[62] solving situations that 'are not penalized by more specific provisions but nevertheless go against the aims of the Treaty'.[63] Loyalty in its conceptual understanding developed in Section 3 below, is also a *reason* for taking a purposive approach to the interpretation of the EU Treaties and hence plays an important role in the integration-friendly case law of the CJEU. The CJEU's reading, which reasons from the objectives and the effectiveness of EU law, allows these considerations to influence the interpretation of all organizational principles and specific rules of EU law.

2.3 Limits

Since the entry into force of the Lisbon Treaty, the general principle of sincere cooperation has been grouped in Article 4 TEU together with the principles of conferral and the duty to respect national identity, which impose limits on sincere cooperation. An illustrative example of potential tensions between the principles of sincere cooperation and conferral is the doctrine of implied external powers, which is originally derived from the principle of sincere cooperation and allows the EU to act without express powers in the Treaties, where this serves to attain an objective under the Treaties.[64] In practice, the doctrine of implied powers limits the capacity of the principle of conferral to set clear boundaries for Member States' obligations flowing from sincere cooperation.

The Union's obligation to respect the 'national identities' and 'essential State functions' of the Member States aims to reserve scope for national sovereignty by protecting it from Union interference. This includes 'ensuring the territorial integrity of the State, maintaining law and order and safeguarding national security ... [as] [...] the sole responsibility of each Member State'. This is also a legal means introduced under primary law to reign in the Court, who is mandated to interpret and apply primary law, but cannot question its validity.[65] In particular, the references to core elements of state sovereignty, such as 'territorial integrity', demonstrate the fundamental nature of this limit.

Ultra vires action, where the overstepping of competences is obvious, qualifies as a breach of the duty to cooperate in good faith. The German Federal Constitutional Court (GFCC) in its 2009 Lisbon judgment elaborated on the purpose of principles, such as respect for national identities, sincere cooperation, subsidiarity, and proportionality, to ensure that the powers conferred at European level are exercised in such a way that the competences of the Member States are not unduly affected.[66] The GFCC opposed the principle of sincere cooperation and the duty to respect national identities in a way that imposes limits on the obligations flowing from the former. It argued that the duty to respect national identities justifies the review powers of national courts[67] and that sincere cooperation applied to the Member States could not exclude review by national courts. Codified limits of EU powers have continuously been strengthened in the past rounds of Treaty amendments. Examples are the introduction of the duty to

[62] ibid, para 11. [63] ibid.

[64] Opinion 1/03 (Lugano Convention) [2006] EU:C:2006:81, para 124. The landmark case on implied powers, ERTA, explicitly refers to sincere cooperation, see Section 4.1 below.

[65] See for the interpretation of national identity: Case C-42/17, *MAS, MB* (*Taricco II*) [2017] EU:C:2017:936.

[66] See also: BVerfG, 2 BvE 2/08, para 304 (Treaty of Lisbon judgment).

[67] ibid, para 240.

respect national identities, but also the yellow and orange card procedures[68] to give the subsidiarity principle more bite.[69] These formal legal limits vest national courts with additional arguments and legitimacy when they set limits to EU powers, as well as the Court's interpretation of sincere cooperation.

The scope of Union law may further appear prima facie as a logical limit to organizational principles of Union law. Post-Lisbon, the scope of EU law has played the most important role in the context of the application of the Charter, whose scope of application is identical to the scope of Union law, which is considerably broader than situations of implementation in the strict sense (*Fransson*).[70] The Swedish legislation at stake did not implement EU law; yet it was intended to further the purpose of EU law, that is, of preventing conduct prejudicial to the EU's financial interests. This also seems in line with pre-Lisbon case law,[71] which established two ways by which Member State action falls within the scope of EU law: when they implement EU law[72] and when they derogate from provisions of EU law.[73] Advocate General Villalón proposed in *Fransson* that the CJEU should review fundamental rights compliance by Member States when there is 'a *specific interest of the Union* in ensuring that that exercise of public authority accords with the interpretation of the fundamental rights by the Union'.[74] He supported this point essentially with reference to the effectiveness of EU law within the national legal order. Because EU law takes primacy, the lawfulness of public authority within the Union could be at stake if Member States' compliance with fundamental rights were not ensured when they give effect to EU law *objectives*. The limits of this purposive reading of the notion of 'scope of EU law' was illustrated by the case of *Willems*, where a Member State was using data collected under an EU regulation for purposes outside that regulation. This was not considered acting within the scope of EU law.[75]

The scope of Union law is wider than the scope of Union competences because the objectives of the Treaties are attained through action not only of the Union itself but also of the Member States.[76] As we have seen, it has been argued to stretch as far as the Union's interest in compliance with the Union interpretation of fundamental rights. Sincere cooperation also carries meaning beyond the Union's competences, whether exclusive or shared and exercised. However, it serves more directly the purpose to protect Union interests, irrespective of the objectives pursued. In this way, it goes beyond the scope of EU law. Actions of the Member States, either individually or collectively,

[68] National parliaments have the powers to scrutinize and issue reasoned opinions on the compliance of draft legislation with the principle of subsidiarity. If a third issues a negative opinion, this is a yellow card. If a simple majority issues a negative opinion, this is an orange card. The consequences of both are set out in art 7(2) and (3) of Protocol 2, respectively.

[69] See art 4(2)TEU and protocol 2, respectively.

[70] Case C-617/10, *Åkerberg Fransson* (n 41) paras 19–21. The later cases of Case C-206/13, *Cruciano Siragusa* [2014] EU:C:2014:126 and Case C-198/13, *Hernandéz and Others* [2014] EU:C:2014:2055 did not shed more light on the scope of EU law. Most recently, this approach was confirmed by: Case C-390/12, *Pfleger* [2014] EU:C:2014:281, in particular para 36.

[71] Michael Dougan, 'Judicial Review of Member State Action Under the General Principles and the Charter: Defining the "Scope of Union Law"' (2015) 52 CML Rev 1201.

[72] Case 5/88, *Wachauf* [1989] EU:C:1989:321.

[73] Case C-260/89, *Elliniki Radiophonia Tileorassi* [1991] EU:C:1991:254.

[74] Case C-617/10, *Åkerberg Fransson* [2012] EU:C:2012:340, AG Villalón, para 40.

[75] See Case C-446/12, *Willems* [2015] EU:C:2015:238; Council Regulation (EC) 2252/2004 on standards for security features and biometrics in passports and travel documents issued by Member States [2004] OJ L 385/1.

[76] Allan Dashwood, 'The Limits of European Community Powers' (1996) 21 EL Rev 113 (at the time with regard to the Community).

are affected by their duty of loyal cooperation whenever such actions have a bearing on the Union's ability to pursue its objectives, interests, or on existing or future EU law. In Section 4 below we will see that this is particularly broad in scope in the context of external relations, where the Union pursues a wide range of objectives and where Member State action is particularly susceptible of having a negative impact on the pursuit of these Union objectives, interests, or law. To conclude, the circumstances in which the duty of loyalty comes into play are not limited to the scope of EU law.

When applied to the EU institutions, sincere cooperation itself may have the ability to protect the reserved competences of the Member States. Loyalty is not as such centralizing. It requires *mutual* respect, not only of the interests but also the autonomy of the different units. Loyal cooperation is a necessary requirement of federalism.[77] It applies to the individual units in relation to each other and to the individual units' relationship with the overall political construction. It applies to all actors, including all national civil servants. Loyalty requires federate entities to demonstrate loyalty towards the federal system even if they disagree with the substance or exercise of a federal action in a particular policy area. Within the flexible and dynamic division of competences of a federation, loyalty can also be interpreted as a counterbalance to effectiveness. It serves the purpose of avoiding the risk that effectiveness considerations eat away at the reserved competences of the federate entities and ultimately threaten the power balance that characterizes a federation and ensures its legitimacy. Loyalty aims to protect the scope for autonomous decision-making of both the Union and the Member States. However, loyalty does not necessarily protect an autonomous position of Member States on the international plane. The next section sets out the conceptual features of loyalty, which also illustrate different implications within the relationship of those connected by loyalty and vis-à-vis third parties.

3. Beyond the Law: What is Loyalty?

The differences between loyalty, good faith, and sincere cooperation are not purely semantic. I argue that loyalty requires a voluntary commitment to give normative priority to the relationship between the 'loyal person' and the 'object of loyalty'. Loyalty introduces a higher cause or purpose, which is not present in the concepts of (sincere) cooperation or good faith. It is voluntary and purposive. In order to investigate the possibility that this reading is appropriate to conceptualize cooperation duties under EU law, this section will engage with loyalty from a conceptual rather than a legal perspective.

3.1 A conceptual approach

Josiah Royce's philosophical engagement with the notion of loyalty remains the leading work in the field. He defines loyalty as '[t]he willing and practical and thoroughgoing devotion of a person to a cause'.[78] 'Willing' refers to Aristotle's commander, who is not motivated by fear or trickery. The cause is hence a cause to which the loyal person *chooses* to devote herself. 'Practical' expressions of loyalty require the loyal person to *act* with a sense of devotion to a cause (objective element), rather than just nourishing

[77] Anna Gamper, 'On Loyalty and the (Federal) Constitution' (2010) 4 ICLJ 157, 169. See the Introduction for a conceptualization of federalism.

[78] Josiah Royce, *The Philosophy of Loyalty* (Macmillan 1908) 16–17 (hereafter Royce, *Loyalty*).

emotions (subjective element). 'Thoroughgoing' indicates that any such emotion and course of action must be of a certain duration and continuity and have some relevance for the person in a deeper sense, going beyond the specific action in question.

Royce further explains that '[s]ince loyalty is a relative term, and always implies some object, some cause, to which any given loyalty is to be shown, we must consider what are the fitting objects of loyalty'.[79] Loyalty relates a subject (the loyal person) to an object (the cause). This relational aspect of loyalty is closely related to its durability aspect. Loyalties only emerge as a result of relationships. Loyalty requires the loyal person to feel sufficiently closely bound to call the cause their own. This presumes that the person expects their relationship with the cause to be of some duration. My loyalties are to *my* friends, *my* family, *my* profession, or *our* country, not yours, unless yours are also *mine*. Loyalties are the result of an identification that binds the success, failure, fate, or well-being of the objects of loyalty to one's own. As a result, '[w]e identify and feel shame or pride in their doings. We will take risks or bear burdens for them.'[80] This implies that loyalty is a commitment that *changes one's interest*. Supporting the object of loyalty becomes one's own interest. An important aspect is that loyalty as a relational emotional band influences both behaviour and (the perception of) own interests. The objective act of demonstrating loyalty to a cause and hence privileging it above other causes for the subjective reason of a relational link usually requires taking an action that—without loyalty—would not be fully motivated and justified by one's own interest.

The relational aspect of loyalty has even been used for the moral argument that loyalty is a central and intrinsic feature of the 'historical self', defined by relationships grown in the course of our personal history.[81] Prima facie it seems difficult to justify any departure from an impartial morality[82] by reference to loyalty relationships, which may also vary considerably in nature (individual relationships within a family or belonging to a group such as the people of a country). The significance of relations for the morality debate cannot be further discussed in the present context. The debate, however, demonstrates the underlying understanding that being loyal is a *character trait* and hence somewhat entrenched and durable; that loyalty arises only in the context of *durable* relations; that it has not only an *objective* but also a *subjective* element; and that identity is not only relevant to loyalty but that loyalty itself has identity-forming consequences. The work of philosophers on moral obligations flowing from relationships may help us to think about the relevance of individuality and identity; in short, 'the idea that individuals are not inter-substitutable'.[83] The objective element of loyalty is that the loyal person decides to serve the cause because she sees that the cause has value beyond her own interest. Taken to the extreme, loyalties may 'lead people to suspend judgment about right and wrong'.[84] In a less extreme form they impact on the considerations and may change judgment. This implies that loyalty may lead to actions that cannot be justified without reference to this loyalty.

[79] ibid, 14–15.

[80] See similarly the definition of loyalty in the *Stanford Encyclopedia of Philosophy* http://plato.stanford.edu/entries/loyalty/.

[81] See above all: George Fletcher, *Loyalty: An Essay on the Morality of Relationships* (OUP 1993) (hereafter Fletcher, *Morality of Relationships*).

[82] Fletcher considers impartial morality an 'unrealistic utopianism'. ibid, 170.

[83] Bernard Williams, *Moral Luck: Philosophical Papers 1973–1980* (Chapter 'Persons, character and morality', CUP 1981) 15.

[84] Fletcher, *Morality of Relationships* (n 81) 36.

In its strongest form, loyalty has the ability to bring together the totality of a loyal person's actions and direct them towards one unified cause. This cause, in turn, then provides priority and direction and allows the individual to escape the paradoxical tendencies of self-realization. It tells the loyal person what to do and frees her from hesitancy.[85] Loyalty hence has an ordering function, ultimately with the potential to trigger an identity-creating dynamic. This ordering function can also be found in the etymological origin of the word loyalty. Loyalty, just as law, stems from the Latin word 'lex' and the French word 'loi'.[86] Both loyalty and the law are understood in a binary way: either one acts lawfully or unlawfully, either one is loyal or disloyal. This is the sustained ordering function that loyalty shares with the law. This ordering function explains why loyalty, understood as a subjective understanding of a relationship that is expressed in an objective action, has the potential of creating or transforming the relationship between the subject and the object of that loyalty in a fundamental and durable fashion. This ability of loyalty to vest the loyal person with a unity of purpose explains the transformative potential of loyalty.

3.2 Institutional loyalty

Institutional loyalty is instrumental to ensuring the sustainability of associational affiliations.[87] It allows long-term commitments even where a particular social institution temporarily fails to deliver the goods for which the loyal person connected to it in the first place. Loyalty is a mechanism that ensures, at least temporarily, that an association with an institution or political body is honoured despite it falling short of supplying the goods that were expected from it. It creates a commitment beyond short-term interest to work towards ensuring that the institution or political body delivers the goods it promised. Institutional loyalty also ensures that efforts within that association relationship are made to ensure compliance with the common standards, for example, show the same commitment.[88] These commitments only cease to exist where it becomes clear that the institution is no longer capable of delivering such goods. Institutional loyalty does not rule out interventions by loyal contestants. The loyal person may oppose or contest the course required by loyalty but remain loyal, that is, such contestation must take place within a framework of continuous cooperation.

'Loyalty' in political and legal relations is usually used in the relationship between the individual and the polity of which they are part. The classic example of loyalty between the individual and the polity is the devotion that a patriot feels who dies for her country. Indeed, loyalty of the individual towards their nation, that is, patriotism, is a central theme in loyalty research. The subjects of loyalty are hence usual individuals. However, loyalty obligations also exist among different entities within one polity. In particular the duty not to jeopardize the common endeavour, that is, the functioning of the polity as such, is present in one form or other in all federal structures. Examples are the *Bundestreue* in Germany[89] and loyalty in the United States of America.[90] At its core, *Bundestreue* is, for example, 'an obligation directed to the federal and federate

[85] Royce, *Loyalty* (n 78) 22.
[86] Brian Byron, *Loyalty in the Spirituality of St. Thomas More* (Nieuwkoop De Graaf 1972) 25.
[87] Albert Hirschman, *Exit, Voice, and Loyalty: Response to Decline in Firms, Organizations and States* (HUP 1970).
[88] ibid for more generally on the mechanism of loyalty in different contexts.
[89] Albert Bleckmann, 'Zum Rechtsinstitut der Bundestreue—Zur Theorie der subjektiven Rechte im Bundesstaat', [1991] JuristenZeitung 900 (hereafter Bleckmann, 'subjektiven Rechte').
[90] Mark Tushnet, 'What Then Is the American?' (1996) 38 Ariz L Rev 873.

level not to infringe the general interest and the interests of the other federate units, when they exercise their competences;'[91] yet it also entails softer and more far-reaching duties of cooperating sincerely,[92] including specific norms of conduct.[93] It goes further than what can be litigated and determines inter alia how the broad supervisory powers should be exercised at the federal level.[94] EU loyalty between the Member States and the Union is a comparable form of loyalty among institutional entities.

3.3 Framing force and limits

Loyalty has a particular meaning that denotes more than the obligation of either taking action or refraining from taking action. It has a relational, subjective dimension that is not present in the concept of 'sincere cooperation' or 'good faith' in that it refers to and requires a certain commitment to a common cause that shapes the loyal person's understanding of the world. Loyalty has the ability to transform relationships. Sincere cooperation, while potentially contributing to building a relationship, does not as such transform the nature of a relationship. By using the framing of 'loyalty', the Treaties, the CJEU, Advocate Generals, legal scholars, and parties before the Court add a *relational, subjective* element to the objective legal obligations that govern the actions and interactions within the EU legal order. This framing reminds the involved parties of their *voluntary decision* to be loyal since all of them agreed and ratified the Treaties and (largely) accepted the case law of the CJEU on sincere cooperation as part of their Union membership. It also has the important function of making the sustainability of the cause (shared purpose of the European integration project) part of the justification of the particular legal obligations that flow from the principle of sincere cooperation.

The CJEU applies loyalty considerations most prominently in cases in which the exercise of the Member States' powers exclusively in accordance with their own interests would adversely affect the others or the Union as a whole. The cause to which Member States are required to be loyal is the realization of the Union's objectives and interests, including effectiveness of EU law and external unity in international representation. Loyalty emphasizes the relational element that Member States are *members* of the EU, which places them in a *durable* relationship with each other as part of the whole EU. The loyalty frame focuses attention on the shared objectives, the polity as the framework for the relationships of the involved actors, as well as on the distinction between internal and external relations. Internally, that is, within the EU decision-making structures, EU rules determine the interactions and the possibilities for contestation. Externally, the interest of the polity is to act in a concerted way. The latter goes to the core of what loyalty is: a reason to privilege the relationship of loyalty, that is, the internal EU relations.

EU law acknowledges a special relationship of loyalty of the individual towards their Member State.[95] It does not have the same means to generate identification, such as social solidarity networks and direct services, such as education or safety. It cannot in the same sense impose duties on individuals, either. It has only very limited means to

[91] The German original reads: 'das an Bund und Länder gerichtete Verbot, bei der Ausübung ihrer Kompetenzen die Allgemeininteressen und die Interessen der anderen Bundesländer zu verletzen'.

[92] BverfGE 12, 205, 255ff.

[93] BverfGE 34, 216, 232 (JZ 1973, 361) (Coburg-Fall).

[94] Bleckmann, 'subjektiven Rechte' (n 89) 903–04.

[95] Most clearly expressed in Case C-270/13, *Iraklis Haralambidis* [2014] EU:C:2014:1358, Opinion of AG Wahl, para 43, speaking of a 'special relationship of allegiance' and explicating that 'a person generally has stronger feelings of loyalty, trust and devotion towards the country to which he, his family and his roots belong'.

ensure that individuals adhere to the rules that protect Union interests,[96] as states can require individuals to adhere to constitutional principles, for example, in the naturalization process. In short, the EU cannot provide the services of an administrative apparatus financed by taxation as a state does, nor does it benefit from having a monopoly on the legitimate use of force or on the decision of who is an EU citizen. The loyalty relations between individuals and the EU remain weaker than those between individuals and their state,[97] which however, as mentioned above, have Europeanized. Overall, both have been found to have weakened.[98]

The CJEU requires institutional loyalty from the Member States. Loyalty justifies privileging one course of action over another, even if the latter better serves one's immediate interest. EU loyalty may require Member States to act in the best interest of the Union even if that may not seem to be in the best national interest. Member States would need to justify this vis-à-vis their citizens. If individuals are not also loyal to the Union or at least see the justification for their state, this may create tensions. In other words, the need for justification, inherent in every public action,[99] places a political limit on EU loyalty. If individuals see themselves only as national citizens and not also as EU citizens,[100] they are likely to consider the constraints that EU loyalty places on national decision-making as more relevant than any increase of autonomy of the Union on the international plane. If the experienced constraints are not outweighed by a sense of gaining something, it is likely that individuals contest EU loyalty and put pressure on national governments either to better justify EU membership or use their internal influence to contest or reduce (the obligations flowing from) EU loyalty, including through litigation. At least in the long run, the EU can only command loyalty that Member States can justify within the national political structures and that is able to survive scrutiny from 'a certain distance'.[101]

Rainer Forst distinguishes three different dimensions of justification: an ethical, a moral, and a third dimension that justifies loyalty and belonging to a group.[102] EU loyalty requires justification in the sense of this third dimension. Hence, this justification does not have to be but forward in ethical or moral terms. The decisive point in the context of loyalty is that particularly where, in the individual case, it may go against the (perceived) national interest, the reasoning would likely (have to) be (at least also) based on the *common interest* or even the *purpose* of the Union.[103] Furthermore, internal channels of voice permissible under EU loyalty, that is, scope for politics, must be strong enough to put this purpose, as well as Union actions, up for debate, not only within the institutions but also among EU citizens. If internal politics are too weak, significantly some citizens may strive for exit.

[96] Defining crimes under art 83(1) TFEU offers only very limited means to protect Union interests by EU law.

[97] Ewald Wiederin, 'Staatsbürgerschaft in Europa: Elemente and Entwicklungen' (2009) 64 ZÖR 421, 429ff. See also Eurobarometer Spring 2018 at pp. 35–37, Eurobarometer Spring 2016 at p. 20 and Eurobarometer Autumn 2013 at p. 34: the vast majority (approx 90%) of EU citizens consistently see themselves as primarily or solely national citizens. Only a consistently tiny minority (7–8%) consider themselves as primarily or solely European citizens.

[98] ibid. eg Eurostat http://ec.europa.eu/eurostat/web/products-datasets/-/tsdgo510.

[99] See Section 4.1 in Chapter 1, relying primarily on the work of Jürgen Habermas.

[100] See ibid for an understanding of individuals as dual sovereign, that is, national and EU citizens.

[101] A point Adam Smith made with regard to moral beliefs (*The Theory of Moral Sentiments*, III. I. 2, 1759).

[102] Rainer Forst, *Recht auf Rechtfertigung. Elemente einer konstruktivistischen Theorie der Gerechtigkeit* (Surhkamp Verlag 2007) 28–29.

[103] See Section 4.3 in Chapter 1 for a discussion on democratic representation in external relations as a purpose of the Union.

The here-developed concept of loyalty is a deontological concept. Subordination to EU law and acceptance of their own role as EU Member States by the Member States is voluntary. In 2001, Joseph Weiler argued that the obedience of the Member States to EU law results from 'an autonomous voluntary act, endlessly renewed on each occasion, of subordination, in the discrete areas governed by Europe to a norm which is the aggregate expression of other wills, other political identities, other political communities'.[104] EU loyalty is a horizontal legal concept, applicable not only across all these policy areas but even beyond the scope of EU law. It is also part of the legal structures of justification and bonding, in which the voluntary submission of Member States provides the potential for justification by the Union and the Member States towards their citizens. It offers the opportunity to explicate the common cause and interest that this submission serves. Such explication would also allow emphasizing the pragmatic aspect of EU loyalty that lies in the fact that, within the interlocking embrace of the Union and its Member States with high interconnected stakes, any sharp distinction of interests becomes unconvincing.[105] The next section reflects on EU loyalty in the specific context of external relations and develops the particularly far-reaching legal consequences in this context.

4. Loyalty and External Relations

Unity and coherence remain a challenge for the EU in the context of external relations. The main reason for this is that the EU consists of 29 different entities, which all have international personality and are able to pursue their own interests under international law. Sincere cooperation has, in this context, the important task of allowing for coherent action, irrespective of whether the EU's competence is exclusive, shared, or parallel. It must ensure that multiple international actors, who do not stand in a hierarchical relationship towards each other, do not contradict each other and jeopardize the common interest and position. Actions under international law are also more easily susceptible to jeopardizing the common interest in a more far-reaching manner. This is the case because Member States are legally able to act in ways under international law that contradict EU law; international law entrenches positions because it is more cumbersome to amend than domestic law, be it national or EU secondary law; and often third parties are involved that do not share the high common interest in the functioning of the EU legal order.[106]

4.1 Exclusivity and pre-emption

The case of *ERTA/AETR*[107] is the foundational case for the doctrine of implied external competences of the Union. It also established an obligation to abstain from national action, where this endangers the effectiveness of Union law. This includes situations in which the exercise of national competences does not directly conflict with Union law, but which could nonetheless jeopardize the attainment of Union objectives.[108] In

[104] Joseph Weiler, 'Federalism and Constitutionalism: Europe's Sonderweg' (2001) Jean Monnet Working Paper 10/2000, 53.

[105] See Section 3.2 of Chapter 1 on interconnected stakes.

[106] See also the Conclusions for more details on why external Member State actions, eg under international law, pose a greater threat to the EU legal order than internal Member State actions, eg under EU or national law.

[107] Case 22/70, *Commission v Council* [1971] EU:C:1971:32 (hereafter Case 22/70, *ERTA*).

[108] See also: Case C-467/98, *Commission v Denmark* [2002] EU:C:2002:625, para 82; Case C-476/98, *Commission v Germany* [2002] EU:C:2002:631, para 108.

ERTA, the *existence* of Union competence was linked to a host of arguments, such as the Union's legal personality, other Treaty provisions, and secondary law.[109] The *pre-emptive effect* of preventing Member States from taking parallel measures (exclusivity) was, by contrast, centrally based on a combined reading of a Treaty objective and the principle of sincere cooperation.[110]

Later the CJEU explicated that the 'ERTA-effect' of prohibiting Member States from taking unilateral international action where this could 'affect common rules or alter their scope',[111] extended to the adoption of positions within international organizations.[112] In the case at hand, the Union was not a member of the international organization (International Maritime Organization (IMO)), because the IMO only allowed states to become members. However, the Union effectively had competence to implement the measures adopted within the international organization.[113] Greece had wanted to discuss a proposal within the internal institutional framework and pursuant to the internal rules;[114] yet such discussion had not taken place. The Court held that irrespective of whether the Commission had infringed its own duty to cooperate sincerely, for example, by failing to put the proposal up for discussion, the Member State attempting to initiate the internal decision-making process would have to continue acting loyally.[115] This case highlights a core characteristic of loyalty. Loyalty is not subject to reciprocity.[116] It is loyalty to a common cause, even if others act at times against the common cause.

Post-Lisbon, Article 3(2) TFEU incorporates and codifies a specific obligation originally flowing from the general principle of sincere cooperation (exclusivity of implied external powers).[117] Despite suggestions to depart from the Court's *ERTA* doctrine, the actual wording of Article 3(2) TFEU is very similar to that doctrine. In *ERTA*, the Court had stated that 'the Member States cannot, outside the framework of the [Union] institutions, assume obligations which might affect [...] [Union] rules or alter their scope'. Article 3(2) 3rd condition TFEU reads: 'The Union shall also have exclusive competence for the conclusion of an international agreement [...] in so far as its conclusion may affect common rules or alter their scope.' Hence, 'might' has become 'may' and 'so far as' was added. Textually, this is more restrictive; yet the slight change in wording has not changed the understanding of the doctrine by the Court.[118] At the time of *ERTA* (1970), the duty of sincere cooperation was 'the only appropriate Treaty

[109] Case 22/70, *ERTA* (n 107) paras 12–16.

[110] ibid, paras 17–22, in particular 20–22.

[111] See art 3(2) TFEU.

[112] Case C-45/07, *Commission v Greece* (n 9).

[113] SOLAS Convention and Parliament and Council Regulation (EC) 725/2044 on enhancing ship and port facility security [2004] OJ L 129/6.

[114] See art 10(4) Regulation (EC) 725/2044, ibid.

[115] Case C-45/07, *Commission v Greece* (n 9) paras 24–26.

[116] Joined Cases 90–91/63, *Commission v Luxembourg and Belgium* [1964] EU:C:1964:80. Belgium and Luxemburg tried to invoke the *exceptio non adimplendi*, arguing that the Council did not fulfil its obligations, and therefore they would not fulfil their obligations either. The Court did not accept this and held that the Treaty obligations are not reciprocal but that a new legal order required that all involved parties meet their obligations without exception.

[117] The Union shall also have exclusive competence for the conclusion of an international agreement when its conclusion is provided for in a legislative act of the Union or is necessary to enable the Union to exercise its internal competence, or insofar as its conclusion may affect common rules or alter their scope.

[118] Case C-399/12, *Germany v Council (OIV)* [2014] EU:C:2014:2258 (hereafter Case C-399/12, *OIV*), para 43, where the Court held that art 3(2) TFEU establishes exclusive external competences of the EU, 'since [the draft recommendations in question] [were] likely to affect common EU rules'. See also Chapter 4 on the legal basis for more details on this case.

provision in force [...] to achieve, in combination with the Treaty objective, such far-reaching implications for the treaty-making authority of the Member States'.[119] Post-Lisbon, the codification in Article 3(2) TFEU remains an expression of loyalty.

In Opinion 1/13, the Court held that the acceptance of the accession of a third country to the Hague Convention of 25 October 1980 on the Civil Aspects of International Child Abduction falls within the exclusive competence of the Union, irrespective of the fact that it needs to be expressed by the Member States on behalf of the Union. It relied on Article 3(2) 3rd condition TFEU and held that the risk of affecting or altering does not presuppose that the areas covered by the international commitments and those covered by the EU rules must fully coincide. The CJEU further pointed out that 'EU rules may be affected by *international* commitments even if there is no possible contradiction between those commitments and the EU rules'.[120] This seems to imply that external commitments constitute a greater risk than internal rules of affecting or altering internal rules. This is also confirmed by the considerations of Advocate General Jääskinen, who clarified that 'the purpose of the conferral of exclusive external competence on the European Union in every area in which it has adopted rules in the exercise of its internal competence is, in particular, to ensure that the Member States do not undermine or undo action taken by the EU by means of action taken outside the EU' and emphasized that 'sincere cooperation is all the more necessary where, as in the present case, the power to conclude an international agreement in the area in question lies solely with the Member States'.[121] Furthermore, it is interesting that the Advocate General contemplated 'the foreseeable future development of EU law' and hence interpreted the principle of loyalty to require a certain action in the present in order to avoid a potential future conflict.[122] In Opinion 1/13, the CJEU and its Advocate General confirm that they interpret Article 3(2) TFEU broadly and in the spirit of EU loyalty.

4.2 Mixed agreements: differences between internal and external actions

The internal increasing interlocking between national and EU law and the close embrace of national and European actors in adopting and implementing policies cannot easily be transferred to external relations. The closest attempt to do so is mixed agreements.

Mixed agreements are the most vivid illustration at what length the EU has to go legally to ensure international action as a united actor. They originate within the Euratom Treaty[123] and continue to be a common choice for the Union and the Member States, including after the entry into force of the Lisbon Treaty. They are in

[119] Klamert, *Principle of Loyalty* (n 4) 75.

[120] Opinion 1/13 [2014] EU:C:2014:2303, para 86 (hereafter Opinion 1/13), referring to Opinion 2/91 (ILO Convention) [1993] EU:C:1993:106, para 37 (hereafter Opinion 2/91) paras 25–26; and Case C-114/12, *Commission v Council* [2014] EU:C:2014:2151, para 71 (hereafter Case C-114/12, *Commission v Council*) (emphasis added).

[121] Opinion 1/13 [2014] EU:C:2014:2292, View of AG Jääskinen, para 99 (hereafter Opinion 1/13, View AG Jääskinen).

[122] ibid, para 100. See on this point also the discussion on the BIT cases in Section 4.4 below.

[123] Art 102 Euratom Treaty: 'Agreements or contracts concluded with a third State, an international organization or a national of a third State to which, in addition to the Community, one or more Member States are parties, shall not enter into force until the commission has been notified by all the Member States concerned that those agreements or contracts have become applicable in accordance with the provisions of their respective national laws.'

principle concluded when international agreements fall both within the competences of the Union and Member States. However, a tendency towards 'facultative' mixed agreements, even where the Union could (and should[124]) act alone, has made mixed agreements even more common. Quantitatively, about one-fifths of all Union agreements are identified to be mixed agreements.[125]

Mixed agreements are seen as 'a creature of pragmatic forces—a means of resolving the problems posed by the need for international agreements in a multi-layered system'.[126] They offer a political and legal construction that allows the Union and the Member States to act jointly. However, behind this creative political construction ensuring the continuous presence of Member States on the international plane hides a centralizing force.

Both the EU institutions and Member States must act in accordance with the principle of sincere cooperation when they negotiate, conclude, or fulfil obligations under international agreements.[127] The principle is particularly relevant in the intricate context of mixed agreements, where the legal construction avoids explicating the formal division of powers between the Union and its Member States. It extends cooperation obligations of the Member States beyond the scope of the Union's formal powers or even the scope of EU law to broadly protect the Union's international interest and ensure the attainment of its objectives.

When the Union and its Member States are jointly members to an international organization and have to coordinate their actions in a continuous manner within a durable legal framework in which they interact with third countries, the duty of loyalty plays a particularly important coordinating role. The interventions of the Commission in Opinion 2/13 are instructive as to the potential impact of sincere cooperation within an international organization and in particular in the context of an international dispute settlement mechanism. The Commission argued that sincere cooperation requires 'representation of the Member States before the European Court of Human Rights (ECtHR) by a single agent, a requirement which should be included in the internal rules'[128] and that 'the EU and the Member States [are] to act in a coordinated manner when they express their views or cast their votes on the execution of a judgment of the ECtHR delivered against the EU or against a Member State establishing a violation of the European Convention on Human Rights (ECHR) in proceedings to which the EU was a co-respondent'.[129]

The *PFOS* case exemplifies the strict interpretation of the principle of sincere cooperation in the context of mixed membership.[130] The Court ruled in this case that Sweden had breached the principle of sincere cooperation when it unilaterally proposed adding a new substance[131] to Annex A of the Stockholm Convention on Persistent Organic Pollutants. The Court held more specifically that even though the subject matter of the Convention did not fall within the exclusive competence of the Union, Sweden had departed from a 'concerted common strategy' on the matter.

[124] See Chapter 5.

[125] Armin von Bogdandy, Felix Arndt, and Jürgen Bast, 'Legal Instruments in European Union Law and Their Reform' (2004) 23 YEL 91, 107.

[126] Case C-243/15, *Lesoochranárske zoskupenie VLK* [2016] EU:C:2016:491, Opinion AG Kokott, para 56.

[127] Opinion 2/91 (n 120). [128] Opinion 2/13 (n 27) para 84. [129] ibid, para 77.

[130] Case C-246/07, *PFOS* (n 21). Marise Cremona, 'Case C-246/07, *Commission v Sweden* (PFOS), Judgment of the Court of Justice (Grand Chamber) of 20 April 2010' (2011) 48 CML Rev 1639.

[131] Perfluoroctane sulfonate—PFOS.

In areas of exclusive EU competence, the Member States may not embark on international actions at all. In areas of shared competence, Member States are limited by the duty of sincere cooperation as soon as the Union has taken any steps towards a concerted action. *PFOS* demonstrates that the actual specific obligation of refraining from taking action may be very similar, irrespective of whether it concerns an area of shared or exclusive competence.[132] It is not clear whether there is a difference in timing, that is, whether, if the Member State has tried to initiate an internal decision-making process or reached a common position and failed, it may after a reasonable period of time take unilateral external action. Marise Cremona argues that if the duty of sincere cooperation 'is to be kept conceptually separate from pre-emption, as a restraint on but not a denial of Member State competence, this obligation is best seen as a "best efforts" obligation rather than requiring Member States to refrain from acting until agreement is reached'.[133] It seems conceptually logical that in areas of shared competences Member States should continue to have the right to take unilateral external action if they have met the requirements imposed by the duty of sincere cooperation, for example, by sincerely attempting for a reasonable period of time to agree on a Union position. This of course begs the question: how long would a Member State have to refrain from external action if the decision-making within the Council has ground to a halt?

The ruling of the Court in *PFOS* contains both elements that indicate that the Court might have considered a limitation of the duty of sincere cooperation possible under different circumstances and elements that indicate that it would not have accepted such a limitation even if decision-making in the Council had come to a complete halt. On the one hand, the Court engaged with Sweden's allegation that the situation in the Council amounted to a 'decision-making vacuum' in the sense that the waiting period became equivalent to the absence of a decision.[134]. On the other hand, the Court pointed out that under 'the decision-making process provided for by that convention [...] the unilateral proposal has consequences for the Union'.[135] The decision-making procedures of the Swedish Convention, after a unilateral proposal of a Member State, either allow the Union to vote 'against that proposal, thus depriving the Member State making the proposal of the possibility of defending its own proposal [...]' or allow the 'Member State [to] exercise its right to vote in favour of its own proposal, thus depriving the Union of the possibility of exercising its right to vote with the number of votes equal to the number of its Member States'.[136] In sum, the detailed elaborations on the negative consequences that a unilateral proposal would have for the Union's (and the Member States') ability to act autonomously and credibly on the international plane seem to indicate that the Court would not easily accept these consequences, even after a reasonable period of time. The CJEU's case law may, in fact, lead to a situation of paralysis. If internally the EU cannot reach a common stand on a matter that falls within the exclusive competences of the Union, Member States cannot represent their position externally.[137] *PFOS* extends this to shared competences. In the words of Advocate General Maduro: 'Member States must not be caught in a never-ending process, in which a final decision by the [Union]

[132] See also two cases on transport agreements for inland waterways on the same issue: Case C-519/03, *Commission v Luxembourg* [2005] EU:C:2005:234; Case C-433/03, *Commission v Germany* (n 23).

[133] Cremona, 'Cooperation and Compliance' (n 41) 168.

[134] Case C-246/07, *PFOS* (n 21) para 87.

[135] ibid, para 92.

[136] ibid, para 94.

[137] See also: European Commission, 'Procedural Framework for the Adoption of Community or Common Positions for IMO Related Issues and Rules Governing Their Expression in the IMO', SEC (2005) 449.

is postponed to the point of inaction'.[138] The paralysis continues even if the EU institutions, namely the Commission, breach their duty of sincere cooperation by failing to facilitate internal discussion and decision-making.[139] As explained above, EU law in general and compliance with the duty of sincere cooperation are not subject to reciprocity. After the passing of a reasonable period of time, a conceivable course of action for a Member State in the position of Sweden in the case of *PFOS*, would be to bring an action against the Council. Yet, while bringing the case to the CJEU does not go against the duty of loyalty, it does not appear very promising in light of the Court's case law, for example, in the above-discussed case of *Commission v Greece*.[140]

The *PFOS* ruling is interesting as regards the consequences of Sweden's action on the EU internal decision-making process. Advocate General Maduro in particular was concerned that a Member State might use external competences, or at least the threat of using them, to influence internal decision-making. He argued that this might disturb 'the internal balance of power of the Community decision-making process'.[141] This is in line with the Commission's argument that Sweden's action unilaterally pre-empted further discussion in the Council. In the worst-case scenario, external actions may lead to accomplished facts that may involve high costs to renounce. It is the objective of the duty of loyalty to prevent this from happening. It requires that all influence on the internal decision-making process must follow the internal rules and does not involve third parties. In the end, this may even establish a duty only to act in a concerted fashion that is in principle applicable to both the Member States and the Union institutions.

Furthermore, *PFOS* demonstrates how the Union's participation in international regimes can restrict Member States from exercising powers externally that they would have been able to exercise internally. The Court examined the argument of whether Sweden could propose a substance under the Stockholm Convention because this would constitute a more stringent measure and Article 193 TFEU specifically allows for more stringent measures. It argued that actions that have no impact on the Union if they are taken under national law, such as the introduction of more stringent standards, could nonetheless have consequences for the Union if they are taken externally, for example, by proposing an additional substance within the context of an international environmental regime. Hence, the problem was that Sweden submitted its proposal to the 'institutional and procedural framework' of the Stockholm Convention[142] and that this directly limited the Union's margin of manoeuvre. The Court concluded that it was unclear whether the rule disallowing concurrent exercise of rights by the EU and its Member States allowed the EU to opt out from a proposal that was suggested by one of its Member States.[143] It concluded that the proposal would give rise to 'legal uncertainty' and, therefore, 'has consequences for the Union'.[144] The Court literally concluded that '[t]he Union could be bound by an amendment to an Annex to the Stockholm Convention whereas it is not bound by national measure.'[145] The Court's considerations demonstrate that the procedural rules of the multilateral framework are relevant to the interpretation of the duty of sincere cooperation.[146]

[138] Case C246/07, *Commission v Sweden (PFOS)* [2010] EU:C:2009:589, Opinion of AG Maduro, para 56 (hereafter *PFOS*, Opinion AG Maduro), para. 57.
[139] Case C-45/07, *Commission v Greece* (n 9). [140] ibid.
[141] *PFOS*, Opinion AG Maduro (n 138) para 56.
[142] Case C-246/07, *PFOS* (n 21) para 103. [143] ibid, paras 98–99.
[144] ibid, para 101. [145] ibid, para 102.
[146] In *PFOS*, both the Advocate General and the Court paid attention to this, see ibid, para 93.

PFOS also demonstrates that the Union's participation in the international regime had the consequence of restricting the ability of the Member States to exercise their powers. The case of *OIV*, discussed in detail in Chapter 4, demonstrates however that, even when the Union does not formally participate in the international regime, EU membership in combination with an exercise of Union competences can impose far-reaching constraints on Member States internationally.[147] This can be logically supported by the fact that the Union remains an international actor that is constituted of and inseparably interlinked with its Member States. For it to be taken seriously by the other international actors, it must be able to act autonomously from the Member States. EU loyalty protects this autonomy.

4.3 Information and communication obligations

The duty of loyalty imposes information and communication obligations on the Member States and the EU institutions, in the exercise of their own, as well as delegated powers. These obligations have been developed by the Court with particular clarity in the context of mixity and are sometimes agreed between the institutions in 'codes of conduct'.

Codes of conduct often set out detailed communication and information duties. They also demonstrate a different nuance of a point made above, namely that cooperation between the institutions concerns cooperation between the Union and the Member States in disguise. The Arrangement between the Council and the Commission regarding preparation for *Codex Alimentarius* is an illustration of this point. It sets out, for example, that *Member States* will refrain from answering directly to *Codex Alimentarius* Letters when the Commission indicates that it will prepare a common reply, but that instead they raise their issues internally with the Commission.[148] These communication and information duties also exemplify that the Member States are subject to a duty of *loyalty* that is different from the duty of good faith under public international law. Member States must allow the Commission to act as the external spokesperson. They may not act unilaterally externally but are bound by the higher meta-objective of the Union's 'unity of action' to only voice their issues and concerns internally. They have a right to be taken seriously and given a justification but they cannot circumvent any internal decision-making structure, in which they were not able to make their position the position of the Union. They cannot use the external powers that they have under international law if internal decision-making is still ongoing or if the Union has come to a concerted position.

The CJEU also accepted that *EU institutions* lay down in interinstitutional agreements rules and obligations that may be seen as specifying in a *legally binding manner* what the duty of loyalty requires in a particular institutional context. The leading case on this point is the *FAO* case,[149] which concerned voting rights on an agreement

[147] Case C-399/12, *OIV* (n 118); see Section 4.3 of Chapter 4 for more details on this case.

[148] See eg Arrangement between the Council and the Commission regarding preparation for Codex Alimentarius (Annex III to Council Decision (EC) 2003/822 on the accession of the European Community to the Codex Alimentarius Commission [2003] OJ L209/14, Section 2.2. See for duties of the Commission vis-à-vis the Member States Section 2.3.

[149] See Case C-25/94, *Commission v Council (FAO)* [1996] EU:C:1996:114 (hereafter Case C-25/94, *FAO*). See also J Heliskoski, 'Internal Struggle for International Presence: The Exercise of Voting Rights Within the FAO' in Alan Dashwood and Christophe Hillion (eds), *The General Law of EC External Relations* (Sweet & Maxwell 2000).

negotiated within the Food and Agriculture Organization (FAO).[150] There was no dispute on the coordinated common position of the Union and its Member States throughout the negotiations. The Council and the Commission had concluded an interinstitutional agreement that regulated the exercise of voting rights within FAO. The Court found the agreement in the specific circumstances binding on EU institutions. It ruled that from the specific terms of the agreement, the parties had intended to make the agreement a binding commitment and that it was a specific expression and fulfilment of sincere cooperation.[151] The Court was also prepared to enforce the agreement.

The Court found further that loyalty justified general obligations of keeping the other institutions informed or, depending on the circumstances, even consulting them well in advance with a view to allowing them to share information or voice concerns. However, these obligations seemed limited in that the institutions are not required to keep an open mind as to their final position until after the consultation. In the *ITLOS* case (2015), the Court ruled that the Commission is competent to submit a written statement on behalf of the European Union to the International Tribunal for the Law of the Sea (ITLOS) and that it does not require the approval of the content of that statement by the Council.[152] The Commission explicitly argued that it had acted pursuant to 'the principle of *loyal* cooperation', when it 'sent the Council a working document outlining the main lines of the Union submission in case ITLOS 21'. It further explained how it understood the limits of this principle, namely that the Council was 'to be informed' and that it 'look[ed] forward to taking in the utmost account any suggestions and advice from Member States to make the Union's case more solid'.[153] The Commission hence limited the influence of the Council and the Member States to strengthening 'the Union's case' as the Commission had set it out. It indirectly excluded that it would change its position following the input of the Council and the Member States. The Court explicated that the principle of sincere cooperation requires the Commission to 'consult the Council beforehand if it intends to express a position' before an international court and found that the Commission had complied with this obligation.[154] The Court interpreted the sincere cooperation duty of the Commission fairly narrowly; it did not expect the Commission to remain open to reconsidering the Union's position.

Information and consultation obligations flowing from the duty of loyalty exist for all actors, Member States and EU institutions. These obligations are also enforceable. Yet the case law confirms the impression that the Court approaches the Member States with higher loyalty standards than the EU institutions. This seems to stand in tension with the understanding of loyalty as a shared commitment to a common cause.

4.4 Unity of international representation as an independent source of distinct obligations

Unity in the international representation of the Union is one expression of sincere cooperation in external relations.[155] The CJEU uses this concept often to justify specific

[150] An agreement to promote compliance with international conservation and management measures by vessels fishing on the high seas.

[151] Case C-25/94, *FAO* (n 149) paras 49–50. See on the relevance on intention: Thomas Beukers, *Law, Practice and Convention in the Constitution of the European Union* (doctoral thesis University of Amsterdam, defended on 21 April 2011) 212, 242.

[152] Case C-73/14, *Council v Commission* (n 30).

[153] ibid, para 28.

[154] ibid, paras 86–87.

[155] Case C-66/13, *Green Network SpA* [2014] EU:C:2014:156, Opinion of AG Bot, para 103.

cooperation obligations of the Member States.[156] In fact at times, the CJEU appears to use unity as a rationale for the *existence* of the duty of cooperation rather than *as its objective*.[157] When the EU concludes a mixed agreement, the duty of loyalty and the specific obligations not to jeopardize Union action may even extend to non-participating Member States.[158] Furthermore, the unity of international representation also comes into play, when the Union is not a member of the international regime.[159]

EU loyalty regulates how competences can be legally exercised. In principle, loyalty is not meant to create competences or give rise to independent obligations of the Member States beyond those arising from the Treaties.[160] However, under certain circumstances, the principle of sincere cooperation may be an independent source of distinct legal duties.[161] Member States can be found to abuse their powers even in the sphere of their own competences. Indeed, even expressly reserved powers of the Member States, such as the possibility to withhold information regarding essential interest in national security matters in Article 346 TFEU, must be interpreted in light of the principle of sincere cooperation.[162] It confirmed that derogations must be interpreted strictly, and that the provision cannot be understood in such a way as to confer on Member States a power of derogation on grounds of national security concerns that can be exercised without coordination, consultation, and the taking into account of the common interest.[163] Furthermore, settled case law confirms that the duty of loyalty requires Member States, even where they retain the right to enter into agreements with third States, not to hinder the Union in the exercise of its powers. In particular they must not jeopardize the attainment of the objectives of the Treaties, for example, by concluding conflicting international agreements when a concerted decision has been taken and the Commission has been mandated to conduct negotiations[164] or by taking actions in the context of their participation in international organizations that may run counter to the Union's position.[165] The latter may also apply when only (some of the) Member States are members of the international organization. This came to the fore in the *OIV* case, in which the CJEU implicitly made an argument of unity of international representation without expressly mentioning the unity of international representation

156 Opinion 2/13 (n 27); *Commission v Council* (n 96); Opinion 2/91 (n 120) para 36; See also: *PFOS*, Opinion AG Maduro (n 138) para 37.

157 Opinion 2/91 (n 120) para 36. The principle of sincere cooperation for Member States was codified at the time in art 5 EEC Treaty.

158 Marise Cremona, 'External Relations of the EU and the Member States: Competences, Mixed Agreements, International Responsibility, and Effects of International Law' (2006) EUI Working Paper 22/2006, 5 on the position of Denmark in the context of the Lugano II Convention.

159 Case C-399/12, *OIV* (n 118); see Section 4.3 of Chapter 4 for more details on this case.

160 Case C-176/15, *Riskin* [2016] EU:C:2016:488, para 36, referring to the order of 19 September 2012 in Case C-540/11, *Levy and Sebbag* [2012] EU:C:2012:581, not published, paras 27–29.

161 Klamert, *Principle of Loyalty* (n 4) 233ff.

162 Panos Koutrakos, 'Public Security Exceptions and EU Free Movement Law' in Catherine Barnard and Okeoghene Odudu, *The Outer Limits of European Union Law* (Hart Publishing 2009).

163 Case C-337/05 *Commission v Italy* [2008] EU:C:2008:203; Case C-157/06 *Commission v Italy* [2008] EU:C:2008:530; Case C-284/05 *Commission v Finland* [2009] EU:C:2009:778; Case C-294/05 *Commission v Sweden* [2009] EU:C:2009:779; Case C-372/05 *Commission v Germany* [2009] EU:C:2009:780; Case C-409/05 *Commission v Greece* [2009] EU:C:2009:782; Case C-461/05 *Commission v Denmark* [2009] EU:C:2009:783; Case C-378/05 *Commission v Italy* [2006] EU:C:2006:581; and Case C-239/06 *Commission v Italy* [2009] EU:C:2009:784; Case C-615/10 *Insinööritoimisto Ins Tiimi Oy* [2012] EU:C:2012:324.

164 Case C-45/07, *Commission v Greece* (n 9) paras 29–30. See also discussion in Section 2 above.

165 Opinion 1/13, View AG Jääskinen (n 121); Eleftheria Neframi, 'Renforcement des obligations des États membres dans le domaine des relations extérieures' [2009] Revue trimestrielle de droit européen 601ff; and Opinion of AG Sharpston in Case C-114/12, *Commission v Council* [2014] EU:C:2014:224, para 98.

or sincere cooperation but requiring Member States to act on the Union's behalf.[166] Both examples illustrate the impact of the loyalty duty on the ability of Member States to autonomously exercise their powers.

Ultimately, the duty to cooperate sincerely may even require a relatively particular action of Member States in the fields that fall under their reserved competences.[167] This is the case in circumstances where the EU and the Member States have competence to regulate different fields in different (parts of the) agreement(s) 'which are inextricably interlinked'. In particular in the context of mixed membership (World Trade Organization (WTO)), the CJEU emphasized the significance of the duty to cooperate in order to ensure 'unity of action',[168] which as the Commission pointed out is necessary to protect the Union's negotiating power.[169] The Commission even more explicitly referred to the 'unity of action vis-à-vis the rest of the world'.[170] However, while the Court acknowledged the relevance of unity of action it did not attach legal consequences to it in the specific Opinion.[171] In fact it confirmed that the principle of sincere cooperation cannot change the competence division as it is set out in the Treaties.[172]

However, very far-reaching specific obligations may develop under certain circumstances. Where respective rights and obligations under mixed agreements are indivisible, EU Member States may for example be obliged under EU law to conclude the agreement if the Council, on a proposal from the Commission, decides to participate in the Union's interest. This may even be the case if a Member State does not have a national interest in the agreement or—even more far-reaching—if the Member State can argue that justified reasons stand in the way, such as incompatibility with substantive national law. The principle of loyalty may in such circumstances require the Member State to place the common interest, for example, in unity of international representation or uniform application of Union law, above the national interest. An example of such compulsory conclusion is the amending Protocol to the Paris Convention of 29 July 1960 on Third Party Liability in the Field of Nuclear Energy.[173] It contradicted inter alia the local responsibility under Austrian law with regard to responsibility for nuclear accidents. However, in principle all Member States would have had to conclude the amending Protocol in the name and in the interest of the Union, which had exclusive jurisdiction for only one Article relating to territorial jurisdiction and recognition and enforcement of judgments. An exception was stipulated in the (non-binding[174]) recitals of the relevant Council decision,[175] setting out why non-participation by certain Member States was exceptionally permitted. Particularly in such circumstances where the exclusive competence of the Union for a very limited part of the agreement could require Member States to participate in an international agreement, of which the absolute greatest part remains national competence, the ripple effect of mixity and loyalty becomes most apparent.

Through the framing of cooperation obligations as EU loyalty, Member States are also asked to make Union interests their own when they act on behalf of the Union.

[166] Case C-399/12, *OIV* (n 118); see Section 4.3 of Chapter 4 for more details on this case.
[167] Opinion 1/94 (WTO agreement) [1994] EU:C:1994:384, para 19 (hereafter Opinion 1/94).
[168] ibid, para 108. [169] ibid, para 106. [170] ibid. [171] ibid, para 107.
[172] ibid, 106–07.
[173] Recitals 8 to 10 of Council Decision 2004/294 [2004] OJ L 97/53 set out that Member States 'should' ratify the protocol. They also explain specifically why three of the Member States are not under this obligation.
[174] Case C-290/12, *Della Rocca* [2013] EU:C:2013:235, para 38, with further references.
[175] ibid.

A classic example of where Member States act on behalf of the Union is when the Union is competent in a particular field but cannot join an international organization active in this field because the rules of this international organization do not allow non-state members.[176] It is important to realize that this situation is particular to external relations and that it is one of the constellations that illustrates why the EU struggles with the 'requirement of unity in the international representation'[177] at a different level than federal states. It is also a constellation in which the *active* obligations under Article 4(3) TEU become particularly relevant. Marise Cremona phrased this situation as Member States acting 'as trustees of the Union interest'.[178]Member States may be required to make their best endeavours to facilitate amendments of an international convention in order to enable the Union to accede to it.[179]

The precise meaning and the consequences flowing from the requirement for unity in the international representation of the EU and the principle of sincere cooperation are interpreted very differently by the different actors. This became apparent in the *Air Transport Agreement* case (2015).[180] The case concerned the adoption of the decision on the signing, on behalf of the Union, and the provisional application of the Air Transport Agreement between the USA as one party, the Union and its Member States as the second party, and Iceland and Norway as the third and fourth parties, respectively. The Council and the representatives of the Member States had taken this decision jointly (called a hybrid decision). The Commission took 'the view that the adoption of hybrid decisions [was] likely to "blur" the independent personality of the EU in international relations, whereas in the Council's opinion, hybrid decisions [were] the ultimate expression of cooperation between the EU and the Member States'.[181] The CJEU concluded that close cooperation under the principle of sincere cooperation in the context of mixed agreements cannot justify that the Council sets 'itself free from compliance with the procedural rules and voting arrangements laid down in Article 218 TFEU'.[182] It found that the Member States had illegally interfered with the contested Council decision. Additionally, while not referring to the concept of unity of international representation, the Court confirmed the necessity of institutional autonomy by upholding the procedural requirements of the Treaties. The EU institutions are hence obliged by the principle of sincere cooperation to maintain vis-à-vis the Member States their institutional autonomy given to them under the Treaties.[183]

Advocate General Mengozzi's distinction in this case between internal and external aspects of the Commission's plea[184] is helpful to categorize the different interests that sincere cooperation aims to protect. Externally, a distinction can be made between on the one hand obligations under international law, that is, under international

[176] The most well-known example is probably the International Labour Organization (ILO) and the International Maritime Organization (IMO), see also Opinion 2/91 (n 120) para 37.

[177] eg ibid, para 36; Opinion 1/94 (n 167) para 108 (Competence of the Community to conclude international agreements concerning services and the protection of intellectual property); Case C-25/94, *FAO* (n 149) para 48.

[178] Marise Cremona, 'Member States as Trustees of the Union Interest: Participating in International Agreements on Behalf of the European Union' in Anthony Arnull and others (eds), *Constitutional Order of States: Essays in EU Law in Honour of Alan Dashwood* (Hart Publishers 2011) 435; Robert Schütze, *Foreign Affairs and the EU Constitution: Selected Essays* (CUP 2014) 336.

[179] In the case of the International Convention on civil liability for oil pollution damage.

[180] Case C-28/12, *Commission v Council* [2015] EU:C:2015:282.

[181] Case C-28/12, *Commission v Council* [2015] EU:C:2015:43, Opinion of AG Mengozzi, para 59 (hereafter Case C-28/12, *Commission v Council*, AG Mengozzi).

[182] Case C-28/12, *Commission v Council* (n 180), para 55.

[183] ibid, paras 41–42.

[184] Case C-28/12, *Commission v Council*, AG Mengozzi (n 181) para 40.

agreements and potential responsibility for not fulfilling these obligations, and on the other the unity of representation, that is, representation of interests and the impression of third parties of who is in charge. Internally, the greatest concern is a departure from the procedures under the Treaty and a changing of the balance of powers between the institutions and between the institutions and the Member States. Any decision on the correct internal procedure and legal instrument also has external consequences. However, the unity of representation should not be able to affect the internal institutional power balance.

A decisive factor in the considerations is that actions, either of the institutions or of the Member States, may not be 'liable to weaken the EU as a full player on the world stage by concealing its independent and autonomous international personality'.[185] Allowing the EU to act as a 'full player' on the world stage, despite the fact that international law regards it as an international organization, which does not have the same rights as states, is the most important objective of the concept of unity in international representation. The Union's horizontal external objectives take a global approach and confirm that the Union's overarching objective is to be a credible and powerful international actor.[186] The EU institutions and the Member States are bound by EU loyalty to cooperate in achieving the Union's objectives, to abstain from undermining such action, and to ensure consistency between the Union's different policies. Prima facie, this appears to subordinate national interests at times to the common Union interest. This is precisely where loyalty should be used as a structure of justification (and bonding) in order to give reasons and put this juxtaposition of interests up for debate. This would also allow politics, understood as deliberation but also at times political struggle, to come to the fore within these legal structures.

4.5 Protecting autonomous actions of the Union in the future

Article 351(2) TFEU on Member States' duties to renegotiate or even denounce prior international agreements is, as explained above, a specific codified expression of the principle of sincere cooperation. It is particular to external relations, in that it concerns prior international obligations that are not displaced by conflicting EU law by the primacy of EU law. This specific constellation leads to far-reaching obligations of Member States that may even require them to avoid potential conflicts of their international obligations with future legislative action of the Union.

A series of enforcement proceedings were brought against Member States for keeping in force bilateral investment treaties (BITs) concluded prior to their accession to the EU, because these BITs did not allow for restrictions on the free movement of capital and could therefore potentially conflict with restrictive measures (sanctions) imposed by the EU.[187] The Court found even a clause referring to the laws of the contracting parties insufficient to ensure compliance with EU law.[188] In effect and even if it has remained limited to the specific circumstances of urgent (and in several ways exceptional[189]) restrictive measures, this line of cases imposes an obligation on Member

[185] ibid, para 87. [186] Art 21 TEU.

[187] See the Bilateral Investment Treaty cases (Case C-205/06, *Commission v Austria* (n 13); Case C-249/06, *Commission v Sweden* [2009] EU:C:2009:119; Case C-118/07, *Commission v Finland* [2009] EU:C:2009:715; see also eg Case C-170/98, *Commission v Belgium* [1999] EU:C:1999:411; Case C-84/98, *Commission v Portugal* [2000] EU:C:2000:359; Case C-62/98, *Commission v Portugal* [2000] EU:C:2000:358.

[188] Case C-118/07, *Commission v Finland*, ibid.

[189] Christina Eckes, 'The Law and Practice of EU Sanctions' in Steven Blockmans and Panos Koutrakos (eds), *Research Handbook on CFSP* (Edgar Elgar 2019, *forthcoming*).

States to avoid potential future incompatibility and eliminate even the risk of conflict before such conflict has occurred. Advocate General Maduro, while concluding that the BITs were not as such incompatible with the provision on the Union's power to adopt restrictive measures, argued in favour of a breach of EU loyalty.[190] His reasoning was based on a parallel with the Court's case law on EU directives for which the transposition period has not yet expired. He also pointed to the exceptional and urgent nature of restrictive measures. The Court emphasized the need for a common attitude of the Commission and the Member States and concluded that international obligations of the Member States may not amount to an obstacle to the (potential) exercise of Union powers.

The BIT cases go exceptionally far in imposing positive loyalty obligations of Member States. They also support that these obligations go further in the external context than in the internal context. The Advocate General referred to the implementation of directives as a parallel internal scenario. Yet the obligation not to jeopardize the objectives of directives during the period of transposition goes less far. First of all, it is a negative obligation, not to interfere with the objectives of the directive. Second, the directive is a concrete internal legal instrument, that is, concretization of the Union's position in secondary law, triggering this obligation. In the BIT cases, Member States were obliged to take specific action (renounce the BITs). Furthermore, this obligation was not triggered by a specific internal legal instrument, Treaty provision, or position but simply by the existence of a general Treaty provision vesting the Union with the competence to adopt restrictive measures. In conclusion, the BIT cases also demonstrate that Member States' obligations to avoid future conflicts with EU law are externally more stringently interpreted.

In the context of EU loyalty, this also raises the question of whether or not prior international obligations of the Member States could and should equally be considered by the EU institutions when exercising their powers under the EU Treaties. In other words, the EU institutions should also act loyally towards the Member States in these circumstances. The next section reflects, in the light of the far-reaching obligations here presented, on the transformative effects of EU loyalty in the context of external relations.

5. The Transformative Effect of EU Loyalty

The CJEU has constructed the cooperation obligations under the EU Treaties based on an underlying understanding of a duty of EU loyalty. This has particularly in external relations resulted not only in a comprehensive net of specific obligations, but arguably affects the (self-)conception of the EU Member States as *members of the Union*. This section identifies the nature and specific features of EU loyalty and examines whether and to what extent the CJEU's construction of cooperation duties as loyalty is inevitable. Is the construction itself and are the strict obligations flowing from this construction justified in light of EU primary law and the nature of the Union?

[190] Case C-118/07, *Commission v Finland* [2009] EU:C:2009:525, Opinion of AG Maduro, paras 23ff.

5.1 Loyalty: justified choice

EU loyalty expresses the deeper rationale of creating an open-ended relationship among the Member States and between the Union and its Member States. It forms part of operationalizing the 'ever-closer Union among the peoples of Europe'.[191] EU loyalty serves the 'higher' purpose of ensuring the functioning of the EU legal order, the effectiveness of its law and the Union's capacity as an autonomous international actor. Even if some of the specific cooperation obligations imposed in the EU context and those imposed by good faith under public international law may resemble each other,[192] the higher purpose of serving the Union justifies a conceptual distinction of EU loyalty from good faith under public international law. This purpose is most explicitly expressed in the reference to loyalty but inherent in different ways in the Treaties and the entire body of case law of the CJEU on specific cooperation obligations. The context and overall nature justify speaking of a 'duty of loyalty' in the EU context, while such terminology would be misplaced in the context of public international law.

Loyalty requires a particular commitment to an overarching purpose (the object of loyalty). EU loyalty requires the Member States to commit to the common endeavour, as set out in the European Treaties. Member States have expressly and repeatedly committed to the Union as an autonomous and effective international actor in every single Treaty amendment since the Community's inception. The Union can only act according to this mandate if Member States refrain from jeopardizing the Union's actions aimed at attaining the agreed objectives on the international plane. This is in particular the case because Member States are comparatively more powerful under international law than the Union. International law recognizes only states as primary architects of the international legal order and as actors benefiting from territorial sovereignty, that is, under international law, states have the power of the last word over their territory.

This connects to the binary application that loyalty shares with law.[193] Either one is loyal or one is not loyal. In this sense, loyalty, just as autonomy,[194] is an ordering principle and not a matter of balancing. This is also what distinguishes it from other classic principles, such as subsidiarity and coherence, which operate on balance.

In particular, in the external relations context, it emphasizes the difference between on the one hand the internal relations between the Union and the Member States and among the Member States, which are governed by loyalty, and on the other external relations with non-EU actors, which are not governed by loyalty. Internally, disagreement can be voiced, legal actions may be brought, and information must be exchanged. Relationships characterized by loyalty must be prioritized over relationships that are not characterized by loyalty, within the former voice must be possible. The Union offers Member States a strong voice through the European Council and the Council, both in internal legislative procedures but also in determining the direction and focus of internal and external actions. Finally, Member States are privileged applicants before the CJEU and can at all times seek the Court's opinion on internal acts, as well as envisaged international agreements.

Loyalty also explains the application of internal (EU law) rather than external rules (international law) between the Member States. Primacy determines that inter-se agreements are subject to EU law, irrespective of whether they were concluded earlier

[191] Art 1(2) TEU. [192] De Baere and Roes, 'EU Loyalty' (n 6).

[193] See Section 3.1 above.

[194] See Section 3.1 of Chapter 1 and Chapter 6. See similarly to autonomy: Marcus Klamert, 'The Autonomy of the EU (and of EU Law): Through the Kaleidoscope' (2017) 6 EL Rev 815.

or later than the accession of the Member States in question or the EU Treaties. This is a general rule, which finds particular expression in so-called disconnection clauses, which are the 'substantive counterpart of Article [344 TFEU]'.[195] At the same time, sincere cooperation also applies beyond the scope of EU law. As examined above, actions within the reserved powers of the Member States, exercised outside the scope of EU law, may, to the extent that they have an impact on the Union's interests and ability to achieve its objectives, very well be subject to obligations flowing from sincere cooperation.

Within the Union, EU loyalty is a powerful tool for translating objectives and even interests into legally binding and judicially enforceable obligations. The fact that Member States take action is as such sufficient to breach the principle of sincere cooperation. The CJEU does not engage in an assessment of whether the action actually had any negative effects on the position of the Union.[196] It hence takes a deontological approach to sincere cooperation: Member States are under a *duty* not to assume new obligations under international law, irrespective of the result, that is, consequences of their actions. The deontological approach, focusing on the action rather than its effects, is justified by the commitment to the Union as an autonomous actor. It is also justified based on a consequentialist reasoning that the entrenching and at times irreversible effects of international law, present in particular when non-EU actors are involved, make waiting for actual consequences of Member States' actions a risk to the position of the Union.

Many scholars examine, in particular in the context of the *PFOS* case discussed earlier, whether the duty of sincere cooperation amounts to a duty of best endeavours or a duty of reaching a specific result.[197] However, in some cases the two simply become a matter of how long a Member State is required to wait until it can externally take a course of action for which it has tried to establish a common position internally but did not manage. The question whether at some point Member States could take external action in situations like the one in *PFOS*, however, does not connect well to the distinction of the obligation of best endeavours or obligation of result, as it is used in civil law. I would argue that EU loyalty is always subject to a deontological logic. It creates a duty either to act or to refrain from action, but this duty is not subject to further considerations of the *actual result* in the specific situation. Member States must take or refrain from action in all situations, including based on considerations of the result that could *reasonably be excepted*. The duty to act loyally does not cease at any point except if loyalty as such is withdrawn

EU loyalty is not bound to the existence of legally binding obligations. It already comes into play, for example, before the EU has concluded an agreement. The CJEU specifically held that '[t]he adoption of a decision authorising the Commission to negotiate a multilateral agreement on behalf of the Community marks the start of a concerted Community action at international level and requires for that purpose, *if not a duty of abstention on the part of the Member States, at the very least a duty of close cooperation* between the latter and the Community institutions in order to facilitate the achievement of the Community tasks and to ensure the coherence and consistency of

[195] Cremona, 'Cooperation and Compliance' (n 41) 143.

[196] Case C-266/03, *Commission v Luxembourg* [2005] EU:C:2005:341, para 60 (hereafter Case C-266/03, *Commission v Luxembourg*); Case C-433/03, *Commission v Germany* (n 23). See also Piet Eeckhout, *EU External Relations Law* (2nd edn, OUP 2011) 248.

[197] See eg Cremona, 'Cooperation and Compliance' (n 41); Hillion, 'Duty of Cooperation' (n 50) 21.

the action and its international representation.'[198] EU loyalty vests internal action of the institutions during the decision-making process, which do not address or otherwise directly affect the Member States, with legally relevant effects and limits the Member States' powers beyond what could be concluded from the law on a literal reading. This is justified in order to protect the internal decision-making procedure, where Member States have carefully weighted influence which is subject to legitimizing procedural requirements. Legal autonomy from political forces, that is, that politics becomes law only through predetermined formal procedures, ensures a certain level of distance, stability, and objectivity.

Furthermore, in the context of external relations, EU loyalty also protects, under certain circumstances, potential future action by the Union, even before any legal instrument or common position is adopted. Loyalty in these strictly circumscribed circumstances hence has effects without being anchored in a specific act concretizing the Union's position. It protects the capacity of the Union to take action, including in the future.

Overall, the careful construction of the Union as an internal legal order in which citizens are represented both as EU citizens and national citizens can only be protected if Member States cannot resort to international law to put pressure on this construction in a context where they enjoy the formal power to act as sovereign entities unfettered by EU law. Furthermore, Member States' unambiguous choice to strengthen the Union as an autonomous international actor entails a commitment not to undermine the Union's ability to fulfil this mandate at the same time. In short, the legal construction of the Union requires loyalty, in particular in external relations. However, loyalty also applies to the Union and its institutions. Loyalty also requires that Member States enjoy a reasonably effective way of voicing their disagreement and concerns internally. The Court seems to have emphasized the duty of loyalty above all for the Member States. However, while loyalty is not reciprocal continued loyalty of all parts depends not only on the success of the joined endeavour but also on the overall commitment of all actors.

This section summarized and explicated why it is justified to understand the detailed (and sometimes technical) obligations flowing from the principle of sincere cooperation as part of an overall duty of EU loyalty. The next section contrasts internal and external obligations flowing from EU loyalty and argues that it is not only reasonable but also rational that loyalty imposes more stringent obligations in the external context. In fact, this is the very nature of loyalty.

5.2 Stricter EU loyalty in external relations

Loyalty is more stringently interpreted and applied in the external than in the internal context, in particular where the autonomy or the unity of the EU legal order is at stake.[199] This flows from the deontological nature of loyalty that imposes particular duties vis-à-vis specific actors, but could also be established from a consequentialist perspective. The underlying rationale is that departure from the unity of international representation has more far-reaching negative consequences externally than internal contestation or even disobedience. Internally, the primacy of EU law

[198] Case C-266/03, *Commission v Luxembourg* (n 196) para 60; Case C-433/03, *Commission v Germany* (n 23) para 66.

[199] Case C-459/03, *Mox Plant* (n 14); Joined Cases C-300-392/98, *Dior* (n 37); Hillion, 'Duty of Cooperation' (n 50) 21.

requires disapplying a rule of national law that infringes EU law. Externally, a rule that infringes EU law cannot simply be disapplied as this would result in a breach of public international law, with the possibility of the non-EU state bringing an action in an international dispute settlement mechanism, potentially resulting in the international responsibility of the disapplying Member State. Internally, sincere cooperation is to a larger extent subject to a balance of interests. The effectiveness of EU law acts as an overshadowing omnipresent meta-consideration but it is not absolute. The unity of international representation, while serving at least also the effectiveness of the Union as an international actor, is a conceptual framing that emphasizes the binary nature of loyalty. As a result, it often makes a balance of interests impossible but requires absolute loyalty.

An understanding of the principle of sincere cooperation as loyalty also inherently justifies why it imposes stricter obligations externally than internally. It is the essence of loyalty, not to take internal disagreements outside, because the unity of representation of the internal actors towards the outside is seen as a common cause. Over time this has transformative effects on the self-understanding of the actors and their own interests. Loyalty translates into serving the overarching purpose of ensuring the functioning and autonomy of the Union and the effectiveness of EU law. This results in a hierarchical reading of the relationship between the EU and its Member States, which becomes particularly apparent in external relations.[200] The centralizing effect, for example, of the Treaty objectives, which have been considerably extended by the Lisbon Treaty, lies in their obliging force when they are read in light of EU loyalty. This leads to a hierarchical ordering of multiple foreign policy commitments and objectives of the Member States, in which the EU objectives are given priority over other motivating national objectives or interests.

Generally speaking, EU loyalty gives rise to stricter duties if more cooperation is necessary to ensure attainment of the objectives. In other words, the closer the competences of the EU and the Member States are intertwined, the more the exercise of competences depends on the cooperation of the others, the higher are the demands imposed by the principle of sincere cooperation on the behaviour of all parties. This explains why externally sincere cooperation is interpreted more strictly. It also explains why it plays such a particularly important role in the context of mixed agreements. In the comparison between the effects of sincere cooperation internally and externally, it is relevant to note that loyalty does not limit the political discretion of Member States within the EU institutions. They do not have to work towards a compromise in the Council.[201]

This is not to say that the implications of EU loyalty for the Member States internally and in particular in administrative law are negligible. In administrative law, loyal cooperation has had the implication of redefining the internal distribution of power and relations between core state institutions. It has even been criticized for subverting relations of loyalty within the state apparatus.[202] Furthermore, more situations and hence more cases arise internally than externally.[203] In particular, there are situations where Member States are required to act 'on behalf of' or as 'trustees' of the Union

[200] Pierre Pescatore already wrote in 1970 about the hierarchical relationship, see 'Das Zusammenwirken der Gemeinschaftsrechtsordnung mit den nationalen Rechtsordnungen' [1970] Europarecht 207.

[201] Joined cases C-63-67/90, *Portugal and Spain v Council* [1992] EU:C:1992:381, paras 52–53.

[202] Case 103/88, *Costanzo* (n 45).

[203] I would like to thank Filipe Brito Bastos for discussing this point with me.

externally. Exceptionally, this may also be the case internally. Under the Common Agricultural Policy, for example, the CJEU held that national authorities may be considered to act 'as agent of' the Union even though this is not required by the text of the relevant legislation.[204] However, the limited capacity of the Union under international law, as compared to the Member States, makes such 'on behalf'-action necessary in a much broader and more structural fashion.

In terms of quality rather than quantity, it is still correct to conclude that loyal co-operation imposes more far-reaching restrictions in the context of external relations on the Member States, their scope to act autonomously, their international visibility, and their relations with the rest of the world. This also becomes apparent in the context of reserved competences of Member States. While internally Member States are also required to comply with general principles of Union law, for example when they exercise their reserved competences for education, they may not discriminate;[205] externally the obligations are much more specific, in particular when positive obligations are concerned. The most drastic example remains the compulsory conclusion of an international agreement.[206] Because of the 'outside-in' effect, most visible in the *PFOS* case, as well as in the *OIV* case, where regulatory measures within an international organization are susceptible of imposing constraints and obligations on the Union, the need for unity is externally higher than internally.[207] It is difficult to see how loyalty alone could internally oblige Member States to similarly specific actions. Ultimately, this can be explained with the absence of primacy of EU law vis-à-vis non-EU actors.[208]

Loyal behaviour requires raising criticism and contesting decisions pursuant to the internal rules and shielded from third parties. This also entails specific procedural obligations to raise potential issues of conflict internally, such as, information and consultation obligations, but also ultimately an obligation of abstention, for example, not to bring a dispute to an international quasi-judicial forum. With its focus on internal conflict resolution, loyalty is meant to allow the EU to speak with a single voice. The ultimate objective of the duty of loyalty when applied in external actions is to allow the EU to develop its true added value of amplifying the voices of the Member States on the international plane. Loyalty binds Member States to place this overarching goal above their individual interests, ultimately because overall and in the longer term this should also be in their best national interest. The precise idea of converging interests was expressed by the Court in its Opinion 1/75, in which it speaks of 'the defence of the *common interests* of the Community, within which the particular interests of the Member States must *endeavour to adapt to each other*'.[209] Loyalty is ultimately pragmatic. The purpose and greater ability of the Union to ensure the voice of both Member States and EU citizens in the international context makes it rational for the Member States to comply with EU loyalty, including the far-reaching obligations flowing from the CJEU's interpretation of sincere cooperation in the external relations context.

Under a federal logic, EU loyalty does not require the Union and its institutions to ensure the Member States' continuous visibility and influence externally. An adequate

[204] Court of First Instance, Case T-94/95, *Landyut v Commission* [1998] EU:T:1998:23, para 30 and Case T-93/95, *Laga v Commission* [1998] EU:T:1998:22, paras 33–45.

[205] See eg Bruno de Witte, 'Exclusive Member State Competences: Is There Such a Thing?' in Sacha Prechal and Inge Govaere (eds), *Division of Competences* (Hart Publishing 2017) 59.

[206] See Section 4.4 above.

[207] Case C-246/07, *PFOS* (n 21); Case C-399/12, *OIV* (n 115); see Section 4.3 of Chapter 4 for more details on this case.

[208] Christina Eckes, 'EU Loyalty: External Relations as a Constitutional Challenge' CYEL 2019 *forthcoming*.

[209] Opinion 1/75 [1975] EU:C:1975:145 (emphasis added).

influence and voice internally are sufficient both to ensure their autonomous political existence and to allow the Union to draw from the indirect legitimacy through the representation of individuals as national citizens.

6. Conclusions

EU loyalty is the appropriate term to refer to an overarching duty of all EU actors that finds expression in specific obligations, enshrined in the Treaties and developed by the CJEU. 'Loyalty' frames the relationship between Member States and the EU in a particular way and exercises an ordering and meaning-giving force on that legal and factual relationship.[210] Loyalty justifies specific negative and positive obligations. Ultimately, the negative obligations involving refraining from taking action that may put the common cause in danger may be even more central to the concept of loyalty than positive obligations.

EU loyalty is inherent to the formally agreed Treaty framework, including specific provisions on sincere cooperation, as well as a general agreement by Member States in favour of membership in a Union that requires loyalty. This is the voluntarist, consensual dimension. It is also based on a deontological, normative dimension that complying with the *duty* of loyal is the 'right' thing to do. On the grounds of both the tacit agreement to the nature of Union membership and the normative pull of the joined endeavour, Member States, while they have formally agreed (only) to sincere cooperation set out in the Treaties, are obliged by the Court to comply with more far-reaching obligations flowing from a conceptual understanding of relations between the Union and its Member States and among Member States as EU loyalty. This in turn imposes independent, autonomous obligations, for example, to ensure unity in the external representation and to help the Union to attain its (external) objectives. The restraining force of loyalty on the legal and political autonomy of the Member States is particularly stringent in external relations. It is reflected in the fact that they can no longer decide on signing and concluding an international agreement, including in fields of reserved competence, without taking the interests of the other parties into account. Coordination obligations flowing from EU loyalty are nowhere more apparent than in the context of mixed agreements and mixed membership, where Member States must further EU interests even if the subject matter falls within Member States' reserved competences.

The duty of loyalty is not limited to areas of Union competence, nor by 'the scope of Union law', already broadly defined by the CJEU. In principle, any interference with EU objectives is susceptible of triggering the duty of loyalty. It is overarching and even extends into the reserved competences of the Member States, where these actions affect the attainment of the Union's objectives or even the effectiveness of EU law. One reason for the transformative effect of EU loyalty is this very far-reaching scope of application in external relations.

EU loyalty imposes federal discipline by introducing gradual, negative, and positive, obligations. Member States are obliged not to undermine the EU's external actions and ensure unity in international representation in all areas of EU competences, including both exclusive and shared competences. Hence, one could assume that the more stringently loyalty is interpreted vis-à-vis the Member States, the more EU law

[210] This idea is widely accepted in legal-sociological and legal-political studies, see Maarten Hajer and David Laws, 'Ordering through Discourse' in Michael Moran and others (eds), *Oxford Handbook of Public Policy* (OUP 2006).

and the CJEU limit the permissible conduct of Member States. Taken to its utmost extreme, this would mean that EU Member States are no longer in a position to take international action, which is independent or even contradictory to the EU position. Their influence would be limited to voicing admissible opposition within the internal decision-making structures of the EU. This highlights the dilemma set out in the introduction: How can the Union act effectively internationally without triggering ever further integration?

Loyalty obligations should be read more explicitly in the spirit of federalist theory. The need and objective of protecting the indirect legitimacy of the Union should form part of the considerations that determine the case-by-case interpretation of what loyalty means. Ultimately, this pleads in favour of strengthening the loyalty obligations of the EU institutions.

Besides its integrative forces, loyalty may also serve as bonding structure that plays a relevant role in the processes in which individuals give meaning to their social and political relations. It shapes citizens' understanding of what matters. Inherent tensions or contradictions between different understandings of the world and one's position within it, including one's relations to others, stand in dialogue with each other and may develop transformational powers if one understanding grows more dominant over time, for example, because it seemingly better reflects reality. EU loyalty has, on an institutional level, also the power to give meaning to participation in the Union and to give priority to the common cause.

As a structure of bonding, EU loyalty does not only require justification, it also offers a framework for justification. EU loyalty appeals to an extra-legal concept to justify legal obligations. This as such entails the danger of lifting the common cause above politics and shielding it from political discourse or struggle. Obligations flowing from EU loyalty should be reasoned in light of the purpose and added value of Union actions but also EU membership.

In particular, the notion of unity in international representation offers opportunities to develop structures of bonding. It offers opportunities to develop and tell the narrative of the purpose of the Union to allow self-determination in times of globalization. Loyalty requires a voluntary commitment to a common cause. Explicating this and making visible that the legal principles and structures that govern the functioning of the EU legal order are built on this is a chance to connect this justification to EU citizens. It also offers the possibility to engage in a discourse and create scope for politics. Justification and engagement in a discourse with its citizens directly benefits the Union's *legitimacy*, which is understood as justifiability or worthiness of recognition. EU loyalty is justified by reference to the common cause of the functioning and effectiveness of the common normative order. This cause in the context of EU loyalty should be related to a discourse on the Union's ability to solve transnational problems and to determine one's own position and course of action internationally.

Finally, the principle of *effectiveness*, that is, the effectiveness of EU law, which should be distinguished from the ability to problem-solve effectively, originates in sincere cooperation. It continues to be one of the explicit objectives of the duty of loyalty. The common cause of EU loyalty is the well-functioning of the EU legal order, whose most unique feature is the effectiveness of its law. In short, loyalty aims to ensure effectiveness. Effectiveness is a central underlying concern when EU loyalty is invoked to orchestrate external actions. While the anchor of external loyalty duties is often the unity in international representation, which offers a different conceptual frame than effectiveness, this unity also at least serves effectiveness. It serves to strengthen the Union's capacity to act effectively as one unified international actor.

The particular need of bringing together a multitude of international actors and bridging the mismatch between internal competences and international rules explains the special relevance of sincere cooperation in external relations. The autonomy of the Union is more vulnerable on the international plane than the autonomy of the Member States. Depending on the severity of an internal conflict taken outside, it undermines the trust of third parties in the EU as a capable and autonomous external actor and ultimately leads to a preference of dealing with the Member States rather than the Union.

3

Organizational Principles Under External Pressure

Subsidiarity, Primacy, and Coherence

1. Introduction

Organizational principles ensure the well-functioning of the complex relationships of cooperation within the EU legal order. They govern the conduct of the different actors within the EU's institutional and constitutional structure and organize the relations between the Union and the Member States, among the EU institutions, and among the Member States. 'Organizational principles', also sometimes called 'structural principles', partially overlap with but should be distinguished from 'general principles'.[1] By contrast with the latter, organizational principles do not include principles that directly define the legal situation of individuals, such as fundamental rights.

Organizational principles are tools to develop the law and fill the relations and interactions with substance. They are horizontally applicable across the whole range of EU law. The principles explored in this book are all codified. They function as aids for constitutional interpretation and are grounds for judicial review. The book focuses not so much on the gap-filling function of organizational principles but their transformative potential, including as structures of bonding (*Bindungsstrukturen*).[2]

The specific question addressed in this chapter is: What happens to the logic of organizational principles when the Union takes external action? It focuses on three illustrative examples of organizational principles: first, the principle of subsidiarity, which addresses the federal question of at what level should a shared competence be exercised, that is, who should exercise it; second, the principle of primacy, which vests EU law with its prevailing status vis-à-vis national law; and third, the principle of coherence, which has been tremendously strengthened under the Lisbon Treaty and enjoys particular relevance in the area of external actions. These principles are selected for the following reasons: they go to the core of the division of powers between the Union and its Member States; they have a significant impact on bonding structures; and they are particularly relevant in the context of external relations. The principle of sincere cooperation, better understood as EU loyalty, would squarely fall within the definition of organizational principles in this chapter. Because of its great relevance, in particular for external relations, it was separately examined in Chapter 2.

The chapter demonstrates that when policy-making happens in external relations this tends to strengthen the EU's position. The external relations context also changes the interpretation of the underlying structures of bonding. At least potentially, it

[1] See for a detailed explanation of the function and functioning of general principles: Koen Lenaerts, Jose Gutiérrez-Fons, 'The Constitutional Allocation of Powers and General Principles of EU Law' (2010) 47 CML Rev 1629.

[2] See Chapter 1 for a conceptualization of bonding structures.

creates new possibilities for the formation of such structures. The chapter argues in favour of using these possibilities and strengthening the potential of these structures.

Formal structures of bonding are relevant to allow individuals to feel co-authorship of public decisions. The principles of subsidiarity, primacy, and coherence all interact with the structures of bonding within the EU legal order. Subsidiarity has the potential to serve as a structure of justification and bonding. Primacy enhances effectiveness of EU law and strengthens the potential of formal legal structures—as does coherence by potentially enhancing effectiveness, and the ability of citizens to adequately comprehend lines of representation, reasons for action, and divisions of powers.

This chapter is structured as follows. Section 2 addresses the role of subsidiarity in the context of external actions. How is subsidiarity interpreted when the EU acts externally? Evidence exists, for example, that the simple fact that EU law gives effect to international agreements has at times been deemed sufficient to justify that the Union rather than the Member States take action. International environmental law in particular gives us a glimpse of the vanishing relevance of the subsidiarity principle in a globalizing world, both factually and legally. This presumption that external action of the Union meets the requirements of subsidiarity can and should be argued on the grounds that the Union is better placed to represent the interests and positions of EU citizens externally. Justifying Union action because of the Union's greater ability to contribute to the democratic legitimacy of external relations also uses subsidiarity as a formal structure of justification and bonding. Section 3 examines how the interpretation of the principle of primacy is affected when policy-making happens under international law. It discusses in particular how national (constitutional) courts and the EU Courts engage with each other's positions and how their positions may influence each other when international law obligations play a role. It demonstrates the relevance of primacy for the effectiveness and legitimacy of EU law, which are core to the potential of bonding structures. Section 4 addresses, in the context of external relations, the influence of the principle of coherence on the interpretation of the power division between the EU and its Member States. Coherence post-Lisbon is in many ways characterized by blurred delimitations. This creates ambiguity, which above all empowers the Court, results in constitutionalization, and removes issues from the political discourse. At the same time, coherence contributes to predictability, which is highly relevant for the expectations, engagement, and sense of ownership of EU citizens. A certain level of coherence is hence a precondition for the realization of the potential of bonding structures. Section 5 concludes and links the findings of the chapter to bonding structures, autonomy, effectiveness, and legitimacy.

2. Subsidiarity Under External Pressure

2.1 Constitutional framework and interpretation

The principle of subsidiarity requires that, 'in areas which do not fall within its exclusive competence, the Union shall act only if and in so far as the objectives of the proposed action cannot be sufficiently achieved by the Member States, either at central level or at regional and local level, but can rather, by reason of the scale or effects of the proposed action, be better achieved at Union level'.[3] It expresses a preference for decentralization

[3] Consolidated Version Treaty on European Union [2016] OJ C 202/01 (hereafter TEU), art 5(3).

and 'embedded authority'.[4] It is consciously phrased as a one-directional principle, placing a burden of justification on the Union for exercising shared competences. It was introduced under the Maastricht Treaty as one of the means to contain 'creeping EU competences' and to counterbalance the revolutionary creation of the Union and the extension of its competences into areas of deep political significance.[5] However, scholars have fundamentally criticized its ability to have any actual effect on containing the exercise of powers by the Union, not only for reasons of lack of judicial enforcement but also for structural reasons of how subsidiarity is operationalized.[6] Within the context of external relations, subsidiarity is by definition even less useful as a means of containing the increasing (exercise of) Union powers. The international level of action and the involvement of non-EU actors are regularly read as indicating that the Union is better placed to exercise a particular competence.

Subsidiarity forms part of the triumvirate of the principle of conferral, subsidiarity, and proportionality, which are all three intended to contain EU law-making.[7] The principle of conferral determines that the Union can only act where it has competence. The principle of proportionality among others protects individual rights and Member States by ensuring that they are not subject to interference by public (Union) actions unnecessarily.[8] Finally, subsidiarity complements these two principles by offering a framework to resolve the question of 'who' should take action to pursue a particular objective in specific circumstances in areas of shared competences, taking into account this objective, as well as the geographical scope and nature of the issue to be regulated. It is phrased as a limitation of the Union's right to exercise its competences. Applying a federal lens, Robert Schütze refers to subsidiarity as giving the answer to the question of whether the Union legislator has unnecessarily restricted national autonomy.[9] Indeed, subsidiarity limits the Union's ability to *exercise* existing competences and aims, in its one-directional formulation, to protect the autonomy of the federate units (Member States). While it may influence the interpretation of EU law in a way that results in an expansion of Union competence, subsidiarity as such cannot expand Union competence.[10] This would go against its very rationale.

Subsidiarity is meant to give effect to two concerns that may at times pull in different directions: effectiveness and democratic legitimacy.[11] First, subsidiarity promotes

[4] Maria Cahill, 'Sovereignty, Liberalism and the Intelligibility of Attraction to Subsidiarity' (2016) 61 AJJ 109.

[5] Deborah Cass, 'The Word that Saves Maastricht? The Principle of Subsidiarity and the Division of Powers within the European Community' (1992) 29 CML Rev 1107. See also Derrick Wyatt 'Could a "Yellow Card" for National Parliaments Strengthen Judicial as well as Political Policing of Subsidiarity?' (2006) 2 Croatian Y Eur L & Pol 1, 6.

[6] Gareth Davies, 'Subsidiarity: The Wrong Idea, in the Wrong Place, at the Wrong Time' (2006) 43 CML Rev 63 (hereafter Davies, 'Subsidiarity').

[7] Post-Lisbon, the more stringently formulated obligation of the Union to respect national identity in art 4(2) TEU serves a similar function.

[8] Fundamentally: Jürgen Schwarze, *European Administrative Law* (Sweet & Maxwell 2006) 678ff. For the protection of Member States' powers, see eg Case C-84/94 *UK and Northern Ireland v Council (Working Time Directive)* [1996] EU:C:1996:431 or C-426/93, *Germany v Council* [1995] EU:C:1995:367.

[9] Robert Schütze, 'Subsidiarity After Lisbon: Reinforcing the Safeguards of Federalism?' (2009) 68 CLJ 525, 529.

[10] Koen Lenaerts and P van Ypersele, *Le principe de subsidiarité et son contexte: Étude de l'article 3B du Traité CE* (Cahiers de droit européen, 1994) 3, argue unconvincingly in favour of competence extension. AG Toth, 'The Principle of Subsidiarity in the Maastricht Treaty' (1992) 29 CML Rev 1079, 1082 agrees that this is not possible.

[11] See more generally for a discussion of the underlying normative concerns: Andreas Follesdal, 'The Principle of Subsidiarity as a Constitutional Principle in International Law' (2013) 2 Global Constitutionalism 37, 41–46. For more details on the legitimacy debate: Antonio Estella, *The EU*

comparative effectiveness by prioritizing the level of decision-making that attains at least sufficient (Member States; sufficiency test) or greater (Union; added value test) effectiveness; and second, it promotes (democratic) legitimacy by introducing a presumption in favour of greater proximity of government, as well as an obligation to justify distancing decision-making from those governed. Subsidiarity is an attempt to operationalize the latter concern, which is also clearly expressed in the binding codification of Article 1(2) TEU ('decisions are taken [. . .] as closely as possible to the citizen'). Post-Lisbon this becomes most apparent in the procedural role of national parliaments in protecting subsidiarity.[12] Subsidiarity protects collective (group) autonomy in the decision-making process,[13] rather than individual rights from specific measures (which is the aim of proportionality). This establishes a link between subsidiarity and popular sovereignty, understood as collective autonomy of the national people through their national parliaments.

The Lisbon Treaty attempted to vest subsidiarity with additional procedural and judicial 'teeth' in the legislative procedure. Protocol 2 requires '[t]he Commission [. . .][to] forward its draft legislative acts and its amended drafts to national Parliaments at the same time as to the Union legislator'.[14] Any draft legislative act must justify why the principle of subsidiarity is met and to substantiate the reasons for concluding that a Union objective can be better achieved at Union level by qualitative and, wherever possible, quantitative indicators.[15] The EU institutions, usually the Commission, and national parliaments can enter into a reasoned exchange on whether any given piece of draft legislation complies with the principle of subsidiarity.[16] The Protocol further makes the principle of subsidiarity explicitly justiciable[17]—a possibility that the Court of Justice of the European Union (CJEU) has confirmed.[18] The role of national parliaments, however, remains limited to the political process; they cannot independently bring a case to the CJEU.

Even with these procedural 'teeth', subsidiarity remains difficult to operationalize. Subsidiarity struggles to impose clear limits to Union actions, for example in the context of Article 114 TFEU.[19] The very objective of creating and maintaining the functioning of the internal market seems to require Union action. At an abstract level, all differences in regulation may potentially constitute an obstacle to trade.[20] Subsidiarity has also had the less explicit effect of guiding the CJEU's approach and reasoning on Union action in the area of the internal market. This guiding influence appears to prioritize Union action.[21] Internally, the cross-border nature of an issue was for a long time the touchstone of the Union's ability to harmonize.[22] In short, 'Member States

Principle of Subsidiarity and Its Critique (OUP 2002) Chapters 2 and 3 (hereafter Estella, *Principle of Subsidiarity*).

[12] Protocol 2; see discussion below.

[13] See for the link to the Aristotle's *Politics* and the relevance of groups: Estella, *Principle of Subsidiarity* (n 11) 77.

[14] Art 4(1) of Protocol 2. [15] Art 5 of Protocol 2. [16] Art 7 of Protocol 2.

[17] Art 8 of Protocol 2.

[18] eg Case C-58/08, *Vodafone and Others* [2010] EU:C:2010:321 (hereafter Case C-58/08 *Vodafone*), paras 72–79; Case C-176/09, *Luxembourg v Parliament and Council* [2011] EU:C:2011:290, paras 73–83.

[19] Consolidated Version of the Treaty on the Functioning of the European Union [2008] OJ C115/47 (hereafter TFEU); Davies, 'Subsidiarity' (n 6) 68–75.

[20] Case 8/74, *Procureur du Roi v Benoît and Gustave Dassonville* [1974] EU:C:1974:82, para 5.

[21] See Thomas Horsley, 'Subsidiarity and the Court of Justice: Missing Pieces in the Subsidiarity Jigsaw?' (2012) 50 JCMS 267, 269–71.

[22] Some nuances are necessary after the Court's case law on citizenship, which does not require a cross-border element at all times. See eg Case C-34/09, *Gerardo Ruiz Zambrano v Office national de l'emploi (ONEm)* [2011] EU:C:2011:124.

[…] cannot ensure cooperation and coordination by acting alone, […] by reason of its territorial and personal scope, [this can] be better achieved at the Union level'.[23] It would be impossible to argue that Member States acting alone could sufficiently meet the objective of harmonization.[24] In fact, the Netherlands once tried to argue that international action by the Member States may be just as effective as EU harmonization.[25] The Court rejected this argument. Furthermore, Gareth Davies concludes that 'once the [Union] announces that it wishes to pursue one of the objectives which comprise the functional competence, since these competences are defined in terms creating uniformity, and Member States clearly cannot achieve this alone, subsidiarity no longer applies'.[26] He argues, relying on internal market examples, that whether or not subsidiarity can be invoked depends on how the policy objectives are framed.

In 1992, the European Council set out guidelines for the application and implementation of subsidiarity.[27] These guidelines were codified in a protocol to the Amsterdam Treaty[28] and given judicial relevance.[29] Since the entry into force of the Lisbon Treaty, the Amsterdam protocol has been repealed.[30] As a consequence, the *substantive* guidelines intended to help operationalizing subsidiarity are no longer codified. However, they continue to be helpful in understanding considerations underlying the principle of subsidiarity. The guidelines inquired 'whether the issue under consideration has transnational aspects which cannot be satisfactorily regulated by action by Member States; and/or whether actions by Member States alone or lack of Community action would conflict with the requirements of the Treaty […] or would otherwise significantly damage Member States' interests; and/or whether action at Community level would produce clear benefits by reason of its scale or effects compared with action at the level of the Member States'.[31]

The problem with these substantive guidelines as they were previously codified is that they focused on the effectiveness dimension and thereby diverted attention away from the democratic legitimacy concern. This also becomes apparent in the formulaic reference to the 'scale and effects' of the action.[32] The way the Commission examines

[23] Parliament and Council Regulation (EU) 2017/2394 on cooperation between national authorities responsible for the enforcement of consumer protection laws and repealing Regulation (EC) No 2006/2004 [2017] OJ L 345/1, recital 53.

[24] Davies, 'Subsidiarity' (n 6) 74 referring also to the argument of AG Fennelly in Case C-376/98, *Federal Republic of Germany v European Parliament and Council of the European Union (Tobacco Advertising)* [2000] EU:C:2000:324 (hereafter Case C-376/98, *Tobacco Advertising*).

[25] Case C-377/98, *Netherlands v EP and Council (Biotechnology Directive)* [2001] EU:C:2001:523. See also Juliane Kokott and Thomas Diehn, '*Kingdom of the Netherlands v European Parliament and Council of the European Union*, Case C-377/98. 2001 ECR I-7079' (2002) 96 AJIL 950.

[26] Davies, 'Subsidiarity' (n 6) 75.

[27] European Council, 'Conclusions adopted at Edinburgh European Council, Annex 1 to Part A: Overall Approach to the Application by the Council of the Subsidiarity Principle and Article 3b of the Treaty on European Union' (Bulletin of the European Communities, 12-1992).

[28] Protocol (no 30) on the application of the principles of subsidiarity and proportionality [1997] OJ C 321/308, provide for an authoritative definition of subsidiarity.

[29] Judicial relevance of the subsidiarity guidelines: Case C-491/01, *British American Tobacco (Investments) and Imperial Tobacco* [2002] EU:C:2002:741, para 178; Case C-58/08, *Vodafone* (n 18) paras 72–74.

[30] Art 9 of Protocol No 1 to the Treaty of Lisbon, amending the protocols annexed to the Treaty on European Union, to the Treaty Establishing the European Community and/or to the Treaty Establishing the European Atomic Energy Community, states: The following Protocols shall be repealed: […] (g) Protocol on the application of the principles of subsidiarity and proportionality (1997), which shall be replaced by a new Protocol with the same title.

[31] European Council, (n 27)

[32] eg Parliament and Council Decision (EU) 1386/2013 on a General Union Environment Action Programme to 2020 'Living well, within the limits of our planet' [2013] OJ L 354/171, recital 38: 'Since the objective of this Decision, namely to set up a General Union Environment Action

subsidiarity as part of its impact assessments in the pre-legislative stage further marginalizes the 'national policy and autonomy interests'.[33]

The procedural rules introduced by the Treaty of Lisbon, which strengthen the position and influence of national parliaments, should be read as a reaction and as an attempt to bring the democratic legitimacy concern back to the fore, even though they also express a preference for quantifiable indicators. Jürgen Habermas identifies that 'the principle of subsidiarity [...] serves to maintain the organizational structure of the member states and protect national ways of life' as a relevant element to establish and maintain a divided sovereignty, in the sense that citizens act as EU citizens and as national citizens at the same time.[34] This entails that the Member States' respective autonomies and the democratic achievements of the founding nation states are protected. Indeed, while more recent writings of Jürgen Habermas concentrate above all on ways to strengthen the European dimension of the dual-sovereign,[35] this should not lead us to forget his explicit acknowledgement that Member States are and should also be one of the sources of normative legitimacy within the EU.

The effectiveness dimension of subsidiarity has led to a wealth of economic considerations entering the subsidiarity debate. This becomes problematic, for example, where the democratic legitimacy dimension is factored in as 'heterogeneity of preferences'.[36] This economic concept does not grasp the full spectrum of the normative underpinning of democratic legitimacy and collective autonomy as part of subsidiarity. Proximity of government to citizens is about the better knowledge of and ability to consider the preferences and conditions of those governed. Yet proximity of government is also about transparency,[37] ability to participate, trust in public institutions, and the possibility of feeling represented, as seeing decisions as one's own.

For the discussion of the potential of subsidiarity as a structure of justification and bonding, it is important to keep in mind that any public debate on subsidiarity is preceded by a process of selection. Subsidiarity can only be observed in action, that is, in secondary law or case law, when at least the Commission has positively decided on the question of Union's ability to exercise its competence. Only if the Commission makes a proposal does the subsidiarity debate reach the public domain. Otherwise, if the Commission does not make a legislative proposal, subsidiarity is not publicly debated. This subsection sketched the background against which the following two subsections demonstrate that the effectiveness-focused interpretation of subsidiarity in the context of external relations favours Union action. Yet they also argue that the democratic legitimacy dimension of subsidiarity speaks in favour of external action by the Union and that the Union should use subsidiarity to explicate and justify its ability to represent EU citizens on the international plane.

Programme setting out priority objectives, cannot be sufficiently achieved by the Member States but can rather, by reason of the scale and effects of that action programme be better achieved at Union level'.

[33] Davies, 'Subsidiarity' (n 6) 76.

[34] Jürgen Habermas, 'Democracy in Europe: Why the Development of the EU into a Transnational Democracy is Necessary and How It is Possible' (2015) 21 ELJ 546. See also Section 4.1 of Chapter 1.

[35] Jürgen Habermas, *Zur Verfassung Europas. Ein Essay* (Suhrkamp 2011).

[36] Josephine van Zeben, 'Subsidiarity in European Environmental Law: A Competence Allocation Approach' (2014) 38 Harvard EL Rev 415 (hereafter Van Zeben, 'Subsidiarity in European Environmental Law').

[37] Art 1(1) TEU.

2.2 A revealing example: externalities in environmental law

Environmental law is particularly illustrative for the changing interpretation of subsidiarity when policy-making is internationalized. The Union's exercise of environmental competences has greatly increased since the beginning of Union action in that area.[38] Environmental law is a shared competence; subsidiarity is hence applicable. The principle of subsidiarity even originates in the area of environmental law. It was introduced into the Treaties by the Single European Act in 1986 as part of the new provision on Community powers in environmental matters stating that '[t]he Community shall take action relating to the environment to the extent to which the [specific] objectives [...] can be attained better at Community level than at the level of the individual Member States'.[39] At the same time, it has been argued that 'in the area of the environment, it should be easy to substantiate the reasons for Community action'.[40] This is due to the potential geographic reach of many environmental problems, which by definition do not respect jurisdictional boundaries. The prime example is climate change. A significant reduction of greenhouse gases in the atmosphere could only be achieved in a collective, if not in a concerted effort. This leads to an inherent presumption that environmental concerns with transboundary effects can be better dealt with by the EU.[41] For other environmental problems however, such as local air quality, a presumption that they can only be addressed effectively on a European scale seems prima facie more difficult to establish. Nonetheless, secondary law has been justified with the general argument that the objectives of improving 'environmental quality and human health cannot be sufficiently achieved by the Member States but can rather, by reason of their scale and effects, be better achieved at Union level'.[42]

Externalities form part of the considerations that are taken into account in a subsidiarity test. They are mentioned by the Treaties as 'reasons of [...] effect'. At an abstract level, interlocking regulatory regimes and interconnecting markets increase externalities between Member States and for non-EU parties. These increased externalities of policy-making support prima facie action at the more inclusive Union level. This may—again prima facie—reduce the effectiveness of subsidiarity as a means to contain the Union's exercise of competences. However, in the *Tobacco Advertising* case the CJEU was clear that abstract considerations are not sufficient to justify the choice of a legal basis, but that concrete and specific effect on the internal market must be demonstrated.[43] The same should apply in the context of the subsidiarity test. General potential 'safe haven' or 'race to the bottom' arguments should not therefore be sufficient. Additionally, and more importantly, while externalities seem in practice to justify cementing the rebuttable presumption that Union action is *better* in the context

[38] See the first Environmental Action Programme in 1973 [1973] OJ C 112.

[39] Art 130 r (4) s 1 EEC. See also the Environmental Action Programme, ibid.

[40] Koen Lenaerts, 'The Principle of Subsidiarity and the Environment in the European Union: Keeping the Balance of Federalism' (1994) 17 Fordham ILJ 846. See for a further discussion: Jonathan Golub, 'Sovereignty and Subsidiarity in EU Environmental Policy' 1996 XLIV Political Studies 686.

[41] See eg Parliament and Council Regulation (EU) 2017/852 on mercury, and repealing Regulation (EC) No 1102/2008 [2017] OJ L 137/1, recital 34: 'by reason of the transboundary nature of mercury pollution and the nature of the measures to be taken, be better achieved at Union level'.

[42] Parliament and Council Directive (EU) 2015/2193 on the limitation of emissions of certain pollutants into the air from medium combustion plants [2015] OJ L 313/1, recital 33.

[43] Case C-376/98, *Tobacco Advertising* (n 24), in particular 84.

of environmental matters,[44] they are only part of the considerations that feed into the subsidiarity test.

The externality considerations in the context of environmental matters, also in the non-EU context, drive the tendency towards international law-making. This in turn shifts these matters into the realm of EU external relations, rather than internal EU environmental law. Substantive considerations of externalities come together with international law-making and both are translated in the context of subsidiarity into a presumption in favour of Union action. Examples for this are the references to subsidiarity in the Emissions Trading System (ETS) Directive, with which the EU aims to meet the obligations under the Kyoto Protocol[45] and in the Ship-Source Pollution Directive.[46] Both refer to the fact that the EU instrument gives effect to international standards as the reason why the subsidiarity requirement is fulfilled and why, therefore, the EU is the right actor to adopt this policy. At face value, these legal instruments hence appear to take the position that action is justified because (and seemingly only because) there is a transnational aspect to the policy-making. Cross-border effects or externalities were not mentioned in either instrument, even though both greenhouse gas emissions and ship-source pollution have externalities. Nor did the Union legislator engage with the democratic dimension of subsidiarity. No argument was made that the Union could have an added value in representing the interests and position of EU citizens externally.

Globalizing dynamics are omnipresent in the form of increasing interconnectedness and interdependencies. The EU is also a response to globalization rather than only an allegory of it. It creates a high level of interconnectedness and interdependencies internally, but it also addresses externalities and strengthens public rule in the face of global challenges. This becomes most apparent in external relations. Dealing with unavoidable externalities and representing both the Member States and EU citizens in the world is one of the core added values of the Union or arguably even its *raison d'être*.[47] Where global environmental problems cannot be addressed by unilateral national action and large multinationals have so much power that they can decide to defy public rule in an individual country the Union could make a convincing explicit argument in favour of Union action based not only on effectiveness but also democratic considerations. By limiting justification to effectiveness considerations, the Union neglects the potential of subsidiarity to connect to and justify the European dimension

[44] Van Zeben, 'Subsidiarity in European Environmental Law' (n 36) 419, questioning the rationale for this presumption of centralization.

[45] 'Since the objective of the proposed action, namely the establishment of a link between the Kyoto project-based mechanisms and the Community scheme, cannot be sufficiently achieved by the Member States acting individually, and can therefore by reason of the scale and effects of this action be better achieved at Community level, the Community may adopt measures, in accordance with the principle of subsidiarity as set out in Article 5 of the Treaty.' Parliament and Council Directive (EC) 2004/101 amending Directive 2003/87/EC establishing a scheme for greenhouse gas emission allowance trading within the Community, in respect of the Kyoto Protocol's project mechanisms [2004] OJ L 338/18, para 19.

[46] 'Since the objectives of this Directive, namely the incorporation of the international ship-source pollution standards into Community law and the establishment of penalties—criminal or administrative—for violation of them in order to ensure a high level of safety and environmental protection in maritime transport, cannot be sufficiently achieved by the Member States and can therefore be better achieved at Community level, the Community may adopt measures, in accordance with the principle of subsidiarity as set out in Article 5 of the Treaty.' Parliament and Council Directive (EC) 2005/35 on ship-source pollution and on the introduction of penalties for infringements [2005] OJ L 255/11.

[47] See Section 4.3 of Chapter 1 for more details.

of the divided sovereignty. Wide-spread dynamics of globalization and increasing international law-making confer broader relevance on the finding, that giving effect to public international law in institutional practice seems to establish a presumption as such that Union action is better. The next section broadens the examination of the role of subsidiarity in EU external relations beyond environmental law.

2.3 Rebuttable presumption that Union action in external relations is needed?

Subsidiarity is not an issue that is brought up very often before the CJEU in the context of EU external relations law.[48] The limited relevance of subsidiarity is due to a number of factors that limit its formal application within the external context.

First, subsidiarity is formally applicable to non-exclusive competences.[49] Internally, it is usually considered in the context of shared competences. However, other types of non-exclusive competences, such as parallel competences (eg the Common Foreign and Security Policy (CFSP) or humanitarian aid) also fall, in principle, within the realm of subsidiarity. Bilateral actions may be preferred to Union actions. At the same time, the continuing ability to take national measures makes the subsidiarity issue less pressing.

Second, the possibility of implied *exclusive* competence for the conclusion of international agreements under Article 3(2) TFEU is a mechanism that may draw internally shared competences within the realm of exclusive external competences. This excludes the application of the principle of subsidiarity. The development is illustrated by the Court's dynamic interpretation of exclusive Union competences in Opinion 2/91 on the International Labour Organization. The CJEU ruled in this opinion that '[t]he exclusive or non-exclusive nature of the Community's competence does not flow solely from the provisions of the Treaty but may also depend on the scope of the measures, which have been adopted by the Community institutions for the application of those provisions and which are of such a kind as to deprive the Member States of an area of competence, which they were able to exercise previously on a transitional basis'.[50] The opinion exemplifies how every exercise of Union internal competences can hence exclude external actions by the Member State and how it allows the Union 'to escape the reach of the subsidiarity principle'.[51] In other words, implied external competences leave the decision on the scope of 'application of the constitutional principle of subsidiarity to a legislative decision by the [Union]'.[52] Either the Union has legislated internally and becomes exclusively competent or it has not done so and the Member States remain free to act internationally.

Third, the procedural enforcement mechanisms of Protocol 2 only apply to legislative acts. In the context of non-legislative action, for example, in the area of CFSP,

[48] In four cases with the 'subject-matter' 'external relations' in the categories pre-defined by the CJEU, one of the parties brought up the principle of subsidiarity. The Court did not discuss it in any of these four cases. In one external relations case, the court stated that a reference to the principle of proportionality is not necessary, referring to a prior case in which it held the same for subsidiarity. Search on curia.eu on 4 April 2018.

[49] Art 5(3) TEU.

[50] Opinion 2/91 (ILO Convention) [1993] EU:C:1993:106 (hereafter Opinion 2/91) para 9.

[51] Robert Schütze, *From Dual to Cooperative Federalism: The Changing Structure of European Law* (OUP 2009) 306.

[52] ibid, 341.

where legislative action is excluded,[53] the principle of subsidiarity remains a guiding principle on how to answer the federal question but loses its procedural 'teeth'.

Fourth, mixed agreements are a particular form of joint Union and Member State action, where the core federal question of who should take action is precisely avoided by taking action together. This makes subsidiarity considerations futile.

De Baere argues that both mixed agreements and implied external powers are an expression of subsidiarity.[54] Mixed agreements because they involve the Member States and implied powers because if external action is justified under Article 216(1) TFEU this meets the criteria of subsidiarity. I do not think that the first argument on the subsidiarity rationale for mixed agreements can convince. Mixed agreements specifically avoid answering the federal question of who is in charge.[55] Moreover, mixed agreements are neither a choice for effectiveness, nor for democratic legitimacy—the two interests that the principle of subsidiarity aims to further. Dual democratic legitimacy that can be traced back to individuals as EU and as national citizens, requires the need to put citizens in the position to be able to adequately know what they are voting on (eg as national citizens in national referenda) and whom they are electing to do what (both in national and European elections).[56] In fact, subsidiarity entails a choice between different levels of action: national or European. In the external relations context, the level of action is always international. The remaining core element on which subsidiarity may have an influence in the external relations context is: who represents whose interests and who has a say in what the international action is. In the particular external relations context, the democratic legitimacy dimension of subsidiarity hence becomes even more relevant.

De Baere's argument is prima facie more convincing for implied exclusive external powers. The different alternatives of Article 216(1) TEU seem to express arguments that would also be considered in a subsidiarity test. One core element is effectiveness. Implied competences arise, inter alia, when internal objectives cannot effectively be achieved without a corresponding external power. This is particularly relevant where it concerns competences with purposive language because effectiveness is always related to certain objectives stated within the legal bases. Yet similar to the considerations on mixed agreements, the democratic legitimacy dimension is irrelevant for the establishment of implied powers but should be considered in the context of subsidiarity.

Applying the above-cited substantive guidelines to external relations,[57] 'clear benefits by reason of scale' are almost inevitable when the Union concludes international agreements, rather than individual Member States. Often a reference to the 'international character' of the regulated subject matter is presented as satisfying subsidiarity.[58] Much depends therefore on whether all three criteria must be met or only

[53] Art 24(1) TEU.

[54] Geert de Baere, 'Subsidiarity as a Structural Principle Governing the Use of EU External Competences' in Marise Cremona (ed), *Structural Principles in EU External Relations Law* (OUP 2018) Chapter 5.

[55] See also on mixity Chapters 2, 4, and 5.

[56] The Dutch referendum on the EU–Ukraine Association Agreement on 6 April 2016 is a case in point. Based on the media coverage, it was impossible for Dutch citizens to understand that their vote as national citizens only concerned a very small part of the agreement. See on this point, in particular, Chapter 5.

[57] See n 27 and accompanying text above.

[58] eg Parliament and Council Regulation (EU) 1257/2013 on ship recycling and amending Regulation (EC) No 1013/2006 and Directive 2009/16/EC [2013] OJ L 330/1, recital 22: 'cannot be sufficiently achieved by the Member States due to the international character of shipping and ship recycling, but can rather by reason of its scale and effects, be better achieved at Union level'.

one. In the original formulation of the guidelines in Edinburgh 'and/or' was used to indicate that meeting one of the criteria should be considered sufficient. This was dropped in the Amsterdam protocol, which could be read to indicate that a cumulative reading was later favoured.[59] Even more importantly, the literal reading of Article 5(3) TEU supports a cumulative reading. Criteria one and two, specifying what is meant by 'cannot be sufficiently achieved by the Member States', require a closer examination, including in the context of external relations. Bilateral action may also be able to achieve the objectives in question. In the context of the internal market much depends on the framing of the objectives of the adopted legal instrument.[60] In the context of external relations, the international dimension and the involvement of non-EU actors is automatically present. This is not a matter of framing. External relations always concern transnational interaction of jurisdictions. If this alone suffices to justify action by the Union under the subsidiarity principle—and this seems to be the case in the internal market context—the involvement of non-EU parties seems to be sufficient, in principle, to satisfy the subsidiarity test. This seems also to be the rationale behind the a priori exclusive Union competences for the construction of a customs union and the common commercial policy.[61]

At the same time, the exclusion of abstract considerations[62] by the CJEU in *Tobacco Advertising*[63] (in the context of the choice of the legal basis) should also exclude a general conclusion in the context of subsidiarity that the involvement of non-EU parties and the need to demonstrate unity in international relations as such justifies action at Union level. An argument in favour of 'better Union action' in the external relations context should be based on specific substantive reasons of scale and scope and of addressing externalities.

More importantly, an argument for preserving collective autonomy and self-determination could be made in the context of external relations, which also demonstrates why the inward-looking quantification of 'heterogeneity of preferences' does not encompass the full reach of the democratic legitimacy rationale of subsidiarity. The Union is regularly better placed to represent EU citizens externally. It has greater economic bargaining power, offers a larger market, and has better resources to bring to the negotiation table. In several ways, the effectiveness and the democratic legitimacy points here mutually reinforce each other. With the European Parliament being informed, involved in the negotiations behind the scenes, and having a veto power for the conclusion of international agreements, it may institutionally be in the position to offer a more direct channel of democratic legitimation to EU citizens on the international plane than national parliaments.[64] This argument of representation would justify a presumption in favour of Union action in external relations. Any such arguments should however be made more explicitly. This would contribute to the justifiability of Union action. It would also make the external relations argument in favour of Union action subject to public deliberation—both within the institutions and in public discourse.

By way of conclusion, the ability of the principle of subsidiarity to confine the Union's exercise of powers is even more limited in the external relations context than in the context of internal law-making. At times, it is presumed that international relations

[59] Arguing in favour of a cumulative reading: Jacob Öberg, 'Subsidiarity as a Limit to the Exercise of EU Competences' (2016) 36 YEL 1 https://papers.ssrn.com/sol3/papers.cfm?abstract_id=2876866.
[60] See above Section 2.1. [61] Art 3(1)(a) and (e) TFEU.
[62] The distortion must be *real*. [63] See above text accompanying n 42.
[64] See Section 2 of Chapter 1, as well as Chapter 5.

as such satisfy the subsidiarity test. Furthermore, subsidiarity is one of the formal legal contexts in which the EU institutions, above all the Commission, should give good reasons for European as opposed to Member State action. It has the potential to function as a structure of justification and bonding. In fact, subsidiarity is in its core an obligation to give reasons. Reducing these reasons to effectiveness considerations does not do justice to the rationale of subsidiarity. In order to deploy the potential of subsidiarity as a bonding structure, the EU institutions should engage with the Union's ability to ensure democratic self-determination of its citizens when giving reasons in the context of the subsidiarity test. Elaborating on the democratic reasons for Union action would directly benefit the legitimacy of that Union action.

The next section turns to primacy as another organizational principle that is pivotal for the power relationships between the Union and the Member States. Other than subsidiarity, primacy does not deal with the possibility and justifiability of taking Union action, when the Union is competent. It deals with the formal legal relationship between EU law and national law. The next section is more indirectly linked to the discussion of structures of bonding than this section. The potential of structures of bonding between the Union and EU citizens directly depends on the unique effectiveness of EU law. Primacy is one of the principles that centrally contributes to the formal ability of EU law to be effective in the national legal orders.[65] If external pressure resulted in a withdrawal of national support for the primacy of EU law, this would immediately have negative consequences, not only for the effectiveness of EU law but also for the potential of all bonding structures between the Union and EU citizens.

3. Primacy Under External Pressure[66]

3.1 Meaning and interpretation within the EU

The EU and national conceptions of the primacy of EU law are very different. Starting from an understanding of autonomous validity of EU law, the CJEU interprets primacy to mean that 'all EU law has absolute and unconditional precedence and should always be given precedence over all conflicting provisions of national law'.[67] All instruments of EU law enjoy primacy vis-à-vis conflicting national law at all levels of the national legal hierarchy, irrespective of their nature or time of adoption.[68] The *effect* of primacy is that the national rule must be set aside. EU law will govern the factual situation. While the term primacy etymologically refers to the condition of being first in rank[69] and may therefore be read to imply hierarchy, the CJEU does not claim that

[65] See Section 3 of Chapter 1 for more details on the relationship between primacy and effectiveness.

[66] This section draws on the article: Christina Eckes, 'Protecting Supremacy from External Influences: A Precondition for a European Constitutional Legal Order?' (2012) 18 ELJ 230.

[67] Monica Claes, 'The Primacy of EU Law in European and National Law' in Anthony Arnull and Damian Chalmers (eds), *The Oxford Handbook of European Union law* (OUP 2015) 178 (hereafter Claes, 'The Primacy of EU Law').

[68] Case 6/64, *Costa v ENEL* [1964] EU:C:1964:66; Case 11/70, *Internationale Handelsgesellschaft mbH v Einfuhr- und Vorratsstelle für Getreide und Futtermittel* [1970] EU:C:1970:114; Case 9/65, *Acciaierie San Michele SpA (in liquidation) v High Authority of the ECSC* [1965] EU:C:1965:63; Case 48/71, Commission of the European Communities v Italian Republic [1972] EU:C:1972:65; Case 34/73, *Fratelli Variola S.p.A. v Amministrazione italiana delle Finanze* [1973] EU:C:1973:101.

[69] See also René Barents, 'The Precedence of EU Law from the Perspective of Constitutional Pluralism' (2009) ECL 421, 423. Some make a distinction between supremacy (relating to the hierarchy of norms) and primacy (a conflict rule relating the application of norms), see Damian Chalmers and others, *European Union Law* (CUP 2006) 196–201.

incompatibility with EU law renders national law invalid. It does not have the formal power to declare national law invalid.[70] Moreover, it does not stand in an institutional hierarchy in relation to national courts that would allow it to repeal their decisions. Another effect of primacy is that national law must be interpreted in conformity with EU law. One could of course argue that norms of the same rank should also be interpreted in conformity with each other; however, EU law is not interpreted in conformity with national law, only vice versa. It hence concerns a one-directional demand to conform. Primacy may only be limited by other organizational principles of *EU law*, such as proportionality,[71] and not by national law. This reflects the underlying understanding of the absolute and unconditional priority of EU law.

Virtually all national constitutional actors, most prominently national constitutional courts, start from the understanding that the primacy of EU law is ultimately founded in national constitutional law.[72] This logically makes a unilateral withdrawal from the EU possible and hence from the primacy of EU law. It also makes primacy conditional upon meeting the requirements imposed by national constitutional law. While a number of national constitutional courts have not addressed the issue and others have seemingly accepted the CJEU's conception,[73] others have prominently put forward their reading of the limits of the primacy of EU law.[74] The EU conception of primacy and the conceptions of the majority of national constitutional courts are irreconcilable. The former is based on the autonomous validity of EU law, which is precisely what the latter deny. While mutual engagement with each other's autonomous and self-referential reasoning may contribute to flexibility, increase mutual understanding, and raise the willingness and ability to avoid conflict, the different positions cannot be conceptually resolved or even approximated. In addition, judicial dialogue on conceptual points is made very difficult by the linguistic, doctrinal, socio-political, and institutional particularities and constraints that put fetters on the free movement of legal arguments between jurisdictions. Overall, a trend can be observed that more and more constitutional courts engage more and more explicitly in the debate on the limits of EU primacy imposed by their national constitutions.[75] The reasons for such a trend cannot be identified in the context of the present study. Any study of the reasons would, however, not only have to take into account the increase of the number and heterogeneity of national constitutional systems and courts within the EU legal order, but also the increase of Union powers and their exercise, as well as the attempts to create protected spaces of national autonomy.[76]

The objective of primacy is to ensure effectiveness, as well as the uniform interpretation and application of EU law.[77] A strict interpretation of primacy lies at the core of

[70] See also Thomas Vandamme, *The Invalid Directive, the Legal Authority of a Union Act requiring Domestic law Making* (Europa law Publishing 2005) 126–27.

[71] Ultimately, this may allow for the application of a conflicting rule: Joined Cases C-10-22/97, *Ministero delle Finanze v IN.CO.GE.'90* [1998] EU:C:1998:498, para 21.

[72] See for more details: Claes, 'The Primacy of EU Law' (n 67).

[73] Monica Claes counts five Member States, in which no clear view on primacy has emerged and five Member States, in which courts appear to have accepted an unconditional conception of EU law: Monica Claes, 'The Validity and Primacy of EU Law and the "Cooperative Relationship" between national Constitutional Courts and the Court of Justice of the European Union' (2016) 23 MJECL 1, 157; see also for differences in approach of different Member States and for (some of) the reasons for such differences, ibid, 188ff.

[74] Above all the German Constitutional Court.

[75] See also Section 3 of Chapter 1.

[76] See Chapter 1 for examples of attempts to contain EU powers in the context of external relations. Other examples are the national identity clause in art 4(2) TEU and art 53 of the Charter of Fundamental Rights.

[77] eg Case 166/73, *Rheinmühlen-Düsseldorf v Einfuhr- und Vorratsstelle für Getreide und Futtermittel (Rheinmühlen II)* [1974] EU:C:1974:3, para 2.

the Union's ability to vest its own law with effect in the national legal orders. Overall, the Union has managed to oblige and convince national actors to give better effect to EU law than to international law.[78] The CJEU has taken a pragmatic approach to primacy, avoiding any formal showdown but maximizing the effects of EU law on the ground through low-profile accommodation of national concerns. Ultimately, it prioritizes effectiveness over dogmatic considerations, with the aim of making non-compliance impossible to the extent that this is within its powers.

3.2 A revealing case of external pressure: UN counter-terrorist sanctions

Counter-terrorist sanctions imposed by the United Nations (UN) and given effect through EU restrictive measures (EU sanctions) have been the subject of countless scholarly pieces on human rights, EU external relations, and the relationship between international and EU law.[79] They are a particularly illustrative example of how the primacy of EU law may come under external pressure. In the widely discussed case of *Kadi*, concerning a challenge to the EU legal instrument giving effect to UN counter-terrorist sanctions, the CJEU strengthened the principle of primacy.[80] It acted as the guardian of the Union's 'foundations', including fundamental rights, and agreed to review all European law measures irrespective of their origin.[81] The Court decided in line with its narrative of a distinct and autonomous EU legal order, in which it has absolute control over the interpretation of EU law.[82]

Even though UN sanctions against private individuals are exceptional in their specificity and direct interference with fundamental rights, they demonstrate a very real problem, which gains broader relevance with the increasing role of the individual within the international legal order. Ultimately, the EU institutions (including the CJEU) and the Member States have to develop a mutually acceptable approach to deal with their obligations under international law. In light of the complexity of the European legal order and the delicate balance of powers on which it is based, this seems to require squaring the circle.

In *Kadi*, the Court of First Instance (CFI; now: General Court) and the CJEU made very different attempts to resolve the underlying conflict between Member States' international law obligations and EU fundamental rights obligations.[83] The CFI chose to confer primacy to Member States' obligations under the UN Charter,[84] including within the EU legal order. This ensured compliance with international law but

[78] See Section 3 of Chapter 1 for more details.

[79] Christina Eckes, *EU Counter-Terrorist Policies and Fundamental Rights: The Case of Individual Sanctions* (OUP 2009).

[80] Joined Cases C-402 and 415/05 P, *Kadi and Al Barakaat v Council* [2008] EU:C:2008:461 (hereafter Joined Cases C-402 and 415/05 P, *Kadi*).

[81] See on the latter point: Bjorn Kunoy and Anthony Dawes, 'Plate Tectonics in Luxembourg: The Ménage à Trois Between EC Law, International Law and the European Convention of Human Rights Following the UN Sanctions Cases' (2009) 46 CML 73.

[82] See Chapter 1.

[83] Case T-306/01, *Yusuf and Al Barakaat International Foundation v Council and Commission* [2005] EU:T:2005:331; Case T-315/01, *Kadi v Council and Commission* [2005] EU:T:2005:332; Joined Cases C-402 and 415/05 P, *Kadi* (n 80); see on the Court of First Instance's ruling: Christina Eckes, 'Judicial Review of European Anti-Terrorism Measures: The Yusuf and Kadi Judgments of the Court of First Instance' (2008) 14 ELJ 74; on the CJEU's ruling: Christina Eckes, 'A Test Case for the Resilience of the European Union's Constitutional Foundations' (2009) 15 EPL 351.

[84] More specifically under a Security Council resolution adopted under Chapter VII of the UN Charter.

excluded judicial review in light of fundamental rights guarantees under EU law and left the applicants without effective protection of their rights under EU law. On appeal, the CJEU prioritized the Union's autonomy, agreed to review the EU instrument that gave effect to the UN obligations, and made clear that obligations under international agreements can neither 'affect the allocation of powers fixed by the Treaties,'[85] nor can they 'have the effect of prejudicing the constitutional principles of the EC Treaty'.[86] It reviewed and annulled the EU legal instrument giving effect to the obligations under the UN Charter for breaching fundamental rights. Prima facie, the CJEU's ruling set the clocks back to normal after the CFI's disconcerting ruling: the Union remains an autonomous legal order and EU law enjoys primacy over national and international law. Yet this is where national courts come in.

The worst-case scenario from a fundamental rights perspective would have been if the highest national courts of the Member States had followed the CFI. The worst-case scenario from an institutional European Union perspective would have been if national supreme courts had challenged the primacy of European law in order to ensure an acceptable fundamental rights protection in their own legal order. Neither of the two happened. None of the highest courts of the EU Member States ruled on the legality of national measures giving effect to UN sanctions in the period between the CFI's and the CJEU's ruling in *Kadi*. Hence, none of the highest courts of the EU Member States followed the CFI's approach. However, a seeming contradiction remains. The CJEU demands in its settled case law that national courts accept the primacy of EU law while it refuses to defer to 'prevailing' obligations under the UN Charter.[87] Indeed, the *Bundesverfassungsgericht* used the CJEU's ruling in *Kadi* as an argument to justify the rejection of the absolute primacy of EU law vis-à-vis German law.[88] It argued that 'similar' to the Court of Justice it had placed 'the assertion of its own identity as the legal community above the commitment that is otherwise respected'.[89]

The UK Supreme Court was the first highest Member State court to rule on *national* measures giving effect to UN counter-terrorist sanctions (case of *Ahmed*).[90] It simply disregarded EU law. While the lower UK courts had held that a merits-based review of the listings was possible,[91] the Supreme Court held that there was no effective judicial remedy, either at the time of designation or at the time of the proceedings.[92] This might recall the CJEU's conclusion in *Kadi* that 'the rights of the defence [...] were patently not respected'[93] and it could 'do no other than find that it is not able to undertake the review of the lawfulness of the contested regulation'.[94] However, even though the two courts drew very similar conclusions about the infringement of the right to a fair trial,[95] the underlying messages of the two judgments are very different. The UK Supreme Court's main concern was the separation of powers.[96] Lord Hope, giving the leading judgment, used strong words: 'Conferring an unlimited discretion on the executive as

[85] Joined Cases C-402 and 415/05 P, *Kadi* (n 80) para 282. [86] ibid, para 285.

[87] See art 103 UN Charter: 'In the event of a conflict between the obligations of the Members of the United Nations under the present Charter and their obligations under any other international agreement, their obligations under the present Charter shall prevail.' The prevailing force is consequently formally limited to obligations under international agreements.

[88] BVerfG, 2 BvE 2/08 (Treaty of Lisbon judgement) para 340. [89] ibid.

[90] *HM Treasury v Ahmed* [2010] UKSC 2 (hereafter UKSC 2 *Ahmed*). This is further explored in the following section.

[91] *A, K, M, Q, G v HM Treasury* [2008] EWCA Civ 1187.

[92] UKSC 2 *Ahmed* (n 90) para 78, per Lord Hope.

[93] Joined Cases C-402/05 P and C-415/05 P, *Kadi* (n 80) para 334. [94] ibid, para 351.

[95] See also Lord Brown at UKSC 2 *Ahmed* (n 90) para 203.

[96] The orders were made in Council based on the UN Act 1946. ibid, para 4.

to how those resolutions, which it has a hand in making, are to be implemented seems to me wholly unacceptable. It conflicts with the basic rules that lie at the heart of our democracy.'[97] The CJEU, by contrast, had focused on the relationship between the UN Charter and the EU legal order, as well as procedural rights of those sanctioned. For the CJEU, the question had not been *which internal constitutional actor* could restrict fundamental rights to the extent required by the Security Council resolution, but *whether* (only because Security Council resolutions require this) rights could be reduced to that extent *at all*.

Ultimately, Member States remain responsible *under international law* for giving effect to UN Security Council resolutions. They could encounter international responsibility for failing to do so. This might also have been one of the reasons for the UK Supreme Court's choice to mention the CJEU's ruling in *Kadi*,[98] but reject its relevance, predominantly on the grounds that the CJEU had found the Union[99] not to be bound by the UN Charter, which allowed it to avoid the conflict rule in Article 103 UN Charter, setting out that obligations under the UN Charter prevail over obligations under other international agreements.[100] Taking the position that the Union is not bound by the UN Charter made the situation at the same time easier and more complicated. It was easier for the CJEU to avoid addressing the status of UN obligations within the EU legal order but it also left this complex question for later and to some extent for others (national constitutional courts) to resolve. National courts cannot do what the CJEU did. They cannot as easily avoid the binding obligations of their state flowing from the UN Charter and turn to a reasoning based on domestic law only. This being said, a strictly dualistic approach also allows Member States to avoid conflicts of norms by removing domestic norms from the reach of potentially prevailing norms of international law—albeit at the risk of encountering state liability.

By way of conclusion, the UK Supreme Court followed neither the CJEU's nor the CFI's line. It certainly did not hide behind Union law. Even though the facts were strikingly similar there are many fundamental legal differences between the two judgments. First, the CJEU did not find obligations under the UN Charter binding on the Union, while the UK is bound by the UN Charter. Second, the way human rights are protected in the UK is different from the way human rights are protected within the EU legal order. While the EU relies on internal standards (foundations of EU law), in the UK fundamental rights are protected to the extent that is required by the European Convention on Human Rights (ECHR),[101] which is an international treaty that could fall under the conflict rule in Article 103 UN Charter, with the effect that obligations under the UN Charter would prevail over rights guarantees under the ECHR. In any event, and irrespective of these differences, the UK Supreme Court's ruling contains a message on the importance of Union law (or lack thereof) and the CJEU's position on the implementation of UN resolutions in the UK.

[97] ibid, para 45 per Lord Hope. [98] ibid, paras 67ff.

[99] At the time of the judgment this was still the European Community.

[100] See UKSC 2, *Ahmed* (n 90) para 71 (per Lord Hope), para 104 (per Lord Philips), and para 203 (per Lord Brown).

[101] *R (Quark Fishing Ltd) v Secretary of State for Foreign and Commonwealth Affairs* [2006] 1 AC 529, paras 33–34: The UK Human Rights Act 1998 (HRA) was intended to 'bring rights home' by providing 'a remedial structure in domestic law for the rights guaranteed by the Convention'. This led the House of Lords to conclude that the territorial scope of the HRA was 'intended to be coextensive with the territorial scope of the obligations of the UK and the rights of victims under the Convention'. See also art 21(1) HRA, defining the European Convention 'as it has effect for the time being in relation to the United Kingdom'.

Prima facie, the Court of Justice's ruling could be criticized for applying double standards: requiring Member States to respect the primacy of Union law while denying the prevailing force of obligations under the UN Charter. However, any analysis must also consider what perceivable alternatives the CJEU had. It appears equally unlikely that national courts would accept that the 'checkpoint' on the bridge between EU law and international law is abolished (as suggested by the CFI) and that UN Charter obligations that blatantly infringe domestic fundamental right guarantees would simply enter the EU legal order and hence be vested with the unique effectiveness of EU law. If there was no mechanism (except for review on the basis of *jus cogens*) to review Union law giving effect to UN Charter obligations, national courts, by accepting the primacy of Union law, would surrender fundamental rights protection to the UN. The CJEU, however, sketched out another potential solution to normative conflict between Union law and international obligations of the Member States. In *Kadi*, the Court reminded both the European institutions and the Member States in clear words of the foundations of European law. Indeed, it introduced the 'foundations of the [EU] legal order' expressed in Article 6 TEU as a new layer of law that is hierarchically superior to the rules expressed in the Treaties.[102] These foundations are based on the ECHR and the constitutional traditions of the Member States. Hence, they take into account what is considered most fundamental, in both national and international law. These foundations, as identified by the CJEU and post-Lisbon necessarily linked to the EU Charter of Fundamental Rights, could over time be further developed into a common set of core principles and rights, shared by the EU and the Member States, that cannot be violated under any circumstances. This may strengthen the normative appeal of the primacy of EU law to national courts.

3.3 Primacy: relevance for external relations

Primacy has an external dimension. It is in particular relevant for protecting the EU legal order and the cooperation of the CJEU and national courts from direct, unfiltered external pressure. UN counter-terrorist sanctions may be a particularly revealing example of conflicting international and EU law obligations. However, with increasing EU external relations and more generally with the increasing constraints that international law imposes on the law of states and on individuals directly, the examples of conflicts may increase. The uniform application of EU law and the functioning of the EU legal order, however, depend on the protection of the principle of primacy from law originating outside the Union, particularly in conflict situations.

Furthermore, the primacy of EU law is crucial to ensuring that Member States cannot use international rules to justify derogation from EU law. Member States' executives are—as Lord Hope pointed out in *Ahmed*—the authors of international obligations and hence in a different direct or less direct fashion at the origin of the obligation. The development of the external dimension of primacy, for example, in *Kadi*, is in line with the Court of Justice's previous restrictive interpretation of Article 351 TFEU, preventing Member States from relying on prior treaty obligations as a justification to derogate from European law.[103] It excludes more clearly than previously that Member States can use the UN or other international forums to circumvent EU law.

[102] Joined Cases C-402 and C-415/05 P, *Kadi* (n 80) para 304. See also Chapter 6.

[103] Christina Eckes, 'Case C-188/07, *Commune de Mesquer v Total France and Total International Ltd.*, Judgment of the Court (Grand Chamber) of 24 June 2008 [2008] ECR I-4501; Case C-301/08, *Irène Bogiatzi v Deutscher Luftpool*, Société Luxair, European Communities, Luxembourg, Foyer

Moreover, while from the standpoint of the CJEU, international agreements of either the Union or the Member States—or both—cannot directly challenge the autonomy or primacy of EU law. Member States, for example, could not enter into an international agreement that gives primacy to international law over EU law without breaching their obligations under EU law. Bodies created under international agreements, such as international courts or tribunals (ICTs), are not bound by EU law and their rulings are not predictable in the same way as a clause in an international agreement. Some ICTs follow the internal EU line, accepting for example that EU law 'would prevail over the [Energy Charter Treaty] in case of any material inconsistency'.[104] Others dismiss it, taking the position that 'EU law does not and cannot "trump" public international law'.[105] This as such is contrary to the CJEU's standpoint. External actors are not part of the same game and do not have the same stakes in the game. They may challenge and have challenged the autonomy and primacy of the EU legal order at lower costs.[106] Chapter 6 will develop this point in more detail.

This section explained how and why primacy may come under particular pressure in the context of external relations. National constitutional courts could be placed in the position to choose between their EU law obligations and their international law obligations. They have and could use the CJEU's dualist position towards international law to reject the primacy of EU law vis-à-vis national law. If, however, they challenged the primacy of EU law as a matter of practice rather than only its origin,[107] this may have far-reaching consequences beyond the context of external relations. It would undermine EU law's unique effectiveness and weaken the potential of the Union to connect with EU citizens through formal legal structures of bonding.

The next section turns to the principle of coherence. It develops its particular relevance in external relations, including the delimitation between CFSP and TFEU policies, and highlights its influence on bonding structures: on the one hand, coherence contributes to predictability and stable expectations. This strengthens the potential of bonding structures. On the other hand, the way the Treaties aim to achieve coherence by blurring delimitations empowers the Court with the result that issues settled by the Court are removed from the political discourse. This makes it more difficult for citizens to experience ownership.

4. Coherence Through Ambiguity

4.1 Constitutional framework and interpretation

EU primary law emphasizes the importance of coherence more explicitly and more often than any other principle or value.[108] Article 7 TFEU is the most general expression of the principle of coherence, reminding us of its relative nature, having to be interpreted in light of the EU's objectives and being limited by the formal powers of

Assurances SA, Judgment of the Court (Fourth Chamber) of 22 October 2009' (2010) 47 CML Rev 899.

[104] *Electrabel S.A. v Hungary*, ICSID CASE NO ARB/07/19, [2012], para 4.191 https://www.italaw.com/sites/default/files/case-documents/italaw1071clean.pdf.

[105] *RREEF Infrastructure (G.P.) Limited, RREEF Pan-European Infrastructure Two Lux S.à r.l.*, ICSID Case No. ARB/13/30 [2016], para 87 https://www.italaw.com/cases/2317.

[106] ibid. [107] See Section 3 of Chapter 1.

[108] The English version refers to 'consistency' while the French and German versions make reference to 'cohérence' and 'Kohärenz' respectively. I use the term coherence.

the institutions. Beyond this, the Treaties contain numerous references to coherence *within* specific policy areas;[109] *between* different policy areas;[110] in external actions;[111] of external actions with other policies;[112] between the actions and statements of the different EU actors;[113] and of enhanced cooperation with Union law.[114] In the particular context of CFSP, the Treaty refers to the Union's ability to act as 'a cohesive force in international relations'.[115] Furthermore, integration clauses, such as Articles 8 (equal treatment), 11 (environment), 12 (consumer protection), 13 TFEU (animal welfare) TFEU should be regarded as indirect expressions of the principle of coherence. Coherence is hence relevant in the relationship between Member States and the Union, between institutions and within institutions.

The formal Treaty rules on coherence—as agreed by the Member States (with limited involvement of the institutions)[116] in the Lisbon Treaty—have opened up more space to disagree on the specific institutional prerogatives and rules that apply in the particular case. Disagreement about the interpretation of ambiguous provisions leads to cases before the Court. This juridification of EU external relations moves certain constitutional choices to the CJEU as a supranational EU actor, including the dividing line between intergovernmental areas, where Member States are relatively more powerful, and supranational areas, where the EU actors are relatively more powerful.

4.2 Coherence in external relations

Coherence is for several combined reasons particularly relevant in the context of external relations. Internal decision-making is complex and involves numerous actors, including the European External Action Service (EEAS), one of whose specific *purposes* is to ensure coherence. Additionally, the continuous relevance of the distinction between CFSP and TFEU policies, with different procedures and a different division of powers between the actors involved, makes coherence particularly relevant for external relations as well as for the power division between the institutions. Speaking externally with one voice or 'unity in international representation' is difficult to ensure but seen as a necessary, albeit not sufficient, condition for effectiveness and potentially even actorness of the Union. Both the Union and its Member States are subjects of international law and often retain the competence to act in parallel.

Marise Cremona (2008) suggested a three-level analysis of the coherence of the Union's external relations. At the first level, she identified conflict avoidance through rules of hierarchy; at the second, avoiding duplication and gaps through rules of delimitation; and at the third, establishing synergies between norms, actors, and instruments through principles of cooperation and complementarity.[117] The changes under the Lisbon Treaty have largely been aimed at coherence at the third level. Besides the lists of competences delimitating EU and Member States competences (second level), the Treaties have introduced new institutional and procedural ambiguities that create space for cooperation and complementarity and that may lead to synergies between norms, actors, and instruments (third level).

[109] Art 42(7) TEU; art 196(1) TFEU; art 212 TFEU; art 214 TFEU.
[110] Art 13 TEU; art 7 TFEU.
[111] Art 16(6) TEU; art 18(4) TEU; art 26(2) TEU.
[112] Art 21(3) TEU.
[113] Art 13 TEU; art 16(6) TEU; art 18(4) TEU; art 26(2) TEU.
[114] Art 329(2) TFEU.
[115] Art 24(3) TEU.
[116] See art 48 TEU.
[117] Marise Cremona, 'Coherence Through Law: What Difference Will the Treaty of Lisbon Make?' (2008) 3 Hamburg Rev Soc S 11.

The Lisbon Treaty has not only added a new body, the EEAS, and increased the powers of certain institutions (Parliament and European Council). It has also focused on the institutional set-up and the principles that govern it, such as the explicit introduction of the inter-institutional duty of sincere cooperation,[118] to ensure that the allocation of powers and differences in procedures does not stand in the way of coherence and cooperation. If anything, the high priority given to coherence and cooperation, blurs the contours of prerogatives of the different institutions and makes the identification of their specific roles and responsibilities in the institutional balance more difficult. The Lisbon Treaty notably pursued coherence by refraining from clear-cut delimitations, creating space for convergence and synergies between different policies and powers of different actors, and by leaving many details to be determined through interpretation and application by the Council, but also increasingly the Court.

The two major structural changes introduced by the Lisbon Treaty to achieve greater substantive coherence are examples of ensuring coherence through ambiguity: first, the introduction of common horizontal objectives; and second, the abolishment of any hierarchy between the two Treaties and hence between the CFSP and TFEU policies.[119] The delimitation of competences along Treaty lines has become less clear and the (same) actors are vested with competences both under the CFSP and under the TFEU. The most prominent examples of how the Lisbon Treaty aims to ensure coherence through institutional ambiguity is the position of the High Representative and creation of the EEAS. The principle of coherence is applicable across the board to all Union action, including CFSP and between different policy areas, including between TFEU policies and the CFSP. Ambiguity is *intended* to generate political space, guided and confined by legal principles in which a coherent position can be found. However, as will be discussed below, it also works against transparency, reduces the ability of citizens to know who is in charge, and empowers the Court as a supranational actor that benefits from very little democratic legitimacy. This works strongly against politics and ownership.

4.3 Institutional ambiguity

The EU, as a single legal entity, has taken over all pre-existing international agreements and obligations of the Community. This is perhaps the most fundamental step towards coherence in external relations. From an external perspective, bringing CFSP and TFEU policies within the competence of one entity or even one body has advantages. From the perspective of third countries, a fragmented institutional landscape on the EU side makes a bilateral country-to-country approach more attractive than dealing with the Union as one actor, in particular in certain policy areas, such as Area of Freedom Security and Justice (AFSJ). However, despite the Union's succession to the Community and the 'partial depillarisation',[120] formal procedural and institutional differences prevail that make a distinction between CFSP and TFEU external policies necessary. In the area of CFSP, Union competences are parallel competences;[121] the Council may not adopt legislative acts;[122] the flexibility clause of Article 352 TFEU does not apply;[123] the roles and involvement of the Commission and the Parliament are

[118] Art 13(2) TEU. [119] Arts 1(1) and 40 TEU.

[120] Marise Cremona, 'Implementation of the Lisbon Treaty, Improving Functioning of the EU: Foreign Affairs, Updated Study for the AFCO Committee' (European Parliament: Directorate-General for Internal Policies. PE 571.373, 2015) 11.

[121] See Chapter 1. [122] Arts 24(1) and 31(1) TEU; Declaration 41 [2012] OJ C 326/1.

[123] See art 352(4) TFEU.

limited; and the jurisdiction of the Court is limited. In short, the dividing line between CFSP and TFEU external policies has become more difficult to identify; however, it has by no means become less significant.

At an institutional level, Member States' (and to a limited degree the EU institutions') choice of pursuing coherence through ambiguity becomes particularly apparent in the establishment of the EEAS. This is the case in two ways: First, the EEAS is only mentioned once in Article 27(3) TEU and its composition, powers, and relations with the EU institutions had to be devised following the entry into force of the Lisbon Treaty. Second, one of the core reasons for establishing the EEAS was to improve coherence.[124] The EEAS was called 'the natural administrative expression of the European Union's desire to give greater force and coherence to its external policies'.[125] Its institutional set-up is intended to ensure better coordination between Union and Member States' actions. Even though the EEAS provision is part of the Title on CFSP, its services cover a much broader scope of action. The EEAS is functionally and institutionally dependent on and answerable to the High Representative, who holds a truly cross-Treaty post;[126] chairing the Council of Foreign Affairs (TFEU tasks), being a vice-president of the Commission (TFEU tasks) and representing the Union on matters of CFSP.[127] The fact that the High Representative takes on multiple roles that go far beyond CFSP matters is reflected in the evidence that Baroness Ashton gave to the House of Lords in 2011: she did not explicitly mention the term 'CFSP' at all.[128]

Naturally, the different functions and tasks of the High Representative determine the scope of action of the EEAS.[129] By concentrating external actions, both in TFEU and in CFSP policy fields, into one hierarchical branch of actors (High Representative, EEAS in Brussels, EU delegations), the Lisbon Treaty has broadened the scope where it is not necessary to specify whether or not a certain act or position falls within the CFSP. A network of 141 EU Union delegations and offices is connected to the EEAS. They cover both CFSP and TFEU functions, including, for example, development cooperation.

Channels of communication to the delegations are shared between the Commission and the EEAS. 'The Commission and the EEAS will agree on detailed arrangements relating to the issuing of instructions from the Commission to delegations. These should provide in particular that when the Commission will issue instructions to delegations, it will simultaneously provide a copy thereof to the Head of Delegation and to the EEAS central administration.'[130] Chains of command run from High Representatives to the Heads of Delegation.[131] In principle, information that goes up and down in the organization is separated by Chinese walls.

[124] Art 21(3) TEU and Council Decision 2010/427 establishing the organization and functioning of the European External Action Service [2010] OJ L 201/30, recital 2 and arts 2(1) and 3 (hereafter EEAS Decision).

[125] Quote of Mr Brendan Donnelly, Director of the Federal Trust at: House of Commons, 'Foreign Affairs Committee Foreign Policy Aspects of the Lisbon Treaty' (Third Report of Session, 2007–08) 63.

[126] Art 18 TEU.

[127] Art 2(2) EEAS decision (n 124) further states that the EEAS should assist the Commission as a whole.

[128] Revised transcript of evidence taken before House of Lords, The Select Committee on the European Union, Evidence Session with Baroness Ashton of Upholland, High Representative for Foreign Affairs and Security Policy, Vice-President of the European Commission (Evidence Session No 1, 14 June 2011) http://www.parliament.uk/documents/lords-committees/eu-select/transcripts/ceus20110614ev1.pdf.

[129] See also recital 1 of the EEAS Decision (n 124).

[130] ibid, recital 13.

[131] ibid, art 5(3).

The functional indivisibility of foreign policy had already led to a gradual erosion of the pillar structure even before the Lisbon Treaty entered into force.[132] The creation of the EEAS and the fact that the Treaties no longer establish a hierarchy between the different areas[133], further facilitate the integration of different policy areas leading to the development of an amorphous post-pillar foreign policy. The difficulty in delimitating competences at all levels has clearly influenced the wording of the EEAS Council decision, stating that the EEAS has the task to support the High Representative in her capacity 'as President of the Foreign Affairs Council, *without prejudice to the normal tasks of the General Secretariat of the Council*' and 'as Vice-President of the Commission [...], *without prejudice to the normal tasks of the Commission services*'.[134]

The EEAS is largely a support service and many of its actions remain internal acts[135] that cannot easily become subject to litigation. This finds confirmation in the fact that it is *not* vested with legal personality, but only with 'legal capacity'.[136] Assistance to national diplomatic services (Article 3 EEAS decision) is largely of a non-legal nature. However, this does not exclude the possibility that the participation of the EEAS in preparatory work could be seen as 'affecting' the tasks of the Commission within the meaning of Article 40 TEU. The preparatory stage is the stage in which the EEAS can best achieve its main objective of ensuring coherence between different policies. Closer coordination may also mean 'affecting' the policy outcome on the other side. Whether a particular individual EEAS act has legal effects and could as a result be brought before the CJEU would have to be established in the individual case. As a matter of principle, it is very difficult to challenge preparatory acts under Article 263 TFEU for example.

However, that it is possible to bring ambiguous EEAS institutional arrangements, as well as its decisions, before the Court is exemplified by the *Union Delegation* case.[137] The order is interesting for two reasons. First, the General Court, when ruling on the admissibility of the action, did not consider whether Union delegations fall outside the jurisdiction of the EU Courts because they fall under CFSP. [138] Second, the General Court discussed in detail the relationship between Union Delegations, the EEAS, and the Commission. It held that the Union Delegation (to Montenegro) 'is an integral part of the hierarchical and functional structure of the [EEAS] and is merely a division of that service, whereas the latter is clearly designated as an independent body of the European Union, holding the legal capacity to carry out its missions'.[139] Delegations have hence a 'link of organic dependence with the EEAS'. They also have 'a functional subordination [...] to the Commission, in the implementation of the budget of the European Union'.[140] The Commission has the power of the purse—at least for

[132] Stephan Stetter, 'Cross-Pillar Politics: Functional Unity and Institutional Fragmentation of EU Foreign Policies' (2004) 11 JEPP 720.

[133] See both arts 18 and 40 TEU.

[134] EEAS Decision (n 124) recital 3 and art 2(1).

[135] Commentary to art 3: 'the EEAS is primarily conceived to work for and with other actors ...' in Steven Blockmans and Christophe Hillion (eds), 'EEAS 2.0: A Legal Commentary on Council Decision 2010/427/EU Establishing the Organisation and Functioning of the European External Action Service' (2013) EUI Working Paper 03/2013 https://www.eui.eu/Documents/DepartmentsCentres/AcademyofEuropeanLaw/Publications/AEL201303.pdf.

[136] Art 1(2) EEAS Decision (n 124).

[137] Case T-395/11, *Elti d.o.o. v Delegation of the European Union to Montenegro* [2011] EU:T:2012:274 (hereafter Case T-395/11, *Elti*), para 46.

[138] The same is true for the Court's order concerning damages against the EU delegation to Turkey: Case T-369/11, *Diadikasia Symbouloi Epicheiriseon A v Commission and EU Delegation to Turkey* [2011] EU:T:2012:425.

[139] Case T-395/11, *Elti* (n 137) para 35.

[140] ibid, para 37.

operational expenditure.[141] Delegations are hence subject to a split rather than shared control and their legal status in its entirety is subject to the Court's jurisdiction, irrespective of their CFSP component.

Similarly, the case of *Elitaliana* demonstrates that the notion of '*acts adopted on the basis of [CFSP] provisions*' in Article 275(1) TFEU is not clear cut.[142] The case concerned the award of a public service contract for a project involving helicopter support of the European Union Rule of Law Mission in Kosovo (hereafter 'EULEX Kosovo'). The defendant argued that the Court had no jurisdiction to review the legality of the measures, because it was an act adopted on the basis of CFSP provisions. The General Court had declined jurisdiction on the ground that EULEX Kosovo did not have the capacity to act as a defendant.[143] It consequently did not have to engage with the scope of its jurisdiction. The CJEU considered the case to fall within its jurisdiction, essentially on the ground that despite the fact of EULEX Kosovo having been established pursuant to the CFSP, the award of the public contract on helicopter support gave rise to expenditure charged to the Union budget[144] and therefore subject to non-CFSP rules.[145] The Court essentially followed its Advocate General Jääskinen that acts such as the contested measures, which involve expenditure charged to the Union budget and which relate to management of the functioning of CFSP entities, must be distinguished from acts adopted under the CFSP provisions in the Treaties, as well as from acts adopted by bodies created under the provisions which relate and apply to the CFSP: jurisdiction exists in respect of the former but not in respect of the latter.[146]

The case of *H*,[147] concerning the review of legality of a decision to re-deploy an Italian magistrate to a regional of office of the European Union Police Mission, raised similar issues concerning the delimitation of the Court's jurisdiction. The General Court had denied jurisdiction because the contested measures fell within the scope of the CFSP. The CJEU by contrast found that the contested acts were '*acts of staff management*'[148] and as a consequence were not acts adopted on the basis of the provisions relating to the CFSP in the sense of the first paragraph of Article 275 TFEU. It essentially developed a coherence argument, stating that EU staff in this situation would have been subject to its jurisdiction and that therefore national staff seconded to the institutions should also be subject to its jurisdiction, in order to avoid 'irreconcilable'

[141] Art 8 (1) EEAS Decision. See also for this split responsibility the new financial regulation and in particular art 65(6) of the Parliament and Council Regulation (EU, Euratom) 966/2012 on the financial rules applicable to the general budget of the Union and repealing Council Regulation (EC, Euratom) No 1605/2002 [2012] OJ L 298/39.

[142] Case C-439/13 P, *Elitaliana v Eulex Kosovo* [2015] EU:C:2015:753 (hereafter Case C-439/13, *Elitaliana*).

[143] See the order of the Order of the General Court of 4 June 2013 in Case T-213/12, *Elitaliana v Eulex Kosovo*, [2013] EU:T:2013:292.

[144] According to art 41(2)1 TEU '[o]perating expenditure to which the implementation of this Chapter [on the CFPS] gives rise shall also be charged to the Union budget, except for such expenditure arising from operations having military or defence implications and cases where the Council acting unanimously decides otherwise'.

[145] Council Regulation (EC, Euratom) 1605/2002 of 25 June 2002 on the Financial Regulation applicable to the general budget of the European Communities [2002] OJ L 248/1. See for the Court's explanation: Case C-439/13 P, *Elitaliana* (n 142) para 49.

[146] Opinion of AG Jääskinen in Case C-439/13 P, *Elitaliana v Eulex Kosovo* [2014] EU:C:2014:2416, para 42.

[147] Case T-271/10, *H v Council* EU:T:2014:702 and, on appeal, Case C-455/14 P, *H v Council and Commission* EU:C:2016:569.

[148] ibid, Case C-455/14 P, *H v Council and Commission*, para 55.

decisions.[149] *H* is hence an example of how an argument of coherence may extend the CJEU's jurisdiction into CFSP-related matters.

The EEAS may end up and has ended up before Court. The Court may and has been asked to determine the boundaries of its own jurisdiction and the dividing line between CFSP and TFEU policies. These cases demonstrate how the institutional integration of CFSP and TFEU policies has created grey areas that are neither purely CFSP, nor purely TFEU and as a consequence extended the Court's jurisdiction into these grey areas. They also demonstrate that judicial challenges place the Court in the position to determine detailed rules, where primary and even secondary law remain ambiguous. The next section further develops how the choice to pursue coherence through ambiguity, made by the Member States (and the institutions) in the Treaties, results in litigation. It develops this point for CFSP more broadly, that is, not limited to the EEAS but very well applicable to the EEAS, with the expressed caveats.

4.4 Ambiguity triggers litigation and extends jurisdiction

4.4.1 Mutual non-affection clause

The 'mutual non-affectation clause' of Article 40 TEU is probably the most specific reflection of the changed relationship between the Treaties, which was meant to create more coherence but which also raises numerous questions of what such coherence means in practice. Until the entry into force of the Lisbon Treaty, the separation provision (ex-Article 47 TEU) was understood to protect the *acquis communautaire* from policies under the second and third pillar.[150] The Court of Justice's pre-Lisbon rulings in *Airport Transit Visa* (1998)[151] and *Environmental Crime* (2005)[152] emphasized the role of ex-Article 47 TEU as a preserver of the powers of the Communities and held that *if* a subject matter *can be* governed by Community measures, it *must* be dealt with under Community law.[153] Post-Lisbon, Article 40 TEU abolishes the default priority given to the former *acquis communautaire*, now-TFEU policies. It excludes any substitution or replacement between the CFSP and the Union's powers under the TFEU, and any legal hierarchy between the two.[154] The two fields are competing at eye level and the outcome is uncertain.

Article 40 TEU hence protects both sides *equally*. Yet applying the *Environmental Crime* approach to both sides is not logically possible. Asking the question whether a measure 'can be' adopted as a TFEU measure and then asking whether it 'can be' adopted as a CFSP measure as well is likely to result in two affirmative answers in many cases. The abolishment of hierarchy requires a new interpretation and makes disagreement on whether a policy falls within the CFSP or the TFEU policies more

[149] ibid, para 57.

[150] In combination with the principle of sincere cooperation, art 4(3) TEU. Case 44/84, *Hurd v Jones (Her Majesty's Inspector of Taxes)* [1986] EU:C:1986:2; Cases C-63/90 and C-67/90, *Portugal and Spain v Council* [1992] EU:C:1992:381; Case C-70/90, *Spain v Council* [1992] EU:C:1992:382 and Case C-71/90, *Spain v Council* [1992] EU:C:1992:383.

[151] Case C-170/96, *Commission v Council (Airport Transit Visa)* [1998] EU:C:1998:219.

[152] Case C-176/03, *Commission v Council (Environmental Crime)* [2005] EU:C:2005:542.

[153] For *Airport Transit Visa*: Maria-Gesella Ketvel, 'The Jurisdiction of the European Court of Justice in Respect of the Common Foreign and Security Policy' (2006) 55 ICLQ 91; Piet Eeckhout, *External Relations of the European Union* (2011). For *Environmental Crime*: Ester Herlin-Karnell, *The Constitutional Dimension of European Criminal Law* (Hart Publishing 2012) 77ff.

[154] Similarly, with regard to ex-art 47 TEU: Ricardo Gosalbo Bono, 'Some Reflections on the CFSP Legal Order', (2006) 43 CML Rev 337, 351.

likely. Indeed, since the entry into force of the Lisbon Treaty, the Court has already ruled several times on the matter.[155] In particular, the first of these cases (*UN Sanctions* (2012)), concerning a dispute about the correct legal basis of an EU law instrument giving effect to UN counter-terrorist sanctions, is highly illustrative of how the choice to pursue coherence through ambiguity in Article 40 TEU has increased the CJEU's role as a constitutional court in the field of CFSP.[156] In this case, the CJEU permitted, as a matter of principle, the use of a cross-Treaty joint legal basis, but excluded it again by requiring a level of procedural similarity that does not exist between CFSP and TFEU policies. This case is an example of how the case law of the Court has not reduced the level of ambiguity by introducing more detailed and clearer rules, but how the Court has contributed to further ambiguity and potentially opened the door for more litigation.[157]

Article 40 TEU further confirms that the CFSP can only affect the Union's power under the TFEU where this is expressly provided. Article 215 TFEU, which is a 'hybrid CFSP/TFEU provision' that requires a prior CFSP decision under the TEU for the Union to take action under the TFEU (the adoption of restrictive measures, that is, sanctions) in order to protect political discretion of the Member States, is an example of such an exceptional express provision. The underlying CFSP decisions can *explicitly* determine both the objective and the content of the TFEU measures adopted on the basis of Article 215 TFEU in the context of this particular procedure. What the CFSP cannot do is *implicitly* determine the scope of Union law under the TFEU.[158] Furthermore, while the Treaty of Lisbon has given the Court jurisdiction to arbitrate on 'encroachment' by TFEU policies on CFSP territory, the absence of specific CFSP objectives explored in the following section ironically makes it more difficult to defend that territory.

4.4.2 Horizontal objectives

Coherence was also the aim pursued by the introduction of *one list* of *horizontal* objectives for *all* the Union's external relations policies in Article 21 TEU. CFSP has as a result lost post-Lisbon one of its most important distinctive features: its *specifically conferred objectives*.[159] Treaty objectives do not generally serve to create or delimit

[155] Case C-263/14, *Parliament v Council (Tanzania)* [2016] EU:C:2016:435 (hereafter Case C-263/14, *Tanzania*); Case C-658/11, *Parliament v Council (Piracy Agreement I (Mauritius))* [2014] EU:C:2014:2025 (hereafter C-658/11, *Piracy Agreement I (Mauritius)*); Case C-130/10, *Parliament v Council (UN Sanctions)* [2012] EU:C:2012:472 (hereafter Case C-130/10, *UN Sanctions*).

[156] ibid, Case C-130/10, *UN Sanctions*.

[157] See Section 4.2 of Chapter 4 on the legal basis.

[158] The concept of implicit amendments of Community law is highly controversial. In favour: Matthias Pechstein, 'Die Justiziabilität des Unionsrechts' (1999) 5 EuR 1; excluding the possibility of implicit amendments: Maastricht decision of the German Federal Constitutional Court, BVerfGE 89, 155 (196).

[159] Pre-Lisbon these were already so broad that any delimitation would have been difficult. However, for example, they did not include trade, specific economic objectives, or the environment.

> Art 11(1) TEU: The Union shall define and implement a common foreign and security policy covering all areas of foreign and security policy, the objectives of which shall be:
> — to safeguard the common values, fundamental interests, independence and integrity of the Union in conformity with the principles of the United Nations Charter,
> — to strengthen the security of the Union in all ways,
> — to preserve peace and strengthen international security, in accordance with the principles of the United Nations Charter, as well as the principles of the Helsinki Final Act and the objectives of the Paris Charter, including those on external borders,

competences; however, in the specific context of the delimitation between CFSP and TFEU policies, they are used to serve this purpose. The introduction of horizontal objectives consequently complicates the determination of what is CFSP.

Ironically, it also complicates the Court's mandate under Article 40 TEU, to defend political discretion under CFSP from TFEU encroachment. The Court has hence post-Lisbon an extended mandate and a more difficult task.[160] The list of horizontal objectives renders it impossible to conduct the same objectives-based analysis that the Court deployed pre-Lisbon in common commercial policy cases[161] and in *ECOWAS*,[162] and that was also suggested in *UN Sanctions*. In *ECOWAS*, the Commission challenged a CFSP measure for encroaching upon Community law. The case concerned the question of whether financial and technical aid to the Economic Community of West African States fell under the CFSP or the former Community pillar. Advocate General Mengozzi suggested distinguishing between 'preserving peace and/or strengthening international security' (CFSP) and 'social and economic development' (development cooperation). Post-Lisbon, this distinction would no longer resolve any border conflict between ordinary EU external relations and the CFSP: both would fall under the general objectives of the Union's external action, under Articles 21(2)(c) and 21(2)(d) TEU, respectively. Nevertheless, Advocate General Bot argued post-Lisbon in *UN Sanctions* that EU action on the international stage 'which pursues one or more of the objectives referred to in Article 21(2)(a) to (c) TEU, in particular the objective of preserving peace and strengthening international security, must be regarded as falling within the sphere of the CFSP'.[163] This led him to the conclusion that the 'contested regulation was correctly adopted on the basis of Article 215(2) TFEU on account of its CFSP dimension'.[164] In his view, any 'other legal basis would run counter to Article 40, paragraph 2, TEU'.[165] He hence gave Article 40 TEU the role of a dividing line between the two groups of objectives in Article 21 TEU. This seems to disregard the very intention of introducing horizontal objectives pursued by all external action by the Union. In the second dispute on the division between CFSP and TFEU policies, the *Piracy Agreement 1* case, Advocate General Bot in fact relied on the pre-Lisbon division (the objectives in ex-Article 11 TEU) to justify the dividing line.[166]

In conclusion, the horizontal objectives in Article 21 TEU, while aiming to achieve coherence, have made the division between CFSP and TFEU competences more problematic than before the entry into force of the Lisbon Treaty. Articles 21 and 40 TEU create a situation of living together apart. Encroachment upon each other's policies is excluded but one joint set of objectives is to be pursued. Further, while CFSP and TFEU are kept strictly apart at the level of primary law by Article 40 TEU and while secondary law cannot in practice[167] be based on a joint cross-treaty legal basis, the

— to promote international cooperation,
— to develop and consolidate democracy and the rule of law, and respect for human rights and fundamental freedoms.

160 Pre-Lisbon, the objectives were already so broadly phrased that any delimitation would have been difficult. Yet, for example, they did not include trade, specific economic objectives, or the environment.

161 See Chapter 4 on legal basis.

162 Case C-91/05, *Commission v Council (ECOWAS)* [2008] EU:C:2008:288.

163 Case C-130/10, *UN Sanctions* [2012] EU:C:2012:50, Opinion of AG Bot, para 64. The case concerned the choice of the correct legal basis for restrictive measures (sanctions) as hybrid CFSP/TFEU or TFEU only acts. It is also discussed in Chapter 4.

164 ibid, para 72. 165 ibid, para 67.

166 Case C-658/11, *Parliament v Council (Piracy Agreement I (Mauritius))* [2014] EU:C:2014:41, Opinion of AG Bot, para 87.

167 Chapter 4 on the legal basis.

Treaty of Lisbon has created a cross-treaty institutional branch under the authority of the High Representative. Ultimately, it is left up to the Court to draw the line between the TFEU, which constitutes a more constitutionalized EU sphere, and the realm of CFSP, which is characterized by greater discretion of the national executives. This depoliticizes this decision and removes it from the public discourse, but potentially—with a growing body of case law—creates greater legal certainty and predictability, which is also relevant for the Union's ability to connect to its citizens.

4.4.3 Procedural prerogatives before the court

Procedural coherence has been enhanced by the choice for one general procedure to conclude international agreements under Article 218 TFEU. The Member States (and the institutions) strengthened in the Lisbon Treaty the role of the European Parliament in the conclusion, and in a more limited fashion, in the negotiation of international agreements (Article 218 TFEU).[168] However, special rules for CFSP remain, which for example limit the powers of the European Parliament when the Union concludes CFSP-only agreements. Because of procedural differences, inter-institutional disputes concerning the protection of institutional prerogatives are the most important context, in which the delimitation between CFSP and TFEU powers may become an issue before the EU Courts. In the *Piracy Agreement 1* case, Parliament challenged the Council's decision on the signing and conclusion of an agreement with Mauritius concerning the treatment of suspected pirates and associated seized property.[169] The central point of contention arose precisely in the context of the post-Lisbon general procedure to conclude EU international agreements. Article 218(6) TFEU requires the consent or consultation of Parliament for the conclusion of international agreements, with the exception of agreements that relate exclusively to CFSP, where Parliament is excluded. The issue was whether the agreement in question related exclusively to CFSP and would hence fall under the exception. This dispute exemplifies how the search for greater procedural coherence between CFSP and TFEU policies under Article 218 TFEU may trigger litigation. Article 218 TFEU is subject to the jurisdiction of the Court, including where CFSP is concerned.[170] Increased litigation strengthens the Court's grip over external relations, including CFSP.

The Court's involvement and willingness to apply constitutional principles, has made these principles more relevant for the exercise of external relations, including CFSP. This also increases coherence across all Union actions in all policy fields. An example is the second issue in the *Piracy Agreement 1* case, concerning the scope of Parliament's right to be informed during all stages of the procedure (Article 218(10) TFEU).[171] The CJEU confirmed that this right exists across all policies, including CFSP.[172]

Coherence is also a matter of perception. The Lisbon Treaty's choice to pursue coherence by integrating different policies, applying general procedures and objectives, and by freeing space to coordinate politically, increases the risk that EU policy-making is perceived as not following clear rules and potentially that the application of these rules is incoherent in itself. Coherence should not only apply to substantive policy-making but also to the procedural aspects of policy-making, as well as to the image that

[168] See Chapter 5 for more details.

[169] Case C-658/11, *Piracy Agreement I (Mauritius)* (n 155). See Section 3.4 of Chapter 5 on power shifts for more details on this case.

[170] ibid, para 73.

[171] See for more details Chapter 5.

[172] Case C-658/11, *Piracy Agreement I (Mauritius)* (n 155), paras 83–86.

the general public has of the exercise of EU external powers. Parliament's right to be informed across all policy fields is important in this regard. Parliament is directly elected by EU citizens. It offers a classic channel of input legitimacy, but also is a central actor in Habermas' communicative legitimacy.[173] For the objective of coherence and also transparency, it is important that Parliament's rights stretch across CFSP.

The more difficult it is to identify the dividing line both legally formally and in practice, the more difficult it is to explain to the public why Parliament is informed about certain agreements or parts of agreements, but not about others. This renders the representation through and influence of Parliament as limited in a technical manner that is difficult to convey. It also artificially limits Parliament's ability to act as a window of the public. To be worthy of recognition (*Anerkennungswürdigkeit*), both the legal order and the individual decision also depend on the adequate possibility of citizens to understand and access the institutional framework and to attribute responsibility. At least within the consciously created grey area, where a decision between CFSP and TFEU policies is not required, the information requirements should apply.

4.4.4 Enforceability and constitutionalization

Pursuant to Article 275(2) TFEU jointly with Article 40 TEU, the Court of Justice remains competent to review the relationship between CFSP and TFEU policies, and hence competent to determine the scope of its own jurisdiction, which is largely identical to the scope of the TFEU. At the same time, the Court has to police the border looking in both directions. Article 40 TEU and the new Treaty framework more generally enables the Court to review cases, in which instruments and procedures of external relations policies under the TFEU are used to the detriment of CFSP instruments and procedures. Parallelism instead of pre-emption remains a core feature of CFSP and indeed one of its core differences with the ideal type of TFEU policies. Hence, if the Union exercises its CFSP competences, Member States are not prevented from taking national actions on the same subject matter,[174] as far as their actions do not undermine the Union's position and infringe on the principle of sincere cooperation.[175] In the area of CFSP, however, the Commission cannot bring an enforcement action to the Court even if a Member State arguably undermines the position of the Union. Hence, even if a Member State acted illegally it would be difficult to *directly* confront it with *legal, rather than political* consequences. The principle of coherence is applicable to the CFSP and may be determinative for an action brought under Article 40 TEU. Because of the particular way Member States' powers and interests are protected under the CFSP and the limited jurisdiction of the Court it seems prima facie that the principles of coherence, at least where the dividing line between CFSP and TFEU policies are concerned (Article 40 TEU), may more easily deploy effects in the CFSP context than, for example, the principle of sincere cooperation.

One consequence of the Lisbon Treaty's choice to pursue coherence through ambiguity is an empowerment of the CJEU. This leads to a judicialization of external relations, which also breeds constitutionalization, that is, application of constitutional

[173] See Section 4 of Chapter 1 for more details. [174] Declarations 13 and 14.

[175] Sincere cooperation is generally codified in art 4(3) TEU and specifically sharpened and applied to CFSP in art 24(3) TEU: 'The Member States shall support the Union's external and security policy actively and unreservedly in a spirit of loyalty and mutual solidarity and shall comply with the Union's action in this area. [...] The Council and the High Representative shall ensure compliance with these principles.' See Chapter 2.

principles to CFSP that were developed under the TFEU. In fact, the case law of the CJEU is the most visible form of self-feeding dynamics of constitutionalization within the European Union.

The argument is that the ambiguity of constitutional procedures triggers judicial challenges. However, constitutional procedures are not self-serving, but serve a substantive purpose, such as democratic legitimation and the protection of fundamental rights. Furthermore, any judicial ruling on procedural issues has an influence on who is in charge of determining substantive policies, who may give input, and who is excluded. This ultimately also impacts on the actual substantive policy that is adopted. Finally, one consequence of constitutionalization is entrenchment. In the EU, a combination of the sizable majorities necessary to amend the Treaties, the primacy of EU law, and the strong role of the CJEU vest the Court of Justice with the power to create law at the constitutional level, which requires a particularly high threshold to be amended. This has an effect that was termed 'overconstitutionalization' by Dieter Grimm.[176]

An increase of the jurisdiction of the CJEU in the context of external relations hence allows the Court to establish procedural rules that are strongly entrenched, that is, difficult to change, and that necessarily have an effect on the division of power. Such constitutionalization through case law raises democratic concerns. To the extent that the Court ensures the observance of procedures, the institutional balance, or even strengthens the role of the European Parliament, it could be seen as ensuring the framework conditions for democratic deliberation in the Habermasian sense.[177] However, constitutionalization by courts remains at least susceptible to undermining democratic legitimacy, as well as the ability of citizens to understand themselves as authors of the rules that govern their legal situation and relations. This would limit the potential of any structures of bonding between the Union and its citizens.

5. Conclusions

Organizational principles can either serve as structures of bonding (and justification) or have a direct or indirect effect on the potential of legal structures of bonding, for example, by contributing to the effectiveness of EU law or increasing the ability of citizens to develop an adequate understanding of reasons for action, responsibilities, and powers. Organizational principles also empower the Court, in particular where they are widely phrased and lack concretization into specific (procedural) rules. This triggers juridification, including in the highly political salient field of external relations. Furthermore, the relevance and interpretation of organizational principles may change when they are applied in the context of external relations rather than internal law-making. This has itself consequences for the internal power division.

Subsidiarity directly contributes to the effectiveness of substantive policies. Effectiveness is one of the express objectives of subsidiarity. The other is ensuring and protecting embeddedness of decision-making and democratic legitimacy. When policy-making takes place under international law, the Union is always the entity that

[176] See for example: Dieter Grimm, 'The Democratic Costs of Constitutionalisation: The European Case' (2015) 21 ELJ 460 (hereafter, Grimm, 'Democratic Costs'). See also in the introduction to this book.

[177] See Section 4 of Chapter 1 for more detail. See also Christina Eckes, 'Common Foreign and Security Policy: The Consequences of the Court's Extended Jurisdiction', (2016) 22 ELJ 492–518.

represents more people, a larger territory, and more economic power. This already satisfies several of the criteria of the subsidiarity test. To put it more crudely, external relations as such may justify that the Union is better placed to take action. However, an additional argument can be made that the institutional structures of the Union allow better representation of the interests of EU citizens in external relations. This democratic legitimacy dimension of subsidiarity has the potential of being used as a structure of bonding. In other words, explicating the argument that the Union may be in a better position to represent EU citizens on the international plane opens up a formal structure of bonding. Whether this could result in actual bonding of citizens is a different question that is not decisive for the existence of such structures.

The basis of the *primacy* of EU law is contested. However, primacy is broadly applied in practice as a conflict rule that ensures the uniform application of EU law within national legal orders. This contributes to the effectiveness of EU law, rather than necessarily effective substantive policies or effective decision-making. Primacy is further closely related to and can only be maintained based on (the CJEU's narrative of) the autonomy of EU law, including in the international relations context. Primacy, while also requiring a high level of legitimacy, contributes to the effectiveness of EU law. When international law imposes obligations on the Member States and potentially also the Union, primacy comes under pressure. Maintaining the autonomy and primacy of EU law, based on a dualist logic vis-à-vis international law, ensures the Union's ability to guarantee compliance of its law with the foundations of Union law, including fundamental rights. However, it leaves Member States potentially in a position where they have to choose between complying with EU or with international law. Internally, the CJEU has taken a rather pragmatic approach to primacy, which may not be best-suited to dealing with external sources of law. If the Court pursues a more rigid approach externally—which arguably seems to be the case—this, as such, will result in greater tension than in purely internal situations, where it has been able to create scope for national concerns, at least to a certain extent. Primacy directly contributes to or is even a precondition for the effectiveness of EU law. This in turn strengthens the potential of bonding structures linking the Union to its citizens.

The Lisbon Treaty's choice for *coherence* through ambiguity is not limited to external relations, but it is particularly pronounced in this area. Coherence is also an even greater challenge in external relations than in other areas. In particular, the relationship between CFSP and TFEU policies has become subject to stricter formal requirements of coherence; at the same time, the line between the two has become even more difficult to establish. Substantively, CFSP and other policies could never be neatly separated; post-Lisbon, however, this has become even more difficult. A formal separation, for example, based on who is acting, will inevitably result in inconsistencies and substantive overlap of formally distinguishable acts. The Lisbon Treaty creates room for greater flexibility and politics internally, while imposing a high threshold of substantive coherence in external relations. First, it opted for less hierarchy by placing CFSP and TFEU policies on an equal footing. Second, it created the EEAS as a cross-cutting autonomous body. Third, it consciously left decisions legally open to allow for later political agreement. This translates into legal rules and provisions that are open to interpretation and that can lead to a power transfer that is only inherent in the legal text as one of several possible interpretations. This has and will trigger further litigation and vest the CJEU with a far-reaching power to determine the rules of the game and the division of tasks, obligations, and powers between the institutions and between the EU and the Member States.

Generally, it is presumed that a higher level of coherence between and within policies and between the decisions of different actors results in a higher level of effectiveness. Coherence also contributes to legal certainty and more indirectly to citizens' ability to comprehend the law. Not only the formal division of competences but also the ability to legally exercise them must necessarily be adequately comprehensible in order for a polity and its actions to be worthy of recognition by its citizens. Coherence in principle contributes to visibility, clarity, and accessibility of structures of bonding. Even in its most limited form, as absence of contradictions, it creates better circumstances for the development of structures of bonding. If, however, formal rules are constructed in a way that aims to leave room for coherence at the level of policy-making, this entails a risk of making these choices less transparent and less comprehensible from a citizen's perspective. Moreover, if the definition of what coherence means in practice is left to the Court, this interferes with the role of constitutional rules to offer 'the framework for politics, not the blueprint for all political decisions'.[178] If judicialization goes too far, the Court is in danger of depoliticizing fundamental political choices, including who should be in charge.

[178] Grimm, 'Democratic Costs' (n 176) 460.

4

Consequences of Choosing an External Legal Basis

1. Introduction

Within the European Union, the choice of legal basis has constitutional significance.[1] It is the legal manifestation of an omnipresent political struggle of who is in charge. In external relations, this struggle has been becoming considerably more vigorous post-Lisbon. Advocate General Kokott's observations in May 2018, discussing an action for annulment brought by the Commission against the Council, illustrates this point:

> Both sides put forward their respective arguments with astonishing passion. The Council and some of its interveners make the underlying allegation that the Commission wished to do everything possible to prevent international action by the Member States, while the Commission alleges that the Council is compulsively looking for legal bases that always permit participation by the Member States alongside the Union.[2]

The choice of legal basis is highly relevant within the EU legal order because the Union may only act within the competence conferred to it.[3] The choice of legal basis also determines the division of tasks and influence of the EU institutions.[4] It may be perceived as less openly political than the institutional balance; yet it determines the institutional balance in individual cases. In external relations, the choice of legal basis also determines whether the Union may act alone or together with the Member States. This chapter focuses on how the choice of legal basis subjects Member States' actions to the forces of European Integration.[5] The strongest form of this subjection is pre-emption, that is, because the EU exercises its powers,[6] Member States may no longer exercise theirs. Softer forms occur, where Member State action is still possible but subject to EU principles and rules. The different effects are determined by the choice of legal basis.

Basing secondary legal acts on an 'external' legal basis triggers more different consequences in terms of pre-emption and restrictions on reserved national competences than using an 'internal' legal basis. This chapter does not focus on whether or not the EU has competence to take action (principle of conferral). Instead, it focuses on how much scope for manoeuvre the Member States continue to have after the Union has

[1] Post-Lisbon, this was confirmed eg in Opinion 2/00 (Cartagena Protocol) [2001] EU:C:2001:664 (hereafter Opinion 2/00), para 5; Case C-263/14, *European Parliament v Council* [2016] EU:C:2016:435, para 42 (hereafter Case C-263/14, *Tanzania Pirates Agreement)*; C-600/14, *Germany v Council (COTIF)* [2017] EU:2017:935, para 80.

[2] Joined Cases C-626/15 and C-659/16, *Commission v Council* [2018] EU:C:2018:362, conclusion of AG Kokott, para 75.

[3] Consolidated Version Treaty on European Union [2016] OJ C 202/01 (hereafter TEU), art 5(2).

[4] Art 13(2) TEU.

[5] See Introduction for a definition of integration.

[6] The term 'competences' refers to the formal legal ability to take action within the legal bases framework of the Treaties. The term 'powers' is understood to go beyond this and include the scope for autonomous determination of the course of action by the EU institutions and Member States.

taken action and, in particular, how this scope changes when the Union acts externally as compared to internally.

The choice of legal basis is the formal legal expression of the understanding that in a multilevel representative democracy it must be clear which political institutions are responsible for what, who may claim credit for a particular policy, and who is to blame for a failure. The whole concept that one 'can throw the scoundrels out'[7] in elections, only works if it is reasonably possible to know who the scoundrels are. Furthermore, formal legal structures of reference and bonding between the Union and its citizens can only work if the division of powers between the Union and the Member States is reasonably predictable and transparent. Similarly, the worthiness of recognition of the exercise of public power (*Annerkennungswürdigkeit*)[8] also requires reasonable justification of who exercises power within a pre-established institutional and procedural framework.

This chapter is structured as follows. Section 2 explains how the correct legal basis is determined within the EU legal order. It sets out why the choice of legal basis is highly relevant and contested and gives some examples of this contestation. Section 3 highlights consequences and functions of the choice of legal basis in external relations. Section 4 sets out constellations in which the choice to use either an internal or an external legal basis determines the scope to manoeuvre of the Member States. The choice of an external (rather than an internal) legal basis regularly imposes furthergoing limits on Member States' powers. Section 5 turns from consequences of the choice of legal basis to external pressures on the Union's internal structures, including the choice of legal basis. It concentrates in particular on the dividing line between the Common Foreign and Security Policy (CFSP) and policies set out under the TFEU[9] and demonstrates how international cooperation and external actions of the Union put pressure on this dividing line. It also highlights who wins and who loses power when the line is seemingly disregarded. Section 6 demonstrates how international obligations of the Member States are vested with the same bite as EU law, when the question of who should take action, which is at the centre of the choice of legal basis, is avoided by concluding a mixed agreement. Participation of the Union in an international agreement limits the scope of manoeuvre of Member States as international actors. The Conclusions offer some further reflection and place the findings of this chapter within the main arguments of this book, by explicating the relevance of the discussion on the consequences of choice of legal basis for emerging structures of bonding and the justifiability of Union action.

2. Choice of Legal Basis: Relevance and Principles

The principle of conferral in Article 5(1) s 1 and (2) TEU is the foundation of the division of competences between the EU and its Member States. The Union is competent only if and to the extent that powers are conferred upon it under the European Treaties, as written and ratified by the Member States. The revisions of the founding

[7] Ian Shapiro, *Democracy's Place* (Cornell UP 1996) 96; 'To Be a European Citizen: Eros and Civilization' in Joseph Weiler, *The Constitution of Europe: 'Do the New Clothes Have an Emperor?' and Other Essays on European Integration* (CUP 1999) 329.

[8] See Section 4.1 of Chapter 1.

[9] Consolidated Version of the Treaty on the Functioning of the European Union [2008] OJ C115/47 (hereafter TFEU).

Treaties all take place pursuant to procedures set out in the European Treaties. Since the entry into force of the Lisbon Treaty, the Parliament has a greater say in these procedures, but Member States remain the determinative actors. All revision procedures continue to require unanimity. Treaty amendments also require ratification by the Member States.[10] In other words, Member States collectively have determined and continue to determine the scope of Union competences.

The Lisbon Treaty has introduced significant textual changes aiming to improve transparency and coherence of the division of competences between the EU and its Member States. Examples are the lists of competences,[11] a horizontally applicable list of external relations objectives,[12] and the codification of the doctrine of implied external powers.[13] Yet even after the entry into force of the Lisbon Treaty, the allocation of powers remains in practice difficult to predict.[14] Any Treaty amendment also naturally raises the question of whether and how it affects the competence division between the Union and the Member States. Several Advocates General have taken the explicit position that the Lisbon Treaty largely codified the external powers of the Union and the doctrines of how they should be exercised as they existed before under the case law of the Court of Justice of the European Union (CJEU).[15] The Council, which should in this context be seen as also expressing the position of the Member States, by contrast took the position that 'since the entry into force of the Lisbon Treaty, the exclusive external competence of the European Union is viewed in a more restrictive manner'.[16] It also explicitly argued that the Union should not take external actions where, in areas of shared competence, internal rules have not yet been adopted.[17] This position is a clear departure from the case law of the CJEU, for example in Opinion 1/03.[18] Since the entry into force of the Lisbon Treaty, a high number of inter-institutional disputes have reached the CJEU in the context of external relations, particularly on competence and legal basis grounds.[19] Several Member States have brought cases and many Member

[10] In some Member States, the formal requirements under the limited simplified revision procedure under art 48(6) TEU are less strict. The simplified revision procedure was used in Council Decision (EU) 2011/199 amending art 136 of the Treaty on the Functioning of the European Union with regard to a stability mechanism for Member States whose currency is the euro [2011] OJ L 91/1 and judicially reviewed in Case C-370/12, *Pringle v Ireland* [2012] EU:C:2012:756.

[11] Arts 2–6 TFEU. [12] Art 21 TEU. [13] Arts 216(1) and 3(2) TFEU

[14] See also Chapter 3 on organizing principles for the choice for consistency through ambiguity.

[15] Opinion 1/13 (The Hague Convention) [2014] EU:C:2014:2392, Opinion of AG Jääskinen, para 63. Case C-66/13, *Green Network SpA v Autoritá per l'energia elettrica e il gas* [2014] EU:C:2014:156, Opinion AG Bot, para 33.

[16] Summarized by the Court in Case C-114/12, *Commission v Council (Broadcasting Organisations)* [2014] EU:C:2014:2151.

[17] Council Decision (EU) 2015/798 Authorizing the European Commission to Negotiate, on Behalf of the European Union, Amendments to the Vienna Convention for the Protection of the Ozone Layer and the Montreal Protocol on Substances that Deplete the Ozone Layer [2015] OJ L 127/19.

[18] Opinion 1/03 (Lugano Convention) [2006] EU:C:2006:81 (hereafter Opinion 1/03).

[19] Case C-130/10, *Parliament v Council (UN Sanctions)* ECLI:EU:C:2012:472 (hereafter Case C-130/10, *UN Sanctions*). Case C-28/12, *Commission v Council* [2015] EU:C:2015:282. Case C-114/12, *Commission v Council* [2014] ECLI:EU:C:2014:2151. Case C-137/12, *Commission v Council (Services Convention)* [2013] EU:C:2013:675. Case C-377/12, *Commission v Council* [2014] ECLI:EU:C:2014:1903. Case C-660/13, *Council v Commission* [2016] ECLI:EU:C:2016:616. Case C-26 3/14, *Tanzania Pirates Agreement* (n 1). Case C-425/13, *Commission v Council (Emission Trading System)* [2015] EU:C:2015:483. Case C-389/15, *Commission v Council (Lisbon Agreement on Appellations of Origin and Geographical Indications)* [2017] EU:C:2017:798. Case C-687/15, *Commission v Council (CMR-15)* [2017] ECLI:EU:C:2017:803. Joined Cases C-626/15 and C-659/16, *Commission v Council* (pending). Those where the choice of legal basis is of relevance for the power division between the EU and the Member States are explored here. Chapter 5 on inter-institutional

States have intervened in the inter-institutional disputes.[20] Almost all of these cases were decided by a Grand Chamber.[21]

The CJEU is a powerful arbiter, which establishes what the Union can and cannot do within the Treaty framework. It has repeatedly emphasized that the choice of legal basis has high constitutional significance and must be carried out pursuant to objective criteria that are susceptible to judicial review.[22] The correct choice between two or multiple potential legal bases is in principle identified pursuant to the centre of gravity test.[23] According to this test, a measure that pursues two or more objectives or has two or more components and where one of these objectives or components is identifiable as the main one, while the others can be seen as merely incidental, then a single legal basis is sufficient for the adoption of that measure, namely the basis required by the main objective or component. Other potential legal bases should not be added except when a measure simultaneously pursues a number of objectives or has several components which are inseparably linked without one being incidental to the other. Such a measure will have to be founded, exceptionally, on the various corresponding legal bases. Recourse to a dual legal basis is not possible where the procedures laid down for each legal basis are incompatible with each other, for example, the consultation procedure combined with the ordinary legislative procedure.[24]

The choice of legal basis determines that the Union is competent to act, the involvement of different political institutions, the geographical scope of the adopted measure, potential pre-emption of Member State action, jurisdiction of the Court, and the nature of the EU's competence, that is, whether it is exclusive or shared. The nature of the competence in turn determines whether the principle of subsidiarity is applicable.[25] The legal basis requirement is intended to guarantee that all actors involved remain within their powers and do not act *ultra vires*. The case law may give the impression that the CJEU is particularly respectful of the involvement of the Parliament[26] and would give preference to a legal basis that places Parliament in a stronger position.

power shifts further explores the details of those cases that relate more closely to the power division between the institutions.

[20] Case C-399/12, *Germany v Council (OIV)* [2014] ECLI:EU:C:2014:2258. Case C-600/14, *Germany v Council* [2017] ECLI:EU:C:2017:935. Case C-656/11, *United Kingdom v Council* [2014] ECLI:EU:C:2014:97 (Third Chamber). For Member State interventions see ibid, Case C-28/12, *Commission v Council*: 12 intervening Member States. Case C-137/12, *Commission v Council*: 5 intervening Member States. Case C-263/14, *Tanzania Pirates Agreement*: 3 intervening Member States; Case C-425/13, *Commission v Council*: 8 intervening Member States. Case C-389/15, *Commission v Council*: 12 intervening Member States.

[21] ibid, Case C-28/12, *Commission v Council*; Case C-137/12, *Commission v Council*; Case C-263/14, *Tanzania Pirates Agreement*; Case C-425/13, *Commission v Council*; Case C-389/15, *Commission v Council*.

[22] See eg Case 45/86, *Commission v Council* [1987] EU:C:1987:163, para 11; Case C-300/89, *Commission v Council (Titanium dioxide)* [1991] EU:C:1991:244, paras 10ff (hereafter Case C-300/89, *Titanium dioxide*); Opinion 2/00 (n 1) para 5; Case C-411/06, *Commission v Parliament and Council* [2009] EU:C:2009:518, para 46 (hereafter Case C-411/06, *Commission v Parliament and Council*).

[23] For internal legal acts, see eg ibid, Case C-300/89, *Titanium dioxide*, para 10 and Case C-295/90, *Parliament v Council* [1992] EU:C:1992:294, para 13. For external actions, see eg Case C-91/05, *Commission v Council (ECOWAS)* [2008] EU:C:2008:288 (hereafter Case C-91/05, *ECOWAS*). See rather exceptionally: Case C-376/98, *Federal Republic of Germany v European Parliament and Council of the European Union (Tobacco Advertising)* [2000] EU:C:2000:324.

[24] Paraphrasing: Case C-155/07, *Parliament v Council (European Investment Bank Guarantees)* [2008] EU:C:2008:605, paras 35–37.

[25] See Chapter 3 for the effects on subsidiarity of taking policymaking outside.

[26] This is confirmed in: Case C-300/89, *Titanium dioxide* (n 22), paras 17-21. See also Case C-91/05, *ECOWAS* (n 23)

In a nuanced analysis, however, Pieter Jan Kuijper demonstrated that the latter conclusion is too blunt in light of case law to the contrary.[27] This is confirmed by a post-Lisbon ruling, in which the CJEU accepted that a specific legal basis in the Euratom Treaty had been chosen, which limited the role of Parliament to being consulted, rather than the more general legal basis under the TFEU,[28] which would have involved Parliament under the ordinary legislative procedure. The CJEU held that the framers of the Treaties made this option available and that the institutions could hence choose it. The case also confirms the general rule that the principle of sincere cooperation under Article 13(2) TEU governs the manner in which powers, validly established under other Treaty provisions, are to be *exercised*, but that it cannot create self-standing obligations where no powers exist or change existing powers.[29]

The choice of an external legal basis is, in principle, guided by the same principles and rules as the choice of an internal legal basis. One difference is that the Treaties set out fewer explicit legal bases for external actions than for internal actions, even if the Lisbon Treaty has increased the number of the former. This makes the doctrine of implied powers, which complements and arguably complicates the rule that every secondary legal instrument requires a legal basis in the Treaties, more powerful in the context of external relations. The doctrine of implied external powers was established in a line of cases, starting in the 1970s with the landmark case of *ERTA/AETR*.[30] It allows the Union to take action in order to achieve the objectives in the Treaties, even where the Treaties do not vest it with express powers. Post-Lisbon, the judge-made concepts of and principles on the existence and nature (exclusive or shared) of Union powers have been codified in Articles 216(1) and 3(2) TFEU. Article 216(1) TFEU also ties external competences to internal objectives.

Internally, the Treaties codify a clear distinction between the existence of a Union competence and its nature.[31] The Treaties establish for several policy fields a priori exclusivity of Union competence.[32] The exercise of a shared competence by the Union results in what is sometimes called 'conditional exclusivity',[33] which leads to pre-emption.[34] Opinion 1/03, besides allowing for external action if there is a need to act internally and externally at the same time, confirmed this distinction between existence

[27] Pieter Jan Kuijper, 'The Case Law of the Court of Justice of the EU and the Allocation of External Relations Powers. Whither the Traditional Role of the Executive in EU Foreign Relations?' in Marise Cremona and Anne Thies (eds), *The European Court of Justice and External Relations—Constitutional Challenges* (Hart Publishing 2014) 95ff, referring inter alia to Case C-327/91, *France v Commission* [1994] EU:C:1994:305.

[28] Art 192(1) TFEU.

[29] See in this regard, eg C-73/14, *Council v Commission* [2015] EU:C:2015:663, para 84 and the case law cited.

[30] Case 22/70, *Commission v Council (ERTA)* [1971] EU:C:1971:32. See also above all: Opinion 1/03 (n 18).

[31] Arts 2–6 TFEU. [32] Art 3 TFEU.

[33] Paul Craig and Gráinne de Búrca (eds), *The Evolution of EU Law* (2nd edn, OUP 2011) 79.

[34] Pre-emption under EU law has attracted considerable scholarly attention but remains a somewhat indeterminate principle of EU law. See, for example, Robert Schütze, 'Supremacy Without Pre-Emption? The Very Slowly Emergent Doctrine of Community Pre-Emption' (2006) 43 CML Rev 1023. Some deny that it is a principle separate from loyalty and Union interest: Marcus Klamert, *The Principle of Loyalty in EU Law* (OUP 2014), Chapter 5. Others treat pre-emption as a dimension of supremacy: S Krislov, C Ehlermann, and J Weiler, 'The Political Organs and the Decision-Making Process in the United States and the European Community' in Mauro Cappelletti, Monica Seccombe, and Joseph Weiler (eds), *Integration Through Law: Europe and the American Federal Experience* (Vol 1, De Gruyter 1986) 90.

and nature for implied external competences.[35] Post-Lisbon, the distinction between the existence and the nature of EU competence also becomes apparent in the rather different approach that the CJEU takes to the very similar wordings of Articles 216(1) and 3(2) TFEU. This is illustrated by Opinion 1/13 on the EU's competence in relation to the 1980 Hague Convention on civil aspects of international child abduction. When establishing the existence of a Union competence, the CJEU simply asserted that the Union had internal competence and that it had exercised this competence.[36] When establishing the exclusive nature of the EU competence, the CJEU carried out a detailed analysis of the internal regulation on the matter and The Hague Convention to determine whether the latter could be said to 'affect' or 'alter the scope' of the former.[37]

By way of conclusion, the CJEU has established that the choice of legal basis should be subject to 'objective' criteria and explicated these criteria in the centre of gravity test. However, legal challenges of this highly relevant choice demonstrate that in individual cases the application may often be the subject of hot contestation. The next section zooms in on the choice of legal basis for external actions.

3. Consequences and Function of (External) Legal Bases

Some external legal bases are subject to particularities. Others are different in nature from their substantive internal counterparts. In certain constellations, the choice of legal basis is relevant to the non-EU party of an EU international agreement, for example, when it determines the geographical scope of the measure. In the external context, a legal basis sends a signal of competence and responsibility to non-EU actors and EU citizens. This section demonstrates the high significance and different consequences of the choice of *external* legal bases, by examining their pre-emptive quality, geographical scope, and signalling function.

3.1 Parallel competences in external relations

Parallel competences allow Member States to continue to act in a particular policy field and on a particular issue, even after the Union has taken action. Parallel competences are not limited to, but particularly common in, external relations. Article 4(3) and (4) TFEU set out that competences for research, technological development, and space, as well as development cooperation and humanitarian aid are parallel in nature, that is, that Member States remain able to act even if the Union has taken action on the particular issue. One of the objectives of this parallelism is to protect national competences from pre-emption when the Union agrees on certain measures in an international agreement, for example, in order to further the development in a third country.[38] In addition, the Union competences for development cooperation and economic, financial, and technical cooperation, in Articles 209(2) 2nd sentence and 212(3) 3rd sentence TFEU respectively, explicate that Union action does not prejudice

[35] Opinion 1/03 (n 18); Marise Cremona, 'External Relations of the EU and the Member States: Competences, Mixed Agreements, International Responsibility, and Effects of International Law' (EUI Law No 2006/22, EUI 2006) 3 (hereafter Cremona, 'External Relations').

[36] Opinion 1/13 (n 15), para 68. See also Opinion 1/03 (n 18) para 134.

[37] ibid, Opinion 1/13, para 68.

[38] See the Introduction for other attempts to protect national powers from the Union's external actions.

Member States' power to negotiate within international bodies and conclude international agreements. This could, in the light of Article 4(3) and (4) TFEU, be seen as redundant repetition when the Union agrees on technological or development co-operation based on Article 212 or 209 TFEU; yet it expresses a particular concern of Member States that when the Union acts externally this will, despite all internal parallelism, bind their hands externally. The specific clauses introducing parallelism protect Member States from seeing their hands bound by formal pre-emption. Member States remain—irrespective of any clauses of parallelism—subject to the principle of sincere cooperation, which may also prevent them from taking action.[39]

Furthermore, some grey zones may remain in practice, in which it is not immediately clear whether Member State action is pre-empted. This is illustrated by the post-Lisbon case concerning the choice of the legal basis for the Partnership and Cooperation Agreement (PCA) with the Philippines.[40] The CJEU (Grand Chamber) annulled the Council's decision to sign this PCA,[41] because the Council had based this decision on Articles 91 and 100 TFEU (transport), 79 (3) TFEU (readmission of third-country nationals), and 191 (4) TFEU (environmental protection) in addition to the two core legal bases Articles 207 (common commercial policy (CCP)) and 209 (development cooperation) TFEU. The Commission had argued that the legal bases of Articles 207 and 209 TFEU would have been sufficient to cover the entire scope of the PCA.

The main controversial issue was whether Article 209 TFEU was externally, in the development context, sufficient to adopt the policies that were internally covered by more specific legal bases. The Court sided with the Commission and found the legal bases of Articles 207 and 209 TFEU sufficient because the purpose of the agreement was development cooperation and the specific policies were means deployed to attain this purpose.[42] The means deployed in the agreement did not pursue any separate, additional purpose within the specific policy fields. The Union may therefore enter into development cooperation agreements using means from any specific policy field, including in the event internal Union competence has not yet been exercised in that field. Yet the choice of limiting the legal basis to development cooperation also entails consequences for the pre-emption of national action. Because of the parallel nature of Article 209 TFEU—or Articles 212 or 217 TFEU for that matter—Member States are not pre-empted to adopt national measures in such a field.

By way of conclusion, particularly in the field of external relations, the Treaties set out parallel competences that allow the Member States to continue to act after the Union has taken action. In the context of these—often general—external competences, the adding or omitting of additional legal bases—usually covering more specific policy fields—that trigger the pre-emption set out in Article 2(2) TFEU is significant for the remaining national powers. This point highlights not only the relevance of the choice of the specific legal basis or bases, but also of the Court's centre of gravity test, which

[39] See Chapter 2 on EU loyalty.

[40] Case C-377/12, *Commission v Council* [2014] EU:C:2014:1903. See also: Friedrich Erlbacher, 'Recent Case Law on External Competences of the European Union: How Member States Can Embrace Their Own Treaty' (2017) CLEER Working Paper Asser Institute 02/2017. See also: Laurens Ankersmit, 'The Boundaries of the Development Cooperation Legal Basis: What to Make of the Court's "Centre of Gravity" test?' (*Europeanlawblog*, 13 June 2014) http://europeanlawblog.eu/tag/centre-of-gravity-test/.

[41] ibid, Case C-377/12, *Commission v Council*.

[42] See also: Joined Cases C-132/14 to 136/14, *European Parliament and Commission v Council* [2015] EU:C:2015:813, where the Court accepted art 349 TFEU as a sufficient (general) legal basis.

limits in most cases the number of legal bases. It also draws attention to this difference in consequences flowing from general external legal bases as opposed to more specific internal legal bases. Parallel competences protect Member States' scope for external actions and the Court has demonstrated that it is willing to protect this scope. The next section concentrates on the geographical scope of measures adopted on different legal bases and highlights why a potential change of the choice of legal basis is even more problematic in the external context.

3.2 Geographical scope

The choice of a particular legal basis also has specific geographical consequences. It determines whether exceptions negotiated and agreed by certain Member States are applicable. While this is also highly relevant for internal policy-making, in the external context non-EU actors have a legitimate interest in knowing in advance the geographical reach of any agreement that they negotiate with the Union.

The UK has, under Protocol 21, the right not to take part in measures adopted within the Area of Freedom, Security and Justice (AFSJ). It therefore matters for the applicability of that protocol and for the legal position of the UK whether (an amendment to) an association agreement is adopted based on a specific legal basis in the context of the internal market, that is, Article 48 TFEU, or a legal basis within the AFSJ, namely, Article 79(2)(b) TFEU.[43] In a 2014 case concerning the Association Agreement with Turkey, the CJEU concluded that the contested Council decision, amending the implementing provisions giving effect to the agreement, should have been adopted on the joined legal basis of Articles 217 TFEU and 48 TFEU. This was because the measures were intended to give effect to an association agreement, that is, did not concern purely internal measures, as well as being intended to coordinate social security systems.[44]

The CJEU however did not annul the contested decision, which had been solely based on Article 48 TFEU, because the addition of Article 217 TFEU would not have affected the content or the procedure by which the decision had been adopted. In any event, Protocol 21 would have been immaterial as neither legal basis falls within the AFSJ. However, if the particular set of objectives and measures had been different, a change in the geographical scope could, in principle, have occurred as a consequence of a ruling by the Court requiring a different (joined) legal basis. The conclusion that the addition of a parallel competence to an ordinary shared competence would not formally change the measure, may also be read as indirectly confirming that such addition would not result in parallelism. Or, in other words, the pre-emption triggered by Article 48 TFEU is not affected by the parallelism of Article 217 TFEU.

The fact that a change of an internal procedural decision, that is, the choice of the basis, may trigger a change of the geographical reach of a policy is a unique consequence of the compound nature of the Union that requires a high level of flexibility and differentiation internally. The possible link between the choice of legal basis and the geographical scope of the measure highlights the complexity of the consequences of the former. Externally, however, it additionally confronts non-EU actors with the

[43] See the three cases, all concerning association agreements: Case C-81/13, *United Kingdom v Council* [2014] EU:C:2014:2449 (hereafter *United Kingdom v Council*); Case C-656/11, *United Kingdom v Council (Switzerland-EEA Social Security Coordination)* [2014] EU:C:2014:97 (hereafter *United Kingdom v Council*); Case C-431/11, *United Kingdom v Council* [2013] EU:C:2013:589.

[44] ibid, Case C-81/13, *United Kingdom v Council*, paras 62 and 63.

consequences of this internal differentiation in a way that may put into question the Union's ambition of being a credible, reliable, and powerful international actor. This relates to the signalling function of legal bases discussed in the following section.

3.3 Signalling function

Externally, the legal basis also has a signalling function towards non-EU actors. This was recognized in some cases by the CJEU.[45] In other cases, however, the Court emphasized that the distribution of competences between the EU and the Member State was a purely internal matter[46] and should not concern third parties. Attributing a signalling function to the choice of legal basis stands in open contrast to the tendency of the Union and its Member States to opt for mixed agreements.[47] Mixity is a construction, which intentionally blurs any indication of responsibility both externally, that is, in relation to non-EU actors, but also internally, that is, in relation to EU citizens. Such a signalling function also seems to clash with the spirit and purpose of legal constructions, such as the co-respondent mechanism in the draft accession agreement on EU accession to the European Convention of Human Rights (ECHR), which specifically avoids the need for allocation of responsibility.[48] The choice of legal basis is a formal and public published indication of what competence division was assumed; yet it is not a fully reliable source of what the division of competences is formally.[49]

Non-EU actors have an interest in knowing who—the EU or the Member States—is responsible for which part in the negotiation, conclusion, and implementation of an international agreement. This is also apparent and acknowledged in the adoption of declarations of competences.[50] Furthermore it is vis-à-vis for EU citizens (and Member States) relevant and desirable to clearly establish competence and as a result responsibility for a measure. The Union is constructed as a representative democracy with formal channels of direct (link between EU and citizen) and indirect (via Member States) democratic legitimation.[51] In other words, decision-making in the EU draws democratic legitimacy from several channels that exist in parallel but are intertwined and act together. Such a compound construction requires that citizens can make informed choices about whom they vote into office to represent them for what. To put it differently, the democratic deficit of the Union widens when it remains unclear—or even consciously veiled—whether EU institutions or national actors are responsible for particular political choices. Individuals voting as EU and national citizens in the elections of national and European parliaments do not even have the formal possibility of knowing which parts of which international agreement or what external policy is decided by which parliament. This makes the Habermasian concept of citizens acting as dual sovereign[52] inaccessible to citizens and undermines their ability to exercise power and feel represented as EU citizens. Particularly in the context of facultative mixity,

[45] Case C-94/03, *Commission v Council (Rotterdam Convention)* [2006] EU:C:2006:2, para 55 (hereafter Case C94/03, *Rotterdam Convention*).

[46] This is the reading of Cremona, 'External Relations' (n 35) 10, of Opinion 2/00 (n 1), para 17, considering the purpose of now-art 218(11) TFEU.

[47] See also Chapter 2 (mixity and sincere cooperation) and Chapter 5 (facultative mixity).

[48] Art 3 of the Draft Accession Agreement of 5 April 2013 https://www.coe.int/t/dlapil/cahdi/Source/Docs2013/47_1_2013_008rev2_EN.pdf.

[49] See also: Cremona, 'External Relations' (n 35) 22.

[50] Most interesting is the procedural approach in UNCLOS Annex IX, which tries to protect in general the Union's autonomy and dynamic competence division, while offering third parties a means to obtain clarity in the individual case.

[51] See Section 2 of Chapter 1.

[52] See Section 4.1 of Chapter 1.

when political considerations rather than legal competence and legal basis arguments are made to explain the choice of mixity, this is highly problematic.[53] The choice of the correct legal basis raises similar problems, perhaps in a less apparent manner. In principle, it should be reasonably foreseeable for an interested and reasonably informed person who will take core decisions in any given policy field.

Yet it is not only a question of whether the Union and its institutions on the one hand or the Member States on the other are in charge. A similar argument of foreseeability applies to all the consequences of the legal basis. When policies are publicly deliberated, the following questions are relevant: Are national or EU institutions in a position to decide? Can stricter national rules be adopted in that particular field? Are Member States pre-empted from taking national action? All these questions (should) have an influence on citizens' informed evaluation of the performance of the representatives, whom they voted into office: Did they represent their political position on the subject matters for which they are responsible well? Citizens should then also be in the position to 'throw the scoundrels out',[54] that is, to punish those who do not represent their positions well. In principle—even though the public debate is seldom at this level of clarity of detail—the argument can also be made for procedural consequences of the choice of legal basis, which determine whether Member States have a veto or not and whether the European Parliament has the powers to amend, needs to consent, or is only consulted on a particular policy.

The consequences of failing to allocate responsibility and understand ownership become apparent in the context of the conclusion of mixed agreements. In 2016, the German Federal Constitutional Court (GFCC) ruled on a number of challenges against the German role in the signing, conclusion, and provisional application of the EU–Canada Comprehensive Economic and Trade Agreement (CETA).[55] It held that *under international law Germany could unilaterally terminate the provisional application of CETA*, a mixed agreement of which only a very small part falls under national competence.[56] The GFCC did not examine under whose competence the parts fell that were provisionally applied. These parts did not include the provisions on investment protection, which would at least also fall under the competence of the Member States. In fact, the GFCC did not engage with the competence and hence division of responsibility between the Union and the Member States at all. The Court's conclusion that Germany, and hence any Member State, could terminate the whole agreement, irrespective of the division of competences and hence irrespective of the fact that Member States were only competent for a very small part of the agreement,[57] is the correct interpretation of international law. Furthermore, in the minutes of the Council meeting on CETA, several Member States explicitly stated that they consider that they, as a

[53] See also Section 4 of Chapter 5 on consequences of facultative mixity.

[54] Shapiro, 'Democracy's place' (n 7).

[55] Comprehensive Economic and Trade Agreement between the EU and its Member States on the one hand and Canada on the other. See for the particular issue of investor state dispute settlement and the investment court system Chapter 6.

[56] 2 BvR 1368/16, 2 BvR 1444/16, 2 BvR 1482/16, 2 BvR 1823/16, 2 BvE 3/16, Verfassungsbeschwerden und Organstreitverfahren betreffend die Unterzeichnung, die vorläufige Anwendung und den Abschluss des Freihandelsabkommens zwischen Kanada einerseits und der Europäischen Union und ihren Mitgliedstaaten andererseits (Comprehensive Economic and Trade Agreement—CETA), para 38: 'Die vorläufige Anwendung des Abkommens kann nach einer den anderen Vertragsparteien zu notifizierenden Erklärung der Bundesregierung gemäß Art. 30.7 Abs. 3 Buchstabe c CETA-E jederzeit von einem Mitgliedstaat beendet werden (vgl. unten Rn. 72). Die Entscheidung in der Hauptsache kommt deshalb nicht zu spät.'

[57] See the discussion of Opinion 2/15 in Section 3.2 above and Section 4.2 below.

party to CETA, have the powers to exercise 'their' right under Article 30.7(3)(c) of CETA, concerning the termination of its provisional application.[58] They all, however, acknowledged that any exercise of this right would take place in accordance with EU procedures.

The GFCC's conclusion and the Member States' declarations in the Council's minutes run counter to the division of competences under EU law and the ability of the Union to autonomously exercise its exclusive competence for external trade. In light of this competence division, it is problematic if a national constitutional court rules and the political representatives of Member States declare that all parties to the agreement, that is, all Member States and the Union unilaterally, can simply terminate the agreement's provisional application at any point in time, irrespective of the fact that the lion's share of the agreement falls under exclusive Union competence. This is in particular the case because only these parts that fall under exclusive Union competence were provisionally applied. Relying on a right under international law, in disregard of the internal competence division, contributes to blurring the division of responsibility and stands in the way of putting citizens in the position to adequately know and understand which body, institution, or polity is in charge of what. The consequences of the blurred division of powers also became very apparent in the debates surrounding the Dutch referendum on the Ukraine Association Agreement. The absolute largest share of the public debate did not even consider the fact that the Member States, and hence also the Netherlands, had a say in a very small part of the agreement, while the lion's share fell within the exclusive competences of the Union. As a result, the absolute majority voting in the referendum did not know what exactly they were voting on, cast their vote with regard to the whole agreement, and had false expectations with regard to the effects of a negative outcome of the referendum.[59]

The mismatch between Member States' formal powers under international law and their competences under EU law, which allow them to undermine Union powers in a binding form under international law and hence override the Union's exercise of trade competences, also demonstrates why Member States' action under international law is particularly powerful if used against the Union. Any such international measures directly affect the Union's ability to exercise its powers, it binds the Member States and potentially also the Union, and creates facts from which it is difficult to step back. Internally, the Union could simply adopt secondary law, including after a Member State has adopted national legislation. In the event of a conflict, the primacy of EU law would result in a disapplication of national law. Furthermore, the Commission could bring an infringement action under Article 258 TFEU against the Member State and the Court could ultimately fine the Member State for a breach of EU law.

Bonding structures allow individuals to relate to the exercise of public power, but only to the extent that it is adequately understandable who exercises what power in the name of whom. In law, the delimitation of powers is captured by the choice of the correct legal basis. It is hence reasonable to attribute a signalling function to the choice

[58] 'Comprehensive Economic and Trade Agreement (CETA) between Canada, of the one part, and the European Union and its Member States, on the Other Part—Statements of the Council Minutes' 13239/16 WTO 288 SERVICES 25 FDI 21 CDN 21 http://data.consilium.europa.eu/doc/document/ST-13463-2016-REV-1/en/pdf, paras 21 (Germany and Austria), 22 (Poland), 37 B (Belgium). Art 30.7(3)(c) s 1 of CETA reads: 'A Party may terminate the provisional application of this Agreement by written notice to the other Party.'

[59] It led to the adoption of European Council Conclusions on 15 December 2016, agreeing on an interpretation of the agreement, which is binding under EU law http://www.consilium.europa.eu/media/24151/15-euco-conclusions-ukraine.pdf.

of legal basis vis-à-vis EU citizens. It is also reasonable to consider that non-EU parties have an interest in knowing who is in charge, the geographical scope of an agreement, as well as whether Member States can legally continue to take parallel action. The following section focuses on (hidden) consequences of the scope of manoeuvre of Member States triggered by choosing an external rather than an internal legal basis in a given policy field, such as the environment and CCP. It also argues in favour of explicating and justifying these consequences.

4. Integrating Effects of Union External Actions

With the Union's external objectives of promoting multilateral solutions and working towards international cooperation,[60] the EU institutions have received a broad mandate to pursue policies outside the EU legal order. The mandate is, of course, not open-ended; rather, it is linked to the Union's competences and EU law principles, such as the principle of conferral and sincere cooperation. The European Treaties set out a number of explicit external competences, for example Article 207 TFEU on the CCP in Part 5 of the TFEU, Title 5 of the TEU on CFSP, but also, within specific policy areas, such as Article 191(1) 4th indent TFEU on international cooperation on environmental matters. For policy areas where an explicit external competence is missing, Article 216 (1) TFEU acts as a bridge from 'internal to external' competencies.[61] This section examines in turn how minimum harmonization becomes maximum harmonization in the external context, how trade agreements introduce harmonization through the back door, and how the Union's position affects the exercise of Member States' powers in an international organization, even if the Union is not a member of this organization.

4.1 The case of environmental law: minimum or maximum harmonization?[62]

The division of powers between the EU and its Member States is very complex. It also depends on the choice of legal basis. The European Treaties mention, for example, the environment as a shared competence in Article 4(2)(e) TFEU. A large part of EU environmental policy further consists of minimum standards, rather than maximum harmonization, for example, Article 193 TFEU. If no other treaty provisions are involved, stricter national measures are possible without further requirements. While Member States have to comply with the other provisions of the EU Treaties, when they derogate for example from the free movement provisions, stricter national environmental measures do not even have to comply with the European law's principle of proportionality.[63] Furthermore, the accepted understanding is that competence to introduce minimum standards internally cannot lead to exclusive competence externally.[64] Member States

[60] Art 21 TEU.

[61] Case C-81/13, *United Kingdom v Council* [2014] EU:C:2014:2114, Opinion of AG Kokott, para 104.

[62] This section draws from: Christina Eckes, 'Environmental Policy "Outside-In": How the EU's Engagement with International Environmental Law Curtails National Autonomy' (2012) 13(11) Ger LJ 1151. It focuses on the implications of the choice of legal basis for the scope of manoeuvre of the Member States. The implications of the choice of legal basis for the inter-institutional power relations is further explored in Chapter 5.

[63] Case C-6/03, *Deponiezweckverband Eiterköpfe* [2005] EU:C:2005:222, paras 61–64.

[64] Jan Jans and Hans Vedder, *European Environmental Law: After Lisbon* (ELP 2012).

remain competent to agree on stricter international standards or even lower international standards if it is clear from the international agreement that it sets a minimum standard only.[65] In areas where the Union is competent to adopt rules of minimum harmonization, the non-exclusive external competence results in the adoption of mixed agreements. Indeed, in the field of environmental policy, virtually all conventions to which the Union is a party are mixed agreements, including the Stockholm Convention and the Aarhus Convention.[66]

Furthermore, many environmental measures have the additional objective, or at least the consequence, of regulating trade and the internal market. In principle, a single legal basis should be chosen, but if a measure pursues several objectives, and if the different components are indissociably linked, without having one dominant objective, the measure can be based on a dual legal basis.[67] Internally, the dual legal basis would consist of Articles 192 and 114 TFEU for environmental measures with an internal market objective or vice versa.[68] Externally, it would be Articles 192 and 207 TFEU. In practice, both dual legal bases, Articles 192 and 114 TFEU[69] and Articles 192 and 207 TFEU,[70] are used.

In the present context, it is interesting to analyse the consequences that these two combinations of provisions present. They have different implications for whether Member States are allowed to adopt stricter national measures. For measures adopted under Article 114 TFEU, the procedure in Article 114(4)–(6) TFEU applies, which allows Member States to derogate from EU law after providing notification of national measures that maintain or introduce a standard that is incompatible with the Union standard. By contrast, the CCP under Article 207 TFEU is an exclusive Union competence, which means that Member States are not allowed to adopt any parallel national measures. Hence, in principle, Member States may adopt more stringent measures when the EU adopts internal environmental law instruments based on Article 192 TFEU (Article 193 TFEU), irrespective of whether they act internally or externally. However, where international conventions are concerned, the Union and the Member States usually conclude mixed agreements. Mixity then limits Member States' scope of manoeuvre through the back door.[71]

[65] Opinion 2/91 (Convention No 170 of the Int'l Labour Org. concerning safety in the use of chemicals at work) [1993] EU:C:1993:106, para 18.

[66] For an overview of international environmental agreements to which the EU is a Party or a Signatory, see http://ec.europa.eu/environment/international_issues/agreements_en.htm. On the consequences of concluding mixed agreements, see Christophe Hillion and Panos Koutrakos, *Mixed Agreements Revisited: The EU and its Member States* (Hart Publishing 2010).

[67] See Section 2 above on the centre of gravity test. See also: Case C-178/03, *Commission v Parliament and Council (Dangerous Chemicals)* [2006] EU:C:2006:4 (hereafter Case C-178/03, *Dangerous Chemicals*).

[68] In Case C-300/89, *Titanium dioxide* (n 22), the CJEU ruled out a joined legal basis of then-arts 100A and 130S EEC because the adoption procedures foreseen in the two provisions were considered to be incompatible. This is no longer the case for arts 192(1) and 114 TFEU. Art 192(2) TFEU specifically states that any measures under this paragraph should not negatively affect the powers under art 114 TFEU.

[69] eg Commission Regulation (EC) 842/2006 on certain fluorinated greenhouse gases [2006] OJ L 161/1; Council Directive (EC) 2006/66 on batteries and accumulators and waste batteries and accumulators and repealing Directive [2006] OJ L 266/1.

[70] The combined legal basis of arts 192(1) and 207 TFEU is possible. See Case C-178/03, *Dangerous Chemicals* (n 67) paras 58–59. However, it remains rather exceptional, eg Council Regulation (EEC) 3254/91 prohibiting the use of leghold traps in the Community and the introduction into the Community of pelts and manufactured goods of certain wild animal species originating in countries which catch them by means of leghold traps or trapping methods which do not meet international humane trapping standards [1991] OJ L 308/1.

[71] See for more details Chapter 2 on mixity and sincere cooperation and Section 6 below.

The Member States' scope for action is immediately more limited when the EU instrument is based on a dual legal basis. This is also the case where the difference between an internal and external legal basis becomes most apparent: while the combination of Articles 192 and 114 TFEU for internal measures still allows for more stringent national measures, the combination of Articles 192 and 207 TFEU for external measures excludes more stringent measures.

Pre-Lisbon, the Court of Justice ruled several times on the correct legal basis for measures that pursue an environmental objective but also regulate trade between the EU and third countries.[72] In the *Chernobyl I* case (1990),[73] concerning the importation of agricultural products that might be radioactively contaminated, the Court ruled that trade rules, which also pursue environmental objectives, should be based on the CCP legal basis (now-Article 207 TFEU). Similarly, in the *Energy Star Agreement* case (2002),[74] the Court held that an international agreement with the United States opening the EU market to the US Energy Star Program (a specific label for energy-saving fridges and dishwashers) must be correctly based on the now-Article 207 TFEU, despite the environmental dimension of the agreement. It concluded:

> It is true that in the long term, depending on how manufacturers and consumers in fact behave, the program should have a positive environmental effect as a result of the reduction in energy consumption which it should achieve. However, that is merely an *indirect and distant effect*, in contrast to the *effect on trade* [...] which is *direct and immediate*.[75]

This distinction between direct and immediate effects on the one hand and long-term effects on the other hand appears to introduce a logical bias for a trade legal basis. Measures that have the long-term objective of protecting the environment will often have immediate effects on ongoing trade. In light of the more restrictive consequences of Article 207 TFEU on the ability of Member States to adopt more stringent national measures, as compared to Article 114 TFEU, the choice of an environment or trade legal basis is even more relevant externally than internally. The tendency to prioritize short-term (trade) consequences over long-term (environmental) objectives ultimately imposes additional limits on Member States' powers.

In Opinion 2/00 on the correct legal basis for the conclusion of the Cartagena Protocol on Biosafety to the Convention on Biological Diversity,[76] the CJEU equally considered the delimitation between an environment and a trade legal basis. It applied the centre of gravity test and came to the conclusion that only an environment legal basis (now-Article 192(1) TFEU) was necessary and sufficient. Eight years later, in the case of *Commission v Parliament and Council* (2009),[77] concerning Regulation 1013/2006 on shipments of waste, the Court referred to its *Cartagena Protocol* Opinion, again applied the centre of gravity test, and came to the same conclusion that the Commission's call for a dual legal basis was unfounded and that now-Article 192 TFEU sufficed.

Finally, three years earlier in between these two cases, in the *Rotterdam Convention* case (2006),[78] concerning a prior informed consent procedure for hazardous chemicals

[72] Opinion 2/00 (n 1).

[73] Case C-70/88, *Parliament v Council (Chernobyl I)* [1990] EU:C:1990:217.

[74] Case C-281/01, *Commission v Council (Energy Star Agreement)* [2002] EU:C:2002:761.

[75] ibid, paras 40–41 (emphasis added).

[76] Opinion 2/00 (n 1). The Cartagena Protocol was negotiated under the Convention on Biological Diversity. It governs the trans-boundary movement of living biotechnologically modified organisms that might have adverse effects on the conservation and on biological diversity.

[77] Case C-411/06, *Commission v Parliament and Council* (n 22).

[78] Case C-94/03, *Rotterdam Convention* (n 45).

and pesticides in international trade, the CJEU recognized that a joint legal basis of environment and trade (now-Articles 192(1) and 207 TFEU) was necessary. The Court referred to its ruling in the *Energy Star Agreement* and used the concept of 'direct and immediate effect on trade' but came to the conclusion that 'the Convention includes, both as regards the aims pursued and its contents, two indissociably linked components, neither of which can be regarded as secondary or indirect as compared with the other, one falling within the scope of the CCP and the other within that of protection of human health and the environment'.[79] The Court concluded that, in accordance with earlier case law, 'the decision approving that Convention on behalf of the [Union] should therefore have been based on the two corresponding legal bases, namely, in this case, [ex-]Articles 133 and 175(1) EC [now-Articles 207 and 192(1) TFEU], in conjunction with the relevant provisions of [ex-]Article 300 EC [now-Article 218 TFEU]'.[80]

Even though all these cases concerned the choice between legal bases in environment and trade, they concerned very different factual situations. A general conclusion is hence difficult to draw. However, it is fair to conclude that the CJEU's approach has become more nuanced over time. The Court looks carefully into both the intention and the effects of any such measure and does not easily accept disguising measures predominantly aimed at protecting the environment as trade. This is relevant for the present argument that external environmental measures that are based on a trade legal basis have a stronger limiting effect on Member States' powers to adopt stricter (parallel) measures than those based on an environmental legal basis. In cases in which the CJEU accepts the environmental legal basis as sufficient for measures that also pursue an economic objective, in principle more stringent national measures remain possible, irrespective of whether the Union acts internally or externally. Where, however, the CJEU focuses on the short-term economic effects and accepts a (joint environmental) trade legal basis, Member States are precluded from adopting more stringent national measures.

4.2 Common commercial policy: ever more inclusive?

International agreements cannot change the competence division between the Union and the Member States. Yet the exercise of the Union's competence to conclude international agreements may nonetheless have an impact on this competence division. This is particularly true in the area of trade, in which the Union adopts a new generation of deep and comprehensive trade agreements that cover or at least touch upon an unprecedented range of subject matters. The possibility of such power-expanding effects is indirectly acknowledged by Article 207(6) TFEU.[81] They are possible because of a combination of factors. Importantly, international agreements concluded by the EU rank in the hierarchy of norms of the European legal order between primary and secondary law. Additionally, as part of the EU legal order, they enjoy primacy over national law.[82] In particular, CCP is an exclusive external competence, which in combination with the comprehensive list of horizontal objectives, is capable of pulling shared competence into the realm of exclusive competences. This goes beyond the specific constellations discussed where trade measures pursue environmental objectives.

[79] ibid, para 50. [80] ibid.

[81] See Chapter 1 on Member States' attempts to contain the expansion of the Union's external powers.

[82] See Chapter 1 on the hierarchy of norms in the EU legal order.

In several post-Lisbon cases, the CJEU adopted a wide understanding of what is covered by the CCP. In 2013 in the *Broadcasting rights* case, the CJEU for example accepted that a CCP legal basis was sufficient for adopting an international agreement that was intended to extend to third countries the internal market *acquis,* that is, the regime established in Directive 98/84/EC for the protection of conditional access broadcasting rights.[83] This case referred to the earlier *Daiichi Sankyo* case, in which the CJEU held, departing from Advocate General Cruz Villalón, that the CCP covered rules on patentable subject matter in Article 27 of the Trade-Related Aspects of Intellectual Property Rights (TRIPS) Agreement.[84] The Court emphasized that the TRIPS Agreement pursued the objective of reducing distortions of international trade by ensuring, in the territory of each member of the World Trade Organization (WTO), the effective and adequate protection of intellectual property rights and that it set a framework with which all EU internal market measures must comply.[85] Hence, even though patentability is only indirectly relevant to trade and would internally fall under the shared competence of Article 114 TFEU, when trade with third countries is concerned it falls under the exclusive CCP competence of the Union.

The definition of trade in *Daiichi Sankyo* consists of two elements: first, the measure must essentially *intend* to promote, facilitate, or govern trade, and second, have direct and immediate *effects* on trade.[86] As long as this is the case, other effects do not have a consequence for the choice of the correct legal basis. In other words, *Daiichi Sankyo, Broadcasting rights*, and Opinion 2/15 are a line of cases that illustrate that, post-Lisbon, the CJEU will interpret the EU's international trade policy in a way that makes it capable of meandering into other competences, which are in principle shared with the Member States and result in harmonization or where harmonization is excluded in the exercise of internal competences. Potentially at least, such harmonization of policy areas may have the effect of occupying the field and ultimately even of making functional succession possible and hence allow the Union to replace its Member States in international forums and conventions. The CJEU, however, does not apply the doctrine of functional succession lightly.[87]

In Opinion 2/15, the CJEU addressed in a more general manner how CCP has changed post-Lisbon and demonstrated its broad and objective-oriented approach to CCP. The Court examined the Union's CCP competence in the light of its foreign policy objectives and held that the chapter of the EU–Singapore Free Trade Agreement (FTA) concerning sustainable development, which primarily deals with environmental and labour standards, fell within the CCP. The CJEU further stated that 'the [TFEU] differs appreciably from the EC Treaty previously in force, in that it includes new aspects of contemporary international trade in that policy', that the 'extension of the field of the [CCP] by the [TFEU] constitutes a significant development of primary EU law', and that 'the objective of sustainable development' was from now on to be seen 'as an integral part of the [CCP]'.[88]

[83] Case C-137/12, *Commission v Council* (*Broadcasting Rights*) [2013] EU:C:2013:675, paras 64–65, referring to Case C-414/11, *Daiichi Sankyo and Sanofi-Aventis Deutschland* [2013] EU:C:2013:520, paras 58 and 60 (hereafter Case C-414/11, *Daiichi Sankyo*).

[84] ibid, Case C-414/11, *Daiichi Sankyo*, para 60.

[85] ibid, paras 58 and 59.

[86] ibid, para 51.

[87] One should rather say adequately restrictively, see the landmark ruling in Joined Cases 21 to 25/72, *International Fruit Company and Others v Produktschap voor Groenten en Fruit* [1972] EU:C:1972:115, para 18. See also: Case 38/75, *NV Nederlandse Spoorwegen* [1975] EU:C:1975:154, para 21.

[88] Opinion 2/15 (EU–Singapore Free Trade Agreement) [2016] EU:C:2017:376, paras 141 and 147.

It is interesting to contrast the Court's approach to CCP with its approach to the notion of 'development' in the case discussed above on the Philippines PCA.[89] For the definition of development, the Court referred to the European Consensus on Development (2006) and the financing instrument for development cooperation that cast development objectives of the Union in a legal form. The CJEU noted the connection between Article 208 TFEU (development cooperation) and the Union's external action objectives in Article 21 TEU and concluded that the Union's development cooperation should be conducted within the framework of these objectives, including the 'fostering the sustainable economic, social, and environmental development of developing countries, with the primary aim of eradicating poverty'.[90] While also oriented towards the Article 21 TEU objectives, this reading appears considerably narrower than the Court's reading of CCP.

A remarkable point in Opinion 2/15 is the relevance of the Union's horizontal foreign policy objectives in Article 21 TEU. They prove to be highly significant for the delimitation between different competence areas. The CJEU explicitly departed from the opinion of Advocate General Sharpston, who had argued that 'Articles 3(5) and 21 TEU [...] are not relevant to resolving the issue of competence' and 'cannot affect the scope of the [CCP] laid down in Article 207 TFEU'.[91] It recalled that Article 207(1) TFEU explicitly states that the CCP 'shall be conducted in the context of the principles and objectives of the Union's external action' and engaged with the specific objectives of development and the environment.[92] This is one of the features that formally distinguish the Union's CCP competence from its internal market competence. Article 114 TFEU does not refer to the Union's objectives. In the end, while AG Sharpston concluded that the sustainable development chapter still fell under the competences shared with the Member States, the Court found it covered by the exclusive EU competence of CCP.

CCP, in its broad and objective oriented interpretation, includes measures regulating intellectual property rights and services, as well as labour rights and environmental aspects. The CJEU's interpretation is susceptible of drawing a wide range of internal market and other policies into the CCP, as long as the measures are related to trade with third countries. EU FTAs may hence regulate a very broad scope of policies in a deep, that is, detailed and invasive, fashion.

After Opinion 2/15, EU FTAs without involvement of the Member States are likely to become the new default, potentially supplemented by a mixed investment agreement. Post-Lisbon, foreign direct investment is explicitly covered by Article 207 TFEU. Yet Opinion 2/15 also drew a line in the sense that broader Investor State Dispute Settlement mechanisms and portfolio investment can only be established under a mixed agreement, requiring ratification by the Member States. The EU–Singapore FTA, for example, is split into two agreements, each following its own adoption procedure: one EU–Singapore only, which covers matters that fall under EU exclusive competence, and an EU–Singapore Investment Protection Agreement, which is adopted as a mixed agreement.[93]

[89] Case C-377/12, *Commission v Council* (n 40).

[90] ibid, para 37.

[91] Opinion 2/15 [2016] EU:C:2016:992, Opinion of AG Sharpton, para 495.

[92] Opinion 2/15 (n 88) paras 142–45.

[93] This is the line that the Commission takes after Opinion 2/15, see http://ec.europa.eu/trade/policy/in-focus/eu-singapore-agreement/agreement-explained/.

CCP measures are further capable, not only of framing internal EU policy-making, but also of harmonizing national law.[94] Several Member States argued that Article 207(6) TFEU provided that the exercise of the Union's CCP competences shall not affect the delimitation of competences between the Union and the Member States, and shall not lead to harmonization of legislative or regulatory provisions of the Member States in so far as the Treaties exclude such harmonization.[95] Opinion 2/15 hence also demonstrates that the Treaty attempts to neutralize the risk of competence creep through the CCP did not have the effect that Member States might have expected or at least hoped when they included such containment clauses.[96]

Member States are required to exercise their powers, including in areas of reserved national competences, in compliance with the international obligations flowing from international agreements of the Union. The considerable constraining effects that this may have in practice became particularly apparent in Opinion 2/15,[97] in which the CJEU reminded Member States that the carving out of the regulation of property rights as a national reserved competence in Article 345 TFEU 'does not mean that those rules are not subject to the fundamental rules of the European Union'.[98] In light of the far-reaching provisions in the investment chapter,[99] effects on specific aspects of the system of property ownership are in fact to be expected. In the case of FTAs, this means for example that considerations of public order, security, or other public interests, which remain reserved national competences, must be interpreted in light of trade commitments and cannot create obstacles to free trade without further consideration of these trade commitments.[100]

FTAs do not directly regulate the levels of labour and environmental protection within the legal orders of the contracting parties. They govern trade between the contracting parties and pursue the objective of trade liberalization. Yet the liberalization of trade is subject to the condition that the contracting parties comply with their other international obligations, including those that concern social protection of workers and environmental protection. As a consequence, international commitments of the Union (and the Member States) in the field of international trade frame the exercise of other competences, including shared competences when there is no internal EU secondary law.

The competences of determining levels of social and environmental protection are internally shared. Hence, where the Union is exclusively competent to conclude FTAs that indirectly determine levels of social and environmental protection, these competences become exclusive Union competences through the back door, as the Union determines which international obligations are referred to and what principles are mentioned.[101] The next section demonstrates, however, that positions taken on behalf of the Union under international law also have internal effects, even if the Union is not a contracting party to the agreement or a member of the international organization.

[94] Case C-137/12, *Commission v Council (Broadcasting Rights)* [2013] EU:C:2013:441, Opinion of AG Kokott, paras 66–67.

[95] See the Court's discussion of this argument in para 164 of Opinion 2/15 (n 88).

[96] See for more details on the containment clauses the Introduction.

[97] Sacha Garben, 'Opinion 2/15: Competence Creep Through International Trade?' (*Europe and the World: A Law Review blog*, 30 May 2017 http://blogs.ucl.ac.uk/europe-and-the-world-journal/2017/opinion215-competence-creep.

[98] Opinion 2/15 (n 88) para 107, referring to: Cases C-105-107/12, *Essent and Others* [2013] EU:C:2013:677, paras 29 and 36.

[99] See Chapter 6 on more details on Investor State Dispute Settlement provisions in FTAs.

[100] Opinion 2/15 (n 88) para 103.

[101] ibid, paras 164–66.

4.3 Ripple effect of Union positions in international organizations

A position taken on the Union's behalf in an international organization may pre-empt Member States from acting internally, even if neither the EU nor all Member States are parties to the international organization. This is a very specific but potentially far-reaching effect of decisions adopted on the Union's position on policies discussed within international standard-setting organizations.

In a case concerning the International Organisation of Vine and Wine (OIV),[102] the CJEU addressed two points: first, the possibility of the Union to adopt a position within an organization to which neither the Union itself nor all Member States are a party; and second, the legal effects of the decisions of that organization. On the first point, the CJEU held that, as long as it falls within a field in which the Union has competence, nothing prevented the Union from adopting a position to be defended in a body set up by an international agreement on its behalf through the Member States, which are party to that agreement, acting jointly in its interest.[103] The position in question had been adopted pursuant to Article 218(9) TFEU and the CJEU interpreted this provision fairly widely, holding that it did not require that the Union is a member of the 'body' in question. In light of the fact that the Union is not a member of many international organizations, this point may not have been entirely new[104] but has far-reaching consequences.

On the second point, the Court held that the fact that acts 'are capable of decisively influencing the content of [EU] legislation' is sufficient for them to be considered as having *legal effects* within the meaning of Article 218(9) TFEU,[105] which gave the Council the powers under this provision. In its reasoning, the Court made a general and seemingly widely applicable point. While the EU had largely regulated the particular sub-area of the Common Agricultural Policy (CAP), that is, the common organization of the wine markets, the CJEU did not clearly limit its ruling to situations where the Union had exercised its competences internally, but referred to the CAP as an example.[106] An extension to areas of shared competences that are not fully regulated, is squarely in line with the CJEU's case law on implied external powers,[107] but also gives a broad reading to 'legal effects' and widens the field of application of the Court's interpretation of Article 218(9) TFEU—to other international organizations and to issues where no internal legislation exists.

In the context of international standard-setting organizations, such as the OIV or the *Codex Alimentarius*, the rules adopted may have the same harmonizing effects as internal EU legislation. The adoption of a Union position pursuant to Article 218(9) TFEU in the context of such organizations that 'carry out standardization activities, and [contribute] to international harmonization of existing practices and standards and, as necessary, to the preparation of new international standards'[108] may internally have pre-empting effects. The *OIV* case hence leads to the conclusion that the exercise of external powers in the particular context of organizations, even in the absence of internal rules and in organizations to which neither the EU nor all Member States are

[102] Case-399/12, *Germany v Council (OIV)* [2014] EU:C:2014:2258.

[103] ibid, paras 48–55.

[104] See Opinion 1/13 (n 15), para 43.

[105] ibid, paras 63–64.

[106] See ibid, para 52: '… falls within a competence of the European Union, such as the one mentioned in the preceding paragraph' and para 51: 'the [CAP] and, more specifically, the common organisation of the wine markets, an area which is regulated for the most part by the EU legislature in the exercise of its competence under Article 43 TFEU'.

[107] Opinion 1/03 (n 18).

[108] Case-399/12, *Germany v Council (OIV)* (n 102) para 59.

party, may pre-empt Member States from adopting internal measures that would go against the Union's position under Article 218(9) TFEU. The *OIV* case was brought by Germany, supported by seven other Member States. Besides the outlined potential effects of this decision, the case is also one example of several[109] of the above-mentioned deeper unease of Member States about the fettering effects of a combination of the Union's post-Lisbon external relations competences and the CJEU's doctrines in that area on their ability to decide externally and internally on their own course of action.

After highlighting integrative forces *resulting* from the choice of legal basis, the next section turns to specific examples of *external pressure on* the Union's choice of legal basis. First, the Union's external actions put pressure on the Union to simplify and harmonize its complex and differentiated decision-making system, in which CFSP and TFEU policies are adopted in different procedures and with different involvement of the EU institutions (Section 5.1). Second, Member States put pressure on the Union by exercising more powers than a prima facie reading of the Treaties would indicate in the specific area of restrictive measures. In this very specific context, they determine through a CFSP decision (adopted by unanimity in an intergovernmental procedure) every detail of a regulation under the TFEU (Section 5.2).

5. External Pressures on the Foundations

5.1 Legal bases for cross-Treaty policies[110]

International cooperation may stand in tension with the internal power division of the European Union. Pre-Lisbon, a particularly illustrative example of such tension was international cooperation that touched both upon third pillar policies (now the AFSJ) and the first pillar, which were subject to different rules and procedures with a different involvement of the Member States and the institutions. The Treaty of Lisbon abolished the distinction between the first and the third pillar and with it to a large extent the existing tensions. However, CFSP, the former second pillar, remains a policy apart and some of the problems of cross-pillar international cooperation continue.

5.1.1 Pre-Lisbon third pillar cases

To appreciate fully the influence of external relations on the internal division of powers, it is worth recalling the Union's uneasy cross-pillar approach to international agreements that touched upon first and third pillar policies. Two illustrative examples[111] are the UN Convention against Transnational Organized Crime (Palermo Convention)[112] and the above-discussed passenger name record (PNR) agreements.[113] As to the first,

[109] See case law cited in nn 19 and 20.

[110] This section draws from: Christina Eckes, 'Common Foreign and Security Policy: The Consequences of the Court's Extended Jurisdiction' (2016) 22 ELJ 492 and 'The Common Foreign and Security Policy and Other EU Policies: A Difference in Nature?' (2015) 20 EFA Rev 535 (hereafter Eckes, 'Difference in Nature').

[111] See also: Marise Cremona, 'EU External Action in the JHA Domain: A Legal Perspective' in: Marise Cremona, Jörg Monar, and Sara Poli (eds), *The External Dimension of the European Union's Area of Freedom, Security and Justice* (Peter Lang 2011) 85.

[112] United Nations General Assembly resolution 55/25 of 15 November 2000 Convention against Transnational Organized Crime. It entered into force on 29 September 2003 http://www.unodc.org/unodc/treaties/CTOC/index.html.

[113] Council Decision (EC) 2004/496 on the conclusion of an Agreement between the European Community and the United States of America on the processing and transfer of PNR data by Air

two of the protocols to the Palermo Convention, on smuggling of migrants and on trafficking of persons respectively, were concluded by the then Community, based on its competences under different parts of the first pillar, that is, development co-operation[114] and migration policy.[115] Because of the procedural differences of the two policy areas, the Community concluded each of the protocols in two separate decisions 'in so far as the provisions of [the respective] Protocol [fell] within the scope of' either of the two policy areas.[116] To add to the confusion, a third protocol, on illicit manufacturing and trafficking of firearms, required a separate conclusion since this issue fell at least partially under the Member States' competence for security.[117] In addition to the Community's conclusion of certain aspects of this third protocol,[118] the Council agreed a common strategy on those aspects that fell under what was then the third pillar.[119] The need to adopt six different legal instruments to conclude three protocols to an international convention in two different Council formations and the uncertain scope of these instruments 'in so far as the provisions [fell]' within a particular policy field demonstrate the mismatch between taking uniform external action and fragmented internal policy-making powers. Necessarily, this is not only an obstacle to uniform external action, it also pressures the Union to unify its internal approach. The abolishment of the pillars in the Lisbon Treaty was in fact an attempt to achieve a higher level of unity. However, the pillars continue to cast their shadows in the remaining procedural differences. The division of policies into different pillars with very different roles for political actors and different control of Member States also makes it significantly more difficult for the Union (and the Member States) to communicate adequately to individuals, both as EU citizens and as national citizens, who exercises power where and how on their behalf.

The second example concerns the PNR agreements. The pillar structure made not only the adoption more complex but also resulted in a successful legal challenge of the first PNR agreement.[120] This agreement was originally concluded on the basis of Article 95 EC (now 114 TFEU)—largely because this was the legal basis of the earlier adopted Data Protection Directive, which determined the legal requirements for data

Carriers to the United States Department of Homeland Security, Bureau of Customs and Border Protection [2004] OJ L 183/83 (hereafter EU–US PNR Agreement).

[114] Ex-arts 177ff TEC (now-arts 208ff TFEU).

[115] Part III, Title IV TEC (ex-arts 61ff TEC).

[116] See eg Council Decision (EC) 2006/616 on the conclusion, on behalf of the European Community, of the Protocol Against the Smuggling of Migrants by Land, Sea and Air, supplementing the United Nations Convention Against Transnational Organised Crime concerning the provisions of the Protocol, *in so far as the provisions of this Protocol fall within the scope of Articles 179 and 181a TEC* [2006] OJ L 262/24; and Council Decision (EC) 2006/617 on the conclusion, on behalf of the European Community, of the Protocol Against the Smuggling of Migrants by Land, Sea and Air, supplementing the United Nations Convention Against Transnational Organised Crime concerning the provisions of the Protocol, *in so far as the provisions of the Protocol fall within the scope of Part III, Title IV of the TEC* [2006] OJ L 262/34 (emphasis added).

[117] Ex-art 296 TEC (now-art 346 TFEU).

[118] Council Decision (EC) 2001/748 concerning the signing on behalf of the European Community of the United Nations Protocol on the illicit manufacturing of and trafficking in firearms, their parts, components, and ammunition, annexed to the Convention against transnational organized crime [2001] OJ 280/5.

[119] Common Position (JHA) 2000/130 on the proposed protocol against the illicit manufacturing of and trafficking in firearms, their parts and components, and ammunition, supplementing the United Nations Convention against transnational organized crime [2000] OJ L 37/1, based on ex-art 34(2)(a) TEU.

[120] Joined Cases C-317 to 318/04, *Parliament v Council and Commission* [2006] EU:C:2006:346 (hereafter Joined Cases C-317 to 318/04, *Parliament v Council*).

exchange between EU carriers and US authorities. However, the Court struck down the Council decision concluding the agreement.[121] It considered the PNR agreement to fall outside the scope of the Data Protection Directive and consequently also outside Article 95 EC, because the agreement concerned 'processing operations concerning public security and the activities of the State in areas of criminal law'.[122] The Union had to conclude a new agreement under what was then the third pillar.[123] This excluded Parliament from acting as a co-legislator and it also limited the CJEU's powers to rule on the agreement for the years to come.[124]

Post-Lisbon, the joined legal basis of the new PNR agreement is Article 218(6) TFEU in combination with Articles 82(1)(d) and 87(2)(a) TFEU, AFSJ legal bases governing police and judicial cooperation. The latter two provisions are also the legal basis for the 2016 PNR Directive.[125]

Furthermore, in certain instances third country preferences seem to have had a direct impact on the choice of legal basis within the EU. In a case concerning the European Economic Area (EEA) social security coordination with Switzerland, a proposed third pillar legal basis which would have resulted in a UK opt-out,[126] was not acceptable to the third country (Switzerland) and was replaced by a first pillar legal basis. The attempt by the UK to challenge this choice of legal basis was unsuccessful.[127]

As is well known, the particular difficulties of drawing lines between first and third pillar competences have disappeared with the Lisbon Treaty. Much of the decision-making in the AFSJ has become subject to the ordinary legislative procedure.[128] Ending the need to adopt international agreements through a multitude of legal instruments following different procedures and involving different actors was certainly a welcome side effect of the integration of the third pillar. Nonetheless, the dividing line between CFSP and the rest, including the AFSJ, remains in place[129] and the Union will still have to bridge this split to accommodate external demands. The next subsection demonstrates that the problems of multiplication of conclusion instruments, the arguable influence of third countries on the choice of legal basis, and the difficulties in determining the dividing line continue to exist.

5.1.2 Cross-Treaty legal basis post-Lisbon

The choice of the correct legal basis for cross-Treaty policies has become[130] and will remain a hotly contested issue in inter-institutional relations. The requirements of international cooperation cannot be neatly fitted into the Union's internal treaty structure but continue to pressure the Union to neglect the less prominent policy field

[121] EU–US PNR Agreement (n 113).

[122] Joined Cases C-317 to 318/04, *Parliament v Council* (n 120) para 56.

[123] Based on ex-arts 24 and 38 TEU. See (n 113) for the second EU–US PNR agreement.

[124] The case was decided in 2006 and only since 1 December 2014 the CJEU had full jurisdiction over the former third pillar.

[125] Parliament and Council Directive (EU) 2016/681 on the use of PNR data for the prevention, detection, investigation, and prosecution of terrorist offences and serious crime [2016] OJ L 119/132.

[126] Protocol 21.

[127] See Case C-656/11, *United Kingdom v Council (Switzerland-EEA Social Security Coordination)* (n 43) paras 47–66.

[128] Arts 77ff TFEU.

[129] Eckes, 'A Difference in Nature' (n 110).

[130] Case C-130/10, *UN Sanctions* (n 19); Case C-658/11, *Parliament v Council (Piracy Agreement (Mauritius))* [2014] EU:C:2014:2025, argument of Sweden in para 42; Case C-72/15, *Rosneft* [2017] EU:C:2017:236, paras 84–93 (hereafter Case C-72/15, *Rosneft*); Case C-263/14, *Tanzania Pirates Agreement* (n 1) para 42 on the jurisdiction of the Court.

in the choice of legal basis or to opt for a cross-Treaty legal basis in tension with the Court's case law, ruling out the combination of incompatible adoption procedures. Post-Lisbon the mutual non-affection clause (40 TEU)[131] and the extended external competences of the Union will only increase the need for clarification.

Pre-Lisbon the leading case on the distinction between CFSP and then-Community law was *ECOWAS*.[132] In this case, the CJEU came to the conclusion that effectively the policy to incentivize people to turn in their small arms and light weapons after the civil wars in West Africa could fall under both CFSP and development policy. Yet it excluded the possibility of using a joint CFSP/Community law basis and decided that because of the priority given at the time to the former first pillar, the measure should have been a Community measure.[133] Post-Lisbon, the CJEU by contrast accepted in the *UN Sanctions* case (2012) the combination of a CFSP and a TFEU legal basis as a matter of principle.[134] In *UN Sanctions*, Parliament had challenged the legal basis chosen by the Council to give effect to UN Security Council resolutions imposing sanctions against terrorist suspects. The Council had based the sanctions on Article 215 TFEU, which is an exceptional 'hybrid CFSP-TFEU provision' requiring a prior CFSP decision (under the TEU) for the Union to take action under the TFEU. Parliament argued that the correct legal basis would have been Article 75 TFEU, which provides for the adoption of counter-terrorist sanctions as part of AFSJ.[135] Legal instruments based on the latter provision are adopted pursuant to the ordinary legislative procedure, while Article 215 TFEU only requires that Parliament be informed. The Court accepted the Council's preference for using a hybrid CFSP-TFEU provision, Article 215 TFEU, rather than the 'pure' TFEU competence in Article 75 TFEU.

The *UN Sanctions Case* is interesting because of what the Grand Chamber said both explicitly and implicitly. It first spent a lengthy section, which was not even strictly necessary to give a ruling in the case at hand, on the question of whether and under which conditions different legal bases can be combined. As is often the case, the starting point of the CJEU allows drawing conclusions regarding the broader viewpoint of the Court. The Court explained that the correct legal basis is to be determined pursuant to the centre of gravity test,[136] including where a CFSP provision is considered an option.[137] Most relevant in the present context is that the Court *did not rule out* the use of a *cross-Treaty joint legal basis* (CFSP-TFEU) as matter of principle but assumed that the choice of legal basis follows the same rules as within the TFEU. Implicitly, the Court hence assumed that the nature of CFSP does not stand in the way of a cross-Treaty joint legal basis. It herewith acknowledged the efforts of the Lisbon Treaty to approximate the TEU and the TFEU.[138] At the same time, applying these general rules (centre of gravity test) results in an exclusion of a cross-Treaty joint legal basis. In *UN Sanctions*, the Court explicitly held that the ordinary legislative procedure cannot be combined with a provision where Parliament is only informed.[139] The underlying reason is that a combination of legal bases may not encroach upon the prerogatives of

[131] See for more detail Section 4.4.1 of Chapter 3.
[132] Case C-91/05, *ECOWAS* (n 23).
[133] ibid, para 75ff. See also, Geert de Baere, *Constitutional Principles of EU External Relations* (OUP 2008) 295ff.
[134] Case C-130/10, *UN Sanctions* (n 19).
[135] See for an in-depth discussion of the choice of legal basis, Christina Eckes, 'EU Counter-Terrorist Sanctions Against Individuals: Problems and Perils' (2012) 17 EFA Rev 113.
[136] See Section 1 above on more details on the centre of gravity test.
[137] This was already established in Case C-91/05, *ECOWAS* (n 23) paras 60, 73, and 75.
[138] See Chapter 3 on coherence.
[139] Case C-130/10, *UN Sanctions* (n 19) para 47.

any of the institutions. Article 31 TEU stipulates that '[CFSP d]ecisions [...] shall be taken by the European Council and the Council acting unanimously, except where this Chapter provides otherwise'.[140] Parliament is not mentioned at all.[141] The provision further specifies how a Member State can abstain and sets out the exceptions to the general decision-making rule in which 'the Council shall act by qualified majority'.[142] The exceptional qualified majority vote is further subject to an 'emergency break'. Where a Member State sets out 'vital and stated reasons of national policy' 'the Council may, acting by a qualified majority, request that the matter be referred to the European Council for a decision by unanimity'.[143] This differs considerably from the ordinary legislative procedure under the TFEU, not only as regards the involvement of Parliament but also in the described procedural particularities that protect decisions that are democratically legitimized through national channels and hence ultimately national political discretion. These differences are greater than the differences in the combination that the Court explicitly excluded. Hence, a cross-Treaty legal basis should be excluded. This should ultimately require splitting up comprehensive international agreements along their substantive content into CFSP and TFEU agreements if both components are equally prominent. Alternatively, the usually less prominent CFSP component will simply be adopted—in line with the centre of gravity text—under a TFEU legal basis, which formally hides the CFSP component.

The Lisbon Treaty has made CFSP part of the Union's *one* legal order but preserved the particular protection of national political discretion and the looser control of EU constitutional mechanisms and actors. In *UN Sanctions,* the Court has adopted a similarly mixed approach. On the one hand, it approximated CFSP to other policies by opening the door for speculations that a cross-Treaty legal basis is possible and framed the choice of legal basis under CFSP in the same constitutional terms as other policies. On the other hand, it protected national political discretion by accepting the choice for a CFSP legal basis and making a cross-Treaty legal basis procedurally impossible. The former reveals the Court's view of CFSP as part of the Union's legal order, which is subject to the same basic EU constitutional rules and principles. Whether the extended jurisdiction of the Court will, in practice, lead to the Court applying and enforcing constitutional principles more intensively under CFSP remains to be seen.

5.1.3 International treaties

Pre-Lisbon, only the distinction between the first and the third pillar had given rise to significant litigation, not the distinction between the second and the third pillar. Logically, a cross-Treaty joint legal basis between the former Union pillars (second and third) was possible before Lisbon.[144] Post-Lisbon, the dividing line between the AFSJ

[140] See also art 24(1) TEU sets out that the adoption of a CFSP measure 'is subject to specific rules and procedures. It shall be defined and implemented by the European Council and the Council acting unanimously, except where the Treaties provide otherwise.'

[141] Formally Parliament has a limited role under CFSP see in particular arts 36 and 41(3) TEU, which require Parliament to be consulted.

[142] Art 31(2) TEU. [143] ibid.

[144] See in particular Case C-355/04 P, *Segi and Others* [2007] EU:C:2007:116; and Case T-338/02, *Segi and Others* [2004] EU:T:2004:171 and Council Decision (CFSP) 2007/551 on the signing, on behalf of the European Union, of an Agreement between the European Union and the United States of America on the processing and transfer of PNR data by air carriers to the United States Department of Homeland Security (DHS) (2007 PNR Agreement) [2007] OJ 204/16. The chapter on the former third pillar referred to the CFSP provision on the conclusion of international agreements; see also

(former third pillar policies, now part of the TFEU) and CFSP is more pronounced but the Union will still have to bridge this split to accommodate external demands. In total the Union has concluded 115 international agreements that at least also relate to CFSP.[145] The potential for cross-Treaty (TEU/CFSP and TFEU) action becomes apparent in the fact that some of these 115 agreements, despite their link to foreign and security policy, are based on TFEU legal bases only.[146] Adopting (and hence making invisible) the CFSP component may on the one hand protect TFEU policies from CFSP influence. It avoids explicating that economic cooperation and trade (TFEU policies) are dependent on the compliance of the third country with certain security requirements, for example, non-proliferation, or more broadly, no trade in weapons of mass destruction (CFSP). On the other hand, making such links invisible does not, in practice, avoid the substantive dependencies. It also works against making structures of responsibility transparent and adequately accessible to citizens. The complexity of a joined legal basis may not be particularly accessible either; yet not explicating certain components in the choice of legal basis only further highlights the general difficulty of making the Union decision-making procedures transparent and accessible.

Furthermore, many CFSP only agreements were concluded since the entry into force of the Lisbon Treaty. In particular many agreements were concluded concerning the protection of classified information,[147] but also, for example, agreements concerning piracy,[148] and concerning participation in the EU's crisis management operations,[149]

Christina Eckes, 'How Not Being Sanctioned by a Community Instrument Infringes a Person's Fundamental Rights: The Case of SEGI' (2006) 17 King's College LJ 144.

[145] Search in the EU Treaties Database on 15 February 2018 for 'Foreign and Security Policy' http://ec.europa.eu/world/agreements/searchByActivity.do?parent=8521&xmlname=760&actName=Foreign%20and%20Security%20Policy&printAcrivity=.

[146] See eg Council Decision (EU) 2016/1888 on the signing, on behalf of the Union, and provisional application of the Agreement between the European Union and Solomon Islands on the short-stay visa waiver [2016] OJ L 292/1 and Council Decision (EU) 2016/437 on the signing, on behalf of the European Union, and provisional application of the Agreement between the European Union and the Republic of Peru on the short-stay visa waiver [2016] OJ L 78/2, based on art 77 TFEU. Council Decision (EU) 2016/2220 on the conclusion, on behalf of the European Union, of the Agreement between the United States of America and the European Union on the protection of personal information relating to the prevention, investigation, detection, and prosecution of criminal offences [2016] OJ L 336/1, based on art 16 TFEU.

[147] In total (pre- and post-Lisbon) the EU has concluded 21 agreements on the exchange of classified information until 15 February 2018. Recent examples are: Council Decision (CFSP) 2017/2322 concerning the signing and conclusion of the Agreement between Canada and the European Union on security procedures for exchanging and protecting classified information [2017[] OJ L 333/1; Council Decision (CFSP) 2017/718 concerning the signing and conclusion of the Agreement between the European Union and the Republic of Moldova on security procedures for exchanging and protecting classified information [2017] OJ L 106/1; Council Decision (EU) 2016/1946 concerning the signing and conclusion of the Agreement between the European Union and Georgia on security procedures for exchanging and protecting classified information [2016] OJ L 300/1; Council Decision (EU) 2016/402 concerning the signing and conclusion of the Agreement between the Council of Ministers of the Republic of Albania and the European Union on security procedures for exchanging and protecting classified information [2016] OJ L 74/1.

[148] Council Decision (CFSP) 2010/199 on the EU–Montenegro Agreement on the participation of Montenegro in the European Union military operation to contribute to the deterrence, prevention, and repression of acts of piracy and armed robbery off the Somali coast (Operation Atlanta) [2010] OJ L 88/1; Council Decision (CFSP) 2011/640 on the EU–Mauritius Agreement on the conditions of transfer of suspected pirates and associated seized property from the European Union-led naval force to the Republic of Mauritius and on the conditions of suspected pirates after transfer [2011] OJ L 254/1.

[149] Council Decision (CFSP) 2011/133 on the signing and conclusion of the EU–Montenegro Agreement establishing a framework for the participation of Montenegro in European Union crisis management operations [2011] OJ L 57/1; Council Decision (CFSP) 2011/318 on the US-EU

the maintaining of police missions,[150] the participation of third countries in EU missions,[151] and the logistic cooperation of military services.[152]

Finally, an example of post-Lisbon agreement with a cross-Treaty legal basis is the partnership agreement between the EU and its Member States and New Zealand, based on Article 37 TEU and Articles 207 and 212 TFEU.[153] The general procedure for the conclusion of EU agreements, that is, both CFSP and TFEU, is Article 218 TFEU. The Council decision, signing, and agreeing provisional application were adopted with unanimity. Since New Zealand is not an accession state, this voting requirement was due to the CFSP component of the agreement. Cross-Treaty legal bases immediately raise the question of procedural compatibility. Both Articles 207(2) and 212(2) TFEU require the ordinary legislative procedure. Article 37 TEU only expresses the Union's ability to conclude international agreements under CFSP and is usually used 'in conjunction with' Article 218(5) and (6) sub 1 TFEU. In this combination, the Council alone sets the guidelines and authorizes the opening of negotiations and the signing of CFSP agreements. The cross-Treaty legal basis of the partnership agreement with New Zealand seems to depart from the compatibility requirement as formulated by the CJEU in *UN Sanctions*. The next subsection discusses in detail whether and how CFSP could affect TFEU policies when the Union takes external actions.

5.2 European sanctions as an exceptional bridge between CFSP and TFEU policies

EU restrictive measures (sanctions) are a specific and exceptional example of where Member States exercise powers through CFSP over the detailed content of a TFEU regulation beyond what becomes apparent from a prima facie reading of the Treaties. Here, the Union's external actions under the CFSP, in an expanding field of action pursuing international peace and security objectives, lead to a tightening of the grip of the Member States over law-making of the EU institutions under the TFEU.

The case of *Rosneft*, concerning the adoption of restrictive measures under Article 215 TFEU, specifically concerned the encroachment of CFSP on TFEU policies.[154] The CJEU carried out an analysis of the CFSP decision and the TFEU Regulation against the background of the mutual non-affection clause in Article 40 TEU. One

Framework Agreement on the participation of the United States of America in European Union crisis management operations [2011] OJ L 143/1; Council Decision (CFSP) 2012/315 on the EU–New Zealand Agreement establishing a framework for the participation of New Zealand in European Union crisis management operations [2012] OJ L 160/1.

[150] Council Decision (CFSP) 2016/1783 on the signing and the conclusion on behalf of the Union of the Agreement in the form of an Exchange of Letters between the European Union and the Islamic Republic of Afghanistan on the extension of the agreement on the status of the European Union Police Mission in Afghanistan (EUPOL AFGHANISTAN) [2016] OJ L 273/1.

[151] Council Decision (CFSP) 2016/602 on the signing and conclusion of the Participation Agreement between the European Union and the Swiss Confederation on the participation of the Swiss Confederation in the European Union Advisory Mission for Civilian Security Sector Reform Ukraine (EUAM Ukraine) [2016] OJ L 104/1.

[152] Council Decision (CFSP) 2016/2360 on the signing and conclusion of the Acquisition and Cross-Servicing Agreement between the European Union and the United States of America [2016] OJ L 350/1.

[153] Council Decision (EU) 2016/2079 on the signing, on behalf of the European Union, and provisional application of the Partnership Agreement on Relations and Cooperation between the European Union and its Member States, of the one part, and New Zealand, of the other part [2016] OJ L 321/1.

[154] Case C-72/15, *Rosneft* (n 130) paras 84–93.

issue was whether the Council encroached, by defining 'the Union position on the restrictive measures [...] in excessive detail' in the CFSP decision, 'on the joint power of proposal of the High Representative [...] and the Commission'.[155] In other words, it was controversial whether the Council by exercising its CFSP powers under the TEU encroached on the powers and procedures provided under the TFEU. The Court pointed out that it will assess the alleged encroachment in the specific context of Article 215 TFEU,[156] which builds an explicit bridge between the TFEU and the TEU and should therefore be read as an exception to the general mutual non-affection of the two Treaties. Consequently, the CJEU's considerations are not easily transferrable to other policy areas.

However, the CJEU again pointed out that 'the wide scope of the aims and objectives of the CFSP, as set out in Article 3(5) TEU and Article 21 TEU and in the specific provisions relating to the CFSP, in particular, in Articles 23 and 24 TEU' should be taken into account and that these aims and objectives vested the Council with 'a broad discretion' in determining restrictive measures.[157] It referred to Article 215 TFEU as 'a bridge between the objectives of the EU Treaty in matters of the CFSP and the actions of the Union involving economic measures falling within the scope of the FEU Treaty'.[158] It should, however, be added that Article 21 TEU sets out horizontal objectives, which apply to all Union external relations and cannot be divided into categories of CFSP and other external relations objectives.[159] Hence, arguably all Union external relations under the TFEU may pursue all objectives listed in Article 21 TFEU, as may CFSP measures.

The Court emphasized that the aim of the CFSP Council Decision was to establish restrictive measures in a technical field and that it could not be criticized for predetermining in excessive detail the content of the TFEU Regulation.[160] Finally, the CJEU rejected the argument that the CFSP Council decision constituted a legislative act, which would be contrary to Articles 24 and 31 TEU, by relying on the purely formal definition that a legislative act is an act adopted pursuant to the legislative procedures of the TFEU.[161] This is in line with the Court's position more generally, for example, when distinguishing delegating and implementing acts; yet it seems to render the prohibition of legislative CFSP acts void of purpose. CFSP decisions adopted pursuant to CFSP procedural rules could never be legislative acts in formal terms, even if in their substantive nature they are generally applicable, detailed, and in essence substantively indistinguishable from legislative acts adopted under the TFEU.

Sanctions are the exception, where the Court interprets Treaty provisions in a way that allows a CFSP decision (with Member States in a comparatively powerful role) to give determinative guidance for the content of TFEU measures (subject to the ordinary legislative procedure). This particular influence of the Member States through the more intergovernmental CFSP may, however, be due to the above-discussed bridge function of Article 215 TFEU. No general conclusion for CFSP should be drawn from this particular example.

[155] ibid, para 84. [156] ibid, para 86. [157] ibid, para 88.
[158] ibid, para 89 with a reference to: Case C-130/10, *UN Sanctions* (n 19) para 59.
[159] See for more detail Chapter 3. [160] Case C-72/15, *Rosneft* (n 130), para 90.
[161] ibid, paras 91–92.

6. Vesting International Obligations with the Bite of EU Law: The Case of the Aarhus Convention

The international law obligations of the Member States remain, in principle, the same irrespective of whether they are the only contracting parties or whether the Union is also a party to the international agreement. Yet the EU's participation has significant implications for the Member States' obligations *under EU law*. This in turn reduces their scope of manoeuvre as international actors.

'Mixed agreements have the same status in the [Union] legal order as purely [Union] agreements.'[162] Both the EU institutions and the Member States are obliged to ensure compliance with agreements concluded by the Union (Article 216(2) TFEU). This also makes mixed agreements binding in their entirety on the Member States. They become part of the EU legal order and enjoy primacy over national law. As a consequence, a Member State breaches both EU law and international law when it acts contrary to aspects of a mixed agreement that fall within the competences of the Union.[163]

Member States fulfil a particular obligation not only in relation to the non-EU state concerned 'but also and above all in relation to the [Union] which has assumed responsibility for the due performance of the agreement'.[164] The 'effect in the [Union] may not be allowed to vary according to whether their application is in practice the responsibility of the [EU] institutions or of the Member States and, in the latter case, according to the effects in the internal legal order of each Member State which the law of that State assigns to international agreements concluded by it'.[165] International obligations become EU law obligations for Member States and their room for manoeuvre is significantly limited, including in areas where they formally remain competent to act on the international plane. The CJEU has also assumed jurisdiction for mixed agreements in their entirety.

The Union has consequently *the legal means* to hold Member States to account under EU law for mixed agreements in their entirety.[166] By potentially enforcing international obligations of Member States against Member States, the Union widens the scope in which it directly confers rights on individuals. This increases the scope for EU law to be directly relevant to citizens and creates potential bonding structures.

6.1 *Slovak Bears*

The Aarhus Convention is a particularly illustrative example of the effects that Union participation in international legal regimes, that is, making them mixed agreements,

[162] Case C-459/03, *Commission v Ireland (Mox Plant)* [2006] EU:C:2006:345, para 169 (hereafter Case C-459/03, *Mox Plant*). See also: Case C-240/09, *Lesoochranárske zoskupenie VLK* [2011] EU:C:2011:125 (hereafter Case C-240/09, *Slovak Bears*).

[163] Case C-239/03, *Commission v France (Étang de Berre)* [2004] EU:C:2004:598 (hereafter Case C-239/03 Étang de Berre) paras 29–30 See Pieter-Jan Kuijper, 'Case C-239/03, *Commission v French Republic*' (2005) 42 CML Rev 1491; Marise Cremona, 'Defending the Community Interest: The Duties of Cooperation and Compliance' in Marise Cremona and Bruno de Witte (eds), *EU Foreign Relations Law: Constitutional Fundamentals* (Hart Publishing 2008) 125.

[164] Case C-104/81, *Hauptzollamt Mainz v Kupferberg* [1982] EU:C:1982:362, para 13.

[165] Case 181-73, *R. & V. Haegeman v Belgium* [1974] EU:C:1974:41, para 14.

[166] See eg: Case C-13/00, *Commission v Ireland (Berne Convention)* [2002] EU:C:2002:184, paras 13-19; Case C-239/03, *Étang de Berre* (n 163) paras 29–30. Both discussed at Eleftheria Neframi, 'The Duty of Loyalty: Rethinking Its Scope Through Its Application in the Field of EU External Relations' (2010) 47 CML Rev 323, 333.

may have not only on the rights of individuals but also on the question of who determines these rights.[167] The Aarhus Convention contains three broad themes of procedural rights in environmental matters: access to information, public participation, and access to justice, as well as a number of important general features. It is particularly specific and detailed in its procedural requirements. Yet the Aarhus Convention shows deference to national legal culture and is intended to establish minimum standards to be achieved.

Because the Aarhus Convention is a mixed agreement, Member States' obligations under the Aarhus Convention become EU law obligations. As a consequence, Member States lose their margin of discretion, which other parties to the Aarhus Convention enjoy under international law, on how to give domestic effects to international obligations. Under EU law, not only the international agreement itself is binding, but also its interpretation by the CJEU. This is true for all EU agreements but has particular consequences in the context of the Aarhus Convention, because of its subject matter—procedural rights—and its great detail.

In the *Slovak Bears* case,[168] for example, the Court of Justice was asked in a preliminary ruling to determine whether Article 9(3) of the Aarhus Convention has direct effect.[169] This provision is implemented by EU law with regard to access to justice against decisions of the EU institutions;[170] yet legislative attempts to extend the EU Regulation to Member States' decisions were not successful.[171] The Court stated that, as a matter of principle, it would 'be for the courts of [the] Member States to determine, on the basis of national law, whether individuals could rely directly on the rules of [the] international agreement' if the Union had not yet exercised its powers to implement the obligations under the provision in question.[172] If, however, the Union had exercised its power to implement the obligations under Article 9(3) it would be for the CJEU to determine whether the provision enjoys direct effect.[173] This reflects the general rule of parallelism between internal and external competences, in which external competences in principle depend on internal competences but not vice versa.

However, rather than focusing on the *procedural* obligation flowing from Article 9(3), the CJEU turned to the issues at stake in the main proceedings before the national court that had referred the case to the CJEU. The main proceedings in *Slovak Bears* concerned the question of whether an environmental protection association may be a 'party' to administrative proceedings, in which derogations are determined to a system of protection for species. The species in question was subject to a system of strict protection under the Habitats Directive,[174] from which derogation was only

[167] Since 18 May 2005, the EU has been a party to the Aarhus Convention. See Council Decision 2005/370, OJ [2005] L 124/1.

[168] Case C-240/09, *Slovak Bears* (n 162). *See* Damian Krawczyk, 'Case Note: The Slovak Brown Bear Case: The ECJ Hunts for Jurisdiction and Environmental Plaintiffs Gain the Trophy' (2012) 14 Env L Rev 53.

[169] Art 9(3) obliges 'each Party [to] ensure that, where they meet the criteria, if any, laid down in its national law, members of the public have access to administrative or judicial procedures to challenge acts and omissions by private persons and public authorities which contravene provisions of its national law relating to the environment'.

[170] Parliament and Council Regulation (EC) 1367/2006 on the application of the provisions of the Aarhus Convention on Access to Information, Public Participation in Decision-making, and Access to Justice in Environmental Matters to Community institutions and bodies [2006] OJ L 264/1.

[171] See European Commission, 'Proposal for a Directive of the European Parliament and of the Council on Access to Justice in Environmental Matters' COM (2003) 624 final. The proposal did not find a majority in the Council.

[172] Case C-240/09, *Slovak Bears* (n 162) para 32.

[173] ibid, para 33.

[174] Council Directive (EEC) 92/43 on the conservation of natural habitats and of wild fauna and flora [1992] OJ L 206/7.

possible under that Directive. Based on this, the Court came to the conclusion that 'the *dispute in the main proceedings* falls within the scope of EU law'.[175]

The CJEU further acknowledged that the Union's declaration of competences explicated that the application of Article 9(3) to national proceedings fell within the competence of the Member States *until the Union implements these obligations*.[176] Nonetheless, the Court ruled that 'a *specific issue* which has *not yet been subject to EU legislation* may fall *within the scope of EU law* if it relates to a field covered in large measure by it'.[177] The Court then stressed the importance of uniform application of provisions that sometimes apply to the national context and sometimes to the EU law context and concluded that it had jurisdiction to determine the direct effect of Article 9(3). The Court arguably departs here from its decision in *Merck Genéricos*,[178] to which it referred in the judgment and in which it had made the competence to determine the direct effect of any particular provision of an international agreement dependent on whether that provision fell within an area in which the EU had legislated.

The broad (and substantive) focus of the CJEU on a field covered in large measure by EU law drew Article 9(3) within the scope of EU law, disregarded the wording of the declaration of competences to the Aarhus Convention, and blurred the distinction between substantive environmental protection and procedural rights. From the perspective of environmental protection, this blurring might be considered positive because it potentially vests international environmental law with teeth (no direct effect of Article 9(3) though).[179] Yet it also exemplifies how the EU's external actions, that is, becoming part of the Aarhus Convention, may have consequences for the internal powers of the Member States.

First, the Court filled some of the regulatory void that was left by the failed attempts to legislate on the issue of access to justice against Member States' decisions with an environmental impact and assumed the role of the legislator. Second, taking into account 'downstream' legislation, that is, the listing of a species in a directive on substantive, rather than procedural protection, is 'random and arbitrary' and results in a fragmentation of the interpretation of Article 9(3) depending on the substantive environmental issue at stake,[180] for example, what species is concerned in the particular case.

In *Slovak Bears,* the CJEU came to the conclusion that Article 9(3) does *not have direct effect within the EU legal order*, but that it is for the legal systems and the courts of each Member State to *interpret national law in a way that is consistent* with Article 9(3) and makes the exercise of rights under the Habitats Directive effective.[181] It hence vested parts of the Aarhus Convention that were actually not implemented under EU law with additional effect under EU law by giving concrete guidelines to the national court that essentially prescribed interpretation of national law consistent with the Aarhus Convention. Specifically, while the Aarhus Convention, as well as the

[175] Case C-240/09, *Slovak Bears* (n 162) para 38 (emphasis added).

[176] Declaration under art 19 of the Aarhus Convention. Council Decision (EC) 2005/370 on the Conclusion, on Behalf of the European Community, of the Convention on Access to Information, Public Participation in Decision-Making and Access to Justice in Environmental Matters [2005] OJ L 124/1.

[177] Case C-240/09, *Slovak Bears* (n 162) para 40 (emphasis added).

[178] Case C-431/05, *Merck Genéricos* [2007] EU:C:2007:496.

[179] See Christian Walter, 'Internationalisierung des deutschen und Europaeischen Verwaltungsverfahrens- und Verwaltungsprozessrechts—am Beispiel der Aarhus Konvention' (2005) 40 Europarecht 302, 316 (arguing with regard to the particular example of the Aarhus Convention that substantive and procedural law can no longer be separated).

[180] Case C-240/09, *Slovak Bears,* Opinion of AG Kokott [2010] EU:C:2010:436, para 70.

[181] ibid, paras 42–43.

implementing EU regulation, defers to national law, by, for example, making access subject to 'meeting any requirements under national law', the requirement of consistent interpretation of the CJEU considerably limits Member States' scope of discretion.

6.2 Further case law

Another series of cases in which the CJEU applied the Aarhus Convention concern access to justice in the form of the *locus standi* conditions for non-governmental organizations (NGOs). Several Member States had made declarations and reservations to the Aarhus Convention.[182] Sweden, for example, limited the scope of Article 9(1) and (2) 'with regard to access by environmental organizations to [. . .] court [. . .] concerning such decisions [. . .] that require environmental impact assessments'.[183] However, the position taken by the CJEU in *Slovak Bears*, as well as in the case of *Djurgarden* and *Bund für Umwelt und Naturschutz*, limit the effects of such a declaration. In the case of *Djurgarden*[184] concerning the Swedish implementation of an EU Directive giving effect to the Aarhus Convention,[185] the CJEU assumed jurisdiction and found that the Swedish requirements were too restrictive. In *Bund für Umwelt und Naturschutz*[186] equally concerning Article 9(2), an environmental NGO challenged the partial permit for building a coal-fired power station in Germany and relied on a rule designed to protect individual interests, rather than one that protects the general public interest.[187] The CJEU ruled that by having to rely on a rule that protects individual interests, environmental NGOs were deprived of the role that is granted to them under EU law and the Aarhus Convention. In fact, the Court opened the door for collective actions in environmental matters.[188]

The fact that the Union is a party to the Aarhus Convention has empowered the CJEU to enforce the detailed rules of the Aarhus Convention against Member States. The CJEU obliged Member States to give effect to the Aarhus Convention in a way that Member States were not obliged to do under international law and had not done under national law. The Aarhus Convention has taken an increasingly important role before the Court of Justice in preliminary reference proceedings, in direct actions, and even in one enforcement action.[189] The body of case law of the EU Courts dealing with the Aarhus Convention is rapidly growing. It touches on fundamental issues that go to the core of reserved national competence, with great economic and security

[182] Those Member States are Austria, Denmark, Finland, France, Germany, Netherlands, Norway, Sweden, and the UK.

[183] https://treaties.un.org/Pages/ViewDetails.aspx?src=IND&mtdsg_no=XXVII-13&chapter=27&clang=_en#EndDec.

[184] Case C-263/08, *Djurgården-Lilla Värtans Miljöskyddsförening* [2009] EU:C:2009:631.

[185] Council Directive (EEC) 85/337 on the assessment of the effects of certain public and private projects on the environment [1985] OJ L 175/40, amended by Parliament and Council Directive (EC) 2003/35 providing for public participation in respect of the drawing up of certain plans and programmes relating to the environment and amending with regard to public participation and access to justice [2003] OJ L 156/ 17.

[186] Case C-115/09, *Bund für Umwelt und Naturschutz Deutschland* [2011] EU:C:2011:289.

[187] Wolfgang Durner and Martin Paus, 'Die erweiterten Klagerechte der Umweltverbände in der verwaltungsgerichtlichen Praxis' (2012) 34 Natur und Recht 325.

[188] ibid.

[189] In the national context, France sticks out with five cases in 2011 concerning the Aarhus Convention.

implications.[190] Questions even arise concerning the applicability of the Aarhus rules to the national legislative process and relevance of national security concerns.[191]

The Aarhus Convention is exceptional in its direct and detailed impact on the procedural rights of individuals. At the same time, we can increasingly observe that international agreements are of a quasi-legislative nature, in that they govern in a detailed manner the legal position of individuals.[192] As a consequence, it may become a broader phenomenon that the CJEU enforces international obligations of the Member States against the Member States in a detailed manner that goes further than what they agreed to under international law. This moves power to the CJEU and hence the Union.

Furthermore, the CJEU seems to apply stricter rules to the Member States than it applies within the EU legal order. This becomes apparent in the context of standing requirements, which are by many considered to be very (too?) restrictive within the EU legal order.[193] In fact, the Aarhus Convention Compliance Committee (ACCC) has found in 2017 the Union in breach of its obligations under Article 9(3) and (4) 'with regard to access to justice by members of the public because neither the Aarhus Regulation, nor the jurisprudence of the CJEU implements or complies with the obligations arising under those paragraphs'.[194] The Commission objected to the findings of the ACCC on the EU's non-compliance and the findings and recommendations of the ACCC were changed as a result.[195] This puts into question the Court's emphasis in *Slovak Bears* on uniform application in the EU and in the national context. It also makes the strict enforcement of international obligations vis-à-vis the Member appear prima facie even more difficult to justify.

The Union has *an interest* in holding Member States to their obligations under mixed agreements. All provisions of a mixed agreement are fully binding on the Union both under international law and under EU law. In principle, state responsibility is engaged by conduct incompatible with the international obligations of the state in question, irrespective of the level of administration or government at which the conduct occurs. This is also true for federal states, which are, in principle, responsible for the exercise of power by whatever authority and at whatever level within the framework of the state,[196] including the conduct of their federate units. For the EU and the Member

[190] See Council Directive 2003/87, 2003 OJ L 275/32. See Case C-524/09, *Ville de Lyon (trading emission allowances)* [2010] EU:C:2010:822; Case C-71/10, *Office of Communications (mobile phone base)* [2011] EU:C:2011:525.

[191] Request for a preliminary ruling from the Cour constitutionnelle (Constitutional Court, Belgium) lodged on 7 July 2017—Case C-411/17, *Inter-Environnement Wallonie asbl, Bond Beter Leefmilieu Vlaanderen vzw v Conseil des ministers* (pending).

[192] Wyn Rees, 'Cooperation on Counter-Terrorism and the Internationalisation of Law Enforcement' in Marise Cremona, Joerg Monar, and Sara Poli (eds), *The External Dimension of the Union's Area of Freedom, Security and Justice* (Peter Lang 2011) 389; Marise Cremona, 'Justice and Home Affairs in a Globalised World: Ambitions and Reality in the Tale of the EU–US SWIFT Agreement' (2011) Institution for European Integration Research Working Paper 04/2011, sec 4; Christina Eckes, Elaine Fahey, and Machiko Kanetake, 'International, European and US Perspectives on the Negotiation and Adoption of the Anti-Counterfeiting Trade Agreement (ACTA)' (2013) 20 Currents ITLJ 20 (hereafter Eckes and others, 'ACTA').

[193] Case C-50/00 P, *Unión de Pequeños Agricultores v Council (UPA)* [2002] EU:C:2002:462, para 41. Whether the preliminary ruling procedure is indeed sufficient is very contested, see for example Ewa Biernat, 'The Locus Standi of Private Applicants under Article 230 (4) EC and the Principle of Judicial Protection in the European Community' (2012) Jean Monnet Working Paper 03/2012.

[194] UNECE Aarhus Convention Compliance Committee, 'Findings and recommendations of the Aarhus Convention Compliance Committee with regard to Communication ACCC/C/2008/32 (Part II) concerning compliance by the European Union' (17 March 2017) para 123.

[195] See Chapter 6 for more details, in particular Section 2.3.2.

[196] See LaGrand (*Germany v United States of America*) (*Provisional Measures*) [1999] ICJ Rep 9, para 28.

States, mixity results in a situation where often both the EU and its Member States are jointly and severally liable for all obligations under an international agreement. In short, irrespective of who has infringed the provisions of the mixed agreement, the Union could face international responsibility.[197]

The great advantage and the great danger of mixed agreement is that they allow the Union and the Member States to avoid clearly determining the division of competences. Mixed agreements do not contain a list of competences setting out which part falls within Union competence and which part does not. Declarations of competence made by the EU in the context of mixed agreements often simply refer to the dynamic division of competences under EU law[198] and are not vested with great force by the CJEU.[199] The combination of keeping a decision on the competence division pending and obliging all involved parties to work together loyally is intended to avoid discussions to determine whether any given matter falls within the competences of the Union or the Member States.

By way of conclusion, mixed agreements are the prototype of an outside-in effect of external relations. They are a legal construction to allow circumventing supposedly clear legal rules on the division of competences, when acting externally. They allow the Member States (and the Union) to politically pretend that they have the power to legally conclude the whole agreement.[200] This 'potential for ambiguity',[201] however, is not without internal consequences. Mixed agreements illustrate how international obligations can have implications for the internal power division.

7. Conclusions

Generally, the understanding is that external powers develop in parallel with internal powers. This is also the case. This chapter focused on the opposite. It highlighted how the choice of an external legal basis or a mixed agreement may trigger power shifts between the different actors. It also shed light on external pressure on the internal division of powers. The particular focus was on constellations where the exercise of external powers by the Union has an influence on the powers of the Member States (and in one exceptional case the other way around).

This chapter brought a number of examples of 'outside-in' effects to light. Under certain circumstances, minimum harmonization becomes maximum harmonization when a policy is adopted as an external action rather than an internal one. Adopting measures under the CCP, including those regulating (elements of) policies that are internally shared, makes these policies fall within the exclusive powers of the Union. Difficulties of fitting international cooperation into post-Lisbon Treaty structures may lead to a formal disappearance of CFSP components and hence allow the Union to determine the content of more intergovernmental policies through more-Unionized

[197] See also Case C-53/96, *Hermès International* [1998] EU:C:1997:539, Opinion of AG Tesauro, para 21.

[198] Case C-246/07, *Commission v Kingdom of Sweden (PFOS)* [2010] EU:C:2010:203, leaving open the voting arrangements.

[199] Case C-240/09, *Slovak Bears* (n 162).

[200] Interesting in this regard was the political debate surrounding the referendum on the Association Agreement with Ukraine. See Chapter 5 for more details.

[201] Joni Heliskoski, 'Adoption of Positions under Mixed Agreements (Implementation)' in Christophe Hillion and Panos Koutrakos (eds), *Mixed Agreements Revisited: The EU and Its Member States in the World* (Hart Publishing 2010) 138.

procedures. The case law shows that the horizontal external relations objectives in Article 21 TEU has made the objective-oriented approach of the Court in determining the correct legal basis very difficult. In the exceptional context of restrictive measures, adopted in a combination of CFSP-TFEU legal instruments, the Court by contrast accepted a far-reaching pre-determination of the TFEU component by the CFSP decision. This strengthens the control of the Member States over the imposition of restrictive measures.[202] When the Union and the Member States conclude mixed agreements, the CJEU is on the one hand in the position to ensure that individuals are actually able to enjoy the rights, which states have agreed to give them under international law. On the other, mixed agreements blur the division of competences and hence of responsibilities in a way that does not allow citizens to develop an adequate understanding of who is in charge and represents them, and allows the Court to interpret Member States' international law obligations.

The link between the choice of legal basis and legal structures of bonding may prima facie appear tenuous. The choice of legal basis is a rather technical issue that does not translate into identification by or even expectations of citizens. Yet the significance of the legal basis debate is not limited to the technical legal domain or the procedural consequences of adopting a measure based on one or the other provision. Legal bases have a broader ordering function.

Being able to identify political responsibility chains is a central building block of representative democracies. The choice of legal basis also has a signalling function. In the context of international agreements, such a signalling function may potentially be identified vis-à-vis third parties. In our context more importantly, it is relevant and necessary for the participation of individuals in a representative democracy that they are at least, in principle, in the position of being able to know who is in charge of what. This lies at the heart of representation and the ability of those represented to vote for those who represent them out of office. Predictability and transparency of who is in charge and which institutions have influence is consequently relevant to the abstract legal potential of structures of bonding, for example, those created between the European Parliament and EU citizens.[203]

The choice of the correct legal basis also offers room for justification of Union action. By explicating objectives and the legal basis to pursue them, the EU institutions should also have EU citizens in mind and their justified interest in understanding why the Union takes external actions that limit the scope of manoeuvre of Member States further than internal actions. These consequences should be part of the public debate on the desirability of Union action. Clear and predictable responsibilities ultimately limit the ability of Member States and national politicians to participate in decision-making in the EU context but avoid taking responsibility for participation in Union actions vis-à-vis individuals as national citizens.

Even potentially, citizens can only be able to experience their role within the Union decision-making process as co-authors if the participation of the different channels of representation in the Council and the European Parliament can still be traced, understood, and explained. They can only experience the exercise of power by the Union as worthy of recognition if it can be explained on the basis of pre-established and hence reasonably predictable principles and rules.

[202] This is also confirmed by Case C-130/10, *UN Sanctions* (n 19), further discussed in Chapter 5 on institutional power shifts.

[203] See also Chapter 5, Institutional Powers in External Relations.

Furthermore, not so much the choice of legal basis itself but repeated judicial challenges of the legal bases used for EU external relations, gives room for the 'us' and 'them' narrative of EU domination and competence creep. This may in particular be the case where high-profile FTAs are concerned and of course even more so when at least parts of the agreement, for example, the provisions on adjudication, are controversial. The 'us' and 'them' narratives may be more likely in cases where large numbers of Member States are litigants or at least act as interveners, as it has been the case post-Lisbon.[204]

[204] See case law in nn 19 and 20.

5

Institutional Powers in External Relations

1. Introduction

The common understanding of what happens to internal power as the result of international law-making is that it shifts towards the executive. Going beyond this common understanding, the present chapter sheds light on more subtle and hidden ways in which power moves in the context of external relations.

The inner institutional decision-making powers, that is, the level of involvement of the different EU institutions, changes when the EU concludes international agreements, as compared to when it adopts internal legislation. Power shifts towards the executive. This is the case within national legal orders, but also within the EU legal order, which is already characterized by a form of governance that is regularly labelled as 'executive federalism', in which decision-making takes place shielded from the public rather than in the form of an 'argumentative conflict of opinions with the broad public'.[1] This shift takes place as a shift towards the Council and perhaps in a less obvious way towards the European Council. However, under certain circumstances, power also shifts towards the European Parliament (EP).

The European Parliament's formal legal and also factual powers give EU citizens a voice in international relations. Parliament, with all its flaws, draws on a source of direct democratic legitimation that is independent and separate from the EU Member States. Parliament's ability to reject the conclusion of EU international agreements vests these agreements with a legitimacy that is not ultimately rooted in the Member States, but in the Union's direct link to its citizens. The core argument is that the EP's independent representation of EU citizens in external relations creates formal legal structures of bonding[2] that formally have the potential of shifting identification and making the (self-) conception as *EU* citizens part and parcel of the (self-)conception of national citizens.

Parliament's empowerment in external relations goes hand in hand with an increasing democratization of foreign relations more broadly. The need for a democratization of EU external relations is exacerbated by the trend of concluding ever-deeper and more comprehensive free trade agreements with regulatory content, containing institutional structures that allow further delegated exercise of regulatory powers by semi-autonomous bodies, as well as international adjudication. This is the background that facilitates and will continue to facilitate the use of Parliament's formal powers in practice and increase their factual relevance.

Article 13(2) TEU is interpreted by the Court of Justice of the European Union (CJEU) to reflect the principle of institutional balance, which constitutes a characteristic of the institutional structure of the European Union and requires that each of the institutions must exercise its powers with due regard for the powers of the other

[1] Jürgen Habermas, *The Crisis of the European Union: A Response* (Polity Press 2012) 6.
[2] See Chapter 1 for a conceptualization of structures of bonding.

EU Powers Under External Pressure: How the EU's External Actions Alter its Internal Structures.
Christina Eckes © Christina Eckes 2019. Published 2019 by Oxford University Press.

institutions.[3] Any power shifts in the context of external relations must be identified by reference to the internal institutional balance established by the Treaties,[4] the case law of the CJEU, and inter-institutional practices.

This chapter is structured as follows. Section 2 sets out the formal legal powers of the EU institutions in external relations since the entry into force of the Lisbon Treaty. It briefly introduces the executive dominance (Section 2.1), as the necessary background for focusing on the role of Parliament in the conclusion of international agreements (Section 2.2). Finally, the Common Foreign and Security Policy (CFSP) is outlined as a particular case of external relations (Section 2.3). Section 3 turns to the consequences of these power changes in practice. It sets out several occasions on which Parliament refused to give consent to prominent international agreements (Section 3.1), discusses the influence of Parliament after these visible acts of contestation (Section 3.2), concentrates on Parliament's external visibility (Section 3.3), and finishes by discussing the particularities of CFSP agreements (Section 3.4). It highlights how the practice of external relations strengthened the position of Parliament, as compared to a prima facie reading of the Treaties. Section 4 focuses in on the specific issue of facultative mixity, that is, where mixed agreements are concluded as a political choice rather than a legal necessity. It discusses how facultative mixity affects the institutional roles and powers of the different actors, as well as how it hampers attributing responsibility. Facultative mixity stands in a way of allowing citizens to be appropriately able to understand how they are represented in the decision-making process. Section 5 evaluates the role and powers of Parliament. It conceptualizes representation as structures of bonding (Section 5.1), explains the symbolic function of parliamentary representation (Section 5.2), reflects on the EP's ability to represent as compared to national parliaments (Section 5.3) and engages with the implications of the role and powers of the EP (Section 5.4). Section 6 concludes and places the findings in the context of conceptual considerations on the effectiveness of EU law, structures of bonding, and their potential consequences for the justifiability of EU action.

2. Shifting Powers Within a Setting of Executive Dominance and Institutionalized Diffusion

Any inter-institutional power struggle within the European Union, which reveals a direct dispute about the division of power between the institutions, can only be fully understood in the context of the division of powers between the Union and the Member States. Member States and their interests are formally represented in the Council and the European Council, while the Commission and Parliament are in different ways formally more independent and one step further away from the control of the Member States. The European Council and the Council act as *EU institutions*. However, because they are comparatively more controlled by the Member States than the Commission and Parliament, it is still correct to interpret any power shift from the Commission or Parliament to the European Council or the Council also as a power

[3] See similar formulations in a number of post-Lisbon judgments: Case C-73/14, *Council v Commission (ITLOS)* [2015] EU:C:2015:663, para 61; Case C-425/13, *Commission v Council (ETS)* [2015] EU:C:2015:483, para 69; Case C-660/13, *Council v Commission (Memorandum of Understanding* [2016] EU:C:2016:616, para 32.

[4] See in particular Title III TEU setting out the primary roles and tasks of the institutions. Consolidated Version Treaty on European Union [2016] OJ C 202/01 (hereafter TEU).

shift towards the Member States. To put it differently, the European Council represents a Union of States, while the European Parliament represents a Union of citizens. Both structures can be traced back to the individuals as citizens of their states and citizens of the Union.[5] This chapter focuses on inter-institutional power shifts in this light.

2.1 External relations as the domain of the executive

The European Council and the Council are the two greatest institutional concentrations of *national* executive powers within the Union.[6] The European Council cannot adopt secondary legislation[7] and its decisions do not generally have legally binding force. Yet, its decisions give direction to the political and legislative course of the EU. References are made to its conclusions in recitals of secondary legislation.[8] They are tools for a persuasive interpretation of secondary legislation.[9] The Lisbon Treaty has strengthened the European Council in several ways.[10] It benefits from a strong position across all policy fields; yet, its influence is particularly apparent in the context of external relations. It determines the general guidelines in the area of CFSP and the Common Security and Defence Policy (CSDP)[11] and has formally become the strategic driver behind *all external policy fields*.[12] The European Council, with its President, is further an executive power largely unfettered by parliamentary control.[13]

Along with the European Council, the Council is a platform where national interests are exchanged and brought to a compromise by representatives of the executives of the Member States. The Council remains a very powerful institution in external relations. CFSP may be the clearest example but also, in the context of concluding EU agreements, the Council authorizes the opening of negotiations, adopts negotiating directives, authorizes the signing, and concludes the agreements, acting, subject to exceptions, by qualified majority.[14]

International agreements rank between primary and secondary law. This means, in principle, that they cannot be reviewed in the light of secondary law and that secondary law is interpreted in line with international agreements. Exceptions could be argued, for example, where secondary law gives specific expression to a general principle of EU law.[15] This means further, in principle, that the executive could, subject

[5] Jürgen Habermas, *Zur Verfassung Europas—Ein Essay* (Suhrkamp 2011), 66–70 (hereafter: Habermas, *Zur Verfassung Europas*). See also Christian Callies, *Die neue Europäische Union nach dem Vertrag von Lissabon* (Mohr Siebeck 2010), 71. See Chapter 1 for more details on this point.

[6] Deirdre Curtin, 'Challenging Executive Dominance in European Democracy' (2014) 77 ML Rev 1. See also Deirdre Curtin, *Executive Power of the European Union: Law, Practices, and the Living Constitution* (OUP 2009).

[7] Art 15(1) TEU.

[8] eg Recital 16 of Parliament and Council Regulation (EC) 1905/2006 establishing a financing instrument for development cooperation [2006] OJ L 378/41, providing for implementation of thematic programmes including migration.

[9] eg Community Charter of Fundamental Social Rights of Workers, adopted at the European Council meeting held in Strasbourg on 9 December 1989; Case C-222/14, *Konstantinos Maïstrellis v Ypourgos Dikaiosynis, Diafaneias kai Anthropinon Dikaiomaton* [2015] EU:C:2015:473; The Court and its Advocate Generals referred to the European Council in 122 cases in the 5 years since the entry into force of the Lisbon Treaty; 112 times in all the years before (1975–2009).

[10] It is now uncontroversial that the European Council is an institution of the Union (art 13 TEU), meeting at least twice in six months (art 15(3) TEU)—in practice much more often. See also the role of its President: art 15(5) TEU.

[11] Art 26(2) TEU. [12] Art 22 TEU. [13] Arts 15 and 22 TEU; art 15(6) TEU.

[14] Consolidated Version of the Treaty on the Functioning of the European Union [2008] OJ C115/47 (hereafter TFEU), art 218.

[15] See Case C-555/07, *Seda Kücükdeveci v Swedex GmbH & Co. KG* [2010] EU:C:2010:21.

to principles of coherence and sincere cooperation, conclude international agreements even if they are contrary to secondary law adopted by the European Parliament and the Council acting as co-legislators on a proposal of the Commission. To put it more crudely, there is room not only for the Member States but also for the Council to change the level playing field by going outside and having the Commission negotiate different rules with a third country.[16]

The Commission, while arguably holding diffused executive, legislative, and also quasi-judicial powers,[17] is the purest form of *supranational* EU executive power. It counterbalances the intergovernmental executive power of the Council. It, for example, represents the Union within the fields of TFEU powers (Article 17(1) TEU). It is subject to the political control of the European Parliament when exercising its external relations powers, including in areas that fall under CFSP. The inter-institutional exchanges of Parliament and the Commission on the Commission's Work Programme tools and the discharge procedure further allow a considerable level of influence. The next subsection demonstrates that the powers of Parliament have increased tremendously and the hypothetical scope for bypassing internal institutional procedures and secondary law by turning to international law has, as a consequence, shrunk. Parliament has, post-Lisbon, the right to consent to the conclusion of most international agreements, for example, in all areas where it would have been involved as a co-legislator under the ordinary legislative procedure. As a consequence, it can veto the conclusion of these agreements.

The way the institutions interpret the division of powers is regularly challenged before the CJEU. Inter-institutional challenges usually aim to protect institutional prerogatives.[18] Intergovernmentalism within the European Union is always not only a power shift towards the Member States but often also a shift away from Parliament and hence towards executive power within the EU. The Court has a strong role in protecting the institutional balance. One of the post-Lisbon Grand Chamber rulings on the power division in external relations, in which the Council was supported by 12 Member States, dealt with the permissibility of a power shift in practice towards the Member States. It concerned the challenge of a Council decision adopted by the Council and the Member States jointly on the conclusion and provisional application of an international agreement (*Air Transport Agreement*).[19] The Commission, supported by Parliament, sought annulment of the Council decision on grounds that the Council had illegally derogated from the procedural requirements of the European Treaties (e.g. majority voting) by taking the contested decision jointly with the Member States. The CJEU ruled that the participation of the Member States was indeed illegal because it resulted in circumventing the qualified majority voting requirement in Article 218(8) TFEU. Member States do not have competence to take a decision on the signing and the provisional application of the international agreement. The joint decision convoluted decisions of the Council with decisions of the representatives of the Member States in the eyes of the Court.[20] Additionally, several organizational principles of EU law govern the exercise of Union powers, in particular in external relations: the

[16] For the Member States: For the Council see the discussion of the PNR agreement below.

[17] The Commission has, for example, the legislative powers to initiate legislation (art 17(2) TEU) and to exercise delegated legislative powers (art 290 TFEU). It exercises quasi-judicial powers under art 258 TFEU.

[18] See Chapter 4 on the choice of legal basis.

[19] Case C-28/12, *Commission v Council* [2015] EU:C:2015:282, concerning the Air Transport Agreement between the US, the EU, Norway, and Iceland.

[20] ibid, see paras 44–57; Case C-377/12, *Commission v Council* [2014] EU:C:2014:1903.

principle of conferral, the principle of institutional balance, and the principle of sincere cooperation.[21] They may impose different and far-reaching obligations on the institutions.[22] Yet, the CJEU emphasizes in its settled case law that these principles (of course!) cannot change Treaty powers. In particular, 'sincere cooperation [...] is exercised within the limits of the powers conferred by the Treaties on each institution'.[23]

2.2 Counterbalancing the executive: Parliament's increased role in external relations

Foreign relations have undergone a general process of democratization.[24] International trade agreements have been subject to a tremendous intra-parliamentary and extra-parliamentary debate.[25] Within the European Union, these democratization and politicization dynamics have both triggered formal Treaty change and been driven by formal Treaty change.

Three different forms of linking decisions to citizens can be distinguished: first, acceptance of a law by the fact that it is not changed. This argument is often made in favour of Member States' acceptance of the case law of the CJEU: they could have—if reaching consensus between national governments and majority ratification by all national parliaments, most likely including referendums in several Member States—changed the Treaty to overrule the Court. If this argument stands at all, this is a very weak form of democratic legitimacy. The second form of democratic support for a decision is consent—an affirmative decision, a thumbs-up or -down affair, with binary choices for the decision-maker. This is the formal power of the European Parliament when the Union concludes international agreements. The third and strongest form is authorship. This is the actual writing of the law, in an affirmative, constructive, and proceduralized manner that gives influence over every detail.

This section argues that the European Parliament has not only been vested with the significant formal powers to convey the second form of democratic legitimacy (consent). It has also been adept at exercising these powers, for example by vetoing controversial international agreements and bringing challenges before the CJEU to confirm a favourable reading of its formal information rights in the negotiation of international agreements. In practice, Parliament, while not being involved in any proceduralized manner, has been able to exercise its powers over the content of EU international agreements affirmatively and constructively.

[21] All expressed in art 13(2) TEU. See Chapter 2 for an argument that sincere cooperation is particularly stringently applied in external relations and Chapter 3 for an argument that the principle of coherence plays a particular role in external relations.

[22] Case C-660/13, *Council v Commission* [2016] EU:C:2016:616, para 20.

[23] Case C-48/14, *Parliament v Council* [2015] EU:C:2015:91.

[24] Pieter Jan Kuijper, 'The Case Law of the Court of Justice of the EU and the Allocation of External Relations Powers. Whither the Traditional Role of the Executive in EU Foreign Relations?' in Marise Cremona and Anne Thies (eds), *The European Court of Justice and External Relations: Constitutional Challenges* (Hart Publishing 2014) 95ff.

[25] Gabriel Siles-Brügge and Ferdi de Ville, *TTIP. Wie das Handelsabkommen den Welthandel verändert und die Politik entmachtet* (Transcript Verlag 2016); Niels Gheyle and Ferdi de Ville, 'How Much Is Enough? Explaining the Continuous Transparency Conflict in TTIP' (2017) 5 Politics and Governance.

2.2.1 *Formal Treaty powers*

The greatest formal increase of power by the European Parliament is its increased role in the general procedure for the conclusion of international agreements in Article 218 TFEU. While the Council may remain the most powerful institution in the context of the conclusion of international agreements, Parliament, benefiting from a direct legitimacy that can be linked back to EU citizens rather than the Council or national parliaments, has become an actor that cannot be ignored. It is important to distinguish between the initiation and negotiation stage on the one hand and the signing and conclusion stage on the other. Parliament is not formally involved in the negotiations but has the right to be informed during all stages of the procedure[26] and, as we will see, has been able to assert this right. At the conclusion stage, it can be involved in two ways: consultation or consent. The latter is required for policy fields falling under the ordinary legislative procedure,[27] which is applicable in the vast majority of cases.

Parliament furthermore increased its formal powers in a range of more specific policy areas. From not even being mentioned in the provisions on trade in the founding EEC Treaty (1957), the powers of the European Parliament have gone through a tremendous development. Until the entry into force of the Lisbon Treaty, Parliament's powers to participate in the conclusion of international agreements were very limited. Since Lisbon, this has changed for all policy fields governed by the ordinary legislative procedure. About eighty policy fields, including the Area of Freedom, Security and Justice (AFSJ) and internal market issues, are now subject to the ordinary legislative procedure. By comparison, before Lisbon only about forty policy fields required the old co-decision procedure (post-Lisbon renamed ordinary legislative procedure). The President of the European Parliament self-confidently expressed: 'the European Parliament is a body through which you can be heard as you elect your representatives to defend your key interests. And we want to listen to you'.[28]

The common commercial policy (CCP) is a pertinent example of the strengthened position of Parliament. Post-Lisbon, the CCP requires the ordinary legislative procedure (Article 207(2) TFEU) for the definition of the framework of its implementation. Pre-Lisbon, under ex-Article 133 EC and its predecessors, Parliament was excluded from participating in the shaping of this core EU external relations policy, although the Council regularly consulted Parliament on a voluntary basis.[29] This meant that the chosen external legal basis for trade (CCP) often also had direct consequences for the involvement of Parliament. The internal legal basis for internal market measures (ex-Article 95 EC (now-Article 114 TFEU)) by contrast gave Parliament co-decision rights. Hence pre-Lisbon, the involvement of non-EU actors, that is, third countries, required a legal basis for trade and excluded Parliament. Similarly relevant was the choice for the residual competence in ex-Article 308 EC (now-Article 352 TFEU), which only gave Parliament an advisory role. This has also changed under the Lisbon Treaty. This increase in Parliament's powers under the CCP is particularly relevant because of the wide field of policies that nowadays falls under the CCP.[30] While traditionally the

[26] Art 218(10) TFEU.

[27] Art 218(6)(a) TFEU (explaining that art 218(6)(a)(v) includes agreements that fall within the policy fields in which the ordinary legislative procedure applies).

[28] Preface by Martin Schulz, at the time the President of the EP, in 'The European Parliament: The Citizen's Voice in the EU' (Publications office of the EU, 2015) http://www.europarl.europa.eu/pdf/divers/QA0214324EN1.pdf.

[29] Stated in the Preamble of numerous pre-Lisbon CCP legal acts.

[30] See Chapter 4 on the consequences of the choice of legal basis. See also Marise Cremona, 'A Quiet Revolution: The Common Commercial Policy Six Years After the Treaty of Lisbon', SIEPS Paper

CCP focused on trade in goods, the Union has gradually also come to be in charge of regulating services and intellectual property (Treaty of Amsterdam 1999) and foreign direct investment (Lisbon Treaty 2009). The Commission argued on the basis of the latter competence that the Union should be able to conclude deep and comprehensive free trade agreements, such as EU–Canada Comprehensive Economic and Trade Agreement (CETA) as EU-only agreements.[31]

2.2.2 Information is power: formal rules

The rationale of strengthening Parliament's role under Article 218 TFEU is to increase the democratic control over international agreements. Democratic control can only be ensured if Parliament is involved not only at the conclusion stage (consultation or consent), but also at the negotiation stage. Advocate General Bot seemed to make a similar point, when he argued that Parliament's right to be informed under Article 218(10) TFEU applies during all stages of the procedure and across all policies, but is particularly extensive where Parliament's consent is required for the conclusion of the agreement under Article 218(6) TFEU.[32] If Parliament's involvement is limited to the final conclusion stage, it is not in the position to exercise one of its core parliamentary tasks of deliberating in an informed manner in order to search for a majority and offer a window for public involvement. It simply cannot properly deliberate and participate in a public discourse if it is not well informed. Furthermore, if it does not receive the relevant information on time during the negotiations, it loses the opportunity to informally influence the negotiations. This is also acknowledged in the Framework Agreement on Relations between the EP and the Commission of October 2010, which strengthens Parliament's role in the negotiation of international agreements beyond the strict wording of the Treaty.[33] The Framework Agreement, for example, adds that 'Parliament shall be immediately and fully informed at all stages of the negotiation and conclusion of international agreements, *including the definition of negotiating directives*. The Commission shall act in a manner to *give full effect* to its obligations pursuant to Article 218 TFEU, while respecting each institution's role in accordance with Article 13(2) TEU'.[34] It further specifies that the information 'shall be provided to Parliament *in sufficient time for it to be able to express its point of view if appropriate, and for the Commission to be able to take Parliament's views as far as possible into account*'.[35]

More specific rules on international agreements are included in Annex III to the Framework Agreement, setting out that '[t]he Commission shall inform Parliament about its intention to propose the start of negotiations *at the same time* as it informs the Council;' the Commission 'shall at the same time present [draft negotiating directives] to Parliament' as to the Council; '[t]he Commission shall take due account of Parliament's comments throughout the negotiations'; and it 'shall keep Parliament *regularly* and promptly informed about the conduct of negotiations until the agreement

2017:2 http://www.sieps.se/en/publications/2017/a-quiet-revolution-the-common-commercial-policy-six-years-after-the-treaty-of-lisbon-20172/.

[31] The Court gave a more nuanced reply in Opinion 2/15 (EU–Singapore Free Trade Agreement) [2016] EU:C:2017:376. See Chapter 4.

[32] Case C-658/11, *Parliament v Council* [2014] EU:C:2014:41, Opinion of A-G Bot, paras 142–44.

[33] Institutional Agreements, Framework Agreement on relations between the European Parliament and the Commission [2010] OJ L 304/47, Annex 11 (hereafter Framework Agreement between Parliament and Commission).

[34] ibid, at III (ii)(23) (emphasis added).

[35] ibid, at III (ii)(24) (emphasis added).

is initialled, and *explain* whether and how Parliament's comments were incorporated in the texts under negotiation and if not why'. Furthermore, for international agreements the conclusion of which:

> requires Parliament's consent, the Commission shall provide to Parliament during the negotiation process *all relevant information that it also provides to the Council* [...]. This shall include draft amendments to adopted negotiating directives, draft negotiating texts, agreed articles, the agreed date for initialling the agreement, and the text of the agreement to be initialled. The Commission shall also transmit to Parliament, as it does to the Council [...], *any relevant documents received from third parties*, subject to the originator's consent.[36]

The originator's consent rule (ORCON), which makes any further sharing of information, including with other EU institutions, dependent on the consent of the originator, becomes particularly relevant in a negotiation context, where the input on international law-making originates outside the EU.[37]

The detail of the rules aiming to ensure that Parliament can make use of its information rights in practice is conspicuous. In particular, the requirements to submit information in a timely manner and to justify why the EP's comments were not incorporated have great practical relevance. The obligation of justification is remarkable when compared to national systems. These procedural requirements offer structures for justification and aim to give room for a substantive exchange of arguments. Exclusion of effective parliamentary intervention has happened when the executive acts under high time pressure in external relations and when representatives of the Member States act within and alongside the European legal order, that is, within the Council of the European Union, within the European Council, or in meetings in the margins of official meetings of the EU institutions. The strength of the executive remains its ability to act quickly. This strength is at times imperative but can also be deployed to escape parliamentary influence. The requirement to *explain why* the EP's comments were not *incorporated* at least aims to explicate the reasons for not including Parliament's views. This automatically introduces a reasonableness check on the views that the other institutions can take.

As Advocate General Kokott emphasized, the EP's right to be immediately and fully informed on all stages of the procedure is a 'reflection of the fundamental democratic principle applying to any decision-making process at EU level', an element of 'democratic control', and 'has inherent value' that goes beyond the limited rights of being consulted and giving consent.[38] This particular relevance of Parliament's involvement for the 'fundamental democratic principle that the people should take part in the exercise of power through the intermediary of a representative assembly' has been acknowledged by the Court previously, expressly in the context of internal legislative procedures.[39] Institutional balance and sincere

[36] ibid (emphases added).

[37] The agreement between Council and Parliament also confirms ORCON as the basic principle of handling classified information. art 3(4) of the Interinstitutional Agreement between the European Parliament and the Council concerning the forwarding to and handling by the European Parliament of classified information held by the Council on matters other than those in the area of the common foreign and security policy [2013] OJ C 353 E/159 (annex to Parliament Decision 2012/2069): 'the Council may grant the European Parliament access to classified information which originates in other Union institutions, bodies, offices or agencies, or in Member States, third States or international organisations only with the prior written consent of the originator'. See also Maarten Hillebrandt, *Living Transparency* (PhD thesis University of Amsterdam, defended on 10 March 2017), Chapter 9.

[38] Case C-263/14, *Parliament v Council (Pirates Agreement II (Tanzania))* [2015] EU:C:2015:729, Opinion of AG Kokott.

[39] Case C-65/93 *European Parliament v Council* [1995] EU:C:1995:91, para 21.

cooperation[40] further require the other institutions to share information actively rather than to leave the initiative of requesting information to Parliament.

2.2.3 Parliament's dual role

Parliaments serve a particular role at the intersection of *institutional* politics and *extra-institutional* politics. The European Parliament's institutional role is to take part in the formal exercise of power by the EU institutions jointly and the power struggles between the institutions, as well as between the EU and the Member States. Parliament's extra-institutional role as a representative but through this process of representation also an interpreter of (the interests and wishes of) EU citizens[41] becomes apparent, among others, in the way in which it is, like other parliaments, the target of lobbying by particular constituencies, as well as by public and private interest groups.

The lasting focus on increasing Parliament's powers in all Treaty amendments is a direct consequence of 'the ideological concern for democratic legitimacy'.[42] It was meant as a response to the democratic deficit concerns, including of national governments. Indeed, 'the idea shared among national public opinions that there is a democratic deficit, which opens a window of opportunity for reform (without inevitably strengthening the EP); the predisposition of national leaders to "parliamentarize" the EU because they are familiar with the parliamentarist matrix, [. . .]; and the absence of any other credible scenario to address the democratic deficit'.[43] It is ultimately meant to enhance the Union's link with its citizens through an actor that combines an institutional with an extra-institutional role and so allows EU citizens to be and feel directly represented in the institutional structures of the Union.

2.3 CFSP as a policy apart

CFSP formally remains an institutional world apart, in which the powers of the European Parliament, the Commission and the Court are strictly limited. 'High politics' conducted by the High Representative and the European External Action Service (EEAS) under CFSP remain protected from parliamentary control. Even the very establishment of the EEAS, giving the mentioning of this new 'service' in the Treaties form and function, took place by Council decision, with the Parliament only being consulted.[44] However, Parliament wielded considerable power on the substance of the Council Decision by making it dependent on agreement on the flanking budget and staff regulations.[45] The Commission had to give consent to the EEAS decision, but in general its role under CFSP is formally limited. In practice, it remains well informed.

[40] See ibid, where the Court also developed the link between Parliament's consultation rights and sincere cooperation.

[41] Johan Olsen, *Organized Democracy: Political Institutions in a Welfare State—The Case of Norway* (Universitetsforlaget 1983).

[42] Mark Pollack, 'Delegation, Agency and Agenda Setting in the European Community' (1997) 51 International Organizations 99, 106–07.

[43] Olivier Costa and Nathalie Brack, 'The Role of the European Parliament in Europe's Integration and Parliamentarization Process' in Oliver Costa, Stelios Stavridis, and Clarissa Dri (eds), *The Parliamentary Dimension(s) of Regionalization and Globalization* (Palgrave 2013) 45–46.

[44] Art 27(3) TEU. Council Decision (EU) 2010/427 establishing the organization and functioning of the European External Action Service [2010] OJ L 201/30.

[45] Leendert Erkelens and Steven Blockmans, 'Setting Up the European External Action Service: An Act of Institutional Balance', 8 EU Const (2012), 246–79.

The CJEU's role in external relations is formally limited in the area of CFSP. This is particularly relevant because in the context of TFEU policies, the CJEU's case law has been instrumental for the establishment of the Union as an external actor. The Treaties give the CJEU, with regard to 'envisaged' international agreements, the power to find these agreements incompatible with the Treaties *before* they become legally binding (Article 218(11) TFEU). This procedure vests the CJEU with the power of considering, *in abstracto* and without being limited by the facts of any specific case, the legality of increasingly broad agreements. Indeed, the new generation of free trade agreements concluded by the Union are unprecedented in terms of regulatory depth and width. This puts the Court in a particularly powerful position to protect and develop the meaning of the institutional balance within the meaning of the Treaties.

In the context of the present chapter, it is important to explicate that each and every decision of the CJEU that relates to the exercise of the Union's external relations or the relation of international and EU law has immediate consequences for the division of powers between the institutions and often directly or in any event indirectly for the division of powers between the EU and its Member States. Because of its limited jurisdiction over CFSP, the Court is less capable to protect not only fundamental rights but also the Union's position as an autonomous actor in this field.

3. Affirming Powers in Practice: The European Parliament

The Treaty of Lisbon has empowered the European Parliament as an institutional actor in EU external relations. Yet having powers and exercising them are a very different matter. When an institution has been formally constitutionally empowered it must still conquer this new space in reality, it must still develop internal practices and procedures to be in the position to fill this space. Additionally, its different members and parts must come together in an understanding of their ability, rights, and purpose to develop political significance.

Parliament has successfully affirmed its powers and prerogatives through practices that vest the increased formal powers under the European Treaties with meaning and establish an actual influence of Parliament. It has interpreted its rights broadly and given them substance by taking procedural and judicial action and mobilizing particular political positions. The European Parliament may have developed into the most powerful parliament in Europe in the conclusion of international agreements and external relations more broadly.[46] This section will concentrate on the role of the European Parliament in the conclusion of international agreements as an illustrative example of the potential of structures of bonding.

3.1 Refusal of consent

Since the entry into force of the Lisbon Treaty, Parliament has refused to give its necessary consent under Article 218(6) TFEU to two high-profile agreements: The Terrorist Finance Tracking Programme (TFTP) agreement with the US and the multilateral Anti-Counterfeiting Trade Agreement (ACTA). This has attracted much attention,

[46] Guri Rosén, 'The Impact of Norms on Political Decision-Making: How to Account for the European Parliament's Empowerment in EU External Trade Policy' (2016) 24 JEPP 1450.

both in the media and in academic circles.[47] Most voices have criticized the secretive negotiations and the exclusion of Parliament, as well as the potential difficulties that the Union might face as an international actor if, at the last minute, it cannot legally conclude a negotiated agreement. These are valid criticisms. Yet in the particular context of this book, other institutional and constitutional dynamics and effects are more relevant.

3.1.1 TFTP agreement

Shortly after the Lisbon Treaty entered into force, Parliament showed its newly established teeth by vetoing the first EU–US TFTP agreement.[48] The agreement falls within an area where, pre-Lisbon, Parliament did not have any say in the process cumulating in the conclusion of international agreements in the former third pillar.[49] Since Lisbon, the policies formerly falling within the third pillar are part of the Union's AFSJ. The greatest share of AFSJ provisions apply the ordinary legislative procedure. This means, as explained, that Parliament has the right to be informed during all stages of the negotiations and needs to consent to the conclusion of international agreements. The EU–US TFTP I agreement had been signed on the eve of the entry into force of the Lisbon Treaty. It provided for the transfer of large volumes of transaction information from the Society for Worldwide Interbank Financial Telecommunication (SWIFT) to the US for the purpose of counter-terrorist surveillance.[50] This naturally raised a multitude of data protection concerns. In the course of the negotiations of the TFTP I agreement, Parliament had been completely excluded from the information flow.[51] Indeed about two and a half months before the entry into force of the Lisbon Treaty, Parliament had adopted a resolution setting out minimum conditions the agreement should satisfy, stating that it had to do so in abstract because it had been provided with so little information that it could not engage with the existing draft.[52] Three months after the entry into force of the Lisbon Treaty (the agreement had already provisionally entered into force),[53]

[47] eg Valentina Pop, 'Sighs of Relief as EU Parliament Approves "Swift" Deal' (*euobserver*, 8 July 2010) http://euobserver.com/foreign/30447; Benjamin Fox, 'Acta in Tatters After MEPs Wield Veto' (*euobserver*, 4 July 2012) http://euobserver.com/political/116866; Deirdre Curtin, 'Official Secrets and the Negotiation of International Agreements: Is the EU Executive Unbound?' (2013) 50 CML Rev 423; Marieke de Goede, 'The SWIFT Affair and the Global Politics of European Security' (2012) 50 JCMS 214.

[48] Agreement between the European Union and the United States of America on the processing and transfer of Financial Messaging Data from the European Union to the United States for purposes of the Terrorist Finance Tracking Program [2010] OJ L 8/11.

[49] Ex-arts 24 and 38 TEU. First Justice and Home Affairs and then Police and Judicial Co-operation in Criminal Matters.

[50] SWIFT is an inter-service banking company, which is used in roughly 80 per cent of all international transactions. See also Gloria Fuster, Paul De Hert, and Serge Gutwirth, 'SWIFT and the Vulnerability of Transatlantic Data Transfers' (2008) 22 I Rev LCT 191.

[51] Christian Kaunert, Sarah Leonard, and Alex MacKenzie, 'The Social Construction of an EU Interest in Counter-Terrorism: US Influence and Internal Struggles in the Cases of PNR and SWIFT' (2012) 21 ES 474, 488.

[52] Parliament Resolution on the envisaged international agreement to make available to the United States Treasury Department financial payment messaging data to prevent and combat terrorism and terrorist financing (P7_TA(2009)0016, 17 September 2009).

[53] The agreement provisionally entered into force on 1 February 2010.

Parliament then refused to consent, by a vote of 378 to 196 (with 31 abstentions).[54]

Although the refusal was ostensibly aimed to protect the data protection rights of EU citizens, it was also widely seen as a political move.[55] Former President of the EP Buzek explained: 'The Lisbon Treaty [...] has given MEPs a right of veto over international agreements [...]. The same governments must accept that the EP will use this power in a way which reflects its own assessment of the concerns of Europe's citizens'.[56] There are two elements to President Buzek's statement. First, he specifically calls on the Member States' governments to accept the Parliament's new role, rather than on the Council and the Commission, which were in practice the actors that had not taken sufficient note of Parliament's new powers concerning international negotiations. An opinion of the Parliament's legal service stated, for example, that the Council had made it 'impossible for practical reasons for Parliament to react' by delaying the formal submission of the agreement to Parliament due to 'translation problems'.[57] Parliament was left with only one week to draft a response.[58] Second, and in the present context most importantly, President Buzek emphasized that Parliament will act according to *its own assessment* and in order to reflect *the concerns of Europe's citizens*. This demonstrates Parliament's *self-conception* as an independent voice of EU citizens within the EU structures and its intention to make this claim explicit with the intention to have this claim recognized by EU citizens.

Despite this first refusal to consent, Parliament then issued a recommendation for a negotiation mandate to the Council for the development of a long-term TFTP agreement and thus recognized the importance of such an agreement. It also submitted recommendations regarding the content of the TFTP,[59] and in May 2010 the Council authorized the Commission to (re-)start the negotiations on a second TFTP agreement, which was swiftly signed as a slightly amended version of the original TFTP agreement.[60] Changes introduced after Parliament voted it down include, for example, vetting by Europol.[61] After taking into account the considerations of the various

[54] European Parliament, 'SWIFT: European Parliament votes down agreement with the US' (Press release, 11 February 2010) http://www.europarl.europa.eu/sides/getDoc.do?pubRef=-//EP//TEXT+IM-PRESS+20100209IPR68674+0+DOC+XML+V0//EN.

[55] eg Jörg Monar, 'The Rejection of the EU–US SWIFT Agreement by the European Parliament: A Historic Vote and Its Implications' (2010) 15 EFA Rev 143 (hereafter: Monar, 'The Rejection of the EU–US SWIFT Agreement').

[56] European Parliament, 'EP President Jerzy Buzek on the rejection of the SWIFT interim agreement by the European Parliament' (Press release, 11 February 2010).

[57] European Parliament, 'Legal Opinion of the Legal Service of the EP' (D(2010)5811, 2 February 2010) http://www.statewatch.org/news/2010/feb/ep-libe-cttee-opinion-legal-service-eu-usa-swift.pdf. Compare with the above-discussed Framework Agreement on relations between the EP and the Commission of October 2010.

[58] This failure to involve Parliament is also the background to a legal action brought against the refusal to grant access to documents relevant to the negotiation of the TFTP I agreement: Case T-529/09, *Sophie in 't Veld v Council* [2012] EU:T:2012:215 (hereafter Case T-529/09, *Sophie in 't Veld I*).

[59] Parliament Resolution on the Recommendation from the Commission to the Council to authorize the opening of negotiations for an agreement between the EU and the USA to make available to the US Treasury Department financial messaging data to prevent and combat terrorism and terrorist financing (P7_TA(2010)0143, 5 May 2010).

[60] Agreement between European Union and the United States of America on the processing and transfer of Financial Messaging Data from the European Union to the United States for purposes of the Terrorist Finance Tracking Program [2010] OJ L 195/5, signed on 28 June 2010.

[61] Oversight by Europol was accepted as a compromise. The EP originally wanted control by a public judicial body. See Sergio Carrera, Nicholas Hernanz, and Joanna Parkin, 'The "Lisbonisation" of the European Parliament assessing progress, shortcomings and challenges for democratic accountability in the area of freedom, security and justice' (*CEPS*, 9 September 2013) 18 (hereafter: Carrera and others, 'Lisbonisation of the European Parliament').

committee opinions, Parliament gave its consent to an amended TFTP II agreement on 8 July 2010,[62] with the agreement entering into force shortly thereafter on 1 August 2010. Parliament's consent to an agreement that contained only very few changes seems to confirm that the original rejection was at least partially motivated by the fact that Parliament was kept out of the loop during the negotiations.

3.1.2 ACTA

A second case where Parliament refused to consent to an agreement because it was not sufficiently included in the negotiations, is the attempted conclusion of ACTA. About a year and a half after the entry into force of the Lisbon Treaty, the Commission published a proposal[63] and the Council swiftly adopted the appropriate decision to conclude ACTA.[64] As in the case of the TFTP II agreement, Parliament had to give its consent for ACTA to enter into force. Yet, even though the agreement was deemed necessary to improve the enforcement of anti-counterfeiting law internationally, the report of the parliamentary rapporteur of the Committee on International Trade advised Parliament to refuse its consent because of 'the potential threats to civil liberties'.[65] Furthermore, Parliament experienced unprecedented direct lobbying by thousands of EU citizens, in street demonstrations, emails to Members of the EP (MEPs), and calls to their offices, as well as by 2.8 million citizens worldwide, who signed a petition—all urging Parliament to reject the agreement. Public and parliamentary support for the agreement was dwindling.[66] After the mounting public controversy and rather late in the negotiations, DG Trade recognized the need to give both the public and Parliament more information. It published online a digest of all the answers that it had given to all the questions tabled by MEPs. On US Independence Day of 2012, Parliament declined to give its consent, in line with the recommendation made by its rapporteur.[67] According to Parliament's legislative resolution, the explicit reasons for the rejection included the failure of the Council and the Commission to inform Parliament adequately and on time. Hence, beside the issues concerning the controversial substantive content

[62] Monar, 'The Rejection of the EU–US SWIFT Agreement' (n 55).

[63] European Commission, 'Proposal for a Council decision on the conclusion of the Anti-Counterfeiting Trade Agreement between the European Union and its Member States, Australia, Canada, Japan, the Republic of Korea, the United Mexican States, the Kingdom of Morocco, New Zealand, the Republic of Singapore, the Swiss Confederation and the United States of America' COM (2011) 380 final.

[64] Council Decision (EU) 12195/2011 on the conclusion of the Anti-Counterfeiting Trade Agreement between the European Union and its Member States, Australia, Canada, Japan, the Republic of Korea, the United Mexican States, the Kingdom of Morocco, New Zealand, the Republic of Singapore, the Swiss Confederation, and the United States of America (2011/0167 (NLE), 23 August 2011).

[65] Parliament Recommendation on the draft Council decision on the conclusion of the ACTA Agreement (A7-0204/20126, 22 June 2012) http://www.europarl.europa.eu/sides/getDoc.do?pubRef=-//EP//NONSGML+REPORT+A7-2012-0204+0+DOC+PDF+V0//EN.

[66] Max Rowlands, 'Support for ACTA Wanes Following Mass Protests' (2011) 21 Statewatch J http://database.statewatch.org/print.asp?aid=31752&.

[67] Parliament Resolution on the draft Council decision on the conclusion of the Anti-Counterfeiting Trade Agreement (P7_TA(2012)0287, 4 July 2012). See also European Parliament, 'European Parliament rejects ACTA' (Press release, 4 July 2012) http://www.europarl.europa.eu/news/en/pressroom/content/20120703IPR48247/html/European-Parliament-rejects-ACTA. And, Charles Arthur, 'Acta down, but not out, as Europe votes against controversial treaty' (*The Guardian*, 4 July 2012) http://www.guardian.co.uk/technology/2012/jul/04/acta-european-parliament-votes-against/.

of ACTA,[68] one reason for the refusal to consent was again that Parliament had been denied access to a range of key documents. In particular, the negotiating mandate was not shared with Parliament.[69] The Union never concluded ACTA.

In the analysis of the EP's role in international negotiations, it is crucial to point out that the *negotiations* regarding the TFTP I agreement took place *before* the entry into force of the Lisbon Treaty, while only the conclusion took place thereafter. Hence, while being a notorious case, the TFTP I agreement is not representative for the involvement of Parliament at the negotiation stage *after* its increased powers under the Lisbon Treaty. It rather highlights the broader problem of parliamentary exclusion in international negotiations. The negotiations for ACTA took place both pre- and post-Lisbon. They demonstrate that with the entry into force of the Lisbon Treaty there was no immediate change but that Parliament had to take action to ensure that its post-Lisbon position under the Treaties resulted in a more meaningful inclusion in practice.

3.2 'Business as usual': information, influence, and inter-institutional cooperation post-Lisbon

Parliament's role in international negotiations has changed. Post-Lisbon practice seems to indicate that Parliament is involved in a more meaningful way and that the Commission informs Parliament in line with the Framework Agreement on Relations between the EP and the Commission of October 2010.[70] In other words, the EP seems in ordinary practice no longer side-lined in the conclusion of EU international agreements. While its Treaty powers remain formally focused on the final stage of actual conclusion and limited to consent in most but not all cases. Informally, Parliament has been able to exercise considerable influence on the content of post-Lisbon international agreements of the EU.

3.2.1 Institutional involvement: EU–US Personal Name Record (PNR) Agreement and new generation free trade agreements

The greater involvement of the EP is demonstrated by the fourth EU–US PNR agreement, which concerns equally controversial and rights-relevant issues, but has been negotiated under different conditions. The need for a new, fourth EU–US PNR agreement arose out of the entry into force of the Lisbon Treaty. The previous, third PNR agreement dated back to 2007 and required parliamentary approval for it to remain in force. Parliament had long-standing concerns about privacy and other civil liberties, which indeed date back to the first PNR agreement in 2004. As a consequence, it postponed its vote on the fourth PNR agreement until it had explored the options for potential arrangements on the use of PNR data that were in line with EU law and met the concerns expressed in its earlier resolutions.[71] Following this postponement, the Commission issued a recommendation to the Council for the opening of negotiations

[68] Christina Eckes, Elaine Fahey, and Machiko Kanetake, 'International, European and US Perspectives on the Negotiation and Adoption of the Anti-Counterfeiting Trade Agreement (ACTA)' (2013) 20 Currents ITLJ 20 (hereafter Eckes and others, 'ACTA').

[69] Case T-301/10, *Sophie in 't Veld II* [2013] EU:T:2013:135 (hereafter Case T-201/10, *Sophie in 't Veld II*). The same MEP, who personally challenged the secrecy surrounding the TFTP agreement, Sophie in 't Veld, challenged the refusal by the Council to give access to this mandate under the regulation on public access to documents.

[70] Framework Agreement between Parliament and Commission (n 33).

[71] See Parliament Resolution on the launch of negotiations for Passenger Name Record (PNR) agreements with the United States, Australia, and Canada (P7_TA(2010)0144, 5 May

for a new EU–US *data protection* agreement.[72] Furthermore, in September 2010, the Commission issued a communication on the global approach to transfers of PNR data to third countries[73] and Parliament responded by issuing a second resolution explaining its general position on the transfer of PNR data to third countries.[74] In this second resolution concerning the fourth PNR agreement, Parliament noted that the Commission's communication and recommendation regarding PNR reflected important elements contained in previous resolutions of the EP on the subject.[75] After reiterating its position concerning proportionality, data mining, and other PNR-related issues, Parliament addressed its own role in the forthcoming negotiations. In point 8 of the resolution, it highlighted 'the need to be fully informed on all PNR-related and relevant developments in order to be able to consider giving its consent'.[76]

The Council authorized the Commission to negotiate the new agreement on 2 December 2010.[77] About one year later, the Commission initialled the agreement on behalf of the EU[78] and the Council signed this fourth EU–US PNR agreement in December 2011.[79] Two months after the Council's approval, the EP's rapporteur for the Civil Liberties, Justice and Home Affairs (LIBE) Committee, Sophie in 't Veld,[80] submitted her recommendation to Parliament to withhold its consent to the EU–US PNR agreement.[81] She argued that the agreement did not meet the criteria set out in the two 2010 resolutions of the EP and was contrary to existing EU law.[82] In particular, the agreement infringed EU and national data protection legislation. However, the rapporteur did not voice criticism of the level of involvement of Parliament in the negotiations of the fourth EU–US PNR agreement. This may be read as an indirect confirmation that Parliament was sufficiently involved. The Committee did not follow

2010) http://www.europarl.europa.eu/sides/getDoc.do?pubRef=-//EP//TEXT+TA+P7-TA-2010-0144+0+DOC+XML+V0//EN.

72 European Commission, 'European Commission seeks high privacy standards in EU–US data protection agreement' (Press release, IP/10/609, 26 May 2010). NB: this recommendation was partly declassified on 23 July 2010, though the operative part of the recommendation is still unavailable.

73 European Commission, 'On the global approach to transfers of Passenger Name Record (PNR) data to third countries' COM (2010) 492 final.

74 Parliament Resolution on the global approach to transfers of passenger name records (PNR) data to third countries, and on the recommendations from the Commission to the Council to authorize the opening of negotiations between the European Union and Australia, Canada, and the United States (P7_TA(2010)0397, 11 November 2010) http://www.europarl.europa.eu/sides/getDoc.do?pubRef=-//EP//TEXT+TA+P7-TA-2010-0397+0+DOC+XML+V0//EN.

75 ibid, indent 7. The Parliament lists its previous resolutions on previous PNR agreements.

76 ibid.

77 See European Commission, 'New EU–US agreement on PNR improves data protection and fights crime and terrorism' (Press release, IP/11/1368, 17 November 2010).

78 ibid.

79 Council, 'Council gives green light for the new EU–US agreement on Passenger Name Records (PNR)' (Press release, 184454/11, presse 490, 13 December 2011) http://www.consilium.europa.eu/uedocs/cms_data/docs/pressdata/en/jha/126892.pdf.

80 Appointed 5 December 2011.

81 Parliament Recommendation on the draft Council decision on the conclusion of the agreement between the United States of America and the European Union on the use and transfer of Passenger Name Records (PNR) to the United States Department of Homeland Security (rapporteur Sophie in 't Veld, 17433/2011 – C7-0511/2011 – 2011/0382(NLE), 3 April 2012) (hereafter Parliament PNR Recommendation).

82 ibid. For more detailed arguments, see Gerrit Hornung and Franziska Boehm, 'Comparative Study on the 2011 draft Agreement between the Unites States of America and the European Union on the use and transfer of Passenger Name Records (PNR) to the United States Department of Homeland Security' (The Greens and European Free Alliance, 14 March 2012) http://www.statewatch.org/news/2012/mar/eu-usa-pnr-study-green-group.pdf.

the rapporteur's recommendation and suggested that Parliament give its consent.[83] Parliament approved the agreement, by a vote of 409 to 226, with 33 abstentions.[84]

Parliament also seems to have been adequately involved in the negotiations for the 2011 permanent[85] PNR agreement with Australia.[86] After a Commission recommendation to authorize the opening of negotiations, the Council quickly adopted its authorization and after equally swift negotiations, the Council signed the EU–Australia PNR agreement on 29 September 2011.[87] Following a positive recommendation by the LIBE Committee, Parliament consented on 27 October 2011.[88] With regard to the involvement of Parliament, rapporteur in 't Veld noted that cooperation between Parliament, the Commission, and the Council worked well. She stated that 'this example demonstrated that if the institutions work together, Europe is a force to be reckoned with'.[89] She saw the agreement with Australia as a chance to establish a new trend, hoping to reach better agreements also with the US and with Canada. In 2015, Parliament, following a proposal by ALDE,[90] asked the CJEU to give an opinion on the compatibility of the EU–Canada PNR agreement with EU law.[91] This resulted in the Court declaring the agreement in Opinion 1/15 incompatible with the EU Charter of Fundamental Rights and arguably establishing high privacy and data protection standards that the internal PNR legislation does not even meet.[92] The agreement, however, with its lack of purpose limitations and the absence of a link between the purpose and the counterterrorism goal, allowed the use of data for other purposes, which went beyond what is possible under the 2016 Data Protection Directive. The EU–Canada PNR agreement is hence also an example of an *earlier* international agreement upholding a lower standard of protection than the later piece of internal legislation. In the context of the EU–Canada PNR agreement, Parliament did not veto the agreement but protected non-economic interests through its reference to the Court.

While the examples so far discussed may seem particularly susceptible to raise political controversy because they deal with core civil liberties and security issues, free trade agreements (FTAs) are no longer seen as uncontroversial technical matters either. In fact, it has become trite to state that international agreements, and in particular FTAs, have become more and more regulatory and political in nature. They regulate not only trade but labour, and environmental and social conditions.[93] Under the label of deep

[83] Parliament PNR Recommendation (n 81).

[84] European Parliament, 'Parliament gives green light to air passenger data deal with US,' (Press release, 19 April 2012) http://www.europarl.europa.eu/sides/getDoc.do?type=IM-PRESS&reference=20120419IPR43404&secondRef=0&language=EN.

[85] In 2008 a provisional agreement had been signed.

[86] See also European Commission, 'on the importance of a global approach to PNR data transfers with third countries' COM (2010) 492 final.

[87] See Council, 'Signature of the EU–Australia agreement on Passenger Name Records (PNR)' (Press release, 14664/1, PRESSE 330, 29 September 2011).

[88] Parliament Resolution on the draft Council decision on the conclusion of the Agreement between the European Union and Australia on the processing and transfer of Passenger Name Record (PNR) data by air carriers to the Australian Customs and Border Protection Service (09825/2011—C7-0304/2011—2011/0126(NLE), 27 October 2011).

[89] See interview http://pr.euractiv.com/pr/eu-australia-pnr-agreement-get-green-light-91621.

[90] Alliance for Liberals and Democrats for Europe (ALDE) of which Sophie in 't Veld is a member.

[91] Opinion 1/15 (EU–Canada PNR Agreement) [2017] EU:C:2017:592.

[92] Parliament and Council Directive (EU) 2016/680 on the protection of natural persons with regard to the processing of personal data by competent authorities for the purposes of the prevention, investigation, detection or prosecution of criminal offenses or the execution of criminal penalties, and on the free movement of such data, and repealing Council Framework Decision 2008/977/JHA [2016] OJ L 119/89.

[93] See also Chapter 4 on the harmonizing effects of international agreements.

and comprehensive FTAs, the EU pursues a path of closer regulatory integration with its trade partners, which makes them much more politically salient and controversial.

International negotiations, despite the greater involvement of parliaments more generally, continue to have difficulties meeting the requirements of robust democratic legitimacy. The EP has become one of the forums where the political controversy of FTAs has played out. This is formally due to the exclusive competence of the Union for international trade (CCP). It is also facilitated by the fact that within the EP, party cohesion is relatively less strong than in national parliaments because Parliament relies heavily on committee work internally and MEPs are not usually bound to vote in accordance with their party affiliation. This allows the EP to focus more easily on matters that are controversial to the public. This has allowed it to profile itself as 'a champion of the environment, consumers, women, and other diffuse but electorally popular causes'.[94]

Parliament is an institutional forum where political ideas challenging the market-driven focus that is prevalent in the politics of the European institutions could be articulated and deliberated without deepening party partisan divisions. Parliament is the best forum in which to articulate that also non-mainstream non-neoliberal (leftish) objectives are best—or perhaps can only be—pursued in a European (transnational) context, that is, that, in a globalized world, European integration and cooperation are also a necessity for the successful realization of non-market-driven politics. The European Parliament is in this sense in an exceptional institutional position to contribute to 'agonistic politics',[95] that is, to allow for a struggle between substantive political positions without leading to a destructive fight.

3.2.2 Veto powers, institutional involvement, and substantive influence

The European Parliament has the power to veto international agreements. It does not have the formal power to amend them. The majorities in the European Parliament result from direct elections, and are independent from and do not coincide with national elections. The majorities in the Council and in Parliament consequently emerge and change independently and at different times. This formally places Parliament in the role of the opposition rather than a governing role.[96] The situation is somewhat comparable to Parliament's position and powers under the co-decision procedure between the entry into force of the Maastricht Treaty and the entry into force of the Amsterdam Treaty. In this first version of co-decision, the European Parliament could only veto or consent to the draft law in the third reading. This placed the European Parliament in a much weaker negotiating position than the Council because when the two institutions failed to reach an agreement, the Council could always return to its original position and offer it to Parliament in the third reading as a 'take-it-or-leave-it' final offer.[97] This was seen to at least potentially incentivize the Council not to negotiate in good faith, but to approach things in a way that would stir the draft law into a third reading. At that stage, the only option for Parliament was to block the proposal all together. [98]

[94] Mark Pollack, 'Representing Diffuse Interests in EC Policymaking' (1997) 4 JEPP 580–81.

[95] Chantal Mouffe, *The Democratic Paradox* (Verso 2009); see also Chantal Mouffe, *On the Political* (Routledge 2005). See also Section 4 of Chapter 1.

[96] Eckes and others, 'ACTA' (n 68).

[97] See for more details on this take-it-or-leave it dynamics: Mark Pollack, *The Engines of European Integration: Delegation, Agency, and Agenda-Setting in the EU* (OUP 2003) 225.

[98] In George Tsebelis, 'The Power of the European Parliament as a Conditional Agenda Setter' (1994) 88 APSR 128, the author argues that this made the Council effectively the agenda-setter.

This nuclear option is difficult for Parliament to realize because it represents so many and diffuse interests. There is a danger of a split of Parliament, when MEPs are asked to choose between yes and no based on their own assessment. Because Parliament remained the weaker part in this first version of the co-decision procedure, the Treaty of Amsterdam promoted Parliament to a true co-legislator also in the third reading.

At the same time, if the EP is able or even forced to keep a distance from the negotiations, it can more easily voice controversial views and raise citizens' concerns that are not reflected within the institutional power constellation in the same way as in public opinion. This observation stands in direct tension with its objective and its opportunity to influence the content of agreements at the negotiation stage. Again, in a comparison with the internal legislative procedure, Parliament's role to take an opposition position on any given issue has been diminished by its involvement in internal negotiations within the trialogue process, which is focused on seeking consensus *within* the institutional structures of the EU, rather than bringing controversies to light. Also, in practice, single reading has become the norm. In fact, trialogues have often been criticized for undermining the democratic legitimacy of the co-decision procedure and in particular of the European Parliament's role therein.[99] They have tilted the balance between the EP's institutional and extra-institutional role towards the former, by isolating it from the public. This has weakened its extra-institutional embedding and brought it firmly within the internal circle of exchanges of institutional actors. Involvement of Parliament at an early stage is still the best way to improve democratic legitimacy and an appropriate discourse; yet, it comes potentially at the price of more institutional cooperation behind the scenes, that is, less visibility of Parliament and more difficult conditions for developing the potential of the formal representation structures as structures of justification and bonding.

Parliament has had a considerable influence on shaping trade policy post-Lisbon.[100] An example of Parliament exercising its influence are its resolutions on the Transatlantic Trade and Investment Partnership (TTIP), in which it expressly recalls that TTIP would have had to be ratified by the EP and twenty-eight national parliaments, where it makes specific recommendations to the Commission and also to the Member States.[101] The overall tone points out the limitations of the Commission's negotiating mandate and the need of the Commission and the Council to take the EP's position into account if they want the EP to consent in the end. Specifically, on the controversial arbitration clauses, the EP outlined in its resolution on TTIP that the existing Investor-State Dispute Settlement (ISDS) system should be replaced 'with a new system for resolving disputes between investors and states'.[102] It highlighted that 'judges' should be 'publicly appointed' and that 'the jurisdiction' of the EU and national courts and the 'right to regulate' should be respected. These are exactly the building stones of the Commission's 2015 proposal to introduce an Investment Court

[99] Achim Hullermann and Joan Debardeleben, 'Democratic Dilemmas in EU Multilevel Governance: Untangling the Gordian Knot' (2009) 1 EPSR 229, 238.

[100] Marika Armanovica and Roberto Bendini, 'The role of the EP in shaping the EU's trade policy after the entering into force of the Treaty of Lisbon' (European Parliament Think Tank, 9 July 2014).

[101] Parliament Resolution containing the European Parliament's recommendations to the European Commission on the negotiations for the Transatlantic Trade and Investment Partnership (TTIP) (2014/2228(INI), 8 July 2015) http://www.europarl.europa.eu/sides/getDoc.do?pubRef=-//EP//TEXT+TA+P8-TA-2015-0252+0+DOC+XML+V0//EN.

[102] Christilla Roederer-Rynning, 'Parliamentary Assertion and Deep Integration: The European Parliament in the CETA and TTIP Negotiations' (2018) CRIA (hereafter Roederer-Rynning, 'Parliamentary Assertion'), citing *The Parliament Magazine*, 29 May 2015.

System (ICS).[103] The influence of Parliament also depends on the recognition and reaction of the other institutions. All involved actors, above all the Commission as the negotiator of EU international agreements, have an interest in insisting on involving Parliament throughout the negotiation, for reasons of their own credibility in relation to third parties. In the ISDS context, the Commission's strategy was to include Parliament in the final rewriting.[104] Here, Parliament was involved and had influence throughout the process.

In the CETA negotiations, the Commission effectuated a last-minute change to the ISDS provisions in order to allow for establishing an ICS. While—despite the fact that the agreement has been provisionally applied since February 2017—many details still need to be settled and many voices remain critical of the ICS, the process demonstrates the EP's powers to influence the content of international agreements during the negotiations, despite its lack of formal amendment powers. This was also in different ways confirmed by the previously discussed negotiations. The ICS provisions of CETA are also a vivid example of the EP's role and ability to act as the voice of EU citizens, to channel and amplify public pressures, and to effectively bridge the institutional realm with the extra-institutional realm. CETA is also an example of national parliaments establishing their voice in EU external relations, with Belgium referring a question on the compatibility of the ICS provisions to the CJEU.[105]

Parliament's increased involvement also has more subtle consequences for the content of agreements. The Union is not a unitary actor. Not only the Member States but also the EU institutions participating or influencing the negotiating of international agreements prioritize different interests and positions of the Union. The European Parliament was, for example, identified to have played a more active role than the Commission in promoting rights in the negotiation of the FTA negotiations with Vietnam.[106] The ideational basis of the respective units or even institutions also shifts over time.[107] This may have an influence on their prioritization of certain points over others. However, while these shifts occur and may have an influence, Parliament has demonstrated repeatedly that it acts as an advocate of non-economic interests in negotiations.

At the same time, an assessment of Parliament's strengthened role in law and in practice in the negotiation and conclusion of international agreements cannot ignore the broader issue of Parliament's limited access to confidential information and how this restrains, in the context of external relations, its ability to deliberate as an institution and conduct a public debate. The above-introduced Framework Agreement on Relations between the EP and the Commission (2010) has given Parliament, inter alia, a right to be fully informed in a timely manner that goes beyond what is codified in the European Treaties. Such an agreement is an expression of what is required by

[103] For more details see Chapter 6. Highlighting the same link: Siles-Brügge and de Ville, *Handelsabkommen* (n 25) 21.

[104] Roederer-Rynning, 'Parliamentary Assertion' (n 102).

[105] Opinion 1/17, pending at time of writing. See also Chapter 6.

[106] Daniela Sicurelli, 'The EU as a Promoter of Human Rights in Bilateral Trade Agreements: The Case of Negotiations with Vietnam' (2015) 11 JCER 230.

[107] Lachlan McKenzie and Katharina Meissner, 'Human Rights Conditionality in European Union Trade Negotiations: the case of the EU–Singapore FTA' (2017) 55 JCMS 832, 837, speak of a shift from 'the trade development nexus towards the growth agenda that prioritizes commercial interests', cited by: Clair Gammage, 'A Critique of the Extraterritorial Obligations of the EU in Relation to Human Rights Clauses and Social Norms in EU–Free Trade Agreements' (2018) Europe and the World: A Law Review.

the duty of sincere cooperation and could be enforced before the CJEU.[108] However, the Council's insistence that public awareness of internal, that is, inter-institutional, disputes can negatively influence international negotiations and its emphasis on the discretion of the executive to decide whether access to information may harm international relations[109] is not unreasonable. The debate illustrates that transparency requirements and judicial safeguards, which a democratic society offers with regard to the internal law-making process, cannot be taken for granted when such law-making is moved outside the domestic framework. Furthermore, when access is granted only to a few MEPs and under very restrictive circumstances this is very problematic for the EP's core role as a window to the public. It divides MEPs into 'ins' and 'outs' and gives the former a sense of inclusion and power. The problems are comparable to agreements hammered out behind closed doors that are then passed at first reading within the ordinary legislative procedure.[110] This practice has indeed been severely criticized for lack of openness.[111]

In other words, the EP is not side-lined in the conclusion of EU international agreements. Informally, Parliament has been able to exercise considerable influence on the content of post-Lisbon international agreements of the EU, including, for example, in the case of the failed TTIP. At the same time, Parliament and non-trade values remain comparatively less well represented in the adoption of international FTA than in the adoption of internal market regulation, where Parliament is a co-legislator.

3.3 Struggle for (external) visibility

Parliament has also demonstrated its awareness of obstacles to potential (structures of) bonding. Three years after it was generally elected for the first time, it expressed that 'European unification will only be achieved if Europeans want it. Europeans will only want it if there is such a thing as a European identity. A European identity will only develop if Europeans are adequately informed. At present, information via the mass media is controlled at national level.'[112] The struggle for media attention for European issues is still ongoing. In 2014, the creation of *Spitzenkandidaten* was publicly motivated with the intention of bringing political struggle (politics) to the fore within the EU structures. It was also an attempt to raise media attention for the EP elections and make different political positions visible—with limited success.

External relations, however, have over time become more visible. In the 2014 elections to the European Parliament, a post-election poll of the Eurobarometer identified '[t]he role of the EU in the international scene' as the fifth most important issue that motivated the respondents who voted.[113] There are also signs that the Union's

[108] Case C-25/94, *Commission v Council (FAO)* [1996] EU:C:1996:114, paras 49–50. The Council and the Commission had concluded an inter-institutional agreement that regulated the exercise of voting rights within FAO, which was found to be binding on the EU institutions. The Court deduced the binding force of this agreement from the intention of the parties and from the duty of sincere cooperation. See on the relevance on intention T Beukers, *Law, Practice and Convention in the Constitution of the European Union* (PhD thesis, University of Amsterdam 2011) 212 and 242.

[109] Case T-201/10, *Sophie in 't Veld II* (n 69).

[110] See for more details: Council, 'Guide to the ordinary legislative procedure' (Publications Office of the EU, 2016) https://www.consilium.europa.eu/media/29872/qc0415816enn.pdf.

[111] For many references see Carrera and others, 'Lisbonisation of the European Parliament' (n 61) 24–31.

[112] Parliament Resolution of 1982 (EP doc 1-1013/81-8, 1982).

[113] Under 'What is at stake in the vote' in European Parliament, 'Post-election survey 2014 European Elections 2014, Socio-Demographic Annex, Section 2.3' (Directorate-General for Communication, Public Opinion Monitoring Unit, 2014) 38 http://www.europarl.europa.eu/pdf/eurobarometre/

negotiation partners acknowledge that Parliament is an actor to be reckoned with in the negotiation of international agreements. The Obama Administration agreed to renegotiate some elements of the 2007 PNR agreement, 'largely in recognition of the fact Parliament was unlikely to approve the existing 2007 agreement'.[114]

An important note of caution is in order. It remains open whether and to what extent Parliament will be able to profile itself as the voice of EU citizens in the international context in the future. Better inter-institutional arrangements have been agreed and when Parliament has the opportunity to participate fully in the negotiation stage, it is better positioned to fulfil its core function of deliberating and framing the issues in the internal political arena. Much of Parliament's considerable visibility in the examined examples was triggered by its earlier exclusion. It could *legitimately* take a public stance *against* international agreements at the final stage *because* it was excluded from their negotiation. This was a visible and public rejection of what the other institutions and the involved third countries had agreed, which will become much less likely if Parliament is involved and listened to behind the scenes. Also, journalists report conflict situations more easily and extensively than consensual situations.[115]

However, there are signs that the EP will keep up its visibility in external relations. The LIBE Committee, for example, published a report on the US NSA surveillance programme in December 2013[116] and asked Edward Snowden to testify by video link.[117] The report expressed strong condemnations of bulk surveillance and proposes much stronger EU privacy protections, including halting agreements on personal data sharing with the US. Both the report and the invitation of Snowden were picked up by the US media.[118]

3.4 CFSP agreements

The conclusion of CFSP agreements constitutes an exception where the role and participation of Parliament are much more limited than for international agreements falling under TFEU policies. In the *Piracy Agreement 1* case, Parliament challenged the Council's CFSP decision on the signing and conclusion of an agreement with Mauritius concerning the treatment of suspected pirates and associated seized property.[119] Parliament aimed to defend its increased prerogatives under Article 218 TFEU. Compliance with the procedures under Article 218 TFEU falls under the jurisdiction of the Court, including where the conclusion of a CFSP agreement is contested, because the provision is part of the TFEU.[120] Requiring the consent or consultation of

2014/post/post_ee2014_sociodemographic_annex_en.pdf. The percentage of those who considered the EU's role in the world as a relevant issue was even slightly higher in the 2009 elections.

[114] Kristin Archick, 'The European Parliament' (Congressional Research Service, 19 May 2014) 14 (hereafter Archick, 'The European Parliament').

[115] Bo Laursen, 'Transparency in the Council of the European Union: Why Journalists Don't Get the Full Picture' (2012) 14 Journalism 771.

[116] Parliament Report on the US NSA surveillance programme, surveillance bodies in various Member States and their impact on EU citizens' (rapporteur Claude Moraes, 2013/2188(INI), 23 December 2013) (hereafter Parliament NSA report).

[117] Nikolaj Nielsen, 'Snowden Set for EU Parliament Video Link' (*euobserver*, 10 January 2014) http://euobserver.com/justice/122687.

[118] Dan Bilefsky, 'E.U. Panel Invites Snowden to Testify on Privacy Breaches' (*The New York Times*, 9 January 2014) http://www.nytimes.com/2014/01/10/world/europe/eu-panel-invites-snowden.html?_r=0.

[119] Case C-658/11, *Parliament v Council (Piracy Agreement I (Mauritius))* [2014] EU:C:2014:2025.

[120] ibid, para 73.

Parliament for the conclusion of many international agreements, it also sets out an exception for agreements that relate exclusively to the CFSP, where the EP has no say. The right to be informed however is also applicable to CFSP. The central point of contention in the *Piracy Agreement 1* case was whether the agreement related *exclusively* to CFSP and would hence fall under the exception. The CJEU found the CFSP legal basis the correct choice. Hence, Parliament did not win the case as regards its claims of how the agreement should have been *concluded* in this particular case. However, the CJEU explicitly confirmed that Parliament's right to be informed during the *negotiations* cuts across all different procedures, including procedures that culminate in the conclusion of CFSP agreements.[121] This can only be seen as a procedural victory for Parliament. As a result, not only Parliament's extended involvement in the conclusion of international agreements but also its information rights are a new avenue for the Court to exercise jurisdiction over CFSP matters.

However, after the broad reading of Parliament's information rights in *Piracy Agreement 1 case*, the CJEU specified the content of this right in the following *Piracy Agreement 2 case*.[122] First, it emphasized that Parliament's information right 'covers, in particular, the negotiation phase'.[123] Second, however, the Court held that in the area of CFSP, where participation of the Parliament in the negotiation and conclusion of international agreements is 'specifically excluded', the 'information requirement does not extend to stages that are part of the internal preparatory process within the Council'.[124]

By way of conclusion, the Lisbon Treaty has done much to ensure parliamentary involvement and consent in the negotiation and conclusion of international agreements. Parliament has established its new powers with prominent acts of contestation. It has consolidated better involvement among the institutions. In high-profile cases, Parliament has been able to call the executives' position into question and take an active stand against (secretly) negotiated international agreements. The notorious cases of parliamentary exclusion and the veto of the TFTP agreements and ACTA have attracted most attention, both in the media and by scholars. Parliament has put itself on the map of international relations. Yet above all, these cases illustrate the limited role of Parliament pre-Lisbon and its effective way of bringing its strengthened post-Lisbon powers to the attention of the other institutions, the public, and the EU's negotiating partners. Indeed, it has been able to effectively claim an internal and external role in the negotiation and conclusion of international agreements.

4. Facultative Mixity

Mixity is a widely spread phenomenon in EU external relations law,[125] including in cases in which the international agreement falls within the competences of the Union and hence does not strictly legally speaking require the involvement of the Member States. The CJEU's Chapter for Chapter and Section for Section examination of the Free Trade Agreement with Singapore in Opinion 2/15 could be read as indicating that

[121] ibid, paras 54 and 80–86.

[122] Case C-263/14 *Parliament v Council (Piracy Agreement II (Tanzania))*, EU:C:2016:435.

[123] ibid, para 70. [124] ibid, para 77.

[125] See Chapter 2 for EU loyalty in the context of mixed agreements, and Chapter 4 for the restraining effects of mixed agreements on the room for manoeuvre of Member States (example of the Aarhus Convention).

the Court at least aims for a purely legal approach to the question of mixity. Yet, the Court did not address the situation where the competence division does not give rise to such mixity. It did not explicitly rule out facultative mixity,[126] because in the case at hand, the law required the agreement to be concluded as a mixed agreement.

When the Commission and the Council agree to mixity, even though the competence division between the Union and its Member States does not prescribe such mixity, this changes the institutional balance. Parliament's post-Lisbon powers are undermined if a mixed agreement is chosen without the legal need for mixity. This is particularly obvious in areas that fall squarely under the exclusive competences of the Union. It is particularly problematic in the scenario in which the European Parliament gives its consent, while any of the twenty-eight national parliaments would be in the position to cancel out this consent with their negative vote. Yet it is also problematic in the scenario in which the European Parliament refuses its consent. While it still has the power to derail the agreement, the political power relations have changed. It is already politically problematic for inter-institutional relations if Parliament refuses—at least repeatedly—its consent to an agreement that the Commission has negotiated and the Council has signed. A rejection would be even more difficult if a large number or even all twenty-eight national parliaments had already approved the agreement. It would be close to impossible for the European Parliament to claim that it speaks for EU citizens if large numbers of national parliaments representing the same individuals as national citizens have already agreed to it. This would pitch the two direct forms of representation of individuals as national citizens and as EU citizens against each other. On a conceptual level this is particularly problematic in the context of mixity—and arguably even more so if no legal reason prescribes mixity—because the division of competences is usually left undetermined in the context of mixed agreements.

Facultative mixity leads to confusion as to the personality of the European Union in international relations and the powers which it has to adopt a decision by itself in that field. When the involvement of Member States as separate international actors is not legally warranted, not only their formal powers but also their claims to represent their citizens in the negotiation and conclusion process make responsibilities and representation less comprehensible from a citizens' perspective. The EU institutions, by permitting the Member States to be involved in carrying out a procedure that falls within the competences of the Union, weaken the institutional framework of the European Union. This may arguably stand in tension with their obligation to cooperate sincerely under Article 13(2) TFEU. Furthermore, they weaken the potential of formal structures of reference and bonding that could allow individuals to understand themselves *as EU citizens* as the authors of Union legal action. To put this more strongly, it goes against the basic aspect of democratic legitimacy that those represented are not in the position to discern which act or part of an act reflects the will and competence of the EU institutions, including the Parliament, and which act or part of an act reflects the will and competence of the Member States. It makes it more difficult to feel represented by the European Parliament.

This begs the question of why the EU institutions agree or at least do not challenge this. For the Council, this is explicable through the strong representation of Member States' interests. For the Commission and Parliament, the answer is less apparent.

[126] Allan Rosas, 'The European Union and Mixed Agreements' in Alan Dashwood and Christophe Hillion (eds), *The General Law of E.C. External Relations* (Sweet & Maxwell 2000). See Laurens Ankersmit, 'Opinion 2/15 and the Future of Mixity and ISDS' (*European law blog*, 18 May 2017) https://europeanlawblog.eu/2017/05/18/opinion-215-and-the-future-of-mixity-and-isds/.

Relying on mixed agreements may prima facie appear to enhance democratic legitimacy of the agreement by relying on the approval of national parliaments representing individuals as *national citizens*. The negative consequences for representation of individuals as *EU citizens* may be less immediately apparent. Moreover, the decision to conclude a mixed agreement is a common way of avoiding explicating the competence division. It may also often form part of a political compromise to opt for a mixed agreement.

Power shifts triggered by political decisions, not only unwarranted by but arguably contrary to the law, would not meet the requirements of delegation. The CJEU has established limits to delegation in its settled case law, both between EU institutions[127] and from the EU institutions to national authorities.[128] The Court explicated in that case law that powers within the area of trade policy can only be exercised by national authorities if these powers have expressly been delegated to the Member States.[129] In the context of facultative mixity, no specific powers are delegated; rather the entire agreement is concluded and ratified by both the Union and the Member States. This lack of specificity excludes reading the explicit agreement of the EU institutions as a form of delegation.

Additionally, such a shift away from the European Parliament to the national parliaments is problematic for the identification of EU citizens with the European Parliament as their voice in external relations. On the one hand, one could argue that the need for ratification by national parliaments strengthens the democratic legitimacy of mixed agreements, as compared to EU-only agreements. After all, national parliaments are arguably even more strongly democratically legitimized than the European Parliament, also because the turnout in the elections to the EP is much lower than the median turnout in national elections. On the other hand, the described blurring of lines of responsibilities hinders effective representation of citizens in either forum. Moreover, the legally unwarranted involvement of Member States as parties and national parliaments as legitimacy-givers undermines the democratization of the EU process of (negotiating and) concluding international agreements, as intended by the Lisbon Treaty.

The German Federal Constitutional Court (GFCC) engaged in its Lisbon Treaty judgment (2009) in detail, both with the limitations of the parliamentary function of the EP and with the role of national parliaments. It drew redlines of which important areas of competence Germany has to retain in order to remain an independent sovereign state. These areas were relevant to the (constitutional) identity of Germany; yet, this as such does not mean that the German parliament must necessarily be finally responsible. In practice however, reserving these areas to national action means that the European Parliament could not sufficiently legitimize them. External relations did not as such fall within these redlines. The GFCC's position starts from the position that sovereignty and hence also full parliamentary representation of a people is necessarily linked to the state.[130] This is not the understanding in this book. This book explicitly commits to the necessary legitimizing role and function of Member States within the EU legal order and the need to protect this role. However, this can also be realized within the Union. Reliance on Member States for indirect legitimacy

[127] Case 9-56, *Meroni & Co., Industrie Metallurgiche, SpA v High Authority of the European Coal and Steel Community* [1958] EU:C:1958:7.

[128] Case 41/76, *Donckerwolcke* [1976] EU:C:1976:182.

[129] See on this point also: Pieter Jan Kuijper, 'Post-CETA: How we got there and how to go on' (*ACELG*, 28 October 2016) https://acelg.blogactiv.eu/2016/10/28/post-ceta-how-we-got-there-and-how-to-go-on-by-pieter-jan-kuijper/.

[130] See Chapter 1.

does not necessarily require external visibility of the Member States, nor ratification of agreements in any particular area by national parliaments. To be more specific, national parliaments could internally be strengthened through a revamped institutional involvement of COSAC, the 'Conférence des organes parlementaires spécialisés dans les affaires de l'Union'. They could jointly be given a greater role of consultation and input-giving, not limited to but including the final stage of conclusion. If information is shared with the European Parliament, a presumption could kick in that COSAC should also have access to that information. This is very different from formal national ratification of international agreements by national parliaments, which circumvents and undermines the role of the European Parliament and allows national parliaments to make claims towards their electorates to powers that they do not formally have.

5. The European Parliament's Acts of Contestation as Claim to External Representation

The European Parliament has been assertive in exercising its post-Lisbon external powers in a way that has made a real difference in the institutional practice of treaty conclusion. This section examines how these practices can be read as a claim made by the European Parliament to represent EU citizens in international relations. [131]

5.1 Representation as structures of bonding

The European Union is a representative democracy.[132] Representation was defined by Hanna Pitkin as 'the making present *in some sense* of something which is nevertheless *not* present literally or in fact'.[133] In representative democracies, representatives are elected by secret ballot and by a large number of individuals. The combination of the large number of individuals constituting the electorate and the fact that they do not explicate their motivations for electing one representative rather than another or none at all, make it impossible to make the views and wishes one-for-one 'present'. This makes the mandate of representatives open to interpretation and both requires and allows them to give meaning to their role.[134] Representatives cannot act differently than put forward and continuously adapt certain 'claims' about those they represent, both concerning their wishes, but also their identity.[135] However, representation is a circular process. Representatives are elected. They must make claims in the political process about whom and what they represent. Those represented must recognize themselves and their wishes within that claim.[136]

[131] Many thanks to Kathalijne Buitenweg, whose PhD thesis has made me engage with the concept of claim-making of the European Parliament. Kathalijne Buitenweg, *The European Parliament's Quest for Representative Autonomy: An Internal Perspective* (PhD thesis University of Amsterdam, Eleven International Publishing 2016) (hereafter Buitenweg, *Representative Autonomy*). See in particular Chapter 2: 'The Concept of Representative Autonomy'.

[132] See the slightly roundabout formulation in art 10(1) TEU: 'The functioning of the Union shall be founded on representative democracy'.

[133] Hanna Pitkin, *The Concept of Representation* (ECP 1967) 8–9 (hereafter Pitkin, *The Concept of Representation*).

[134] See also Michael Saward, 'The Representative Claim' (2006) 5 CPT 297, 68 (hereafter Saward, 'The Representative Claim').

[135] ibid. See also Pitkin, *The Concept of Representation* (n 133) 209 on the responsiveness of representatives.

[136] Andrew Rehfeld, 'Towards a General Theory of Political Representation' (2005) 68 JP 1, 4. See for Saward's criticism of Rehfeld: Saward, 'The Representative Claim' (n 134) 56.

The recognition of the electorate does not have a formal place in the election process. However, when citizens go to vote it matters whether they feel represented—most obviously, because it is much more likely that they will choose not to go to vote for a body that they do not feel represents them. Low voter turnout for the European Parliament remains an obvious concern in this regard. Moreover, also in day-to-day political processes, recognition by those formally represented does matter. Only if the representatives can at least to some extent make a plausible claim of representation, are those formally represented at least in principle in the position to perceive themselves as the authors of the decisions of the representing body.[137] Only then are these political structures of representation and the decisions taken in them adequately worthy of recognition.

One aspect of political representation is that those represented are not only mandate givers, but also the *object* of the claim-making of those representing them.[138] Unity of the group of those represented comes about in a process and as a *consequence* of political construction and representation. Unity in this context is a process,[139] not a given prior to representation. The development, application, and interpretation of specific rules can act as vehicles for claim-making by the Parliament about those whom they represent. They offer opportunities to create formal bonding structures, which have not only the potential of relating EU citizens to Parliament but also allowing them to recognize each other as part of a group. This is the potential of bonding structures of representation.

Furthermore, recognition usually comes about in a circular and interactive process, in which representatives continuously adapt their claims to the actions and reactions of those represented. Ultimately, the European Parliament, that is, representatives as a group, can only remain articulate about representing EU citizens and their interests in inter-institutional exchanges, when their claims are at least to some extent recognized by those they claim to represent.

Three strands of theoretical perspectives on the democratic legitimacy of Parliament and the Union can be distinguished. First, the strand takes a communitarian perspective. This is the strand, in which the position that the EU lacks a 'demos' and cannot therefore reach full democratic legitimacy as a polity or for the exercise of certain core state powers.[140] This strand of literature turns to national constitutional law as sources of legitimation. This is also often their point of reference to justify the close link between demos and democratic legitimacy. National constitutions are often textually explicit about their parliaments representing the nation as a unity.[141] A second strand of scholars, arguably on the opposing end of the spectrum, relies for the legitimacy of the Union and its actions on to its technocratic capacity to generate output.[142] Finally, a third strand focuses on overarching shared norms and argues that these can legitimize

[137] See Chapter 1, Section 4.

[138] The focus of Buitenweg in *Representative Autonomy* (n 131).

[139] Nadia Urbinati, *Representative Democracy. Principles and Genealogy* (UCP 2006).

[140] David Miller, *On Nationality* (OUP 1999) 257; Dieter Grimm, *Soveränität: Herkunft und Zukunft eines Schlüsselbegriffs* (BUP 2009); Stefan Haack, *Verlust der Staatlichkeit* (Mohr Siebeck 2007).

[141] Examples are: art 42 of the Belgian Constitution: 'The members of the two Houses represent the Nation, and not only those who elected them'; art 50 Dutch Constitution: the Dutch States General represents the 'entire Dutch people'; art 38(1) of the German Constitution: members of parliament 'are representatives of the entire people'; art 67 of the Italian Constitution: members of parliament represent 'the Nation'.

[142] Giandomenico Majone, *Dilemmas of European Integration: The Ambiguities and Pitfalls of Integration by Stealth* (OUP 2005); Fritz Scharpf, *Governing in Europe: Effective and Democratic* (OUP 1999). See also Section 4.1 of Chapter 1.

supranational policy-making.[143] Habermas' model of EU democracy falls into the third category.[144] It is based on a subjectless, intersubjective understanding of popular sovereignty in which 'communicatively generated power' springs from 'the interactions between legally institutionalized will-formation and culturally mobilized publics'.[145]

All three highlight different ways in which public power can find legitimation. In particular, the third perspective (common norms) accepts as a basic premise that the Union, including in its actions, also builds and depends on the legitimizing structures of the Member States. It therefore does not require an entirely self-standing legitimation. Yet also the first (identity) and the second (technocracy) strand are reconcilable with the concept of dual legitimation resting both on individuals as national citizens via state structures and individuals as EU citizens via EU structures. The constitutions of many Member States, while they may serve as a textual point of reference for the first identity strand, also express a particular commitment and link to the European integration project. This privileging of the Union and European integration in national constitutions could be interpreted as a reflection of the acceptance of the fact that nation states increasingly transform into EU Member States in their own legal obligations.[146] It also, at least potentially, allows for an argument that (emerging) structures of bonding between the EU and individuals as EU citizens find at least indirect recognition in national constitutions as well.

The European Parliament's increased influence and voice in external relations are relevant for the ability of citizens to identify with the Union and see their interests represented in international relations. Parliament vests the EU's position in international relations with a popular backing. Institutionally, Parliament with its independent legitimacy base is in the position to offer a strong form of representation to citizens that is not subject to party discipline and loyalty bonds with national governments. External relations are also the most apparent situation in which the European Parliament represents EU citizens as such. While Parliament always represents EU citizens, internal politics are often portrayed in a divisive fashion. Representation vis-à-vis the interests of non-EU countries and citizenries has at least the potential of a unifying effect.

John Steward Mill stated, when discussing representative democracy, that the whole people exercise the 'ultimate controlling power' through representatives.[147] Despite the limitations of a veto right, in the conclusion of (most) international agreements the EP has the ultimate power to make the agreement fail. Arguably, Parliament also holds this ultimate controlling power for the whole EU citizenry internally; yet more often than not conflicts or at least contrasts of interests are internally (portrayed as) occurring along lines of nationalities. This diminishes the potential of the 'we-perspective'.

5.2 Parliament's symbolic function

Parliaments have institutional and symbolic functions.[148] Their institutional function relates to their effectiveness: Parliaments justify their existence when they are effective

[143] Francis Cheneval and Frank Schimmelfennig, 'The Case for Demoicracy in the European Union' (2013) 51 JCMS 334; Jürgen Habermas, *Zur Verfassung* (n 5).

[144] See Section 4 of Chapter 1 for more details.

[145] Jürgen Habermas, 'Three Normative Models of Democracy' (1994) 1 Constellations 1, 10.

[146] See in particular Chapter 2 on EU loyalty.

[147] John Steward Mill, *Betrachtungen über die repräsentative Demokratie* (Paderborn 1971) 89.

[148] Marcus Obrecht, *Niedergang der Parlemente? Transnationale Politik im Deutschen Bundestag under der Assemblée Nationale* (Ergon 2009) 16 (hereafter Obrecht, *Transnationale Politik*) with reference to Werner Patzelt, *Einführung in die Politikwissenschaft: Grundriss des Faches und studiumbegleitende Orientierung* (Rothe 2003) 63.

and useful. The symbolic function focuses on the imagined link with their electorate. Parliaments meet the symbolic function if they can create and maintain a fiction of representation and legitimacy.[149]

The EP is directly elected since 1979 and is formally independent from national democratic representation. Article 10(1)2 TEU expresses *tout court*: 'Citizens are directly represented at Union level in the EP.' In practice, it claims to represent EU citizens as a collective, transcending national boundaries. At the same time, the EP struggles to connect to its electorate. This struggle is reflected both in opinion polls and in the tragically low turnout in the elections for the EP, which has been on the decline ever since 1979.[150] While the problem is nearly universally recognized, the evaluation differs: both an emerging *demos* or 'sovereign people' of Europe, and hence a change in the future, and the impossibility of ever establishing any such collectivity have been argued.[151] The core argument here is that if Parliament could successfully claim to represent EU citizens as a group in external relations this might indeed be relevant for the EP's symbolic function. Citizens may *feel* better represented through the EP than through their national parliaments.

Apart from the increase in formal powers and its ability to establish them in practice, Parliament is the institution that offers real European politics, rather than bargains based on national interests (like the Council). Party cohesion is the most significant factor. Most MEPs vote along the lines of transnational European party groups rather than on the basis of nationality.[152] Much has also been done to improve the accountability link between Parliament and the Commission. However, neither increased powers nor political debate have so far solved the gap between the Parliament and EU citizens. At least at present, the EP cannot be said to fulfil the symbolic function to the same extent as national parliaments.

In the external context, the EP has recently voiced a strong claim of representation that may convince in a different way because it does not oppose European and national democratic representation, which overlap in the sense that the same individual is represented in both contexts. Internally, the EU context, including the EP, is often perceived as the 'other' opposing the national context, with which individuals identify more strongly when this opposition is put to the test. Externally, Parliament offers direct, effective, and visible European representation in a context where individuals are largely represented only in a more indirect and less visible fashion through their national governments (and in the EU context their national representative in the Council).[153] Both the role of the EP and national parliaments has been strengthened under the Lisbon Treaty, largely for the same reason: to increase democratic control and legitimacy of

149 'Repräsentations- und Legitimations*glaube*'.

150 The turnout of the European Parliament elections was in 1979: 61.99%; 1984: 58.98%; 1989: 58.41%; 1994: 56.67%; 1999: 49.51%; 2004: 45.47 2009: 42.97%; 2014: 42.61%. See for more statistics the European Parliament website on the elections http://www.europarl.europa.eu/aboutparliament/en/000cdcd9d4/Turnout-(1979-2009).html. Some theories of democracy consider the opportunity to vote as sufficient to ensure democratic legitimacy.

151 Neil MacCormick, 'Sovereignty and After' in Hent Kalmo and Quentin Skinner (eds), *Sovereignty in Fragments: The Past, Present and Future of a Contested Concept* (CUP 2011) 167. Habermas, *Zur Verfassung Europas* (n 5). See for a very different perspective the German Federal Constitutional Court (GFCC) in the Maastricht and Lisbon Treaty decisions (BVerfG—2 BvR 1877/97 [1998]; DE:BVerfG:1998:rs19980331.2bvr187797; BVerfGE 123, 267, 2BvE 2/08 [2009]. DE: BVerfG:2009:es20090630.2bve000208).

152 Simon Hix, Abdul Noury, and Gerard Roland, *Democratic Politics in the European Parliament* (CUP 2007) 3–5. Yet an increase of MEPs coming from anti-European national parties is also perceivable in the EP.

153 Art 10(2) TEU.

EU decision-making. Yet, only the EP has been able to establish an external voice, that is, speak for the EU citizens in the EU's external relations, while the improved position of national parliaments is largely limited to the internal sphere, that is, internal EU decision-making. Parliament credibly gives EU citizens a voice in international relations that, with all its flaws, draws on, as defined in Article 10(1) TEU, a source of democratic legitimation that is independent and separate from the EU Member States.

Parliament's new external role raises questions as to how international recognition and effective external representation of EU citizens interacts with the continuing internal symbolic weakness. Can the former compensate for the latter? Will citizens *feel* better represented? At present there is a mismatch between the weak fiction and Parliament's strong external acts of contestation, namely, its claim to give an external voice to EU citizens. Power without fiction may be potentially unstable and require a qualitative change. Edmund Morgan eloquently explained the tension between fiction and the real world in his influential book *Inventing the People*:

> The political world of [fictions] mingles with the real world in strange ways, for the [fictitious] world may often mould the real one. In order to be viable, in order to serve its purpose, whatever that purpose may be, a fiction must bear some resemblance to fact. If it strays too far from fact, the willing suspension of disbelief collapses. And conversely, it may collapse if facts stray too far from the fiction that we want them to resemble.[154]

Fiction and reality must hence sufficiently resemble and confirm each other to be maintainable. Where they differ to the extent that one challenges and undermines the other, a qualitative transformation is looming. There are two potential ways of adjusting the mismatch. Either EP's influence on the EU's external relations generates greater popular interest and a sense of being represented or the tension between the weak internal fiction of popular sovereignty through the Parliament and its ability to affirm external representation may at some point become so great that it requires a legal adjustment. What might work in favour of a sense of being represented is that in the external sphere there is no longer a notion of 'we', the national self, against 'them', the bigger European collective. 'Being' and 'becoming' a self, having a self-understanding, requires an encounter with the 'other'—an external reflection of oneself.[155] An effective external representation has at least the potential to create the 'we' as the European collective,[156] which is confronted by non-EU actors, who offer this reflection. And by that, it may have a different influence on the perception of the 'human figuration', that is, the structured and changing pattern of interdependence and collectivity within Europe.[157] This may be particularly relevant in the external context because, as will be addressed in the following section, in the international context the EP seems to offer greater visibility and influence than its national counterparts.

[154] Edmund Morgan, *Inventing the People: The Rise of Popular Sovereignty in England and America* (Norton 1988) 14.

[155] For more nuanced (and different) views on the relationship between self-identity and self-realization: Charles Taylor, *Sources of the Self: The Making of the Modern Identity* (HUP 1992); Kenneth Wright, *Mirroring and Attunement: Self-Realisation in Psychoanalysis and Art* (Routledge 2009) and Anthony Giddens, *Modernity and Self-Identity: Self and Society in the Late Modern Age* (SUP 1991).

[156] See on the broader point of a duality of identity which allows individuals to feel allegiance to several groups, the 'double coding of citizenship': Jürgen Habermas, 'The European Nation-State: On the Past and Future of Sovereignty and Citizenship' (1998) 10 Public Culture 397, 404; see also Habermas, *Zur Verfassung Europas* (n 5).

[157] Compare Abram de Swaan, *In Care of the State: Health Care, Education and Welfare in Europe and the USA in the Modern Era* (Polity Press 1988) 2.

5.3 Is the European Parliament the better alternative?

The EP has found its voice in the context of external relations. It has asserted a meaningful role in the conclusion of international agreements—arguably more meaningful and certainly more visible than national parliaments.

The general understanding is that national parliaments lose control through Europeanization and globalization ('*Entparlamentarisierung*').[158] The debate has so far given more attention to Europeanization processes than to international law.[159] Indeed, within the internal sovereignty discussion the focus has been on the decrease of Member States' powers as a result of Europeanization and in particular the steady empowerment of the EP.[160] This may also explain the strengthened position of national parliaments under the Lisbon Treaty and the fact that some of them have actively claimed greater influence, for example, the Finnish and Dutch parliaments.[161] In Germany, the *Lisbon Treaty* decision of the GFCC also prodded the national parliament to take up a more active role in the EU context.[162] Yet, when national parliaments exercise indirect influence by holding their representative in the European Council and in the Council accountable or even direct influence by controlling compliance with the subsidiarity principle, this is likely to have a more limited effect of enhancing the public visibility of national parliaments. If there is any public debate it often does not go beyond that particular Member State.

In most states, ratification of international agreements requires parliamentary approval. The UK and the US are exceptions where certain comprehensive international agreements are negotiated as executive agreements.[163] Also in France not all international agreements require parliamentary approval.[164] In Germany, for example, the

[158] Annette Elisabeth Töller, *Europapolitik Im Bundestag. Eine Empirische Untersuchung Zur Europapolitischen Willensbildung Im Eg-Ausschuß Des 12. Deutschen Bundestages* (Peter Lang 1995) 50.

[159] eg: Philipp Dann, *Parlamente Im Exekutivföderalismus* (Springer 2004); John O'Brennan and Tapio Raunio (eds), *National Parliaments Within the Enlarged European Union: From 'Victims' of Integration to Competitive Actors?* (Routledge 2007); Philip Giddings and Gavin Drewry (eds), *Britain in the European Union Law, Policy and Parliament* (Palgrave Macmillan 2004).

[160] eg Marlene Wind, *Sovereignty and European Integration: Towards a Post-Hobbesian Order* (Palgrave Macmillan 2001) 159. See also for a concern about the erosion of sovereign power, including because of the involvement of Parliament: UK Government, 'Foreign policy report: review of the balance of competences between the United Kingdom and the European Union' (Foreign and Commonwealth Office, 28 November 2012) https://www.gov.uk/government/consultations/foreign-policy-report-review-of-the-balance-of-competences.

[161] See eg art 10(2) TEU, which emphasizes national parliaments' role in legitimizing the national representatives in the European Council and the Council and Protocol 1 to the Lisbon Treaty, which gives national parliaments as a collective a control function over the correct interpretation of subsidiarity in the EU legislative process. The position of the Dutch parliament in EU matters has arguably decreased since Lisbon.

[162] See for examples of legislative implementation of the GFCC's guidelines: Gesetz über die Zusammenarbeit von Bundesregierung und Deutschem Bundestag in Angelegenheiten der Europäischen Union (EUZBBG), of 4.07.2013 (BGBl. I S. 2170). This law repeals the EUZBBG of 12.03.1993 (BGBl. I S. 311, 1780), which had been changed three times to extend the control powers of the German parliament, including after the GFCC's Lisbon Treaty decision and after the GFCC's ESM Decision, see Gesetz zu dem Vertrag vom 2. März 2012 über Stabilität, Koordinierung und Steuerung in der Wirtschafts- und Währungsunion vom 13. September 2012 (BGBl. II S. 1006) and Gesetz zur Änderung des EUZBBG vom 22. September 2009 (BGBl. I S. 3026).

[163] This was the case for the TFTP agreement, the PNR agreement and ACTA, see Archick, 'The European Parliament' (n 114) 15 and Eckes and others, 'ACTA' (n 68).

[164] Only the categories enumerated in art 53 of the French Constitution. The constitutional amendment of 1992 has improved the position of the *Assemblée nationale* (AN). It gave 60 members of the AN and 60 members of the Sénat the power to refer treaties to the Conseil constitutionnel for constitutionality review and strengthened the role of AN in the EU decision-making process, see art 88-4 C. See also Obrecht, *Transnationale Politik* (n 148) 177ff.

parliament (*Bundestag* and depending on the subject matter also the *Bundesrat*) has to approve the conclusion of international agreements in the legislative procedure if these agreements govern the political relations of the German Federation or concern a subject matter that falls under federal competence.[165]

In practice, however, the actual control and the ability to contest the actions of the executive differ. In parliamentary democracies, the particular relationship between governments and parliaments is characterized by support of the majority of parliamentarians for the government in office. This is not necessarily the case in presidential systems. In both systems parliaments legally are in the same position: they can deny approval to an international agreement. However, in the parliamentary system effective control by the majority is politically less likely and the majority logic of parliaments makes it difficult for the opposition to exercise effective control. A strict application of the majority rule in committees and rapporteur allocation, for example, marginalizes the minority parties behind the scenes.[166] Parliamentary inclusion, information sharing with Parliament, and a more open debate are more problematic in the parliamentary systems, while presidential systems, such as the US, may resemble the EU more here.

Furthermore, at least within the EU Member States (not so much the US), limited resources place great constraints on parliaments' involvement in foreign policy-making.[167] A comparison of the ratification processes of the Constitutional Treaty and of the Lisbon Treaty seems to indicate that national parliamentary approval of comprehensive and controversial international agreements does not usually pose problems (as opposed to the popular rejection in referendums).

By contrast, the power spectrum across party lines in the Council and within the EP develop independently of each other. In the EP, majorities and minorities form according to the outcome of direct elections. These elections happen every five years and are formally entirely unconnected to national elections, even if in practice they take place on the basis of national lists and voters may use them to punish national parties. The political powers in the EP are disconnected from the spreading of political powers in the Council, which shifts more frequently. The division between government majority and opposition does not play out in the EP in the same way as in national parliaments. The main task of the majority in the EP is not to keep an executive in the saddle. With the Commission, the EP has a relationship of confidence and cooperation, while the EP's relationship with the Council and the European Council has an opponent character. Both sides have their own independent democratic legitimation and also define its positions in contrast with each other. This distance from its intergovernmental counterparts gives the EP more room to manoeuvre than national parliaments in parliamentary systems usually have vis-à-vis the executive.

In short, Parliament offers a true political counterweight to the Council and the European Council. Furthermore, its connection to the Commission remains comparatively loose. Elections to the EP are taken into account but they do not directly determine the composition of the Commission.[168] After a proposal by the European Council,[169] the EP elects the President of the Commission[170] and the Commission as a whole is responsible to Parliament.[171] It must, for example, reply to questions

[165] Art 59(2) GG: '1(a) für Verträge, welche die politischen Beziehungen des Bundes regeln und 2(b) für Verträge, die sich auf Gegenstände der Bundesgesetzgebung beziehen.'

[166] 1990ff at Assemblée Nationale, 'Statistique de l'activité législative' http://www.assemblee-nationale.fr/connaissance/recueil-lois.asp.

[167] Obrecht, *Transnationale Politik* (n 148) 264–65.

[168] Art 17(7) TEU.

[169] ibid.

[170] Art 14(1) TEU.

[171] Art 17(8) TEU.

of Parliament or individual MEPs[172] and the EP can send the Commission home by means of a motion of no-confidence. The Lisbon Treaty has hence strengthened the EP's control over the Commission but the two remain less intimately connected than in parliamentary democracies. Moreover, the Council and the European Council hold more executive power in political terms than the Commission.

In practice, the EP has post-Lisbon achieved an exceptional visibility and influence in external relations. It has established itself as an independent and influential political force in the conclusion of international agreements. Several reasons can be pointed out that contributed to Parliament's ability to establish visibility in external relations. First, within the European legal order, people seem to feel more naturally that they belong to their national group and are represented by their national political forces, heads of government, ministers, and national parliaments. Externally, the opposition of the national context of one EU Member State versus that of another falls away.

Second, even though the EU is in a similar position to its Member States as regards executive dominance and secrecy in external relations, post-Lisbon, ordinary practice, and the recognition by third countries confirms that Parliament exercises some effective democratic control over the EU's external relations. It works in the EP's favour that it is not directly intertwined with the political composition of the Commission and Council. This gives it greater independence from the EU executive and has contributed to the EP's visibility.

Third, in the instances of the TFTP agreement and ACTA, Parliament was placed in the position to either vote ay or nay. It chose to confront the other EU institutions in public with the real-life consequence that the agreements could not be concluded. Rejecting high-profile international agreements at conclusion stage is highly visible. It has allowed Parliament to step out of the shade of inter-institutional cooperation and take the position of an internationally visible player. With the improved cooperation arrangements, Parliament may lose part of its newly established external visibility. Participating in the negotiations, and being involved before a deal is struck with the third country involved, remains behind the scenes and hence is by definition less visible. When Parliament is involved behind the scenes, all participants—at least on the EU side—have often reached a joint position by the time the agreement appears in the media. How this will play out in the future remains to be seen. At the same time, it is the strength and duty of Parliament to allow for and display politics, including antagonistic politics, that is, true and potentially irreconcilable political struggles. It must avoid at all costs ending up in situations where the political arguments come down to 'there is no alternative' because of the high costs of vetoing an international agreement at a very late stage. Such arguments are often used in the EU, in particular in the context of the financial and economic crises, and they shut out politics in a way that undermines democracy.

Finally, Parliament is strongest when an institutional issue is concerned (asserting its strengthened role in external relations) and when MEPs feel that they can politically profile themselves with a politically salient issue. After all, the majority within the EP depend on the political issue (much lower party cohesion, as discussed above). This was the case in the data protection issues that were at stake in the most visible instances of parliamentary contestation. If, by contrast, Parliament acts to establish access to power and information motivated (only) by institutional concerns, rather than for substantive reasons, it may be more difficult for it to connect with its electorate. A democratic

[172] Art 230(2) TFEU.

voice still needs to make a substantive point. Much depends on the arguments—how the parts of Parliament present them and how they are picked up by the media. One element that could help is a certain amount of competition between representation through the European Parliament and through national parliaments, in particular in the specific context of mixed agreements, parliaments could demonstrate their ability to represent views and interests in the issues discussed, the questions asked, and the reasoning provided by members of (European) Parliament for their vote. However, Parliament would have to be careful in communicating its strengths. As in any competition, there is a danger that it may also ultimately be to the detriment of the EP because national parliaments have shorter lines to their citizens. As mentioned above, in the case of CETA, the Wallonian parliament took a prominent place in the media and motivated the Belgian parliament to refer the question of whether the ICS provisions in the agreement were compatible with EU law.

Moreover, this discussion of course leaves open the sociological question that in the end Parliament is better at actually representing the *substantive* interests of the majority of EU citizens. It also leaves open whether Parliament's claim-making will actually appeal to voters or have some success in promoting a possible vision of self-determination as EU citizens to individuals. At present it remains the case that most individuals' identification with the European Union and their role as EU citizens is considerably weaker than their identification with their state and their role as national citizens.[173]

5.4 Potential implications of Parliament's claim

The EP's claim to representation in external relations may not only strengthen the institutional potential for EU citizens to feel represented through the EP but also have additional qualitative effects on the legitimacy of the EU's claim to exercise original (sovereign) rights. It could lend popular backing to the CJEU's construction of EU law as an autonomous legal order.[174] Meshing instrumental power dynamics, normative force of argument, and symbolic appeal effectively enhanced Parliament's substantive influence beyond its formal constitutional involvement.

Neil Walker identifies sovereignty 'as a speech act' and argues that:

> its capacity to make a difference to the world depends upon its plausibility and its acceptance as a way of knowing and ordering the world, which in turn depends upon its status as an 'institutional fact'—a fact whose authenticity and credibility depends upon the internalisation by key actors of a complex of rules and expectations which support and subscribe to the sovereign claim.[175]

[173] Feelings of European citizenship are at an all-time high: 70% of EU citizens feel a sense of EU citizenship (Eurobarometer 89, *European Citizenship*, Spring 2018 at p. 29 http://ec.europa.eu/commfrontoffice/publicopinion/index.cfm/ResultDoc/download/DocumentKy/83538) compared with 64% in Spring 2016 (Eurobarometer 85, *European Citizenship*, Spring 2016 at p. 14 https://ec.europa.eu/commfrontoffice/publicopinion/index.cfm/ResultDoc/download/DocumentKy/75905P) and its lowest point since Lisbon of 59% in Autumn 2013 (Eurobarometer 80, *European Citizenship*, Autumn 2013 http://ec.europa.eu/commfrontoffice/publicopinion/archives/eb/eb80/eb80_citizen_en.pdf). However, this belies the fact that the vast majority (approx 90%) of EU citizens consistently see themselves as primarily or solely national citizens. Only a consistently tiny minority (7–8%) consider themselves as primarily or solely European citizens (see Eurobarometer Spring 2018 at pp. 35–37, Eurobarometer Spring 2016 at p. 20, and Eurobarometer Autumn 2013 at p. 34).

[174] Most explicitly making the link to sovereignty: Francis Jacobs, *The Sovereignty of Law: The European Way* (The Hamlyn Lectures 2006, CUP 2007). See the lecture version http://socialsciences.exeter.ac.uk/media/universityofexeter/schoolofhumanitiesandsocialsciences/law/pdfs/9780521878876_HAML_Jacobs.pdf.

[175] Neil Walker, 'Late Sovereignty in the European Union' in Neil Walker (ed), *Sovereignty in Transition: Essays in European Law* (Hart Publishing 2006) 7.

External relations are outside the realm, in which both the Member States in the national context and the EU, notably the CJEU, have for many years interpreted the sovereignty relations in their own constitutional terms.[176] In the *Lisbon Treaty* ruling, the GFCC effectively denied as recently as 2009 that the European Parliament could make a meaningful claim to be a full parliament representing EU citizens.[177] By involving international actors in the game, Parliament can seek external recognition of its claim to power and the ability to represent EU citizens. This is a way of consolidating and perpetuating its position beyond the reach of the Member States. Parliament's strategy seems to work. The US has demonstrated an increased interest in the EP that comes with its power to stop international agreements.[178] Not only the above-discussed TFTP, the PNR agreement (up for renewal in 2019), and ACTA, but also the Transatlantic Trade and Investment Partnership (TTIP), which seems off the table for the moment,[179] and the EU–US agreement on personal data protection (so-called Umbrella Agreement, signed in 2016), were and are subject to consent by Parliament. With the US accepting Parliament's relevance in international relations, one key actor has adapted its expectations, accepted the institutional reality post-Lisbon, and confirmed the relevance of the Parliament's powers. Furthermore, having a voice in external relations has become more and more important to maintain effective representation of citizens in an interconnected world, where internationally agreed decisions directly determine the position of individuals.

Until the EP's refusals, the most well-debated act of contestation of an EU institution with external consequences has been the CJEU's rulings in the first *Kadi* appeal of 2008.[180] In *Kadi*, the Court annulled the EU legal instruments that gave effect to a UN Security Council Resolution. It was an act to protect the rule of law within the EU legal order, but it was not backed by democratic will. The EP's acts of contestation are of a different political order. Parliament formally represents EU citizens and by making its powers politically relevant it has given them a voice in external relations. Furthermore, they are not aimed at protecting specific individuals, but assert the right to engage in general policy-making. Since the beginning, the link between the EU and its citizens has been central to the CJEU's narrative of original rights. In a very positive reading of this narrative, direct effect and primacy have taken '[Union] law out of the hands of the politicians and bureaucrats and to give it to the people' and to 'enable ordinary men and women to savour the fruits of integration'.[181] Only this has remained largely a legal narrative. A strengthened and prominent role of the EP in external relations offers a formal legal structure that could allow for more bonding and the potential of feeling represented (structures of bonding). Representation can only take place within a constitutive procedural and normative framework, it is not the simple accumulation of individual preferences. Post-Lisbon, the European Treaties offer a framework for such representation through the EP in the conclusion of international agreements.

[176] See Section 3.4 of Chapter 1.

[177] GFCC, Lisbon Treaty decision (n 151).

[178] Archick, 'The European Parliament' (n 114); see also Benjamin Fox, 'US Enthusiastic About Trade Deal Despite Culture Opt-Out' (*euobserver*, 24 June 2013) http://euobserver.com/economic/120604.

[179] Talks with the US have been reported to have failed by different national politicians.

[180] Cases C-402 and 415/05 P *Kadi and Al Barakaat v Council and Commission* [2008] EU:C:2008:461 confirmed in Joined Case C-584, 593, and C-595/10 P, *Commission, Council and UK v Kadi* [2013] EU:C:2013:518.

[181] Giuseppe Federico Mancini and David Keeling, 'Language, Culture and Politics in the Life of the European Court of Justice' (1994–95) 1 Colum J Eur L 397. At the same time, it is worth acknowledging that in practice few private individuals (or public interest groups) bring direct actions against EU institutions and that preliminary references depend on the goodwill of national courts and do not allow for third party interventions.

6. Conclusions

The EU differs from international organizations not only internally with regard to the effectiveness and intensity with which it determines the legal position of its subjects (both in scope and in quality), but also with regard to the quality of its international presence, confirmed by its state-like position in certain functional legal regimes. External relations are one of the areas in which Parliament's powers have increased the most. Post-Lisbon, the European Parliament has voiced loudly on the international plane its (subjective) claim to speak for 'a European polity'.

Despite the limitations of the legitimacy of Parliament, within the EU, Parliament is *the* formal institutional manifestation of direct democratic legitimacy within the European polity.[182] The increased role of Parliament in the conclusion of international agreements constitutes a conscious departure from the prevalent executive dominance in external relations agreed by the Member States (and the institutions) in the Treaty amendment procedure. Constitutional constraints in the EU Charter of Fundamental Rights and in the European Convention on Human Rights (ECHR), combined with a stringent judicial review by the CJEU, back Parliament's claim to be a legitimate actor and thereby contribute to its institutional capacity to represent its citizens in an autonomous manner. A combination of Article 10(2) TEU and Article 218 TFEU[183] vest Parliament with the formal legal capacity to represent *EU citizens*. In other words, the formal legal structures are in place. However, it must still realize the potential of these bonding structures fully in practice. Besides the strategic vetoes of the past and the greater influence behind the scenes, Parliament as such, for example, in its mission and tasks as outlined in its communication with the public, and MEPs, for example, in their election communication strategies, should make the claim that they represent EU citizens in international relations. This has only happened to a very limited extent in the elections to the European Parliament up to those held in 2014. It may also make it potentially advisable to challenge the choice to opt for mixity, where this is not legally prescribed, in strategic (inter-institutional) litigation.

Parliament's claims of (better) representation through explicit communication and acts of contestation may strengthen Parliament's capacity to establish the link of representation with EU citizens. They draw attention to the formal legal structures of bonding and fill them with practice. As such, they add a qualitative different aspect to the CJEU's claim that the EU is autonomous and directly connected to its citizens. They also take this differentness beyond the internal debate to be experienced by external actors. The US, as an important third country, has already demonstrated an increased interest in the position of the EP. At the same time, the strengthened role of Parliament does not achieve a substitution of bargaining by deliberation, because Parliament formally can only take or leave the final agreement—even if this gives it some leverage at the negotiation stage. Parliament must keep in mind its political role when linking to its citizens. Some measure of politics, that is, political struggle, is not only desirable but *inevitable* for the Union to succeed as a polity that *also draws from autonomous and direct democratic legitimation*. The objective of structures of bonding is justification, in a way that explicates arguments and puts them forward in a discourse for an exchange of arguments and reasonable disagreement.

[182] 'Direct' refers to the direct link between Parliament and individuals as EU citizens, as opposed to the 'indirect' legitimation of the Union by individuals as national citizens through their Member States. See Section 2.3 of Chapter 1.

[183] In particular art 218(6)(a) and (10) TFEU.

When the EP, with its formally independent source of democratic legitimacy, is vested with the powers to exercise effective control over the Union's external actions, this creates a formal legal framework that has the potential of allowing EU citizens to feel represented by the EP in the international relations context. When the EP puts this into practice, makes claims of representation, and brings in the voice of EU citizens in contrast to the representatives of national citizens, this may be a powerful tool. In a positive reading, the EP could offer external political autonomy to EU citizens and give them a hitherto lacking ability to contest international law-making. The link between EU citizens and the EP may in particular be reinforced by the relative absence of representation by national parliaments in the international context and by the absence of opposing national contexts, which may allow individuals to identify with their 'Europeanness'. Ultimately, this strengthens the popular element in the CJEU's narrative that the EU possesses original sovereign power. External visibility should not be underestimated. It has always been a core concern within the EU sovereignty debate.

6

International Courts or Tribunals and the Autonomy of the EU Legal Order

1. Introduction

International Courts or Tribunals (ICTs) have become the litmus test of the autonomy of the EU legal order vis-à-vis international law.[1] The CJEU has repeatedly been asked to evaluate the compatibility of EU commitment to ICTs with EU law.[2] In 2014, the Court rejected the EU's planned accession to the European Convention on Human Rights (ECHR).[3] A request for an opinion on the compatibility of the Investment Court System (ICS) in the EU's Free Trade Agreement with Canada (CETA) is pending.[4] At the same time, the Lisbon Treaty has, as is well known, made EU accession to the ECHR possible and, arguably, made it an obligation for the EU institutions. It has also extended the EU's competences concerning foreign direct investment.[5] This has led the Commission to argue that the EU could also set up Investor-State Dispute Settlement (ISDS) mechanisms in international agreements concluded by the Union alone.[6] The Court, however, rejected this reading in Opinion 2/15.[7] It held that ISDS did not fall within the exclusive competence of the EU and cannot therefore be set up without the Member States' consent. The Commission continues to remain committed to ICTs and generally endeavours to replace ISDS with an ICS.[8] It has also, as did Parliament, confirmed its commitment to further pursue EU accession to the ECHR after Opinion

[1] See Chapter 1 on the meaning and construction of the autonomy of the EU legal order.

[2] Opinion 1/91 (creation EEA I) [1991]EU:C:1991:490 (hereafter Opinion 1/91); Opinion 1/92 (creation EEA II) [1992] EU:C:1992:189; Opinion 2/94 (Accession by the Community to the European Convention for the Protection of Human Rights and Fundamental Freedoms) [1996] EU:C:1996:140; Opinion 1/09 (European and Community Patents Court) [2011] EU:C:2011:123 (hereafter Opinion 1/09); (Opinion 2/13 (Accession to ECHR) [2014] EU:C:2014:2454 (hereafter Opinion 2/13); Opinion 1/17 (Request for an Opinion on CETA) not yet reported (hereafter Opinion 1/17).

[3] Opinion 2/13 (n 2).

[4] Opinion 1/17 (n 2).

[5] Consolidated Version of the Treaty on the Functioning of the European Union [2008] OJ C115/47 (hereafter TFEU) art 207(4).

[6] This is, in any event, the interpretation of the Commission. European Commission, 'Investment in TTIP and beyond—the path for reform' (concept paper, 5 May 2015) http://trade.ec.europa.eu/doclib/docs/2015/may/tradoc_153408.PDF.

[7] Opinion 2/15 [2015] EU:C:2017:376 (hereafter Opinion 2/15) on the EU's competence to conclude the Free Trade Agreement with Singapore (EUSFTA). Member States have concluded about 1,500 bilateral investment treaties, all of which contain similar provisions on investment protection and ISDS. The EU has, so far, only concluded a Free Trade Agreement with Canada (CETA) and EUSFTA with ISDS. Based on two criteria (market potential and need for better protection of foreign investments), the Commission has compiled a list of five countries and one regional entity (Canada, China, India, Mercosur, Russia, and Singapore) which will be privileged partners in the negotiation of the first investment agreements.

[8] See European Commission, 'Commission proposes new Investment Court System for TTIP and other EU trade and investment negotiations' (Press release, 16 September 2015) http://europa.eu/rapid/press-release_IP-15-5651_en.htm (with further links) (hereafter Commission, ICS press release).

EU Powers Under External Pressure: How the EU's External Actions Alter its Internal Structures. Christina Eckes © Christina Eckes 2019. Published 2019 by Oxford University Press.

2/13.[9] While the EU and the Commission in particular actively support some ICTs, the Commission has also recently proposed rejecting the draft findings and recommendations of the Aarhus Convention Compliance Committee (ACCC),[10] arguing that these findings ignore the very nature of the system of judicial protection within the EU.[11] This chapter examines the internal constitutional consequences of the EU's submission to ICTs. It pays particular attention to three ICTs in which individuals or the public play a role and that have been seen as problematic by the Court of Justice or the Commission. These are the European Court of Human Rights (ECtHR), ISDS/ the ICS, and the ACCC. Finally, this chapter explicates how the autonomy debate in the context of ICTs relates to the effectiveness of EU law, the emerging structures of bonding, and the legitimacy of Union action.[12]

Section 2 introduces ICTs in general and then concentrates on the ECtHR, ISDS/ the ICS, and the ACCC. Section 3 examines how ICTs could undermine the autonomy of the EU legal order, based on the same examples. Section 4 is dedicated to the EU's accession to the ECHR, which raises additional problems, in particular for structures of bonding and legitimacy, because of the nature of fundamental rights and the relevance of the ECHR within the EU legal order and in the EU integration process. Section 5 categorizes ICTs and explains which features may be particularly problematic not only for the autonomy of the EU legal order, but also its effectiveness. Section 6 concludes and links the autonomy of the EU to different forms of legitimacy. In addition to the concern for the (absolute) legal autonomy of the EU, it argues that a certain degree of political autonomy is necessary to develop legal structures of bonding and legitimacy. It also raises the question of whether submission to the jurisdiction of ICTs is justifiably more problematic for the EU than for nation states.

2. International Courts or Tribunals

ICTs are institutionally and contextually very different. The EU has committed to a number of ICTs, which usually are not seen as problematic for the autonomy of the EU legal order. An example is the dispute settlement system of the World Trade Organization (WTO). The Agreement Establishing the WTO is a mixed agreement, with both the EU and all its Member States being parties to the agreement. Within the WTO, however, this mixed nature has, in practice, been replaced by EU dominance.

[9] European Commission, 'Staff working document of 15 May 2017 on the Application of the EU Charter of Fundamental Rights in 2016 Accompanying the document Communication from the Commission to the European Parliament, the Council, the European Economic and Social Committee and the Committee of the Regions on 2016 Report on the Application of the EU Charter of Fundamental Rights' (SWD/2017/0162 final); European Parliament resolution of 16 September 2015 on the Commission Work Programme 2016 (2015/2729(RSP)).

[10] UNECE Aarhus Convention Compliance Committee, 'Draft Findings and Recommendations of the Compliance Committee with regard to Communication ACCC/C/2008/32 (Part II) Concerning Compliance by the European Union' https://www.unece.org/fileadmin/DAM/env/pp/compliance/C2008-32/Findings/C32_EU_Findings_as_adopted_advance_unedited_version.pdf.

[11] European Commission, 'Proposal for a Council Decision on the position to be adopted, on behalf of the European Union, at the sixth session of the Meeting of the Parties to the Aarhus Convention regarding compliance case ACCC/C/2008/32' COM (2017) 366 final, 5 (hereafter COM (2017) 366 final) https://ec.europa.eu/transparency/regdoc/rep/1/2017/EN/COM-2017-366-F1-EN-MAIN-PART-1.PDF.

[12] See chapter 1 for a conceptualization of 'effectiveness', 'structures of bonding', and 'legitimacy' within the EU.

The EU rates as one of the most active users of the WTO dispute settlement system.[13] It routinely acts as a complainant and respondent, including in cases brought by a third state against an EU Member State.[14] To make the picture complete, it should be added that the CJEU holds decisions of the WTO dispute settlement body at arm's length by not conferring direct effect on them.[15] They are binding but cannot be enforced against the EU by private parties. The CJEU reasons in its settled case law that the 'nature and structure' of the WTO agreement do not justify vesting the agreement with direct effect. It also concludes that decisions of the dispute settlement body equally lack direct effect.[16] The WTO example also has wider significance, as some bilateral agreements, such as the EU–Singapore FTA (EUSFTA), have included ICTs modelled on the WTO (or NAFTA[17]) system.[18]

In line with its approach to the WTO system, the Court has not taken issue with the EU being a contracting party to the UN Convention on the Law of the Sea (UNCLOS). While at the very beginning the Commission took a rather ambivalent attitude towards the International Tribunal for the Law of the Sea (ITLOS) established under UNCLOS,[19] only a year later Chile and the EU agreed to establish a special Chamber of ITLOS.[20] Similar to WTO law, the CJEU found that UNCLOS does not have direct effect because of its 'nature and broad logic'.[21] The CJEU has not so far ruled on the direct effect of decisions of a Chamber of ITLOS, but in line with its WTO case law, these decisions may be expected not to have direct effect, because UNCLOS does not.

Other ICTs, such as the ECtHR and ISDS, raise serious concerns for the autonomy of the EU legal order in the eyes of the Court.[22] In Opinion 1/91 on the European Economic Area (EEA Opinion), the Court confirmed as a matter of principle that the EU can be a party to international agreements that set up judicial disputes mechanisms and that the CJEU would consider itself bound by that judicial mechanism's

[13] Allan Rosas, 'The EU and International Dispute Settlement' (2017) 1 Europe and the World: A Law Review 1, 2–3 http://discovery.ucl.ac.uk/1559541/1/Rosas%20article.pdf.

[14] Christina Eckes, 'The European Court of Justice and (Quasi-) Judicial Bodies of International Organizations' in Ramses Wessel and Steven Blockmans (eds), *Between Autonomy and Dependence* (Asser Press 2013); World Trade Organizations, 'Disputes by Country/Territory' www.wto.org/english/tratop_e/dispu_e/dispu_by_country_e.htm.

[15] Ibid. See also Anne Thies, 'EU Membership of the WTO: International Trade Disputes and Judicial Protection of Individuals by EU Courts' (2013) 2 Global Constitutionalism 237.

[16] Case C-377/02, *Van Parys* [2005] EU:C:2005:121, para 39 ff.

[17] North American Free Trade Agreement (NAFTA) Chapter 20 https://www.nafta-sec-alena.org/Home/Texts-of-the-Agreement/North-American-Free-Trade-Agreement?mvid=1&secid=ed3bd8c9-2d73-45fb-9241-d66364f8037a.

[18] See eg Chapter 15 of the EU–Singapore FTA http://trade.ec.europa.eu/doclib/press/index.cfm?id=961. Chapter 20 of NAFTA offers a mechanism similar in scope and jurisdiction to the WTO's Dispute Settlement Understanding. Chapter 19 of NAFTA (antidumping and countervailing duty cases) incorporates a more limited scope and operates under national law.

[19] The Commission proposed to the Council in 1999 that no preference should be expressed for any of the three dispute settlement procedures provided for in UNCLOS, namely ITLOS, an arbitral tribunal, or a special arbitral tribunal. The Council never formally decided on the line proposed by the Commission, and the Commission withdrew the proposal in 2004.

[20] In 2000, the EU brought the case before the WTO early in the year. Both cases remain suspended at the time of writing.

[21] Case C-308/06, *Intertanko* [2008] EU:C:2008:312, para 65.

[22] Opinion 2/13 (n 2); Case C-284/16, *Slovak Republic v Achmea BV* [2018] EU:C:2018:158 (hereafter Case C-284, *Achmea*). See also Niilo Jääskinen and Alicja Sikora, 'The Exclusive Jurisdiction of the Court of Justice of the European Union and the Unity of the EU Legal Order' in Marise Cremona, Anne Thies, and Ramses Wessel (eds), *The EU and International Dispute Settlement* (Hart Publishing 2016) (hereafter Jääskinen and Sikora, 'The Exclusive Jurisdiction of the Court of Justice').

interpretation of the international agreement.[23] The greatest obstacle to the EU's participation in such a judicial dispute mechanism remains that such participation cannot alter the tasks or authority of the CJEU.[24] Examples of the Court's struggles are Opinion 1/76 on the European Laying-up Fund for Inland Waterway Vessels;[25] EEA Opinion;[26] Opinion 2/94 on the accession of the Community to the ECHR;[27] Opinion 1/00 on the European Common Aviation Area;[28] the case of *Mox Plant*;[29] Opinion 1/09 on the creation of a unified patent litigation system;[30] and Opinion 2/13 on the accession of the EU to the ECHR.[31] Scholars have agreed[32] and disagreed[33] with the CJEU's conclusion in Opinion 2/13 that the EU's accession to the ECHR threatens the autonomy of the EU legal order and whether the agreed co-respondent mechanism and the prior involvement mechanism sufficiently protect the CJEU's judicial monopoly over EU law. In any event, Opinion 2/13 is an unequivocal expression of the CJEU's standpoint that EU submission to the jurisdiction of the ECtHR threatens the autonomy of the EU legal order. The basic point that ICTs could at least potentially threaten the autonomy of the EU legal order was also confirmed by other institutional actors, for example, during negotiations on the draft agreement for EU accession to the ECHR and by Belgium's request for an opinion on the ICS in Chapter F of CETA.[34] The Commission also specifically rejected the draft findings and recommendations of the ACCC on access to justice under EU law (2017) with a reference to the particularities of the EU legal order. The remainder of this section outlines the three ICTs that, for different reasons, have raised problems for the autonomy and

[23] Opinion 1/91 (n 2) paras 39-40: The EU's 'capacity to conclude international agreements necessarily entails the power to submit to the decisions of a court which is created or designated by such an agreement as regards the interpretation and application of its provisions'.

[24] The Court's opinions and rulings have been examined in great detail in the literature: Ramses Wessel and Steven Blockmans (eds), *The Autonomy of the EU Legal Order from International Organizations* (Asser Press/Springer 2013); in particular the chapter by Jan Willem van Rossem, 'The Autonomy of EU Law: More is Less?'. See also Adam Lazowski and Ramses Wessel, 'When Caveats Turn into Locks: Opinion 2/13 on Accession of the European Union to the ECHR' (2015) 16 Ger LJ 179 (hereafter Lazowski and Wessel, 'Opinion 2/13'); Piet Eeckhout, 'Opinion 2/13 on EU Accession to the ECHR and Judicial Dialogue: Autonomy or Autarky?' (2015) Jean Monnet Working Paper 01/2015 (hereafter Eeckhout, 'Opinion 2/13').

[25] Opinion 1/76 (Draft Agreement establishing a European laying-up fund for inland waterway vessels) [1977] EU:C:1977:63. In this case, the CJEU rejected the establishment of a fund tribunal consisting of six of its own judges. It expressed concern about the possibility of a conflict of jurisdiction in the event of two parallel preliminary ruling procedures on the interpretation of the agreement (one before the fund tribunal and one before the CJEU) and on the impartiality of those judges that sit on both judicial bodies.

[26] Opinion 1/91 (n 2).

[27] Opinion 2/94 (Accession by the Community to the European Convention for the Protection of Human Rights and Fundamental Freedoms) [1996] EU:C:1996:140.

[28] Opinion 1/00 (Proposed agreement between the European Community and non-Member States on the establishment of a European Common Aviation Area) [2002] EU:C:2002:231, paras 21, 23, and 26.

[29] Case C-459/03, *Commission of the European Communities v Ireland (Mox Plant)* [2006] EU:C:2006:345.

[30] Opinion 1/09 (n 2) paras 73–89.

[31] Opinion 2/13 (n 2).

[32] Daniel Halberstam, '"It's the Autonomy, Stupid!" A Modest Defense of Opinion 2/13 on EU Accession to the ECHR, and the Way Forward' (2015) 16 Ger LJ 105.

[33] Lazowski and Wessel, 'Opinion 2/13' (n 24); Eeckhout, 'Opinion 2/13' (n 24).

[34] Opinion 1/17 (n 2). 13 observations were submitted to the CJEU in Opinion 1/17, with Slovenia and Greece defending the autonomy of the EU legal order, while the remaining Member States (NL, GER, FR, Council, EST, SK, FIN, LIT, AT, ESP) and the Commission defending ICS in CETA.

legitimacy of the EU legal order: the ECtHR post-accession, ISDS/the ICS, and finally the ACCC.

2.1 The European Court of Human Rights

2.1.1 Relevance of EU accession to the European Convention on Human Rights

The ECtHR rules on human rights violations in all policy fields. It reviews compliance with the European Convention on Human Rights (ECHR) which, within Europe, is the prime example of an international agreement vesting individuals with specific, enforceable rights. The ECHR is one of the sources of the general principles of EU law[35] and its constitutional status is codified in the European Treaties.[36] Where rights protected under the EU Charter of Fundamental Rights 'correspond to rights guaranteed by' the ECHR 'the meaning and scope of [these] rights shall be the same' as those under the ECHR.[37] The CJEU has further extended this particular point to the case law of the ECtHR, holding that Charter rights 'must therefore be given the same meaning and the same scope as [the corresponding right] of the ECHR, as interpreted by the case law of the [ECtHR]'.[38] The ECHR is in many ways the prime source of the EU's understanding of human rights. Even if accession to the ECHR is not a formal written requirement to become a Member State of the EU, it has become a de facto accession requirement.[39] In short, the ECHR has been exceptionally determinative for the protection of fundamental rights within the EU legal order. The status and legal force of the Convention and the case law of the ECtHR within the EU legal order goes beyond what contracting parties commonly confer to the ECHR.

Accession would constitute something of a constitutional revolution. The EU would take external responsibility for its acts under an international law framework that allows individuals to hold the EU to account. There is no precedence for this. Opinion 2/94 highlighted the fundamental institutional implications and the constitutional significance of the EU's accession to the ECHR. It is also reflected in the procedural rules in Article 218(8) (and (6)(ii)) TFEU that require not only a unanimous decision of the Council and consent of the Parliament but also approval by the Member States 'in accordance with their respective constitutional requirements'. An inherent tension exists between the accession obligation in Article 6 TEU and the express codification of a static division of competences in Article 6 TEU and in Protocol 8. EU fundamental rights competences and EU responsibility under the ECHR are seen as a potential means for the EU to acquire creeping influence over Member States' actions.[40]

[35] Art 6(3) TEU. [36] Art 6(2) and (3) TEU and art 53 CFR.

[37] Art 52(3) CFR. The CFR enjoys the same legal value as the Treaties (art 6(1) TEU).

[38] Case C-400/10 PPU, *JMcB v LE* [2010] EU:C:2010:582, para 53. Douglas-Scott interprets 'correspond' as 'the same' or 'identical'. Sionaidh Douglas-Scott, 'The European Union and Human Rights After the Treaty of Lisbon' (2011) 11 HRLR 655, 655–56. This seems to be an overly strict reading. Indeed, the explanations to the Charter offer a list of 'corresponding rights'. This appears to provide a good interpretation of the scope of the Court of Justice's ruling.

[39] Christina Eckes, 'EU Accession to the ECHR: Between Autonomy and Adaptation' (2013) 76 MLR 254 (hereafter Eckes, 'EU Accession to the ECHR').

[40] This becomes apparent in the tug-of-war between the CJEU and national constitutional courts in cases concerning fundamental rights (see Chapter 1). It is also the reason for the adoption of Protocol 30, the Declaration on the EUCFR, Declaration 53 (Czech Republic), Declarations 61 and 62 (Poland).

After accession, the jurisdiction of the ECtHR would extend to all EU policies, including those falling within the highly politicized ex-Union pillars, now called the Area of Freedom, Security and Justice (AFSJ) and the Common Foreign and Security Policy (CFSP). The ECtHR's review would also extend to secondary EU law adopted pursuant to the legislative procedures of the EU. Furthermore, judicial review of (autonomous) political decision-making always raises questions whether it (potentially) undermines democratic legitimacy. This is also the case for the direct and indirect input of individuals as EU citizens and as national citizens that vests the institutional structure with legitimacy. Yet, the ECtHR largely aims to protect the autonomous political choices of the contracting parties, using the legal concept of a 'margin of appreciation' which reserves space for political decisions that will not be subject to judicial review.[41] As regards political choices, after accession the Union would be in an equivalent position to that of the other contracting parties to the ECHR. The main difference between the position of the Union and States does not pertain to substantive policy choices but rather to the particularities of the EU's institutional judicial framework, which make it, as a matter of principle, possible that the CJEU has not had the chance to rule on cases concerning EU law[42] and the ECtHR's ability to make a binding determination of the nature of Union law and relations between different legal spheres.[43]

2.1.2 Draft accession agreement and Opinion 2/13

The draft accession agreement proceduralized and hence postponed many choices on the precise relationship between the EU and its Member States and between EU and national law. The prior involvement mechanism treats the EU as a quasi-federal structure in which the CJEU should have the final say rather than as a conglomerate of sovereign entities, in which the Member States could decide that EU law is not relevant. The prior involvement mechanism gives the CJEU the opportunity to interpret and rule on an issue of EU law before it reaches the ECtHR.[44] This is intended to avoid situations, in which a case concerning EU law may reach the ECtHR, after all national remedies have been exhausted, without having given the CJEU the opportunity to interpret EU law, because national courts have failed to refer a relevant question to the CJEU.

The co-respondent mechanism and the default of joint responsibility by contrast reflect the involvement of several sovereign entities, which are given the room to have their own say in the procedure and determine the precise division of responsibility outside the courtroom. There is a tension between these different arrangements. Future decisions of the ECtHR and the EU administration (in which cases would they intervene as co-respondent?) would still be decisive in determining these relationships. While the ECtHR would not attribute responsibility as standard practice (only in

[41] While the ECtHR has used the concept of the 'margin of appreciation' for a long time, Article 1 of Protocol No. 15 to the ECHR amended the Preamble to the ECHR to confirm that contracting parties 'enjoy a margin of appreciation' (open for ratification since 24/06/2013).

[42] The requirement of exhaustion of domestic remedies (art 35 ECHR) would be met by national courts. It does not require a preliminary reference to the CJEU. See, however, the next section on the prior-involvement mechanism under the Draft Accession Agreement of 5 April 2013 https://www.coe.int/t/dlapil/cahdi/Source/Docs2013/47_1_2013_008rev2_EN.pdf.

[43] This point is fully developed in Sections 3 and 4 below.

[44] See art 3(6) of the Draft revised Agreement on the Accession of the European Union to the Convention on Human Rights and Fundamental Freedoms, (Final Report to the CDDH 47+1 (2013) 008rev2, 10 June 2013) 4–12 (hereafter DAA).

exceptional cases), an internal arrangement for compliance with the ruling has to be found. The allocation of responsibility for execution and compliance (remedy a breach and guarantee non-repetition within the meaning of Article 46 ECHR) would need to be established and necessarily raises questions about the division of competences. This would further place EU institutions in a position where they may have to ensure that Member States comply with the ECHR when acting within the scope of EU law.[45] This could deeply affect the relationship between the Union and its Member States, between EU law and national law, and ultimately between both the Union and the Member States on the one hand and the individual on the other. By definition, fundamental rights relate any such shifting responsibilities and power to the individual. Furthermore, postponing the final decision on how rules would be interpreted to the application stage requires a high level of mutual trust that any interpretation respects common sense and is based on good faith. Furthermore, the ECHR, as fundamental rights typically do, leaves considerable room for reasonable disagreement on what its provisions mean when applied to an individual case.

In 2014, the CJEU rejected the draft agreement on EU accession to the ECHR for the core reason that it threatened the autonomy of the EU legal order.[46] Furthermore, in particular, the CJEU identified that the co-respondent mechanism did not (fully) exclude the ability of the ECtHR to rule on the division of responsibility between the Union and its Member States. It took issue with the fact that accession would place the ECtHR in the position of ruling on CFSP, from which the CJEU is itself largely excluded. It considered that mutual trust and recognition among Member States would be threatened by requirements imposed by the ECtHR. The Court further saw its monopoly of jurisdiction set out in Article 344 TFEU undermined. Currently and despite the legal obligation under the Treaties, EU accession to the ECHR has been moved to the unforeseeable future. The Court's position of protecting the autonomy of EU law creates an obstacle to Union accession towards a well-regarded and reasonably well-functioning regional human rights regime. This makes it impossible for the Union to draw legitimacy from submitting itself to the authority of the ECtHR. It does not affect the Union's and the CJEU's ability to rely on the ECtHR's case law in its reasoning and to indirectly draw legitimacy from the ECHR.

2.2 Investor-State Dispute Settlement and the Investment Court System[47]

In practice, ISDS mechanisms are arguably more relevant to the EU than accession to the ECHR. Since the late 1960s, bilateral investment treaties have included ISDS

[45] See Section 4.2 below for more details.

[46] Opinion 2/13 (n 2). See also Jääskinen and Sikora, 'The Exclusive Jurisdiction of the Court of Justice' (n 22); Tobias Lock, 'The Not So Free Choice of EU Member States in International Dispute Settlement' in Marise Cremona, Anne Thies, and Ramses Wessel (eds), *The EU and International Dispute Settlement* (Hart Publishing 2016). See for more background: Vasiliki Kosta, Nikos Skoutaris, and Vassilis Tzevelekos (eds), *The EU Accession to the ECHR* (1st edn, Hart Publishing 2014); JP Jaqué, 'The Accession of the European Union to the European Convention on Human Rights and Fundamental Freedoms' (2011) 48 CML Rev 995; Tobias Lock, 'EU Accession to the ECHR: Implications for Judicial Review in Strasbourg' (2010) 35 EL Rev 777; Lazowski and Wessel, 'Opinion 2/13' (n 24); Eeckhout, 'Opinion 2/13' (n 24).

[47] ISDS systems exist in very different shapes and forms and ISDS tribunals take very different positions on core legal concepts and principles. This section focuses on ISDS/the ICS in agreements between the Union (and its Member States) on the one hand and non-EU states on the other. It does not engage with intra-EU BITS between Member States.

mechanisms in order to protect investors from developed countries from risks caused by the domestic political and judicial systems of developing countries.[48] Over time, ISDS mechanisms have 'develop[ed] into a mechanism of global governance with arbitral tribunals crafting and concretizing treaty-overarching standards of investment protection with prospective effects on host states and investors',[49] as well as public policy-makers. Their very *purpose* is to contribute to economic development by managing political risks or, more specifically, limiting the (regulatory) powers of the host state in order to protect foreign investors from arbitrary or discriminatory actions (but arguably also beyond this). The creation and multiplication of ISDS mechanisms were met by an exceptionally low level of public trust, including by civil society,[50] and the criticism of many scholars,[51] as well as the European Parliament[52] and the EU Commission.[53]

2.2.1 Investment Court System

In response to the critical voices, the Commission presented in September 2015 its proposal to move to an 'Investment Court System' (ICS) that would replace existing ISDS mechanisms in all ongoing and future EU investment negotiations.[54] The ICS is considered by some as the start of 'a new generation of FTAs'.[55] CETA was the first

[48] The 1968 BIT between the Netherlands and Indonesia was arguably the first that gave investors the possibility of initiating arbitral proceedings against host states to claim violations of contracts or the BIT itself.

[49] Stephan Schill, 'International Investment Law and Comparative Public Law: An Introduction' in Stephan Schill, *International Investment Law and Comparative Public Law* (OUP 2010) 4 (hereafter Schill, 'International Investment Law').

[50] See the Commission, ICS Press release (n 8).

[51] See above all: Gus van Harten, *Sovereign Choices and Sovereign Constraints: Judicial Restraint in Investment Treaty Arbitration* (OUP 2003); Muthucumaraswamy Sornarajah, *Resistance and Change in the International Law on Foreign Investment* (CUP 2015); see also: Barnali Choudhury, 'Recapturing Public Power: Is Investment Arbitration's Engagement with the Public Interest Contributing to the Democratic Deficit?' (2008) 41 VJTL 775; David Schneiderman, *Constitutionalizing Economic Globalization: Investment Rules and Democracy's Promise* (CUP 2008).

[52] European Parliament, 'Report on the Future of European Investment Policy' (2010/2203(INI)). Available at www.europarl.europa.eu/sides/getDoc.do?pubRef=-//EP//NONSGML+REPORT+A7-2011-0070+0+DOC+PDF+V0//EN. See G:

> whereas after the first dispute settlement cases of the 1990s, and in spite of generally positive experiences, a number of problems became clear because of the use of vague language in agreements being left open for interpretation, particularly concerning the possibility of conflict between private interests and the regulatory tasks of public authorities, for example in cases where the adoption of legitimate legislation led to a state being condemned by international arbitrators for a breach of the principle of 'fair and equitable treatment.

See for a rather positive assessment of ISDS, Pieter Jan Kuijper and others, 'Investor-State Dispute Settlement (ISDS) Provisions in the EU's International Investment Agreements' (European Parliament, D-G for External Policies, 'Investor-State Dispute Settlement (ISDS) provisions in the EU's international investment agreements', Vol 1—Workshop).

[53] See the Commission, ICS Press release (n 8).

[54] ibid. At face value this departs from the Council Directives for the negotiation on the Transatlantic Trade and Investment Partnership between the European Union and the United States of America of 17 June 2013 http://data.consilium.europa.eu/doc/document/ST-11103-2013-DCL-1/en/pdf.

[55] Steffen Hindelang and Teoman Hagemeyer, 'In Pursuit of an International Investment Court. Recently Negotiated Investment Chapters in EU Comprehensive Free Trade Agreements in Comparative Perspective' (European Parliament, D-G for External Policies 2017) 15 (hereafter Hindelang and Hagemeyer, 'Investment Chapters in Comparative Perspective').

FTA to set up an ICS, following a last-minute move by the Commission.[56] The criticism levelled at ISDS challenged different aspects all related to its very limited legitimacy, including the lack of judicial independence, predictability and consistency of decisions, as well as transparency. To address (some of) the criticism, the ad hoc arbitration of traditional ISDS was replaced by the ICS.

The ICS in CETA is composed of a tribunal of first instance and an appeal tribunal, operating with relatively independent arbitrators[57] with high-level legal qualifications comparable to those required for the members of permanent international courts, such as the International Court of Justice and the WTO Appellate Body. The tribunal[58] has fifteen members; five from Canada, five from the EU, and five from a third country. Members of the tribunal must possess professional qualifications[59] and adhere to an ethics code.[60] The arbitrators are allocated to a case on the basis of drawing from a roster, 'ensuring that the composition of the divisions is random and unpredictable, while giving equal opportunity to all Members of the Tribunal to serve'.[61] An Appellate Tribunal reviews the decisions of the tribunal.[62] This is aimed at ensuring a greater predictability of outcomes and consistency of decisions. Further, it addresses the criticism that in traditional ISDS mechanisms the first decision is final.[63] The ICS also aimed to reduce the bias towards investors by limiting the financial incentives to act as an arbiter, for instance by providing a retainer fee, as well as a random allocation of cases.

The Commission's proposal is part and parcel of a broader trend towards judicialization of adjudication in EU FTAs.[64] It moves ISDS mechanisms on the scale between arbitration and institutionalized judicial bodies towards the latter. It improves the internal coherence of investment law and the independence of arbitrators. It also reduces the private autonomy bias of arbitration that is part of the current system. The latter helps to frame investor-state disputes as what they are: a claim by an individual that the public exercise of power is incompatible with the principles and norms by which the public authority is bound. This is, and should be, different from finding a pragmatic outcome for a dispute between two private parties. In *Achmea*, the CJEU

[56] Commission, ICS Press release (n 8). The complete text of CETA was published in August 2014. On 29 February 2016, the Commission announced that the EU and Canada had agreed to replace the ad hoc ISDS with a permanent institutionalized construction (the ICS).

[57] The Commission used at the hearing for Opinion 1/17 (26 June 2018) the term 'hybrid' to characterize the ICS, despite its name, as neither ISDS nor a court system.

[58] Art 8.27 EU–Canada Comprehensive Economic and Trade Agreement (CETA) [2017] OJ L11/23.

[59] Art 8.27(4) CETA: 'The Members of the Tribunal shall possess the qualifications required in their respective countries for appointment to judicial office, or be jurists of recognised competence. They shall have demonstrated expertise in public international law. It is desirable that they have expertise in particular, in international investment law, in international trade law and the resolution of disputes arising under international investment or international trade agreements.'

[60] Art 8.30 CETA.

[61] Art 8.27(7) CETA; see also Hindelang and Hagemeyer, 'Investment Chapters in Comparative Perspective' (n 55) 15. See by contrast, the EUSFTA, under which the parties appoint the arbitrators in principle themselves, no mandatory roster exists to assign cases; and fewer qualification requirements apply: art 9.18(2), (3) and (6) EUSFTA, text June 2015 http://trade.ec.europa.eu/doclib/press/index.cfm?id=961.

[62] Art 8.28 CETA.

[63] See also the EU's new trade and investment strategy: European Commission, *Trade for all—Towards a more responsible trade and investment policy* (Foreword by Cecilia Malmström, European Union Publications Office 2015) 21 http://trade.ec.europa.eu/doclib/docs/2015/october/tradoc_153846.pdf.

[64] See already Ignacio Garcia Bercero, 'Dispute Settlement in European Union Free Trade Agreements: Lessons Learned?' in Lorand Bartels and Federico Ortino (eds), *Regional Trade Agreements and the WTO Legal System* (OUP 2006). The author is now the chief negotiator of the TTIP.

made a distinction between ISDS mechanisms and commercial arbitration;[65] yet, the precise scope of what the Court meant and to what extent the latter may also cover disputes in the context of the International Centre for Investment Disputes (ICSID) remains unclear.[66] The framing of disputes is crucial to justify decisions, which may ultimately require the use of public taxpayer money to pay large awards to private parties.

2.2.2 Remaining criticism

Some of the points of criticism continue to remain valid for ICS. First of all, it is an inherent function of law to frame disputes.[67] Law determines what facts are legally relevant and irrelevant and only the former have a direct impact on the ruling. Because of their disconnection from permanent judicial systems, ISDS mechanisms frame disputes in an isolated economic sphere. Furthermore, they disembed the conflicts from their concrete institutional, legal, and factual context, which would allow making communal choices about common goods and constitutional principles relevant for how these conflicts are settled. ICS does not re-embed the conflicts. Their settlement continues to take place in a framework, where non-economic interests compete on an unequal footing with economic interests.[68] This may in principle affect all policy choices to protect non-economic issues, such as public health, the climate, the environment, or labour standards.

Second, on an abstract level CETA addresses the lack of balance between investors' rights and a state's responsibility (obligation[69]) and right to regulate.[70] It has limited the scope of application as compared for example to EUSFTA, which allows 'goodwill' to fall under the term investment,[71] gives investors a right to legitimate expectations,[72] and contains an umbrella clause that requires the parties not to 'frustrate or undermine' a specific and clear commitment in a contractual obligation owed to a foreign investor.[73] The absence of an umbrella clause helps to rebalance interests to some extent. Umbrella clauses favour investors by incorporating other state obligations into the foreign investor's rights and allowing recourse to ISDS with regard to these obligations.[74] However, an investor's interests continue to benefit from strong protection because

[65] Case C-284/16, *Achmea* (n 22) paras 54-55. See more generally on the ruling: Christina Eckes, 'Don't Lead with Your Chin! If Member States continue with the ratification of CETA, they violate European Union law' (*Europeanlawblog*, 23 March 2018) (hereafter Eckes, 'Don't Lead with Your Chin!') https://europeanlawblog.eu/2018/03/13/dont-lead-with-your-chin-if-member-states-continue-with-the-ratification-of-ceta-they-violate-european-union-law/.

[66] See the website for ICSID for more details on procedures and institutional set-up https://icsid.worldbank.org/en/.

[67] See on the phenomenon of framing, eg Mariely Lopez-Santana, 'The Domestic Implications of European Soft Law: Framing and Transmitting Change in Employment Policy' (2006) 13 JEPP 481.

[68] Alessandra Arcuri, 'The Great Asymmetry and the Rule of Law in International Investment Arbitration' in Lisa Sachs, Lise Johnson, and Jesse Coleman (eds), *Yearbook on International Investment Law and Policy* (OUP 2018).

[69] eg established by the Paris Agreement 2015 https://unfccc.int/sites/default/files/english_paris_agreement.pdf.

[70] Art 8.9 CETA. The relevance of the right or scope to regulate has been acknowledged by the CJEU in Joined Cases C-46 and 48/93, *Brasserie du Pêcheur SA* [1996] EU:C:1996:7, para 45 (hereafter Joined Cases C-46 and 48/93, *Brasserie du Pêcheur*): The '[. . .] exercise of the legislative function must not be hindered by the prospect of actions for damages whenever the general interest of the Community requires legislative measures to be adopted which may adversely affect individual interests'.

[71] Art 9.1 (1)(g) EUSFTA. [72] Art 9.4 (2)(e) EUSFTA. [73] Art 9.4 (5) EUSFTA.

[74] Gus Van Santen, 'The EU's Emerging Approach to ISDS: A Review of the Canada–Europe CETA, EU–Singapore FTA, EU–Vietnam FTA' (2016) 1 UBL Rev 138, 158.

CETA gives broad access to dispute settlement in other ways. It takes for example an 'asset-based' approach to 'investment', including 'claims to money',[75] and does not further define 'fair and equitable treatment'.[76] The overall criticism of an asymmetrically strong protection of an investor's interests hence remains valid.

Third, the ICS remains separate from domestic judicial structures, including the CJEU, while relying on them for enforcement. Investment chapters in FTAs usually contain provisions aimed at preventing parallel proceedings before an ISDS mechanism and the domestic judiciary. A U-turn, of moving from ISDS to domestic litigation in an ongoing dispute, is usually excluded. However, exceptionally, CETA allows recourse to domestic remedies if the ISDS mechanism dismisses the claim because it is obviously ill-founded or the claimant withdraws the claim within a certain time.[77] At the same time, CETA not only requires a disputing party to '*recognise and comply with an award without delay*', it also ensures that an award is given the status of an award under both the ICSID and the New York Conventions.[78] This means that there is no or limited scope for judicial review of such awards and that execution can also be sought in states other than that of the party against which the award was issued.[79]

In short, both traditional ISDS mechanisms and the ICS lack an institutional connection to the domestic judiciary and do not possess any comparable constitutional guarantees of rights, principles, democratic legitimacy, or independence.[80] Even if the ICS may possibly offer a higher level of internal coherence,[81] it remains disjointed from the domestic constitutional structures. In fact, the creation of an ICS strengthens the development of investment arbitration growing into a quasi-precedent system that creates a separate system of treaty-overarching standards of investment law.[82] Hence, ISDS allows *reasoning* and *taking binding decisions outside any constitutional framework*, with very limited possibilities to appeal against the ISDS decisions to the domestic judicial system. Moreover, ISDS awards, while determining monetary damages, touch upon the social fabric of society. The risk of high damages and the perception that policy choices could be found to be 'illegal' by an international tribunal are likely to

[75] Art 8.1 CETA 'definitions': '[...] investment means every kind of asset that an investor owns or controls, directly or indirectly, that has the characteristics of an investment, which includes a certain duration and other characteristics such as the commitment of capital or other resources, the expectation of gain or profit, or the assumption of risk'. Some claims to money are then excluded, see art 8.1 CETA for more detail.

[76] Art 8.10 CETA. This is similar to art 9.4(1) EUSFTA.

[77] Hindelang and Hagemeyer, 'Investment Chapters in Comparative Perspective' (n 55) 14.

[78] Art 8.41 (2) CETA. 'New York Convention' refers to the 1958 UN Convention on the Recognition and Enforcement of Foreign Arbitral Awards.

[79] Art 8.41 (4–6) CETA. Art 54(1) ICSID stipulates: 'Each Contracting State shall recognize an award rendered pursuant to this Convention as binding and enforce the pecuniary obligations imposed by that award within its territories as if it were a final judgment of a court in that State'. See, however, the formulation of art 30(2) 'Enforcement of awards' of the Commission's proposal of 16 September 2015 http://trade.ec.europa.eu/doclib/docs/2015/september/tradoc_153807.pdf.

[80] See on conflicts of interests of ad hoc appointed arbitrators who want to continue a career in any given commercial environment or within the arbitration business itself: Cecilia Olivet and Pia Eberhardt, 'Profiting from Crisis. How Corporations and Lawyers are Scavenging Profits from Europe's Crisis Countries' (TNI CEO 2012) http://corporateeurope.org/sites/default/files/profiting-from-crisis_0.pdf.

[81] This should not be immediately concluded, as Ingo Venzke rightly argues in 'Investor-State Dispute Settlement in TTIP from the Perspective of a Public Law Theory of International Adjudication' (2016) 17 JWIT 374, inter alia, pointing out that the appellate instance also introduces a new dynamic of (increased) judicial law-making and does not solve the question of *who* decides.

[82] Schill, 'International Investment Law' (n 49) 20.

affect governance choices (regulatory chill).[83] An ISDS decision that finds a policy decision in breach of the international investment treaty is likely to affect the perception of the legitimacy of these choices by the public. This is precisely the reason why they should be evaluated in the context of the constitutional principles and institutional structures of the affected society. Union participation in ISDS/the ICS supports the choice of an economic bias and sanctions the decoupling of conflict resolution from shared principles and objectives. Potentially, it submits Union policy decisions to this economic review and may ultimately place the Union in the position that it has to justify, not only participation in these mechanisms, but also compliance with its decisions regarding Union citizens. It is difficult to imagine how such justification would not reinforce the (perceived) economic bias and hence affect the legitimacy of Union actions.[84]

2.2.3 The future of ISDS and the ICS

In Opinion 2/15, the CJEU held that setting up ISDS did not fall within the exclusive competence of the EU and cannot therefore be set up without the Member States' consent, including because ISDS remove disputes from national courts. This brings a politically controversial issue within the realm of the ratification powers of national parliaments and triggers all the institutional difficulties that mixed agreements bring with them.[85] In Opinion 2/15, the CJEU also explicated that its position on the competences of the EU 'is entirely without prejudice to the question whether the content of the agreement's provisions is compatible with EU law'.[86] The Court specifically referred to this statement in the section on ISDS,[87] which may at an abstract level already raise doubts about the compatibility of the CJEU's position on ISDS with EU law.

In March 2018, the CJEU ruled in the case of *Achmea* that the ISDS mechanism in the bilateral investment treaty between the Netherlands and Slovakia (NL-SK-BIT) was *incompatible* with EU law.[88] This raises further doubts about the legality not just of ISDS in BITs between Member States (intra-EU BITs) but also of the ICS model introduced in CETA. Two arguments are usually presented to distinguish the ICS in CETA from the ISDS in BITs: first, ICS meets higher rule of law standards. As discussed above, this is true as such. Yet, the CJEU did not declare in *Achmea* that the ISDS was incompatible with EU law on rule of law grounds. The CJEU introduced its ruling with eight paragraphs of principled considerations on the autonomy of the EU legal order before turning to questions about the compatibility of the ISDS mechanism with EU law. The autonomy of EU law, referred to by the CJEU as justified 'by the essential characteristics of the EU and its law',[89] is what makes EU law a legal order. EU law depends for its constitutional character and its ability to ensure the effectiveness of EU law on its autonomous character, that is, its self-referential nature of not depending on national and international law for its validity and interpretation.

[83] Kyla Tienhaara, 'Regulatory Chill in a Warming World: The Threat to Climate Policy Posed by Investor-State Dispute Settlement' (2017) 7 TEL 22.

[84] See below for more details.

[85] See Chapter 5 for a discussion of the issues that mixity raises in terms of political responsibility.

[86] Opinion 2/15 (n 7) para 30.

[87] ibid, para 290.

[88] Case C-284/16, *Achmea* (n 22). This section draws from: Eckes, 'Don't Lead with Your Chin!' (n 65).

[89] *Achmea*, ibid, para 33. See Section 3 of Chapter 1 for a detailed conceptualization of the autonomy of EU law.

The Court found the ISDS in *Achmea* to be in conflict with this autonomy. This is in line with its settled case law which holds that EU submission to ICTs, while it remains possible as a matter of principle, may threaten the very nature and existence of the EU as an autonomous legal order. The CJEU has held that no field of EU law may be removed from the substantive reach of the preliminary reference procedure. The *potential effects* of an international institutional arrangement must be considered when deciding whether such a removal takes place. CETA ensures that foreign investors must choose to bring proceedings either before domestic courts or before an ICS tribunal. If they choose the ICS tribunal they are required to discontinue domestic proceedings or refrain from starting them (fork in the road clause).[90] This provision thus effectively ensures that investment tribunals will be the sole arbitrator. It thus undermines the powers of domestic courts to hear similar claims. Both in relation to the ISDS mechanism in the EUSFTA and with regard to intra-EU BITs, the CJEU has already held that the investment chapter '*removes disputes from the jurisdiction of the courts of the Member States*'. [91] In *Achmea*, it argued that the autonomy of the EU legal order can only be preserved by an internal EU judicial system that is able 'to ensure the consistency and uniformity in interpretation of EU law'.[92] The EU judicial system would be undermined if disputes could be removed from it by bringing them before arbitral tribunals, which, besides the fact that they are not subject to an exhaustion of domestic remedies rule, do not form part of the EU judicial system and consequently cannot ask the CJEU preliminary questions.[93] The removal of potential questions about EU law from the preliminary ruling procedure is not limited to situations in which the arbitral tribunal actually strictly speaking interprets EU law. Questions about EU law can also arise from prima facie purely national legal issues, because they fall within the widely defined scope of EU law or because they touch upon the Union's interest. These fundamental concerns of the CJEU seem to apply in the same way to the ICS under CETA.

Second, in *Achmea* the Court ruled on a bilateral investment agreement between two EU Member States. CETA is an FTA between the EU and all 28 Member States as one party and a third country as the other. If anything, this makes the situation more problematic. In *Achmea*, the CJEU rejected that an arbitral tribunal established under an international agreement between two Member States could be considered part of the judicial system of the EU.[94] The same conclusion applies even more obviously to an arbitral tribunal established in a multilateral agreement involving a third country. The Court's *reasoning* in *Achmea* confirms that the threat to autonomy is not averted by the CETA provision that aligns the interpretation of EU law by the arbitral tribunal to the 'prevailing interpretation' of the CJEU and stipulates that 'any meaning given to domestic law by the Tribunal shall not be binding upon the courts or the authorities of that Party'.[95] Section 3.5 below discusses the effects of provisions classifying domestic law as facts. *Achmea* made apparent the tangible probability that the Court may find fault with CETA in Opinion 1/17.

[90] Art 8.22 (1)(f) and (g) CETA.
[91] Citation from Opinion 2/15 (n 7) para 292. See also: Case C-284/16, *Achmea* (n 22) paras 50–52.
[92] *Achmea*, ibid, para 35. [93] ibid, paras 50–52. [94] ibid, para 45.
[95] Art 8.31 CETA; nearly identical for example: Section 3, art 16(2) of the EU–Vietnam Free Trade Agreement.

2.3 Aarhus Convention and its compliance committee

The ACCC is a non-judicial body mandated to review compliance of the parties with their obligations under the Aarhus Convention.[96] It is an 'optional arrangement[] of a non-confrontational, non-judicial and consultative nature',[97] whose powers are limited to examining compliance issues and making findings and recommendations.[98] This non-confrontational nature becomes apparent in the recommendations it addresses and the limitation of potential means: usually it issues its recommendations to the Meeting of the Parties, rather than to the party concerned.[99] Neither the ACCC nor the Meeting of the Parties can issue fines, or order cessation or compensation. In practice, the Meeting of the Parties adopts the position of the ACCC and endorses its findings and recommendations. The Meeting of the Parties is then responsible for agreeing upon appropriate measures in order to bring the non-complying party into full compliance with the rules of the Aarhus Convention.[100] The ACCC must allow for appropriate public involvement, which may include 'communications' from the public.[101] This has given a voice to particular interlocutors in the debate, in particular non-governmental organizations (NGOs) and individual members of the public.

2.3.1 Reception and rejection of ACCC findings

The ACCC has produced a considerable body of case law interpreting the Aarhus Convention.[102] The CJEU has given quite some attention to the findings of the ACCC.[103] At the same time, it has shown considerable restraint when confronted with questions on the compatibility of EU law with the Aarhus Convention. A preliminary ruling from France presented the CJEU with the question of whether the Environmental Information Directive was applicable to trading information of emission allowances under the ETS.[104] Advocate General Kokott argued in favour of relying on the explanatory memorandum for the Commission proposal of the directive and

[96] UNECE, 'Meeting of the Parties to the Convention on Access to Information, Public Participation in Decision-making and Access to Justice in Environmental Matters' (Report of the First Meeting of the Parties, Addendum, Decision I/7, Review of Compliance, UN Doc. ECE/MP.PP/2/Add. 8, October 2002) section VI (hereafter UNECE (United Nations Economic Commission for Europe), Convention on Access to Information). In addition, a party may make a submission about compliance by another party or about its own compliance and the secretariat may also make a referral to the Committee.

[97] 15 United Nations Economic Commission for Europe Convention on Access to Information, Public Participation in Decision-Making and Access to Justice in Environmental Matters [1998] 2161 UNTS 447.

[98] Decision I/7 (n 96) para 37.

[99] The Committee may make recommendations directly to the party concerned only with the party's agreement.

[100] Decision I/7 (n 96) para 37. Decision 1/I sets out the rules of procedure of the Meeting of the Parties MoP, see para 35 of UNECE, Convention on Access to Information (n 96) Decision I/1. Generally, every effort shall be made to reach a decision by consensus, but if this is not possible the MoP can decide on substantive issues by a three/fourth majority.

[101] The Bern Convention has also introduced a so-called 'case-file system' which allows complaints to be filed by NGOs, although this system is more based on passive monitoring than the proactive role of the ACCC in issuing recommendations.

[102] A Andrusevych and S Kern (eds), *Case Law of the Aarhus Convention Compliance Committee (2004–2014)* (3rd edn, Edition RACSE 2016).

[103] See eg Opinion of AG Kokott in Case C-260/11, *Edwards v Environment Agency* [2012] EU:C:2012:645.

[104] See Case C-524/09, *Ville de Lyon* [2010] EU:C:2010:822.

the Implementation Guide for the Aarhus Convention.[105] The Court did not follow its Advocate General but ruled that the Environmental Information Directive is not applicable to 'trading information'.[106] The Aarhus Convention, as an international agreement of the EU, ranks between primary and secondary law. Secondary law should, if not reviewed, be interpreted in light of the Convention.[107] A consistent interpretation of the directive with the Convention would have arguably led to a broad understanding of 'environmental information'.

A particular issue under EU law continues to be participation and standing requirements. The General Court ruled in the *Stichting Natuur en Milieu* case that the rules on participation and access to justice in the 2006 Regulation, which limit access to the internal review procedure to 'measure[s] of individual scope', are incompatible with Article 9(3) of the Aarhus Convention.[108] On appeal,[109] the CJEU cited *Slovak Bears* and reiterated that Article 9(3), because 'only members of the public who "meet the criteria, if any, laid down in ... national law" [were] entitled to exercise the rights provided for in Article 9(3), that provision [was] subject, in its implementation or effects, to the adoption of a subsequent measure'[110] and that it therefore did not have direct effect. The Court further rejected with regard to the rules on participation and access to justice in the 2006 Regulation, the *Fediol* or *Nakajima*[111] exceptions that allow for review of EU law in light of the GATT/WTO if secondary EU law either explicitly refers to or implements specific GATT obligations.[112] While the specific rules on participation and access to justice do not refer to the specific obligations under the Aarhus Convention, the 2006 Regulation was expressly focused on giving effect to the Aarhus Convention. Another appeal is pending before the CJEU against a 2016 ruling of the General Court, inter alia, for applying an incorrect and impossible burden of proof on NGOs bringing challenges under Articles 10 and 12 of the Aarhus Regulation on behalf of the environment.[113]

The Union, as a party to the Convention, is obliged under international law to comply with its rules. Beyond this, a coherence argument can be made that the CJEU should submit Union law to the same interpretation of the Aarhus Convention as national law. Such an argument is supported by the prominent role of coherence in the European Treaties and in *Slovak Bears*.[114] That is, with regard to law enforcement by

[105] See Case C-524/09, *Ville de Lyon* [2010] EU:C:2010:613, Opinion of AG Kokott, paras 37, 42, and 64.

[106] ibid. [107] ibid.

[108] Case T-338/08, *Stichting Natuur en Milieu v Commission* [2012] EU:T:2012:300.

[109] Joined Cases C-404 and 405/12 P, *Council and Commission v Stichting Natuur en Milieu* [2015] EU:C:2015:5 (hereafter Joined Cases C-404 and 405/12 P, *Stichting Natuur en Milieu*).

[110] ibid, para 47. See also: Case C-470/16, *North East Pylon Pressure Campaign Limited Maura Sheehy v An Bord Pleanála Minister for Communications, Climate Action and Environment, Ireland Attorney General, Ireland and Joined party EirGrid Plc* [2018] EU:C:2018:185.

[111] Case C-70/87, *Fediol v Commission* [1989] EU:C:1989:254; Case C-69/89, *Nakajima* [1991] EU:C:1991:186.

[112] Joined Cases C-404 and 405/12 P, *Stichting Natuur en Milieu* (109) paras 50–51. Joined Cases C-401/12 P to C-403/12 P, *Council and Others v Vereniging Milieudefensie and Stichting Stop Luchtverontreiniging Utrecht* [2015] EU:C:2015:4 (hereafter Joined Cases C-401/12 P to C-403/12 P, *Vereniging Milieudefensie*)

[113] Appeal brought on 14 February 2017 by TestBioTech eV, European Network of Scientists for Social and Environmental Responsibility eV, Sambucus eV against the judgment of the General Court (Fifth Chamber) delivered on 15 December 2016 in Case T-177/13: Case C-82/17 P, *TestBioTech eV, European Network of Scientists for Social and Environmental Responsibility eV, Sambucus eV v Commission.*

[114] Case C-243/15, *Lesoochranárske zoskupenie VLK (Slovak Bears)* [2016] EU:C:2016:838. See Section 6 of Chapter 4 for more details on this case.

the Union and the national authorities, environmental NGOs should be placed in the same position before the EU Courts as before national courts.

2.3.2 Deference and bite of the ACCC

The ACCC has shown great deference to the CJEU by waiting for the CJEU's rulings in at least three cases: one on standing under Article 263(4) TFEU after the entry into force of the Lisbon Treaty; one on standing rules in light of the EU's accession to the Aarhus Convention; and one on the validity of the Aarhus Regulation.[115] However, it is also an international body (here discussed as an ICT, even if it is expressly non-judicial) that has most directly and strongly confronted the EU judicial system on fundamental grounds. In 2011, the ACCC was asked to decide whether the standing requirement of 'individual concern' before the EU Courts was in compliance with the provisions of the Aarhus Convention. [116] The applicant had addressed this as a general point, focusing on the CJEU's case law in the main rather than the relevant provisions or particular decisions, while including a number of specific cases in its analysis.[117] The ACCC focused on *WWF-UK*,[118] the first decision of the General Court after the Aarhus Convention entered into force for the EU. It showed great deference to the EU Courts[119] but, at the same time, reached a rather critical conclusion. The ACCC declined to rule on the question of whether the *WWF-UK* case in itself amounts to non-compliance with the Convention and avoided any direct finding that the EU is in breach of the Aarhus Convention. However, it concluded that 'with regard to access to justice by members of the public, the Committee is convinced that if the jurisprudence of the EU Courts, as evidenced by the cases examined, were to continue, unless fully compensated for by adequate administrative review procedures, the [EU] would fail to comply with Article 9[(3) and (4)]'.[120] The ACCC also recommended 'that a new direction of the jurisprudence of the EU Courts should be established in order to ensure compliance' and 'that all relevant EU institutions within their competences take the steps to overcome the shortcomings reflected in the jurisprudence of the EU Courts'.[121]

In 2017, the ACCC found that the EU had failed to comply with Article 9(3) and (4) 'with regard to access to justice by members of the public because neither the Aarhus Regulation, nor the jurisprudence of the CJEU implements or complies with

[115] ibid; Case C-530/11, *European Commission v United Kingdom (WWF-UK)* [2014] EU:C:2014:67; Joined Cases C-404 and 405/12 P, *Stichting Natuur en Milieu* (n 109) and Joined Cases C-401/12 P to C-403/12 P, *Vereniging Milieudefensie* (n 112).

[116] UNECE, 'Findings and Recommendations of the Compliance Committee with Regard to Communication ACC/C/2008/32 (Part I) Concerning Compliance by the European Union' (14 April 2011) (hereafter UNECE, 'Findings and Recommendations') http://www.unece.org/fileadmin/DAM/env/pp/compliance/C2008-32/DRF/C32Findings27April2011.pdf. See also Charles Poncelet, 'Access to Justice in Environmental Matters: Does the European Union Comply with its Obligations?' (2012) 24 J Env L 287; Teresa Weber, 'Die Umsetzung der Aarhus-Konvention beim direkten Vollzug von Unionsrecht' (2012) 20 JPR 137.

[117] Joined Cases T-236/04 & T-241/04, *European Environmental Bureau (EEB) and Stichting Natuur en Milieu v Commission of the European Communities* [2005] EU:T:2005:426. Case T-37/04, *Região autónoma dos Açores v Council* [2008] EU:T:2008:236; Case C-444/08, *Região autónoma dos Açores v Council* [2009] EU:C:2009:733. Case T-338/08, *Stichting Natuur en Milieu v Commission* [2012] EU:T:2012:300.

[118] See Case T-91/07, *WWF-UK Ltd. v Council* [2008] EU:T:2008:170; Case C-355/08, *WWF-UK Ltd. v Council* [2009] EU:C:2009:286.

[119] See eg UNECE, 'Findings and Recommendations' (n 116) paras 7, 10, 59, and 63, which demonstrate deference and limitation to the main allegation.

[120] ibid, para 88.

[121] ibid, paras 97–98.

the obligations arising under those paragraphs'.[122] The Commission objected to the findings of the ACCC on the EU's non-compliance with its obligations under that treaty on the ground that the ACCC's findings 'do not recognise the EU's special legal order' because the findings 'neither acknowledge the central role of national courts as ordinary Court of EU law, nor recognise the system of preliminary rulings under Article 267 TFEU as a valid means of redress'.[123] Moreover, it concluded that the findings 'challenge constitutional principles of EU law that are so fundamental that it is legally impossible for the EU to follow and comply with the findings'.[124]

In practice a compromise was struck requiring the amendment of the draft recommendations on a number of issues.[125] The findings of the ACCC would, for example, no longer be 'endorsed' but 'take[n] note of' by the Meeting of the Parties. Furthermore, significant parts of the recommendations were deleted and the EU was only required to 'consider' the recommendations. On this basis, the Union would have been able to accept the decision. Yet, the non-EU signatories to the Convention refused to adopt the EU's position at the Meeting of Parties in September 2017. The decision was ultimately postponed until the next Meeting of Parties in 2021.[126]

This was the first time that a contracting party of the Aarhus Convention proposed not to endorse a decision of the Meetings of Parties that was based on the findings of the ACCC. None of the EU institutions has made a claim that the ACCC constitutes a threat to the autonomy of EU law. However, the open rejection of the findings of the ACCC stands in direct tension with the Union's explicit external objective of committing and contributing to international rule-based multilateralism as a way of strengthening the rule of law principles under international law.[127]

3. Is the Autonomy of the EU Legal Order Under Pressure?

This section examines in five sections the potential effects of EU submission to the jurisdiction of ICTs on the EU legal order, including the institutional and constitutional basis of the Union's claim to autonomy as set out in Chapter 1, such as the preliminary ruling procedure and the competing narratives of autonomy and sovereignty. Sections 5 and 6 below draw further conclusions on consequences for emerging structures of bonding, legitimacy, and effectiveness of the EU legal order.[128]

[122] UNECE Aarhus Convention Compliance Committee, 'Findings and recommendations of the Aarhus Convention Compliance Committee with regard to Communication ACCC/C/2008/32 (Part II) concerning compliance by the European Union' (17 March 2017) para 123.

[123] COM (2017) 366 final (n 11) 2, 7. Laurens Ankersmit, 'Judging International Dispute Settlement: from the Investment Court System to the Aarhus Convention's Compliance Committee' (2017) ACELG Working Paper 04/2017 https://www.researchgate.net/publication/321496769_Judging_international_dispute_settlement_from_the_Investment_Court_System_to_the_Aarhus_Convention%27s_Compliance_Committee.

[124] ibid, 5.

[125] See ibid. Council Decision (EU) 2017/1346 on the position to be adopted, on behalf of the European Union, at the sixth session of the Meeting of the Parties to the Aarhus Convention as regards compliance case ACCC/C/2008/32 [2017] OJ L 186/15.

[126] European Parliament, 'Implementing the Aarhus Convention Access to justice in environmental matters' (briefing, October 2017) http://www.europarl.europa.eu/RegData/etudes/BRIE/2017/608753/EPRS_BRI(2017)608753_EN.pdf.

[127] See European Commission, 'Reflection Paper on Harnessing Globalisation' COM (2017) 240 https://ec.europa.eu/commission/sites/beta-political/files/reflection-paper-globalisation_en.pdf.

[128] See Chapter 1 for more details on these concepts.

3.1 Contestation from the inside

International agreements do not regulate the issue of dualism and monism. This remains a decision made by the contracting parties under domestic law, even if international agreements can claim self-executing force or direct effect. However, if ICTs—in decisions binding on the Union—classify EU law as international law, they formally deny EU law and the CJEU the possibility of taking a dualist approach to international law and allow national courts to challenge the CJEU's dualist position within the framework of EU law. As a consequence, the self-referential nature of EU law, that is, the separation of the logical frameworks for legal reasoning, would be put under pressure. This self-referential nature, however, is the very foundation of the autonomy of EU law.

The ECtHR, for example, sees the EU as an 'international organization' to which states 'have transferred part of their sovereignty'.[129] It refers to EU law as 'international legal obligations' of the contracting parties.[130] Indeed, this is the core of the argument in the case of *Bosphorus*, in which the ECtHR established the presumption of equivalent protection, on the basis of which it exercises full judicial review *only if* the protection under EU law proves to be 'manifestly deficient' in the individual case. The *Bosphorus* presumption is based on a view of the CJEU as 'international machinery for supervising fundamental rights'.[131] Hence, the ECtHR's deference to the CJEU is based on its understanding that EU law is of an international nature and that the CJEU is an international court.

Post-accession, the *Bosphorus* doctrine would, logically, no longer be applicable to the EU.[132] The general and abstract presumption that equivalent protection is provided simply cannot apply to a specific opinion of the CJEU under the prior involvement procedure foreseen in the draft accession agreement. After receiving the CJEU's opinion on a particular (aspect of a) case, the Strasbourg Court would have to rule whether the Convention has been breached. It would have to decide whether or not the specific interpretation of the CJEU violates the Convention, but it could not logically refer to the abstract *Bosphorus* presumption that the human rights protection in the EU legal order is generally sufficient. However, there is no logical reason why the ECtHR would change its reading of EU law as international law.

The draft agreement on the EU's accession to the ECHR states that the term 'domestic' in Article 35(1) ECHR also relates, *mutatis mutandis*, to the internal legal order of the EU.[133] In Opinion 2/13, the Commission used this point together with the fact that '[w]ith regard ... to the prior exhaustion of domestic remedies, ... the draft agreement guarantees that remedies before the Courts of the EU must be exhausted before an application against an act on the part of the EU can be validly brought before the ECtHR' in order to argue that the CJEU should be seen as a *domestic* court. It also referred to the fact that 'proceedings before the Courts of the EU are not to be understood as constituting "procedures of international investigation or settlement"',[134] nor, in fact, as means of dispute settlement within the meaning of Article 55 of the ECHR.

[129] *Bosphorus Hava Yollari Turizm veTicaret AS v Ireland* App no 45036/98 (ECtHR, 30 June 2005) para 154 and following case law (hereafter *Bosphorus*).

[130] ibid.

[131] *Michaud v France* App no 12323/11, 6 December 2012.

[132] Eckes, 'EU Accession to the ECHR' (n 39) 280. Considering the application of *Bosphorus* post-accession as uncertain: Leonard Besselink, 'The Protection of Fundamental Rights post-Lisbon: The Interaction between the EU Charter of Fundamental Rights, the European Convention on Human Rights (ECHR) and National Constitutions' (*FIDE*, 2012). Available at www.fide2012.eu/index.php?doc_id=94.

[133] Art 1(5) second indent of the DAA; see also Opinion 2/13 (n 2) para 89.

[134] ibid.

The draft accession agreement also established that '"national law", "administration of the State", "national laws", "national authority", or "domestic" [...] [in] the Convention [...] shall be understood as relating also, *mutatis mutandis*, to the internal legal order of the European Union as a non-State party to the Convention and to its institutions, bodies, offices or agencies'.[135] This, however, does not guarantee that the ECtHR would drastically change its understanding on the nature of EU law. The accession agreement places the CJEU in a special position as compared to domestic courts of other contracting parties. The prior involvement procedure, which allows the ECHR to hold proceedings in order to ask for the CJEU's interpretation of EU law, treats the CJEU differently from the constitutional courts of the other contracting parties, which do not enjoy such privilege. This complicated approach of treating the CJEU as a domestic court, while granting it special privileges, is an acknowledgement of the compound judicial structure of the EU, in which the CJEU stands in a cooperating relationship with national courts, without having the power of repeal.[136] It could also be read as attempting the impossible by asking the ECtHR to apply the Convention to the EU in the same way as it is applied to the other contracting parties, precisely *despite the fact* that EU law is international law. This would explain the formulation of provisions 'understood as relating to' and '*mutatis mutandis*', which allow necessary alterations to be made to adapt to the fact that EU law is international law while not affecting the main point of the review procedures.

The Commission seems to be keenly aware of the challenges of protecting the autonomy narrative of the CJEU and herewith the understanding that EU law is domestic law and can take a dualist approach to international law. It suggested that an explicit clause is included in international trade agreements that EU law is domestic law, for example, in the case of CETA.[137] In principle, ISDS arbitrators may consider EU law as international law, domestic law, or fact.[138] An example where ISDS arbitration explicitly found EU law to be subordinate to international investment law is the *AES* case, in which Hungary claimed that the tariff reductions that allegedly infringed the fair and equitable treatment standard of an investment treaty were required by EU law.[139] Establishing an explicit understanding that the EU is domestic law and that it can take a dualist position, vis-à-vis international law that is binding both on the ICTs and the Member States, may help to address this particular threat to the EU's autonomy. It would, however, have to be even more explicit than the formulations under the draft accession agreement.

In principle, when the EU is a contracting party to an international agreement establishing an ICT, the Union, including the CJEU, and the Member States, including national courts, are bound under EU law by the ICT's interpretations.[140] This allows national courts to rely—also vis-à-vis the CJEU—on these interpretations by the ICT, including the interpretation that EU law is international law and hence subordinated to general rules of international law. These interpretations give national courts

[135] Art 5 of the DAA.

[136] See Section 3.2 of Chapter 1 on the preliminary ruling procedure.

[137] See art 8.31(2) CETA: 'The Tribunal shall not have jurisdiction to determine the legality of a measure, alleged to constitute a breach of this Agreement, under the *domestic* law of the disputing Party' (emphasis added).

[138] The latter is how international courts, including the ECtHR, see domestic law.

[139] *AES v Hungary* Case No ARB/07/22 (Award) (ICSID, 23 September 2010) para 7.6.6; see Mathew Parish, 'International Courts and the European Legal Order' (2012) 23 EJIL 141, 148.

[140] Art 216 TFEU. The binding force of decisions of ISDS may be excluded for the interpretation of EU law, see eg art 8.31 CETA.

valid arguments to challenge the narrative of the CJEU of the autonomous EU legal order within the framework of norms legally binding on the Union.[141] A challenge to the CJEU's autonomy narrative by national courts poses a threat to the EU legal order for two reasons. First, national courts do not form part of *one* judicial pyramid with the CJEU. The CJEU cannot annul the decisions of national courts but depends on their willingness to apply and follow its decisions. National courts have the formal power to boycott and challenge the system.[142]

Second, the domestic nature of EU law is as such contested. This is different for national law. As a consequence, national courts could rely on rulings of ICTs that are binding on the CJEU to justify that EU law is international law. As a knock-off effect, they could argue that EU law should as such be seen as binding *on* the national legal order, rather than being binding *in* the national legal order enjoying primacy and direct applicability. They could also argue that EU law is, for example, subordinate to UN Security Council resolutions under Chapter VII.[143]

Ultimately, the intensity of the threat to the EU's autonomy is determined by the question of how integrated and irreversibly interlocked the EU and national legal orders—above all their judicial systems—really are. A confirmation by a well-respected external judicial authority such as the ECtHR that the EU is international law and should be treated as such (no dualism vis-à-vis international law; dualism by Member States vis-à-vis EU law) would be a trump card in the judicial relationship between the CJEU and national courts.

Martti Koskenniemi concluded in more general terms: 'to reduce one [EU law or international law] into the other or to set them in a hierarchical relationship will distort the image of both'.[144] The threat to the autonomy of the EU legal order is a concretization of this distortion of this relationship.

The autonomy of EU law vis-à-vis national law can often be best preserved by voluntary adaptation. The interdependencies between the national legal orders and the European legal order are much higher than the interdependence between the European legal order and any international regime setting up an ICT, including the ECHR. The willingness to adapt in order to preserve the status quo of multiple narratives of autonomy is very high among national courts and the CJEU. ICTs, by contrast, are not part of this interlocking relationship with interdependent stakes. Their commitment to preserving the internal validity of the different autonomy narratives may not be expected to run as high. This is a particular expression of the general point that external relations are different from the internal relations within the EU: between EU law and national law, between the CJEU and national courts, and between the EU institutions and national governments, and between EU citizens the joint interdependent stakes are extraordinarily high. This results in a much greater willingness to cooperate and recognize the common cause of a functioning EU legal order.

3.2 Article 267 TFEU

The CJEU argues that, in particular, any changes to 'the essential character of [the] powers' of the judiciary would have an 'adverse effect on the autonomy of the EU legal order'.[145]

141 See Section 3.1 of Chapter 1 for a detailed development of the CJEU's autonomy narrative.
142 See Section 3.3 and 3.4 of Chapter 1 for more details on this point.
143 See below the hypothetical scenario of the *Kadi* case after EU accession to the ECHR.
144 Martti Koskenniemi (ed), *International Law Aspects of the European Union* (Brill 1997) vii–viii.
145 Opinion 2/13 (n 2) para 183.

Most importantly, the EU legal order consists of 29 judicial systems, connected via a preliminary ruling system in which the courts of the 28 jurisdictions of the Member States can ask the CJEU to rule on the interpretation and validity of EU law, which is vested with effect in these 28 judicial systems via primacy and direct effect. The preliminary ruling procedure is hence the pivotal connection between these judicial systems.[146] It is crucially important for the functioning of the EU legal order and the effect of EU law within the national legal orders. If disputes are brought before ICTs, which do not have the power of referral and which are hence removed from this formalized judicial discourse and cooperation mechanism, this interrupts this pivotal connection and stands in the way of EU law developing its *unique effectiveness within* the national legal order.[147] Removing disputes creates bubbles in which the uniform application of EU law can no longer be ensured. This likely consequence was flagged by the Commission in the context of intra-EU BITs.[148] Ultimately, this weakens the bonding potential of this structure which connects the Union to its citizens as rights holders.[149]

3.3 Policy choices and division of competences

In principle, one could argue that challenges to the legitimacy and the substantive choices of the legal order affect state parties to ISDS mechanisms in the same way as the Union. However, in several respects the Union and the CJEU may nonetheless be particularly vulnerable to these challenges.

As mentioned above, regulatory chill is one of the concerns that speaks against ISDS/the ICS. In this context, it is worth recalling that in the past the CJEU expressly aimed to avoid such an effect. It held that the 'exercise of the legislative function must not be hindered by the prospect of actions for damages whenever the general interest of the [Union] requires legislative measures to be adopted which may adversely affect individual interests'.[150] Hence, the CJEU's case law is at present on the opposite of a scale from what is feared to be the effect of ISDS/the ICS.

It is furthermore noteworthy that the CJEU remains a *supranational* court that depends to a high degree on the willingness of national courts. This is different for the highest national courts, which can repeal decisions of lower national courts. The Member States (with a limited involvement of the institutions) introduced in the Lisbon Treaty a new appointment procedure aimed at raising the standards for judicial qualifications and the independence of the CJEU's judges.[151] Yet the CJEU, as a supranational court, may arguably be built on a less solid basis of public support and fundamental institutional trust than national courts.[152] In turn, the EU Courts would

[146] See also Section 3.2 of Chapter 1.

[147] See the CJEU's reasoning in *Achmea* in Section 2.2.3 above.

[148] *European Commission, Amicus Curiae submission in European American Investment Bank AG (EURAM) v Slovak Republic* (13 October 2011); *European Commission, Amicus Curiae submission as quoted by the arbitration tribunal in Achmea B.V. v The Slovak Republic* (UNCITRAL, PCA Case No 2008-13, award on jurisdiction 7 December 2012) https://www.italaw.com/sites/default/files/case-documents/ita0309.pdf.

[149] See Section 2 of Chapter 1 for a conceptualization of bonding structures.

[150] Joined Cases C-46 and 48/93, *Brasserie du Pêcheur* (n 70) para 45.

[151] Arts 253 and 254 TFEU. See Michal Bobek (ed), *Selecting Europe's Judges: A Critical Review of the Appointment Procedures to the European Courts* (OUP 2015).

[152] See however the 'Standard Eurobarometer 87—Public opinion in the European Union' on trust in institutions, showing interview data that more citizens tend to trust the EU than their national governments and national parliaments (42% as opposed to 37% and 36%, respectively) http://ec.europa.eu/commfrontoffice/publicopinion/index.cfm/Survey/getSurveyDetail/instruments/STANDARD/surveyKy/2142.

be more easily affected by legitimacy problems of ICTs, to whose decisions they give effect, than national courts, which form part of the national constitutionally established judiciary.

Moreover, the legitimacy concerns that ISDS mechanisms raise with regard to deliberative democracy, as well as the economic framing of disputes, correspond to two weak spots of the EU. The difficulties of democratically legitimizing decisions within the EU political and legal order are well known[153] and the EU has long been criticized for prioritizing the liberalist economic perspective.[154] Hence, where EU international agreements set up ISDS, which result in less transparency and an economic bias, this weakens the EU's legitimacy in areas where the EU already struggles to be perceived as legitimate. This may be one of the reasons why the Commission has, more clearly than the EU Member States, expressed its intention to improve transparency and independence of investment arbitration, make it subject to stricter rules, protect domestic value choices, and bring it closer to the domestic judiciary.

In addition, pursuing strategies of holding ISDS/the ICS at arm's length similar to the strategies that the CJEU's pursues with, for example, WTO law by denying it direct effect within the EU legal order, may be difficult. In light of the settled case law of the CJEU and the Commission's ICS proposal[155]—particularly, in light of the ICSID and New York Conventions, which oblige domestic courts to enforce international awards— this seems not to be a viable strategy.

Finally, investment arbitration may interfere with the CJEU's exclusive competence to give a 'definite' interpretation of EU law. Investment arbitration does not usually require the exhaustion of local judicial remedies. This may result in a situation in which the CJEU has not had the opportunity to rule on the EU law issues at stake.

The imposition of investment awards, even though it concerns questions of responsibility rather than competence, may require a consideration of the division of competence between the EU and the Member States. In Opinion 2/15, the CJEU held that ISDS mechanisms did not fall within the exclusive competence of the EU and cannot therefore be set up without the Member States' consent.[156] The Commission pursues a practice of splitting FTAs into a general EU–only agreement and a mixed agreement for ISDS/the ICS.[157] Mixed agreements, in principle, specifically avoid a clear determination of the division of internal competence.[158]

Hence, even though the *interpretation of EU law* in the context of investment arbitration is not directly authoritative or binding within the EU legal order, it applies pressure to define competences, including competences whose definition has been consciously left open, for example, by the choice for a mixed agreement. This is why attempts have been made to avoid ICTs rulings on the division of competences by referring the decision to an internal procedure of determination between the Union and

[153] See literature on the EU's democratic deficit. eg Andreas Follesdal and Simon Hix, 'Why There is a Democratic Deficit in the EU: A Response to Majone and Moravcsik' (2006) 44 JCMS 533. See also Chapter 1, Section 4.

[154] Gareth Davies, 'Democracy and Legitimacy in the Shadow of Purposive Competence' (2015) 21 ELJ 2.

[155] See Commission, 'ICS proposal' (n 82).

[156] Opinion 2/15 (n 7) in which the Commission asks the Court whether the Union has the requisite competence to sign and conclude alone the Free Trade Agreement with Singapore.

[157] See for the Commission's reaction to Opinion 2/15 http://ec.europa.eu/trade/policy/in-focus/eu-singapore-agreement/agreement-explained/.

[158] Chapter 2 on Sincere Cooperation.

its Member States[159] or to require that investment arbitrators request guidance from the CJEU in cases where an interpretation of EU law is necessary. The Union has addressed this point with the adoption of the Financial Responsibility Regulation, which regulates the conditions of financial responsibility and sets out criteria for determining the respondent in ISDS cases.[160] EU agreements containing some form of ISDS also provide that, in principle, the EU and not the arbitration tribunals determine the respondent to the cases by foreign investors.[161] However, this does not fully rule out that investment tribunals take a position with regard to the division of powers between the Union and its Member States.[162]

3.4 Standing

The 'complete system of legal remedies', in which the preliminary ruling procedure complements the annulment procedure under Article 263 TFEU, satisfies the right of access to justice in the eyes of the CJEU.[163] The CJEU justifies, in this complete system of remedies, the strict rules on the standing of non-privileged applicants under the annulment procedure by reference to the alternative route of challenging EU law under the preliminary ruling procedure. Irrespective of whether this combination of different judicial routes starting in different jurisdictions provides appropriate judicial protection (there are good reasons to argue that it is not sufficient!), relying heavily on the preliminary ruling procedure for the pursuit of individual justice gives this formalized mechanism of judicial dialogue and cooperation a central place. This in turn contributes to the frequent use of the preliminary ruling procedure, which leads to an even closer interlocking embrace of national and European law, and ensures the unique high level of effectiveness of EU law in the national legal order. This reliance on the preliminary ruling procedure or, to be more precise, the restrictive standing requirements under the annulment procedure may create a particular problem in the context of ICTs.

First, a case could arise in which a foreign investor is denied standing and brings a case to the ICTs. In fact, 'there have been numerous cases where actions brought by economic operators or associations thereof have been declared inadmissible by the Community judicature', as the Commission submitted to the ACCC.[164] An example

[159] An attempt to proceduralize the competence question is the Declaration of Transparency under art 26.3.b(ii) of the Energy Charter Treaty which reads: 'The Communities and the Member States will, if necessary, determine among them who is the respondent party to arbitration proceedings initiated by an Investor of another contracting party. In such case, upon the request of the Investor, the Communities and the Member States concerned will make such determination within a period of 30 days.'

[160] Parliament and Council Regulation (EU) 912/2014 establishing a framework for managing financial responsibility linked to investor-to-state dispute settlement tribunals established by international agreements to which the European Union is party [2014] OJ L 257/121. See Laurens Ankersmit, 'Dispute Settlement in the Current Generation of Trade and Investment Agreements of the EU: Foregoing the Days of Caution and Restraint?' (2018 *forthcoming*) SYEL 22–24.

[161] See for instance Art 8.21 CETA.

[162] Hannes Lenk, 'Issues of Attribution: Responsibility of the EU in Investment Disputes under CETA' (2016) TDM 1.

[163] Case C-50/00 P, *Unión de Pequeños Agricultores v Council (UPA)* [2002] EU:C:2002:462, para 41. Whether the preliminary ruling procedure is indeed sufficient is very much contested, see for example Ewa Biernat, 'The Locus Standi of Private Applicants under article 230 (4) EC and the Principle of Judicial Protection in the European Community' (2012) Jean Monnet Working Paper 03/2012.

[164] European Commission, written submissions of the EC in ACCC/C/2008/32 (11 June 2009), para 35 and the Appendix http://www.unece.org/env/pp/compliance/compliancecommittee/32TableEC.html accessed 10 January 2018. The Commission listed 37 cases where economic operators or associations thereof were denied standing before the courts.

is the case of *Telefónica v Commission,* in which a multinational telecommunications company was denied standing to challenge a Commission decision addressed to Spain declaring an aid scheme (tax breaks) partially incompatible with the internal market.[165] The CJEU argued that Telefónica could have brought the rejection of its application for the scheme before the national courts.[166] Another example is the case of *T & L Sugar,* in which a group of sugar cane refiners was denied standing to challenge a series of Commission acts that prioritized beet sugar over cane sugar.[167] The CJEU held that the applicants were not directly concerned because they produced cane rather than beet sugar and the measures related to the latter. It further argued that the required rubber stamping by national authorities qualified as national implementation within the meaning of Article 263(4) TFEU.[168] Both cases illustrate that it is a very reasonable scenario that actors, who are economically affected within the wide definitions of investment treaties, could be denied standing before the CJEU. This in turn places tribunals of the ICS in the position to rule on situations on which the CJEU has not had the opportunity to rule and award damages to applicants who would not have had standing before the EU Courts.

A second scenario has in fact already occurred. The ACCC found that the complete system of legal remedies does not meet the requirements of the right of access to justice as guaranteed under the Aarhus Convention. It held, in particular, that the preliminary ruling procedure, which relies on national courts for challenges against EU acts, cannot compensate for the strict standing requirements for direct actions before the CJEU.[169] The findings of the ACCC were highly problematic for the EU. Yet, because of the non-confrontational nature of the ACCC, discussed above, the problem was more of a legitimacy problem than a formal legal challenge to the EU legal order. The Commission suggested rejecting the findings under the Aarhus procedures. However, a rejection also comes at high political costs for the credibility and legitimacy of the EU as a reliable actor in multilateral structures.

From the perspective of justice, it may be very desirable that the Union is submitted to external evaluation mechanisms, because they bring to light flaws in the EU legal order that result in a denial of justice, as did the ACCC. At the same time, any such an evaluation has internal effects that should be explicated and discussed. The negative opinion of the ACCC puts pressure on the legitimacy of the EU judicial system. If the ECtHR took a position similar to the ACCC on the standing rules before the EU Courts, which is as such not unlikely, this should be welcomed as an even more authoritative and horizontal external evaluation, that is, across all policy fields, rather than limited to environmental matters.

At the same time, it would put considerable pressure on the EU to extend the scope for direct actions against EU measures. The consequences of such an amendment of the European system of remedies should be carefully considered. It would likely shift certain disputes from the interactive preliminary ruling procedure to the annulment procedure, in which only EU Courts are involved. While at first glance the evaluation of the legality of EU acts falls outside the scope of jurisdiction of national courts, disputes that would otherwise end up before national courts are perceivable, for example, where national implementation is perceived to only rubber stamp EU law.[170] When

[165] Case C-274/12 P, *Telefónica SA v Commission* [2013] EU:C:2013:852.

[166] ibid, paras 27–36, 59.

[167] Case C-456/13 P, *T & L Sugars Ltd and Sidul Açúcares, Unipessoal Lda v Commission* [2015] EU:C:2015:284.

[168] ibid, paras 41–50.

[169] UNECE, 'Findings and Recommendations' (n 116) para 90.

[170] See eg the discussion of Case C-456/13 P, *T & L Sugar* case above.

national courts implement CJEU rulings under Article 267 TFEU, the effects within the national legal order are immediate and benefit from the authority and legitimacy of national courts. This ensures a high level of effectiveness. When an EU legal act is annulled under Article 263 TFEU, the effects under national law are more indirect and require additional action by national authorities.

A binding ECtHR decision, relevant for all policy fields and enjoying broad and deep social legitimacy among political actors, the judiciary and the public, in which the ECtHR holds that the level of judicial protection in the EU is not only deficient in an individual case but structurally violates the ECHR, would arguably put pressure not only on the Member States and the CJEU to amend or interpret differently the EU Treaties, but also on national courts to disapply EU law. From an EU perspective, it would be even more problematic if one of the ICTs did not rule that *the EU* failed to comply with the right of access to justice but that *the Member State* did so when it accepted that EU law, which it ratified and implemented, is only open to be challenged via the indirect route of a preliminary ruling. In fact, this point speaks in favour of focusing evaluation on the EU rather than the Member States. It consequently supports EU submission to the jurisdiction of ICTs in order to put pressure on the EU system to be amended rather than pressure on national courts to challenge it.

The effects of submitting weak points of the EU legal order, such as the standing requirements, to an external evaluation are complex and cannot easily be classified as reducing or enhancing legitimacy. The discussion has shown that any such exposure to an external evaluation mechanism has effects on the EU and that these effects are likely to reduce the effectiveness of EU law. This may, however, be a cost to be borne for gains in terms of justice and legitimacy.

3.5 EU law as fact

Some international agreements stipulate that the respective ICT shall treat domestic law of the parties, that is, also EU law, as facts. The ECtHR, in principle, treats the domestic law of the contracting parties as facts. The ICS under CETA assesses EU law 'as a matter of fact'.[171] As discussed above, CETA additionally requires that ICS follow the 'prevailing interpretation' of EU law given by domestic courts and excludes that the CJEU is bound by the tribunal's interpretations.[172]

This consideration of EU law as facts may, on the one hand, avoid legally binding decisions by the ICT that make a claim to an authoritative interpretation of EU law. On the other hand, it may negatively affect the full effectiveness of EU law, as EU law may not be applied altogether or at least not fully. For instance, where domestic courts may be required to interpret legal acts in light of principles of EU law, the ICT would be prevented from doing the same because EU law is not given authoritative legal value.[173] Furthermore, a certain tension appears to exist between the 'domestic law as facts' approach and procedural mechanisms of giving deference to domestic political decision-making, such as the margin of appreciation.

[171] The determination of law as a matter of fact originates from a judgment from the Permanent Court of International Justice (PCIJ) in *German Interests in Polish Upper Silesia* from 1925. See German Interests in Polish Upper Silesia: *Germany v Poland* PCIJ (ser. A) No 6 (August 1925).

[172] Art 8.31 (3) CETA. See Section 2.2.3 above.

[173] Case C-283/81, *Srl CILFIT and Lanificio di Gavardo SpA v Ministry of Health* [1982] EU:C:1982:335, para 16.

Similarly, the view of an ICT of what the prevailing interpretation of EU law is may not necessarily be in line with the actual position of the CJEU on that matter. At the same time, the ICT's interpretation makes a—non-binding—claim of correct interpretation that the CJEU is not in the position to rebut, since it can—as any court—only act when a question is addressed to it.

In conclusion, the strategies of normatively disconnecting EU law and the CJEU from ICT decisions (EU law as facts; CJEU not bound by ICT decision) or normatively connecting ICT to EU law (ICTs must follow prevailing interpretation of EU law) do not fully address the potential effects of EU submission to the jurisdiction of ICTs. However, they may mitigate the actual effects to an extent that they do not significantly interfere with the effectiveness of EU law. In any event, none of these strategies addresses the removal of disputes from the institutional backbone of the autonomy and effectiveness of EU law: the preliminary ruling procedure, as discussed above.

4. The Special Case of the ECHR

The ECHR is the international agreement that has had the broadest and deepest impact on the definition of individuals' rights within the European legal order. The special position and the binding obligation of the Union to accede to the ECHR[174] are the reasons for focusing on the CJEU's autonomy concern in the specific context of EU accession to the ECHR and for considering hypothetical post-accession scenarios.

4.1 Elevated status within the European legal order

EU fundamental rights, which are interpreted in line with the ECHR and the case law of the ECtHR,[175] are part of the 'foundations' of EU law. In the appeal case of *Kadi I,* the CJEU scrutinized the right of Member States to derogate from EU law under Article 351 TFEU. The Court held that all derogations must under all circumstances comply with the foundations of EU law, that is, that the Member States' right of derogation is limited by these foundations.[176] This allows the conclusion that they rank above 'ordinary' primary law if they limit Treaty rights of the Member States, namely, that they constitute a layer of law that is hierarchically superior to the rules codified in the Treaties. The present argument is different from claiming that the ECHR formally enjoys primacy over EU primary law, but it nonetheless makes the ECHR the main source of inspiration for a layer of EU law (the foundations) that enjoys such primacy.

This reading of an informal legal hierarchy, in which the ECHR is seen as a means of interpretation ranking above EU primary law, is confirmed by two pre-Lisbon cases: the *Cresson* case[177] and the *Ocalan* case.[178] In both cases, the CJEU effectively reviewed the compatibility of primary EU law with the ECHR. In the first case, the

[174] Art 6(2) TEU. See Section 2.1 above. [175] Art 52(3) CFR.

[176] Joined Cases C-402 and 415/05 P, *Yassin Abdullah Kadi and Al Barakaat International Foundation v Council of the European Union and Commission of the European Communities (Kadi I)* [2008] EU:C:2008:461, paras 303–04 (hereafter Joined Cases C-402 and 415/05 P, *Kadi I*). See also Section 3.2 of Chapter 3.

[177] Case C-432/04, *Commission v Édith Cresson* [2006] EU:C:2006:455, para 112 (hereafter Case C-229/05, *Édith Cresson*).

[178] Case C-229/05 P, *Osman Ocalan, on behalf of the Kurdistan Workers' Party (PKK) and Serif Vanly, on behalf of the Kurdistan National Congress (KNK) v Council* [2007] EU:C:2007:32, conclusion in para 83 (hereafter Case C-229/05, *PKK and KNK*).

Court declared that Mrs Édith Cresson acted in breach of the obligations arising from her office as a Member of the Commission, for the purposes of Article 213(2) EC.[179] Mrs Cresson argued in the proceedings that her rights of defence and effective judicial protection were violated by the fact that if the Court decided to impose a penalty she would not possess a legal remedy to challenge that finding.[180] The Court then considered whether Article 213(2) EC was in conformity with Article 2(1) of Protocol 7 to the ECHR, which provides that everyone convicted of a criminal offence by a court or tribunal has the right to have his or her conviction or sentence reviewed by a higher court or tribunal. The Court questioned whether Article 2(1) applied to proceedings based on Article 213(2) EC, but in the context of the Court's reasoning this question referred to substantive reasons and not to the question of whether EU primary law could be not just interpreted but reviewed in the light of the ECHR. The latter was simply an underlying assumption of the Court. The Court then concluded that there was no breach because this 'right may be subject to exceptions in cases, inter alia, where the person concerned was tried in the first instance by the highest court or tribunal'.[181]

The second case concerned Mr Ocalan's appeal against a ruling of the General Court (GC) that he could not bring proceedings on behalf of the Kurdistan Workers' Party (PKK). The CJEU set the GC's ruling aside and declared Mr Ocalan's application admissible. On the merits of the grounds of appeal, the Court considered whether admissibility under now-Article 263 TFEU was interpreted so restrictively that the provision conflicted with the ECHR.[182] The Court explained that it 'draws inspiration from the constitutional traditions common to the Member States and from the guidelines supplied by international instruments' and that '[t]he ECHR has special significance in that respect'.[183] It then referred to ex-Article 6(2) EU, which provides that '[t]he Union shall respect fundamental rights, as guaranteed by the [ECHR]'. On this basis, the Court considered Article 34 ECHR and the ECtHR's interpretation of who is a victim within the meaning of that provision in the *Segi* case.[184] It concluded that the case at hand was very similar to the *Segi* case and that the case law of the [ECtHR] appeared to indicate that the applying organization would not enjoy the status of a victim within the meaning of Article 34 ECHR and would hence not be able to bring an action before the Strasbourg Court. The CJEU concluded that '[c]onsequently, in the circumstances of the present case no conflict between the ECHR and [Article 263(4) TFEU] [...] [had] been established'.[185]

Hence, while the CJEU would not accept a direct challenge brought under Article 263 TFEU based on an alleged incompatibility of EU primary law with the Convention, the Court has conducted a review of EU primary law in the light of the Convention in other contexts. Arguably, this does not create a formal hierarchical relationship between the ECHR and EU primary law. However, the review that the CJEU carried out in *Cresson* and *Ocalan* goes further than the classic approach, in which provisions of different legal instruments, for example, European Treaties and ECHR, should be interpreted consistently, irrespective of their hierarchical relationship. It goes beyond consistent interpretation, which neither requires nor allows reviewing compatibility.

179 And the identical art 126(2) EA.

180 Case C-229/05, *Édith Cresson* (n 177) para 111.

181 ibid, para 112.

182 Case C-229/05, PKK and KNK (n 178) para 75.

183 ibid, para 76.

184 ibid, para 80; referring to *Segi and Gestoras Pro-Amnistia and Others v 15 States of the EU* (decision) App Nos 6422/02 and 9916/02 (ECtHR, 23 May 2002).

185 ibid, para 83.

4.2 Triangle of ECHR, EU law, and national law post-accession

In several national constitutions, EU law enjoys a privileged status as compared to international law.[186] However, this status does not establish a hierarchy between the ECHR and EU law. If after accession the CJEU is directly bound by the ECHR as interpreted by the ECtHR (in cases to which the EU is a party) and it continues to construct a hierarchical relationship between the ECHR and EU primary law, national courts may simply follow this reading. This would affect their obligations under EU law, for example, in the AFSJ, where at present mutual trust and recognition obligations exceed what the ECHR would allow.[187] In other words, and potentially desirable from a rights perspective, national courts may understand the ECHR to trump and set aside EU law obligations within national legal orders.

Furthermore, the EU would, as a result of accession, be placed in a position where it enforces obligations under the Convention against the Member States.

> [T]he ECHR [...] does not constitute, *as long as the European Union has not acceded to it*, a legal instrument which has been formally incorporated into European Union law. Consequently, European Union law does not govern the relations between the ECHR and the legal systems of the Member States, nor does it determine the conclusions to be drawn by a national court in the event of conflict between the rights guaranteed by that convention and a rule of national law.[188]

This would change after EU accession to the ECHR. The CJEU would interpret and enforce the ECHR and the case law of the ECtHR. Article 2 s.2 of Protocol 8 would not prevent this by stipulating that: 'nothing [in the accession agreement] affects the situation of Member States in relation to the European Convention'. Additionally, in light of the CJEU's far-reaching interpretation of the duty of sincere cooperation[189] and the Union's new role in Strasbourg, Member States would be subject to new European law constraints in relation to the ECHR.[190]

States receive decisions of the ECtHR in very different ways. The German Federal Constitutional Court (GFCC), for example, explicitly ruled that the Convention, as any other binding international law in Germany, has the same status as ordinary laws (*Gesetzesrang*).[191] In the UK, the ECHR is given effect by the Human Rights Act 1998. However, the Human Rights Act does not require Parliament to legislate compatibly with the Convention nor does it oblige courts to disregard national laws that are incompatible with the Convention. In the case of *Horncastle*,[192] the UK Supreme Court

[186] See eg art 23 of the German Constitution (*Grundgesetz*); arts 88-1 to 88-7 of the French Constitution (*Constitution de la République française*), and art 7(2) of the Constitution of the Slovak Republic (conferring primacy on EU law).

[187] Christina Eckes, 'Protecting Fundamental Rights in the EU's Compound Legal Order: Mutual Trust Against Better Judgment?' in Loïc Azoulai, Nehal Bhuta, and Marise Cremona (series eds) *Collected Courses of the Academy of European Law* (OUO 2018, *forthcoming*) preprint https://papers.ssrn.com/sol3/papers.cfm?abstract_id=2850465. This was also one of the underlying reasons that led the CJEU to reject the DAA in Opinion 2/13 (n 2).

[188] Case C-617/10, *Åkerberg Franson* [2013] EU:C:2013:105, para 44 (emphasis added), with a reference to Case C-571/10, *Kamberaj* [2012] EU:C:2012:233, para 62. This established this exception to the primacy of EU law when an alleged interference with an ECHR right as far as the *Simmenthal* (n 35) principle is concerned.

[189] See for more detail Chapter 2 on EU loyalty.

[190] Compare also the discussion of the Aarhus Convention in Section 6 of Chapter 4.

[191] GFCC, Decision of 14 October 2004—2 BvR 1481/04—(*Görgülü; ECHR decision*). See more recently: GFCC, Decision of 4 May 2011,- 2 BvR 2365/09; 2 BvR 740/10; 2 BvR 2333/08; 2 BvR 1152/10; 2 BvR 571/10—(*Preventive Detention*). See for more details Eckes, 'EU Accession to the ECHR' (n 39).

[192] *R v Horncastle and others (Appellants) (on appeal from the Court of Appeal Criminal Division)* [2009] Michaelmas Term [2009] UKSC 14 (hereafter *R v Horncastle*).

explained what was meant by 'taking the Strasbourg jurisprudence into account'[193] and ruled that on 'rare occasions where [it] has concerns as to whether a decision of the Strasbourg Court sufficiently appreciates or accommodates particular aspects of [the UK] domestic process' 'it is open to [the UK Supreme Court] to decline to follow the Strasbourg decision, giving reasons for adopting this course'.[194] It effectively declared that—under narrow circumstances—it is not obliged to follow the ECtHR. This position is compatible with the Human Rights Act.[195] In the Netherlands, with a (moderate[196]) monist tradition, individuals can by contrast rely upon provisions of international treaties even if they are incompatible with the national constitution.[197] Decisions of the ECtHR can be directly invoked before national courts and the ECtHR de facto functions as the highest human rights court of the land since the Dutch *Hoge Raad* does not have the power of constitutional review.

In many ways, the situation in Germany and in the UK allows courts to do the same as the CJEU has been doing in the pre-accession era: to 'domesticate' the Convention and its interpretation by the Strasbourg Court on domestic terms and create in this way some distance between the specific interpretation in Strasbourg and the application within the EU legal order. In the Netherlands by contrast, the situation is similar to the situation as it would be in the EU post-accession. Within the scope of EU law, international obligations of the EU become obligations of all the Member States with the same force and status as EU law. This would effectively lead the CJEU to enforce Convention rights as it enforces EU law, that is, with absolute primacy.[198] In Member States, such as Germany and the UK, which in practice accept the primacy of EU law, but not of the Convention, the impact would be felt the most. It would change the reception of the Convention and vest it with the same effects as EU law. Individuals could—pursuant to the conditions established by EU law—directly rely on the Convention in national courts.

In short, EU accession to the ECHR would fundamentally change the relationship between EU law and the ECHR, and the role of the EU institutions in enforcing it, but—at least in certain Member States—also the reception of the ECHR within the national legal orders. This would have consequences for the cooperation between the CJEU and national courts. It would also widen structures of bonding of citizens as rights holders under EU law. At the same time, it may reasonably widen the expectation-delivery gap as the CJEU is not equipped to act as a general human rights court as the ECtHR.[199]

[193] See S.2 of the UK Human Rights Act 1998: 'A court or tribunal determining a question which has arisen in connection with a Convention right must take into account any ... judgment ... of the European Court of Human Rights'.

[194] *R v Horncastle* (n 192) para 11.

[195] UK Human Rights Act, s 2 (1): 'A court or tribunal determining a question which has arisen in connection with a Convention right must *take into account* any—(a) judgment, decision, declaration or advisory opinion of the European Court of Human Rights, [...] whenever made or given, so far as, *in the opinion of the court or tribunal*, it is relevant to the proceedings in which that question has arisen' (emphasis added).

[196] It is considered moderate because international customary law has internal effect but does not take precedence over a conflicting rule of Dutch law (HR 6 March 1959, NJ 1962, 2 (Nyugat)).

[197] Except for provisions of international agreements that are not binding on everyone ('een ieder verbindend'), art 94 of the Dutch Constitution.

[198] See Section 3 of Chapter 3 on primacy.

[199] Christina Eckes, 'Integrated Rights Protection in the European and International Context: Some Reflections About Limits and Consequences' in Sasha Garben and Inge Govaere (eds), *Interfaces between EU and International Law* (Hart Publishing 2019 *forthcoming*) preprint https://papers.ssrn.com/sol3/papers.cfm?abstract_id=3048781.

4.3 ECHR accession and the autonomy of the European legal order

In Opinion 2/13, the CJEU found that the agreement setting out the legal framework for EU accession to the ECHR was incompatible with EU law, essentially because it endangered the autonomy of the EU legal order.[200] The CJEU confirms in Opinion 2/13 that it treats the autonomy concern as a second-order reason in the Razian sense of a meta-consideration that displaces all first-order reasons.[201] In other words, in the view of the CJEU, the protection of the autonomy of the EU legal order must be ensured, not as a balance of interests but as an existential question.

What would change post-accession is the binding force and status of the ECHR and the case law of the ECtHR within the EU legal order. The ECHR and rulings of the ECtHR may be expected to become legally operative norms at an elevated level. The ECtHR's rulings in cases to which the EU is a party would become directly binding on the EU. Direct effect would be difficult to deny since the entire ECHR deals with the rights of individuals; indeed, it serves the purpose of allowing individuals to challenge the compatibility of the exercise of public power with human rights.

For the Member States, in addition to their international legal obligations, the ECHR would within the scope of EU law become binding as a matter of EU law. National courts may enforce the ECHR and the binding decisions of the ECtHR under the current interpretation of the CJEU above EU law. At the same time, the CJEU would, of course, continue to hold the monopoly of judicial interpretation over the EU fundamental rights and the foundations of EU law. Technically, this would allow the CJEU to insist on an interpretation that differs from the position of the ECtHR. Yet, in the light of the clear choices of Article 6(3) TEU and Articles 52(3) and 53 CFR as well as its previous case law, it would be difficult for the CJEU to change its position on the elevated status of the ECHR.

Besides the substantive interpretation of human rights, any ruling of the ECtHR engaging with the relationship between EU law and international law or the relationship between EU law and national law would enjoy exceptional status within the EU legal order. Its formal legal value on points of EU law, including the relationships between legal orders, is technically limited by the understanding of the Strasbourg Court of EU law as fact. However, the persuasive force of these EU law-related parts of an ECtHR ruling can hardly be overestimated. The analysis of human rights and the attribution of responsibility may not only be based on a particular understanding of how the EU legal order works and interrelates to other legal spheres, these considerations may in fact be inseparable with the legal analysis of the human rights violation. The potential challenge to the judicial monopoly—and ultimately the authority—of the Court of Justice resulting from a ruling of the ECtHR picked up by national courts would be of a very different quality than any potential challenge presented by national courts purely within the logic of their own national legal framework. The ECHR would work as the missing common conceptual point of reference that allows integrating the different legal orders logically within one hierarchy.[202] This would undermine the CJEU's ability to maintain its unconfirmed narrative of autonomy and hence the pluralist autonomous sources of legitimacy on which the Union's legitimacy depends.

[200] See literature cited above (n 30).
[201] See Section 3.1 of Chapter 1.
[202] See on the missing point of reference Section 3 of Chapter 1.

4.4 Post-accession scenario: 'what-if?'-considerations

The CJEU takes a strong stand that no international obligation can prejudice the constitutional principles of EU law and in particular that all EU acts must respect fundamental rights, even if they give effect to obligations under the UN Charter (*Kadi*, 2008).[203] Post-accession, the CJEU would no longer be able to maintain its dualist position in *Kadi* and would ultimately no longer be able to protect fundamental rights guaranteed under EU law.[204]

In *Kadi*, the CJEU reviewed the domestic EU implementing measures giving effect to UN Security Council resolutions in the light of general principles of EU law.[205] The situation was in some ways unusual because the EU is not a member of the UN and hence not directly bound by UN Security Council resolutions.[206] Yet the CJEU also clarified that even if it had been bound under international law, the obligations flowing from Chapter VII UN Security Council resolutions would have had the same status as all international law within the EU legal order, which is between primary and secondary law.[207] The CJEU's reasoning in *Kadi* is based on and only possible if one accepts the autonomy and domestic nature of EU law, which allows relying on a dualist logic. As we have seen, however, the ECtHR understands EU law to be international law and hence denies the technical possibility of understanding the relationship between EU law and international law as dualist.

The ECHR, despite being largely accepted as a 'constitutional instrument of European public order',[208] is interpreted to be an international convention rather than a domestic legal order, including by the ECtHR itself. As such it is subject to the conflict norm in Article 103 UNC, pursuant to which obligations under the Charter prevail over obligations under any other international agreement. Hence, logically under this formal hierarchy of norms, the ECHR could not protect individuals from Security Council resolutions adopted under Chapter VII of the UN Charter.

The ECtHR was asked to rule on the relationship between Convention rights and UN Security Council resolutions in the context of a detention during a military mission (*Al Jedda*) and in the context of sanctions imposed on natural and legal persons (*Nada*).[209] In neither case did the Strasbourg Court explicitly reject the possibility of an institutional hierarchy or explicitly accept it. In *Al Jedda*, it merely determined that in the case at hand there was no conflict between the Convention and UN Charter obligations of the UK[210] and that therefore the relevant Convention right was 'not displaced'.[211] The Court did not *exclude* the possibility that an obligation stemming from a UN Security Council resolution under those circumstances *could displace* human rights under the Convention. In *Nada* by contrast, the ECtHR found a conflict

[203] Joined Cases C-402 and 415/05 P, *Kadi I* (n 176) para 285. See Section 3.2 of Chapter 3 for more details on this case.

[204] Even less a ruling like *Medellín v Texas*, 552 US 491 (2008).

[205] For a discussion see Christina Eckes, 'International Sanctions Against Individuals: A Test Case for the Resilience of the European Union's Constitutional Foundations' (2009) 15 EPL 351.

[206] See also Chapter 3, Section 3 on primacy.

[207] Christina Eckes, *EU Counter-Terrorist Policies and Fundamental Rights: The Case of Individual Sanctions* (OUP 2009) Chapter 4.

[208] See *Loizidou v Turkey* (Preliminary Objections) App no 15318/89 (ECtHR, 23 March 1995) para 75; *Bosphorus* (n 129); *Behrami & Behrami v France* App No 71412/01 (ECtHR, 2 May 2007; *Saramati v France, Germany and Norway* App No 78166/01 (ECtHR, 13 June 2006) para 145.

[209] *Nada v Switzerland* App No 10593/08 (ECtHR, 12 September 2012) and Joined Cases C-402 and 415/05 P, *Kadi* (n 176) concerned nearly identical measures.

[210] *Al-Jedda v UK* App no 27021/08 (ECtHR, 7 July 2011) para 109.

[211] ibid, para 110.

between Switzerland's Convention and UN Charter obligations. Yet, the Court did not consider it necessary in that particular case to decide upon this conflict.[212] It regarded it as sufficient to rule that Switzerland had acted in violation of the Convention by not doing all it could to adapt the implementation of the UN Security Council resolution, as far as possible, to the specific circumstances and aim to maintain the Convention rights to the greatest extent possible.

Kadi is also unusual because it concerned very specific obligations under a Chapter VII Resolution of the Security Council. While consensus appears to have emerged in doctrine that the Security Council's exercise of power is subject to certain limits,[213] in practice the enforcement of any limits is very difficult. What can be concluded is that domestic courts are, in principle, in the best position to impose any limits on the *effects* of Security Council resolutions. Yet if the CJEU were no longer in the position to act as a 'domestic court' and limit the effects of Security Council resolutions within the EU legal order understood as a 'domestic legal order', individuals would be left without protection from EU law.

Furthermore, national courts could only protect individuals from EU law by rejecting the primacy of EU law.[214] In this scenario the protection of human rights would happen at the expense of the functioning of the EU system, which has no influence on the decisions taken in the UN context but would no longer be able to shield its legal order from them. If cases similar to *Nada* and *Al Jedda* were first decided by the CJEU but later ended up in Strasbourg, this could directly test the situation. This scenario is not all theoretical since the two most prominent forms of global governance exercised by the Security Council are peacekeeping missions and sanctions, including counter-terrorist sanctions. The latter are, in practice, nearly exclusively given effect by EU law, and in the context of the former the EU is increasingly taking a prominent role.

5. Relevant Characteristics of International Courts or Tribunals

Several characteristics of ICTs seem to be—at least potentially—relevant when we assess whether these ICTs constitute a threat to the autonomy of the EU legal order. First and foremost, it seems relevant whether the ICTs allow *individuals* to bring disputes or whether they operate on a purely inter-state basis.

The EU is not, so far, subject to the jurisdiction of any binding ICT that allows individuals to act as parties or directly receives complaints from individuals, except the Energy Charter ISDS mechanism. The ACCC is required to consider communications from the public; yet, it does not treat individuals as parties to the case.

Furthermore, the EU's own history of integration and ability to achieve a unique level of effectiveness of EU law within the national legal order has largely been triggered by and hinges on the decentralized enforcement of EU law by individuals. The particularly problematic constellation of individuals bringing disputes with the EU before an ICT should be understood against the background of the contested foundations of the autonomy of the EU legal order and the preliminary ruling procedure

[212] ibid, para 197.

[213] R Bernardt, 'Article 103' in Bruno Simma and others (eds), *The Charter of the United Nations: Volume II* (2nd edn, OUP 2002) 1292–1302.

[214] See also Chapter 3, Section 3 on primacy and the position of national constitutional courts towards the CJEU's decision in *Kadi I*.

within the EU as being at the heart of judicial cooperation.[215] Indeed, under EU law, direct actions of individuals before the CJEU were much less relevant in the transformation of EU law than the ability and willingness of national courts to give effect to EU law and to refer questions to the CJEU under the preliminary ruling procedure. This explains why removing disputes from the preliminary ruling procedure and hence precluding the CJEU from giving the final interpretation of EU law is very problematic for the sustainability of the otherness and autonomy narratives of the CJEU.[216]

Additionally, challenges brought by individuals require the ICT to evaluate specific legal situations rather than general policies. While ruling on a general policy may have a powerful influence on the margin of discretion of the political branches, a specific violation of an individual right requires direct addressing. It cannot easily be held at bay by 'taking account of' the findings. Adapting the interpretation of law may not be enough: specific changes may be necessary to remedy the violation. For all these reasons, ICTs that receive complaints from individuals are prima facie more problematic for the autonomy of the EU legal order than inter-governmental ICTs.

A distinction is in order; some ICTs are potentially or effectively very invasive. Yet, not every form of invasiveness poses a threat to the autonomy of the EU legal order. The autonomy of EU law comes under pressure, first, when submission to ICTs impairs the ability of the CJEU to ensure the uniformity of EU law, that is, compliance of national courts with the interpretation of the EU law by the CJEU. This is primarily the case when disputes that involve EU law are removed from the preliminary ruling procedure. Second, when the EU and also the CJEU are bound by interpretations of EU law that do not acknowledge its otherness, this enables it to make a claim to dualism and autonomy. This is particularly problematic when these norms enjoy a supreme status. This particular pressure exists in the case of the EU but not in the case of states. First, this is the case because any mechanism of exhaustion of remedies would need to account for the particularities of the preliminary ruling mechanism as a co-operation mechanism that depends on voluntary references by lower courts and does not form part of the formal appeal stages. In principle, remedies may be exhausted without the CJEU having had the opportunity to rule. Second, the difference results from the fact that the EU is a non-hierarchical constitutional judicial construction, whose autonomy is essentially contested, both under national and international law.

Additional considerations are less relevant for the formal legal autonomy of the EU legal order but for the assessment of whether an ICT could cause a threat to the legitimacy of EU law, which is necessary for both its ability to be effective and its claim to autonomy. Firstly, the *substantive field* in which disputes can be brought to the ICT plays a role. Second, the *institutional setup* of the different ICTs matters for its influence on the legitimacy of EU law. Third, their *embeddedness* in the constitutional framework of the participating parties directly connects to their ability to take the common good and shared objectives, as defined by the relevant society, into account. Fourth, the level of *social and normative legitimacy* that they benefit from matters. Finally, it is relevant whether the ICT's decisions are legally binding.

As to the first point, fundamental rights deserve particular attention in this respect. They are, for many reasons, a particularly intense interference with the autonomy or sovereignty of a polity.[217] The CJEU could reasonably expect greater pressure from the highest national courts if it was legally bound and obliged to enforce external

[215] See Section 3.2 of Chapter 1. [216] ibid. [217] See Section 3.3 of Chapter 1.

determinations of fundamental rights standards that clashed with the internal, national, and/or European interpretations of these rights.

As to the second and third points, some ICTs follow a quasi-judicial model of adjudication with institutional safeguards of independence of the judges and a *stare decisis* system.[218] Some act as a mechanism of last resort by requiring the exhaustion of domestic remedies before actually admitting a case.[219] The institutional set-up may impact on the autonomy and legitimacy of the domestic legal order in a nuanced manner. Quasi-judicial models ensure a higher level of legal and procedural legitimacy of the rulings of the ICT, while the exhaustion requirement allows domestic courts a first shot at determining not only the dispute at hand but also the relationship between different legal spheres. It hence allows them to first determine the hierarchy of legal relations. The latter does not guarantee deference of the ICT to the domestic judiciary, but it may allow it to take place in practice. Furthermore, in this context, it should matter whether the ICT can only impose damages, even very high ones, or also order restitution. While high damages may, as discussed, cause a regulatory chill, restitution requires a specific change of the rights and obligations of individuals.

As to the fourth point, ISDS mechanisms determine the common interest within the framework of trade and investment law, in isolation from other normative choices. Some state–state ICTs, such as the WTO-type ICT in the EUSFTA, have been similarly criticized as an example of where the EU demonstrated its willing to prioritize economic interests above its lofty objectives under Article 21 TEU[220] and how ICT procedures in FTAs apply a lens that prioritizes economic interests above other concerns. Provisions on sustainable development in the EUSFTA are, for example, excluded from the arbitration procedures.[221] The fact that they did not lead to any strong forms of contestation or were seen as a danger to the autonomy of the EU, confirms the particularity of ICTs that allow challenges from individuals.

As to the fifth point, some ICTs do not give legally enforceable decisions. Others do. In principle, one would expect that ICTs whose decisions are legally binding may be more problematic. Yet, the Commission's position on the findings of the ACCC demonstrates that even non-binding decisions may be seen to have an impact on the EU legal order.

Additionally, the EU is more vulnerable to certain threats to its legitimacy than states. This is due to reasons largely unrelated to its contested autonomy. The Union's democratic credentials are regularly questioned. It suffers not only from a historic, but also from a structural economic bias. Therefore, even when ICTs do not offer an authoritative and binding interpretation of domestic law, including EU law, they may be seen as negatively affecting the Union's legitimacy.

An example is ISDS/the ICS. Not only does ISDS/the ICS remove disputes from the preliminary ruling procedure, it also suffers from a particularly low level of embeddedness in the domestic constitutional structures and social and normative legitimacy. This may directly undermine the legitimacy of domestic legal orders, which have to take account and potentially even give effect to these decisions. Hence, even if the obligation to pay monetary compensation is not a declaration of invalidity of a domestic policy,[222] enforcement of these obligations seems to endorse them.

[218] eg the ECtHR and the WTO Appellate Body. [219] eg the ECtHR.

[220] Lachlan McKenzie and Katharina Meissner, 'Human Rights Conditionality in European Union Trade Negotiations: The Case of the EU–Singapore FTA' (2017) 55 JCMS 832, 837.

[221] Art 13.16, Chapter 13, EUSFTA.

[222] This may be different for restitution or specific performance. See Angelos Dimopoulos, *EU Foreign Investment Law* (OUP 2011) 119.

In the case of the EU, which struggles to build up social legitimacy, this may be particularly problematic. ISDS decisions that—are perceived to—prioritize interests of big multinational investors, are more damaging to the legitimacy of the EU—which is perceived to suffer from low democracy and an economic bias anyway—than they are to the legitimacy of a state. The ACCC by contrast voiced in its findings of 2011 and 2017 a justified and widely shared critic, the rejection of which is highly problematic for the legitimacy of the Union in a different way—particularly, because concerns for the autonomy of EU law could hardly be argued to be at play in the ACCC context.

6. Conclusions

The autonomy of the EU legal order, its domestic nature, and its relationship with international law are essentially contested.[223] The CJEU's construction of a dualist relationship between EU and international law depends on the self-referential validity of the CJEU's autonomy narrative.

It would be sufficient to threaten the system if a number of national supreme or constitutional courts, such as Germany, Poland, or the Czech Republic, were able to challenge the internal, that is, within the self-referential nature of EU law, validity of the CJEU's autonomy claim. For example, if they relied on rulings of ICTs binding on the EU to make a credible and serious threat that they would withdraw their support of the supreme effects of EU law within their national legal orders.

The fact that some national systems do not pose this threat and may not be in the position to tip the balance of powers, for example, those that do not possess a constitutional court, such as the Netherlands and Sweden, does not challenge the thesis that EU submission to the jurisdiction of ICTs may under certain circumstances pose a threat to EU autonomy. Furthermore, the latter national legal systems may pose other problems, such as in the Netherlands where the ECHR enjoys high status and direct effect and can be used to directly challenge Dutch law. This is the background against which EU commitment to ICTs must be evaluated.

Chapter 1 explained two particularities of the Union: first, numerous formal legal structures have the potential to stimulate bonding between EU citizens and between EU citizens and the Union as a polity, in which they could feel represented (bonding structures). Second, it possesses legal and institutional structures that allow EU law to be uniquely effective within the national legal order. This vest these structures of bonding with particular potential. Both features require legitimation, in order to work and be justifiable.

The CJEU's rejection of the Union's commitment to ICTs stands in the way of the Union's explicit objective and mandate of committing and promoting the development of an international rule-based system that functions according to rule of law principles.[224] In fact, the more the EU shapes international law according to its own objectives and image of effectiveness,[225] the more difficult it is for the EU to participate in these international regimes, because they would threaten the autonomy of the EU legal order. Rejecting EU participation in ICTs is an obstacle for the Union to meet justified expectations raised by the Treaties and its political actors. It is an

[223] See Section 3 of Chapter 1.

[224] See the commitment to multilateral cooperation and solutions in art 21 TEU. See also: Commission Reflection Paper on Harnessing Globalisation (n 118).

[225] See for both Chapter 1.

obstacle to effectively carrying out the Union's mandate under EU law. It also widens the expectation-delivery gap and results in contradictions between the objectives in the Treaties and the capacity of the Union to act within the constraints under EU law as interpreted by the CJEU.

The EU aspires and requires legitimacy, understood as being worthy of recognition, in its own right. This can only be established if the EU institutions enjoy a certain degree of autonomy, that is, have some room to manoeuvre. The CJEU essentially aims to protect the autonomy of the EU legal order from external interference by protecting its own monopoly of jurisdiction over EU law. Prima facie, this may seem an overly narrow conception of autonomy. Furthermore, in the specific context of the EU, the role of the CJEU as guardian of the autonomy of the EU may—because of a combination of primacy, the super-majorities necessary to amend the Treaties, and the powerful position of the CJEU—be particularly problematic from a democratic perspective.[226]

At the same time, the autonomy and domestic nature of EU law are essentially contested. This distinguishes the EU from (federal) states. The CJEU's strict stand may hence be necessary to protect the political and legal choices made within the framework of the EU, which is in turn a necessary element for the direct legitimacy of the EU and its actions. [227] Furthermore, the ability of the Court to take the role of a domestic court is relevant to the level of fundamental rights protection that the Court can offer. If the CJEU were unable to protect rights vis-à-vis international law obligations and EU participation in international regimes vested these obligations with the status and force of EU law, this would be highly problematic not only for the autonomy but also for the legitimacy of EU law. If the Court lost this ability, national constitutional and supreme courts might challenge its position (even more strongly[228]).

Whether participating in and complying with ICTs can increase legitimacy depends to a large extent on the ICT. A rule-based, inclusive international regime offers advantages in terms of equality if compared to the raw state of international relations, in which each international actor may largely do what they want. Participation in systems such as the ECtHR and the ACCC, which are recognized for their ability to contribute to the common good, also offers external structures of control and justification, which in turn strengthen the justification vis-à-vis EU citizens and also non-citizens, who are affected by the externalities of Union decision-making. The Union is perceived as establishing a power bias in favour of economic power. This perceived lack of impartiality makes submission to the jurisdiction of ICTs, which are confronted with the same criticism and popular resentment, particularly problematic.

Rejecting EU participation in a binding ICT draws attention to the tension between a pluralist argument outside the EU (autonomy; dualist approach) and the stronger hierarchical structures within the EU (primacy; effectiveness). On the one hand, this chapter highlighted arguments in defence of the CJEU's position by pointing out the persuasive power of the Court's autonomy concerns with regard to the EU's participation in certain ICTs, in particular the ECtHR and ISDS/the ICS. On the other, this chapter may be seen as defending a constitutionalist perspective with regard to the EU internally by attaching a high value to the CJEU's monopoly of jurisdiction over EU law and by emphasizing the potential threat resulting from the ability of national courts to challenge the authority of the CJEU from within.

[226] Chapter 1 and Dieter Grimm, 'The Democratic Costs of Constitutionalisation: The European Case' (2015) 21 ELJ 460.

[227] See chapter 1.

[228] See Chapter 1 for the existing contestations.

However, the existing plural authoritative claims within the EU legal order are precisely the reason why the EU should fear interference with the institutional backbone of the effectiveness of EU law, that is, the preliminary ruling procedure, as well as binding authoritative determinations from outside that could affect its autonomy, the nature of the EU law, or the role of the CJEU. The very fact that EU law and the CJEU struggle on a daily basis for recognition of their authority by internal judicial and political actors makes the CJEU's concern regarding autonomy from outside claims convincing. The EU legal order is, more than any state, including federal states, vulnerable to challenges by internal actors relying on international law being binding on the Union.

Also, somewhat paradoxically, this chapter, while understanding the CJEU's constitutional construction of the EU as fundamental for the functioning of the EU, places ultimately less trust in the powers of the Court to maintain this construction after accession than many scholars, who disagree with the CJEU's position and argue in favour of accession and EU participation in ISDS/the ICS. The CJEU's autonomy narrative and its strict position of protecting the EU's autonomy from the pressures of ICTs protects the internal fragile equilibrium of pluralist narratives which is the basis of the EU's legitimacy. It also protects internal decision-making structures, by disallowing internal players from using international structures to put pressure on the internal decision-making process.

Moreover, the Court's particular concern with regard to the EU's accession to the ECHR is justified because of the exceptional status and impact of the ECtHR's rulings within the EU legal order that, if exploited by national courts, threaten the delicate power equilibrium within the EU. After accession, the ECtHR would exercise constitutional review over fundamental political choices made by the EU institutions. Human rights under the ECHR would not only allow the ECtHR to make value choices, but with their indeterminacy they even *require* such choices.

Even more relevant for the autonomy of the EU, is the fact that the ECtHR would also rule on the relationship between legal spheres, which is interpreted very differently by the ECtHR (EU law as international law) and the CJEU (autonomous domestic legal order). Post-accession, the ECtHR's interpretation would be *binding on the EU and the CJEU* and in principle even enjoy *an elevated status within the EU legal order*. This would allow national courts to challenge the core relationship between national, international, and EU law from *within the logic of EU law*. This would also allow national courts to undermine the CJEU's monopoly of interpretation of EU law by relying on rulings on the ECtHR, which are part of the EU legal order. Ultimately, this is likely to have a negative effect on the most unique feature of the Union: the autonomy and effectiveness of EU law.

Accession would put the EU's *maturity* as an integration organization to the test. Is it sufficiently integrated to join the ECHR on an equal footing as the other contracting parties, or will it become the victim of its own success because, despite all this integration, it cannot endure the internal tensions that might result from joining an external human rights regime?

Conclusions

Internal Structures Under External Pressure

The European Union's external actions have profound effects on the constitutional structures of the EU legal order. Since the entry into force of the Lisbon Treaty, the Union has increased its external actions in line with its extended competences and raised ambitions.[1] The Union's increased external actions augment the external and internal pressure on the Union as a legal construction, the nature of whose law is essentially contested and contestable.

The Union's increased external actions accelerate, in particular, the integrative dynamics inherent in EU law. When the Union exercises its external relations powers, this imposes a more far-reaching limitation on Member States' scope of manoeuvre than when the Union adopts internal secondary law. This becomes apparent in the context of organizational principles, whose interpretation changes in external relations, such as EU loyalty,[2] subsidiarity, and coherence.[3] It also becomes apparent in the consequences flowing from the choice of an *external* legal basis, rather than an internal legal basis.[4] An illustrative example of this are further mixed agreements, which are a conscious choice not to explicate the division of powers between the Union and the Member States. While seemingly protective of the continuous externals visibility of Member States, mixed agreements ultimately have more centralizing effects than an explicit competence division.

These integrative dynamics are countered by a pushback from the Member States. In legal terms, one indication of this is the increased litigation in the area of external relations brought by Member States before the Court of Justice (CJEU). The Court is increasingly called to rule on the power divisions between the EU institutions and by extension the power division between the Union and the Member States, often with a large number of Member States intervening in addition to the parties of the dispute.[5] The positions of the EU institutions and Member States with regard to the division of powers have become 'much more entrenched'.[6] As the integrative forces of the Union's increased external actions become visible, then an increased and stronger pushback or potentially more fundamental contestation may be reasonably expected. On the one

[1] See in particular the Union's objectives in arts 3 and 21 TEU. [2] Chapter 2.
[3] Chapter 3. [4] Chapter 4.
[5] Case C-130/10, *Parliament v Council (UN Sanctions)* ECLI:EU:C:2012:472. C-658/11, *Parliament v Council (Pirates Agreement I (Mauritius))* [2014] EU:C:2014:2025. Case C-28/12, *Commission v Council* [2015] EU:C:2015:282. Case C 137/12, *Commission v Council (Services Convention)* [2013] EU:C:2013:675. Case C-377/12, *Commission v Council* [2014] ECLI:EU:C:2014:1903. Case C-660/13, *Council v Commission* [2016] ECLI:EU:C:2016:616. Case C-263/14, *Parliament v Council (Pirates Agreement II (Tanzania))* [2016] EU:C:2016:435 (hereafter Case C-263/14, *Pirates Agreement II (Tanzania)*). Case C-425/13, *Commission v Council (Emission Trading System)* [2015] EU:C:2015:483. Case C-389/15, *Commission v Council (Lisbon Agreement on Appellations of Origin and Geographical Indications)* [2017] EU:C:2017:798. Case C-687/15, *Commission v Council (CMR-15)* [2017] ECLI:EU:C:2017:803. Joined Cases C-626/15 and C-659/16 *Commission v Council, pending*. For cases directly brought by Member States see Case C-399/12, *Germany v Council (OIV)* [2014] ECLI:EU:C:2014:2258. Case C-600/14, *Germany v Council* [2017] ECLI:EU:C:2017:935. C-656/11, *United Kingdom v Council* [2014] ECLI:EU:C:2014:97 (Third Chamber).
[6] Joined Cases C-626/15 and C-659/16 *Commission v Council*, AG Kokott, EU:C:2018:362, para 2.

hand, Member States bring judicial challenges before the CJEU. Judicial challenges, even politically motivated ones, are challenges in accordance with the rules of the system (a form of voice).[7] On the other hand, Member States or even national courts could also start challenging the rules of the system themselves by simply (systematically) ignoring EU law (exit). Wide-spread disobediences of national courts would hit the nerves of a system, which is built on close judicial cooperation between the CJEU and national courts, most directly. This would hence be most problematic for the functioning of the core and distinguishing features of the Union.

This book brought to light both potential and actual transformative consequences flowing from EU external actions in numerous institutional and constitutional contexts, such as organizational principles, the choice of legal basis, the conclusion of international agreements, mixity, and EU submission to the jurisdiction of international courts and tribunals (ICTs).[8] Based on the understanding that public action and its foreseeable consequences must be explicated and justified in order to be legitimate, this book also argued why and how the Union should justify its actions and existence in the context of external relations.[9] This concluding chapter synthesises the main findings and themes that run through the different chapters.

External Pressure is Stronger

External relations are a particular challenge for the Union. When the Union acts externally, integrative and transformative forces are not only more powerful but also to a certain extent inevitable. The Union is not a unitary international actor and indeed not a unitary actor at all. The very nature of its legal order and its direct link with individuals are contested. The Union has the ambition to shape international law as an autonomous actor, while the Member States remain international actors in their own right, who may often take parallel measures and remain formally more powerful. In fact, from the perspective of international law, all states are monolithic while the EU can ultimately be dissolved into its Member States. Moreover, the internal division of powers between the EU and the Member States is not identical to the powers of these actors under international law. This, for example, makes mixed agreements necessary.

Internally, unranked and irreconcilable claims of autonomy and authority exist side by side. This pluralism and heterarchy works primarily for two reasons: first, national actors and law interlock with EU actors and law in a tight embrace. This is illustrated by the formalized judicial cooperation between the Court of Justice (CJEU) and the national courts in the preliminary ruling procedure. Second, all actors involved have a high level of interdependent stakes in a well-functioning and effective Union. Indeed, within the EU legal order, any structural non-compliance or fundamental challenge comes at great costs and even those who disobey or challenge the system are aware that a complete collapse would have detrimental consequences, including for them.

Externally, the situation is very different. Non-EU elements (actors, interests, and law) are game changers for the cooperative relations of the Union and its Member

[7] See Chapter 1 for the concepts of 'voice' and 'exit'.

[8] Chapters 2 and 3 on organizational principles; Chapter 5 on the conclusion of international agreements; Chapters 2, 4, and 5 on mixity; and Chapter 6 on international courts and tribunals.

[9] See on justification possibilities: Chapter 2 for EU loyalty; Chapter 3 for subsidiarity and primacy; Chapter 4 when the correct legal basis is chosen; and Chapter 5 for representation of EU citizens through the European Parliament.

States. External actors are not part of the interlocking embrace, for example, not subject to the jurisdiction of the CJEU. They do not share the same interest in the functioning of the European project. Yet they are not only able, under international law, but also more likely to act against the European interest in cooperation and consensus. Crucially, external actors are not subject to the primacy of EU law. While internally, the primacy of EU law requires disapplying a rule of national law that infringes EU law, non-EU actors are under no obligation to disapply an international rule that is contrary to EU law.

Furthermore, Member States and, in particular, national executives are more powerful actors under international law than the Union. They also have more scope for legally permissive action than EU law would permit them to take. Under international law, the Union is seen as an international organization, or at best as a regional economic integration organization (REIO) which, while it enjoys additional rights in certain contexts, is still an international organization. While it can legally bind itself, in principle on eye level with states, only states are fully autonomous subjects of international law. International organizations, and hence also the Union, are 'neither sovereign nor equal'.[10] They are at least partially seen as penetrable in that behind the organization there are still the Member States as the ultimate point of reference. Under international law, Member States retain the legal capacity and formal powers to conclude binding agreements with regard to their territory, even if such agreements are contrary to EU law and undermine the Union's competence.

Additionally, judicial review of foreign relations is traditionally subject to constraints, both under formal law and judicial practice. Courts demonstrate a higher level of deference to foreign relations than to internal policy-making.[11] This means that national executives are vested under international law with more leeway than they have with regard to internal actions either under EU law or under national law, where the CJEU and national courts enforce EU law, including against the national executive. Furthermore, individuals often cannot directly rely on or challenge international agreements in court. This makes the specific judicial cooperation mechanism of the preliminary ruling procedure less effective in the context of external relations and institutionally weakens the Union's ability to ensure the effectiveness of EU law via national courts within the national legal orders.

Moreover, the conclusion of international agreements and in particular mixed agreements already requires the Union and the Member States to agree, present, pursue, or at least not jeopardize a concerted position at the negotiation stage, including when facing new information, negotiations tactics, or political pressure of non-EU actors.[12] Later in the process, the actions of both the Union and the Member States that are required to implement an international agreement are often inextricably interlinked and dependent on each other. This means that, after the agreement is concluded, the Union and the Member States must continue to cooperate closely in order to avoid international responsibility for non-compliance with the obligations under the agreement.

[10] Catherine Brölmann, 'A Flat Earth? International Organizations in the System of International Law' (2001) 70 Nordic JIL 319.

[11] This is often discussed under the label 'political question doctrine', see eg Thomas Franck, *Political Questions Judicial Answers: Does the Rule of Law Apply to Foreign Affairs?* (Princeton University Press, 1992). Pieter-Jan Kuijper et al, *The Law of EU External Relations* (2nd edn, Oxford University Press 2015) at 655. For recent developments in this area see also Sara Poli, 'The Common Foreign Security Policy After Rosneft: Still Imperfect but Gradually Subject to the Rule of Law' (2017) 54 CMLR 1799.

[12] Chapter 2.

International responsibility would, on many occasions, be borne jointly by the Union and the Member States, even if only one of the actors breached their international law obligations.[13] By contrast, in internal law or decision-making processes, each institutional actor and representative of the Member States can in principle voice their position, exchange arguments, and in principle—this may of course also come at a political cost—change their mind in the course of the process. Furthermore, each actor is directly and separately responsible for breaching procedural or substantive EU law obligations.

In addition, while the law-making process within the Union is often perceived as slow and cumbersome, the conclusion of comprehensive international agreements requires even more resources in terms of time and effort.[14] As a result, the legal situation laid down in international agreements is significantly more entrenched and more difficult to amend. The international norms agreed in an international treaty or produced by a body established as part of multilateral cooperation are at the same time difficult to change and difficult to ignore. They are often very influential within the legal and political discourse, including the domestic discourse.[15] These international norms are further largely removed from domestic political struggles ('politics') and can often only be rejected categorically, rather than made subject to debate and amendment. This effect of removing issues from politics also takes place in the EU context; yet, it is even stronger when norms are adopted under international law. Finally, in international negotiations the risk of complete failure (no agreement at all) is significantly higher than within the Union.

International law makes a strong commitment to the sovereignty of states. On the scale between normativity, that is, the rule of law, and state power politics, international law gives considerably more room to the latter than EU law. EU law proceduralizes joined decision-making and submits all state action to the control of (largely) autonomous, supranational institutions, namely, the Court and the Commission. Hence, when law-making takes place in external relations rather than within the EU legal order this strengthens the executive. This is the case despite the fact that the European Parliament possesses formal and factual powers that allow it to represent EU citizens at the conclusion of international agreements rather than its national counterparts.[16]

[13] Pieter-Jan Kuijper, 'International Responsibility for EU Mixed Agreements' in Christophe Hillion and Panos Koutrakos (eds), *Mixed Agreement Revisited: The EU and its Member States and the World* (Hart Publishing 2010). See also Case C-53/96, *Hermès International* [1998] EU:C:1997:539, Opinion of AG Tesauro, para 21.

[14] Multilateral examples are the Arms Trade Treaty which was registered in December 2014 https://treaties.un.org/Pages/ViewDetails.aspx?src=IND&mtdsg_no=XXVI-8&chapter=26&clang=_en or which the General Assembly started seeking views of the UN member states on a legally binding instrument, establishing common international standards for the import, export, and transfer of conventional arms in 2008, see GA Resolution 61/89 and the UN Convention on Contracts for the International Sale of Goods (CISG) 1980, which arose from the conclusions of a working group which was established in 1969.

[15] For example, recommendations and opinions of several International Bodies feature prominently in the discourse around Ireland's recent repeal of its abortion ban. These included not only findings of international (quasi-)judicial bodies, such as the UN Human Rights Committee (UNHRC) in *Mellet v Ireland*, Human Rights Committee, Communication No 2324/2013, UN Doc CCPR/C/116/D/2324/2013, (2016) and *Whelan v Ireland*, Communication No 2425/2014 CCPR/C/119/D/2425/2014, (2017) and the ECtHR in *A, B and C v Ireland* (2011) 53 EHRR 13, but also the World Health Organization (WHO) guidelines (see WHO (2012) Safe abortion: technical and policy guidance for health systems (2nd edn) http://apps.who.int/iris/bitstream/10665/70914/1/9789241548434_eng.pdf.

[16] See below and Chapter 5.

By way of conclusion, non-EU elements (international law, actors and interests) remain outside the political and judicial control of the Union (or the Member States). In particular, non-EU actors are not part of the interlocking embrace that results in an extraordinarily high level of interdependent stakes in the European project functioning well. International law is an arena where Member States are formally legally able to ignore EU law and enter into binding agreements that may have an entrenched and powerful normative force on and within the Union. They can create rights of non-EU actors that are not legally obliged to comply with EU law, are not subject to the primacy of EU law, and do not share the same interest in avoiding conflict and cooperation failure.

Bonding Structures, Autonomy, Effectiveness, and Legitimacy

Behind the question of what the effects of the Union's external actions are on the relationship between the Union and the Member States, there lingers another arguably even more fundamental question: what are the effects of the Union's external actions on the relationship between law and politics?[17] Many specific issues and nuanced consequences discussed in the different chapters primarily connect to the legal relations and interactions between the Union and the Member States.[18] However, in a democracy, the exercise of public power must ultimately be linked to those governed. 'Structures of bonding' do this work. Bonding structures refer to formal legal principles, rules and rights that allow the Union to justify its actions to its citizens and allow individuals to rely on EU law and to participate in its adoption.[19] They connect the discussions on the specific legal issues and consequences flowing from the Union's external actions to individuals as EU citizens. They also connect the legal analysis to politics and raise questions about what the relationship between law and politics is and should be.

The autonomy and effectiveness of the Union and EU law are what make them unique.[20] Autonomy and effectiveness are also a necessary precondition for making it (at all) reasonable to speak of the potential of legal structures of bonding. The Union's enhanced ability to change the legal position of individuals is what makes it not only possible but inevitable for individuals to experience the Union and its law as directly relevant, irrespective of their willingness to engage. Individuals cannot in many situations avoid direct contact with EU law. The autonomy of the EU legal order is an indispensable building block for the Union's effectiveness and legitimacy as a pluralist constitutional legal order. At the same time, the autonomy of EU law rests so strongly on the monopolist position of the CJEU that politics are crowded out. This raises legitimacy problems of its own.

Rulings of the Court solidify positions and choices in an elevated legal fashion and remove issues from the political discourse. The increased litigation in external relations, including on the power division between the Union and the Member States,

[17] I would like to repeat the disclaimer of Chapter 1 that law is (of course?) a product of politics, but that this distinction still makes sense to the extent that it refers to law as a solidified and formalized expression of past political agreement that exercises a particular framing function on current politics (including law-making).

[18] Chapter 5 is the exception.

[19] See Section 2 of Chapter 1 for a conceptualization of bonding structures.

[20] See Section 3 of Chapter 1 for more details.

leads away from the desired politicization of the Union's strong and autonomous international role. Where fewer explicit and clear principles and rules are laid down in the political process, more is left to be settled in judicial procedures that have little potential to engage citizens and create ownership. In addition, the CJEU possess the power to settle any issue, be it constitutional or regulatory, with quasi-constitutional force.[21] It interprets primary law, annuls secondary law and its decisions enjoy primacy over all national law. Its decisions can only be overturned in Treaty amendments, which require consensus among and formal ratification by all the Member States.

In a democracy, politics are necessary for ownership of those governed over the law that governs them. Political discourse (and struggle) takes the place of the unified image of the former sovereign.[22] Politics and, in particular, perceivable and accessible possibilities of influence and contestation are also necessary for loyalty. Only if the internal voice is possible, can exit legitimately be excluded.[23] The legitimacy of the Union has been conceptualized in a number of different ways. The understanding here is that different forms and aspects of legitimacy are largely mutually reinforcing and that, at their core, lies justification of the exercise of Union power.[24] This requires putting specific actions of the Union up for public debate, but also its basic constitutional structures that vest the Union with considerable external ambitions and inevitably trigger integrative forces when the Union takes external actions.

This book identifies where and how the Union could rely on bonding structures to justify its actions and ultimately its existence. Indeed, the Union's greatest challenge might be to adequately justify its purpose and actions towards its EU citizens in a way that is worthy of recognition (*anerkennungswürdig*).[25] However, such justification is inherently necessary to convincingly explain the Union's ability to impose constraints on Member States and individuals. Justification is also inherently necessary for the Union to successfully connect with EU citizens. Justification is not only the basis of (normative) legitimacy of the exercise of public power, but also essential to being perceived as legitimate, that is, it enhances social legitimacy.

Better Representing EU Citizens in External Relations?

This book advocates putting external relations and the Union's ability to offer individuals *as EU citizens* a comparatively high level of self-determination in an interconnected, globalized world, at the front and centre of the debate on the Union's legitimacy, added value, and constraining effects on national autonomy. It argues that the Union's legitimacy and its ability to create structures of bonding with its citizens would benefit from explicating the Union's strengths as an international actor.

Looking outwards helps to create internal communalities. Experiencing yourself as a part of the whole creates a joint experience. A focus on relations within the EU might help individuals to realize the existing high level of *interdependencies*, which might allow them to shift—even from an individualistic perspective—their concern to the integrity of the whole, of which they understand themselves to be part. At the same time, an internal focus stresses the differences between the parts and divides EU citizens into groups of national citizens, as we have seen for example, in the context of the economic crisis.

[21] See the Introduction and Section 3.3 of Chapter 1 for more details.
[22] See Section 2.3 of Chapter 1 for more details. [23] Chapter 2. See also below.
[24] See Chapter 1. [25] Section 4.1 of Chapter 1.

The European Parliament has gained significant formal powers over external relations. It has also been adept at exercising them, for instance, by vetoing controversial international agreements, and bringing challenges before the CJEU to confirm a favourable reading of its formal prerogatives, such as its information rights in the negotiation of international agreements.[26] Parliament's new role in the conclusion and negotiation of international agreements has allowed it to openly and externally contest the position of the other EU institutions. On several occasions, Parliament has credibly given EU citizens a voice in international relations that, with all its flaws, draws on a source of democratic legitimation that is independent and separate from the EU Member States. The strengthened formal and factual role and powers of Parliament enhance the EU dimension of Habermas' divided sovereignty narrative, in which individuals act as dual sovereign, that is, as national and EU citizens, to legitimize the Union's exercise of public power.[27] They also add a popular sovereignty element to the CJEU's narrative that the EU possesses original rights. Parliament represents individuals as EU citizens and gives them an independent voice by positioning itself (to some extent) in opposition to national governments and parliaments, representing national citizens.

The political system of the EU, which is more similar to the US presidential system than to the parliamentary systems of most Member States, vests the European Parliament with considerable powers in external relations. Arguably, it vests the European Parliament with *greater* powers than many national parliaments, even if its formal powers may be more limited. This offers Parliament an excellent opportunity to substantiate and make visible its formal legal powers to represent EU citizens in external relations. In other words, it gives Parliament formal structures that have the potential to allow for identification and bonding of citizens with the Union and among themselves. Whether or not this influences the actual self-conception of citizens as EU citizens remains a different, empirical, sociological matter, that this book does not address.

'Facultative mixity' is flagged as a particularity of EU external relations that raises particular problems for adequate representation.[28] Where the choice of mixity is a political compromise rather than a reflection of the legal division of competences, this blurs channels of influence, representation, and responsibilities. It makes the exercise of public power less accessible for citizens. Post-Lisbon, the increased legal powers of Parliament in the negotiation and conclusion of international agreements are undermined by the political choice of facultative mixity. When the EU opts for mixity in cases where the competence division does not require such mixity, powers shift away from the European Parliament towards national governments and parliaments. It also results in structures of representation, in which individuals are put in a position in which they cannot know who represents them, either as EU citizens or as national citizens, and in which the decision of who is responsible for what is consciously left open. This stands in the way of ownership, responsibility, and adequate justification of Union powers and how they are exercised. It is highly problematic for the legitimacy of Union action and directly interferes with the potential of bonding structures that link the Union with its citizens.

[26] Chapter 5.

[27] Jürgen Habermas, 'Citizens and State Equality in a Supranational Political Community: Degressive Proportionality and the Pouvoir Constituant Mixte' (2017) 55 JCML 171. See Section 4.1 of Chapter 1.

[28] Section 4 of Chapter 5.

Organizational Principles Under Pressure

One conclusion of this book is that the many autonomous legal systems, actors, and plural internal voices require a stringent and predictable application of organizational principles, particularly in external relations.[29] One could speak of an 'essential' tension between the EU's autonomy and (international) actorness and the very nature of Member States as sovereign states. This book demonstrates the particular significance of four organizational principles in external relations and argues how these could and should be interpreted in the context of external relations: subsidiarity, primacy, coherence, and loyalty. It also draws conclusions on how some of these principles could be structures of bonding and allow the Union to explicate and justify its actions and the purpose for its existence as an international actor.

Subsidiarity is guided by extra-legal considerations of effectiveness and democratic legitimacy. In practice, however, effectiveness considerations dominate the subsidiarity test. In the context of external relations, this leads to a presumption in favour of Union action because of its bigger size and scale relative to the Member States. This interpretation and application of the principle of subsidiarity, however, ignores the rationale of proximity of government, that is, that subsidiarity starts from a presumption in favour of taking action at a lower level, closer to those immediately affected. It presumes that closeness makes it easier to allow for input and establish ownership by citizens. Particularly in the context of external relations, the Union could and should emphasize the democratic legitimacy dimension of subsidiarity. It could and should argue that in many instances it is better placed to represent EU citizens externally and can give them a more powerful voice than their Member States. This would explicate and put up for debate that one of the reasons for the Union to take action is that the Union has the ability—in certain circumstances, such as the conclusion of international agreements—to better represent its citizens.

Primacy is essential for the effectiveness of EU law within national legal orders. When international law makes concrete and detailed legal prescriptions that stand in conflict with EU law, the autonomy of EU law protects the ability of the Union to apply an EU legal standard within the EU legal order, for example, fundamental rights as guaranteed by EU law. Primacy of EU law over national law can only be accepted by national courts and national governments if EU law is not immediately and without exception displaced by international law. International legal obligations of the Union are automatically vested with the same force as EU law within the national legal order. If EU law, including primary EU law, were immediately displaced by the Union's and Member States' international obligations, any such international obligation would—without filter—enjoy the same effectiveness within the national legal order as EU law. In situations in which autonomous international bodies adopt legal norms that openly clash with fundamental rights guarantees under EU and national law (*Kadi*-type situations), this would likely lead national courts to reject the particular effectiveness of EU law within the national legal order in order to reject the normative content of the international obligation. Primacy of EU law vis-à-vis national law and autonomy of EU law vis-à-vis international law are hence closely connected and mutually dependant. The latter protects the former. This point demonstrates the fundamental importance of the external autonomy of the EU legal order, that is, from international law, for the internal functioning of the Union.

[29] Chapters 2 and 3.

However, with the Union's increased external actions and participation in international legal regimes, international norms binding on the Union also increase in number. Additionally, the overall trend can be observed that international norms become more and more regulatory and prescriptive and the number of ICTs increases. In combination, this can reasonably be expected to augment the pressure on the Union's autonomy and (national acceptance of) the primacy of EU law. As a knock-on effect, it also puts pressure on (national acceptance of) the unique effectiveness of EU law and hence the potential of legal bonding structures between the Union and its citizens.

The principle of coherence under EU law requires coherence between policies, within policies, between the actions of different institutional actors, and between actions of the Union and its Member States. The European Treaties particularly emphasize the principle of coherence in the context of external relations, where speaking with one voice is seen as a precondition for realizing the Union's potential and achieving its objectives as an international actor. In the Lisbon Treaty, a choice was made to achieve a higher level of coherence by creating scope for political actors within the legal framework to coordinate, cooperate, and find a common line among several legally possible options. The European External Action Service (EEAS) is the most prominent example of the choice to leave fundamental institutional issues open in the Treaties, in principle with the intention to leave these issues to be settled by the Union's political institutions. Procedurally, one of the greatest challenges for the Union is taking action that falls both under the Common Foreign and Security Policy (CFSP) and (one or several) Treaty on the Functioning of the European Union (TFEU) policies. The Lisbon Treaty has, in particular, made it more difficult to establish the dividing line between CFSP and TFEU policies, while the CFSP-TFEU distinction remains procedurally equally relevant post-Lisbon.

The Lisbon Treaty hence opted for achieving coherence through ambiguity, which in practice ultimately empowers the Court as the actor that is called upon when the political actors disagree. In other words, the prominent role given to coherence and the way coherence is pursued in the EU Treaties triggers juridification of external relations. Juridification of external relations strengthens the Court's role as a supranational actor that centrally interprets constitutional principles, which in turn frames or even ends political struggles. In the end, this may lead to the exact opposite of what the choice of the Lisbon Treaty for coherence through ambiguity intended. Rather than political actors finding a way of attaining coherence through coordination in practice, the Court may lay down detailed legal rules that frame the political debate. The Court's rulings then formally prescribe what the Member States did not or could not agree to determine when they amended the Treaties. Ambiguity also hinders citizens from understanding rather than enabling them to understand who is responsible for what. Moreover, understanding responsibilities is inherently necessary for a compound representative democracy, such as the Union, in which individuals are represented both as EU citizens and as national citizens.

The Higher Purpose of EU Loyalty

EU loyalty is the central organizational principle facilitating cooperation within the EU legal order. It is inherent in the Member States' original and ongoing commitment to the EU legal order as established by the European Treaties and interpreted by the CJEU. EU loyalty is reflected in many Treaty provisions and in the overall construction. The higher purpose of creating the framework conditions for the Union as an autonomous and effective international actor is hence anchored and reflected in the constitutional law of the Union and in Member States' ongoing participation and compliance. The duty of loyalty is a tool that can at times take specific legal obligations beyond the letter of the law. It serves cooperation (and integration), which is at the very root of the Treaty.

The legal analysis in this book shows that the CJEU applies EU loyalty more stringently in the context of external relations than within the EU legal order. In particular, the concept of 'unity of international representation' leads to a stringent interpretation of Member States' negative and positive obligations as international actors. This triggers integrative dynamics when the Union acts externally. However, the additional constraining effect of cooperation duties in external relations is justified by the—as explained above—additional and stronger pressures that the EU legal order is exposed to when the Union takes external actions. The different circumstances and formal powers of the Union and its Member States in external relations, as compared to internal cooperation, require a more stringent interpretation of cooperation duties. The reading that loyalty duties are stricter in interaction with those that are not subject to the duty of loyalty (non-EU actors) is also in line with the conceptual understanding of sincere cooperation as EU *loyalty*.

EU loyalty, by definition, requires adequate opportunities for participation and voice, that is, the possibility to internally question and challenge both basic structures and individual actions. Member States can only justify acting loyally to the Union's common interest towards their citizens, including where the common interest prima facie clashes with immediate national interests if internal political influence and ultimately also recourse to the CJEU allow them to adequately represent their citizens *as national citizens within the EU legal order*.

Loyalty is also pragmatic. Only if the Union is ultimately able to make a convincing argument that, as part of a bigger picture, membership of the Union is in the best interest of the Member States and individuals (as EU and national citizens) can it justifiably require loyalty in the longer term. It should openly make a fundamental argument in favour of Union action, based, among other things, upon the formal and factual ability of the European Parliament to better represent the interests and positions not only of the Member States but also of EU citizens in the conclusion of international agreements.

In a globalized world, self-determination and ownership over the procedure and content of decision-making are more and more difficult to establish or trace. Control and ownership have become core concerns of citizens. Political representation in international relations is a very significant part of this ownership. The Union should be able to justify the loyalty that it requires from its Member States with its greater potential ability—as compared to Member States—to represent its citizens and Member States within a globalized world. EU loyalty offers the formal legal framework to explicate the Union's potential and purpose and thus justify demands of loyalty and the resulting limitations on national autonomy.

External Legal Bases Frame Political Power Struggles and Trigger Integration

The choice of legal basis is a formal means to make power structures within the Union visible and also subject to debate. Indeed, discussions about the choice of legal basis are one of the purest forms of legalizing and hence of framing political power struggles. This is not to say that the choice of legal basis is not determined by political motives—on the contrary. However, once a legal basis is chosen, the law has considerable procedural and content-related restraining effects. It determines in a predictable and legally binding manner the procedure and involvement of the different actors, and formally explicates the objectives of the measures, the division of powers, structures of representation, and responsibilities. It also determines whether Member States can still act in parallel or alongside the Union, as well as the geographical scope of the measure. The choice of legal basis also offers a formal legal framework for explicating political arguments, justifying Union action, and engaging with political discourse. Additionally, the choice of legal basis could serve as a formal means to make power structures adequately accessible to citizens. However, these opportunities may be difficult to seize. In practice, the choice of legal basis also bears the risk of legalizing and seemingly objectifying politically motivated choices without explicating them as political and without openly identifying their consequences of allocating responsibilities and framing issues.

Furthermore, the study of the different legal bases in this book reveals the formal consequences of moving policy-making from within the Union into the international sphere. The internationalization of a particular EU policy may be at times unavoidable, in particular in light of the increasing juridification of international relations and the explicit (and justified) commitment of the Union to seek multilateral rule-based solutions to global challenges. However, adopting policy as an *external*, rather than an internal, action has legally prescribed and hence largely inevitable consequences for the power division within the Union. These consequences should be explicated in a transparent and accessible way, both by the Union but also by the Member States, addressing individuals both as EU citizens and as national citizens.

On many occasions, the choice of an *external* legal basis empowers the Union. This empowerment triggers integrative dynamics. The Union, for example, when it concludes comprehensive and regulatory free trade agreements is given exclusive competence through the back door to harmonize policy-making in areas that internally fall under shared competences. This is aggravated by the fact that the Court interprets the common commercial policy (CCP) in very broad terms post-Lisbon, covering different ancillary aspects that would otherwise fall under shared or arguably even reserved competences, such as labour rights and social security matters. Another example of integrative dynamics is that Member States are precluded from adopting more stringent national environmental standards when a policy on the interface between environmental and economic law is adopted as part of the CCP. Furthermore, the CJEU has particularly in the past focused on the short-term economic effects and prioritized the trade legal basis, which falls under the exclusive competences of the Union, rather than shared environmental competences.

A Normative Case for the Autonomy of the European Union

The internal credibility of the autonomy narrative of the CJEU is the lynchpin of the EU legal order. It is essential to the current relationship between EU law and national law, as well as the current relationship between EU law and international law. It allows the CJEU to hold Member States' interpretations of EU law at bay. It also allows the

Court to act as a gatekeeper by applying dualist elements in its approach towards international law, where this is necessary to protect the functioning of the EU legal order or the rights of individuals.

This book does not address the question of whether the EU legal order can make a convincing claim to autonomy. Instead, it traces the additional pressures on the essentially contested autonomy narrative of the Court and argues that the CJEU's autonomy narrative must remain internally valid to ensure the functioning and legitimacy of the Union.

This book also argues that internally binding pronouncements on the interpretation of EU law that question the domestic and autonomous nature of the EU legal order would allow national courts (and Member States) to challenge the CJEU's autonomy narrative from within its own self-referential logic. This would conceptually go further in challenging the Court's narrative than the alternative national and international narratives or the ongoing disobediences by national constitutional courts. If, however, the autonomy narrative did not remain in place and continue to enjoy normative force within the EU legal order, this would threaten the internal pluralist sources of direct and indirect legitimacy that are independent from each other and jointly legitimize the Union's far-reaching normative power to determine the rights and obligations of individuals.

No discussion of the effects of external relations on the internal constitutional structures would be complete without considering the CJEU's autonomy concerns vis-à-vis ICTs. If Member States and, in particular, national courts were given the opportunity to stage legal challenges based on a valid criticism under EU law, for example, because the Union and the CJEU were bound by a ruling of an ICT that denies the autonomy of EU law, they would be given unprecedented legal and conceptual tools to challenge the CJEU's autonomy narrative. The Court's autonomy concerns are consequently plausible as a matter of principle. This, however, does not support the conclusion that all ICTs have the potential to pose the same challenge.

This book demonstrates the potential internal constitutional consequences of the Union's submission to the jurisdiction of three ICTs that have caused the greatest concerns within the EU: the European Court of Human Rights (ECtHR), investor-state dispute settlement (ISDS)/the Investment Court System (ICS) and the Aarhus Convention's Compliance Committee (ACCC).[30] All three have been classified by either the CJEU or the Commission as posing constitutional challenges for the EU legal order.

EU accession to the European Convention on Human Rights (ECHR) would, in particular, be a new qualitative level of EU participation in international functional regimes. The ECHR, as interpreted by the ECtHR, enjoys a supreme status within EU law. There are cases in which the CJEU even reviewed EU primary law in light of the ECHR. After accession, the ECHR would be binding on the EU institutions. Decisions of the ECtHR that involve the Union would be directly formally binding on the EU, but in practice *all of the ECtHR's decisions* would have an even stronger persuasive force than at present. Binding decisions of the ECtHR that challenge the CJEU's perspective of the Union as an autonomous legal order would, after accession, be a powerful conceptual tool in the hands of the Member States and national courts in particular, to drive a wedge into the delicate power balance of the EU legal order.

[30] Chapter 6.

ISDS and the ICS advocated by the EU Commission, although their decisions do not enjoy an elevated status within the EU legal order, also allow individuals to immediately bring claims. This raises particular challenges for the EU legal order because it removes disputes from the preliminary ruling mechanism, which is the 'keystone' on which the Union's ability to ensure and protect the autonomy and effectiveness of EU law is built.[31] It also raises legitimacy concerns of a different nature because ISDS mechanisms are highly contested. This is primarily because they are not embedded in any constitutional system and therefore lack formal legal guarantees of judicial independence and commitment to the fundamental choices of any polity.

The ACCC, by contrast, does not directly allow individuals to act as parties to the procedure. It only takes account of public submissions. So far, however, it has been the international judicial body that has challenged the EU's legitimacy most openly. In one decision, it found the EU in breach of its obligations under the Aarhus Convention because of the EU's restrictive standing conditions. The Commission strongly criticized and first rejected the findings because they failed to 'acknowledge the central role of national courts as ordinary Court of EU law, nor recognise[d] the system of preliminary rulings under Article 267 TFEU as a valid means of redress'.[32] The Commission took as a starting point the CJEU's position that the preliminary ruling procedure is not only the keystone of the autonomy and effectiveness of EU law but it also forms part of a 'complete system of legal remedies' that offers sufficient judicial protection to individuals.[33] This point is highly controversial.[34] With regard to the ACCC, the Commission's rejection seems more motivated by a disagreement on substance rather than by a conceptually defendable concern for the autonomy of the EU legal order.

The CJEU errs on the side of the Union's autonomy, effectiveness, and existence. It does not take any risks but treats the autonomy issue as an existential question. As with the effectiveness of EU law, the CJEU argues that autonomy is inherent in the EU legal order. In other words, there is no need for the EU if it cannot do what it was set up to do and if it is not autonomous it cannot do what it was set up to do. As such, this is plausible in light of the fact that the Union's unique way of functioning depends on the CJEU's ability to interpret EU law autonomously and in last instance unilaterally. However, while the Court's position may be justified vis-à-vis Member States, it remains questionable whether it is also justified vis-à-vis the political institutions in the Union, such as Parliament and the Council, which enjoy direct and indirect democratic legitimacy and can themselves only make a claim to represent citizens if they are not put in a legal straitjacket by the Court. A completely different and difficult but relevant question is whether the CJEU's position on the autonomy of the EU legal order can be justified in the eyes of non-EU actors, who have only very limited stakes in the functioning of the EU legal order and who would have to see the merit of the CJEU's argument against the background of generalizable principles and ultimately international law.

A democratic polity requires a range of control mechanisms of which judicial review is only one. As mentioned above, the position of the Court can be identified

[31] Opinion 2/13 [2014] EU:C:2014:2454, para 176.

[32] NECE Aarhus Convention Compliance Committee, 'Findings and recommendations of the Aarhus Convention Compliance Committee with regard to Communication ACCC/C/2008/32 (Part II) concerning compliance by the European Union' (17 March 2017) para 123.

[33] C-50/00 P, *Unión de Pequeños Agricultores v Council*, ECLI:EU:C:2002:462 para 41.

[34] eg Ewa Biernat, 'The Locus Standi of Private Applicants under article 230(4) EC and the Principle of Judicial Protection in the European Community' (2003) Jean Monnet working paper 12/03.

as problematic within the EU legal order in that it removes issues from politics. Furthermore, the Court's position is at least potentially even more problematic in external relations, which are politically very salient and where Member States also increasingly challenge the Union's autonomous role and exercise of external powers.

Looking outward, the Court's strict stand on autonomy is at times rightly seen as a form of exclusion. Autonomy is about setting up borders, that is, introducing dualist elements, rather than making them permeable. While 'othering' also has a political bonding function that is necessary for representation, it stands in particular tension with the Union's internal normative appeal. Internally, the Union has championed the interlocking embrace and the creation of interrelated stakes in an overall inclusive manner, which does not allow Member States to keep EU law at bay. However, this book demonstrated that autonomy, and at times exclusion of non-EU laws, are precisely what is needed for the Union to maintain its internal effectiveness and inclusiveness. Additionally, a legal form of 'othering' seems potentially desirable in times of Donald Trump's politics of 'America First!' and Xi Jinping's autocratic governing style.

Integrative Force of EU External Relations

The sometimes hidden but far-reaching integrative effects of EU external actions become most apparent in the context of organizational principles and the choice of legal basis. In particular, the construction of EU loyalty, together with the 'unity of international representation', restrict Member States in the exercise of all their foreign relations powers, including in areas of reserved national competences. Furthermore, principles meant to counterbalance the Union's increased competences, such as subsidiarity, are less effective in an international context, where the Union is arguably better placed to represent EU citizens and their interests. Moreover, harmonization may at times be introduced through the back door by way of international agreements, falling under the exclusive competence of the Union, including in areas that internally are shared competences. This is exacerbated by the trend towards concluding increasingly comprehensive and regulatory trade agreements.

The Union takes more and increasingly comprehensive external actions, which require better justification. One way in which the Union can justify its external actions is by making the case that international representation and self-determination in a globalized world form part of the very purpose of its existence. While this point as such should be put forward in the public discourse, it also begs the question of whether it would ultimately lead to a replacement of the Member States by the Union. As international actors? As sovereign states? In other words: where is the threshold to an EU becoming a super-state on the international plane? What is the significance of external relations for the EU's nature more generally?

The Union depends on a two-track legitimation, in which power can be traced back to individuals *as national citizens* and *as EU citizens*. In these two roles, citizens act as the dual sovereign of the European polity. In order to maintain this two-track legitimation, Member States must, as (the) strong(est) bonding communities for national citizens, continue to play a significant role in the proceduralized process of decision-making through discursive interaction. This justifies loyalty and places normative limits on integration and centralization tendencies of EU law and the Union's external actions. However, the two-track legitimation of the Union does not necessarily require Member States' presence, visibility, and action on the international plane. Moreover, it is difficult to square preserving a significant international role for the Member States with allowing the Union to be a strong autonomous international actor.

Union law should internally offer a framework that allows for discursive exchanges of arguments, permits politics, that is, political struggle for the 'better' outcome, while explicating and justifying in the context of external relations the necessary high commitment of Member States to the cause of making the Union an autonomous, effective, and legitimate international actor. The more it seems inevitable that Member States must surrender their autonomy (to a large extent) to the Union in international relations, the more internal politics must engage individuals not only as national citizens but also as EU citizens. Also, Member States, rather than *only* addressing national citizens, should speak to their citizens *also as EU citizens*. The Union and the Member States should allow an exchange of arguments on the *consequences of the Union's autonomous international actorness for the Member States' continuous international presence*. At the same time, emphasizing the role, relevance, and added value of the Union (in external relations) strengthens the political image of the Union itself and entails a certain danger of triggering integration dynamics.

A development towards justification and politicization is needed to make the Union not only an autonomous, but also a legitimate, international actor. The consequences of the Union's external competences and ambitions should be explicated. They should be subject to political discourse and struggles. The internal scope for politics, including regarding the Union's role in international relations, should be enhanced. Bonding structures, and in particular channels of influence for individuals as EU and national citizens, should be structured and presented in a way that places citizens in the position to adequately understand them.

Ways forward to improve the accessibility and transparency of these bonding structures lie more concretely in reducing the use of mixed agreements, explicating motives for conferring competences on the Union, justifying Union action through a democratic reading of the principle of subsidiarity, and explicating Parliament's role and added value in external relations, in particular when it campaigns for votes in elections.[35] Explicating political choices and striving for clarity of political decisions should be understood as having the potential to reduce litigation. Developing specific loyalty obligations of the EU institutions, both in the internal political process and when they act externally, should contribute to avoiding paralysis of the internal political process.

The Union, the National, and the Other

In the political reality of the Union, the relationship between 'the national' and 'the Union' is problematic and widely exploited. Despite the fact that the political and institutional structures of the EU are consciously built on a partial personal union between the governing national elites and EU decision-makers, national politicians and the media portray and (the different national and EU) publics perceive many debates about the EU or European issues as a form of 'othering'. Narratives are regularly based on a distinction between 'us' and our interests on the one hand and 'them' and their interests on the other. 'They' are those in power in the EU, who determine what 'we', in a given Member State must do or cannot do.

Jean-Claude Juncker, the Commission President referred in his State of the Union Address in 2016 to this well-known phenomenon of European politics: the unwillingness

[35] Individual MEPs only campaign to a very limited extent on external relations issues at present. Examples are German MEP and Co-President of the Greens/EFA Group, Ska Keller, who has been a prolific campaigner on a number of external relations issues, especially trade, and French Socialist and Democrat MEP Sylvie Guillaume, Vice President of the European Parliament, who released a number of statements expressing concern about dispute resolution mechanisms in CETA.

of national politicians to own EU decisions.[36] This unwillingness has existed for a very long time. The Brexit vote in the UK has demonstrated in an unprecedented manner the potential consequences that this lack of ownership may have. All, including well-established and even liberal parties, portray the EU and European integration regularly as intruding into national politics, disenfranchising the national voter, interfering with national preferences and interests. This normalization of anti-European rhetoric, including in the founding Member States, and the unwillingness to give credit to the EU for its successes is helped by an unclear delimitation of powers and hidden consequences of Union action.

The use of bonding structures to justify the Union's (external) actions may also help to establish more political links between the Union and its citizens and allow the EU institutions, on the one hand, to develop also a political narrative of the Union's purpose and added value in external relations and, on the other hand, to put this purpose and added value, as well as individual external actions, up for discussion in the public discourse. Despite the series of crises that the Union experiences and that can adequately be characterized as an underlying crisis of democratic legitimacy, the main message of the book is cautiously optimistic. The Union has a purpose and an added value that become particularly apparent in the context of its increased external actions as an autonomous international actor in a globalized world. Explicating this purpose may be seen as stemming the political tide; yet it is an opportunity to justify its existence.[37]

With every Treaty amendment, Member States consistently chose to continue building two parallel paths: they vested the Union with more external powers and strengthened the powers of the European Parliament. In the Lisbon Treaty, these two paths have come together with Parliament's empowerment in external relations. As a result, the Union can make its case that it offers citizens a legal and institutional structure for self-rule in a globalized world better than ever.[38]

The original purpose of the Union was primarily economic and legal interlocking in order to avoid the possibility of transforming relations between Member States into antagonistic relations. The idea of making national citizens of other Member States part of the same group as oneself and making as a result another war in Europe impossible.[39] This objective still stands but may increasingly not be enough to justify the existing level of European integration.[40] Nowadays, the Union can make its case that it offers citizens a legal and institutional structure for self-rule better than ever. Indeed, the Union could and should make a credible case that in the twenty-first century self-rule of EU citizens in a globalized world forms part of the very purpose of its existence.

[36] Juncker, 'State of the Union of 2016' (oral delivery on 14 September 2016): 'in Brüssel laut "Ja" sagen und zu Hause so tun, als wäre man bei der gemeinsamen Beschlussfassung nicht dabei gewesen, ist das Gegenteil von nachvollziehbarer Kohärenz und Konsequenz'.

[37] To some extent, the book hence agrees with Juncker's State of the Union address in 2018: It may be the hour of European sovereignty, if the Union can square the circle of making its sovereignty be born of Member States' national sovereignty without attempting to replace it. See Jean-Claude Juncker, 'The Hour of European Sovereignty' https://ec.europa.eu/commission/news/state-union-2018-hour-european-sovereignty-2018-sep-12_en. See also the revolutionary proposal of the Commission on the same day to move to qualified majority voting in certain CFSP cases http://europa.eu/rapid/press-release_IP-18-5683_en.htm.

[38] In his uncharacteristically bleak perspective for Europe of 10 October 2018, Jürgen Habermas starts by highlighting the diffuse wish of Member States of vesting the Union with additional external relations powers, he does not draw the conclusion that this entails a hidden potential for the future of Europe (https://www.socialeurope.eu/new-perspectives-for-europe).

[39] For example, the Nobel peace prize motivation in 2012: 'for over six decades contributed to the advancement of peace and reconciliation, democracy and human rights in Europe' (https://www.nobelprize.org/prizes/peace/2012/eu/facts/).

[40] For example, in the Spring 2012 Eurobarometer 53% of respondents said peace among the Member States was one of the EU's main achievements. This answer was most popular with those over age 55 (57%) and least popular with those aged 25–39 (39%) (http://ec.europa.eu/commfrontoffice/publicopinion/index.cfm/ResultDoc/download/DocumentKy/63162, p. 16).

Index

Aarhus Convention 140 *see also* **Aarhus Convention Compliance Committee (ACCC)**
access to justice 140–41, 142, 143
binding, as 141
case law 140–45
choice of legal basis 140–45
competences 141, 142, 143–44
direct effect 141, 142–43
EU as party 143–44
interpretation 141, 142
mixed agreement, as 124–25, 140–45
primary law and secondary law, Aarhus Convention as being between 198–99
procedural rights 140–41, 142, 144
Slovak Bears case 140–43, 144, 199–200
standing 143, 144
Aarhus Convention Compliance Committee (ACCC) 198–201
access to justice 144, 187–89, 199, 200, 208
autonomy 12–13, 198–201, 219, 234, 235
Commission's position on ACCC recommendations 185–86, 187–89, 200–1, 207–8, 218, 235
communications from the public 198, 216
deference and bite of ACCC 200–1
direct effect 199
ECHR, accession to 185–86
effectiveness 235
interpretation 198–99
legitimacy 208, 219
Meetings of the Parties 198, 201
NGOs 198, 199
participation 198, 199, 216, 220
preliminary rulings 200–1, 208, 235
public involvement 198, 199, 216, 235
reception and rejection of ACCC findings 198–99
recommendations 198, 201
secondary law, interpretation of 198–99
standing requirements 199, 200, 207–8, 235
access to justice
Aarhus Convention 140–41, 142, 143, 187–89
Aarhus Convention Compliance Committee (ACCC) 144, 187–89, 199, 200, 208
standing 207, 209
Kadi case 31, 94–96, 97, 182, 210, 215, 216, 230
ACTA (Anti-Counterfeiting Trade Agreement) 158–59, 161–62, 170, 180
AFSJ *see* **area of freedom, security and justice (AFSJ)**
agents or trustees of EU, Member States as 75–76
amendments to Treaties *see* **Treaty amendments**
Anderson, Benedict 21–22
Anerkennungswürdigkeit, annerkennungswürdig, *see also* **justifiability** 42, 108, 228
Anti-Counterfeiting Trade Agreement (ACTA) 158–59, 161–62, 170, 180
anti-EU rhetoric, normalization of 238
arbitration 192–94, 195, 197
area of freedom, security and justice (AFSJ) 1, 100–1, 132–35, 190
cross-Treaty policies, legal bases for 136–38
ordinary legislative procedure (OLP) 134, 135, 138, 154, 159 60
pre-Lisbon cases 132–34
Aristotle 54–55
Australia, PNR Agreement with 164
Austria 68
autonomy of EU legal order 2–3, 15, 22 *see also* **legitimacy and autonomy**
ACCC 12–13, 198–201, 219, 234, 235
BITs 70–71
bonding structures 10, 13, 16, 41–43, 227, 228
citizenship 237
constitutional issues 201, 231–32
contested, autonomy as 27, 42
counter-terrorism sanctions 94–95
democratic legitimacy 227, 234
directives, implementation of 71
dual/divided sovereign 42
ECHR 24, 189–91, 214
ECtHR 185–86, 187–91
effectiveness 13, 15, 16, 22, 23–24, 42, 227, 236
exclusion, autonomy as a form of 30–31
existential question, as 214, 235
exit 7–8
federalism 23–24, 27–28, 86
future actions, protection of 70–71
globalization 7
harmonization 5
ICTs 12–13, 23–24, 27, 185–221, 231
institutions 16, 23–24, 25–26, 69
internal autonomy 23–24
international agreements 98
international law 23–24, 233–34
interpretation 22–24, 25, 27–28, 30, 233–34, 235
ISDS/ICS 12–13, 187–89, 191–97, 220, 221, 234
judiciary, changes to powers of 204
justification/justifiability 72
legitimacy 15–16, 19, 42
loyalty 45, 70–72, 74–75, 76–77, 79, 231–32
mixed agreements 65
national courts 25, 27–28, 30, 42, 234
national laws 24, 233–34
normative case 233–36
organizational principles 82, 110, 230

autonomy of EU legal order (*cont.*)
preliminary rulings 16, 22–23, 25, 26, 29–30
pressures 234
primacy 70, 110, 220, 230
purpose, external relations as 40
relative, autonomy as 26–27
self-referential character 24, 27, 202, 219, 234
sincere cooperation, principle of 54, 70, 73–74
sovereignty 23, 28–29, 201
subsidiarity 83, 85–86, 91
Treaties, amendment of 27
unity of international representation 45, 46, 67–68, 69, 70, 77

balance between institutions (institutional balance) 11, 149, 158 *see also* **European Parliament and balance between institutions; executive dominance**
competences 13
cross-Treaty policies, legal bases for 132–38
executive dominance 150–58, 183
facultative mixity 171–72
sincere cooperation, principle of 69–70, 74–75
unity of international representation 69–70
Barroso, Jose 40–41
Belgium 50, 167, 180–81, 187–89
bias 6, 192–94, 195–96
bilateral investment treaties (BITs)
accession, concluded before 70–71
ICTs 204
ISDS/ICS 191–92, 196, 197
loyalty 70–71
Biodiversity Convention, Cartagena Protocol on Biosafety to 126
bonding structures 15, 16–22, 32
accessibility 237
autonomy 10, 13, 15–16, 37–38, 41–43, 227, 228
balance between institutions 149, 150, 183
belonging 15–16
centralization 16, 17, 236–37
choice of legal basis 12, 146
citizens, representation by EP of 173–75, 182
coherence 11–12, 82, 98, 111
control, application of 17
definition 2, 10, 15, 17, 41–42, 227
delimitations 123–24
democratic legitimacy 3–4, 174–75, 229
ECHR, accession to 213
effectiveness 10, 15, 16, 41–43, 109, 227, 231
emerging structures 3, 12–13, 185–86
facultative mixity 171
globalization 3
ICTs 12–13, 185–86
integration 16
interpretation 81–82
justification/justifiability 16, 41–42, 78, 227, 228, 238
democratic representation 13
legitimacy 6–7
legal structures 6, 19–22
legitimacy 6–7, 13, 15–16, 17, 32, 36, 37–38, 41–43
democratic legitimacy 3–4, 174–75, 229
politics 20
loyalty 17, 46, 78, 236–37
mixed agreements 140, 237
organizational principles 3, 81–82, 109
ownership 3
politics 17, 19–22, 227, 237, 238
primacy 82, 91–92, 98, 110
recognition of themselves by represented 173–74
relevance 4, 10, 15
representation 17, 18–19, 149, 173–75
source of rights and obligations, EU law as 17–18
subsidiarity 82, 86, 91–92, 109–10
transparency 3, 237
unique features of EU legal order 10
unity of international representation 78
visibility 168
voice of citizens 3–4, 20
Brexit 32–33, 38, 238
Buzek, Jerzy 160

Canada *see also* **Canada, Comprehensive Economic and Trade Agreement (CETA) with**
Data Protection Directive 164
PNR agreement 164
Canada, Comprehensive Economic and Trade Agreement (CETA) with
awards, status of 195
Belgium 180–81, 187–89
Commission 154–55, 167
competences 122–23
domestic law, EU law as 203
fact, EU law as 209
interpretation 197, 209
Investment Court System (ICS) 167, 180–81, 185–86, 187–89, 192–93, 196
Opinion 1/17 197
umbrella clauses 194–95
CAP (Common Agricultural Policy) 131
CCP *see* **common commercial policy (CCP)**
centralization
bonding structures 16, 17, 236–37
decentralization 7, 9–10, 82–83
hierarchy 6
loyalty 75
mixed agreements 62
national power 7
centre of gravity test 116, 118, 126, 135–36
CETA *see* **Canada, Comprehensive Economic and Trade Agreement (CETA) with**
CFSP *see* **CFSP/TFEU policies; Common Foreign and Security Policy (CFSP)**
CFSP/TFEU policies
AFSJ 136–38
centre of gravity test 135–36
choice of legal basis 138–39, 145–46
coherence 98–99, 100, 104–9
contestation, acts of 170

European Parliament 135–36, 169–32
foundations of EU law, external pressures on 132, 135–36
horizontal objectives 105–6
Lisbon Treaty 135–36, 170
mutual non-affection clause 104–5, 138–39
sanctions 135–36, 138–39, 145–46
Charter of Fundamental Rights of the EU (CFR) 53, 97, 164, 183, 189, 214
choice of external legal basis, constitutional consequences of 113–47
Aarhus Convention 140–45
CFSP/TFEU policies 138–39, 145–46
common commercial policy (CCP) 125, 127–30, 145–46
conferral, principle of 11, 113, 114–15
cross-Treaty policies, legal bases for 136–38
development cooperation 119–20
effectiveness 12
external legal bases, consequences and functions of 113–23, 233
foundations, external pressures on 132–38
framing 232–33
geographical scope of international agreements 117–18, 120
harmonization 124–27, 145–46
integration 113, 124–27, 232–33, 236
internal division of power 12
ordering function 146
parallel competences in external relations 118–19, 145
political power struggles 232–33
pre-emption 113, 116–20
principles 114–18
relevance 114–18
signalling function of legal bases 118, 120–23, 146
standard-setting organizations, ripple effect of EU positions in 131–32
citizens, representation by European Parliament of 173–82, 183
balance between institutions 149
bonding structures 18–19, 173–75, 182
dual/divided sovereign 229
independence of European Parliament 175, 176–77, 179–80, 183–84
international agreements 178–80
national parliaments, EP as better alternative to 178–81
potential implications of EP's claims 181–82
self-conception as citizens 160, 229
substantive interests, representation of 181
symbolic function of European Parliament 175–77
visibility of European Parliament 180
citizenship *see also* **bonding structures; citizens, representation by European Parliament of; dual/divided sovereign, citizens as; voice of EU citizens**
acceptance of law 153
autonomy of EU legal order 237
identification of citizens with the EU 3–4
integration 18
linking decisions to citizens 153, 154
loyalty 58, 74, 78, 232
political autonomy 183–84
referendums 153
self-determination 3
transparency 233
co-decision procedure 154, 165–66
Codex Alimentarius 65, 131–32
codified containment clauses 8
coherence 98–109, 199–200, 230, 231
ambiguity 11–12, 82, 98–109, 110
blurred delimitations 82
bonding structures 11–12, 82, 98, 111
CFSP/TFEU policies 98–99, 100, 104–9
competences 99–100, 111
constitutional framework 98–99
constitutionalization 82, 108–9
cooperation and complementarity, principles of 99
delimitations 98, 99, 100, 103–4, 105–6
divisions of power 82, 99
European External Action Service (EEAS) 99, 100–4, 110, 231
extension of jurisdiction 104–9
hierarchy 99, 100, 110
horizontal objectives 105–6
institutions 98–99, 100–4, 109
interpretation 82, 98–99, 100, 110, 223
judicialization of external relations 99, 108–9, 111, 231
justification/justifiability 11–12
Lisbon Treaty 11–12, 81, 82, 99–101, 108–9, 110, 231
litigation 101–9, 110
loyalty 59, 72
mutual non-affection clause (TEU) 104–5
ownership of citizens, sense of 82, 98, 100
policy-making 98–99, 107–8, 111
predictability 11–12, 82, 98
relevance to external relations 99–100
sincere cooperation, principle of 50–51, 73–74, 100, 108–9
Commission
ACCC, position on recommendations by 185–86, 187–89, 200–1, 207–8, 218, 235
accountability 176
ACTA 161–62
autonomy 23–24
budget 102–3
CFSP 8–9, 138–39, 157
choice of legal basis 113, 119–20
citizens, representation by EP of 179
Council
cooperation with *Codex Alimentarius* over 65
executive dominance 152
democratic legitimacy 179
DG Trade 161–62
ECHR, accession to 185–86
EEAS 101, 102–3, 157
enforcement actions 108
EU loyalty 60, 62, 63–64, 65–66, 67–68, 69, 70–71, 73–74

Commission (*cont.*)
European Parliament 154–56, 166–67
executive dominance 152
Framework Agreement 154–55, 162, 167–68
free trade agreements (FTAs) 154–55
Investment Court System (ICS), proposal for 149, 166–67
executive dominance 150–52
facultative mixity 171–72
free trade agreements (FTAs) 154–55
guardian of the Treaties and primary EU law, as 5
High Representative 101
ICTs 185–86, 204
information and communication obligations 65–66
infringement actions 123
initiative, right of 5
interinstitutional agreements 65–66
Investment Court System (ICS), proposal for 149, 166–67
ISDS/ICS 191–94, 206, 235
Lisbon Treaty 179–80
mixed agreements 62
PNR agreements 162–64
reasons, duty to give 91–92
secondary legislation 5
sincere cooperation, principle of 60
standing 207–8
subsidiarity 84, 85–86, 91–92
TFTP 160
unity of international representation 68, 69
Work Programme 152
Common Agricultural Policy (CAP) 131
common commercial policy (CCP) 127–30
choice of legal basis 125, 127–30, 145–46
competences 8, 125, 127, 129–30, 145
environment 126–27, 128–29, 130
European Parliament 154–55
free trade agreements (FTAs) 129, 130, 165
harmonization 8, 128, 130
horizontal objectives 106
integration 124, 233
internal market 128, 129
international agreements 127–28, 130
Lisbon Treaty 233
objective-oriented approach 129
ordinary legislative procedure (OLP) 154–55
subsidiarity 90–91
succession, doctrine of functional 128
trade, definition of 128
Common Foreign and Security Policy (CFSP) *see also* **CFSP/TFEU policies**
AFSJ 134, 136–38
apart, as a policy 157–58
competences 100
Declarations 8–9
ECHR, accession to 191
ECtHR 190
EEAS 101–4, 157, 231
executive dominance 157–58
foreign policy of Member States 8–9
foundations of EU law, external pressures on 132, 135
free trade agreements (FTAs) 158
High Representative 8–9, 101, 157
integration 1, 124
international agreements 158, 169–70
international organizations, participation of Member States in 8–9
mutual non-affection clause 104–5
police and judicial cooperation 1
purpose, external relations as 40
sincere cooperation, principle of 47, 48
subsidiarity 89–90
common security and defence policy (CSDP) 40, 151
communications *see* **information and communication obligations**
communitarianism 174–75
competences *see also* **divisions of power; exclusive competences; external competences; parallel competences; reserved competences; shared competences**
abuse of powers 67–68
autonomy 27
CFSP 100, 108
codification 189
coherence 99–100, 111
common commercial policy (CCP) 8, 125, 127, 129–30
creep 82–83, 130
declarations 121–22, 142, 145
discrimination 76
ECHR, accession to 189, 190–91
environment 8, 87, 89, 90, 124–25, 130, 233
European Parliament 154–55
existence of EU competences 59–60
facultative mixity 170–71
foreign direct investment (FDI) 185–86
functional competences 84–85
ICTs 205–6
integration 3, 28–29, 124, 236
internal competences 2, 9, 61, 79, 119–20, 128, 141, 142
international agreements 127
ISDS/ICS 196, 206
justification/justifiability 82–83
legitimacy 35, 36–37
Lisbon Treaty 1, 223
list 99
loyalty 46, 59–61
mixed agreements 63–64, 65, 140, 145–46
national competences, conflict with EU of 59–60
pre-emption 118–20
representation 229
signalling function 118, 121–23
sincere cooperation, principle of 52–54, 59–60, 61, 75, 79
standard-setting organizations 131
strengthening competences 7
subsidiarity 82–83, 84–85, 87, 89, 90
ultra vires 52–53
unity of international representation 67–68

competition 180–81
complementarity, principle of 99
conceptual toolkit 10, 15 *see also* **autonomy; bonding structures; effectiveness; legitimacy**
conclusion of international agreements
CFSP 158, 169–70
CFSP/TFEU policies 169–70
choice of legal basis 118–19
citizens, representation by EP of 182
compulsory conclusion 76
European Parliament 154, 162, 167–68, 229
loyalty 76, 77
mixed agreements 62, 225–26
conferral, principle of
autonomy 27–28
choice of legal basis 11, 113, 114–15
executive dominance 152–53
integration 124
Lisbon Treaty 114–15
sincere cooperation, principle of 52
subsidiarity 83
consequentialism 73, 74–75
constitutional issues 1–2
autonomy 201, 231–32, 234
CFSP/TFEU policies 109
choice of external legal basis, constitutional consequences of 113–47
coherence 82, 98–99, 108–9
constitutional construction of EU 221
Constitutional Treaty, ratification of 179
constitutionalism 38–39
constitutionalization 7
counter-constitutionalization dynamics 7
democratic legitimacy 174–75
driving EU apart 7
ECHR, accession to 189, 212, 215
federalist theory 9–10
free movement of persons 18
institutions, role of 1–2
integration 175
internal competences, external competences developing in parallel to 2
internal constitutional structures 3
internal structures 3, 223, 224
interpretation 81
ISDS/ICS 194
Lisbon Treaty 1
national constitutional courts 93, 98
overconstitutionalization 5–6
power-sharing 7
primacy 5–6
subsidiarity 82–86
contestation, European Parliament's acts of 170, 173–82, 183
cooperation, principle of *see* **sincere cooperation, principle of**
Council of Foreign Affairs 101, 102
Council of the EU
ACTA 161–62
annulment of decisions 152–53
balance between institutions 149
CFSP 138–39, 151, 157
choice of legal basis 113, 146
citizens, representation by EP of 178, 179
Commission 65, 152
democratic legitimacy 235
dual/divided sovereign 34
ECHR, accession to 189
European Parliament 154–55, 156, 166–67
executive dominance 150–51, 152–53
facultative mixity 171
international agreements 151, 152–53, 154, 165–66
loyalty 72
national interests 150–51
PNR agreements 163–64
representation 18–19
TFTP 160
unanimity 189
unity of international representation 68, 69
counter-terrorist sanctions 94–97
autonomy 94–95
fundamental rights 94–97
international law 94–97
interpretation 94
mutual non-affection clause 104–5
primacy 94–97
Security Council (UN) resolutions 95–96, 216
surveillance 159–60
UN 94–97
counterfeiting 158–59, 161–62, 170, 180
Court of Justice (CJEU) 149, 185–86, 187 *see also* **judiciary; preliminary rulings**
Aarhus Convention 140–45, 198–201, 207–8
annulment actions 227–28
autonomy 5, 12–13, 22–24, 25, 27–30
balance between institutions 29–30, 158
bonding structures 41–42
centre of gravity test 116
CFSP 104–9, 135–36, 139, 157–58
choice of legal basis 115–18, 147
citizens, representation by EP of 182
coherence 102–9, 110, 231
common commercial policy (CCP) 128–29, 130
competences 77, 117–18
Council 152–53, 235
counter-terrorist sanctions 94–97
deference 200–1, 202
democratic legitimacy 235
development cooperation 129
direct effect 182
dualism 217, 233–34
ECHR, accession to 185–86, 189, 190–91, 210–12, 215
ECtHR 187–89, 190, 202
EEAS 102–4
effectiveness 15, 22–23, 25, 42, 235
environment 89, 91, 127
European Parliament 116–17, 169–70, 229, 235
executive dominance 152–53
fact, EU law as 210

Court of Justice (CJEU) (*cont.*)
facultative mixity 170–71, 172
fines 123
geographical scope of international agreements 120
independence 5, 205–6
information and communication obligations 65–66
institutions 115–16, 235
interpretation
autonomy of EU legal order 235
binding 141
ECHR, EU accession to 190, 214
effectiveness 15, 22–23, 25, 42
ISDS/ICS 206
loyalty 231–32
monopoly 221
primary law 227–28
ISDS/ICS 167, 180–81, 185–86, 187–89, 193–94, 195, 196–97, 205–6
loyalty 57–58, 59–61, 63–64, 71–72, 77, 231–32
mixed agreements 63–65, 140, 145–46
monopolist position 220, 227
national courts 5, 202, 205–6
objectives-oriented approach 145–46
ownership of EU citizens 227–28
politics within institutions, removal of decisions from 5–6, 235
popular sovereignty 229
primacy 92–93, 94–98, 182, 227–28
privileged applicants, Member States as 72
public support 205–6
secondary law 5–6, 227–28
self-referential nature of EU law 24
semi-constitutional status of case law 5–6
signalling function 121–23
sincere cooperation, principle of 47–48, 49–50, 51–52, 57
source of rights and obligations, EU law as 17–18
sovereignty 181–82
standard-setting organizations 131
standing 207–9
subsidiarity 84–85, 89, 91
succession, doctrine of functional 128
supportive parallelism 2
supranational court, as 205–6
Treaty amendments 5–6, 227–28
unity of international representation 66–67, 69
courts and tribunals *see* **Court of Justice (CJEU); international courts and tribunals (ICTs); national courts**
Cremona, Marise 63, 68–69, 99
customs union 90–91
Czech Republic 219

damages 193–94, 195–96, 205, 207–8, 218
Danish Supreme Court 28–29
data protection
Data Protection Directive 133–34, 164
PNR agreements 162–63
TFTP 159–60
third countries, transfer of data to 162–63
Davies, Gareth 84–85
de Baere, Geert 90
deference 200–1, 209, 218, 225
democratic legitimacy
added value 238
autonomy 38, 227, 234
balance between institutions 149, 183
bonding structures 3–4, 174–75, 229
citizens, representation by EP of 181
classic forms of democratic legitimation 36–37
coherence 100, 109
communitarianism 174–75
constitutional issues 38–39, 174–75
decision-making 35
democratic deficit 33, 157
dialectic democracy 34
ECtHR 190
empty space 34
European Parliament 153–54, 156–57, 166, 174–75, 229
fiction, as 175–76
individual rights 36, 234
international agreements 153–54, 156–57, 171–72
intersubjectivity of subjects 34
ISDS/ICS 205, 206, 218–19, 235
justification/justifiability 228, 237
Lisbon Treaty 176–77
nation state, decoupling from 35
politics 20, 237
power from territory, decoupling 35
recognition, being worthy of 228
representation 18–19, 172, 229
shared norms 174–75
signalling function 121–22
social legitimacy 228
standing 209
subjectless form of communication 34
subsidiarity 11–12, 82, 83–84, 85–86, 90, 109–10, 230
technocratic capacity to generate output 174–75
Treaty amendments 157, 183
trialogues 166
voice of citizens 12, 176–77, 229
development
cooperation 118–20, 129, 132–33
European Consensus on Development 129
diplomatic and consular authorities 8–9, 18
direct effect
Aarhus Convention 141, 142–43, 199
ECHR, accession to 214
effectiveness 16, 22
international agreements 202
ISDS/ICS 206
representation 182
source of rights and obligations, EU law as 17–18
UNCLOS 218
directives, implementation of 71

divided sovereign *see* **dual/divided sovereign, citizens as**
divisions of power
bonding structures 81, 114
CFSP/TFEU policies 106
choice of legal basis 12, 113, 114, 124–25, 132
coherence 82, 99, 110–11, 145
common commercial policy (CCP) 127
conferral, principle of 114–15
constitutionalization 109
democratic legitimacy 35
ECHR, accession to 121, 189, 190–91
environment 124–25
executive dominance 150–51, 158, 171
federalism 53, 54
institutions 99, 109, 113, 114, 150–57, 171–72, 223–24
integration 232–33
Lisbon Treaty 110, 115–16
member states 2, 16, 27, 47, 62, 81, 82, 227–28
bonding structures 114
common commercial policy (CCP) 127
conferral, principle of 114–15
environment 124–25
Lisbon Treaty 110
mixed agreements 122–23, 145
mixed agreements 62, 122–23, 145, 171–72, 223, 224
mixity 171, 229
organizational principles 1–2, 109
parallelism 9
policy choices 205–6
primacy 82
sincere cooperation, principle of 11, 68
dual/divided sovereign, citizens as 2, 86, 229, 236–37
autonomy 38, 42, 86
enforcement 27–28
legitimacy 34, 38, 42, 229
representation by EP 229
subsidiarity 86, 88–89
dualism
autonomy 30, 233–34
counter-terrorism sanctions 96
ECHR, accession to 215
ICTs 202, 203, 217
national courts 204
othering 31
primacy 98, 110

ECHR *see* **European Convention on Human Rights (ECHR), EU accession to**
effectiveness of EU law 2–3, 13
ACCC 235
autonomy 13, 15, 16, 22, 23–24, 42, 227, 236
bonding structures 10, 15, 16, 41–43, 101, 109, 227, 231
citizens, representation by EP of 181–82
coherence 99, 111
competences 90
definition 15
direct effect 16, 22
fact, EU law as 209, 210
ICTs 5, 12–13, 204, 216–17, 219–20, 221
implied powers, doctrine of 22
institutions 25–26, 221
integration 16, 22, 24–25, 42, 78
interdependent legal relations 24–25
international law, no dependence on 15
interpretation 22, 25
ISDS/ICS 196, 235
legitimacy 15–16, 32–33
loyalty 57, 59–60, 72, 74–75, 77, 78, 231–32
mixed agreements 12
national courts 22, 230
national law 15, 22
preliminary rulings 16, 25–26, 207, 225
primacy 16, 22, 82, 91–92, 93–94, 98, 110, 230
representation 176–77
sincere cooperation, principle of 22, 50–51, 53, 54, 78
standing 207, 208–9
subsidiarity 11–12, 83–84, 86–87, 90–91, 109–10, 230
uniformity 22, 25
elections to European Parliament
balance between institutions 165–66, 168, 179
coherence 107–8
democratic legitimacy 18–19
information and communication obligations 183
link with electorate 175–77
majorities, tasks of 179
media 168
recognition, worthiness of 174
Spitzenkandidaten, creation of 168
subsidiarity 237
symbolic function of EP 175–76
turnout 21–22, 172, 174, 176
vetoes 165–66
visibility 168
Energy Charter ISDS mechanism 216
environment *see also* **subsidiarity and environmental law**
Aarhus Convention 140–41, 142–43
Cartagena Protocol on Biosafety to Biodiversity Convention 126
collective actions 143
common commercial policy (CCP) 126–27, 128–29, 130
competences 8, 87, 89, 90, 124–25, 130, 233
dual legal basis 125–26
emission allowances 88, 198–99
energy consumption 126
Environmental Information Directive 198–99
free trade agreements (FTAs) 130
Habitats Directive 141–42
harmonisation, minimum and maximum 124–27

environment (*cont.*)
integration 124–27, 233
internal market 125
long-term objectives 126
mixed agreements 124–25
NGOs 141–42, 199–200
procedural rights 140–41, 142–43
proportionality 124–25
regulation of trade 125, 126–27
shared competences 124–25
stricter national measures 125–26, 127, 233
sustainable development 128, 129
third countries, regulation of trade with 126
***ERTA* doctrine** 59–60
EU loyalty 45–79, 230 *see also* **sincere cooperation, principle of; unity of international representation**
active obligations 11
agents or trustees of EU, Member States as 75–76
autonomy 45, 70–71, 74–75, 76–77, 79, 231–32
BITs 70–71
bonding structures 17, 46, 78, 236–37
citizenship 58, 74, 78, 232
CJEU 57–58, 59–61, 71–72, 76, 77, 231–32
coherence 59, 72
competences 46, 59–61, 75, 76, 77, 79
conceptual approach 54–56
conflicts 61, 76, 79
cooperation duties as loyalty 71
definition of loyalty 54–58, 77, 78
deontological concept, as 58–59, 74–75, 77
effectiveness 57, 59–60, 72, 74–75, 77, 78, 231–32
European Parliament 232
ever-closer union 72
exclusivity 59–61
exit 58
federalism 56–57, 76–78
framing 45–46, 57–58, 74–75, 77
globalization 78, 232
good faith 46, 54, 57, 72
higher purpose 231–32
historical self 55
individuality 55
information and communication obligations 46, 65–66, 76
institutions 56, 58, 74, 75–77, 78
integration 11, 45, 77–78, 236
international law 59, 72–73, 74–76
interpretation 61, 74–75
justification/justifiability 11, 33–34, 58, 232
bonding structures 78
choice 72–74
ethical dimension 58
legitimacy 78
moral dimension 58
legitimacy 35, 76, 78
mixed agreements 61–65, 75, 77
mixity 68
morality 55
negative obligations 45, 71, 77–78
non-EU actors 72
objective element 54–55
objectives and interests of EU 57–58, 59–60, 75, 78
ordering principle, as an 72
ownership 232
participation 232
passive obligations 11
politics 228, 237
positive obligations 71, 76, 77–78
potential future action 74
pre-emption 46, 59–61
primacy of EU law 74–75, 76
rationality 24–25, 74
reciprocity 60, 74
relational aspect 55, 57
rule-based framework, as inherent and unnecessary part of 45
self-determination 78, 232
self-realization 56
stricter loyalty 74–76, 232
subjective element 54–55, 57
subsidiarity 72
systematic disobedience 24–25
systemic organizational principle, loyalty as 45
transformation 45, 46, 50–51, 56, 57, 71–76, 78
voice of citizens 58, 76, 232
voluntarism 77
EULEX Kosovo 103
Euratom 61–62, 116–17
European Commission *see* **Commission**
European Consensus on Development 129
European Convention on Human Rights (ECHR), EU accession to 221
Aarhus Convention Compliance Committee 12–13
allocation of responsibility for execution and compliance 190–91
autonomy 24, 187–91, 210–16
binding as matter of EU law, ECHR as 214
bonding structures 213
Charter of Fundamental Rights of the EU 189, 214
CJEU 189, 190–91, 210–12, 214, 215
competences 189, 190–91
constitutional issues 189, 212, 215
co-respondent mechanism 190–91
direct effect 214
draft accession agreement 190–91, 202–3
dualism 215
ECtHR 189–91, 214
elevated status within EU legal order 210–11, 214
foundations of EU law, ECHR as part of 210
hierarchy 210–12, 214, 215
individual rights 210, 214, 216
institutional implications 189, 213, 234
integration 221
interpretation 190, 202, 204, 210–11, 212, 214

national courts, enforcement by 214
Opinion 2/13 190–91, 214
othering 31
post-accession scenario 215–16
primacy 210–12, 216
Security Council (UN) resolutions 215–16
signalling function 121
sincere cooperation, principle of 212
triangle of ECHR, EU law and national 212–13
victim test 211
'what-if' considerations 215–16
European Council
citizens, representation by EP of 179
European Parliament 151, 156
executive dominance 150–51, 152
loyalty 72
national interests 150–51
national parliaments 178
President 151
representation 18–19
subsidiarity 85
Union of States, as representing a 150–51
European Court of Human Rights (ECtHR)
accession to ECHR 189–91, 214
autonomy narrative 185–86, 187–91, 214, 220, 221, 234
case law, status of 214
common goods 220
democratic legitimacy 190
equivalent protection, presumption of (*Bosphorus* doctrine) 202
fact, EU law as 209
international law, EU law as 204
international organization, EU as 202
interpretation 221
margin of appreciation 190
prior involvement procedure 203
secondary law 190
sincere cooperation, principle of 62
sovereignty, transfer of 202
special case, as 210–16
status of rulings 221
European External Action Service (EEAS) 99, 100–4, 110
ambiguity 101–4
CFSP 101–4, 157, 231
delegations 101, 102–3
establishment 101, 157
High Representative 101–2
institutional integration 104, 231
legal capacity, with 102
Police Mission 103–4
preparatory work 102
union delegations 102–3
European Parliament and balance between institutions *see also* **citizens, representation by European Parliament of; elections to European Parliament; international agreements and European Parliament**
ACTA 158–59, 161–62, 180
agonistic politics 165
bonding structures 149, 150, 158, 166, 183, 229
democratic legitimacy 174–75
representing citizens, as 18–19, 173–75
CFSP 8–9, 107–8, 135–36, 157, 169–32
choice of legal basis 146
citizens, forms of linking decisions to 153, 154
CJEU 109, 152–53, 229, 235
co-decision procedure 165–66
Commission 154–56, 166–67
executive dominance 152
Framework Agreement 154–55, 162, 167–68
free trade agreements (FTAs) 154–55
Investment Court System (ICS), proposal for 149, 166–67
competition 180–81
conferral, principle of 114–15
consent to international agreements 153–54, 158–62
contestation, acts of 170, 173–82, 183
controversial agreements 165, 166, 229
Council 154–55, 156, 166–67
democratic legitimacy 149, 183, 235
bonding structures 174–75
consent to international agreements 153–54, 156–57
deficit 157
facultative mixity 171–72
trialogues 166
voice of citizens 229
weak 153
democratization 153
dual role 157
ECHR, accession to 185–86, 189
elections 165–66, 168, 174
Euratom 116–17
executive dominance 152–57, 183
extra-institutional politics 157
facultative mixity 170–72
free trade agreements (FTAs) 164–65, 168
identification of citizens with EU 149, 229
increased role in external relations 153–57
information and communication obligations 154, 155–56, 183
legal mandate 10
legitimacy 34
Lisbon Treaty 107, 154, 158, 162, 182–83
loyalty 57–58
market-driven focus, challenging the 165
national governments 229
national parliaments 171–72, 229
non-economic interests 12, 164, 167
ordinary legislative procedure (OLP) 152, 167–68
party politics 165
PNR Agreements 162–64, 168–69, 181–82
political autonomy for citizens 183–84
politicization 153
powers, affirmation of 158–70, 229
prerogatives 107, 158, 169–70, 229
President 154

European Parliament and balance between institutions (*cont.*)
public opinion 165, 166, 167
refusal of consent to international agreements 158–62, 170, 175
representation 18–19, 149, 166, 173–75, 183
balance between institutions 156–57, 166
contestation, acts of 172–82, 183
secondary law 151–52
Security Council (UN) 182
signalling function 122
sovereignty 183–84
symbolic function 175–77
TFTP 158–61, 170, 180, 181–82
trade policy 166–67
Treaty amendments 153, 157
trialogue process 166
visibility of EP externally 150–58, 166, 168–69, 183
voice of citizens, as 134–35, 149, 175, 177, 178
democratic legitimacy 12, 176–77, 229
negotiations 166, 167, 169
politics 181–82, 183–84
self-conception 160
European Stability Mechanism, Treaty Establishing the 7–8
Europeanization 3, 178
Europol 160–61
ever-closer union 34–35, 72
exclusive competences
choice of legal basis 115–18
common commercial policy (CCP) 127, 129, 130
environment 124–25, 233
facultative mixity 171
integration 236
ISDS/ICS 196, 206
loyalty 59, 61, 62–63, 77–78
mixed agreements 63–64
signalling function 123
sincere cooperation, principle of 53–54
subsidiarity 89, 90–91
unity of international representation 68
executive *see also* **executive dominance; national governments**
executive dominance 150–58, 183
citizens, representation by EP of 180
Commission 150–52
conferral, principle of 152–53
Council 150–51, 152–53
diffusion inside institutions 150–57
division of power between institutions 150–57
European Council 150–51, 152
European Parliament 150–51, 152–57
external relations as domain of executive 151–52
international agreements 151
exhaustion of domestic remedies 190, 197, 202, 206, 217, 218
expectation-delivery gap 213, 219–20
external competences
Aarhus Convention 141
common commercial policy (CCP) 127
competences 3, 124
conferral, principle of 115–16
constitutional challenge of external relations 2
environment 124–25
extended external competences 134–35
implied external competences 59–60
integration 3
mixed agreements 64
parallel competences 2, 9, 119–20, 141, 145
external legal basis *see* **choice of external legal basis, constitutional consequences of**

fact, EU law as 209–10
facultative mixity 61–62, 170–72
balance between institutions 170–72
democratic legitimacy 171–72
ownership of EU citizens 229
personality of EU in international relations 171
political choice, mixed agreements concluded as a matter of 150
signalling function 121–22
fair and equitable treatment (FET) standard 194–95, 203
fear of EU external actions 8–9
federalism
autonomy 23–24, 27–28, 42, 83
executive federalism 149
federalist theory 9–10
legitimacy 36–37, 42
loyalty 56–57, 76–78
mixed agreements 144–45
sincere cooperation, principle of 54
subsidiarity 81, 83, 90
unity of international representation 68–69
Financial Responsibility Regulation 206–7
Finland 178
firearms, manufacturing and smuggling of 132–33
first pillar 132–35
Forst, Rainer 32–33, 58
foundations of EU law, external pressures on 132–38
CFSP/TFEU policies 132, 135–36
choice of legal basis 132–38
cross-Treaty policies, legal bases for 132–38
first pillar 132–35
pillars, abolition of 132–33, 134
sanctions, exercise by member states of more powers in relation to 132
third country preferences 134
third pillar cases (AFSJ) 132–35, 136–38
framing
choice of legal basis 232–33
ISDS/ICS 194
legal relationships 45–46, 57–58
loyalty 45–46, 57–58, 74–75, 77
sincere cooperation, principle of 57, 67–68
free movement of capital 70–71
free movement of persons 18

free trade agreements (FTAs)
CFSP 158
common commercial policy (CCP) 129, 130, 165
competences 233
deep and comprehensive FTAs 127, 154–55, 164–65
environment 130
European Parliament 164–65, 168
ICTs 218
institutions 149
ISDS/ICS 192–94, 195, 206
judicialization 193–94
mixed agreements 206
negotiations 165
new generation 164–65
public order, public security, or other public interests 130
us and them narrative 147
Frontex 27–28
FTAs *see* **free trade agreements (FTAs)**
fundamental rights *see also* **European Convention on Human Rights (ECHR), EU accession to**
Charter of Fundamental Rights of the EU 53, 97, 164, 183, 189, 214
counter-terrorism sanctions 94–97
justification/justifiability 33–34, 35
PNR agreements 162–64
primacy 110, 230
sincere cooperation, principle of 53
UN Charter 94–95

GATT 199
general principles of EU law 151–52, 189, 215
geographical scope of international agreements 117–18, 120
German Federal Constitutional Court (GFCC)
competences 52–53
counter-terrorism sanctions 95
democratic legitimacy 172–73
ECHR 212–13
European Parliament 172–73, 181–82
federalism 56–57
fundamental rights 28–29
integration 28–29
Lisbon Treaty 28–29, 172–73, 181–82
loyalty 56–57
national parliaments, role of 172–73, 178
primacy 219
standard-setting organizations 131–32
state sovereignty 172–73
global financial crisis 32–33, 228
globalization
autonomy 7
collective, influence of 7
Europeanization 3
harmful and unjust consequences 3
integration 41
loyalty 78, 232
national parliaments 178
self-determination 76, 78
subsidiarity 82, 88–89
good faith
international agreements 165–66
international law 45, 72
interpretation 190–91
loyalty 46, 54, 57, 72
sincere cooperation, principle of 45, 48–49, 52–53
governments *see* **national governments**
Gragl, Paul 31
Greece 60

Haas, Ernst 9
Habermas, Jürgen 2, 10, 25n50, 32–33n96, 33n97, 34–36n104, 34n105, 34n106, 34n107, 34n108, 34n109, 35n112, 35n115, 36n118, 36–37n121, 36–37n122, 36–37n125, 36–37n126, 38n129, 38n130, 38–39n132, 38n128, 38n129, 38n130, 39–40n137, 41n147, 42, 58n99, 86n34, 86n35, 107–8, 109, 121–22, 149n1, 150–51n5, 174–75n143, 174–75n145, 176n151, 177n156, 229n27
Habitats Directive 141–42
Hague Child Abduction Convention 1980 61, 117–18
harmonization
autonomy 5
common commercial policy (CCP) 8, 128, 130
foundations of EU law, external pressures on 132
integration 6, 124, 236
maximum 124–27, 145–46
minimum 5, 124–27, 145–46
standard-setting organizations 131–32
subsidiarity 84–85
hazardous chemicals and pesticides, prior informed consent (PIC) **for** 126–27
hierarchy
autonomy 30
coherence 99, 100, 110
ECHR, accession to 210–12, 214, 215
EEAS 101, 102–3
ICTs 204, 218
institutions 92–93
international agreements 127
overconstitutionalization 5–6
preliminary rulings 25–26, 29
primacy 92–93
High Representative for Foreign Affairs and Security Policy 8–9, 100, 101–2, 138–39, 157
human rights *see* **European Convention on Human Rights (ECHR), EU accession to; fundamental rights**
Hungarian constitutional identity 28–29

ICS *see* **investor-state dispute settlement (ISDS)/Investment Court System (ICS)**
ICSID arbitration 193–94, 195, 206
ICTs *see* **international courts and tribunals (ICTs)**

identity
constitutional identity 28–29
cultural identity 21
identification with the EU 3–4, 7, 20, 149, 168, 229
national identity 28–29, 52–53
othering 4, 21
imagined communities 21–22
implied powers, doctrine of 22, 117
in 't Veld, Sophie 163–64
independence
European Parliament 175, 176–77, 179–80, 183–84
ISDS/ICS 192–94, 235
judiciary 26, 218, 235
individual rights *see also* **fundamental rights**
Aarhus Convention 140–41, 144
democratic legitimacy 36, 234
ECHR, accession to 210, 214, 216
international agreements 225
mixed agreements 140
proportionality 83
standing 216–17
information and communication obligations 46, 65–66
balance between institutions 183
CFSP/TFEU policies 169–82
codes of conduct 65
confidential information 167–68
European Parliament 154, 155–56
formal rules 155–56
good faith 65
institutions 65–66
internal communications 46
international agreements 154, 155–56, 167–68
legitimacy 34, 35, 36–37, 107–8
linguistic bonds 36–37
loyalty 46, 65–66, 76
originator's consent rule (ORCON) 156
PNR agreements 162–63
unity of international representation 46
insiders/outsiders *see* **othering**
institutional balance *see* **balance between institutions**
institutions *see also* **Commission; Council; Court of Justice (CJEU); European Council; European Parliament**
ambiguity 99, 100–4
autonomy 16, 23–24, 25–26, 69
balance between institutions, principle of 11, 113, 149
bonding structures 17, 41–42, 81–82, 150
CFSP 150, 157–58
choice of legal basis 113, 114
CJEU 149, 158
coherence 98–99, 100–4, 109
constitutional challenge of external relations 1–2
Council 149
counter-terrorism sanctions 94
democratic legitimacy 12, 149
division of powers 99, 109, 113, 114, 150–57, 171–72, 223–24
ECHR, accession to 189, 213
EEAS 104, 231
effectiveness 25–26, 150, 182–83, 221
European Parliament and balance between institutions 149, 158–70
bonding structures 149, 150, 183
contestation as claim to external representation, acts of 173–82, 183
democratic legitimacy 149, 183
international agreements 12, 149, 183
Lisbon Treaty 182–83
visibility, struggle for external 168–69
executive dominance 150–58, 183
exit 7–8
facultative mixity 150, 170–72
free trade agreements (FTAs) 149
hierarchy 92–93
ICTs 217, 218, 221
integration 104, 124, 231
international agreements 12, 149
interpretation 149
level of involvement 149
Lisbon Treaty 19, 150
loyalty 56, 58, 74, 76–77, 78
media 34
mixed agreements 129
organizational principles 11, 81–82
politics 20
powers in external relations 149–83
practices 3
prerogatives 99, 100, 107, 135–36, 152–53
sincere cooperation, principle of 46, 47, 49–50, 54, 62
social institutions 56
subsidiarity 91
third countries, cooperation with 12
trust 20, 86, 205–6
unity of international representation 69
voice of citizens 7–8
integration 124–27
AFSJ 134
autonomy 23–24, 28–29
bias in favour of EU law 6
bonding structures 16
CFSP 1, 124
choice of legal basis 113, 124–27, 232–33, 236
citizenship 18
clauses 98–99
coherence 98–99, 107–8
competences 3, 28–29, 124, 236
constitutional law 175
EEAS 104, 231
effectiveness 16, 22, 24–25, 42, 77–78
environment 124–27, 233
external competences 3
fear of EU external actions 8
federalism 23–24
free trade agreements (FTAs) 164–65
globalization 41
hierarchical, law as 6
ICTs 204

justification/justifiability 236
law, through 5–6
legitimacy 16, 32–33, 36, 42
Lisbon Treaty 40, 107–8
loyalty 11, 45, 77–78, 236
pre-emption 113
purpose, external relations as 39–41
regional economic integration organization (REIOs) 225
relevance of EU law 4
second pillar 1
sincere cooperation, principle of 51–52, 124
triggering integration 237
unilateral national action 7
interest groups 157
intergovernmentalism 19–20, 48, 99, 145–46, 152–53
internal competences 2, 9, 61, 79, 119–20, 128, 141, 142
internal market
co-decision rights 154–55
common commercial policy (CCP) 128, 129
economic perspective on policymaking 6
environment 87, 90–91, 125
free trade agreements (FTAs) 168
harmonization 8
source of rights and obligations, EU law as 18
subsidiarity 84–85, 87, 90–91
internal structures under external pressure 223–38
autonomy 224, 227, 233–36
bonding structures 227, 228
framing political power struggles 232–33
integration 223, 232–33, 236–37
loyalty 231–32
national, relation with 237–38
organizational principles 223, 224, 230–31
representation of citizens 228–29
stronger, external pressure as being 224–27
international agreements *see also* **Aarhus Convention; Canada, Comprehensive Economic and Trade Agreement (CETA) with; conclusion of international agreements; European Convention on Human Rights (ECHR), EU accession to; free trade agreements (FTAs); international agreements and European Parliament; mixed agreements; negotiation of international agreements; passenger name record (PNR) agreements; refusal of consent to international agreements/vetoes**
ACTA 158–59, 161–62
autonomy 98
CFSP/TFEU policies 169–70
citizens, representation by EP of 178–80
coherence 100–1, 107, 108
common commercial policy (CCP) 127–28, 130
denunciation 70
direct effect 202
dualism 202, 203, 233–34
EU law, ignoring 227
executive dominance 151
fact, EU law as 209
geographical scope of international agreements 117–18, 120
harmonization 236
ICTs 98, 202, 203
individual rights 225
interpretation 151–52, 203–4
ISDS/ICS 206
loyalty 68, 76, 232
national parliaments 178–79
primacy 98, 127, 227
resources 226
secondary law 151–52
self-execution 202
signalling function 146
signing 76, 77
sincere cooperation, principle of 61, 73–74
subsidiarity 82, 91, 230
international agreements and European Parliament
amendment, power of 165–66, 167
balance between institutions 153–56, 158, 226
co-decision procedure 165–66
coherence 107, 108
Commission 166–67
conclusion 154, 162, 167–68, 170, 229
consent 12, 149, 152, 169–70
balance between institutions 153–54, 158–62
democratic legitimacy 153–54, 156–57
consultation 154, 155
contestation, acts of 170
controversial agreements 165, 166, 229
Council 154, 165–66, 169–70
ECHR, accession to 189
facultative mixity 150, 170–72
formal treaty powers 154
information, rights of 154, 155–56, 167–68, 169–70
Lisbon Treaty 170, 172–73
loyalty 232
national parliaments 171–72
negotiations 161–62, 168–70, 229
Commission 166–67
Council 165–66, 169–70
information and communication obligations 154, 155–56, 167–68
opposition position 166
renegotiation 70
ordinary legislative procedure (OLP) 154
prerogatives 107, 169–70
primacy 98
refusal of consent/vetoes
ACTA 161–62, 170
balance between institutions 153, 158–62, 165–66, 229
bonding structures 175
citizens, representation by EP of 181–82
facultative mixity 171
TFTP 159–60, 170, 181–82

international agreements and European Parliament (*cont.*)
signing stage 154
transparency 167–68
visibility 166, 168–69, 180
International Court of Justice (ICJ) 5
international courts and tribunals (ICTs) 185
see also **Aarhus Convention Compliance Committee (ACCC); Court of Justice (CJEU); European Court of Human Rights (ECtHR); investor-state dispute settlement (ISDS)/Investment Court System (ICS)**
Article 267 TFEU, 204–5
autonomy 12–13, 23–24, 27, 185–221, 231, 234
binding decisions 218
bonding structures, emerging 12–13, 185–86
common good 217
competences 205–6
constitutional construction of EU 221
contestation from the inside 202–4
damages 218
deference to domestic courts 218
domestic law, EU law as 203–4, 216
ECHR, accession to 12–13, 185–86, 210–16, 221, 234
effectiveness 12–13, 204, 216–17, 219–20, 221
embeddedness 217, 218, 235
expectation-delivery gap 213, 219–20
fact, EU law as 209–10
ICJ 5
independence of judiciary 218, 235
individuals, standing of 216–17
international agreements 202, 203
international law, EU law as 185–86, 204, 215, 219
interpretation 203–4, 216–17, 218, 219–20
legitimacy 12–13, 185–86, 205–6, 217, 218–19, 220
national courts 203–4, 234
policy choices 205–6
preliminary rulings 201, 204, 216–17
primacy 219, 231
relevant characteristics 216–19
standing 207–9
stare decisis 218
submission to jurisdiction of EU 12–13
substantive field 217
international law *see also* **dualism**
autonomy 23–24
coherence 99
counter-terrorism sanctions 94–97
derogation from EU law 97, 224–25
distinctiveness 30–31
EU law as international law 185–86, 204, 215, 219
EU legal order distinguished 10
good faith 45, 72
hierarchy 204
ICTs 185–86, 204, 215, 219
institutions 12
interpretation 145–46
loyalty 59, 72–73, 74–76
monism 31–32, 202, 212–13
national governments 225
power politics 226
primacy 82, 94–98, 224–25, 230
sincere cooperation, principle of 69–70, 73
state sovereignty 30–31, 226
International Organisation of Vine and Wine (OIV) 131
international organizations
ERTA doctrine 60
EU as international organization 5, 70, 225
EU legal order distinguished 10
mixed agreements 62
regional economic integration organization (REIOs) 225
unity of international representation 69–70
visibility 8–9
international standard-setting organizations, ripple effect of EU positions in 131–32
competences 131
harmonization 131–32
interpretation 131
legal effects of decisions 131
parties to organizations, where EU and member states are not 131
pre-emption 131
International Tribunal for the Law of the Sea (ITLOS) 66, 187
interpretation *see also* **preliminary rulings**
Aarhus Convention 141, 142
Aarhus Convention Compliance Committee (ACCC) 198–99
autonomy 22–24, 25, 27–28, 30, 233–34
balance between institutions 149–50
binding interpretation 141
bonding structures 81–82
coherence 82, 98–99, 100, 110, 223
common commercial policy (CCP) 233
consistent interpretation 142–43
constitutions 81
counter-terrorism sanctions 94
ECHR, accession to 190, 210–11, 212, 214
effectiveness 22, 25
fact, EU law as 209–10
fragmentation 142
good faith 190–91
ICTs 203–4, 216–17, 218, 219–20
institutions 149
integration 6
international law 145–46
ISDS/ICS 197, 206
legitimacy 35–36
loyalty 61, 74–75
organizational principles 3, 11, 109, 223
power division between EU and Member States 2
primacy 82, 92–93, 97
primary law 52, 210–11, 227–28
purposive interpretation 22, 39, 51–52, 53
secondary law 151–52, 198–99

sincere cooperation, principle of 51–53, 62, 64
standard-setting organizations 131
subsidiarity 82–87, 89, 223, 230
teleological interpretation 22
uniformity 93–94
unity of international representation 57
investor-state dispute settlement (ISDS)/ Investment Court System (ICS) 191–97
arbitration 192–94, 197
autonomy 12–13, 187–89, 191–97, 220, 221, 234
awards
competence, division of 206
enforcement 206
payment of large 193–94
bias 192–94, 195–96, 206
BITs 191–92, 196, 197
CETA, Investment Court System (ICS) of 167, 180–81, 185–86, 187–89, 192–93, 196
CJEU 193–94, 195, 196–97, 205–6
CETA 167, 180–81, 185–86, 187–89
interpretation 206
Commission 191–94, 206, 235
common goods 194, 218
competences 185–86, 196, 206
consent to establishment 206
damages 193–94, 195–96, 205
democratic legitimacy 205, 206, 218–19, 235
developing countries 191–92
economic bias 195–96, 206
embeddedness, level of 218, 235
Energy Charter ISDS mechanism 216
facts, domestic law classified as 197
fair and equitable treatment (FET) standard 203
Financial Responsibility Regulation 206–7
framing disputes 194
free trade agreements (FTAs) 192–94, 195, 206
future 196–97
ICSID arbitration 193–94, 206
independence 192–94, 235
interpretation 197, 206
mixed agreements 196, 206
national parliaments, ratification powers of 196
New York Convention 1958 206
preliminary rulings 197, 218, 235
regulatory chill 205
subordinate to international investment law, EU law as 203
TTIP 166–67
transparency 192–93, 206
ISDS *see* **investor-state dispute settlement (ISDS)/Investment Court System (ICS)**

judicialization
coherence 99, 108–9, 111, 231
free trade agreements (FTAs) 193–94
internationalization of policy 233
organizational principles 109
judiciary *see also* **judicialization**
changes to powers 204
cooperation, institutionalized form of 25–26
dialogue 22–23, 93, 224, 225
independence 26, 218, 235
legitimacy 38–39
police and judicial cooperation (third pillar) 1, 132, 133–34, 136–37, 159–60
standards 205–6
Juncker, Jean-Claude 40–41, 238
Justiciability of EEAS actions 101–9, 110
justification/justifiability
Anerkennungswürdigkeit, annerkennungswürdig
autonomy 37–38, 72
bonding structures 6–7, 13, 16, 41–42, 78, 227, 228, 238
choice of legal basis 72–74, 114, 146
coherence 11–12
competences 82–83
democratic legitimacy 6–7, 78, 228, 237
ethical dimension 33–34
European Parliament 156, 166
Forst, Rainer 33n96, 33–34n97, 34n102, 36n116, 58n102
fundamental rights 33–34, 35
group, belonging to a 58
Habermas, Jürgen 2n10, 10, 25n50, 32–33n96, 33n97, 34–36n104, 34n105, 34n106, 34n107, 34n108, 34n109, 35n112, 35n115, 36n118, 36–37n121, 36–37n122, 36–37n125, 36–37n126, 38n129, 38n130, 38–39n132, 38n128, 38n129, 38n130, 39–40n137, 41n147, 42, 58n99, 107–8, 109
information and communication obligations 65
institutions 150
integration 236
legitimacy 10, 15–16, 32–41, 42
autonomy 37–38
democratic 6–7, 78, 228, 237
loyalty 78
loyalty 11, 33–34, 58, 78, 232
moral dimension 33–34, 58
primacy 91–92, 97
reasons, giving of 33–34
'*Rechtfertigungswesen*' (being treated as a being with a right to justification) 33–34
recognition, worthiness of 35
sincere cooperation, principle of 66–67, 74
source of rights and obligations, EU law as 18
'*Sprache der Kritik*' (language of critique) 33–34
subsidiarity 82–84, 86, 88, 91, 237
systematic justification 35
unity of international representation 70

kompetenz-kompetenz 27–28
Koskenniemi, Martti 204
Kosovo 103

Kuijper, Pieter Jan 116–17
law as opposed to politics 5–6, 7, 19–22, 46, 73–74, 227

Lefort, Claude 20
legal basis *see* **choice of external legal basis, constitutional consequences of**
legal certainty 4–5, 64, 111
legal personality of EU 1
legitimacy 2–3, 32 *see also* **democratic legitimacy; legitimacy and autonomy**
  Aarhus Convention 208, 219
  agonistic politics, concept of 36
  bonding structures 6–7, 13, 15–16, 17, 32, 36, 41–43
  coherence 11–12, 107–8
  communicative legitimacy 34, 35, 36–37, 107–8
  competences 35, 36–37
  constitutions 29–30
  different aspects 32–36
  dimensions 10
  dual/divided sovereign 34, 42, 229
  ECHR, accession to 214
  effectiveness 15–16, 32–33
  federal theory 36–37
  fundamental rights 35
  ICTs 12–13, 185–86, 205–6, 217, 218–19, 220
  indirect legitimation 36
  input legitimacy 32–33, 36, 107–8
  integration 16, 32–33, 36, 42
  interpretation 35–36
  justification/justifiability 6–7, 10, 15–16, 32–41, 42
    loyalty and group belonging 33–34, 78
    '*Rechtfertigungswesen*' (right to justification) 33–34
    '*Sprache der Kritik*' (language of critique) 33–34
    recognition, worthiness of 35, 78
    systematic justification 35
  Lisbon Treaty 19
  loyalty 35, 76, 78
  narrative of the Court of Justice 16, 22, 23–24, 27–28, 29–31, 39, 42, 94, 110, 182, 183–84, 203, 204, 214, 216–17, 219, 221, 229, 233–34
  national courts 52–53
  output legitimacy 32–33, 35
  pluralism 29–30
  primacy 82, 110
  procedural legitimacy 34
  public opinion 6–7
  purpose, external relations as 39–41
  reasons 33
  recognition, worthiness of 10, 35, 42, 78, 220
  social legitimacy 32–33, 219, 228
  sovereignty
    dual/divided sovereign 34, 42
    state sovereignty and sovereignty of the people 35
  subsidiarity 86
  throughput legitimacy 33
  transparency 33, 34, 35
legitimacy and autonomy 15–16, 29–30, 37–41, 42, 76–77, 220
  bonding structures 15–16, 37–38
  collective autonomy 38
  conceptual autonomy 37–38
  democratic legitimacy 38
  direct legitimacy 37–38
  federate units 42
  indirect legitimacy 37–38
  individual autonomy 38
  judicial monopoly 39
  justification/justifiability 37–38
  loyalty 76–77
  purposive interpretation 39
  reasonable level 42
  reasons, giving 38
  self-referential validity of law 37–38
legitimate expectations 194–95
LIBE Committee 163–64, 169
linguistic bonds 36–37
Lisbon Treaty
  ACCC 200
  ACTA 161–62
  AFSJ 132, 134, 136–38
  balance between institutions 182–83
  CFSP/TFEU policies 135–36
  choice of legal basis 113, 117
  coherence 11–12, 81, 82, 99–101, 108–9, 110, 231
  common commercial policy (CCP) 233
  competences 1, 223
  conferral, principle of 114–15
  diplomatic legitimacy 86, 176–77
  ECHR, accession to 185–86
  European Parliament 107, 154, 158, 162
  foreign direct investment (FDI) 185–86
  High Representative 100
  institutions 150
  integration 40, 107–8
  legal consequences of exercise of power 7
  legal personality of EU 1
  Member States, constraints on 42–43
  mixed agreements 61–62
  mutual non-affection clause 104–5
  national parliaments 86, 178, 179
  pillars, abolition of 132–33, 134
  PNR agreements 162–63
  ratification 179
  sincere cooperation, principle of 52
  standing 200
  subsidiarity 83–84, 85, 86
  TFTP 159–60, 162
  transfer of powers to EU 1
litigation challenging the post-Lisbon division of powers, *see also* **pushback from Member States 115–16, 223–24**
locus standi *see* **standing**
loyalty *see* **EU loyalty**

MacCormick, Neil 6–7, 29–30
Macron, Emmanuel 40–41

Majone, Giandomenico 9–10, 32–33
margin of appreciation 141, 190, 217
Mauritius, agreement on treatment of suspected pirates and seized property with 169–70
media 34, 168, 170, 180, 237–38
Member States and EU, relations between 3
migrants, smuggling of 132–33
Mill, John Stewart 175
mixed agreements 61–65, 140
  Aarhus Convention 124–25, 140–45
  allocation of responsibility 122–23
  binding, mixed agreements as 140, 144–45
  bonding structures 140, 237
  choice of legal basis 12, 145–46
  common commercial policy (CCP) 129
  competences 63–64, 65, 140, 206–7
    choice of legal basis 145–46
    declarations 145
    division 145–46
  competition 180–81
  conclusion of agreements 62, 225–26
  divisions of power 62, 122–23, 145, 171–72, 223, 224
  effectiveness 12
  environment 90, 124–25
  external actions and internal actions, differences between 61–65
  facultative mixity 61–62, 121–22, 150, 170–72, 229
  federalism 144–45
  free trade agreements (FTAs) 206
  fulfilment of obligations 62
  internal actions and external actions, differences between 61–65, 224
  international law, interpretation of 145–46
  international organizations 62
  international responsibility 225–26
  ISDS/ICS 196, 206
  Lisbon Treaty 61–62
  loyalty 61–65, 75, 77
  negotiations 62, 225–26
  outside-in effect of external relations 145
  ownership of EU citizens 122–23, 230
  political choice 150
  pre-emption 63, 64
  primacy 140
  signalling function 121, 122–23
  sincere cooperation, principle of 62–63
  subsidiarity 90
  unity of international representation 66–67, 68, 69
mixed membership
mixity 65, 68, 121, 125 *see also* **facultative mixity**
monism 31–32, 202, 212–13
Moreno-Lax, Violeta 31
Morgan, Edmund 177
Mouffe, Chantal 36
mutual non-affection clause 104–5, 138–39

national courts *see also* **preliminary rulings**
  ACCC 200–1, 235
  annulment of decisions of 203–4
  autonomy 25, 27–28, 30, 42, 234
  bonding structures 41–42
  CJEU 5
  constitutional courts 25, 28–29, 93, 98, 234
  counter-terrorism sanctions 94–97
  deference 218
  direct applicability 204
  ECHR
    accession to 214
    triangle of ECHR, EU law and national 212–13
  effectiveness 22, 230
  exhaustion of domestic remedies 190, 197, 202, 206, 217, 218
  ICTs 203–4, 234
  ISDS/ICS 195, 196
  legitimacy 52–53
  primacy 11–12, 82, 92–93, 94–98, 204, 230
  pushback 29
  sincere cooperation, principle of 49–50, 52–53
national governments
  balance between institutions 229
  CFSP 106–7
  Council 151
  foreign relations, deference to 225
  institutions 204
  intergovernmentalism 19–20, 48, 99, 145–46, 152–53
  international law 225
  Lisbon Treaty 28–29
  loyalty 50, 58
  primacy 97, 230
  proximity of government, rationale of 83–84, 86, 230
  separation of powers 95–96
  sincere cooperation, principle of 49–50
  Treaty amendments 153
  visibility 176–77
national identity 28–29, 52–53
national laws *see also* **primacy**
  autonomy 233–34
  bonding structures 15
  conflict of laws 22
  effectiveness 15, 22
  EU law as national law 203
  fact, classified as 197
  ICTs 203–4, 216
  integration 22
  overlapping laws 5
national parliaments
  citizens, representation by EP of 178–81
  competition 180–81
  Constitutional Treaty, ratification of 179
  democratic legitimacy 171–72, 176–77
  European Parliament as an alternative 178–81, 229
  Europeanization 178
  international agreements 178–79
  Lisbon Treaty 86, 178, 179
  parliamentary democracies 179
  presidential systems 179

national parliaments (*cont.*)
ratification powers 196
representation 18–19
resources, lack of 179
subsidiarity 84, 86, 178
visibility of national parliaments 178
voice of citizens 134–35, 167, 176–77, 178
national security 67–68, 143–44
nationality 4, 50, 175, 176
negotiation of international agreements
CFSP/TFEU policies 169–82
European Parliament 161–62, 168–70, 229
Commission 166–67
Council 165–66, 169–70
information and communication obligations 154, 155–56, 167–68
opposition position 166
renegotiation 70
free trade agreements (FTAs) 165
mixed agreements 62, 225–26
opposition position 166
PNR agreements 163–64, 168–69
renegotiation 47–48, 70, 168–69
secretive negotiations 158–59
Netherlands
autonomy of EU legal order 219
BITs 196
Brexit 38
ECHR 212–13, 219
harmonization 84–85
monism 212–13
national parliaments 178
Ukraine Association Agreement, referendum on 123
New Zealand, Partnership Agreement with 138
non-governmental organizations (NGOs) 143, 198, 199
nuclear energy 68

Obama, Barack 168–69
opt-outs 64, 134
ordering function of law 5–6
ordinary legislative procedure (OLP)
AFSJ 134, 135, 138, 159–60
CFSP/TFEU policies 135–36
consent to international agreements 154
European Parliament 116–17, 167–68
organizational principles 81 *see also* **coherence; EU loyalty; primacy; subsidiarity**
autonomy 82, 110, 230
bonding structures 3, 81–82, 109
external pressure, under 81–111
gap-filling function 81
general principles 81
horizontal application 81
institutions
action, scope for 11
bonding structures 81–82
conduct 81
formation 81–82
integration 236
interpretation 3, 11, 109, 223
judicial review, grounds for 81
judicialization 109
loyalty 223
policy-making 81–82
purpose 81
sincere cooperation, principle of 81
state sovereignty 230
structural principles 81
transformation 1–2, 81, 224
organized crime 132–33
originator's consent rule (ORCON) 156
othering 30–32
anti-EU rhetoric, normalization of 238
autonomy 30–31, 236
cultural identity 21
dualism 31
ECHR, accession of 31
essentialization 4
fragility 30–32
free trade agreements (FTAs) 147
identity formation 4, 21
international law, distinctiveness from 30–31
media 237–38
monism 31–32
nationality 4
ownership by politicians, lack of 238
pluralism 31–32
politicians 237–38
us and them narrative 21, 147, 237–38
ownership of EU citizens
bonding structures 3
CJEU 227–28
coherence 82, 98, 100
crisis, state of 1
facultative mixity 229
loyalty 232
mixed agreements 122–23
politics 19–20, 228, 232, 238
subsidiarity 230
transparency 100

parallel competences 118–19
Aarhus Convention 141
CFSP 100–1, 108
developing cooperation 118–19
external competences 2, 9, 119–20, 141, 145
grey zones 119
internal competences 2, 9, 119–20, 128
loyalty 59
pre-emption 118–20
shared competences 120
sincere cooperation, principle of 118–19
subsidiarity 89
Paris Convention on Third Party Liability in the Field of Nuclear Energy, 1960 Protocol to 68
parliaments *see also* **European Parliament; national parliaments**
parliamentary democracies 179, 229
presidential systems 179, 229
participation
ACCC 198, 199, 216, 220
bonding structures 3
ICTs 220

loyalty 232
purpose, external relations as 41
subsidiarity 86
passenger name record (PNR) agreements 132–34
Charter of Fundamental Rights of the EU 164
data protection 133–34, 164
police and judicial cooperation 134
privacy 164
passenger name record (PNR) Agreement with US 162–64, 181–82
civil liberties 162–64
consent, refusal of 162–63
data protection 162–63
European Parliament 162–64, 181–82
Fourth Agreement 162–63
information, right to 162–63
Lisbon Treaty 162–63
negotiations 163–64, 168–69
privacy 162–63
Third Agreement 162–63
third countries, transfer of data to 162–63
patriotism 56–57
personality of EU in international relations 171
Philippines, Partnership and Cooperation Agreement (PCA) with 119–20, 129
pillar structure *see also* **area of freedom, security and justice (AFSJ); Common Foreign and Security Policy (CFSP)**
abolition 1, 132–33, 134
cross-pillar approach 132–33
development cooperation 132–33
erosion of pillar structure 102
first pillar 132–35, 136–37
Lisbon Treaty 104, 132, 134, 136–38
migration policy 132–33
opt-outs 134
partial depillarisation 100–1
police and judicial cooperation 1, 132, 133–34, 136–37, 159–60
Pitkin, Hanna 173
PNR agreements *see* **passenger name record (PNR) agreements**
Poland 219
political, the, *see also* **politics**19, 20, 21–22
police and judicial cooperation (third pillar) 1, 132, 133–34, 136–37, 159–60
Police Mission 103–4
policy-making
choices 205–6
coherence 98–99, 107–8, 111
contestation, acts of 182
fragmentation 132–33
geographical scope of international agreements 120
harmonization 233
internal market 6
internationalization 87, 233
ISDS/ICS 191–92
legitimacy 174–75
organizational principles 81–82
primacy 82
resources 179
subsidiarity 87–88, 109–10
politics
agonistic politics 36, 165
autonomy for citizens 183–84
bonding structures 19–22, 227, 237, 238
brute politics 4
choice of legal basis 146, 232–33
citizens, representation by EP of 180–81
creating politics 39
democratic legitimacy 20
dimensions 17
distinction over time, political emerging as a 21–22
extra-institutional politics 157
image of EU 22
imagined communities 21–22
institutions 20
law and politics, relationship between 5–6, 7, 19–22, 46, 73–74, 227
loyalty 228, 237
mixed agreements 150
othering 21, 237–38
ownership 19–20, 228, 238
party politics 165
political as opposed to politics 19, 20
politicization 153, 237
power struggles 232–33
practices of politicians 3
responsibility chains 146
social and personal relations 20
sovereign, taking place of the 228
state-dominated power politics 19–20
state sovereignty 20
symbolism 19
taming national politics 6
Treaties, amendment of 19–20
popular sovereignty 9–10, 83–84, 174–75, 177, 229
predictability
choice of legal basis 114, 146
coherence 11–12, 82, 98
justification/justifiability 11–12
pre-emption
choice of legal basis 113, 116–20
competences 118–20
definition 113
grey zones 119–20
integration 113
loyalty 59–61
mixed agreements 63, 64
parallel competences 118–20
sincere cooperation, principle of 63, 118–19
standard-setting organizations 131
preliminary rulings
ACCC 200–1, 208, 235
autonomy 16, 22–23, 25, 26, 29–30
dialogue 25–26
effectiveness 16, 25–26, 207, 225
exhaustion of domestic remedies 217
fact, EU law as 210
hierarchy 25–26, 29

preliminary rulings (*cont.*)
ICTs 201, 204, 216–17
ISDS/ICS 197, 218, 235
judiciary 22–23, 25–26, 224, 225
keystone of EU judicial system, as 25
religious grounds, discrimination on 29
self-referential character of legal order 25–26
sincere cooperation, principle of 49–50
source of rights and obligations, EU law as 17–18
standing 207, 208
ultra vires 29
uniformity 26
prerogatives
balance between institutions 100
Common Foreign and Security Policy (CFSP) 135–36
division of powers, interpretation of 152–53
European Parliament 107, 158, 169–70, 229
Lisbon Treaty 99
procedural prerogatives 107–8
presidential systems 179, 229
primacy 92–98, 230
autonomy 70, 92–93, 98, 110, 230
bonding structures 82, 91–92, 98, 110
coherence 98–99
conflict of laws 92–93, 97, 110
constitutional law 5–6
counter-terrorist sanctions 94–97
definition 92–93
derogation from EU law 97
dualism 110
ECHR, accession to 210–12, 216
effect of primacy 92–93
effectiveness 16, 22, 82, 91–92, 93–94, 98, 110, 230
fundamental rights 110, 230
hierarchy 92–93
ICTs 204, 219, 231
international agreements 98, 127, 227
international law 82, 94–98, 224–25, 230
interpretation 82, 92–93, 97
justification/justifiability 91–92, 97
legitimacy 82, 110
loyalty 74–75, 76
mixed agreements 73
national conceptions 92–93
national courts 11–12, 82, 92–93, 94–98, 216, 230
national governments 97, 230
objectives 93–94
relevance for external relations 97–98
representation 82, 182
signalling function 123
sincere cooperation, principle of 50
source of rights and obligations, EU law as 17–18
withdrawal of national support 91–92
primary law
Aarhus Convention 198–99
CFSP/TFEU policies 106–7
coherence 98–99
Commission as guardian of primary law 5
ECHR 210–11, 234
interpretation 52, 210–11, 227–28
loyalty 71
Treaty amendments 5–6
principle of sincere cooperation *see* **sincere cooperation** 162–63, 164
public opinion 6–7, 165, 166, 167
pushback from Member States 29, 223–24

qualified majority voting (QMV) 135–36, 152–53

rationality 24–25, 74, 76
Raz, Joseph 22–23, 214
reasons, giving 33, 38, 91–92
***Rechstaat*, principles of modern** 35
reciprocity 60, 74
recognition
selves by represented, of 173–74
worthiness, of 10, 35, 42, 108, 228
referendums 18–19, 153
refusal of consent to international agreements/vetoes
ACTA 158–59, 161–70
balance between institutions 153, 158–62, 165–66, 229
bonding structures 22, 175
European Parliament 153, 158–64, 165–66, 229
facultative mixity 171
PNR agreements 162–64
representation 181–82
TFTP agreement 158–61, 170, 181–82
regional economic integration organization (REIOs) 225
relevance of EU law 4–7, 15, 86, 230
religious grounds, discrimination on 29
representation of citizens 228–29
see also **bonding structures; citizens representation by European Parliament of; unity of international representation**
balance between institutions 149, 183
competences, division of 229
contestation, acts of 173–82, 183
definition 173
democratic legitimacy 18–19, 172, 229
denial of legitimacy 12
direct input 18–19, 190
ECHR, accession to 62
effectiveness 176–77
European Parliament 18–19, 149, 166, 173–75, 183
balance between institutions 156–57, 166
contestation, acts of 172–82, 183
executive dominance 41
facultative mixity 171, 229
fiction, as 175–76, 177
indirect input 18–19, 190
interdependencies 228
justification/justifiability 18–19
primacy 82
self-determination 228, 236
state sovereignty 172–73

subsidiarity 19, 90, 109–10
symbolic function of EP 175–77
visibility 8–9, 166
reserved competences
Aarhus Convention 143–44
common commercial policy (CCP) 130
integration 236
loyalty 11, 76, 77
sincere cooperation, principle of 54
unity of international representation 11, 68
resources 91, 179, 226
restrictive measures *see* **sanctions**
Riker, William 9–10
Royce, Josiah 54–55
rule of law 38–39, 182, 196, 201, 219–20, 226

safeguard-clauses 5
sanctions (restrictive measures) *see also* **counter-terrorist sanctions**
BITs 70–71
CFSP/TFEU policies 135–36, 138–39, 145–46
choice of legal basis 138–39, 145–46
mutual non-affection clause 138–39
powers by Member States, exercise of 132
Security Council (UN) 216
Scharpf, Fritz 32–33
Schütze, Robert 83
second pillar *see* **Common Foreign and Security Policy (CFSP)**
secondary law
Aarhus Convention 198–99
annulment actions 227–28
autonomy 5
choice of legal basis 113
Commission 5
ECtHR 190
interpretation 151–52, 198–99
pre-emption 113
primacy 5–6
signalling function 123
Security Council (UN)
Chapter VII 215–16
counter-terrorism sanctions 95–96, 216
ECHR, accession to 215–16
general principles of EU law 215
peacekeeping missions 216
resolutions 182, 204, 215–16
sanctions 95–96, 216
visibility 8–9
voice of citizens, EP providing a 182
self-conception as citizens 160, 229
self-determination
autonomy 38
bonding structures 3, 17
citizenship 3, 181
globalization 78
loyalty 78, 232
purpose, external relations as 40–41
representation 181, 228, 236
state sovereignty 35
subsidiarity 91
self-referential nature of EU law 15, 24, 27, 37–38, 234
separation of powers 95–96
shared competences
choice of legal basis 116–18
common commercial policy (CCP) 127–28, 130
conferral, principle of 115–16
environment 124–25
free trade agreements (FTAs) 233
loyalty 59, 63, 77–78
sincere cooperation, principle of 53–54
standard-setting organisations 131
subsidiarity 81, 82–83, 87, 89
Ship-Source Pollution Directive 88
signalling function of legal bases 118, 120–23, 146
sincere cooperation, principle of 11, 47–54
abuse of powers 67–68
administrative law 49–50
autonomy 54, 63–64, 73–74
balance between institutions 74–75
best endeavours 63, 73
case law 48–51
CFSP 47, 48, 108
codification 46, 47–48
coherence 50–51, 73–74, 100
competences 52–54, 59–60, 61, 75, 79
conferral, principle of 52
consequentialism 73
deontological approach 73
division of powers 11
ECHR, accession to 212
effectiveness 22, 50–51, 53, 54, 78
emanations of the state 49–50
essential state functions, respect for 52
executive dominance 152–53
framing 57, 68–69
fundamental rights 53
good faith 45, 48–49, 52–53
implied external powers, doctrine of 52
information and communication obligations 65–66
institutions 46, 47, 49–50, 54, 62
integration 51–52, 124
international agreements 61, 70, 73–74, 167–68
international law 69–70, 73
interpretation 51–53, 62, 64
justification/justifiability 66–67, 74
limits 52–54
loyalty 59–60, 61, 75, 81
mixed agreements 62–63
national courts 49–50, 52–53
national identity, duty to respect 52–53
pre-emption 63, 118–19
preliminary rulings 49–50
primacy 50
quality 76
rationality 76
solidarity 48
stricter obligations 74–76, 232
subjects 48–51

sincere cooperation, principle of (*cont.*)
unity of international representation 66–70
within the state, loyalty 50
Singapore, Free Trade Agreement (EUSFTA) with 129, 170–71, 186–87, 194–95, 197, 218
single market *see* **internal market**
Slovakia 196
Snowden, Edward 169
social legitimacy 32–33, 219, 228
Society for Worldwide Interbank Financial Telecommunication (SWIFT) 159–60
source of rights and obligations, EU law as 17–18
sovereignty *see also* **state sovereignty**
European Parliament 176, 181–82, 183–84
international organization, EU as 9
legitimacy 34–35, 42
organizational principles 230
popular sovereignty 9–10, 35, 83–84, 174–75, 177, 229
shared sovereignty 9–10
sincere cooperation, principle of 52
speech act, as 181
visibility 183–84
Spanish Constitutional Tribunal 28–29
spill-over effects 7
standard-setting organizations, ripple effect of EU positions in 131–32
standing 207–9
Aarhus Convention 143, 144, 199, 200, 207–8, 235
access to justice 207, 209
annulment procedure 207, 208–9
burden of proof 199
CJEU 207–9
direct and individual concern 200, 207–8
effectiveness 207, 208–9
individuals 216–17
NGOs 143, 199
non-privileged applicants 207
preliminary rulings 207, 208–9
state sovereignty
autonomy 23, 28–29, 217–18, 230
competences 172–73
democratic legitimacy 20
ECHR, accession to 202
Europeanization 178
integration 40–41
international law 30–31, 226
loyalty 45
power politics 226
rule of law 226
territorial sovereignty 52, 72
transfer 23, 28–29, 30–31, 202, 236
Stockholm Convention on Persistent Organic Pollutants 62–65, 124–25
structure of bonding *see* **bonding structures**
subsidiarity 82–92, 230 *see also* **subsidiarity and environment**
autonomy 83, 85–86
bonding structures 82, 86, 109–10
codification 83–84, 85
competences 82–83, 84–85, 90, 116–17
constitutional framework 82–86
democratic legitimacy 11–12, 82, 83–84, 85–86, 109–10, 230
economic concept, as 11–12
effectiveness 11–12, 83–84, 86, 109–10, 230
impact assessments 85–86
internal market 84–85
international agreements 82, 230
interpretation 82–86, 223, 230
justification/justifiability 82–84, 86, 237
legitimacy
democratic legitimacy 11–12, 82, 83–84, 85–86, 109–10
normative 86
Lisbon Treaty 83–84, 85, 86
loyalty 72
national parliaments 84, 86, 178
ownership by citizens 230
participate, ability to 86
policy-making 109–10
popular sovereignty 83–84
presumption in favour of EU action 82, 87–92, 230
proportionality 83
proximity of government, rationale of 83–84, 86, 230
relevance 82
representation 19, 86, 230
shared competences 81
sincere cooperation, principle of 52–53
transparency 86
who should take action 81, 83
subsidiarity and environment 82, 87–92
autonomy 91
bonding structures 91–92
common commercial policy (CCP) 90–91
competences 87, 89, 90
democracy 88, 90, 91
effectiveness 87–88, 90–91
Emissions Trading System (ETS) Directive 88
framing 90–91
greenhouse gases 87, 88
implied external powers 90
internal market 87, 90–91
international agreements 91
international law-making 88–89
interpretation 87, 89
justification/justifiability 88, 91
Kyoto Protocol 88
mixed agreements 90
policy-making 87–88
reasons, duty to give 91–92
rebuttable presumption that EU action in external relations necessary 89–92
self-determination 91
Ship-Source Pollution Directive 88
transboundary effects 87
succession, doctrine of functional 128
Sweden 62–65, 143, 219
SWIFT 159–60
Switzerland 134, 215–16
symbolic function of European Parliament 175–77

terminology 9
territorial integrity 52
terrorism *see* counter-terrorist sanctions; Terrorist Finance Tracking Programme (TFTP) agreement with US
Terrorist Finance Tracking Programme (TFTP) agreement with US 159–62
  consent, refusal of 159–60
  data protection 159–60
  European Parliament 158–60, 170, 180, 181–82
  Europol 160–61
  Lisbon Treaty 159–60, 162
  media 170
  negotiations 158–60, 162
  SWIFT 159–60
  TFTP II agreement 161–62
TFEU *see* CFSP/TFEU policies
third pillar *see* area of freedom, security and justice (AFSJ)
trafficking of persons 132–33
Transatlantic Trade and Investment Partnership (TTIP) 166–67, 168, 181–82
transparency
  bonding structures 3, 237
  CFSP/TFEU policies 136–37
  choice of legal basis 114, 146
  citizenship 233
  coherence 100
  conferral, principle of 115–16
  European Parliament 167–68
  ISDS/ICS 192–93, 206
  legitimacy 33, 34, 35
  media and institutions, connecting 34
  ownership of EU citizens 100
  subsidiarity 86
transformation 71–76, 224
  bonding structures 3–4, 81
  integration 175
  loyalty 45, 46, 50–51, 56, 57, 71–76, 78
  national courts 216–17
  organizational principle 1–2, 81, 224
  representation 177
Treaty amendments
  autonomy 27
  balance between institutions 165–66, 167
  best endeavours 68–69
  bonding structures 41–42
  CJEU, departure from case law of 5–6
  codified limits on powers 52–53
  competences 3, 115–16
  democratic legitimacy 157, 183
  European Parliament 153, 157
  Lisbon Treaty 7
  loyalty 72
  politics 19–20
  ratification 5–6, 27, 114–15, 227–28
  referendums 153
  sincere cooperation, principle of 52–53
  unanimity 27, 114–15
Treaty on Functioning of EU *see* CFSP/TFEU policies
trialogue process 17–18, 166
tribunals *see* international courts and tribunals (ICTs)
TRIPs 128
Trump, Donald 236
Tuori, Kaarlo 31
Turkey, Association Agreement with 120

Ukraine Association Agreement, Dutch referendum on 123
ultra vires 29, 52–53, 116–17
UN Charter 94–97, 215
UN Convention against Transnational Organized Crime (Palermo Convention) 132–33
UN Convention on the Law of the Sea (UNCLOS) 218
UN Security Council *see* Security Council (UN)
union delegations 102–3
United Kingdom
  AFSJ 120
  Brexit 32–33, 38, 238
  counter-terrorist sanctions 95–96
  ECtHR jurisprudence, taking into account 212–13
  Human Rights Act 1998 212–13
  Netherlands, rights of UK citizens in the 38
  opt-outs 134
  Security Council (UN) resolutions 95–96
  separation of powers 95–96
United States *see also* Terrorist Finance Tracking Programme (TFTP) agreement with US
  Air Transport Agreement, parties to 69
  counter-terrorism surveillance 159–60
  data protection 169, 181–82
  Energy Star Program 126–27
  European Parliament and rejection of international agreements 181–82
  federalism 56–57
  media 169
  passenger name record (PNR) Agreement 162–64, 181–82
  presidential system 179, 229
  surveillance program 169
  SWIFT 159–60
unity of international representation 66–70
  autonomy 45, 46, 67–68, 69, 70, 77
  bonding structures 78
  coherence 99
  competences 67–68, 77–78
  effectiveness 78
  federalism 68–69
  hybrid decisions 69
  independent source of distinct obligations, as 66–70
  information and communication obligations 46
  integration 236
  international organizations
    EU, as 70
    membership of 68–69
  interpretation 232
  justification/justifiability 70
  mixed agreements 66–67, 68, 69

unity of international representation (*cont.*)
mixity 68
national parliaments 174–75
negative and positive obligations 232
process, as 174
reserved competences 11, 68
sincere cooperation, principle of 66–70
stricter loyalty 74 –75
subsidiarity 91
treaties and conventions, accession of EU to 68–69
us and them narrative 21, 147, 237–38
use of force, control over legitimate 27–28

vetoes over international agreements *see* **refusal of consent to international agreements/ vetoes**
Vietnam, free trade agreement (FTA) with 167
visibility
balance between institutions 168–69
citizens, representation by EP of 180
European identity, development of 168
European Parliament 166, 168–69, 177
international organizations 8–9
media 180–81
national parliaments 178
rejection 180
Security Council (UN) 8–9
voice of EU citizens
bonding structures 3–4, 20
democratic legitimacy 12, 176–77, 229
European Parliament 134–35, 149, 175, 177, 178
democratic legitimacy 12, 176–77, 229
negotiations 166, 167, 169
politics 181–82, 183–84
self-conception 160
exit, as form of 7–8
globalization 3
internal exercise 7–8
loyalty 58, 76, 232
national parliaments 134–35, 167, 176–77, 178
politics 181–82, 183–84
TFTP 160
voluntarism 77

Walker, Neil 181
weapons of mass destruction (WMDs) 136–37
Weiler, Joseph 7, 58–59
World Trade Organization (WTO), dispute settlement system of
ACCC 199
CJEU 186–87
direct effect 186–87, 206
dominance of EU 186–87
ITLOS 187
mixed agreement, WTO Agreement as 186–87

Xi Jinping 236